WITHDRAWN
UTSA LIBRARIES

TWILIGHT OF THE COMINTERN, 1930–1935

By the same author

A HISTORY OF SOVIET RUSSIA
in fourteen volumes

**with R. W. Davies*

TWILIGHT OF THE COMINTERN, 1930–1935

E. H. CARR

PANTHEON BOOKS, NEW YORK

LIBRARY
The University of Texas
At San Antonio

Copyright © 1982 by E.H. Carr

All rights reserved under International and Pan-American Copyright Conventions. Published in the United States by Pantheon Books, a division of Random House, Inc., New York, and simultaneously in Canada by Random House of Canada Limited, Toronto. Originally published in Great Britain as *The Twilight of Comintern, 1930–1935*, by Macmillan Ltd.

Library of Congress Cataloging in Publication Data

Carr, Edward Hallett, 1892-1982
Twilight of the Comintern, 1930-1935.

Includes index.
1. Communist International—History.   I. Title.
HX11.I5C34   1983   324'.1   82-14359
ISBN 0-394-52512-4

Manufactured in the United States of America

First Edition

CONTENTS

PREFACE

The original design of my *History of Soviet Russia*, the first volume of which (*The Bolshevik Revolution, 1917–1923*, Vol. 1) was published in 1950, and the last (*Foundations of a Planned Economy, 1926–1929*, Vol. 3) in 1978, did not go beyond the year 1929. My ambition, already vast enough, was to study "the political, social and economic order" which emerged from the revolution. By the end of 1929 Stalin had crushed every opposition to his dictatorship. The first five-year plan was in operation. The trade unions had been well and truly integrated into the apparatus of government. The fateful decision had been taken to collectivize the peasantry. The main structures of the regime had been established.

Another reason which led me to place this chronological limit on my work was the availability of reliable contemporary material. During the nineteen-twenties controversies on major topics had been conducted in congresses and committees, the proceedings of which were published in the daily press and in a multitude of journals. It was not difficult to discover the reasons for any important decision, who had supported it, who had opposed it, and on what grounds. By the end of 1929 this freedom had been slowly eroded. Orthodoxy was the road to promotion, heresy was punishable. The press was rigidly controlled. Congresses and committees met no longer to debate decisions, but to register and popularize them. The historian no longer had a sure foothold.

Thirty years later these arguments need to be qualified. History knows no beginnings and no endings, and what happened in the USSR in the nineteen-thirties grew without a break out of what happened in the nineteen-twenties. Nor is the documentary landscape today as bleak as it seemed in 1950. Dark places remain. But many documents have been published, as well as critical articles by writers having access to party and Soviet archives. In the fifteen years after Khrushchev's disclosures of 1956 past controversies were revived, and Stalin was sometimes held responsible for erroneous decisions. One result of the new evidence has been to modify the traditional picture of an iron dictatorship taking decisions which it then imposed on a subordinate hierarchy of party and state officials.

What emerges is a plethora of unpublished discussions and disputes at all levels; and confusion often resulted when Stalin, cautiously feeling his way, delayed a peremptory verdict.

While engaged on the last instalment of my history, I became acutely conscious of the difficulty of holding together within a single work, on the scale on which I wished to write, so many different aspects of the Soviet scene. Professor R. W. Davies, who collaborated with me in the economic chapters of *Foundations of a Planned Economy, 1926–1929*, came to the same conclusion, and embarked on the study of Soviet economic affairs in the nineteen-thirties, of which two volumes, entitled *The Socialist Offensive: The Collectivisation of Soviet Agriculture, 1929–1930* and *The Soviet Collective Farm, 1929–1930*, have already been published. In the present volume I investigate another corner of Soviet activity in the nineteen-thirties, the work of the Communist International (Comintern). This involves a study of the interaction between Comintern and the Soviet Foreign Office (Narkomindel) and between Comintern and national communist parties. Neither of these topics has hitherto been adequately treated in the literature of the subject. The seventh congress of 1935 marked the culmination of a long process which relegated Comintern to the side-lines of Soviet policy and ideology, and brings this volume to a conclusion. A further volume would be required to narrate the eclipse of Comintern, through the dramatic episodes of the Spanish Civil War and the Munich crisis, to the Soviet–German pact of August 1939, and the final extinction of the institution during the Second World War. I have begun some work on this volume, but feel uncertain how far I shall be able to carry it.

As in the last volume of my *History*, arrangement has been a problem. To narrate what happened in Moscow and what happened in the parties involved some overlapping, which was, however, rarely complete. The charge of "lagging behind" was frequently levelled by Comintern at the parties; but parties sometimes anticipated views later adopted by Moscow. In the present volume the affairs of the central organs of Comintern were so closely intertwined with those of the German party that I have not found it necessary to devote a separate chapter to that party. My choice of parties to be treated separately (out of some sixty belonging to Comintern) has been dictated partly by their importance in this period, and partly perhaps by the availability of significant material. It is not quite identical with the choice adopted in the third volume of *Foundations of a Planned Economy, 1926–1929*.

Problems of transliteration always intrude. I have continued to spell Chinese names in the style current when I embarked on my *History*. The introduction into the present work of the new style of romanization would, I feel, have created confusion for both author and reader.

In the prefaces of successive volumes of my *History*, I recorded my heavy indebtedness to the numerous individuals and institutions in more than one country who have helped me at different stages of my journey. The same ungrudging help has been extended me on many points in the present volume; and I hope that those who have earned my gratitude in this way will forgive me if, without listing names, I tender to them here a comprehensive expression of my warm thanks. I am very conscious of their kindness and cooperation. But, in recalling my labours on this volume over the past three years, I should like particularly to mention Piers Tyrrell of Cambridge University Library, Trevor Kaye of the library of Trinity College, Cambridge, and Jonathan Haslam of the University of Birmingham, who have been indefatigable in identifying and locating out-of-the-way sources which I needed, and in borrowing from other libraries books not available in Cambridge. Finally, Tamara Deutscher's devotion to the spade-work which has gone into the preparation of this volume has increased my sense of obligation to her for support without which it could not have been written.

March 15, 1982   E. H. CARR

LIST OF ABBREVIATIONS

ADGB = Allgemeiner Deutscher Gewerkschaftsbund (General German Trade Union Federation)

BKP = Bulgarskaya Kommunisticheska Partia (Bulgarian Communist Party)

CCP = Chinese Communist Party

CEDA = Confederación Española de Derechas Autónomas (Spanish Confederation of Autonomous Right-wing groups)

CER = Chinese Eastern Railway

CGL = Confederazione Generale del Lavoro

CGT = Confédération Générale du Travail

CGTU = Confédération Générale du Travail Unitaire
= Confederación General del Trabajo Unitaria

CNT = Confederación Nacional del Trabajo (National Confederation of Labour (Anarchist))

Comintern = Communist International

CPGB = Communist Party of Great Britain

FAI = Federación Anarquista Ibérica (Iberian Anarchist Federation)

IFTU = International Federation of Trade Unions ("Amsterdam International")

IKKI = Executive Committee of the Communist International (Comintern)

ILP = Independent Labour Party

KIM = Kommunisticheskii Internatsional Molodezhi (Communist Youth International)

KPD = Kommunistische Partei Deutschlands (German Communist Party)

KPD(O) = Kommunistische Partei Deutschlands, Opposition (German Communist Party, Opposition)

KPÖ = Kommunistische Partei Österreichs (Austrian Communist Party)

KPP = Komunistyczna Partja Polski (Polish Communist Party)

KPZB = Komunistyczna Partja Zachodniej Bielorusi (Western White Russian Communist Party)

KPZU = Komunisticheska Partiya Zachidnei Ukraini (Western Ukranian Communist Party)

MOPR = Mezhdunarodnaya Organizatsiya Pomoshchi Bor'tsam Revolyutsii (International Association for Aid to Revolutionary Fighters, IRH)

MRP = Mezhdunarodnaya Rabochaya Pomoshch' (International Workers' Aid, IAH)

Narkomindel	= Narodnyi Komissariat Inostrannykh Del (People's Commissariat of Foreign Affairs)
NMM	= National Minority Movement
NSDAP	= Nationalsozialistische Deutsche Arbeiterpartei (National-Socialist German Workers' Party, Nazis)
NUWCM	= National Unemployed Workers' Committee Movement
OMS	= Otdel Mezhdunarodnoi Svyazi (International Communications Section (Comintern))
ONR	= Obóz Narodowo-Radykalny (National-Radical Centre)
PCE	= Partido Comunista de España
PCF	= Parti Communiste Français
PCI	= Partito Comunista Italiano
POP	= Parti Ouvrier Populaire
POUM	= Partido Obrero de Unificación Marxista (Marxist Workers' Unity Party)
POW	= Polska Organizacja Wojskowa (Polish Military Organisation)
PPS	= Polska Partja Socjalistyczna (Polish Socialist Party)
Profintern	= Krasnyi Internatsional Professional'nykh Soyuzov (Red International of Labour Unions, RILU)
PSI	= Partito Socialista Italiano
PSOE	= Partido Socialista Obrero Español (Spanish Socialist Workers' Party)
RGO	= Revolutionäre Gewerkschaftsopposition (Revolutionary Trade Union Opposition)
RILU	= Red International of Labour Unions, *see* Profintern
SA	= Sturmabteilungen (Detachments of Storm-Troopers)
SAP	= Sozialistische Arbeiterpartei (Socialist Workers' Party)
Second International	= Labour and Socialist International
SFIO	= Section Française Internationale Ouvrière (French Socialist Party)
SPD	= Sozialdemokratische Partei Deutschlands (German Social-Democratic Party)
SPÖ	= Sozialdemokratische Partei Österreichs (Austrian Social-Democratic Party)
SS	= Schutzstaffel (Elite Defence Corps)
TsIK	= Tsentral'nyi Ispolnitel'nyi Komitet (Central Executive Committee of Congress of Soviets)
TUC	= Trade Union Congress
UGT	= Union General de Trabajadores (General Union of Workers (Socialist))
USSR	= Union of Soviet Socialist Republics
VKP(B)	= Vsesoyuznaya Kommunisticheskaya Partiya (Bol'shevikov) (All-Union Communist Party (Bolsheviks))
WEB	= Western European Bureau (of Comintern)

PART I

THE SCENE IN MOSCOW

CHAPTER 1

THE WORLD ECONOMIC CRISIS

Two crises, whose eventual repercussions were incalculable, coincided in the winter of 1929–1930. A catastrophic collapse on the New York Stock Exchange in October 1929 heralded the breakdown of the whole economic and political order established in western Europe after the First World War; and the USSR, wrestling frantically with the problems of industrialization and the first five-year plan, was overtaken by an acute grain collections crisis, and plunged headlong into the daunting task of the collectivization of the peasantry.

The immediate impact of these events in Moscow was two-fold. On the one hand, the world economic crisis could be hailed as a vindication of the Marxist diagnosis of the mortal sickness of capitalism and a harbinger of the promised revolt of the proletariat. It was agreeable to contemplate the disarray of the capitalist system, and to contrast it with the systematic advance of the five-year plan. On the other hand, the crisis bred more immediate apprehensions, economic and political. It had been recognized for some time that the difficult pursuit of intensive and rapid industrialization called for close economic links with the advanced capitalist countries, in the form both of trade and of technical aid. The crisis contracted capitalist markets for Soviet products, and with them the opportunity of earning the foreign currency necessary to fulfil the programmes of the five-year plan. It fanned animosities between the imperialist Powers, as well as the common animosity against the USSR which united them all, and conjured up visions of coming imperialist wars, which would inevitably involve war against the USSR.

The dilemma thus presented to Soviet policy making was not new. Ever since Brest-Litovsk, the attitude of the Soviet regime to the capitalist world had been compounded of two disparate motives: the promotion of revolution in capitalist countries, and the need, both economic and political, to maintain more or less regular relations with them. Policy was based on an uneasy compromise between the two purposes, represented respectively by the Com-

3

munist International (Comintern) and the People's Commissariat of Foreign Affairs (Narkomindel). But, after the dramatic defeat of the German rising in October 1923, after the minor failures in Estonia and Bulgaria in 1924 and 1925, and after the fiasco in China in 1927, when Comintern, having vigorously supported the bourgeois nationalist revolution, recoiled in embarrassment from the social revolution which should have crowned and completed it, the promotion of revolution no longer occupied a central place in its agenda. World revolution continued to figure in the perorations of Comintern pronouncements on every solemn occasion; it was no longer thought of as the primary condition of the survival of the Soviet regime. "Socialism in one country" had taken its place. In the early nineteen-thirties, the hypothetical contribution of the world economic crisis to the remote and problematical prospect of world revolution was far less actual than its short-term consequences for Soviet prosperity and security. The Soviet regime no longer looked for aid or comfort to the unthinkable event of a world or European revolution. Neither Stalin nor any of the leaders expected such a contingency in any foreseeable future, or even wanted it. Even the less unlikely prospect of sporadic revolutionary risings in Germany suppressed by armed force—a repetition of 1923—would do nothing but inflame hostility to the USSR in the capitalist world, and increase the danger of foreign intervention.

These developments affected Comintern more directly than any other institution, and were the culminating point in a process which had long undermined its original and professed character and purpose. Comintern in the nineteen-thirties continued to use the traditional vocabulary of international revolution. Its debates were conducted in Marxist terms. Its idiom differed markedly from that of Narkomindel. But the difference turned not on the ultimate aim, which was identical for Comintern and for Narkomindel; it turned only on ways and means of promoting the security of the USSR. And, if a theoretical justification was sought in Comintern for this activity, it could be found in the argument that the USSR was the one bulwark of communism in a hostile world, and its defence was therefore a primary and overriding interest of communists everywhere. Article 14 of the "twenty-one conditions" of 1920 had already required from communist parties "unconditional support to every Soviet republic in its struggle against counter-revolutionary forces".[1]

[1] *Kommunisticheskii Internatsional v Dokumentakh* (1933), p. 103.

Differences about ways and means between Comintern and Narkomindel were complicated by a controversy among the leaders of Comintern, which grew sharper with Hitler's rise to power. The hard-liners, firmly entrenched in revolutionary orthodoxy, argued that communist parties could best serve the Soviet cause by inexorably pressing home the threat of revolution against their national governments, which would thereby be incapacitated or deterred from hostile action against the USSR. The more flexible, though they found it difficult at first openly to contest these views, came round slowly to the opinion that communist parties could profitably collaborate with other Left parties opposed to their bourgeois national governments, especially to those of a Fascist complexion, even with parties which did not accept the revolutionary programme of communism. No higher authority intervened to settle the issue between these two conflicting attitudes. Bukharin, the last effective head of Comintern, had been deposed in 1928. Manuilsky was the representative of the Russian party central committee in the Comintern hierarchy, but dared not move far without explicit authority which was rarely forthcoming. Kuusinen, the Finn, represented the international facade of Comintern, but carried no weight. These were the two leading "flexibles". The protagonists of the hard line were Bela Kun, still invested with some prestige as the head of the short-lived Soviet Government of Hungary in 1919, Knorin, an active Russian of Latvian origin,[2] and Lozovsky, the head of Profintern; and at the outset they probably enjoyed majority support in the ramshackle Comintern bureaucracy. Molotov, Stalin's mouth-piece, was silent. Stalin, heavily engaged elsewhere, was not tempted to concern himself with the petty disputes of an institution he had always despised.

The slow process of the "Bolshevization" of foreign communist parties, initiated in the twenty-one conditions of 1920, and proclaimed at the fifth congress of Comintern in 1924, reached its logical conclusion with the consolidation of Stalin's dictatorship. By the end of 1929, long and often bitter struggles within the German, French, Polish, Czechoslovak, British and American parties had been ended by firm decisions of Comintern to cast its mantle over one of the contending factions, and by the expulsion from the party, or removal from the leadership, of those who contested the decisions. After this time, changes in the leadership of parties were

[2] See *Foundations of a Planned Economy, 1926–1929*, Vol. 3, p. 579.

effected by *fiat* from Moscow, and with little pretence of debate or choice within the parties themselves. The parties were firmly bound together by the obligatory acceptance of the supreme duty to defend the USSR against its enemies, who were by definition the enemies of communism. Yet, notwithstanding this apparently total subordination, the persistence of stubborn dissensions within the Comintern hierarchy in Moscow allowed and even encouraged the proliferation of similar dissensions within and between communist parties, and left these parties a certain conditional freedom to air their opinions. The pattern was not uniform. The French, the Austrian and—more hesitantly and with stronger internal opposition—the British, parties moved gradually into the "flexible" camp. The German party was divided; but between communist and social-democratic leaders and many of their followers, mutual animosity was too deep and ingrained to permit of collaboration even when they both became Hitler's victims. Long experience of illegality and persecution made the Italian and Polish parties special cases. It was not until 1935 that the combined forces of Comintern, in the USSR and abroad, were fully mobilized in support of the united popular, anti-Fascist front of resistance to German and Japanese aggression. It would be misleading to depict Comintern and its component parties in the early nineteen-thirties as a monolithic structure responding blindly to the dictates of a single supreme authority.

The most direct concern of Soviet foreign relations at the turn of the year 1929–1930 was, as so often in the past decade, with Germany. The Young plan, which substantially reduced Germany's reparations obligations, had just been negotiated with the western Allies; its signature in January 1930 was sweetened by a promise to withdraw the army of occupation from the Rhineland five years earlier than the date fixed in the Versailles treaty. In Moscow this was read as a continuation of the Locarno policy, which attempted to re-integrate Germany into western Europe, and loosen the ties which bound her to the USSR. What rankled most was that the Young plan had been negotiated by a Left–Centre coalition government headed by a social-democrat Chancellor, Müller. Animosity between KPD and SPD had started from the moment of the foundation of the KPD in January 1919, when social-democrats first abandoned, and then helped to crush, the incipient German revolution; and rivalry continued between them for the allegiance of the German workers. In the middle nineteen-twenties a fresh source of discord emerged. Throughout the Locarno period the SPD became the most loyal and consistent supporter of the western orientation in German foreign policy; besides the KPD, only the parties of the Right showed any enthusiasm for the eastern connexion symbolized by the Rapallo treaty. In 1926 it was the SPD which disclosed and denounced the secret Soviet–German military agreements. By the end of the decade, and especially after the installation in 1928 of the Müller government, the western orientation, and the resulting coolness in Soviet–German relations, constituted in the eyes of Moscow the cardinal sin of the SPD, and was the main source of the righteous indignation of Comintern. This reached its peak with the acceptance of the Young plan. Thälmann in a speech in the Reichstag called the Young plan "a military pact against the Soviet Union".[3] Ample fuel was therefore available for the campaign, prescribed by the sixth congress of Comintern in 1928, of unqualified vituperation of social-democracy. The campaign, though of general application, had been directed primarily against the SPD; the branding of social-democracy as social-Fascism had begun in Germany and was inspired by German conditions.[4] Nowhere was the rift between communist and social-democratic workers driven so deep as in Germany, with much constant encouragement from leaders on both sides.

Bitter animosities spread to the trade unions. Though the movement in Germany was not formally split, as in France and Czechoslovakia, between rival socialist and communist federations affiliated respectively to the Amsterdam International and to Profintern, the KPD kept up incessant pressure to infiltrate and control social-democratic trade union organs. At the end of 1929 it set up an organization called the Revolutionary Trade Union Opposition (Revolutionäre Gewerkschaftsopposition or RGO) to strengthen and systematize resistance to social-democratic domination of the trade unions, and to create a communist centre of power within them.[5] Its president, Merker, who was also the head of

[3] *Verhandlungen des Reichstags*, CCCCXXVI (1930), 3939; the speech is also in E. Thälmann, *Reden und Aufsätze*, ii (1956), 278–304.

[4] See *Foundations of a Planned Economy, 1926–1929*, Vol. 3, Note C, pp. 648–653.

[5] Thälmann's speech at the first national congress of the RGO on November 30, 1929, is in E. Thälmann, *Reden und Aufsätze*, ii (1956), 272–277. Planned on the lines of the National Minority Movement in Great Britain (see *Foundations of a*

the trade union section of the KPD, was an uncompromising supporter of Lozovsky's drive for powerful communist organizations in the trade union movement acting under the aegis of Profintern, and sought to achieve as much independence as he could for the RGO. Early in 1930, in an article on "Lenin and the Political Strike", he called for strikes for economic ends which could readily be transformed into revolutionary struggles for power.[6] Like Lozovsky, Merker would have liked to press on with the formation of Red trade unions in opposition to the reformist unions, but was curbed by official reluctance.[7]

The mood in the KPD at the beginning of 1930 was both complacent and combative. In successive articles the *Rote Fahne* affirmed that the KPD had not, "since 1923, faced such far-reaching revolutionary prospects as at the present time", that the proletariat would not allow itself to be provoked by the bourgeoisie, but would "choose the moment for a decisive fight to the death", and that the German workers were "preparing for a mass political strike".[8] *Pravda* appeared to endorse this mood of optimism, declaring that Germany was one of the "weak links" where "a direct and immediate threat" existed of a break in the imperialist chain.[9] Thus encouraged, the ambitious Merker went beyond his trade union brief, and put himself forward as the exponent on a broader front of the hard-line policies proclaimed by Comintern. In an article entitled "The Next Link in the Chain", which had the first place in the KPD journal for February 1, he boldly asserted the consequences of the American economic crisis for Germany:

> Germany confronts the most violent dissensions between classes, whose extent and force far exceed the struggles of the years 1921–1923, and with iron insistence place on the agenda for the revolutionary proletariat the struggle for the overthrow of the

Planned Economy, 1926–1929, Vol. 3, pp. 332–333), it was more elaborately organized; in July 1930 584 delegates attended a RGO conference in Berlin. Similar organizations existed in Czechoslovakia and Austria (*Protokoll des V Kongresses der Roten Gewerkschaftsinternationale* (1930), ii, 258–259, 263).

[6] *Internationale Presse-Korrespondenz*, No. 5, January 14, 1930, pp. 91–92.

[7] For Lozovsky's campaign see *Foundations of a Planned Economy, 1926–1929*, Vol. 3, pp. 171–175, 252–254; for the more cautious attitude of Stalin and Thälmann see *ibid*. Vol. 3, p. 452, note 208.

[8] *Die Rote Fahne*, January 1, 17, February 1, 1930.

[9] *Pravda*, January 2, 3, 1930.

bourgeoisie and the establishment of the proletarian dictator-ship—if the communist vanguard succeeds in mobilizing and organizing the masses for these gigantic revolutionary struggles. The objective conditions for these struggles are developing at a rapid rate.[10]

A few months earlier Merker's prognostications would have been received in Moscow, perhaps with some private scepticism, but with public applause. Now, in an atmosphere of gathering anxiety, the prospect of an imminent revolutionary situation in Germany provoked alarm, and Merker's activities called urgently for a restraining hand.

Comintern had from an early date shared the general preoccup-ation with the onset of the economic crisis,[11] and quickly fastened on mass unemployment as its major evil. A proposal for an "international day" of demonstrations against unemployment on March 6, 1930, was approved by the political secretariat of IKKI on January 16, and elaborated by a conference of communist parties held on January 31 in Berlin under the auspices of the Western European Bureau of Comintern (WEB);[12] and Pravda, on February 2, 1930, looked to "millions of unemployed" as "the starting-point of mass struggles". The first pronouncement of Comintern on the crisis came from the meeting of an "enlarged presidium" of IKKI which lasted from February 8 to 28, 1930. Manuilsky delivered the main report on "The World Economic Crisis and the Re-volutionary Upsurge". The crisis had stimulated the class struggle; "the radicalization of the masses is no legend." Manuilsky announ-ced the international demonstration of the unemployed to be held on March 6; this would constitute a protest of the workers against attempts by the bourgeoisie to "shuffle off all the consequences of the ripening world economic crisis on to their shoulders". But some later passages in the report struck a more cautious note; and the speaker ended with a discussion of united front tactics in which he

[10] Die Internationale, No. 3, February 1, 1930, p. 65.

[11] Kommunisticheskii Internatsional, 1930, Nos. 2 and 3, carried a series of articles on the economic situation in several important countries, including Germany, France and the United States.

[12] Georgii Dimitrov: Vydayushchiisya Deyatel' Kommunisticheskogo Dvizheniya (1972), pp. 89–90, quoting archives; for WEB see p. 88 below.

dwelt heavily on the importance of supporting workers' "partial demands".[13]

The resolution on the report treated the economic crisis as primarily an American phenomenon, which "liquidates the bourgeois legend of the 'permanent prosperity' of the United States (Hoover), and deals a crushing blow at social-democratic theories of 'organized capitalism'", the last phrase being a hit at Bukharin. Social-democrats were once more branded as "social-Fascists". The "fundamental task" of communist parties was to win over the masses. A complete contrast existed between the "ruinous consequences of the economic crisis for capitalism", and the "economic upsurge" in the USSR, based on the "creative initiative of the proletariat" and "the transition from individual peasant cultivation to large collective cultivation". The parties should engage in "a broad campaign of explanation" about the grandiose achievements of socialist construction. The slogan of "the mass political strike" was to be popularized; and the threat that more parties would soon be placed under a legal ban inspired a demand for "the combination in practice of methods of open and illegal work". The resolution put the number of unemployed in the United States (still the main centre of the crisis) at 6 million, in Germany ("where the economic crisis is only beginning") at 3.5 million, in Britain ("which has not yet entered the crisis phase") at 2 million; throughout the capitalist world 17 million people were unemployed and 60 million (including families) reduced to beggary. But the tone was matter-of-fact and anxious. The resolution was noticeably free from conventional appeals for revolutionary action.[14] Molotov delivered an immensely long report on the achievements of the USSR;[15] and this was greeted in a resolution which ended with the

[13] Manuilsky's report, together with his reply to the debate, was published belatedly in instalments in *Internationale Presse-Korrespondenz*, No. 35, April 23, 1930, pp. 799–803; No. 36, April 25, 1930, pp. 821–824; No. 37, April 29, 1930, pp. 835–843; No. 38, May 2, 1930, pp. 857–861; for an endorsement of the cautious conclusion see his article on "partial demands" (*ibid.* No. 29, March 28, 1930, pp. 693–695). "Partial" or "day-to-day" demands were workers' economic demands which did not have a revolutionary character. For a leading article by Merker on preparations for the "international day" see *ibid.* No. 21, February 28, 1930, pp. 481–482, for reports on it *ibid.* No. 23, March 7, 1930, pp. 543–545, No. 24, March 11, 1930, pp. 577–581.

[14] *Kommunisticheskii Internatsional v Dokumentakh* (1933), pp. 915–925.

[15] This was printed belatedly in several instalments in *Internationale Presse-Korrespondenz*, No. 30, April 1, 1930, pp. 727–731, No. 31, April 4, 1930, pp. 739–740,

exhortation to communist parties to rally to "the defence of the proletarian dictatorship".[16]

The most significant debate of the session, however, related to the affairs of the KPD. Thälmann's report did not stray far from the current orthodoxy of Comintern. He asserted that "the German bourgeoisie, like the bourgeoisie in all other countries, is trying to utilize two methods, the method of social-Fascism and the method of Fascism", and that the latest developments in Germany "demonstrate the progressive growing together of social-Fascism with national Fascism".[17] Gusev in a militant speech described attempts to conciliate social-democrats as "opportunism in practice".[18] The resolution on "the tasks of the KPD" was couched for the most part in conventional terms. A passage on the "revolutionary trade union organization" called on it to intensify its influence over the masses of workers and among the unemployed, but was notably silent on the vexed question of the formation of Red unions. The resolution called for "a mobilization of the masses against the growing threat of a ban on the communist party, and for the struggle for a legal existence". But it also prescribed "a development of broad self-criticism from top to bottom", and ended on the unexpected note of a need to fight against "opportunism, both open (Right) and concealed in 'revolutionary phrases' ('Left')".[19]

It was a long time since a danger from the Left had been signalled in a Comintern resolution. Lenin in the heady days of 1920 had convicted some party members of " 'Left' Infantilism", and had

---

No. 33, April 11, 1930, pp. 759–762, No. 34, April 16, 1930, pp. 777–785. A reference by Gusev (*Kommunisticheskii Internatsional*, 1930, No. 7, p. 34) to remarks made by Molotov "in one of the private discussions" suggests that he was active in the formulation of policy behind the scenes—evidently in a moderating sense.

[16] *Kommunisticheskii Internatsional v Dokumentakh* (1933), pp. 947–951; the customary May 1 manifesto of IKKI in 1930 contained the plea to "protect the first republic of the workers, defend the Soviet Union, your socialist fatherland" (*Internationale Presse-Korrespondenz*, No. 36, April 25, 1930, pp. 817–818).

[17] Thälmann's speech, together with a further speech in the German commission of the session, is in E. Thälmann, *Reden und Aufsätze*, ii (1956), 305–331; substantial extracts from both appeared in *Kommunisticheskii Internatsional*, 1930, No. 7, pp. 24–33, 42–45.

[18] An extract from Gusev's speech, delivered in the German commission, was published *ibid.* 1930, No. 7, pp. 34–41; none of the other speeches in the commission was published.

[19] *Kommunisticheskii Internatsional v Dokumentakh* (1933), pp. 944–947.

come down severely on the "revolutionary phrase".[20] In the autumn of 1929 signs of a Left deviation had been detected in the ever restive German youth movement, and severely repressed.[21] The absence of any reference to a Left deviation or danger in any of the recorded speeches at the enlarged presidium, or in the main resolution, strongly suggests that its appearance at the end of the resolution on the KPD was a last-minute after-thought; and it can hardly have been mere coincidence that the resolution was drafted approximately at the same moment as Stalin's famous letter to the party "Dizziness through Success", in which he called a halt to the headlong process of collectivization, and censured "people who think themselves 'Leftists' ", prescribing "a struggle on two fronts— both against those who lag behind and against those who rush ahead".[22] The party's call for caution, and the very phrases in which it was couched, seeped through from domestic to international policy; the "struggle on two fronts", which appeared for the first time in Stalin's letter, was soon to become a commonplace in Comintern pronouncements. Thorez, in an article written after the sixteenth Russian party congress which he attended in June 1930, described "the 'Left' deviations which made their appearance in the policy of collectivization" as "a reminiscence of Trotskyism";[23] this must have been current talk in Moscow at the time. Left deviations, whether at home or abroad, were likely to be branded as Trotskyism. An article in the Comintern journal bracketed the Russian party with the KPD, the Czechoslovak party and KIM as having "carried out important work in the struggle against the 'Left' twist".[24]

[20] Lenin, *Polnoe Sobranie Sochinenii*, xxxv, 343, 353.

[21] The central committee of the German youth league in December 1929 had dealt not only with a "Right deviation" ("the chief danger"), but with a "Left danger of isolation from the masses", taking the form of "non-application of the united front from below" (*Die Internationale*, No. 3, February 1930, pp. 77–78); in the spring of 1930 the central committee of KIM condemned "sectarianism and Left deviation in the form also of a growth of terrorist-putschist moods" in the youth leagues of Italy, Sweden, Czechoslovakia and Yugoslavia, and "rejection or underestimate of partial demands" in France and Czechoslovakia (*Internationale Presse-Korrespondenz*, No. 39, May 6, 1930, pp. 385–386).

[22] Stalin, *Sochineniya*, xii, 191–199. The session of the enlarged presidium ended on February 28; the letter was published in *Pravda*, March 2, 1930.

[23] *Oeuvres de Maurice Thorez*, II, i (1950), 69.

[24] *Kommunisticheskii Internatsional*, No. 13–14, 1930, p. 11; the word "zagib" means a twist or kink—something less than a deviation.

The warning signal from Moscow was promptly read in Berlin. *Pravda*, commenting on the session of the presidium, sagely observed that the KPD still had much to do before it would be in a condition "to give decisive and victorious battle to the bourgeoisie and to social-democracy".[25] A further article on "The Struggle against Fascism" which Merker had submitted for publication in the party journal in March 1930 was held over; and its place was taken by the first instalment of an article by Remmele under the title "Keep in Step! Why the Struggle Must be Waged on Two Fronts" (Stalin's formula), which eventually spread over three months and four instalments. Remmele, having dismissed Right opportunism in familiar terms, made it clear that his real business was with a "new type of Leftism", characterized by "laudatory, loud-mouthed swaggering over the smallest advances and successes", and by indulgence in talk "without the party having the power to translate this talk into action". The Right opportunists refused to recognize social-Fascism even in the SPD; the Left opportunists admitted no distinctions, and "designate all phenomena of political life as 'social-Fascism'". Without naming Merker, the article quoted Merker's phrase about "the battlefields of the decisive struggles", and retorted indignantly that, to the millions of workers whom the party was seeking to win over, the writer had nothing to offer but "battlefields and revolutionary tribunals". The instalment ended with the call for "*a united front with the workers in the free and in the social-democratic unions and 'beyond that' with the unorganized workers*".[26]

The line having been thus laid down, Thälmann on March 20, 1930, made a major policy speech to the central committee of the KPD, taking the form of a report on the proceedings of the IKKI presidium. It contained a noteworthy characterization of current events in the USSR:

> Not bureaucratically from above, not with revolver in hand, but through the daily exercise of the right of consensus (Mitbestimmung) by the whole population, must the annihilation of the *Kulak* status (Kulakentum) be carried out, though this naturally does not preclude the use of particular measures of compulsion against the *Kulaks*.

[25] *Pravda*, March 1, 1930.
[26] *Die Internationale*, No. 5–6, March 1/15, 1930, pp. 135–138; Merker's second article was published later (*ibid*. No. 8–9, May 1, 1930, pp. 259–266), immediately after Remmele's reply to it (see p. 14 below).

Thälmann quoted a cautious observation of Stalin that "a revolutionary upsurge" did not imply "a leap into an immediately
revolutionary situation". The main target was Merker, who was
still not mentioned by name. In general, "even in Germany the
Right danger should be regarded as the chief danger". But it was
essential "to fight equally with Bolshevik ruthlessness against 'Left'
sectarian deviations in our own ranks". Thälmann quoted passages
from other articles by Merker or his supporters to demonstrate the
conclusion that the "Right opportunist position has unfortunately
of late found a counterpart in the tendency to designate all
phenomena of political life as social-Fascism".[27] The committee
dutifully passed a detailed resolution accusing unnamed "Left
sectarians" of failing to pursue efforts to detach the social-
democratic workers from their leaders, of underestimating the
importance of work in reformist trade unions, and of neglecting the
campaign to preserve the legality of the party. The Leftists had "cut
across revolutionary mass tactics" and "discredited the party line".
Right opportunism could be defeated only "if the party unsparingly
roots out 'Left' sectarianism".[28]

The resolution did not identify the "sectarians", and was adopted
unanimously. But Merker, whose supporters were numerous in the
party, though not among the top leaders, was in no doubt what was
meant, and on March 27 addressed an urgent appeal to IKKI, not
apparently mentioning the resolution, but denouncing Remmele's
article as heretical.[29] If Merker counted on help from his mentor,
Lozovsky, he was disappointed. Lozovsky too had his difficulties,
and was not one to sacrifice himself in a lost cause. The appeal
elicited no response. Meanwhile Remmele published the second
instalment of his article, once more not naming Merker, but quoting
liberally from the central committee's resolution.[30] An article in the
Comintern journal, entitled "The KPD in a Struggle on Two
Fronts", while still referring to the Right as the "chief danger",
devoted itself almost entirely to Merker, whose "sectarian 'Left'
view of the social-democratic workers as a solid reactionary mass"

[27] E. Thälmann, *Reden und Aufsätze*, ii (1956), 332–398; for Stalin's observations
see *Sochineniya*, xii, 189.

[28] *Internationale Presse-Korrespondenz*, No. 29, March 28, 1930, pp. 713–715; for a
report of this session see *ibid.* No. 28, March 25, 1930, pp. 687–688.

[29] The appeal is known only from the politburo resolution of April 5 (see p. 15
below).

[30] *Die Internationale*, No. 7, April 1, 1930, pp. 198–221.

led him to reject or ignore the fundamental task of the party, "the struggle for a proletarian *united front from below*".[31] Finally, on April 5, 1930, the party politburo adopted a long resolution which betrayed the righteous indignation of the KPD leaders at Merker's attempt to enlist support against them in Moscow. It endorsed the terms of the central committee resolution of March 20–21 and of Remmele's article, and declared that Merker's standpoint "differs in principle from the party line". Merker represented a "sectarian Left opportunism which treats the masses of social-democratic workers as class enemies, not as proletarians, instead of freeing them from the influence of their social-Fascist leaders and winning them for the proletarian revolution". It accused him of forming a fraction in defiance of party decisions, and reminded him that such action was "incompatible with membership of the communist party". It did not, however, expel him from the party or even from the central committee, but relieved him of his posts as member of the secretariat and head of the trade union section of the party.[32] A "check" of major party organizations, which "did not have the character of a 'purge'",[33] was evidently a warning to Merker's followers.

Nothing in the controversy suggested any weakening in the determination to brand the SPD and its leaders as social-Fascists and a main prop of the bourgeoisie. But Merker was accused by Remmele of lumping together all hostile elements in the category of social-Fascism; the class enemy was seen as "a uniformly re-actionary mass". This ruled out any effective distinction between the parties of the Centre or the Right and the SPD, or between the SPD leaders and the mass of workers enrolled in the party or in social-democratic unions. The result was a profound pessimism which abandoned hope in the revolutionary role of the proletariat. "National Fascism", represented by the Stahlhelm, Hitler's storm-troopers and similar para-military organizations, scarcely impinged on the discussion. Hitler's National Socialist German Workers' Party (NSDAP or Nazis) was still a small splinter group with 12 seats in the Reichstag, an upstart on the fringe of German politics whose credentials were not taken seriously. It made some headway in provincial and local elections in the winter of 1929–1930; and in January 1930 Frick, one of the Nazi leaders, had become a minister

[31] *Kommunisticheskii Internatsional*, 1930, No. 13–14, pp. 9–11.
[32] *Die Rote Fahne*, April 6, 1930.
[33] *Die Internationale*, No. 8–9, May 1, 1930, p. 267.

in the Thuringian government. But its sensational electoral successes lay ahead. Martynov in an article in the Comintern journal
entitled "Decaying Capitalism and the Fascisization of the Bourgeois State" consoled his readers with the thought that the process
"breeds ever sharper forces of struggle by the revolutionary
proletariat" and was "a necessary condition of its decisive
victory".[34] A subsequent article signed with the initial S was a rare
and early attempt to diagnose the phenomenon of "National
Fascism in Germany", which deserved "the greatest attention" from
communists. It noted in particular that the Nazis treated communism as "only one shade and variety of 'Jewish social-democracy'".[35]
Remmele may claim some credit as the first German communist to
recognize, in the third instalment of his article in May 1930, that the
NSDAP was growing fast and in some districts "substantially
outstripping" the KPD. Merker's slogan, "Strike at social-Fascism,
then you will hit National Fascism", was, he declared, too simple.[36]
But, so long as the main argument turned on the role of the SPD as
the core of social-Fascism, the NSDAP remained a subsidiary
element. Eventually, in July 1930, Merker made a declaration of
submission. The episode was symptomatic of the new note of
caution in Comintern, and perhaps of a reluctance to embark on
action which might lead to clashes with the German authorities,
and exacerbate Soviet-German relations at a critical moment.

The fall of the Müller government at the end of March 1930, and
its replacement by a new coalition under Brüning which excluded
the SPD, was a move to the Right. But the ejection of the SPD was
not likely to excite displeasure in Moscow, where *Pravda* dismissed
the Müller government as "the most hostile German Government
since Rapallo".[37] The change meant that opponents as well as
supporters of the Young plan now sat side by side in the cabinet; and
the trend towards a western orientation would at least be mode-
rated.[38] Curtius, who had succeeded Stresemann as Minister for

[34] *Kommunisticheskii Internatsional*, 1930, No. 5, pp. 31–46.
[35] *Ibid.* 1930, No. 9, 99. 46–56.
[36] *Die Internationale*, No. 8–9, May 1, 1930, p. 255.
[37] *Pravda*, March 29, 1930.
[38] The Soviet Ambassador in Berlin was assured that the change of government
would not affect Soviet–German relations (*Dokumenty Vneshnei Politiki SSSR*, xiii
(1967), 183).

Foreign Affairs in the autumn of 1929, remained in office, and followed Stresemann's formula: an accommodation with the western Powers, such as Locarno or the Young plan, was followed by a balancing gesture of appeasement towards the USSR. On June 14, 1930, after lengthy negotiations, a joint Soviet–German *communiqué* was issued recording the determination of the two governments "to overcome difficulties which have arisen in the spirit of the Rapallo treaty", and "to maintain their mutual relations and proceed to the tasks which may confront them in the future".[39] Three weeks later Litvinov telegraphed to Curtius his congratulations on the ending of the occupation of the Rhineland by Allied troops.[40] At a time when Soviet relations with France were uniformly bad, and relations with the British Labour government were deteriorating, relations with Germany were a matter of supreme importance.

Nor was much excitement aroused in Moscow by the elections to the Saxon Landtag on June 22, 1930, when the NSDAP trebled its previous strength, increasing its votes by 240,000; the SPD lost 54,000 votes, the KPD gained 11,000. An article on the elections in the Comintern news-sheet called the Nazi victory "an alarm-signal for the whole Saxon, and indeed German, body of workers", while pointing out that the Nazi gains had been made entirely at the expense of the bourgeois parties and the SPD.[41] But the NSDAP was not a well organized party with a traditional membership, like the SPD.[42] It seemed inconceivable that it would ever become a serious force. The whole affair was puzzling. Hitler made violent attacks on Bolshevism and on the USSR. But he was quite as ready to denounce capitalism as Bolshevism; and the most popular plank in the Nazi platform was a passionate rejection of all those instruments, from the Versailles treaty to the Young plan, which

---

[39] *Dokumenty Vneshnei Politiki SSSR*, xiii (1967), 354.

[40] *Ibid.* xiii, 374.

[41] *Internationale Presse-Korrespondenz*, No. 53, June 24, 1930, pp. 1168–1169.

[42] Comintern was consistently impressed with the superior strength of the organization of the SPD; as late as August 1931 it wrote in its journal: "The social-democratic organizations are far more solid and more stubborn than the Fascist. Without isolating social-democracy, without destroying its mass influence, the overthrow of capitalism is impossible. Social-democracy is the stronger, more dangerous and more stubborn of these two armies precisely because it has built up its strength in the working class by exploiting the traditions of the pre-war period and the confidence of the masses which it won at that time, and has created a broad system of organization headed by a social-Fascist bureaucracy" (*Kommunisticheskii Internatsional*, 1931, No. 23, p. 5).

embodied Germany's humiliating submission to the western Powers. Like other Right parties, the NSDAP was firmly committed against the western orientation. This alone made it preferable to the spineless SPD. The policy-makers in Moscow continued to count on Hitler's implacable hostility to Versailles and to the Young plan as a welcome counter-weight to the western orientation of the social-democrats.

The sixteenth Russian party congress which met on June 26, 1930, provided a major occasion for a review of the situation, at home and abroad. Stalin opened his political report by juxtaposing the "economic *upsurge*" in the USSR with "the turn towards economic *decline*" in the capitalist world. The section on foreign relations included an ironical reference to the Young plan as an expression of "the spirit of Locarno", and a description of France as "the most aggressive and militarist country of all aggressive and militarist countries in the world". Nevertheless, Stalin cautiously insisted that "our policy is a policy of peace, and of strengthening our trade connexions with all countries".[43] It was left to Molotov to embroider these themes in his report on Comintern. The very existence of the USSR with its planned economy, he observed, "undermines the roots of world capitalism". Since the tenth IKKI a year earlier, a "revolutionary upsurge" could be discerned among the workers of many countries, though "in different forms and not at a uniform tempo". Social-democracy was once more denounced as "social-Fascism". But two errors were detected in the attitude of communists to it. The error of the Right consisted in denying the degeneration of social-democracy into social-Fascism. The "Left" error—to which Molotov devoted far more attention, and of which Merker served as an example—was to declare war on the whole body of social-democratic workers as "rotten elements" hopelessly corrupted by social-Fascism, and to make no distinction between the mass of workers and the "social-Fascist bureaucracy" in the SPD and the trade unions. Molotov briefly referred to "the immense increase in votes of the Fascist party in Saxony" (which Stalin had ignored) as evidence of "the huge offensive of the bourgeoisie against the working class", but offered only the well-worn remedy of "the tactics of the united front from below for an all-out repulse of the offensive of Fascism and social-Fascism".[44]

---

[43] Stalin, *Sochineniya*, xii, 235, 250, 256, 260.
[44] *XVI S"ezd Vsesoyuznoi Kommunisticheskoi Partii (b)* (1930), pp. 407–428.

The speech of Manuilsky, who followed Molotov, was very different in tone. Predictions of future "battles" and "victories" were fewer, and rang hollower. The stabilization of capitalism had been shattered, but not enough to galvanize the masses into revolutionary action. The membership of the German party was frozen at a total of 120,000–130,000. The French party had lost 25 per cent of its peak membership, the British and Czechoslovak parties 50 per cent. Voters for communist candidates in German and French elections far outnumbered members of the parties; only a small fraction of workers who belonged to the Red trade unions in France and Czechoslovakia were party members. Manuilsky attributed all this to deep-seated defects of organization, and made no reference to Left errors.[45] Lozovsky, who spoke on the affairs of Profintern, was mainly concerned to trounce his enemies on the Right, including Tomsky and Yaglom, but found room for a reference to "the other so-called 'Left' view that the economic struggle in present circumstances is hopeless, that one must carry on only a political struggle, and that it is therefore not worth while to engage in economic battles".[46] Khitarov, the youth leader, followed Manuilsky in deploring the declining numbers and floating membership of communist parties, and described the situation in the youth leagues as "completely unsatisfactory". He dilated at some length on the " 'Left'-sectarian moods" prevailing in the leagues, which constituted "a fundamental barrier to the development of our organizations into mass organizations".[47] Nobody attempted to define the content of "Left sectarianism". But it evidently consisted in an undue eagerness to translate revolutionary words into revolutionary action—what in some contexts was labelled "adventurism".

The most significant contribution to the debate was made by the fraternal delegate of the KPD, Neumann.[48] "The central question of the class struggle," he declared, was the struggle against "the transference of the burdens of the Young plan on to the shoulders of the workers". The second question was "the Fascisization of Germany", which marked the transformation of the economic crisis into a political crisis. The petty bourgeoisie in fear of economic ruin

[45] *Ibid.* pp. 428–434.
[46] *Ibid.* p. 443.
[47] *Ibid.* pp. 457–459.
[48] For Neumann see *Foundations of a Planned Economy, 1926–1929*, Vol. 3, pp. 840–841.

stood on the ground, not of the class struggle, but of "patriotism, under the banner and the slogans of the national-Fascist movement." Such successes as those of the Nazis in Saxony "do not indicate that the masses of the petty bourgeoisie are satisfied with capitalism, but that they are dissatisfied with capitalism". In terms which involuntarily recalled the brief and ambivalent flirtation of the KPD with the National-Socialists in 1923 under the catchword of "the Schlageter line", Neumann proposed "an ideological–political struggle to break the Fascist ranks and win over to our side the toiling masses which now follow Fascism". This was to be done "under the slogan of a revolutionary struggle against the Young plan", but was not inconsistent, any more than it had been in 1923, with a campaign in the name of the proletariat against the Fascists. Social-democracy was held responsible for the rise of Fascism, but was not identified with it. Towards the end of his speech, Neumann admitted "the negative effect of all kinds of 'Left' deviations, resulting not so much from Merker's 'theories' as from behaviour of the Merker type"; these "Left-sectarian tendencies and groups" were said to set up "a wire-fence against the masses . . . which we ought to lead".[49]

The resolutions of the congress showed only a faint trace of these anxieties. The main resolution based on Stalin's report referred to "increasing preparation of war against the USSR" as a result of the economic crisis, called for "*a firm and decisive policy of peace and of strengthening the fraternal union and solidarity of the workers and toiling masses of the USSR with the workers and toilers of the capitalist countries and of the colonies*", and ended with the conventional salute to "*the international proletarian revolution*". The much shorter resolution on Molotov's report did justice to the familiar theme of the struggle against social-Fascism, but carefully commended "the struggle on two fronts—both against open Right opportunism, which is the chief danger, and against 'Left' trends, which strengthen this opportunism", and consisted in "a rejection of steady ordinary work and of the daily struggle to win the masses, concealed in 'Left' phrase-making".[50]

The sixteenth party congress was followed, on August 15, 1930, by the fifth congress of Profintern. Kuusinen appeared at the first

    [49] *XVI S" ezd Vsesoyuznoi Kommunisticheskoi Partii (b)* (1931), pp. 438–442; for the episode of 1923 see *The Interregnum, 1923–1924*, pp. 177–186.
    [50] *KPSS v Rezolyutsiyakh* (1954), iii, 11–12, 22, 32–36.

sitting to bring greetings from IKKI and to sound a note of caution, perhaps designed to restrain the ebullient Lozovsky. The danger of "isolation from the masses", as well as "the greater danger of lagging behind the masses", was to be avoided. In countries where independent Red unions did not exist, the scope of the revolutionary trade union movement must be expanded. But "we are against setting a course for the schematic creation of new unions".[51] Lozovsky admitted that Red trade unions in countries where they existed legally (France, Czechoslovakia) suffered from a declining membership, and in countries where they were illegal had "lost their mass basis". In Germany the RGO was growing, but lacked organization in the factories. He reported Right deviations in Germany, Czechoslovakia and France, and Left deviations in Germany (Merker), Cuba, Japan and France, and noted the penetration of Fascism among factory workers in Germany and Austria. Finally he came, with some embarrassment, to the question of new Red unions:

> There are comrades who take the view that new trade unions must and can be created everywhere in whatever circumstances. From no standpoint can this be recognized as correct. . . . We must guard decisively against attempts at a general creation of new unions, as well as against a general denial of the necessity to create new unions where the objective situation demands it.

But his attempts to define the conditions justifying the creation of new unions were wordy and obscure. By way of peroration he repeated the slogan with which he had ended his report at the fourth congress in 1928: "Into the factories! Into the workshops! To the masses!"[52]

The debate threw little further light on conditions in Germany which were the core of the problem. Heckert, who like Lozovsky denounced Merker, sought to probe *"the growth of Fascism and social-Fascism in the workers' movement"*. The slogan "Hit the Fascists wherever you meet them" merely led to "rough-ups between groups of communists and Fascists", in which the latter enjoyed police protection. What was required was *"an ideological struggle with*

---

[51] *Protokoll des V Kongresses der Roten Gewerkschaftsinternationale* (1930), 1, 11.

[52] *Ibid.* pp. 71–99; for the fourth congress see *Foundations of a Planned Economy, 1926–1929*, Vol. 3, p. 178.

the Fascists". In Berlin a "Fascist general", in Munich Hitler, "the leader of the Fascists", had been invited to public debates with KPD leaders. Both had refused. But the implication that more could be hoped for from appeals to Fascist workers than to social-democratic workers was not allowed to emerge. Heckert was severer than Lozovsky in his condemnation of Merker and Left sectarianism, and more forthcoming in his interpretation of the united front.[53] Dahlem, the representative of the RGO, modestly disclaimed any desire to turn it into an independent trade union organization, and deprecated "tendencies" to abandon work in the reformist unions.[54] A Polish delegate defined the dilemma of the creation of new unions. The trade union opposition must be built up on the "old forms", and not on antagonism to them. But he added that "in Germany the old forms are already inadequate for us".[55] Hardly anyone else broached the issue; and Lozovsky in his reply to the debate took refuge in the formula that "the creation of new trade unions cannot proceed according to a schema written up on a wall", and was a question of "the influence of the revolutionary trade union movement among the masses".[56]

The main resolution of the congress firmly repeated the condemnation of the social-Fascists who were at the head of the German and British trade union movements. It denounced both the Right deviation which opposed independent trade union organization and sought compromises with social-Fascism, and the Left sectarianism (of which Merker was "the crassest expression") which refused to distinguish between reformist leaders and the mass of trade union members. It was an error to ignore the circumstances in which "in a number of countries . . . the creation of new revolutionary trade unions was necessary, and will be necessary in the future". On the other hand, nothing could justify "the mechanical creation of new trade unions" where such conditions did not exist.[57] The impression remained that Lozovsky, having abandoned Merker, had made the best of a compromise between his ambition for an aggressive revolutionary trade union movement under the

[53] *Protokoll des V Kongresses der Roten Gewerkschaftsinternationale* (1930), i, 100–123.

[54] *Ibid.* i, 237; according to *Geschichte der Deutschen Arbeiterbewegung*, iv (1966), 273–274, Ulbricht and Florin had spoken in the central committee of the KPD in July 1930 against the formation of Red unions in Germany.

[55] *Protokoll des V Kongresses der Roten Gewerkschaftsinternationale* (1930), i, 464.

[56] *Ibid.* i, 510.

[57] *Ibid.* i, 516–544.

leadership of Profintern and the restraints imposed by party policy speaking through the organs of Comintern.

The autumn of 1930 was a period of increasing tension for the Soviet leaders. The collectivization crisis had been temporarily staved off in the spring, but not solved. Pressures in industry were mounting. Nor was the external prospect any more reassuring. As the economic crisis deepened, and the world drifted slowly towards disaster, anxieties multiplied in Moscow, taking the familiar form of fear that the western Powers would seek to solve their difficulties, and sink their differences, in combined action against the USSR. Denunciation of western imperialists, and especially of France, still thought of as the spear-head of western hostility, filled the Soviet and Comintern press. In November a group of industrial managers were put on trial for industrial sabotage; several of them made confessions, and alleged that the sabotage had been organized and subsidized from French sources. *Pravda*, in an article entitled "International Social-Democracy in the Service of Intervention", contrived to link the trial with imperialist preparations for war against the USSR, fostered by social-democrats.[58] Nor was all well in the party. Lominadze and Shatskin, once prominent figures of the party Left, who had been denounced for some ill-defined offences, and had recanted their errors, at the end of 1929, were now once more accused, in company with Syrtsov, whose sympathies were with the Right, of forming a "'Left'–Right bloc"—apparently the first use of a label which was to become common in party and Comintern terminology—against the party line. Lominadze and Syrtsov were expelled from the party central committee, and Shatskin from the central control commission.[59]

For Comintern the storm-centre of the crisis was in Germany. The German problem was baffling, but inescapable—if only because the KPD could not remain silent. The Reichstag, having

[58] *Pravda*, December 16, 1930; full reports of the trial were carried by *Pravda* in the first half of December. In March 1931 a group of Mensheviks was tried on a charge of a conspiracy hatched abroad for the restoration of capitalism in the USSR.

[59] *Pravda*, December 1, 1930; an article in *Kommunisticheskii Internatsional*, 1931, No. 8, p. 3, commenting on the Syrtsov–Lominadze–Shatskin affair, remarked that "Right and 'Left'" groupings in foreign parties were combining to resist the leadership of Comintern.

refused to accept Brüning's economic programme, was dissolved in July 1930, new elections being fixed for September 14.[60] A manifesto embodying the KPD election programme was published in the *Rote Fahne* on August 24, 1930.[61] The two striking features of the manifesto were the prominence accorded to the motive of national liberation, and the hitherto unaccustomed concentration on "the Fascists (National-Socialists)" as the main target of denunciation. Scorn and contempt were poured on the pretence of the Nazis "that they fight for the liberation of the German people". Only the KPD had consistently opposed the "Versailles robber peace" and its sequel "(Locarno, the Dawes and Young plans etc.)". Everywhere that Fascism was in power, it oppressed "the peoples subject to it (in Italy the Germans and Croats, in Poland the Ukrainians, Belorussians and Germans, in Finland the Swedes etc.)". The Nazis were pointedly reminded that "Hitler and his confederates" had not uttered a word against "the forcible annexation of the South Tirol to Fascist Italy" or "the sufferings of the German peasant population". The social-democrats (the term "social-Fascist" was not used) were relegated to a subsidiary role as "hangman's assistants for the German bourgeoisie" and "voluntary agents of French and Polish imperialism". "Wherever the capitalists and their agents the social-democrats are at the helm, the masses are . . . exploited." Only in the USSR were industry and agriculture advancing, and had unemployment been overcome.

After the rhetoric of the introductory manifesto the programme itself was couched in relatively sober language. It began by recognizing "the full right of self-determination of all nations", and by predicting that, "by agreement with the revolutionary workers of France, England, Poland, Italy, Czechoslovakia etc.", those German territories which so desired would have the possibility of joining Soviet Germany. It proceeded to the familiar indictment of German capitalism, appealed to "all workers who are still under the spell of the inveterate Fascist deceivers of the people" to break decisively and finally with National-Socialism" (the only mention of the Nazis in the programme itself), and concluded with the traditional "Long live the dictatorship of the proletariat! Long live Soviet Germany!" The main authorship can be attributed with

[60] *Ibid.* 1931, No. 5, p. 4.
[61] Reprinted in E. Thälmann, *Reden und Aufsätze*, ii (1956), 530–540.

some confidence to Neumann.[62] It reflected the ideas expressed by him at the Russian party congress two months earlier,[63] being designed to woo for the KPD the votes of those who had been attracted into the Nazi ranks by Hitler's chauvinistic appeals. While the clear tokens of Neumann's personal style refute any suspicion that it was drafted in the Comintern secretariat, Neumann had reason to believe that it would cause no displeasure in Moscow. Nevertheless, by its emphasis on the theme of national liberation and its frank appeal to the petty-bourgeois followers of the NSDAP, it marked a silent departure from the "class against class" ideology of the "third period", and foreshadowed the slogan of a "people's revolution" which Thälmann was to launch some months later.[64] The tone of the programme was echoed in a leading article in *Pravda* denouncing "the bombastic, completely hypocritical, nationalistic campaign" of the "national-Fascists" against the Young plan.

> The basic task now confronting the KPD *in the struggle against national-Fascism* [it continued] consists of *tearing the mask off the national-Fascists as fighters for the national independence of the German people*.[65]

The sensation of the elections of September 14, 1930, was the triumph of the NSDAP, which increased the number of its deputies from 12 to 107, making it the second largest party in the Reichstag. The KPD increased its votes from 3.3 to 4.6 million and the number of its deputies from 54 to 77. Most of the other parties lost ground, the SPD complement of deputies falling from 152 to 143. The *Rote Fahne* confidently announced that "September 14 was the high point of the National-Socialist movement in Germany", and that "what comes after can be only decline and fall"; and Heckert, one of the leaders of the KPD, argued that Hitler's gains represented "only a re-grouping in the bourgeois camp", and called on the party for

---

[62] Thälmann in a major election speech of August 8, 1930, gave far less prominence to the theme of national liberation, and said very little about the Nazis (*ibid.* ii, 486–529).

[63] See pp. 19–20 above; an article by Neumann in *Internationale Presse-Korrespondenz*, No. 69, August 15, 1930, pp. 1677–1678, denounced "the deceitful assertion of the National-Socialists that they are enemies of the Young plan".

[64] See pp. 18–20 below.

[65] *Pravda*, August 17, 1930.

renewed efforts on the basis of the programme.[66] A week later a party writer declared that "the victory of Fascism . . . *carries in its womb the germ of great surprises for the bourgeoisie*".[67] The reaction in Moscow was confused. *Pravda* on September 16, 1930, after celebrating the "electoral victory" of the KPD, admitted that the sensational advance of the NSDAP represented a "temporary success of the bourgeoisie", but noted that the millions of Nazi votes revealed mass disillusionment with the capitalist system and with the Versailles treaty. It hailed the figures as indicating "the dissolution of the bourgeois order in Germany", and "the approach of growing class struggles". IKKI telegraphed its congratulations to the KPD.[68] A leading article in the Comintern journal congratulated the KPD on its "brilliant success", which testified to "the swift revolutionization of the masses", but warned it of the danger of "dizziness through success".[69] The party attempted to form a "non-party proletarian mass organization", called the Union for Struggle against Fascism, under the direction of Remmele. It claimed 100,000 members, but never seems to have been effective.[70]

The alarm caused in western financial circles by the spectacular Nazi gains led to a run on the German currency, and conjured up fears and memories of inflation. No change of government had taken place. But in November 1930 Brüning adopted the practice of emergency legislation by presidential decree which, though it did not infringe the letter of the Weimar constitution, meant the virtual end of government through the Reichstag. The SPD justified its continued support of Brüning on the principle of "lesser evil"—a doctrine which earned it the bitter mockery of the KPD. "The Fascist dictatorship is no longer a threat," declared the *Rote Fahne* on December 2, 1930: "it is already here."[71] But it drew an optimistic

[66] *Internationale Presse-Korrespondenz*, No. 78, September 16, 1930, p. 1940, No. 79, September 19, 1930, pp. 1953–1955.

[67] *Ibid.* No. 81, September 26, 1930, p. 1998.

[68] *Ibid.* No. 80, September 23, 1930, p. 1981.

[69] *Kommunisticheskii Internatsional*, 1930, No. 26, pp. 3–7; an article by Thälmann in the next issue was on similar lines, but admitted some failures which he attributed to "vacillations of a sectarian character" connected with the Merker affair (*ibid.* 1930, No. 27, pp. 16–26). Remmele in the party journal claimed that the KPD was "the only party which must and will be proved right by the objective course of development" (*Die Internationale*, No. 19–20, October 1930, p. 585).

[70] *Geschichte der Deutschen Arbeiterbewegung*, iv (1966), 268.

[71] According to Pyatnitsky's not quite convincing statement to the twelfth IKKI in September 1932, Comintern had at once objected to the *Rote Fahne* article

conclusion: "Never has the revolutionary proletariat had better prospects than now of becoming the real leader of a people's revolution in Karl Marx's sense." The terrorist acts of the Nazis were the death-pangs of German capitalism. The article was written by Neumann, at this time chief editor of the *Rote Fahne*, who now clearly aspired to lead a "Left" or radical movement of revolt in the KPD against the moderate and uninspiring leadership of Thälmann. But Neumann's "Leftism" differed sensibly from that for which Merker had incurred censure. While Merker had appealed to the rank-and-file workers of the SPD, and drew no distinction between the "social-Fascist" leaders of the SPD and the avowed Fascists of the NSDAP, Neumann directed his appeal primarily to the unemployed and unorganized workers outside the ranks of the SPD, many of them members or potential members of the NSDAP. What Neumann wanted from them was precisely what Merker wanted from the rank-and-file of SPD workers: to seduce them from their present allegiance and recruit them as allies in a proletarian revolution led by the KPD. Nor were the violent methods preached and practised by the Nazis uncongenial to his temperament, or to much current thinking in the KPD.[72] The possibility that the party would be deprived of its legal status, and reduced to illegal activities, was frequently canvassed, and even welcomed.

A belief which underlay much party thinking at this time, and lent force to Neumann's campaign, was the confident assumption that the rise of Fascism in Germany was a step on the road to the proletarian revolution, and would hasten its advent. This view had been uncannily foreshadowed by Stalin in a letter written on the eve of the abortive German rising of 1923: "Of course, the Fascists are not asleep. But it is to our advantage to let them attack first; that will

---

identifying the Brüning regime with Fascist dictatorship. Thälmann and Neumann were at this moment on the way to Moscow; on their arrival Neumann obstinately defended the formula, while Thälmann was "not altogether in agreement" with it (*XII Plenum IKKI* (1933), ii, 15). The issue was still being debated at the central committee of the KPD in January 1931 and at the eleventh IKKI in March (see pp. 31, 36 below).

[72] Neumann is said to have enjoyed the support of a large part of the party central committee and almost all the leaders of the youth league (M. Buber-Neumann, *Kriegsschauplätze der Weltrevolution* (1967), p. 332)—a perhaps exaggerated, but not wholly false, picture; the spokesman of KIM at the twelfth IKKI in September 1932 accused him and his supporters of having "tried to set the youth league against the leadership of the party" (*XII Plenum IKKI* (1933), ii, 150).

rally the whole working class around the communists."[73] When the
Nazis early in 1930 began to emerge as a serious force on the
German political scene, Martynov had written in the Comintern
journal that the process of Fascisization was "a necessary condition"
of the victory.[74] A resolution of the central committee of the KPD of
June 4, 1930, diagnosed "the stronger emergence of Fascism in the
present period" as "an unavoidable concomitant of the ripening of a
revolutionary situation".[75] It was the hold of the SPD on a majority
of the organized workers, not the temporary appeal of Nazi
propaganda to the masses, which constituted the obstacle to the
proletarian revolution in Germany. The economic pressures which
accounted for the rise of Nazism would inevitably sharpen the
revolutionary consciousness of the proletariat. This comforting
theory of the rise of Nazism as the pace-maker of proletarian
revolution may in origin have been no more than a desperate
attempt to put the best face on a menacing and baffling
phenomenon. But it continued to flourish, and occupies an
important place among the illusions which paralysed the efforts of
the KPD and of Comintern to find a response to the Nazi offensive.

[73] For this letter, which was not published in Stalin's collected works, see *The
Interregnum, 1923–1924*, p. 187.
[74] For this article see p. 16 above.
[75] *Geschichte der Deutschen Arbeiterbewegung*, iv (1966), 528.

CHAPTER 2

THE ELEVENTH IKKI

Whatever perplexities may have beset the KPD and Comintern in the winter of 1930–1931, the guidelines of Soviet foreign policy, administered by Narkomindel, were sufficiently clear. In France the German Reichstag elections of September 1930 were viewed as proof that the premature evacuation of the Rhineland, far from reconciling the German people to the Versailles settlement, had strengthened the will to overthrow it. But what created consternation in Paris could not be unwelcome in Moscow; *Pravda* rejoined that the Nazi successes created "not a few difficulties for French imperialism", which had no desire to see "a powerful competitor in the form of German neo-imperialism".[1] The economic crisis had increased tension in Soviet relations with France and Britain. A French decree of October 30, 1930, prohibited the importation of certain categories of goods from the USSR.[2] In Britain the inflammatory speeches of Conservative diehards were reinforced by an organized campaign against "Soviet dumping" and against imports from the USSR said to have been produced by "forced labour". But these untoward developments had been balanced by a progressive improvement in official Soviet–German relations. In November 1930 the Soviet and German delegations worked closely together at Geneva in the preparatory commission for the disarmament conference. The replacement of Krestinsky as Soviet Ambassador in Berlin in the autumn of 1930 by Khinchuk, formerly Soviet trade representative to London, was perhaps inspired by the importance attached in Moscow to the maintenance and development of Soviet-German trade; and in February 1931 a large and representative delegation of German industrialists visited the USSR. Negotiations were in progress for the signature of a trade agreement, and of a protocol renewing the Soviet–German treaty of

---

[1] *Pravda*, October 28, 1930.

[2] For a Soviet protest see *Dokumenty Vneshnei Politiki SSSR*, xiii (1967), 566–568; Molotov at the session of TsIK in January 1931 called it "a preparatory step for further and more aggressive action against the USSR" (*SSSR: Tsentral'nyi Ispolnitel'nyi Komitet 5 Sozyva: 3 Sessiya* (1931), No. 1, p. 25).

April 24, 1926, and the Soviet–German conciliation convention of January 25, 1929.[3]

The international situation was reviewed by Molotov in his report to the sixth Union Congress of Soviets early in March 1931. He once more contrasted "the successes of the building of socialism in our country" with "the very deep crisis in the lands of capitalism", dwelt on the Soviet campaign for peace, on the boycott of Soviet goods, and on the threat of armed intervention from abroad. Coming to particular countries, he noted with satisfaction "a certain favourable turn since the middle of 1930 in the relations of the USSR and Germany". In Britain, "the most influential leaders of the Conservative Party and former members of the British Government" were trying to organize "a new intervention against the USSR" and "a new world war". Relations with France in the last two years had been exceptionally difficult, and concealed "an extremely serious and grave threat to the cause of world peace". The report ended with further emphasis on the Soviet devotion to peace. The note of alarm was unmistakable. But its source was found, not in Germany, but in Britain and France.[4] The puzzling developments in Germany had not sensibly modified the international prospect as seen from Moscow. The economic crisis had shaken the stability of the capitalist world. But it had not diminished— it had rather intensified—the anti-Soviet animosities of the western Powers; the policy of "French imperialism" at this juncture was said to be equally "directed against the revolutionary danger in Germany and against socialist construction in the USSR".[5] This made it all the more necessary to cling to the German alliance and to revitalize the spirit of Rapallo. Anything which fanned German

[3] The trade agreement was signed on April 14, 1931, and the protocol on June 24, 1931 (*Dokumenty Vneshnei Politiki SSSR*, xiv (1968), 395–396); for the treaty and the conciliation convention see *Socialism in One Country, 1924–1926*, Vol. 3, pp. 437–438, *Foundations of a Planned Economy, 1926–1929*, Vol. 3, p. 54.

[4] The report was reprinted, in token of its importance for foreign policy, in *Dokumenty Vneshnei Politiki SSSR*, xiv (1968), 124–159; the main points were covered in a resolution of the congress (*S"ezdy Sovetov v Rezolyutsiyakh*, iii (1960), 175–176). A long article by Radek on "Capitalist Slavery and Socialist Organization of Work" (*Internationale Presse-Korrespondenz*, No. 18, February 27, 1931, pp. 465–468, No. 20, March 3, 1931, pp. 531–535) was designed to counter the boycott of Soviet goods produced by "forced labour". The boycott campaign was denounced a few weeks later by the eleventh IKKI (*Kommunisticheskii Internatsional v Dokumentakh* (1933), p. 968).

[5] *Internationale Presse-Korrespondenz*, No. 15, February 20, 1931, pp. 396–397.

resentment against the west, and especially against France and against the Versailles system, earned applause and support.

The KPD presented, as always, the most intractable problem. The party central committee, meeting in January 1931, responded to the growing tension in a resolution on a report by Thälmann which showed few signs of flexibility. Its main novelty was the proclamation of "people's revolution" as "the chief strategic slogan of the party". It was, however, explained that the "people's revolution" was "only a synonym of the proletarian socialist revolution"; conversely, the proletarian socialist revolution was to be conceived as "a genuine people's revolution under the hegemony of the proletariat in the spirit of Marx and Lenin". Economic strikes had "the greatest political significance"; and the struggles of the workers should be linked with "the mass battles of the unemployed". The aim was to organize "a struggle of factory workers and unemployed against the offensive of the employers, a mass struggle of toilers against the realization by the Brüning government of a Fascist dictatorship, and a powerful wave of anti-Fascist mass battles against the murders and the terror of the National-Socialists". Finally:

> The party is confronted with the task of preventing National-Socialism from penetrating the working class, and of tearing away and winning over those National-Socialist workers, employees and toilers generally, who are imbued with anti-capitalist inclinations.

But this also involved the creation of "a united front with social-democratic workers and proletarian members of the Reichsbanner".[6]

The slogan of the "people's revolution", like the party programme of August 1930,[7] was plainly designed to undercut the Nazis by framing demands in "national" rather than in "class" terms,[8] though any hint of unorthodoxy was avoided by its

---

[6] The resolution was published in *Die Rote Fahne*, January 21, 1931, and extensively quoted by Thälmann at the eleventh IKKI (*XI Plenum IKKI* (1932), i, 158, 160, 182, 184); Thälmann's report was published under the significant title *Volksrevolution über Deutschland* (1931).

[7] See p. 24 above.

[8] Hitler was quoted at this time as saying that among the Nazis there were "no citizens, no proletarians, no employers, no catholics or protestants, no monarchists

identification with proletarian revolution, and by constant reference to the proletarian leadership of the movement. The leader of the campaign was once more Neumann, who at this time reached the peak of his influence in the KPD. It derived fresh impetus from the affair of Scheringer, a Reichswehr lieutenant who had joined the Nazis, and been sentenced to nine months' imprisonment for conducting Nazi propaganda in the Reichswehr. In prison he consorted with communist prisoners and read the works of Marx; and on emerging from prison, in a blaze of party publicity, some of which recalled the "Schlageter campaign" of 1923, he announced his adhesion to the KPD.[9] Mixed feelings about the Nazis still prevailed at this time in the KPD; and the widely held belief that Nazi activities were paving the way for the proletarian revolution encouraged both extravagant optimism and aggressive policies.[10] Neumann in the *Rote Fahne* conducted an active campaign on the prospects of revolution, culminating in an article on March 18, 1931, the anniversary of the Paris Commune of 1871, headed "Long Live the Commune", which compared the situation in Berlin with that in Paris on the eve of the Commune, and proclaimed that a proletarian revolution had "become, through the course of history, not only a possibility, but an inescapable necessity". The fault of the Commune had been its failure "to exterminate its enemies".

These demonstrations of militancy were watched with disquiet in Moscow. To denounce the social-democrats, the sworn enemies of German involvement with the USSR, as Fascists and social-Fascists had been perfectly acceptable. But to identify as Fascist the Brüning regime, which was striving to improve German relations with the USSR, was tactless and inopportune. The proclamation of an imminent proletarian revolution in Germany was still more

---

or republicans—only Germans" (*XI Plenum IKKI* (1932), i, 91); Trotsky alleged that Strasser had coined the phrase "people's revolution" in opposition to the Marxist class revolution (*Byulleten' Oppozitsii* (Paris), No. 21–22, May–June 1931, p. 15).

[9] *Internationale Presse-Korrespondenz*, No. 27, March 20, 1931, p. 746; *XI Plenum IKKI* (1932), i, 164–165; for the "Schlageter campaign" see *The Interregnum, 1923–1924*, pp. 179–183.

[10] For an early expression of this view see p. 28 above; it was derided by Manuilsky at the eleventh IKKI (*XI Plenum IKKI* (1932), i, 607). Thälmann admitted as late as the autumn of 1932 that some party members believed that "Hitler must come to power in order to hasten the revolutionary crisis" (E. Thälmann, *Im Kampf gegen die Faschistische Diktatur* (1932), p. 27).

alarming. Many people in Moscow certainly remembered Neumann's responsibility for the Canton commune. Should a similar outbreak occur in Germany, the consequences could be incalculable. An immense hue-and-cry would be raised in the west against the USSR. Military intervention by France in Germany could not be ruled out, and the much vaunted crusade against the USSR to root out communism was on the horizon. On the eve of the eleventh IKKI in March 1931 the Comintern journal published an article by Thälmann apparently designed to soften some of the asperities of the recent party compaign. The January resolution of the KPD had dealt, Thälmann explained, with three "especially decisive problems". First, it had insisted on the prospective *"deepening and sharpening of all the phenomena of the crisis"*; whether or not this would produce a "revolutionary situation" depended on the "subjective factor" of the revolutionary development of the working class. Secondly, the resolution had analysed "the problem of the Fascist development of Germany". The *"bankruptcy of parliamentarianism"* marked *"a definite turning-point"*. But one should speak of *"a ripening, but not yet fully ripe, Fascist dictatorship"*. The Brüning government was *"a government for the promotion of Fascist dictatorship"*. Thirdly, to win a majority of the working class meant "to win the social-democratic workers under the banner of Marxism"; the resolution was "a prelude which marks the beginning of a strong reinforcement of our political activity and of the lively initiative of the party".[11]

The eleventh IKKI, which met on March 25, 1931, a week after the conclusion of the sixth Union Congress of Soviets, and went on for a fortnight, was directed by Manuilsky; Molotov did not appear. The anxiety with which the presidium of IKKI in February 1930 had greeted the first onset of the economic crisis had been intensified; and now that the existence of "Left" as well as Right deviations (though "Left" still usually carried inverted commas) was recognized, directives from Moscow struck an uncertain note. The long report by Manuilsky which opened the proceedings was cautious and elusive. The underlying dilemma which faced the policy-makers in Comintern was apparent. The feature of the past year had been the building up of socialism in the USSR and the

[11] *Kommunisticheskii Internatsional*, 1931, No. 5, pp. 3–17.

deepening of the crisis in the capitalist countries. This change in the
balance of forces had been accompanied by "a strengthening of *the
positions of the world revolutionary movement*". The moment of the
revolutionary crisis (sometime referred to as the "political" crisis)
had, however, not yet arrived; it was an error to treat every minor
local outbreak as heralding the end of the capitalist system. The
delay was due to "*the lagging behind*" of communist parties, which
constituted "*the greatest danger threatening the communist movement*". (In
his reply to the debate Manuilsky again distinguished between the
"objective" factor, i.e. "*the extraordinary favourable objective situation*",
and the "subjective" factor, i.e. "*the lagging behind of the world
communist movement*".) But the conclusion to be drawn from these
premises was embarrassing. Constant attempts since 1928 to
galvanize the parties into positive revolutionary action had been
unsuccessful, and had produced adverse results; and eagerness in
Moscow to hasten the revolutionary crisis in Europe had faded. The
Right danger, which underestimated the prospects of revolution,
and failed to recognize social-democracy ("social-Fascism") as the
principal enemy, was still the chief danger. Manuilsky denounced
the notorious doctrine of the lesser evil, and once more called social-
democracy "the chief social prop of the bourgeoisie". But the
"struggle on two fronts" was also directed against " 'Leftist'
deviations", which overestimated the prospects of immediate
revolutionary action, and failed to draw the line between the social-
democratic leaders and the social-democratic masses. Manuilsky
insisted again and again on the need to pay more attention to the
day-to-day demands of the workers, and to organize "*the united
revolutionary front of the masses from below*".[12] It was a polished
performance. Manuilsky had put the brake on any dangerous
exhibitions of undue revolutionary ardour. But this caution had not
received the formal endorsement of the highest party authorities, and
covert symptoms of divided counsels appeared even during the
session. Lenski and Gottwald, the Polish and Czechoslovak
delegates, insisted strongly on the importance of day-to-day
demands as the way to woo the support of the masses.[13] But Knorin,
the most determined hard-liner in the Comintern hierarchy,[14] and
Lozovsky, while expressing no dissent from Manuilsky, contrived to

[12] *XI Plenum IKKI* (1932), i, 4–83; for the reply to the debate see *ibid*. i, 596–619.
[13] *Ibid*. i, 130, 218.
[14] See p. 5 above.

give a different slant to his conclusions. Knorin quoted Molotov and Stalin, and saw no reason to modify the standpoint of the tenth IKKI in 1929. He attacked Varga for believing in "the automatic collapse of capitalism". Lozovsky thought that the "lagging behind" of the parties "is taking on a highly dangerous character", and wished to spur them to more vigorous action.[15]

The predominant concern of the session was, however, throughout with the KPD, and its pronouncements were motivated primarily by their application to the German problem. Manuilsky had pointed to Germany as the country where "the strengthening of the pre-conditions of a revolutionary crisis" had gone furthest (the KPD was the only major party which had increased its membership). He had described it as the *"central task"* of the KPD to win over a majority of the working class from its allegiance to the social-democrats.[16] Thälmann, in a co-report which, like Manuilsky's report, occupied two whole sittings, closely followed Manuilsky's lead, but sounded more strongly the note of revolutionary optimism. He not only hailed "our electoral victory of September 14", but expressed confidence that September 14 would prove to have been "Hitler's best day, to be followed not by better, but by worse days". He spoke triumphantly of Scheringer's conversion, and of the need to continue the successful campaign to lure Nazi supporters "into the revolutionary class front". The injunction *"we must create a revolutionary situation"* sounded like the cautious modification of a direct call to revolution. The denunciation of social-democracy and "the struggle on two fronts" were not forgotten; and the orator ended by reiterating the slogan of the "people's revolution".[17]

Of the German speakers Neumann was the most self-assured. He praised the slogan of the people's revolution recently adopted by the party central committee, connecting it with the campaign for liberation from Versailles and from the Young plan and with the appeal to recruit the petty bourgeoisie for the KPD. He recognized that Germany was an imperialist Power, as well as a victim of imperialism; this problem could be solved only by the joint action of

---

[15] *XI Plenum IKKI* (1932), i, 398–414, 414–425.

[16] *Ibid.* i, 50–51.

[17] *Ibid.* i, 140–187; predictions of the decline of the Nazi movement were common in KPD literature at the time (see circulars of March and April 1931 quoted in T. Weingartner, *Stalin und der Aufstieg Hitlers* (1970), p. 62, note 156, p. 83, note 219).

the proletariats of Germany and of the major imperialist countries. Neumann dismissed as false the alleged choice between the social-democrats and the Nazis; the main struggle should be directed "against the Fascist bourgeoisie and against its chief social support in the camp of the working class, social-democracy". He endorsed the prevailing optimism about the future. After September 14, some comrades had feared that "the Fascist wave may overwhelm us"; now this danger had been "to a large extent removed". Remmele spoke in much more cautious terms. He admitted a slowing down of the revolutionary tempo. He reproached Varga for seeing only the decay of capitalism, and not the advent of revolution. But he added that revolution was not a process of nature, and depended on the subjective factor of the activity of the working class.[18]

Much of the debate revolved round the analysis of Fascism, primarily in its German incarnation. Manuilsky carefully explained that Fascism was "not some new type of state", but "one of the forms of bourgeois dictatorship in the imperialist epoch". But it was necessary to distinguish different stages in the process of Fascisization; and, while in the debate Thälmann incautiously referred to "the realization of the Fascist dictatorship by the Brüning government", and Neumann called Fascism simply "an organization of finance capital", Manuilsky in his reply spoke of "the bourgeois dictatorship in Germany realized by Brüning and by social-democracy" as being "in process of Fascisization". Thälmann ingeniously explained the rise of Hitler by the theory that the revolutionary movement "through its own higher development" had provoked "a higher stage of counter-revolution"; and Remmele detected a "dialectical process" by which "the pressure applied by the bourgeoisie to the whole mass of workers produces a reverse pressure of revolution".[19] These admissions seemed to go too far in recognizing Nazism as a necessary and perhaps not un-desirable stage in the advance towards proletarian revolution. Manuilsky in his reply to the debate injected a note of stern realism:

> Would it for instance be right to look at the prospect of a people's revolution in Germany without regard to the whole complicated international conjuncture, and above all to the question of the USSR? Can one imagine even for a moment that

[18] *XI Plenum IKKI* (1932), i, 478–491, 560–591.
[19] For the key passages in the debate see *ibid.* i, 35–36, 158, 480, 565.

any powerful revolutionary movement in Central Europe will not bring consequences in its train in the form of a great international struggle?

Manuilsky, while denouncing the doctrine of the "lesser evil" as "the chief channel for the infiltration of the parliamentary illusions of the masses", and "the tendency to underestimate revolutionary perspectives", firmly rejected the "Left" error of supposing that Fascism was either a "historical necessity", or "in its own way an objective 'ally' of the communists, exploding the stability of the capitalist system and destroying the mass basis of social-democracy from the opposite side to the communists". Without naming anyone, he disposed impatiently of theories which treated Fascism as "the father of revolution".[20] Martynov, speaking not in the main debate, but in the debate on the danger of war, described the Brüning government as "the carrier of the Fascist danger" and "the government responsible for introducing Fascist dictatorship".[21] The resolution adopted at the end of the session bore marks of uncertainty and compromise. It was the first pronouncement of Comintern to mention Hitler:

> The Fascists, speculating on the needs and the miseries of the toiling masses, kindling national hate, the imperialist spirit of revenge in the defeated countries, and anti-Semitism . . . disguising their subservience to capitalism with lying anti-capitalist phraseology, paid by finance capital (Hitler), utilize the discontent of the masses in order to strengthen the dictatorship of the bourgeoisie and ruthless oppression of the working class.

It hailed "the rise of the revolutionary upsurge and the growth in a number of countries of the pre-conditions of a revolutionary crisis". But its final paragraph was designed to lower the tension, and set more modest sights:

> Only by carrying on persistent, systematic, daily work, only by sustaining in action the struggle for the daily interests of the workers, by utilizing even the smallest instances of protest by the

[20] *Ibid.* i, 601, 607–610.
[21] *Ibid.* ii, 67–78.

masses against exploitation and Fascist reaction, will communist
parties be able to realize the broadest united front from below,
smash social-democracy, create mass revolutionary trade unions
or a revolutionary trade union opposition, win over a majority of
the working class, and bring the working class to decisive battles
for the proletarian dictatorship.

It was not a clarion call to action, nor did it provide any very precise
guidance to the bewildered KPD.[22]

Though the eleventh IKKI engaged in extensive discussion of the
affairs of the French, Italian, British and Chinese parties,[23] it
produced none of the customary resolutions containing injunctions
to particular parties. The only other resolution was one on the
danger of imperialist war against the USSR. Its adoption was the
sequel of a debate introduced by Cachin, in which delegates of
almost every party expatiated on the theme at tedious length, and it
testified to the continuing anxieties of the Soviet Government: "The
work of Comintern against the danger of imperialist war, and in
defence of the first proletarian dictatorship in the world, has become
one of the most important factors in the preservation of peace
among nations".[24] Manuilsky severely observed that, without "the
historic lagging behind" of the parties, such a debate would have
been unnecessary, since the danger would already have been
removed.[25] At the end of the session thirty full members and twelve
candidates were elected to the standing presidium. The members
included Thälmann, Pieck and Remmele; Neumann was one of the
candidates—a rating which threw some doubt on his standing in
Moscow.[26]

At the first onset of the economic crisis, the presidium of IKKI in
February 1930 had drawn attention to the rise of unemployment,
and March 6 had been celebrated as a day of demonstrations
against it.[27] The results were not impressive. A "comparatively

[22] *Kommunisticheskii Internatsional v Dokumentakh* (1933), pp. 952–966.
[23] See pp. 159–207 (PCF), 239–255 (PCI), 208–238 (CPGB), 319–377 (CCP)
below.
[24] For the resolution see *Kommunisticheskii Internatsional v Dokumentakh* (1933),
pp. 966–972; the debate occupies almost the whole of *XI Plenum IKKI* (1932), ii,
subtitled "The War Danger and the Tasks of Comintern".
[25] *Ibid.* i, 596.
[26] *Ibid.* ii, 246.
[27] See p. 9 above.

small number of the unemployed" had taken part, and united front tactics—between workers and unemployed, and between different parties—had not been adequately utilized. On December 31, 1930, the political secretariat of IKKI decided to repeat the experiment, and fixed February 25, 1931, for another "international day" of protest on behalf of the unemployed. This was duly announced in a joint appeal of the German, French, British, Czechoslovak and Polish parties.[28] *Pravda* in a leading article of February 14, 1931, hailed the prospective event as a "counter-offensive of the working class against hunger, unemployment and exploitation, for work, bread and the power of the proletariat". The demonstrations were duly held with varying degrees of success, and recriminations against social-democrats continued to feature conspicuously in the campaign. The eleventh IKKI a month later reproached communist parties with the weakness of their participation.[29] By the middle of 1931, however, the problem weighed heavily on the whole capitalist world; and the ranks of communist parties began to be swelled by an influx of unemployed workers.[30] It was decided to hold in August 1931 in Prague a conference of communist parties, Red trade unions, and trade union oppositions in capitalist countries, to consider the question. The Comintern news-sheet devoted a special issue to an article by Pyatnitsky reviewing the magnitude of the problem; the statistics quoted included 10 million unemployed in the United States, 5.3 millions in Germany, and 3.5 millions in Britain.[31] The conference met towards the end of August. Ulbricht presided, and delegates of the principal countries made reports. A resolution adopted by the conference noted the absence of unemployment in the USSR, and condemned the temporary remedies proposed by parties of the Second International, but also reproached communist parties with the inadequacy of their efforts.[32]

---

[28] *Georgii Dimitrov: Vydayushchiisya Deyatel' Kommunisticheskogo Dvizheniya* (1972), pp. 90–91; *Internationale Presse-Korrespondenz*, No. 3, January 13, 1931, p. 83.

[29] *Kommunisticheskii Internatsional v Dokumentakh* (1933), p. 964.

[30] The high proportion of unemployed in the KPD had been noticed much earlier (see *Foundations of a Planned Economy, 1926–1929*, Vol. 3, p. 402, note 13).

[31] *Internationale Presse-Korrespondenz*, No. 76, August 4, 1931, pp. 1705–1729.

[32] For brief accounts of the conference see *ibid*. No. 84, August 28, 1931, p. 1886, No. 88, September 11, 1931, pp. 1977–1978; for the text of the resolution *ibid*. No. 87, September 8, 1931, pp. 1958–1960, and of the reports *ibid*. No. 94, September 30, 1931, pp. 2093–2136.

The kaleidoscope of German politics in the spring and summer of
1931 continued to disturb and confuse the leaders of the KPD and of
Comintern. On March 20, 1931, just before the eleventh IKKI met,
the German and Austrian Governments announced an agreement
to conclude a customs union between the two countries. This bold
gesture of independence, fiercely resisted by France, and grudgingly received by her partners, was welcomed by the Soviet press as
a challenge to French domination in Europe.[33] Any chance of its
success was ended by the collapse of important German and Central
European banks less than three months later. In an atmosphere of
financial catastrophe Hoover called for a year's moratorium on
reparations payments, and Brüning had to go cap in hand to the
western Powers for credits. One of the conditions was the abandonment of the customs union. The defeat and humiliation of Germany
were complete. Curtius the Foreign Minister resigned, and was
succeeded by Neurath, the Ambassador in London. That the
Soviet–German protocol renewing the treaty of April 24, 1926, had
at last been signed in the midst of these events[34] was small
consolation to the Soviet Government. The Brüning regime was a
broken reed, and was no more ready than the SPD to resist the
pressure of the western Powers.

The SPD in the summer of 1931 was enmeshed equally with the
KPD in the complexities of the German political situation. On
May 31, 1931, with Germany already under the threat of economic
and financial collapse, the congress of the SPD met at Leipzig in an
anxious mood. It was on this occasion that Tarnow, who made the
principal report, exposed the dilemma in a famous aphorism:

> We are standing *at the death-bed of capitalism*, not only as
> diagnosticians, but also . . . as a doctor who wants to cure? or as a
> cheerful heir who cannot wait for the end, and would like best of
> all to help it along a little with a dose of poison?[35]

Few delegates were eager to answer the question, or to fathom its
implications. The crucial resolution binding the deputies of the SPD
in the Reichstag, as a matter of party discipline, to follow the party
line of support for the Brüning government, was voted after a roll-

---

[33] *Izvestiya*, March 24, 1931.
[34] See pp. 29–30 above.
[35] *Sozialdemokratischer Parteitag in Leipzig* (1931), p. 45.

call by a majority of 324 to 62.[36] Two months later, when all Central Europe faced economic chaos, the Second International held its fourth post-war congress in Vienna. Otto Bauer, the veteran Austrian social-democrat, pointed to the imminent danger of economic collapse and of the victory of Fascism in Germany, and proposed that the congress should call on the western Powers for aid "to overcome the financial crisis in Germany by a rapid and generous act of international solidarity". That a Socialist International should invite capitalist governments to come to the rescue of German capitalism seemed a startling anomaly. Maxton, the leader of the British ILP delegation, urged the German social-democrats to seize the opportunity of overthrowing the German capitalist regime. But the exhortation made little practical sense; and the resolution proposed by Bauer was carried by an overwhelming majority, only the delegates of the ILP, of the Jewish Bund, and of the Polish Left PPS voting against it.[37] But uneasiness continued to haunt the ranks of the SPD. In the autumn of 1931 some of those who had voted in the minority at the Leipzig congress seceded from the party and founded a dissident Socialist Workers' Party (Sozialistische Arbeiterpartei or SAP).[38] The German catastrophe and the rise of Hitler loomed as menacingly over the SPD as over the KPD. But, so long as Comintern stuck to the accepted categories, it was irrefutably established that the SPD, together with the whole Socialist International, was now the saviour and not the destroyer of capitalism, and a traitor to the cause of proletarian revolution. The trouble was that the Nazi movement did not fit these categories; it was difficult to classify it consistently as either the friend or the foe of capitalism.

Other perplexities clouded the view from Moscow of the German scene. In the summer of 1931 the Prussian Government was still a

[36] *Ibid.* p. 187; Knorin called it "the congress of social-Fascists" (*Internationale Presse-Korrespondenz*, No. 67, July 10, 1931, pp. 1503–1504).

[37] *Vierter Kongress der Sozialistischen Arbeiterinternationale* (Zurich, 1932), pp. 552–555; for an account of the proceedings see J. Braunthal, *History of the International* (Engl. transl. 1967), ii, 360–364.

[38] The SAP held a congress in March 1932 and issued a manifesto, which was strongly marked by the influence of Rosa Luxemburg. It condemned the SPD and the Second International for their rejection of the class struggle and involvement in the class system; on the other hand, the KPD and Comintern had abandoned the united front, split the trade unions through the RGO, toyed with petty-bourgeois nationalism, and claimed to occupy a "monopoly position" (*Der Deutsche Kommunismus: Dokumente*, ed. H. Weber (1963), pp. 307–311).

Left–Centre coalition headed by a social-democrat; and the parties of the Right, together with the NSDAP, made a successful demand for a plebiscite on a motion to dissolve the Landtag and hold new elections. The leaders of the KPD decided to abstain; and it is fair to assume that the decision was approved by Comintern.[39] Neumann, still firm in the opinion that social-democrats were more dangerous enemies than Nazis, dissented from the decision. The plebiscite was fixed for August 9; and on July 15 Neumann, allegedly in the name of the party secretariat, though without consulting its other leaders, addressed a letter to the political secretariat of IKKI urging that the KPD should be instructed to support the plebiscite. Neumann had incurred a rebuff from Manuilsky at the eleventh IKKI. But his bolder and more adventurous temperament gave him an advantage over Thälmann; and he certainly had many followers in the party and some powerful friends in Moscow. The requested instruction was sent by telegram on July 20, apparently after a direct intervention by Stalin and Molotov. The central committee of the KPD bowed to the will of Moscow. On the following day it sent an ultimatum to the Prussian Government laying down the conditions for its support; and, when this was automatically rejected, it issued an instruction on July 27 to party members to cast an affirmative vote in the plebiscite, which failed, however, to secure the necessary majority.[40] Thälmann defended the decision on the singularly

[39] "No worker", wrote the *Rote Fahne* on April 10, 1931, "should let himself be misled into marching together with the Nazi murderers and strike-breakers . . . in the present campaign"; Thälmann endorsed this view (*ibid.* April 21, 1931).

[40] The fullest account of this episode is in *Geschichte der Deutschen Arbeiterbewegung*, iv (1966), 300–303, published at a time when Comintern policies in this period were severely criticized and attributed to Stalin's personal misjudgements. According to this account, Neumann's views were shared by "influential members of IKKI and its political commission"; one of these was Knorin, who was said to have "sometimes given recommendations in a sectarian spirit to the German communists" (*Kommunisticheskii Internatsional: Kratkii Istoricheskii Ocherk* (1969), p. 342). An article on the German situation in the journal of Comintern dated August 7, 1931, expressed optimism on the process of winning over the petty-bourgeois masses, but cautiously denied that any revolutionary situation yet existed in Germany, and repeated that "all the forces of the party must be thrown into the struggle against social-democracy". Its concluding paragraphs, which read like an afterthought, presented a confused defence of KPD participation in the Prussian plebiscite (*Kommunisticheskii Internatsional*, 1931, No. 21, pp. 3–15). A later article claimed that the purpose of participation had been "not a united front with Fascism, but a fierce struggle to explain to the toiling masses, deluded by the Fascists and social-democrats, the class character of their parties" (*ibid.* 1931,

unconvincing ground that it "brought confusion into the camp of the bourgeoisie".[41] The incident served as an illustration of the subservience of the KPD to orders from Moscow, and as a culminating example, less significant at the time than it afterwards seemed in retrospect, of collaboration between the KPD and the NSDAP against the SPD. But such collaboration was an implied denial, though nobody in the KPD admitted it as such, of the vaunted identity between social-democracy and Fascism. The eleventh IKKI and its sequel had clarified none of the problems inherent in the uneasy European situation.

The apprehensions and embarrassments of Comintern were accompanied by signs in Moscow, faint and scarcely noticed at first, of a milder attitude to the western Powers. France was still the focus of the anti-Soviet campaign. For two years Franco–Soviet relations had wavered between indifference and open animosity. In April 1931 the French Government, perhaps seeking to hinder the current *rapprochement* between Moscow and Berlin, unexpectedly suggested to the Soviet Ambassador a resumption of the long suspended discussion of a non-aggression pact, and of negotiations for a trade agreement which would suspend the embargo of October 3, 1930, on Soviet products. The overture was cautiously welcomed in Moscow.[42] A visit by Brüning and Curtius to Paris in July 1931, which marked the German surrender on the projected Austro–German customs union, bred fears in Moscow that Germany would be drawn into the western orbit;[43] and anxious Soviet leaders began to contemplate the option of re-insurance in Paris in the event of a further deterioration in Soviet–German relations. By this time Franco–Soviet trade negotiations had proceeded far enough to

---

No. 23, p. 5). The story in M. Buber-Neumann, *Kriegsschauplätze der Weltrevolution* (1967), pp. 309–310, and in B. Gross, *Willi Münzenberg* (Engl. transl. 1974), p. 214, that Neumann, as well as Thälmann and Remmele, opposed participation and bowed to Stalin's decision, evidently came from Neumann himself, and is unconvincing.

[41] *Internationale Presse-Korrespondenz*, No. July 27, 1931, pp. 1639–1640.

[42] *Dokumenty Vneshnei Politiki SSSR*, xiv (1968), 252–254, 266, 290; for the embargo see p. 29 above. In May 1931 the Soviet delegation to the League of Nations commission on European union proposed a protocol on "economic non-aggression" (*Dokumenty Vneshnei Politiki SSSR*, xiv (1968), 342–343).

[43] *Izvestiya*, July 17, 1931.

bring about a withdrawal of the French embargo; and the draft of a non-aggression pact was initialled on August 10, 1931.[44] The French Government wished to make the signature of the pact conditional on the conclusion by the Soviet Government of similar pacts with the neighbours of the USSR; and a Soviet–Polish pact was initialled, apparently as the result of French pressure, on January 26, 1932.[45]

These developments did not directly concern Comintern. But the atmosphere of tension and alarm swelled the anxieties which had been accumulating throughout 1931, and further tilted the balance in favour of restraint. It was a far cry from the days when the Bolsheviks looked to European revolution as the *deus ex machina* which would deliver them from the nightmare of isolation in a hostile capitalist world. The attitude to war had imperceptibly changed. The sixth congress of the Comintern in 1928 had sought to distinguish wars between imperialist Powers from wars directed against a proletarian state. But the view that wars between imperialist Powers should be welcomed as providing communists with an opportunity to transform them into class war and thus hastening the proletarian revolution was no longer tenable and was dismissed as "senseless".[46] Now a revolutionary outbreak in central Europe would provoke French intervention, fan hostility to the USSR, and strengthen the hold of the imperialist Powers over the German bourgeois regime.[47] The world had become too dangerous a place for rash revolutionary adventures.[48]

----

[44] *Dokumenty Vneshnei Politiki SSSR*, xiv (1968), 432, 452–456.

[45] *Ibid.* xv, 57; the Soviet Ambassador in Paris had advised Narkomindel "to utilize French pressure on Poland to obtain a pact" (*ibid.* xiv, 564).

[46] See *Foundations of a Planned Economy, 1926–1929*, Vol. 3, pp. 211–212.

[47] Both Comintern and the KPD continued to fear and expect French military intervention in the event of a revolutionary outbreak in Germany (E. Thälmann, *Der Revolutionnäre Ausweg und die KPD* (1932), p. 27).

[48] The Comintern journal convicted some Baltic communists of an "underestimate of the war danger" based on "the expectation of a war which would facilitate the liberation of toiling masses from the yoke of capital" (*Kommunisticheskii Internatsional*, 1932, No. 21, p. 58); this view was firmly rejected. It was left to a Soviet diplomat, Karakhan, reviewing "the whole global situation" in October 1933 with special reference to Japan, to argue that only a "revolutionary *dénouement*" could halt "unrestrained military adventurism" (*Dokumenty Vneshnei Politiki SSSR*, xvi (1971), 575); the conception of revolution as an antidote to war had completely disappeared from Comintern literature of the period.

CHAPTER 3

THE ROAD TO DISASTER

Two important events occurred simultaneously in September 1931:
the forced abandonment by Britain of the monetary gold standard,
and the military occupation by Japan, following an incident on the
South Manchurian railway, of the whole of Manchuria. The first
marked a culminating point in the crisis of capitalism, and
dramatically confirmed the impression long prevalent in Moscow
that the United States had replaced Britain as the major capitalist
country with which the USSR had to reckon. *Pravda* in a leading
article of September 22, 1931, described it as "not only a weakening
of Britain, but a weakening of international imperialism as a
whole". The immediate threat of the Japanese action to Soviet
interests was obvious; its ultimate repercussions on Soviet relations
with the western world were unforeseen. A flood of protests[1] merely
showed up the impotence of the Soviet forces, while the Japanese
army consolidated its positions in the occupied territory throughout
the autumn of 1931. The mood in Moscow was one of mounting
alarm. Decaying capitalism, Bukharin explained to the seventeenth
party conference in January 1932, would not " 'go away' quietly",
would not die, but would "fire on us with all its guns"; the
international situation was "extremely tense". Molotov harped on
the danger of intervention against the USSR.[2] Fear of war,
obsessive in Moscow since the late nineteen-twenties, now assumed
more immediate and menacing dimensions. The deepening of the
crisis brought nearer the dreaded danger that the imperialist
Powers would seek to reconcile their mutual animosities by a
combined assault on the USSR, and that Germany, crippled and
desperate, would be cajoled or forced into this combination.

Against this background, the complexities of the German
situation continued to preoccupy Comintern, and to dominate its
other anxieties. In the KPD the new mood of caution favoured
Thälmann's unspectacular leadership, and was fatal to the chal-

[1] See pp. 344–345 below.
[2] *XVII Konferentsiya Vsesoyuznoi Kommunisticheskoi Partii (b)* (1932), pp. 80, 156.

45

lenge presented to it by Neumann's more dynamic qualities. Neumann's ambitions were unconcealed. He had induced the political secretariat of Comintern to overrule Thälmann in the affair of the Prussian plebiscite of August 9, 1931; and, if he was right in suspecting that this decision was due to Stalin's intervention, he had reason to think that, with such support, the prize was within his grasp.[3] The high point of Neumann's bid for the leadership was a public meeting in Berlin in September 8, 1931, at which the KPD had invited representatives of the SPD to share the platform—an invitation which was automatically declined. Neumann spoke in terms of studied moderation, putting forward such routine demands of the Left as the nationalization of industry and the banks, the seven-hour day and increased wages; and he argued that the Versailles treaty and the Young plan must be destroyed not through war, but through fraternal cooperation between German, French and Polish workers. But he also declared that "a socialist Germany will be a Soviet Germany" with "a Soviet Government of elected Soviets of proletarians, peasants and other workers".[4] And the *Rote Fahne* under his editorship continued to assert the full rigour of Comintern doctrine: "Brüning's Fascism is not a whit better than Hitler's Fascism. . . . Our chief offensive is against social-democracy.[5]

The issues which divided Neumann and his supporters from the existing leadership were elusive and complex. Ever since the ban on the Frontkämpferbund which had followed the shootings of May 1, 1929,[6] the party had lived under the threat of a legal prohibition. The party central committee had proclaimed in October 1929 that "the illegality of the party is on the agenda", and that preparations

[3] According to M. Buber-Neumann, *Kriegsschauplätze der Weltrevolution* (1967), p. 335, the aim of Neumann and his group was "a palace revolution in the party leadership". Stalin personally preferred Neumann to the colourless Thälmann; when, according to an unsubstantiated but plausible report which reached Trotsky from Moscow, the Polish delegates complained of Thälmann's feeble performance at the twelfth IKKI in August 1932, Stalin replied: "We have got Thälmann only as a legacy from Zinoviev; we can do nothing about it" (*Byulleten' Oppozitsii* (Paris), No. 31, November 1932, p. 23).

[4] *Internationale Presse-Korrespondenz*, No. 89, September 15, 1931, pp. 1995–1997; the story of a speech by Neumann at a Nazi meeting presided over by Goebbels (M. Buber-Neumann, *Kriegsschauplätze der Weltrevolution* (1967), pp. 270–271) is apocryphal.

[5] *Die Rote Fahne*, November 16, 1931.

[6] See *Foundations of a Planned Economy, 1926–1929*, Vol. 3, p. 458.

should be made "up to the last limit" to meet it.[7] During the summer of 1931, with tension increasing on all sides, the danger loomed nearer, and active preparations were made to continue party work underground in illegal conditions.[8] This would involve the party in a directly revolutionary posture; and, however brave a face was put on the prospect, it was unwelcome to Comintern and to the more cautious of the KPD leaders. Willingness to court legal prohibition was associated with reluctance to apply the tactics of the united front with SPD workers or to work actively in the reformist trade unions. These were charges which had been fatal to Merker. The same suspicions now rested on Neumann. Preparation for illegal status was also associated with the cult of physical violence. Neumann's eagerness to appeal to rank-and-file Nazis was not incompatible with an inclination to borrow their methods. The slogan "Hit the Fascists wherever you find them" was attributed to him.[9] His anniversary article on the Paris Commune in March 1931 reproached the Commune with having failed "to exterminate its enemies";[10] and in a speech delivered at the same time he declared that every attack would "cause the ranks of the Bolsheviks to close ever more firmly and aggressively".[11] The rank and file of the party was sharply divided on the issue. Neumann seems to have secured the support of Remmele, formerly active in the denunciation of Merker, but now impatient of Thälmann's leadership.[12] A resolution of the party central committee of November 10, 1931,

---

[7] *Internationale Presse-Korrespondenz*, No. 101, October 29, 1929, p. 2410.

[8] T. Weingartner, *Stalin und der Aufstieg Hitlers* (1970), pp. 94–96, citing party archives; Alpari, the editor of *Internationale Presse-Korrespondenz*, anticipated its closure at any moment, and had prepared "a base for his new enterprises" in Switzerland (J. Humbert-Droz, *Dix Ans de Lutte Antifasciste* (Neuchatel, 1972), p. 47).

[9] M. Buber-Neumann, *Kriegsschauplätze der Weltrevolution* (1967), p. 269. According to Pyatnitsky (*XII Plenum IKKI* (1933), ii, 15), it first appeared in an article in *Die Rote Fahne*, November 5, 1929; Thälmann described it as having "come into use in the spring 1930, when the Nazis were not yet a mass movement" (*XI Plenum IKKI* (1932), i, 156).

[10] See p. 32 above.

[11] *Die Rote Fahne*, March 20, 1931.

[12] Remmele's last contribution to the party journal was an article of June 1931 on the results of the eleventh IKKI (*Die Internationale*, No. 6, June 1931, pp. 241–250), which may have been thought to lay too much emphasis on its routine appeals for revolutionary action; but his speech in the Reichstag denouncing the SPD for its supineness in face of attacks on the working class was reported at length in *Internationale Presse-Korrespondenz*, No. 100, October 20, 1931, pp. 2249–2251.

prohibiting the use of "individual terrorism", was directed against the readiness of Neumann and his supporters to emulate Nazi tactics and to drive the party into illegality and violence.[13] It was said to have spread consternation among the party's fighting organizations, including the successor of the banned Rotkämpferbund.[14]

What happened in Moscow in the last weeks of 1931 is a matter of conjecture. The hard line had its supporters in Comintern. Molotov, who since Bukharin's removal wielded supreme authority, remained silent, and no decisive ruling came from above. The counter-revolutionary character of social-democracy was a recurrent theme; an article by Knorin in *Pravda* on November 7, 1931, was entitled "World Social-Democracy in the Struggle against the Revolutionary Enthusiasm of the Masses". The eighth session of the central council of Profintern in December 1931 found Lozovsky in an intransigent mood. He attacked reformist trade unions as "accomplices of capitalism", and reserved some extra venom for " 'Left' reformists". The British movement and the NMM came in for particularly severe criticism. Smolyansky defended "partial economic struggles", and accused Trotsky and Brandler of regarding them as impracticable. Lozovsky in his reply to the debate declared that work in reformist trade unions "cannot be isolated from the totality of our work among the masses". He cautiously claimed that the formation of Red unions was admissible where "a mass movement is in progress"; everything depended on the concrete situation in particular countries.[15]

It was in relation to the KPD that the embarrassments of indecision were most apparent. Manuilsky, who mistrusted Neumann's radical inclinations, was still the most important official in Comintern, and Pieck, now KPD delegate to Comintern, was also a supporter of Thälmann. Knorin defended Neumann and

[13] *Die Rote Fahne*, November 13, 1931; *Internationale Presse-Korrespondenz*, No. 109, November 17, 1931, p. 2474.

[14] Quoted from archives in T. Weingartner, *Stalin und der Aufstieg Hitlers* (1970), p. 106.

[15] No full record of the session was published; its opening was reported in *Internationale Presse-Korrespondenz*, No. 115, December 8, 1931, p. 2639, Lozovsky's report *ibid*. No. 116, December 11, 1931, pp. 2655–2656, other speeches *ibid*. No. 117, December 15, 1931, pp. 2681–2683, No. 118, December 18, 1931, pp. 2701–2703, other speeches and Lozovsky's reply *ibid*. No. 120, December 30, 1931, pp. 2789–2798. For the British movement see pp. 208–212 below.

Remmele.[16] Neumann was in Moscow in November 1931, and appears to have been well received by Stalin.[17] If so, it was the last mark of favour extended to him; and soon afterwards Stalin must have been induced to withdraw his protection from his former favourite. At the end of the year a long and argumentative article by Thälmann, entitled "Some Errors in our Theoretical and Practical Work and the Way to Overcome Them", appeared in the German party journal. It was certainly not Thälmann's unaided composition, and obviously drew its inspiration from Moscow. The exposure of the first and third errors—weaknesses in the struggle against social-democracy and weaknesses in the struggle against National-Socialism—followed conventional lines: it was necessary to explain why the party had failed to achieve what Thälmann called the "Red united front", comprehensively directed "against the Brüning–Severing system, against the dictatorship of the bourgeoisie and its supporters, against the Hitler party and the social-democratic leadership". The second error related to the application of the slogan of a "people's revolution"—Neumann's old slogan which had been taken over by Thälmann in January 1931 and approved by the eleventh IKKI two months later.[18] The party had allowed itself to be diverted by this slogan from its essential task of winning a majority of the proletariat. The fourth error consisted in "ambiguities" on the question of *individual terror*. Thälmann rejected allegations that the KPD maintained "illegal terror squads", but admitted that some workers, under "the deliberate provocations of the Nazi terror", had consciously or unconsciously "succumbed to the ideology of individual terror, shootings, adventurous operations etc." This he condemned in the light of the view expressed by the eleventh IKKI that "the real immediate revolutionary struggle for power is not yet on the agenda", and that the task of the party was "to ripen rapidly the *pre-conditions* of a revolutionary crisis". He accused the Nazis of seeking to transfer the quarrel "on to the territory of guns and knives", and thus putting pressure on the government to ban the KPD. All this was a scarcely veiled criticism of the provocations of Neumann's group.[19]

[16] *Kommunisticheskii Internatsional: Kratkii Istoricheskii Ocherk* (1969), p. 342.

[17] See p. 52 below.

[18] See p. 31 above; *Geschichte der Deutschen Arbeiterbewegung*, iv (1966), 282, observes that, in propaganda for the people's revolution, "the terms 'Soviet power' and 'a Soviet Germany' were used unconditionally as synonyms for the dictatorship of the proletariat".

[19] *Die Internationale*, No. 11–12, December 1931, pp. 481–509.

The next symptom of what was on foot was the absence of Neumann and Remmele, apparently without explanation or comment, from the session of the KPD central committee which opened on February 19, 1932. Thälmann delivered an immensely long report, in which the few significant passages were buried in a mass of familiar rhetoric. Caution was a keynote of the speech. The SPD was once more denounced as the chief prop of the bourgeoisie; the SPD and the NSDAP were "twins", and "the two most important counter-revolutionary mass parties". The plea that the SPD was the "lesser evil" was again rejected with scorn. While, however, the "chief thrust" of party strategy was directed against the SPD, the dangers of "Hitler-Fascism" should be neither overestimated nor underestimated. Here Thälmann admitted that some party members criticized the campaign for "national liberation" from the Versailles system as incompatible with "proletarian internationalism"; this attitude he refuted with quotations from Lenin. The resolution condemning "individual terror" was defended; but Thälmann admitted that "isolated" members of the party and the youth league dismissed it as a mere tactical manoeuvre. Pieck received extravagant praise in Thälmann's speech, as a model of correct opinions.

The proceedings of the session, other than Thälmann's two speeches,[20] were not published. But Thälmann's reply to the debate showed that many objections were raised. He evaded a discussion of the Nazi menace with the argument that "it is not our task to discuss what situation would arise in case the bourgeoisie should escape from the present cyclical crisis without its coming to a proletarian revolution". But he attempted to answer the many delegates who were conscious of the party's continuing failure to reach the mass of workers, and who had pleaded for a more flexible policy. Some local party organizations were said to have interpreted the united front too widely as permitting direct approaches to SPD organizations. One delegate had argued that the call for political mass strikes damaged the prospects of partial economic strikes; another had defended direct approaches to reformist trade union organizations; another had spoken of "depression" among party workers in the trade unions.[21] The resolution repeated the usual ambiguous

[20] These appeared as a pamphlet, E. Thälmann, *Der Revolutionäre Ausweg und die KPD* (1932).

[21] Pieck long afterwards claimed to have pointed at the session to the danger that Fascism would come to power without the party having offered any serious

formula of the united front, and denounced both "Right opportunist deviations and errors" and "'Left' sectarian dangers in the
party".[22] Nobody mentioned Remmele or Neumann. But the
impression remained of a confused and deeply divided party.

The persistence of what seems in retrospect an extraordinary
complacency and blindness to the Nazi menace could be explained
in part by the fact that this was also a remarkable period of growth
for the KPD. From a fairly steady total of 125,000 in the late
nineteen-twenties its membership rose to 170,000 in 1930, to
240,000 in 1931, and to 360,000 at the end of 1932 on the eve of the
catastrophe. The turnover of members was high, so that a
disquietingly large proportion of members were new recruits.[23] But
the appeal of the KPD, though insignificant in comparison with
that of the NSDAP, was still impressive; and the increase in its
voting power at successive elections encouraged optimism. A false
sense of security was also promoted by Hitler's international
programme. The events of October 1931, when Hitler was received
for the first time by Hindenburg and by his *éminence grise* in the
Reichswehr, Schleicher, and the participation of the NSDAP in the
so-called "Harzburg front" of nationalist Right parties,[24] caused no
stir in Moscow. Hitler's association with the extreme Right,
traditionally the stronghold of opposition to the Versailles system,

resistance (W. Pieck, *Der Neue Weg zum Gemeinsamen Kampf für den Sturz der
Hitlerdiktatur* (1957), p. 27; this was Pieck's report at the subsequent KPD
conference in October 1935). Contemporary evidence is lacking; Thälmann, who
praised Pieck in his report, did not mention him in his reply to the debate. But later
in 1932 Pieck was an active supporter of the "Anti-Fascist Action" (see p. 56
below).

[22] The resolution was not published; for quotations from it see *Geschichte der
Deutschen Arbeiterbewegung*, iv (1966), 326, and E. Thälmann, *Im Kampf gegen die
Faschistische Diktatur* (1932), p. 28.

[23] *Geschichte der Deutschen Arbeiterbewegung*, iv (1966), 310; the membership of the
German Communist Youth League was said to have risen between August 1929
and August 1932 from 20,000 to 57,000, and the members of cells from 250 to 531
(*XII Plenum IKKI* (1933), ii, 133). For earlier figures see *Foundations of a Planned
Economy, 1926–1929*, Vol. 3, p. 403.

[24] For the manifesto of the "front", which denounced both "the bloody terror of
Marxism" and "the policy of submissiveness to the foreigner", and demanded the
formation of nationalist governments in the Reich and in Prussia, see *Geschichte der
Deutschen Arbeiterbewegung*, iv (1966), 557–558.

confirmed belief in his essentially anti-western orientation, and created the impression that both the anti-capitalist and the anti-Bolshevik rhetoric of the Nazi programme could be dismissed as window-dressing. Stalin is said to have asked Neumann in November 1931 whether, if the Nazis came to power in Germany, they would not "concern themselves so exclusively with the west that we can build socialism in peace".[25]

What was not readily recognized in Moscow was that, after the financial collapse of the summer of 1931, no element in the economy of central Europe could resist the domination of the western Powers, and in particular that the survival of capitalism in Germany was bound up with the destinies of western capitalism. Hitler showed a sense of realities when, in December 1931, staking out his claim to head a German Government, he made his first attempts to woo American and British opinion.[26] Secret approaches to France were suspected, but denied.[27] An unusual leading article in *Pravda* on December 21, 1931, expressed the view that no bourgeois German party, "from the Nazis to the SPD", could pursue any policy other than "the policy of submission and fulfilment even of the harshest international obligations". The financial crisis would extinguish "the radical National-Socialist revenge phase" of the NSDAP, and Hitler would be found in the ranks of those whom he had formerly denounced as "slaves of Versailles". But this glimmer of light did not shine far. The article still proclaimed that social-democracy and Fascism were "twins", and rejected with scorn the doctrine of the "lesser evil".

Growing anxieties nevertheless accounted for a gradual stiffening of attitudes towards Germany, both in Soviet diplomacy and in

[25] M. Buber-Neumann, *Kriegsschauplätze der Weltrevolution* (1967), p. 332. Neumann's answer is not on record; but Stalin seems always to have believed that, so long as Hitler was committed against the west, the USSR was secure, and that no German could be mad enough to incur hostility simultaneously on both fronts.

[26] For Hitler's pronouncements and Rosenberg's visit to London see T. Weingartner, *Stalin und der Aufstieg Hitlers* (1970), pp. 117–118; an article in *Internationale Presse-Korrespondenz*, No. 115, December 8, 1931, pp. 2615–2616, was entitled "Hitler on his Knees to World Finance".

[27] See T. Weingartner, *Stalin und der Aufsieg Hitlers* (1970), p. 118; an alarmist article in the Comintern journal asserted that "during the past year the problem of a Franco-German agreement has been very hotly discussed on both sides of the Rhine", and drew the conclusion that "it would be a gross error to deny the possibility of military cooperation between France and Germany against the USSR" (*Kommunisticheskii Internatsional*, 1931, No. 33–34, pp. 35–43).

Comintern. Throughout the nineteen-twenties Germany had been treated by Soviet spokesmen as a victim of the imperialist western Powers; and this convention was observed in denunciations of the Young plan. Occasional criticisms of German imperialism had aroused no enthusiasm in the KPD.[28] But the position was ambiguous. As early as 1927 Bukharin had described Germany as being the *subject* as well as the *object* of imperialism, being "actively engaged . . . on the imperialist political market";[29] and a leading article in the Comintern journal in the spring of 1930, entitled "The Preparation of War against the USSR and German Imperialism", alleged that the "main imperialists" were seeking to draw Germany into an anti-Soviet bloc, and that Germany was trying to sell her services for as high a price as possible "on the imperialist stock market".[30] Thälmann had written in February 1931 of the *"imperialist foreign policy of Germany"*, instancing her opposition to the Young plan, propaganda for rearmament, the chauvinistic campaign of hate against Poland, and—oddly and significantly—"the formation of National-Socialist armed units in Silesia and East Prussia".[31] At the eleventh IKKI in March 1931 he described the project of a German–Austrian customs union, announced a few days earlier, as an example of "the imperialist aggressiveness" of the Brüning government.[32] In the preparatory commission for disarmament at Geneva, a fitful measure of cooperation had been established between Soviet and German delegations.[33] But in January 1932, on the eve of the opening of the disarmament conference, the Comintern press carried an article which bluntly accused the German delegation of hypocrisy; its proposals for

[28] See *Foundations of a Planned Economy, 1926–1929*, Vol. 3, pp. 423–424, 448, note 192.

[29] See *ibid.* Vol. 3, p. 123.

[30] *Kommunisticheskii Internatsional*, 1930, No. 8, p. 4; the repetition of the metaphor of the "imperialist market" suggests that Bukharin may have written the article.

[31] *Kommunisticheskii Internatsional*, 1931, No. 5, p. 13.

[32] *XI Plenum IKKI* (1932), i, 157. Kuusinen, speaking of the "oppressed peoples of Europe", denounced "every kind of national inequality of rights", which sounded like an endorsement of German claims at Geneva; but he did not mention German nationalism, though he condemned "national-Fascists in the Western Ukraine, Macedonia, the Dobrudja etc." (*XI Plenum IKKI* (1932), i, 441, 456).

[33] See *Foundations of a Planned Economy, 1926–1929*, Vol. 3, pp. 116–118, and p. 29 above.

disarmament masked a claim for German rearmament should the other Powers fail to disarm.[34]

These were the first steps in a long process which, in the course of two years, converted the USSR from a champion of the liberation of Germany from the fetters of Versailles to a stout defender of the Versailles system and of the containment of Germany. The deterioration of Soviet–German relations was gradual, and had its ups and downs.[35] A diplomatic contretemps occurred at Geneva, where Litvinov and Brüning were both attending the disarmament conference. April 16, 1932, was the tenth anniversary of the Rapallo treaty; and Litvinov proposed that it should be marked by a Soviet–German lunch, with appropriate speeches. Brüning, anxious not to flaunt an exclusive relation with the USSR in the face of the other delegates, accepted the lunch, but declined the speeches; and Litvinov reviewed the history of the treaty in a statement to the German press, which was no doubt a substitute for the speech he had intended to deliver, leading up to the conclusion that the treaty was significant "not only as a bilateral document, but as an international act, which should serve as a lesson and a model worthy of imitation".[36] The desire on both sides to play down the particular character of Soviet–German friendship was evident, and was read as the symptom of a growing coolness between the two countries. Litvinov went out of his way to express regret to his German colleague at the disarmament conference that "relations between the two delegations differ sharply from those established between Count Bernstorff and myself in the preparatory commission".[37] One source of reassurance was, however, available: the close relations between the Red Army and the Reichswehr. In April 1932 Schleicher and Hammerstein emphatically assured the Soviet Ambassador in Berlin that the Reichswehr would "never tolerate" Hitler as Chancellor or President;[38] and the context showed that

[34] *Internationale Presse-Korrespondenz*, No. 7, January 26, 1932, pp. 157–158; it was followed by an even stronger article alleging that Germany was ready for a military alliance with France if freedom to rearm were conceded (*ibid.* No. 9, February 2, 1932, pp. 220–221).

[35] Stalin, in his interview with the German writer Ludwig in December 1931, sought to allay German fears that the proposed Soviet–Polish pact (see p. 44 above) was directed against Germany (Stalin, *Sochineniya*, xiii, 116–117).

[36] *Dokumenty Vneshnei Politiki SSSR*, xv (1969), 248–250.

[37] *Ibid.* xv, 768, note 142.

[38] T. Weingartner, *Stalin und der Aufstieg Hitlers* (1970), p. 115; the story rests on later reminiscences, but is plausible. In the summer of 1932 the Soviet intelligence

this implied the continuity of the secret military arrangements.

Meanwhile events in Germany had been forcing the pace. Presidential elections were due in the spring of 1932. The SPD put forward no candidate, and prepared on the principle of the lesser evil to vote for Hindenburg in order to keep Hitler out.[39] At the first ballot on March 13, Hindenburg received 18.6 million votes, Hitler 11.4 million, Thälmann 5 million, and Duesterberg, a candidate of the Right, 2.5 million; the Catholic Centre and the SPD formed the core of Hindenburg's support. At the second ballot on April 10, Hindenburg received 19.4 million votes, and Hitler 13.4 million, while Thälmann's vote fell to 4 million. If Hindenburg's increased quota came from former supporters of Duesterberg, it was to be presumed that Hitler's additional 2 million came in part from the KPD.[40] The rising strength of the NSDAP, and the humiliation of the KPD, were underlined by the elections to several provincial Landtags, which took place immediately afterwards. In almost all, the NSDAP emerged as the most numerous party, and reaffirmed its domination of the German political scene.

In this eventful month of April 1932 Comintern was at length galvanized into activity. The KPD leaders were summoned to Moscow to attend a meeting of the political secretariat of IKKI. Neumann and Remmele having been invited to state their case, the "Neumann–Remmele group" was censured as "fractional" and "sectarian", though no formal action was taken against it.[41] This decisive rejection of what was regarded as a deviation to the "Left"

---

agent Krivitsky reported a conversation with a staff officer of the Reichswehr, who was firmly committed to the policy of German–Soviet cooperation, and said of Hitler's rise to power: "Let Hitler come and do his job and then we, the army, will make short work of him"; this report is said to have impressed Stalin (W. Krivitsky, *I Was Stalin's Agent* (1939), pp. 21–22).

[39] Neumann in a speech of March 1, 1932, jauntily predicted that the victor in the coming struggle would be neither Hindenburg nor Hitler, but Bolshevism (*Die Rote Fahne*, March 2, 1932; this seems to have been the last speech of Neumann to be reported in the party press).

[40] The party central committee appealed to party members on March 20 to vote again for Thälmann on April 10 (*Internationale Presse-Korrespondenz*, No. 25, March 26, 1932, pp. 714–715); but an article in the party journal on the results of the first ballot (*Die Internationale*, No. 4, April 1932, pp. 165–174) offered no advice how to vote on the second.

[41] *Geschichte der Deutschen Arbeiterbewegung*, iv (1966), 373.

was a symptom of a changing climate in Moscow. *Pravda*, in an article which called for "a united front with social-democratic workers from below" to defeat the "Fascist and social-Fascist terror", opened the door, if only by a narrow chink, to recognition of a distinction between the SPD and the Nazis:

> Communists do not at all believe that there is no kind of difference between the method of government of social-democracy and the method of government of national-socialism, between a method which besides terror functions *primarily through trickery and a method which besides trickery functions primarily through terror*. But communists explain first of all to the masses that both the social-democrats and the national-socialists carry out, and will carry out, only the will of finance capital.[42]

Thälmann more eagerly branded the "shameful lie" that "it is a matter of indifference to communists whether Hitler comes to power", and announced a "new stage in our *struggle against National-Socialism*".[43] It was decided to draft an appeal to all German workers from the central committees of the KPD and RGO for a united front against "the capitalist robbers and the ever more shamelessly active Fascist gangs". The intention in Moscow was apparently to issue it in advance of the elections to the Prussian Landtag and other provincial Landtags on April 24. By accident or design it was issued only on the day after the elections, and appeared in the *Rote Fahne* two days later still—an error with which the KPD was afterwards reproached.[44]

This document was later cited as the beginning of an "Anti-Fascist Action". But its text scarcely lived up to its title and purpose, and bore witness to the strong inhibitions still prevailing in Moscow. The charges of "terror" and of "strike-breaking" were reserved for the Nazis. But the SPD leaders were convicted of voting for all the repressive measures of the Brüning regime directed against the workers and workers' wages; and their profession of concern for the workers was described as "an electoral manoeuvre". The appeal to SPD workers against the leaders differed only by a slightly milder tone from appeals hitherto made under the rubric of the united front

[42] *Pravda*, April 12, 1932.
[43] *Die Internationale*, No. 5, May 1932, pp. 215, 222.
[44] *XII Plenum IKKI* (1933), ii, 16.

from below.[45] Speeches of Thälmann and Ulbricht in the party central committee on May 24, 1932, unpublished at the time, showed greater realism. Thälmann openly rejected what had hitherto been treated as the core of Comintern and party orthodoxy:

> In the question of the struggle against Fascism, we have often seen a definite identification of Fascism and social-Fascism, of the Hitler party and social-democracy, by way of saying that they are twins. . . . The composition of these parties is quite different. . . . We must formulate the question of the united front quite differently with the social-democratic workers than with the Nazis.

And Ulbricht exclaimed:

> Our task is to talk less of "under the leadership of the RGO", but to realize this slogan in fact, and at the same time to be less frightened of trade union members. . . . Therefore, revolutionary united front tactics and less rhetoric.[46]

A stimulus to the movement may have been given by an incident in the Prussian Landtag on May 25, 1932, when the Nazi deputies, fresh from their electoral triumph, came to blows with the much smaller KPD group.[47] Thälmann, in a leading article in the party journal, associated the campaign with the call for a "people's revolution" leading up to a "workers' and peasants' government".[48] But the appeal to social-democrats was hedged around with conventional reservations; and a note of caution was still sounded in a KPD circular of June 4: "The campaign to win over SPD workers for the joint battles of the Anti-Fascist Action does not mean any weakening of our struggle of principle against the SPD, against social-Fascism."[49] Much evidence can be found of spontaneous enthusiasm manifested in joint demonstrations of rank-and-file SPD and KPD workers arranged by local organizations,

[45] *Die Antifaschistische Aktion* (1965), p. 317; this collection is confined to documents supporting the "action", and does not give a complete picture of KPD attitudes at the time.

[46] For these speeches see *ibid.* pp. 22–30.

[47] For KPD protests see *ibid.* pp. 31–41.

[48] *Die Internationale*, No. 6, June 1932, pp. 261–292.

[49] *Die Antifaschistische Aktion* (1965), p. 77.

but less of contacts between top leaders or of any attempt to formulate concerted action.[50]

These half-hearted gestures of conciliation were accompanied by an equally tentative shift in official attitudes. The Soviet Ambassador in Berlin in April 1932, "without intending to create a panic", reported to Narkomindel that Hitler had spoken publicly of his "task of conducting a struggle with the USSR", and warned Narkomindel that "Germany is not Italy, and Hitler is not Mussolini".[51] A KPD journalist, Neubauer, who was also a Reichstag deputy, wrote an article evidently fresh from the study of *Mein Kampf* and the works of Rosenberg, which reached the unpalatable conclusion that Hitler's hostility to France was negotiable, and the demand for "Raum im Osten" basic to his designs.[52] But this revision of current assumptions stirred no echo in Moscow, and was once more overtaken by dramatic events. At the end of May 1932, Hindenburg dismissed Brüning and, by-passing Hitler, installed as Chancellor a nominee of Schleicher, Franz von Papen. The new Chancellor was eyed with suspicion in Moscow. *Pravda* in a leading article of June 3 concluded that Hindenburg was "organizing a Fascist government by constitutional means, and handing over power to the Nazis"; the KPD remained "the only organization of the masses of workers against Fascist terror". The *Rote Fahne* of June 5, 1932, observed that the Papen government was "holding place-cards for Hitler-Fascism", and noticeably refrained from a direct attack on the SPD. A leading article in the Comintern journal observed that "the centre of gravity" in Germany was "moving from social-democracy as the main social support of the bourgeoisie to the bourgeoisie's own *combat* organization, the terrorist bands of Hitler's mass party", though—the cautious

---

[50] According to a report of the Ministry of the Interior, the "positive successes" of the campaign consisted of "the formation of a united front on the local level, sometimes on the basis of decisions of local trade union federations, the formation of anti-Fascist unity committees and of anti-Fascist defence staffs, joint mass demonstrations etc." (*ibid.* p. 137); the SPD in a circular of June 28, 1932, instructed its organizations to avoid "local negotiations", which produced "only disunity and confusion" (*ibid.* pp. 178, note 1, 185).

[51] *Dokumenty Vneshnei Politiki SSSR*, xv (1969), 287.

[52] *Internationale Presse-Korrespondenz*, No. 41, May 18, 1932, pp. 1253–1256; this was followed by another article from the same hand which may be described as the first serious analysis by a KPD writer of the character and organization of the NSDAP (*ibid.* No. 45, May 31, 1932, pp. 1389–1392). An analysis of the social composition of the NSDAP by another writer followed *ibid.* No. 46, June 3, 1932, pp. 1427–1431.

qualification followed—the social support of social-democracy was still necessary to it.[53]

What, however, created serious alarm in Moscow was the not unfounded suspicion that the Papen government was more inclined than its predecessor to a western orientation in German foreign policy.[54] One of Papen's first public acts was a visit to Lausanne to meet the French Prime Minister, Herriot, ostensibly for the purpose of settling the vexed problem of reparations. A *communiqué* of June 16 referring to Papen's desire to improve relations with France was interpreted in Moscow as a move towards Franco–German military cooperation with a view to intervention against the USSR.[55] These anxieties bred doubts about the Anti-Fascist Action on which the KPD had so tentatively embarked. Hitler's hatred of the west might yet prove an antidote to Papen's pro-western inclinations. Some communists still clung tenaciously, even after Neumann's disgrace, to the line of uncompromising hostility to the SPD, and were disposed to see among members of the NSDAP a more promising source of recruits for the KPD than among the organized social-democratic workers. Some time in June instructions were sent to the KPD—apparently in the form of a telegram signed by Knorin—branding as "opportunist errors" the "open letters" sent to social-democratic organizations with proposals for common action and other forms of fraternization; and the central committee of the KPD, in obedience to this protest, sent a circular letter to its branches and organizations, explaining that the social-democratic workers were not yet ripe for common demonstrations with the KPD, and that meetings between members for the "abstract" discussion of a united front should be discouraged.[56]

[53] *Kommunisticheskii Internatsional*, 1932, No. 16, pp. 3–7.

[54] This view persisted; in a retrospective conversation with the German Ambassador in December 1933 Litvinov dated the decline in Soviet–German relations from "the coming to power of Papen and Hitler" (*Dokumenty Vneshnei Politiki SSSR*, xvi (1970), 740–741).

[55] A report from Lausanne in *Pravda*, July 1, 1932, asserted that military conversations had taken place; an article in *Pravda*, July 8, 1932, on the "Lausanne Bargain" suggested that opposition still existed in Germany to the new policy, and *Pravda*, July 18, 1932, published part of an article by Seeckt in the German press deprecating the *rapprochement* with France and Poland.

[56] The circular letter appears never to have been published, but is known from Guttmann's full account of it at the twelfth IKKI three months later, which did not, however, mention the instruction from Moscow (*XII Plenum IKKI* (1933), ii, 48); for the evidence for Knorin's telegram see T. Weingartner, *Stalin und der Aufstieg Hitlers* (1970), p. 161.

The cautious ambivalence of the new instruction from Moscow was received with mixed feelings in the KPD. It inspired a massive and carefully written article by Thälmann in the party journal. He denied that anything had been changed by the introduction of the Anti-Fascist Action; the party was still faithful to the decisions of the eleventh IKKI, now more than a year old. You could not attack the Fascists without attacking the social-democrats, who were once more branded as social-Fascists; the SPD and the NSDAP were "twin props of bourgeois class rule". Thälmann rejected Trotsky's proposal for a bloc between the KPD and the SPD against Fascism, and condemned "the open champions of a *united front only from above*". What was wanted was *"not and never* a united front policy only from above, but a united front policy from *below"*. This sounded like the repetition of a time-honoured formula. But the qualification "only" implied something more. It "did not exclude" in certain circumstances "united front tactics from below and above in a revolutionary sense". In the trade union movement Thälmann called for "the creation of a broad opposition movement beside the RGO in the free and Christian unions"; and he ended by denouncing "sectarian attitudes" which consisted in an inclination to "extenuate or excuse neglect of the struggle against the Hitler party by some kind of strategic concentration of the main thrust against social-democracy". The conclusion was an appeal, so faint as to be barely audible, for a more tolerant approach to the SPD in the interest of a more decisive "Anti-Fascist Action" against the Nazis.[57] But Thälmann chose about the same time in a party speech to recall Radek's famous Schlageter appeal of 1923, and to summon "the unknown SA soldier" to join "the revolutionary army of freedom against the Young plan and German capitalists".[58] In a desperate and baffling situation every rallying-cry must be tried.

Attempts were made at a higher level to establish contacts between the leaders of the SPD and KPD representatives in the Reichstag. These came to nothing.[59] Things went further in the Prussian Landtag, where Pieck publicly offered to put forward no KPD candidate for the presidium, and to vote for the candidates of the Centre and of the SPD, on the understanding that they would vote with the communists against candidates of the National-

[57] *Die Internationale*, No. 6, June 1932, pp. 261–292.
[58] *Internationale Presse-Korrespondenz*, No. 49, June 14, 1932, p. 1553.
[59] T. Weingartner, *Stalin und der Aufstieg Hitlers* (1970), p. 160.

Socialists and of the nationalists; this offer was rejected.[60] Limited success was achieved at lower levels. An anti-Fascist congress addressed by Thälmann in Darmstadt in June 1932 mustered 1500 delegates. But of these only 44 came from the SPD and 162 from the ADGB.[61] A mass demonstration in the Lustgarten in Berlin was reported on July 3.[62] On July 8 Thälmann met twenty SPD members to answer their questions on the Anti-Fascist Action; and two days later a unity congress was held in Berlin, which adopted a manifesto proclaiming a united front against Fascism.[63] But the SPD leadership held aloof; and most of the members remained faithful to it. Detailed reports were drawn up of "unity committees" and organs of "Red mass self-defence" in different districts; some of these gave numbers of members and even specified a category of "active members".[64] But it is difficult to guess how much spontaneous activity was represented by this organization, and how effective was its appeal to non-communists.

While Comintern and the KPD fumbled and wavered, the instability and violence of the political situation in Germany caused increasing alarm. In the middle of July 1932 a Nazi march through a predominantly communist district of Altona, a suburb of Hamburg, sanctioned by the police, was met by an unauthorized communist counter-demonstration. The police fired on the communist demonstrators, killing eighteen and wounding many more. It did not help that the police-president of the district was a social-democrat.[65] On July 20, 1932, with Reichstag elections pending,

[60] Pieck, who was censured for this overture, defended it in a letter of August 4, 1932, to Florin, the KPD representative in IKKI (*Die Antifaschistische Aktion* (1965), pp. 214–215); for a further similar overture by Pieck see p. 62, note 71 below.

[61] *Internationale Presse-Korrespondenz*, No. 49, June 14, 1932, pp. 1553–1554.

[62] *Ibid.* No. 55, July 5, 1932, p. 1732.

[63] For documents relating to these occasions see *Die Antifaschistische Aktion* (1965), pp. 163–182. Of the 1465 delegates at the Berlin congress, 379 were communists, 954 were non-party, and 132 belonged to the SPD and its subsidiary organizations or to the Sozialistische Arbeiterpartei (SAP); the lumping together of the SPD with the SAP, the splinter group which had broken away from it (see p. 41 above), makes it impossible to guess how many members of the SPD were among the delegates.

[64] *Ibid.* pp. 250–272.

[65] The incident is described in detail in J. Valtin, *Out of the Night* (1941), pp. 309–311; it was referred to by Knorin at the twelfth IKKI (*XII Plenum IKKI* (1933), ii, 68).

Papen staged an important *coup*. Having obtained from Hindenburg full powers as Reichskommissar for Prussia, he removed the restive coalition Prussian Government, and placed Prussia under military rule. The KPD issued an appeal to all German workers and trade unions for a general strike.[66] But this met with no response; and the KPD was criticized by Pyatnitsky at the twelfth IKKI six weeks later for supineness and lack of leadership.[67] At the Reichstag elections on July 31 the NSDAP, with 13.7 million votes, won 230 seats, thus becoming easily the largest party in the Reichstag. The SPD and the Centre parties suffered badly. One of the few other parties to gain was the KPD, which increased the number of its deputies from 78 to 89—a success which enabled Thälmann to make the implausible claim that " the KPD was the only victor of July 31".[68] Knorin in Moscow once more struck a revolutionary note, asserting that "the worker masses have now again become convinced that the offensive of Fascism cannot be defeated by the ballot-box", and that the KPD was ready for "revolutionary action against Fascism and capitalism".[69] Hitler refused an invitation to enter the Papen government, and asked for the Chancellorship. This was still subject to the veto of the Reichswehr,[70] and Hindenburg rejected the demand. When the new Reichstag met on August 30, 1932, Klara Zetkin, as its oldest member, delivered an introductory address, which, though it included an appeal for a united front against Fascism, was politely received. But Göring was elected president of the Reichstag,[71] and soon set out, by constitutional means, to make Papen's position untenable. The KPD issued yet another circular explaining that the election results called for "new methods" of approach to the masses, but offered nothing but the well-worn injunction to "carry the Anti-Fascist Action into

---

[66] *Die Antifaschistische Aktion* (1965), pp. 193–194.

[67] *XII Plenum IKKI* (1933), ii, 17–18; Thälmann accepted unspecified criticisms "in connexion with July 20" (*ibid.* iii, 94).

[68] *Internationale Presse-Korrespondenz*, No. 66, August 9, 1932, p. 2135.

[69] *Internationale Presse-Korrespondenz*, No. 64, August 4, 1932, pp. 2053–2055.

[70] See p. 54 above; Radek in an article of September 1932 argued that the role of the Reichswehr in German politics was so formidable that the NSDAP would never exercise full power even if it secured a majority in the Reichstag (*Internationale Presse-Korrespondenz*, No. 78, September 20, 1932, p. 2490).

[71] Pieck proposed that the KPD should vote on the second ballot for the SPD candidate, provided the Centre did the same, in order to prevent the election of a Nazi (*Die Antifaschistische Aktion* (1965), pp. 213–214); this fell through, since Göring was elected on the first ballot with the votes of the Centre.

the factories".[72] This was the situation when the twelfth IKKI assembled in Moscow on August 27, 1932, to debate the bafflingly complex problems which confronted Comintern and the Soviet Government.

[72] *Ibid.* pp. 217–220.

CHAPTER 4

THE TWELFTH IKKI AND AFTER

The business of the twelfth IKKI, which sat from August 27 to September 15, 1932, and mustered 174 delegates (only 38 of them with voting rights), was carefully arranged. After Thälmann had formally opened the proceedings—a tribute to the importance of Germany in the picture—Kuusinen delivered a massive report on "The International Situation and the Tasks of the Parties";[1] and Thälmann then reported on "The Lessons of Economic Strikes and the Struggle of the Unemployed". The two topics merged and were debated together; and the debate occupied 26 of the 32 sittings, the others being devoted to a report and debate on the Far East,[2] to a report by Manuilsky on socialist construction in the USSR, followed by laudatory comments from other delegates, and to formal business. As at the eleventh IKKI, the absence of Molotov implied that no major policy directive was to be expected, and imparted an indecisive character to the proceedings.[3] Thälmann in his opening address introduced the main themes of the session, all of them reminiscent of those enunciated by the eleventh IKKI eighteen months before: the end of capitalist stabilization, the revolutionary upsurge of the masses, the approach of a new period of revolutions and wars, and the growing danger of imperialist war against the USSR.[4]

Kuusinen in his report reviewed the situation in conventional terms. When he reached the controversial ground of current policy, he paved the way for a cautious approach with an unusually copious fund of quotations from Lenin. Lenin in his theses for the founding congress of Comintern in 1919 had remarked on the danger "that

---

[1] At the eleventh IKKI Manuilsky had made the main report, and Kuusinen spoke only on "colonial" questions; at the twelfth Kuusinen made the main report, and Manuilsky spoke in the debate.

[2] See pp. 353–354 below.

[3] The party was involved at that time in a struggle against another group of dissidents; Ryutin was expelled by a decision of the party central committee of October 9 (*Pravda*, October 10, 1932).

[4] *XII Plenum IKKI* (1933), i, 1–6.

the struggle will be so intense that the consciousness of the working masses will not keep up with such a development", and had expressed the fear that the significance of the Soviets was "not yet clear to the great masses of German workers, reared as they are in the spirit of parliamentarianism and in bourgeois prejudices". Even at this interval of time, mused Kuusinen, one could learn much about "Bolshevik mass policy" from Lenin's words. Lenin had written his pamphlet of 1920 on *The Infantile Disease of "Leftism" in Communism* as a warning against those who would have excluded workers from "mass revolutionary organizations" unless they recognized the dictatorship of the proletariat. In his theses for the second congress of Comintern in the same year, he had said that the task of the moment was "not to hasten the revolution, but to strengthen the preparedness of the proletariat". Stalin's *Foundations of Leninism* could be quoted as recommending "such methods of struggle and such forms of organization as would make it easy for the masses to recognize by experience the correctness of the re-volutionary slogans". Having placed himself on this firm ground, Kuusinen delivered his verdict on the united front, denouncing those opportunists (like "Brandler, Trotsky etc.") who wanted a political bloc with social-democratic leaders, as well as doctrinaire Leftists who attacked all social-democrats as "little Zörgiebels". The emphasis had just perceptibly shifted. The slogan of "independent leadership" was correct; but some comrades in applying it had "committed mistakes amounting to a plain violation of proletarian democracy".

Kuusinen thus belatedly arrived at the German question, which was the underlying theme of the whole debate. Here all was confusion. The KPD had recently effected "a great break-through in expanding the movement for a united front". Mistakes had been made both from the Right and from the Left; but these had been corrected. "The struggle against social-democracy must be con-ducted *in a different way* from the struggle against Fascism or against the other conservative bourgeois parties"; the KPD must "strategically direct the chief blow against social-democracy", but in such a way as "simultaneously to attack Fascism and the big bourgeoisie with full force". At one time the party had under-estimated the Nazi movement. On the other hand, the present regime could not be described as "a complete Fascist dictatorship", since it had not attempted to destroy the workers' organizations; and it was inconceivable that this could be done without an uprising of "the German revolutionary proletariat under the leadership of the communist party". It was "not Marxism" to suppose that "a wave of mass strikes" could be conjured up "on command". Nevertheless an opportunity had been missed on the occasion of the Papen *coup* of July 20 against the Prussian Government. Kuusinen in conclusion returned to generalities with a familiar attack on social-democracy: "Since the bourgeoisie cannot be displaced without overthrowing its principal social prop, it will be correct to say that we should aim our *principal blow* at social-democracy." It would be difficult to imagine a report which more conspicuously evaded the task of giving a clear lead on contentious issues. But the prevailing mood was one of caution and restraint.[5]

The same tactics were pursued by Thälmann, whose report was limited to economic questions, and did not relate specifically to Germany, thus enabling him to ignore the thorny problems of the KPD. His language was entirely conventional. By insisting on the importance of strikes on behalf of the day-to-day demands and grievances of the workers, communists would "harden the will of the masses for the struggle, making them more flexible, more mature, in the decisive battles for the dictatorship of the proletariat". He described the formation of Red trade unions as "an absolutely indispensable and correct step", referring to their achievements in Czechoslovakia and the United States, in France and Poland, and "in part also in Germany". But he admitted that the movement had met with resistance in communist parties, "including the German party", and that Red unions "are in part going through a phase of stagnation, or are on a declining curve". He made one oblique and anonymous reference to "some comrades" (Neumann and his supporters) who were said to prefer "discussion with Nazi workers to discussion with social-democratic workers"; and he ended with the usual call for a "struggle on two fronts—against Right opportunist deviations and against 'Left' sectarianism". It was a less polished performance than Kuusinen's, and even more wordy and repetitive; but it purveyed the same mixture of irresolution and moderation.[6]

[5] *Ibid.* i, 6–41.

[6] *Ibid.* i, 42–77. Humbert-Droz, who was present, later described it as "a serious revision of Lozovsky's policy and a concentration of effort on the reformist unions" (J. Humbert-Droz, *Dix Ans de Lutte Antifasciste* (Neuchatel, 1972), p. 63), but this impression may have been influenced by Humbert-Droz's own leanings.

Lenski, the Polish delegate, and Gottwald, the Czechoslovak delegate, were invited to speak as co-*rapporteurs*. Unlike Thälmann, Lenski plunged straight into the German question, describing Germany, on the basis of a quotation from Stalin, as "*the nodal, decisive point in the very unevenly growing international proletarian revolution*", but also as "the country of the most concentrated proletariat with immense revolutionary traditions". Much of Lenski's language was equivocal. He frequently quoted Kuusinen with approval, and scarcely mentioned Thälmann. But repeated insistence on the advanced state of the revolutionary movement in Poland hinted at an implicit comparison with a laggard Germany. Turning to the strike question, Lenski too found a quotation from Lenin, who in 1912 had hailed "the conjunction of the political and economic strike", pointing to "the genuine character of the movement as a revolutionary upsurge of the masses". In Poland "the new phase of political strikes intertwined with economic strikes" was already beginning. Reproof of the weakness of the KPD or of its leaders seemed to lurk behind fiery invocations of "*the decisive battles for power, for the dictatorship of the proletariat*".[7] Later in the debate Pyatnitsky revealed that Lenski, who was in Berlin at the time of Papen's *coup* of July 20, 1932, had complained to him of the passivity of the KPD on that occasion.[8]

If Lenski, in terms of current Comintern policy, leaned to the Left, Gottwald maintained an impeccable balance. He had risen to power in the Czechoslovak party after a sharp struggle at the fifth party congress in February 1929, which, applying the turn to the Left demanded by the sixth congress of Comintern in 1928, had condemned and ousted the dominant "Right opportunist" group. Party membership, however, fell off disastrously.[9] When the

[7] *XII Plenum IKKI* (1933), i, 78–96. According to a story reaching Trotsky from Moscow, Lenski had asked for a separate debate on Germany; when this was refused, he used his own speech to fill the gap. His speech was loudly applauded, but on the next day he was summoned to the secretariat and rebuked (*Byulleten' Oppozitsii* (Paris), No. 31, November 1932, p. 23). Some slight confirmation of this story may be found in the fact that Lenski, unlike Gottwald, was not given the opportunity to reply to the debate; the second Polish delegate who spoke in the debate went out of his way to be polite to the KPD (*XII Plenum IKKI* (1933), ii, 30–32).

[8] *Ibid.* ii, 17–18; Lenski apparently did not mention this episode in his own speech.

[9] Membership, which is said to have reached a peak of 150,000 in 1928, had fallen in 1931 to 35,000, but thereafter began to recover (for figures from various sources see *American Slavic Review*, xx, No. 4, December 1961, p. 645).

presidium of IKKI in February 1930 detected the danger of Left as well as of Right opportunism, an article in the journal of Comintern asserted that "the 'Left' deviation appeared in its clearest form in the Czechoslovak communist party", where "Left" deviators had demanded "a radical purge of the party".[10] Some change of direction was obviously required. But Gottwald weathered the storm. His report at the sixth Czechoslovak party congress in March 1931 dwelt on such safe and familiar themes as the need to *win a majority of the working class* and the struggle for *the hegemony of the proletariat*, as well as the danger of Fascism and imperialist war and the struggle against social-Fascism.[11]

The congress was followed later in the month by the eleventh IKKI in Moscow. Manuilsky's references in his report to the Czechoslovak party were few and polite, including the claim that the party, "with the cooperation of IKKI", had "liquidated the fall in party membership"; and Gottwald delivered a smooth speech, which provoked one or two sceptical interruptions.[12] During 1932 the Czechoslovak party seems to have moved steadily towards the application of united front policies. A big miners' strike in March–April brought socialist and communist miners together in common action which owed nothing to any initiative by the party leaders. The fifth plenum of the party central committee in July 1932 adopted a resolution on "The Way to Unification of the Working Class for Defence and Offence", and made it clear that the struggle against Fascism called for a united front with workers who had "not yet the class consciousness of the proletarian vanguard", and even with "semi-proletarian and petty-bourgeois strata of the population".[13] Gottwald's good standing in Moscow was confirmed by the invitation to be one of the co-*rapporteurs* at the twelfth IKKI in August; and he used the occasion to pursue, perhaps with slightly greater caution. the same line. Claiming that the strike movement in Czechoslovakia was growing, he hailed it as "the most important path to the masses, chiefly to the social-democratic workers"; and his whole speech could be read as an appeal for a broad

[10] *Kommunisticheskii Internatsional*, 1930, No. 13–14, pp. 10–11.

[11] For Gottwald's report and reply to the debate, a brief record on the proceedings, and an article by Gottwald summarizing the results, see *Internationale Presse-Korrespondenz*, No. 23, March 10, 1931, pp. 621–623, No. 24, March 13, 1931, pp. 669–672, No. 28, March 24, 1931, pp. 772–773.

[12] *XI Plenum IKKI* (1932), i, 76, 216–224.

[13] *Iz Istorii Kominterna* (1970), p. 105, quoting party archives.

interpretation of the united front. He argued that acceptance of communism should be not a condition of the united front, but its aim; and he called for the abandonment of sectarian-dogmatic views of the claim of the communist party to lead the movement. He did not mention Germany.[14]

When the debate was thrown open, Ulbricht stepped into the breach with the first serious attempt to expound the policies of the KPD, though his unwillingness to criticize them set limits to his candour. Quoting Stalin on the identity of social-democracy with Fascism, he explained that the SPD "tries to concentrate the whole attention of the working class on Hitler in order to conceal the support given by it to the establishment of a Fascist dictatorship by the Papen government, which collaborates with the Hitler movement". But, unlike Thälmann, he spoke at length on the Anti-Fascist Action as a "broad united front movement", though he admitted with unwonted frankness that "the fighting movement in the factories is developing at a slow tempo", and that "in the competition between Fascist counter-revolution and the tempo of development of the revolutionary upsurge", the advantage was still with the enemy.[15]

Manuilsky made the most optimistic contribution to the debate. The end of capitalist stabilization had brought the rise of Fascism. But Fascism was "an element in the disintegration of capitalism" rather than "a factor in the consolidation of the class rule of the bourgeoisie". Fascism in Germany was different from Fascism in semi-agrarian Italy or Poland. Germany was "the land of the strongest communist mass party, the land which, of all the leading capitalist countries, stands closest to proletarian revolution". The German bourgeoisie "will not let Hitler come to power", because "it fears that the Hitlerites will still further upset Germany's internal position, will create an extremely tense international situation, and will hasten the ripening of the revolutionary crisis in Germany". As regards the proletariat, "the Papen–Schleicher government will not succeed in fastening a Fascist muzzle on the

[14] *XII Plenum IKKI* (1933), i, 97–112. Trotsky, in an article written before he could have received any report of the twelfth IKKI, quoted a recent article of Gottwald in *Rude Pravo* supporting the united front, and added the comment: "Unfortunately he says nothing directly about the KPD; evidently he cannot bring himself to defend it, but dares not criticize it" (*Byulleten' Oppozitsii* (Paris), No. 32, December 1932, pp. 20–21).

[15] *XII Plenum IKKI* (1933), i, 113–128.

masses, in crucifying them on a 'Hakenkreuz'''; the workers will know how to choose between "war and Fascism on one side, and revolution on the other". While praising the record of the KPD he enquired rather sharply why it had been able to organize so few economic strikes on behalf of the day-to-day demands of the workers. He illustrated subtly changing attitudes in Moscow to the Versailles system: "The preaching of national unity and shared sacrifices is fed by Versailles, so that Versailles not only creates elements of revolutionary crisis, but also creates additional obstacles to its ripening." Like most of Manuilsky's utterances, the speech was clever in detail, but for anyone seeking practical guidance highly elusive.[16]

While every speaker professed conformity to the pronouncements of Comintern, and shared in the denunciation of social-democracy, the course of the debate revealed underlying differences between different spokesmen of Comintern and of the Russian party, as well as between those of different foreign parties. Pyatnitsky was the most outspoken critic of the KPD (as well as of the PCF), severely censuring Neumann's errors, from which he exculpated Thälmann: these were the delay in issuing the initial appeal for the anti-Fascist action, the passivity of the party in face of Papen's July 20 *coup*, and in general the half-hearted application of the united front. He also warned the party to prepare for the contingency of being declared illegal.[17] Knorin stood out as the uncompromising advocate of the hard line. To achieve the aims of the workers, "parliamentary motions are not enough, strikes and demonstrations are not enough"; what was needed (Knorin found a suitable quotation from Lenin in 1915) was "the forcible pressure of a genuine revolution". Most of the speech was devoted to the German question—"the central question at most of our plenums and congresses". The speaker made light of the difference between a Nazi dictatorship and the dictatorship of Hindenburg, Papen and Schleicher; Fascism need not always come in the form of a march on Rome. Formal approval of the united front policies of the KPD was qualified by a sarcastic reference to people who wanted a united front "from below and from above". He recalled Stalin's dictum that social-democracy and Fascism were "not antipodes, but

---

[16] *Ibid.* i, 158–168.

[17] *Ibid.* ii, 14–19; for Neumann's errors see p. 47 above. For Pyatnitsky's criticism of the PCF see p. 177 below.

twins", and ended with a protest against "the passivity of some party workers", and against "an underestimate of revolutionary potentialities" in Germany.[18] Bela Kun less incisively followed the same course, arguing that, with the end of capitalist stabilization, the struggle against social-democracy "acquires a *still more important* place in our tactics".[19] Lozovsky wavered. He still asserted that "the chief danger is undoubtedly the Right danger". But he did not demand the formation of new Red trade unions, and withdrew his earlier description of "reformist unions" as "schools of capitalism".[20]

The same divisions could be found among the non-Russian speakers. Gottwald's plea for the united front was supported by the two other Czechoslovak delegates, Guttmann and the Red trade union leader Šverma, who, bolder than his colleague, directly criticized the KPD for the inflexibility of its united front tactics; and the Netherlands delegate also spoke in favour of the united front.[21] But the Austrian delegate, representing a minute and harassed party, said that, if Gottwald's proposals were accepted, communists would "risk being taken in tow by the social-democrats".[22] Of the KPD delegates Remmele, undeterred by Neumann's disgrace, named as the three principal dangers "Right opportunism", "an underestimate of the readiness of the masses for great revolutionary battles", and "the opportunist cult of legality". Florin steered a more cautious middle course, and thought that the masses had not yet had sufficient experience of "partial" economic struggles.[23] The leaders of the other major foreign parties all spoke at length, but preferred not to involve themselves in these thorny controversies, reciting the well-worn formulas, and obediently attempting to spell out the implications for their own parties.[24]

Gottwald, Thälmann and Kuusinen replied to the debate in that order. Gottwald was brief, and notably refrained from associating himself with Guttmann's and Šverma's strictures on the KPD. Thälmann's speech was as long and discursive as his first, but was

[18] *XII Plenum IKKI* (1933), ii, 63–74.
[19] *Ibid.* ii. 117–128.
[20] *Ibid.* ii, 155–172.
[21] *Ibid.* ii, 43–60.
[22] *Ibid.* i, 180.
[23] *Ibid.* ii, 116, 140.
[24] For the speeches of the French, British and Italian delegates see pp. 177, 220, 249 below.

this time devoted almost entirely to the affairs of the KPD. With more than a touch of irony he cited Gottwald's account of "several, sometimes brilliant, united front actions", but hinted at the dangers of a "schematic" transfer of this experience "to all sections of Comintern". He referred defensively to "the vigilance of the central committee of the KPD", which had corrected "mistakes made in the application of the united front". But he also found several safe targets for attack. He criticized Remmele, who had accused the party leadership of "an insufficiently long perspective" and of underestimating revolutionary prospects. He denounced Trotsky who wanted communists to "stand shoulder to shoulder with the murderers of Liebknecht and Rosa and with Zörgiebel". Finally, on the plea that the question had been raised by "our friends in the Russian party delegation", he embarked on a detailed and pedantic catalogue of Neumann's offences, beginning with his prediction that the Reichstag elections of September 1930 would prove to be the high point of Hitler's fortunes, and ending with his alleged misunderstanding of the significance of Stalin's letter of October 1931 to *Proletarskaya Revolyutsiya*. On the eve of the session the political secretariat of Comintern had decided to relieve Neumann of his position as candidate member of the politburo of the KPD, and to warn him of the consequences of any further "fractional activity". This decision was now—apparently for the first time—announced by Thälmann. The banality of the speech betrayed the plight of a party without a policy in face of insurmountable difficulties.[25] Kuusinen wound up the debate. He dwelt on such grounds as he could find for optimism, repeated the warning against "Right opportunist disbelief in the possibility of mobilizing the masses", and the "Left" danger "masking itself in revolutionary phrases", and raised no fresh issues. He excused himself from saying anything further about the united front, but had an eloquent passage on the rise of "nationalism and chauvinism in Germany", in which he accused the Papen government of seeking to "buy from

[25] *XII Plenum IKKI* (1933), iii, 85–117; according to B. Gross, *Willi Münzenberg* (Engl. transl. 1974), p. 231, Neumann attended the sittings, though he was not allowed to speak, but Remmele absented himself. Marty a year later at the thirteenth IKKI alleged that "at the twelfth IKKI . . . Remmele and Neumann defended a political line opposed to the line of the KPD and of Comintern" (*XIII Plenum IKKI* (1934), p. 565); if so, it happened not in open session, but behind the scenes in the presidium or the political commission. For Stalin's letter see Note A, pp. 428–432 below.

French imperialism" the right to equality in armaments "at the price of an anti-Soviet policy".[26]

The two major resolutions adopted respectively on Kuusinen's and Thälmann's reports did no more than recite the familiar themes. The first once more recorded the crisis of capitalism and the achievements of the USSR. But the note of caution quickly followed:

> The end of the relative capitalist stabilization has set in. But there is as yet no immediately revolutionary situation in the most important and decisive capitalist countries. What is taking place at the present moment is a transition to a new phase of big clashes between classes and between states, to a new phase of revolutions and wars.

The application of the united front from below was not to involve "an opportunist glossing over of differences of principle". The sharpening of class conflict was accompanied by a strengthening of communist parties, especially in Germany. A novel factor of the international scene was the demand in Germany for "the status of an imperialist Power with full rights (annulment of reparations, revision of eastern frontiers etc.)"; Germany, no longer condemned to a passive role, was the centre of "the sharpest and tensest imperialist conflicts in the world". A new imperialist war had become "an *immediate* danger." Nationalist aims could not be excluded from the programme of the KPD, which demanded "a worker-peasant republic, i.e. a Soviet socialist Germany, guaranteeing the voluntary adhesion of the people of Austria and other German regions".[27] The second resolution, while it began by saluting "the growth of the revolutionary upsurge in the sphere of economic struggle", was concerned mainly with the shortcomings of communist organizations. The parties had committed "a number of serious opportunist errors" in applying united front tactics. Work both among the unemployed and in reformist trade unions, in the existing Red unions and in the RGO, had been defective. The usual warning was issued against Right and Left deviations. The resolution was an odd mixture of confident prediction of victory and

[26] *XII Plenum IKKI* (1933), iii, 119–129.
[27] *Kommunisticheskii Internatsional v Dokumentakh* (1933), pp. 973–982; for the injunctions in the resolution on the PCF, the CPGB and the CPI, see pp. 178, 221, 249–250 below.

exposure of specific weaknesses, and afforded little ground for
encouragement.[28] A separate resolution was passed on the war in
the Far East.[29] It was the last Comintern session before the Nazi
take-over in Germany, which now lay only a few months ahead. But
it showed little consciousness of impending disaster. Nothing was
said to advance the cause of the united front. The leaders of the
Russian party and of Comintern were not the only politicians in
Europe who were mesmerized by the rise of Hitler, and found it too
unaccountable to formulate any consistent policy to meet it.

The last days of the session coincided with yet another constitutional crisis in Germany. On September 12, 1932, the Reichstag
by an overwhelming majority passed a vote of no confidence in the
Papen government; and Papen obtained Hindenburg's consent to
another dissolution of the Reichstag. The central committee of the
KPD issued a confident proclamation explaining that the Papen
government could not be overthrown by hostile votes in the
Reichstag: "there is only one way out of the catastrophe—
communism". The leaders of the SPD and the ADGB were
condemned for attempting to negotiate with Strasser and Papen.
The SPD was "the party of Hindenburg, the mortal enemy of the
Red united front, the hanger-on of Fascist reaction".[30] *Pravda* in a
leading article of September 14, 1932, greeted *"the approach of a
revolutionary crisis"*. Having no positive policy to propose, the leaders
in Moscow could only cling to the belief that chaos in Germany was
the prelude to proletarian revolution.

A conference of the KPD met on October 15, 1932, to spell out
the instructions of the twelfth IKKI. The implicit obedience to the
decisions on which Thälmann insisted in his main report served to
bring out their confused character. He repeated the new emphasis
on the imperialism of the German bourgeoisie, supported by "the
nationalist-chauvinist wave in Germany, which has led to the rapid
rise of Hitler-Fascism, and thanks to which the Papen–Schleicher
government has come to power". In addition to rearmament and
the eastern frontier, he mentioned "certain arrangements in the
west, e.g. in regard to Eupen-Malmedy or—in the more tangible

---

[28] *Kommunisticheskii Internatsional v Dokumentakh* (1933), pp. 982–990.
[29] See p. 354 below.
[30] *Internationale Presse-Korrespondenz*, No. 77, September 16, 1932, p. 2456.

future—the question of the Saar territory". All this brought nearer the danger of a German–French or German–Polish war, with its fresh menace to the USSR. He unequivocally maintained the equation between Fascism and social-Fascism, but praised the united front as promoted by the Anti-Fascist Action, and the growing support for recent strikes. He ended with a savage attack on Neumann and his group, whose slogan "Hit the Fascists wherever you find them" had bred "occasional tendencies among the workers to individual terror". On the other hand, Neumann had encouraged those who wanted to bring Hitler to power in order to hasten the revolutionary crisis by calling Hitler "the spring-board of revolution". Thälmann's speech was marked by fulsome expressions of subservience to Comintern; and Florin, the KPD representative in Moscow, delivered a co-report on the socialist achievements of the USSR.[31]

The resolution adopted at the end of the conference was no more than a synopsis of Thälmann's exposition of the decisions of IKKI. The diagnosis of the situation was uncompromising. "The Papen–Schleicher government" had been established "with the help of the Reichswehr, the Stahlhelm and the Nazis"; the Centre and the SPD had "paved the way" for it. The SPD was said to have played the same role in bringing Fascism to power in Germany as the social-Fascists in Poland and Italy; and it was condemned for tolerating the Papen–Schleicher government as a "lesser evil" than a Hitler government. The most striking innovation was the insistence on the "imperialist aggressiveness" of the regime. "The struggle for the imperialist re-armament of Germany" was increasing "the active role of German imperialism in preparing counter-revolutionary war against the Soviet Union". But the call for "a bold, offensive application of the tactics of the united front from below" was qualified by a warning "against opportunist attempts to weaken our struggle of principle against the SPD". Finally, the conference endorsed the censure passed by IKKI on Neumann and his group, who were convicted of "an underestimate of Fascism and a weakening of the struggle of principle against the SPD", and of "a sectarian attitude to social-democratic workers and to work within the trade unions", leading to "a denial of the central importance of

[31] Thälmann's report and concluding remarks are in *Im Kampf gegen die Faschistische Diktatur* (1932), pp. 3–42; Florin's report was published as a pamphlet *Die Wahrheit über die Sowjetunion* (1932).

united front tactics from below". The group was also condemned for carrying on a campaign to discredit the party leadership, and to set the leaders of the youth league against the party.[32]

An open breach was now unavoidable. After the twelfth IKKI Remmele addressed an eighty-page memorandum to Comintern, which constituted "a complete platform". He started from the view that the advent of Fascism to power meant "a change in the state system of capitalism". This led to the hypothesis of a basic opposition between Fascism and bourgeois democracy, and to the conception of a broad united front against Fascism. Remmele, who attacked the KPD leaders as Trotskyists and Luxemburgists, and called his group "Left Bolshevik", postulated a "western communism", which, according to its critics, "rejected the Bolshevization of communist parties, and in practice denied the international character of Bolshevism". At a meeting of KPD leaders on November 16, 1932, Remmele made a partial recantation of his errors, and undertook to end his group activity. Nevertheless, the group continued to function, and Remmele maintained his "group connexions" with Neumann.[33] He was relieved of his post in the party secretariat, and replaced by Ulbricht. Neumann, still perhaps hoping to repair his fortunes, attended a meeting of the party *aktiv* at which Manuilsky reported on the proceedings of the twelfth IKKI, and made due confession of his errors.[34] But this did little to clear up the confusion between the different policies which the KPD professed to pursue simultaneously. An article in the Comintern journal recorded with approval that the KPD during the year had "exposed Right opportunist attempts to push it along the path of a bloc with social-Fascism", and rejected "the liberal line of opposing bourgeois democracy to Fascism", but had "struggled against a simplified piling into one heap of social-Fascism and Fascism".[35]

The long drawn-out agony of Hitler's ascent to power in Germany, which was a turning point in European history and in the affairs of Comintern, began in the autumn of 1932. Following the

[32] *Im Kampf gegen die Faschistische Diktatur* (1932), pp. 42–48.
[33] These particulars come from Marty's report at the thirteenth IKKI a year later (*XIII Plenum IKKI* (1934), p. 565; for this report see p. 108 below).
[34] *Internationale Presse-Korrespondenz*, No. 88, October 25, 1932, p. 2823.
[35] *Kommunisticheskii Internatsional*, 1932, No. 24, p. 49.

dissolution of the Reichstag, fresh elections were fixed for November 6. A few days before the elections the Berlin transport organization, a municipal undertaking, announced a decision to reduce wages in response to the financial emergency. Delegates of the workers met on November 2, and proclaimed a strike, which brought the transport system to a standstill. This apparently spontaneous action was loudly applauded by the communist RGO, but rejected by the SPD union leaders as inopportune. Unexpectedly the Nazis came out actively in support of the strike, so that communist and Nazi organizers appeared side by side to encourage the strikers, and the NSDAP triumphantly claimed to have wrested the leadership of the working class from the KPD. After three days the strike collapsed amid mutual recriminations, the KPD accusing the Nazis of having "disorganized the strikers' front from within".[36]

Whatever the implications of this strange episode, it did not immediately benefit the NSDAP, whose vote in the elections of November 6 declined from 13.7 million in July to 11.7 million, reducing the number of its deputies from 230 to 196, but still leaving it the largest party in the new Reichstag. The KPD did well to increase the total number of its deputies from 89 to 100. The SPD once again lost ground, but retained 121 (as against 133) deputies, so that the combined forces of the SPD and KPD—had they been able to combine—exceeded those of the Nazis. The Comintern and party press again breathed a sigh of relief that the troublesome Nazi movement had now passed its peak;[37] and the KPD issued a manifesto once more celebrating the "victorious advance" of the party.[38] This gleam of hope encouraged the mood of irresolution and procrastination prevailing in Moscow in face of the Nazi menace. A probably apocryphal, but plausible, account of a politburo meeting in Moscow in November 1932 depicted Stalin as dismissing Manuilsky's plea for an alliance with the SPD against Hitler, and insisting that since November 6 the Nazi danger had

---

[36] *Die Antifaschistische Aktion* (1965), p. 297; Thälmann and Ulbricht in retrospective accounts of the strike failed to mention Nazi participation, though Thälmann admitted the "defective ideological struggle against the Nazis" as an error committed by the KPD (*Internationale Presse-Korrespondenz*, No. 99, November 25, 1932, pp. 3181–3185).

[37] *Pravda*, November 10, 1932; *Internationale Presse-Korrespondenz*, No. 93, November 8, 1932, p. 2981.

[38] *Ibid.* No. 94, November 11, 1932, pp. 3025–3027.

disappeared, that the Reichswehr would never allow Hitler to come
to power, and that the principal enemy was still the SPD.[39]

While these hopes proved unrealistic, the impression was widespread at the time of something amiss in the ranks of the NSDAP.
The Papen government had adopted a programme of investment
and job-creation, which contrasted with Brüning's *laissez-faire*
approach to the economy, and temporarily reduced unemployment. Thälmann at the twelfth IKKI scornfully dismissed Papen's
" 'measures to revive the economy', means to overcome the crisis",
as being no more than subsidies to heavy industry and large land-
owners.[40] A KPD commentator on the eve of the elections observed
that "the Papen policy anticipated the Nazi programme", but
claimed that the fall in unemployment had been reversed in
October, and spoke of divisions in the Nazi leadership and
discontent in the ranks of the SA.[41] Some attention was given at this
time in the KPD and in Moscow to the Nazi leader Gregor Strasser,
who was regarded as less reactionary than Hitler, and was said to
have been the author of the radical social clauses in the Nazi
programme. Knorin at the twelfth IKKI in September 1932 quoted
him as having said that 95 per cent of the German people had been
"captured by an anti-capitalist spirit".[42] Immediately after the
November elections, the German Ambassador in Moscow told
Litvinov that, while Hindenburg would not have Hitler in the
government, he might admit "some National-Socialists like, for
example, Strasser"; and the Soviet Ambassador in Berlin reported
"a very persistent rumour that the Chancellorship might be offered,
if not to Hitler himself, to Strasser".[43] Early in December 1932
Izvestiya published a long article on Strasser, who was treated, in

[39] Ypsilon, *Pattern for World Revolution* (1947), p. 164; much of this work falls into
the category of well-informed historical fiction. The conviction that the elections of
November 6, 1932, marked the end of the Nazi menace was equally strong
elsewhere. Blum wrote in the socialist newspaper: "Hitler is henceforth excluded
from power; he is excluded, if I may say so, even from the hope of power" (quoted
in J. Fauvet, *Histoire du Parti Communiste Français*, i (1964), 129); Laski in the *Daily
Herald* of November 19, 1932, ventured on "the safe prophecy that the Hitlerite
movement has passed its apogee".

[40] *XII Plenum IKKI* (1933), iii, 87.

[41] *Internationale Presse-Korrespondenz*, No. 92, November 4, 1932, pp. 2935–2937.
The conjecture that the fall in Nazi votes was connected with the decline in
unemployment is tempting; but the KPD, which like the NSDAP relied heavily on
the support of the unemployed, gained votes.

[42] *XII Plenum IKKI* (1933), ii, 64–65.

[43] *Dokumenty Vneshnei Politiki SSSR*, xv (1969), 604, 620.

contrast with the fanatical petty-bourgeois Hitler, as the "statesman" and realist of the NSDAP.[44]

The elections were followed by Papen's resignation; and at the beginning of December 1932, after the breakdown of further negotiations between Schleicher and Hitler, a new government was installed with Schleicher as Chancellor and without Nazi participation. Schleicher made some parade of the need for a social programme to win the support of the workers; and the implications of the change for the KPD seemed at first obscure. Thälmann greeted the new government with the implausible boast that it was "proletarian class power" which had overthrown Papen, and denounced "demagogic unity talk of an anti-worker front from the Nazis to the social-democrats, who chatter about 'a cabinet of social consensus'". He accurately foresaw that the Schleicher cabinet was "a transitional cabinet . . . to prepare the way for a Hitler coalition or a Hitler government".[45] *Pravda* declared that Schleicher had tried to "disguise Papen's unchanged reactionary-Fascist programme in some trappings of National-Socialist demagogy", and concluded somewhat illogically that this created "a favourable position for a successful struggle by the communists to win over a majority of the working class for decisive revolutionary battles".[46] An article in the Comintern news-sheet diagnosed "a sharpened stage of the Fascist regime, and more intense persecution of the workers' movement and the KPD", and as usual combined denunciation of the SPD with the demand for "proletarian united front action".[47] On December 31, 1932, three Left-wing opposition groups—the SAP, Brandler's KPD(O) and a group calling itself Leninbund (Linke Communisten)—joined in a manifesto under the watchword "Fascism must be beaten before it comes to power", calling for "the creation of a unified defence organization".[48] This attempt, by dissidents from both parties, to build a bridge between SPD and KPD was equally unwelcome to both, and was ignored.

Whatever mixed feelings, however, may have prevailed in the

[44] *Izvestiya*, December 12, 1932; the article, which was signed with a pseudonym, was generally attributed to Shtein, a leading official of Narkomindel. Strasser's ambitions were quickly nipped in the bud by Hitler.

[45] *Die Antifaschistische Aktion* (1965), pp. 318–320.

[46] *Pravda*, December 6, 1932.

[47] *Internationale Presse-Korrespondenz*, No. 102, December 6, 1932, pp. 3243–3246.

[48] *Der Deutsche Kommunismus: Dokumente*, ed. H. Weber (1963), pp. 312–313.

KPD and in Comintern, the advent of Schleicher to the Chancellorship could not be entirely unwelcome in Moscow. No German
Government was likely to be more friendly to the USSR than one
dominated by the Reichswehr. The moment was marked by a
certain détente in Soviet foreign relations. Soviet efforts to counteract a deterioration in Soviet–German relations by a *rapprochement*
with France, and through France with Poland, had persisted for
nearly two years.[49] Signs of a break-through came in the summer of
1932, when the bitterly anti-Soviet Tardieu was succeeded as head
of the French Government by the more flexible Herriot, and when
French apprehensions were sharpened by the rising wave of
nationalism in Germany. On November 27, 1932, the Soviet–Polish
pact, which had been signed on July 25, was ratified;[50] and two days
later the long delayed Franco–Soviet non-aggression pact was
signed in Paris, and greeted hopefully by Litvinov as "the beginning
of a new era in mutual relations between the USSR and the French
Republic".[51] It was a coincidence that these acts were completed on
the eve of Schleicher's installation as Chancellor in Berlin. But it
gave the Soviet Government some sense of security and freedom of
manoeuvre.

Nobody in Moscow doubted, however, that Germany was the
central factor in Soviet foreign relations. When Litvinov had his one
meeting with Schleicher in Berlin on December 19, 1932, he
intimated that, while the Soviet Government had viewed the Papen
government with some mistrust, it had no such scruples in regard to
the Schleicher government. Schleicher was anxious to be reassured
that Soviet pacts with France and Poland implied no change of
attitude towards Germany, declared that his appointment as
Chancellor was a guarantee of the maintenance of firm German–
Soviet relations, and promised an early ratification of the protocol
renewing the Berlin treaty of 1926. He complained of the subversive
activities of the KPD, and hinted at the possibility of a legal ban.
Schleicher had previously assured the Soviet Ambassador that
action against German communists had nothing to do with German
policy towards the USSR. Litvinov now responded by declaring
that measures taken by the German Government against German
communists were no concern of the Soviet Government, and would

[49] See pp. 43–44 above.
[50] *Dokumenty Vneshnei Politiki SSSR*, xv (1969), 436–439; the pact had been
drafted and initialled in January 1932 (see p. 44 above).
[51] *Dokumenty Vneshnei Politiki SSSR*, xv (1969), 637–640, 644–648.

not affect Soviet–German relations.[52] As the new year of 1933 opened, a reassuring balance seemed to have been established in Soviet international relations, the most seriously disturbing factor being the Japanese aggression in Manchuria. On January 23, 1933, Molotov, reviewing the international situation at the session of TsIK, declared with unusual brevity that "Germany occupies a special place in our foreign relations", arising from "the interests of both countries".[53] The same month produced a flood of increasingly shrill protests from KPD organizations against Hitler's openly provocative speeches and murderous attacks by Nazi gangs.[54] But, when Thorez came to Berlin to participate in the annual commemoration of the death of Luxemburg and Liebknecht on January 15, he spoke eloquently of "the anti-capitalist, anti-Fascist front which wages a real struggle against the Versailles treaty and against imperialist war", and apparently did not mention the Nazis at all.[55] Nothing in the climate in the KPD or in Comintern suggested the imminence of an enormous and fateful upheaval in world affairs.

Once again, however, the political situation in Germany refused to remain stable. On January 4, 1933, the banker Schröder arranged a much publicized meeting in his house between Papen and Hitler. Ever since the "Harzburg front" of October 1931,[56] the project of drawing the Nazi movement into an alliance with the industrial, financial and land-owning interests had been on the cards. The alliance was now sealed in conditions far more favourable to Hitler, though the question which would be the predominant party was still open. But the bargain had another significance which was less quickly recognized. Schleicher's would-be radical programme had alarmed the interests for which Papen now spoke; and it was in the last resort Papen, not Schleicher, who had the ear of Hindenburg. The course of events was followed by the KPD and by Comintern with bewilderment and with a plethora of far-fetched conjectures; both resisted the conclusion that the

---

[52] The fullest account of the interview is in *Auswärtiges Amt*, 9496/668964–7; it is briefly recorded in *Dokumenty Vneshnei Politiki SSSR*, xv (1969), 816, note 331, but the telegram of December 20, 1932, in which Litvinov reported on it to Narkomindel, is, perhaps significantly, not included. For Schleicher's earlier assurance see *ibid.* xv, 390.

[53] *SSSR: Tsentral'nyi Ispolnitel'nyi Komitet 6 Sozyva: Seesiya* (1933), No. 1, p. 37.

[54] Some of these are in *Die Antifaschistische Aktion* (1965), pp. 332–356.

[55] *Die Rote Fahne*, January 17, 1933.

[56] See p. 51 above.

downfall of Schleicher, on whom so many hopes had been pinned, was imminent. But long before the end of this fateful month it had become clear that Schleicher could not survive the re-assembly of the Reichstag on January 31. On January 28, he handed in his resignation. Two days later Hitler was summoned by Hindenburg to succeed him.

CHAPTER 5

HITLER IN POWER

It was only in retrospect that Hitler's appointment as Chancellor on January 30, 1933, was seen as the decisive date in his ascent to power. There had been no *coup d'état*, no march on Rome. Of the twelve members of the new cabinet, only three—Hitler, Göring and Frick—were Nazis; the others were representatives of the traditional Right. Germany had long been used to coalitions; and this coalition, which conformed to accepted constitutional conventions, bore no outward symbols of the dictatorship of a single party. The first reaction in *Pravda* on January 31 was to hail Hugenberg, the representative of monopoly capital, as the most important man in the new government; and this view was widely held by other observers, including Trotsky.[1] Nevertheless Hitler's Chancellorship was felt everywhere to mark a new stage. The announcement of Schleicher's resignation on January 29 had inspired a now routine appeal by the KPD to social-democratic workers and organizations for common action against Fascism;[2] and next day the KPD issued a broadsheet calling for a general strike against "this new cabinet of an open Fascist dictatorship".[3] The strike appeal was abortive. It was ignored by the SPD, which issued its own proclamation urging that "the hour demands the unity of the whole working people", but stating firmly that "we conduct our struggle on the basis of the constitution".[4]

This declaration of principle continued to divide the two parties. On February 7, Thälmann spoke at a secret meeting of the KPD central committee of the need for "the security of the party and its maintenance in spite of all assaults of the Fascist terror", and called

---

[1] According to the reminiscences of an eye-witness, the content of the *Pravda* article was dictated by Knorin, who was presumed to have been in touch with Stalin (*Survey*, October 1962, p. 163); for Trotsky's comment see p. 434 below.

[2] *Die Rote Fahne*, January 29, 1933.

[3] *Rundschau*, No. 2, February 1, 1933, p. 23; *Geschichte der Deutschen Arbeiterbewegung*, v (1966), 441–442 (a reproduction of the broadsheet appears among the illustrations in this volume).

[4] *Ibid.* v, 442.

for "a strong campaign to shatter all parliamentary illusions and to educate the masses for an extra-parliamentary mass struggle".[5] During the ensuing weeks public recriminations between KPD and SPD proceeded on familiar lines, though this did not preclude some high-level private contacts[6] and joint demonstrations at lower levels. But events soon overtook these barren exchanges. Acts of violence by Nazis against members or groups of the Left multiplied; and the suspension of newspapers, not unknown under earlier regimes, became a matter of routine. The limits within which legal action was open to parties of the Left were narrowing daily.

Attempts to create an international united front of the Left against Fascism still encountered obstacles. On February 6, 1933, representatives of seven independent Left parties—the British ILP, the German SAP, the French POP, and Polish, Italian, Norwegian and Netherlands independent socialist workers' parties—met in Paris and issued a manifesto addressed to Social-Democrats, Communists and independent Revolutionary Socialists, appealing to "class-conscious workers" to unite against "the common enemy"; telegrams in similar terms were sent to the Second International and to Comintern.[7] The two Internationals were at one, if in nothing else, in their dislike of the intrusion of a third international group of the Left. Both ignored the overture. Not to be outdone, the French, German and Polish communist parties on February 13 appealed to socialist workers to "forge an invincible united front of proletarian struggle".[8] At length, on February 17, the Second International issued its own appeal to workers of all countries "to stop mutual strife and fight together against Fascism",

[5] *Geschichte der Deutschen Arbeiterbewegung*, v (1966), 446–447.

[6] At the Reichstag fire trial in November 1933, Neubauer, a KPD deputy then under arrest, related that Stampfer, a leading SPD deputy, had approached the Soviet Embassy with an overture for cooperation between the two parties against Fascism, and had received the reply that this was not a matter for the Embassy; Neubauer, having learned of this, indicated to the journalist who had given him the information that he was prepared to meet Stampfer. A meeting between Torgler and Neubauer and Stampfer was arranged for February 28, but did not take place owing to the Reichstag fire (*Rundschau*, No. 41, November 3, 1933, p. 1589); for somewhat uncertain evidence of an earlier contact between Torgler and Stampfer see T. Weingartner, *Stalin und der Aufstieg Hitlers* (1970), p. 224. A less credible story appeared in K. Heiden, *Der Führer* (1944), p. 432.

[7] *Kommunisticheskii Internatsional: Kratkii Istoricheskii Ocherk* (1969), p. 351; for the text see *New Leader*, February 10, 1933. For the POP see p. 164 below.

[8] *Humanité*, February 13, 1933.

and offered to enter into negotiations with Comintern to this end.

The belated response to this appeal which came from Comintern on March 5, 1933, showed clear signs of hesitations and divided opinions among its officials. Addressed to the workers of all countries, it began by affirming that the chief hindrance to the united front lay in the policy pursued by the social-democratic leaders of cooperation with the bourgeoisie, known as the policy of the "lesser evil", which had split the unity of the working class, and "led to the triumph of Fascist reaction in Germany". The declaration of February 17 was "in sharpest contradiction" with the line hitherto pursued, and could inspire Comintern and communist parties with no belief in its sincerity. Nevertheless, Comintern was prepared to "recommend" communist parties to approach the central authorities of parties belonging to the Second International with proposals for common action, which should take the form of joint resistance to Fascist attacks and of joint meetings, demonstrations and strikes. Communist parties would also be recommended, during the period of this joint action, to suspend attacks on social-democratic organizations. The proposal for direct negotiations between the Second International and Comintern was ignored.[9] This half-hearted response to a half-hearted appeal was accompanied by a leading article in *Pravda*, which was concerned mainly to heap insults on the record of social-democracy.[10] Notwithstanding its grudging terms, the Comintern "recommendation" was gratefully received by the leading communist parties.[11] On March 14 the KPD, taking its cue from the Comintern appeal, addressed to the leaders of the SPD an open and unqualified proposal of common action and common organization to meet "the unheard of terror of the Hitler–Papen–Hugenberg government and the Hitler-party's SA and SS bands"—a proposal free for the first time of any element of reproach or recrimination.[12] But it came too late, and made no impact. A few days later the executive of the Second International met in Zurich, noted that the Comintern declaration had not even mentioned its offer of negotiations, and instructed its member parties to refrain from separate negotiations

[9] *Pravda*, March 6, 1933, *Rundschau*, No. 4, March 11, 1933, pp. 91–92; the Comintern appeal was followed by an appeal from KIM for a "united fighting front of young workers" (*ibid*. No. 6, March 25, 1933, pp. 151–152).

[10] *Pravda*, March 6, 1933.

[11] For the response of the parties see pp. 182, 224, 250 below.

[12] *Rundschau*, No. 6, March 25, 1933, p. 149.

with communist parties till such time as negotiations had taken place between the two Internationals.[13]

Though Thälmann in his speech of February 7, 1933, had called Hitler "the man who has made a declaration of war on the Soviet Union the guiding line of his policy", the reaction in Moscow to Hitler's Chancellorship was milder. The retention of Neurath as Foreign Minister seemed to promise continuity of policy. *Pravda* consoled its readers with the reflexion that the USSR was the only major country which was not hostile to Germany, and that "only fools on the throne" would want to poison Soviet–German relations and isolate Germany completely.[14] Hitler remained silent on foreign affairs. The two governments continued to transact routine diplomatic business; an agreement on German credits to the USSR was signed in Berlin on February 25.[15] What excited most dismay was the elimination of Schleicher, on whom the Soviet leaders had counted for an assurance of German friendship, and the re-emergence of Papen, whom they suspected of an inclination to seek *rapprochement* with the western Powers. But nothing significant occurred until February 27, when Dirksen, the German Ambassador in Moscow, called on Krestinsky, in charge of Narkomindel during Litvinov's absence in Geneva, and proposed, on instructions from Neurath, "detailed discussions with the Soviet Government on the general state of Soviet–German political relations". Dirksen expressed apprehension at some recent symptoms of a *rapprochement* between the USSR and France, but offered a firm assurance of the constancy of German policy:

> The leading members of the government—Neurath, Schleicher and Papen—have repeatedly declared to responsible representatives of the Soviet Union that the hitherto existing policy of the German Government in relation to the USSR will be fully maintained and continued.

Hitler had told Neurath that "a sharp distinction must be drawn between methods of internal policy in regard to communism in Germany and policy in regard to the Soviet Union", and that he desired no change in the latter. Krestinsky replied rather sourly that

---

[13] J. Braunthal, *History of the International* (Engl. trans. 1967), ii, 393.

[14] *Pravda*, March 4, 1933.

[15] *Dokumenty Vneshnei Politiki SSSR*, xvi (1970), 112–116.

Hitler's statement could have no "binding character", since it "was not made publicly, and not directly to us".[16]

On the evening of the day when this conversation took place in Moscow, the Reichstag building in Berlin was burnt down. An apparently half-witted Dutchman, Van der Lubbe, once a communist, was caught on the spot, and the communists were at once denounced as the perpetrators of the crime. During the night many thousands of communists were arrested. On the following day a presidential decree was issued suspending the liberties and rights guaranteed to individuals by the Weimar constitution; and a reign of terror was inaugurated against the parties and groups of the extreme Left. No attention was paid to a statement issued to the press by the KPD, rebutting all complicity in the Reichstag fire, denying that Lubbe was a member of the Netherlands communist party, and recalling the fraud of the "Zinoviev letter".[17] On March 1 Litvinov, returning from Geneva to Moscow, had an interview with Neurath in Berlin. If the official records, Soviet and German, of the conversation are complete, neither mentioned the Reichstag fire or its sequel. The nearest that Neurath came to an allusion to these events was to remark that, "if he [i.e. Hitler] had recently had to take sharp measures, some pacification will set in after the elections". Neurath repeated the assurance that no change was contemplated in German–Soviet relations, and that "Hitler knows how to distinguish between communism and our state". He added that there were extremists among the Nazis, but that Hitler himself was "a reasonable, practical man and open to conviction". Litvinov, who had just been told by his German colleague at the disarmament conference that Hitler, having taken control of the police, would shortly free himself from the toils of the coalition, may not have been altogether reassured.[18]

Next day Hitler addressed a triumphant mass meeting of his followers. Reverting for the first time since he became Chancellor to his customary style of rhetoric, he fastened responsibility for the Reichstag fire firmly on the "Bolsheviks", and made a violent attack on the domestic policies of the Soviet regime. This was followed by

[16] *Dokumenty Vneshnei Politiki SSSR*, xvi (1970), 117–121.

[17] *Rundschau*, No. 3, March 1933, p. 42; later a more detailed statement, holding Göring personally responsible for the fire, was issued by the communist deputies to the Reichstag (*ibid.* No. 7, March 31, 1933, pp. 170–171).

[18] *Dokumenty Vneshnei Politiki SSSR*, xvi (1970), 134–138; *Auswärtiges Amt*, 2860/562415–8.

official Soviet protests,[19] and by an intensification of violence against German communists. On March 3, Thälmann was arrested; and on March 9, Dimitrov, who was head of the Western European Bureau of Comintern (WEB) in Berlin,[20] was taken into custody with two Bulgarian colleagues, Tanev and Popov, and charged with complicity in the Reichstag fire. Meanwhile elections to the Reichstag had been held on March 5. The Nazis obtained more than 17 million votes, 43 per cent of the total, and, together with the parties of the Right represented in the government, commanded a clear majority. The KPD received 4.8 million votes, the SPD 7 million—creditable figures in the circumstances; the remainder of the minority consisted of the Centre. *Pravda* on March 7 celebrated "The Immense Political Victory of the KPD". Hitler more practically imposed a legal ban on the KPD and on all its institutions and publications; it was excluded from any further part in the proceedings.[21] The SPD escaped for the moment. When the Reichstag met on March 16, the government submitted to it a law conferring absolute powers on the government to legislate and act without the consent of the Reichstag. Great pressure was applied to secure a unanimous vote. The Centre gave way and voted for the law; only the 91 members of the SPD had the courage to vote against it, while continuing to protest that they would act only by constitutional means. In effect, the law-abiding reservation nullified the gesture of the vote. The option of constitutional opposition was not open. The SPD quickly drifted into a posture of refraining from active resistance to the regime in the hope that the regime might be induced to tolerate its continued existence. The trade unions made abortive overtures to Nazi leaders which, if they had been successful, might have secured for them the status of the CGL under Mussolini.

[19] *Dokumenty Vneshnei Politiki SSSR*, xvi (1970), 141–142, 149–150.

[20] Dimitrov, who had worked in Comintern since the Bulgarian disaster of 1923, was appointed to WEB in March 1929, and his vigorous personality seems to have transformed this rather shadowy institution into a busy and effective agency of IKKI, on whose behalf it handled many issues of relations with foreign (not only European) parties; its functions were defined and extended in May 1931 (*Georgii Dimitrov: Vydayushchiisya Deyatel' Kommunisticheskogo Dvizheniya* (1972), pp. 80–82). According to J. Humbert-Droz, *Dix Ans de Lutte Antifaschiste* (Neuchatel, 1972), p. 112, Dimitrov had originally been appointed to this "subordinate" post in order to get him away from Moscow, where he was regarded as a "Right deviationist".

[21] The speech of defiance which Pieck was to have delivered in the Reichstag was published in *Rundschau*, No. 10, April 20, 1933, pp. 268–269.

A single blow had felled the once powerful KPD—the beacon of hope of proletarian revolution in Europe. Most of its leaders who escaped immediate arrest, including Pieck, Ulbricht and Florin, took refuge in Paris, where a rump central committee of the party was quickly constituted. An elaborate organization was set up to maintain contact with such party groups as might still lead a precarious underground existence in Germany. According to a police report, "frontier" posts were established in Amsterdam, Strasbourg, Luxemburg, Copenhagen and Prague; and a centre for illegal organizations in Germany was created in Berlin.[22] How numerous or how active were the underground groups, and how much contact was maintained with them, is difficult to guess. Exaggerated claims were made. But frequent references to the Nazi terror, and reports of arrests of communists, suggest that the repression was in the main effective. Ulbricht towards the end of 1933 admitted that "with most factories in which factory cells existed before January 30 contact has not yet been re-established".[23]

Careful preparations had been made in advance to maintain publishing activities abroad. Since July 1, 1932, the editorial board of *Internationale Presse-Korrespondenz* had published in Basel a monthly journal entitled *Rundschau über Politik, Wirtschaft und Arbeiterbewegung*. Unlike *Internationale Presse-Korrespondenz*, it confined itself mainly to news items and to unsigned articles, reproducing few speeches or articles from other Comintern sources. Otherwise the style and political orientation of the two publications were the same. The appearance of the ninth monthly number (No. 3 of 1933) on March 1, 1933, coincided with the suppression of *Internationale Presse-Korrespondenz* in Germany; and from this date the *Rundschau* transformed itself into a weekly and took on the character of the former news-sheet. Meanwhile issues of a much curtailed *Internationale Presse-Korrespondenz*, as well as of the party newspaper, the *Rote Fahne*, were printed abroad at irregular intervals to be smuggled into Germany. A pamphlet on the Reichstag fire was said to have been printed in 10,000 copies; more dubiously, it was claimed that an appeal to fight against the Hitler government and a May 1 proclamation had been circulated in 200,000 copies.[24] But

[22] *Der Deutsche Kommunismus: Dokumente*, ed. H. Weber (1963), pp. 405–407.
[23] *Rundschau*, No. 46, November 30, 1933, p. 1775.
[24] *XIII Plenum IKKI* (1934), p. 166.

how much party literature and party propaganda slipped through the Nazi net and reached the communist underground remains a matter of conjecture.

The first formal assessment by Comintern of Hitler's victory came at a session of the presidium of IKKI on April 1, 1933. It was imperative to minimize the magnitude of the disaster; for the KPD was, as the Comintern journal still proclaimed, "the vanguard army of revolutionary· Marxism–Leninism in the capitalist world".[25] Heckert delivered a report which was mainly concerned to place the blame for the German catastrophe on the broad shoulders of the SPD. From August 4, 1914, social-democracy had "pursued the policy of *a united reactionary front with the bourgeoisie* against the proletariat". It had come to the rescue of the bourgeoisie in the revolution of 1918–1919. "The bourgeois republic of the Weimar constitution, built by the hands of social-democrats, rested in reality on the same social and economic basis as the Hohenzollern monarchy." The petty bourgeoisie, inflamed by the oppressions of the Versailles treaty and the treachery of the social-democrats, had been engulfed by a wave of chauvinism, which had also not spared some sections of the working class. Only the KPD had stood firmly against Fascism. Terror could not break a party five million strong; and Heckert ended with the prediction that it would "lead the working class to the final victory over Fascism and capitalism". The presidium adopted a resolution which endorsed Heckert's diagnosis, seeking comfort in an argument formerly spurned when it had been propounded by Neumann and his supporters:

> The establishment of an open Fascist dictatorship, which destroys all democratic illusions among the masses, and frees them from the influence of the social-democrats, will hasten Germany's progress towards the proletarian revolution.

It praised the policies of the KPD "before and at the time of the Hitler coup" as "quite correct", and summoned the party "*to prepare the masses for decisive revolutionary battles, for the overthrow of capitalism and for the overthrow of the Fascist dictatorship by an armed rebellion*".[26] In

---

[25] *Kommunisticheskii Internatsional*, 1933, No. 9, p. 13.

[26] *Rundschau*, No. 9, April 12, 1933, pp. 229–231 (resolution), No. 10, April 20, 1933, pp. 261–267 (report); both documents appeared in English in a pamphlet *Why Hitler in Germany?* (1933). For the theory that Nazi successes would promote the cause of proletarian revolution, and Manuilsky's rejection of it, see p. 34 above.

the same spirit an appeal to "the proletarians of all countries", drafted at this time by IKKI for the May 1 celebrations, vehemently denounced social-democracy, which "prefers a united front with the Fascists to defend and preserve capitalism to a workers' united front to overthrow capitalism by a workers' revolution".[27] In May 1933 the rump central committee of the KPD passed a long resolution which endorsed and embroidered the conclusions of the IKKI presidium. It did not omit to condemn "Merker's sectarianism" and "the sectarian policy of the Neumann group". But it added that "the complete exclusion of the social-Fascists from the state apparatus, the brutal suppression of social-democratic organizations and of their press, changes nothing in the fact that they remain as before the chief social prop of the dictatorship of capital".[28]

It could hardly be expected that the smooth verdict delivered in Moscow would heal rifts which had existed in the party before the catastrophe, and which were intensified by the disruptions and humiliations of a party in exile. Remmele, apparently egged on by the now embittered Neumann,[29] replied to the IKKI resolution of April 1, 1933, in a memorandum which asserted that the Nazi seizure of power was "the biggest defeat of the proletariat since 1914"; that "we are passing through a period of Fascism and reaction"; and that "in Germany the whole bourgeois society has sunk to the level of the lumpenproletariat". He called on the party to open a discussion of the situation on the basis of his platform.[30] The invitation was not well received. Other dissident voices were also discounted. Gottwald telegraphed to IKKI on April 9, 1933, urging it to open negotiations with the second International in order to "strengthen activity in favour of the united front from below", and similar opinions were heard in the French and Austrian parties. In Moscow any such overtures were condemned as "inappropriate" in view of the attitude of the leaders of the second International.[31]

---

[27] *Rundschau*, No. 11, April 28, 1933, pp. 300–302.

[28] *Rundschau*, No. 17, June 2, 1933, pp. 541–548.

[29] Neumann wrote to Remmele on March 7, 1933, urging him "to play the role of Rosa Luxemburg" in opposition to the party leaders; this was disclosed by Marty in his indictment of Remmele at the thirteenth IKKI (*XIII Plenum IKKI* (1934), p. 565), and confirmed by Neumann in his recantation of April 1934 (see p. 133 below).

[30] *XIII Plenum IKKI* (1934), pp. 566–567.

[31] *Kommunisticheskii Internatsional: Kratkii Istoricheskii Ocherk* (1969), pp. 353–354.

The controversy provoked a fierce indictment by Trotsky, who pronounced "the strategic judgment of Comintern" to have been "false from beginning to end"; it had consisted in treating social-democracy and Fascism as "akin, if not identical", instead of utilizing the contradiction between reformism and Fascism to weaken Fascism.[32]

In Moscow, censure of social-democracy, eulogy of the KPD and confidence in the future, however unconvincing, served the necessary purpose of avoiding any consideration of the role of Comintern in these events. For many years Comintern had imposed and deposed KPD leaders in the light of its own preconceptions of what was desirable; and the party had been demoralized by being held in a straitjacket of doctrine and policy handed down from Moscow. If the KPD had been blamed for the disaster, the weight of responsibility must have fallen on Comintern. Yet this was not the whole truth. Behind the long record of errors and miscalculations lay the fact that, even in the heady days of the winter of 1918–1919 and again in 1921 and 1923, a majority of German workers had not come out for proletarian revolution. The mood of the majority had not changed in 1933. The difference between the KPD and the SPD was that the former, urged on from Moscow, had a programme of revolutionary action which few of its members were ready to implement,[33] and the latter excused inaction on the plea of its adherence to legality and the constitution.

The respite earned for the SPD by its quiescence was brief. On May 2, 1933, the trade unions were taken over, their buildings occupied and their property seized. On May 10, a mass of communist, trade union, Left-wing and Jewish literature was consigned, amid scenes of enthusiasm, to a vast bonfire in the square in front of the opera house. A week later, when Hitler delivered a speech in the Reichstag demanding a revision of the Versailles treaty and equality of rights for Germany in armaments, the SPD deputies sheepishly voted with the rest in support of the foreign policy of the regime.[34] But the end was now near. On June 22 the SPD was legally banned, its premises were ransacked, and its

[32] *Byulleten' Oppozitsii* (Paris), No. 35, July 1933, p. 3.

[33] Lozovsky had long ago protested against the survival of "legalism" and "constitutionalism" in the KPD (see *Foundations of a Planned Economy, 1926–1929*, Vol. 3, p. 456).

[34] The occasion was reported in an article in *Rundschau*, No. 16, May 26, 1933, pp. 489–490, with the sub-title "The New Shame of the Social-Fascists".

members subjected to the same house-searches and arrests as the communists. Its fate had been anticipated and new party headquarters were set up in Prague. Other parties soon suffered the same fate. The only one to show any resistance was the German National Party, the partner of the Nazis in the coalition of January 30. But this was quickly broken. At the end of June Hugenberg was dismissed from his post in the government; the party was dissolved; and on July 14, 1933, a decree was issued proclaiming the NSDAP "the only political party in Germany". The Nazi dictatorship was absolute.

The KPD and the SPD were now equal victims of the same ruthless persecution. But this companionship in disaster was not enough to heal the mutual bitterness of past antagonisms. The survivors of the rank and file of the KPD still at large in Germany were more realistic than their leaders in exile. An illegal party broadsheet circulated in the spring of 1933, addressed to "Hitler-electors, SA men, workers, employees, officials, small business men", denounced the regime, and its leaders by name, for its depression of the standard of living of the workers and its truckling to "the interests of the exploiter-society", coining the slogan "Hakenkreuz ist Hungerkreuz". It called on Germany to "awake to the struggle against the government of hunger, terror and war", and ended with an appeal for "a struggle for work, bread, freedom, socialism".[35] But among the leaders, isolated from daily experience of the terror, and more directly exposed to pressure from Moscow, the passing mood of reconciliation expressed in the appeal of March 14[36] did not last. The KPD was slower than any other European communist party to accept cooperation with socialist or any other parties in resistance to Fascism. Heckert's report and the resolution of the presidium of IKKI on April 1 had been full of acrimony against the SPD.[37] "The brutal suppression of the social-democratic organizations and press", observed the resolution of the central committee of the KPD endorsing the proceedings of IKKI, "can do nothing to alter the fact that the social-democrats were, and still remain, the chief prop of the capitalist dictatorship."[38] The tone of an open letter of June 20, 1933, to SPD workers appealing for a united front had not significantly changed; it was unambiguously

[35] *Rundschau*, No. 13, May 12, 1933, p. 391.
[36] See p. 85 above.
[37] See p. 90 above.
[38] *Rundschau*, No. 17, June 2, 1933, p. 545; for this resolution see pp. 90–91 above.

directed against the SPD leaders, who were still branded as social-Fascists.[39] On August 1 the four communist ringleaders in the Altona riots a year earlier were executed after a long delayed trial.[40] It was not forgotten that the police-president who had given the order to fire on the communist demonstration was a social-democrat, though he himself had since apparently been killed by the Nazis.

It was in this atmosphere that a conference of the Second International opened in Paris on August 21, 1933. It was inevitably dominated by the German catastrophe. The Russian Menshevik Abramovich accused the SPD of having suffered from a "paralysis of will", due to its determination to observe legality and to avoid the risk of "shedding workers' blood". Everyone attributed the weakness of the Left to the split between the two workers' parties. A substantial minority led by Nenni wished to reopen negotiations with Comintern. In view of past experience a majority rejected this proposal; and the resolution adopted only expressed the intention "to do all in its power to reunite the divided forces of the workers".[41] The proceedings were treated with contempt in a resolution of the central committee of the KPD (misleadingly dated from "Berlin"), which bore the heading, "Proletarians of All Countries! Unite under the Banner of the Communist International".[42]

The main preoccupation in Soviet and Comintern circles in the first months of 1933 was, however, not the fate of the KPD or the eclipse of revolutionary prospects in Europe, but the danger to the USSR which Hitler's tenure of power might entail. A German–Polish incident in Danzig early in March prompted an article by Knorin in the journal of Comintern entitled "The Barometer Points to Storm", which spoke anxiously of "Hitler's open revisionist and war policy" and expressed the fear that Danzig might become "the

[39] *Rundschau*, No. 23, July 7, 1933, pp. 783–787.

[40] *Ibid.* No. 18, June 9, 1933, pp. 587–588, No. 27, August 4, 1933, p. 971, No. 28, August 11, 1933, pp. 1019–1021; for the Altona affair see p. 61 above.

[41] For accounts of the conference see J. Braunthal, *History of the International*, ii (Engl. transl. 1967), 399–402; *Rundschau*, No. 31, August 25, 1933, pp. 1153–1158, No. 32, September 1, 1933, pp. 1206–1209. This was the last major conference of the Second International; the Vienna congress of 1931 (see p. 41 above) had been its last formal congress. It continued for some years to transact business through its executive or a smaller bureau.

[42] *Rundschau*, No. 33, September 8, 1933, pp. 1251–1253.

signal for the unleashing of an imperialist war".[43] At the same
moment Mussolini submitted to the French, British and German
Governments the draft of a four-Power treaty under which the
signatories would be required to reaffirm their peaceful intentions,
but would draw attention to the procedure provided by the
Covenant of the League of Nations for the peaceful revision of
treaties. The *Rundschau*, in an article on "The Rome Pact", noted
that this was the first mention in an official document of a revision of
the treaties, wondered what was being offered to Germany "in order
to moderate Hitler's appetite", and detected "the sharpest war
threat to the Soviet Union".[44] When on March 23 Hitler, perhaps
prompted by Neurath, delivered a speech in which he expressed the
will of his government to maintain friendly relations with the
USSR, and added that the struggle against Bolshevism in Germany
had no bearing on these "state-political" relations, Litvinov
expressed his gratification to the German Ambassador in Moscow.[45]
But *Izvestiya* after some delay published an article entitled "Words
and Facts", which voiced doubts whether these assurances were
compatible with the attitude of the German press and the treatment
of Soviet institutions and nationals in Germany.[46] At a further
meeting with Dirksen, Litvinov expressed his reservations
about Mussolini's draft pact. On April 28, the Soviet Ambassador
was politely received by Hitler in the presence of Neurath; and
Khinchuk took the opportunity to present a memorandum of Soviet
complaints and protests.[47] A few days later, the long delayed
German ratification of the protocol prolonging the Soviet – German
treaty of April 24, 1926, was hailed as a diplomatic event; and,

[43] *Kommunisticheskii Internatsional*, 1933, No. 7–8, pp. 11–18; a translation
appeared in *Rundschau*, No. 5, March 18, 1933, p. 122. For a further incident at
Danzig see p. 259 below.

[44] *Rundschau*, No. 6, March 25, 1933, pp. 130–131. Irritation against Italy was
displayed in a joint appeal of German, Italian, Czechoslovak and Austrian
Communist Parties to workers of the whole world against the enslavement of "the
German population of the South Tirol under the foreign imperialist yoke of Italy"
(*ibid.* No. 6, March 25, 1933, pp. 156–157)—a flagrant attempt to inflame
relations between the two dictators; this did not prevent a strong effort in the
summer of 1933 to improve Soviet–Italian relations (see p. 251 below).

[45] Litvinov's remarks to Dirksen, omitted from the Soviet collection of
documents, are reported in *Auswärtiges Amt*, 2860/562447; for previous assurances
in the same sense see p. 86 above.

[46] For the *Izvestiya* article of March 28, 1933, see *Dokumenty Vneshnei Politiki
SSSR*, xvi (1970), 212–213.

[47] *Ibid.* xvi, 271–274.

though a note of irony crept into comments in the Soviet press, the essential point was once more driven home: "The corner-stone of Soviet foreign policy is the maintenance of peace . . . ; in this spirit the Soviet Union does not wish to alter anything in its attitude to Germany".[48]

While the desire to believe that nothing had fundamentally changed was still strong in Moscow, it was no longer possible to disguise the shock administered to European diplomacy, and in particular to Soviet – German relations, by Hitler's assumption of absolute power. At this moment Radek reappeared in his time-honoured role to fly a kite for policies not yet ripe for official endorsement. On May 10, 1933, an article appeared in *Pravda* over his signature entitled "Revision of the Versailles Treaty". Starting from the familiar denunciation of the Versailles system, he broke new ground in a realistic analysis of the German case for revision, in the colonies and in Europe. "There is no just solution of the national question", declared Radek, either in north-eastern Europe or in the Balkans; conflicting claims could be reconciled only by "revolutionary unification". But, pending this remote solution, he announced conclusions which ingeniously blended old and new:

> It is the Fascist governments which are the standard-bearers of the cry for revision. . . . The path to a revision of the robber peace of Versailles is the path to a new world war. . . . The programme of a revision of the Versailles treaty through the creation of a worse Brest-Litovsk peace . . . is the foreign political programme of German Fascism.

Among the minor nuances of the article was a mention of "the Polish coastal region (known as the 'corridor')"; the contemptuous dismissal of the term "corridor", familiarized by German propaganda ever since 1919, was a friendly gesture towards Poland. In July Radek paid a fortnight-long visit to Poland, where his mother still lived. No mention of his journey appeared either in the Polish or in the Soviet press. But he is said to have visited Danzig and Pomerania (the "Polish corridor"), and he must be assumed to have had some discreet contacts with the Polish authorities and with KPP leaders.[49] If his purpose was to forestall a growing inclination of the

[48] *Izvestiya*, May 6, 1933.

[49] J. Kowalski, *Trudne Lata* (1966), p. 384; according to J. Lipski, *Diplomat in Berlin* (1968), p. 97, note 3, the ostensible purpose of Radek's visit was to return, in his capacity as one of the editors of *Pravda*, a visit paid to Moscow by the editor of *Gazeta Polska*.

Polish Government to seek an accommodation with Berlin, it was a failure.

Provocations from the Nazi camp were, however, not lacking. Rosenberg, the notorious publicist of the Nazi "Drang nach Osten", visited Great Britain in the first half of May 1933 in order to enlist British sympathy for Nazi designs; and an article in the Comintern journal alleged that the Nazis were pursuing a policy of war against the USSR, and hoped to realize their ambitions, however fantastic, with British aid.[50] Some time in May 1933 a report reached Moscow that Papen, on a visit to Rome, had divulged details of the secret Soviet–German military agreements to the French Ambassador; and the report, whether correct or not (Papen seems later to have denied it), bred doubts about the desirability of continuing to implement the agreements and to initiate Reichswehr officers into Soviet military secrets.[51] In the following month Hugenberg submitted to the world economic conference in London a memorandum referring to the German need for "new territories where this energetic race can found colonies and carry out great peaceful works". The text continued:

War, revolution and internal disruption have found a starting-point in Russia, in the vast regions of the east. The process of destruction is still going on. The time has come to stop it.

The words echoed only all too plainly the aggressive doctrines of *Mein Kampf*, and reflected hostile German designs against the USSR. Litvinov, who professed not to have read the memorandum, spoke contemptuously of "ideas which the public in many countries thoughtlessly disregards as fantastic and scatter-brained", and which the German Government officially disclaimed; and the Soviet Ambassador in Berlin protested against the statement as incompatible with the Soviet – German treaty of friendship of April 24, 1926, recently renewed.[52] The Soviet Government was evidently anxious not to make much of the incident. But apprehensions in Moscow about the future course of German policy were mirrored

[50] *Kommunisticheskii Internatsional*, 1933, No. 12, pp. 14–20; the article was signed "N. Rudolf", certainly a pseudonym.

[51] The source for this incident is a despatch from Dirksen reporting a conversation with a member of Narkomindel of August 7, 1933 (*Auswärtiges Amt*, 2860/562513–7); Soviet sources as usual are silent on anything relating to the military agreements. For Papen's alleged denial see *ibid*. 2860/562520–1.

[52] *Izvestiya*, June 20, 1933; *Dokumenty Vneshnei Politiki SSSR*, xvi (1970), 359–361.

in a rapid improvement in Franco – Soviet relations, which in turn
caused uneasiness in German diplomatic circles.[53]

A conversation between Molotov and Dirksen early in August
1933 prior to the latter's recall from Moscow, revealed the slow, but
inexorable decay of the brittle Soviet – German friendship, though
both speakers were plainly reluctant to hasten the process, or to
admit any responsibility for it. Dirksen claimed that there was no
obstacle on the German side to the "normal development of our
former relations". He found nothing to complain of in the recent
Soviet treaties with France and Poland. But he regretted that, while
in the past Soviet opinion had been "categorically" against the
Versailles treaty, revision of the treaty was now qualified as "a
threat of war", and the Soviet press was commenting adversely on
German rearmament. Dirksen feared that "domestic political
affairs, the struggle against communism in Germany, are determin-
ing the foreign policy of the USSR". Molotov replied that the aim of
Soviet policy was "the maintenance and strengthening of friendly
relations with all countries"; this principle applied to relations with
Germany—a cool denial of any special relationship. The USSR
"has pursued, and pursues, a line of non-interference in the internal
affairs of other states". But he had to protest against "arrests,
searches and acts of violence" to which Soviet citizens in Germany
had been subjected, as well as against an alleged speech by Goebbels
who had drawn a parallel between the Versailles and Rapallo
treaties; and he did not accept Dirksen's excuses for the Hugenberg
memorandum. As regards the Versailles treaty, the Soviet attitude
had always been governed by desire "to maintain and strengthen
peace everywhere" and by the principle of "the free national
development of all peoples"; this attitude was unchanged. Molotov
was perhaps right to detect in Dirksen signs of "strong emotion"
during the conversation. He himself remained frigidly polite.[54] At
the same moment an article in the Comintern journal entitled
"Hitler's Foreign Policy" propounded the thesis that the Nazi
ideology was "the genuine reflexion" of "the imperialist plans of the
German big bourgeoisie and big landlords". The bourgeoisie hoped
to realize its anti-Soviet designs "through the National-Socialists";
a "definite historical continuity" could be traced in Nazi foreign

[53] *Ibid.* xvi, 538; for Franco–Soviet relations see pp. 150–151, 184 below.
[54] *Dokumenty Vneshnei Politiki SSSR*, xvi (1970), 476–481; Dirksen's report is in
Auswärtiges Amt, 2860/562498–500.

policy. The implication of this view was that German foreign policy and Nazi ideology could not be distinguished or dissociated from one another.[55]

But, however deep the rift, both sides shrank from any irrevocable step. The German archives contain a record of some remarks made by Hitler at a meeting of officials of the Auswärtiges Amt on September 26, 1933. Hitler observed that "a restoration of the German – Russian relationship was impossible, since the transformation in Germany had destroyed all Russian hopes of bringing about world revolution", and that "a sharper antagonism between Germany and Russia would naturally remain". But he added that he did not wish to break off German – Soviet relations, or "to give the Russians a pretext for such a break".[56] The first symptom of this milder tone was the release of two Soviet journalists who had attempted to attend the Reichstag fire trial just opened in Leipzig, and the decision to admit them to the court-room.[57] When Nadolny was appointed German Ambassador in Moscow at the beginning of November 1933, his instructions, which referred to Hitler's speech of March 23, 1933, to the Rapallo treaty, and to the Berlin treaty of April 24, 1926, were couched in wholly conventional terms. He was instructed "in regard to the present tension" to seek to "restore a better atmosphere", and was reminded that "good German – Soviet relations are of essential importance for Germany". The text continued:

> The fundamental difference of the two state regimes need be no hindrance to the profitable further development of German – Soviet relations. Nevertheless the fundamental principle must be maintained that all attempts by one country to influence the internal affairs of the other (radio, press) must cease.[58]

The ambiguities of the situation nevertheless remained. On October 14 , 1933, Hitler announced the withdrawal of Germany

---

[55] *Kommunisticheskii Internatsional*, 1933, No. 17, pp. 25–33; this article, like its predecessor a few months earlier (see p. 97 above), was signed "N. Rudolf".

[56] *Auswärtiges Amt*, 9464/046218–20.

[57] For Soviet protests see *Dokumenty Vneshnei Politiki SSSR*, xvi (1970), 536–540, for the final settlement *ibid.* xvi, 863, note 252. A provisional settlement was announced in *Izvestiya*, October 3, 1933.

[58] R. Nadolny, *Mein Beitrag* (1955), pp. 143–145; *Auswärtiges Amt*, 9464/046310–3.

from the disarmament conference and from the League of Nations on the grounds of the denial to Germany of equality of rights. Though the USSR, together with Hungary, Poland and Turkey, refused to associate itself with a reply from the conference rejecting the German argument, *Pravda* noted that the German action was not "a step towards the preservation of peace"; Fascist Germany had set its hopes on an increase in armaments, and this was a preparation for "new imperialist wars".[59] Hitler called for fresh elections to the Reichstag and for a specific plebiscite to ratify his decision. On November 12, 1933, out of nearly 44 million votes in the elections, 39.5 million were cast for the Nazi candidates; of 43.5 million voters in the plebiscite, 40.5 millions voted "Yes". It was difficult to find justification for the description of the result in the Comintern news-sheet as "the first great fiasco of the Nazi propaganda machine".[60]

These events were watched by the KPD leaders in exile with a helplessness mitigated, or revealed, by periodical outbursts of rhetoric. A resolution of the party politburo of October 10, 1933, proclaimed that "the blood-and-hunger government of Hitler–Göring–Goebbels", a "government of finance capital and of Junkers", was *"leading Germany towards catastrophe"*. Nevertheless "a huge revolutionary upsurge" was rising in the working class. The prescription was far-reaching:

> *The creation of the united front with SPD workers, the winning over of the Christian workers, of the non-party workers, and of those who have been deceived by the Nazis, is the most important and decisive task of the KPD.*

But the SPD was still not spared: it "continues the policy of splitting the workers' movement and organizing a *counter-revolutionary united front* of the bourgeoisie *against the revolutionary united front* of the proletariat". History now offered the KPD "the possibility of liquidating the mass influence of the SPD".[61] But a commentary on the resolution by Ulbricht, published a month later, significantly softened the tone. *"The tempo of the revolutionary upsurge"* was said to

[59] *Pravda*, October 16, 1933.

[60] *Rundschau*, No. 43, November 17, 1933, p. 1653; a KPD declaration of November 17, 1933, more sensibly pleaded that the plebiscite had been conducted "under the unparalleled terror of the Fascist dictatorship" and praised the courage of those who had voted "No" (*ibid.* No. 46, November 30, 1933, pp. 1773–1775).

[61] *Rundschau*, No. 40, October 27, 1933, pp. 1541–1543.

be *"really dependent on the organization of the working class under the leadership of the KPD,* on the capacity of our party to win the broad *masses of social-democratic workers and former members of the ADGB for the revolutionary united front"*. The formation of joint committees with social-democratic workers for specific ends was commended; and attacks on the record and on the leaders of the SPD were avoided.[62] It would, however, be premature to speak of a change of line. Conflicting voices, or discordant tones of voice, were still audible in Moscow.

In an atmosphere of growing tension the trial of Van der Lubbe, of Dimitrov, Tanev and Popov, and of the leader of the KPD fraction in the Reichstag, Torgler, charged with the burning of the Reichstag, had opened in Leipzig on September 21, 1933. By this time the revulsion and alarm inspired by the methods of the Nazi regime were spreading over western Europe. On the eve of the Leipzig trial, a mock trial was staged in London by a group of lawyers from several countries; this improvised court, on a review of the evidence, acquitted the accused, and pronounced the Nazis themselves guilty of the crime. The international committee against imperialist war and Fascism in Paris issued a cry of protest against "the criminal Leipzig trial".[63] In Leipzig the boldness and ingenuity shown by Dimitrov in pleading his cause and denouncing his judges and his accusers, matching himself with Göring in wit and effrontery, struck the imagination of the world.[64] Dimitrov became overnight an international hero— the first to emerge from the grey ranks of Comintern; and during the next two years his dominant personality, firmly established in popular esteem by the Leipzig trial, was to play an important role in laying the foundations of a common front of communists, social-democrats and western liberals for defence against the Nazi menace; and demonstrations on behalf of Dimitrov took place in

[62] *Ibid.* No. 44, November 18, 1933, pp. 1743–1744, No. 46, November 30, 1933, pp. 1775–1776; the articles were signed "Walter (Berlin)", but were certainly written in Moscow. The resolution of October 10, published as a resolution of the politburo, is here described as a resolution of the central committee; whatever its formal character it was probably the work of the group of KPD *émigrés* in Paris.

[63] *Iz Istorii Mezhdunarodnoi Proletarskoi Solidarnosti,* v (1961), 134–137.

[64] Dimitrov's numerous speeches in court appear in the Bulgarian edition of his works G. Dimitrov, *S'chineniya* (n.d.), ix, 111–287; the most important of them are in G. Dimitrov, *Izbrannye Sochineniya* (1957), i, 315–356.

many western countries.[65] *Pravda* on December 15 published a damning review of the trial and of its prospective "scandalous finale". The trial ended on December 23 with a death sentence on Van der Lubbe and the acquittal, for lack of evidence, of Dimitrov, the two other Bulgarians, and Torgler. They were, however, kept in "protective custody".[66] The future of the Bulgarians was problematical, especially as the Bulgarian Government deprived them of citizenship. Eventually the Soviet Government came to the rescue by conferring Soviet citizenship on them, and applying to the German Government for their repatriation to the USSR.[67] The request was granted, and the three men reached Moscow at the end of February 1934.[68]

The month of November 1933 was marked by another striking event. Litvinov spent the period from November 7 to 25 in Washington; and during this time, after difficult negotiations relating to promises of religious freedom and abstention from hostile propaganda, an agreement was reached for the recognition of the Soviet Government by the United States and an exchange of ambassadors. A common interest in face of the Japanese threat in the Far East was the primary factor in bringing about this accord. But it contributed also to the evolution of Soviet policy in other fields. Establishment of relations with the United States eclipsed any other achievement of Soviet diplomacy in 1933, and encouraged the policy of *rapprochement* with the capitalist world.

In the present international situation [observed Molotov at the session of TsIK in December 1933], it is particularly important that this resumption of relations is likely to have considerable positive significance for the stabilization of international relations as a whole, for the consolidation of peace in general.[69]

[65] *Rundschau*, No. 49, December 21, 1933, pp. 1875–1879; Dimitrov, while in custody before his trial, had already written to Barbusse and Rolland (*S'chineniya* (n.d.), xi, 9–10, 91–92).

[66] Torgler remained in custody till his death ten years later; his submissive behaviour at the trial, where he accepted the advocate assigned to him by the court, discredited him in communist eyes, and he was expelled from the KPD in 1935 (*Rundschau*, No. 73, December 12, 1935, p. 2826, No. 75, December 19, 1935, p. 2896). *Kommunisticheskii Internatsional*, 1935, No. 7, p. 6, described him as "one of those bourgeois who have accidentally strayed into the workers' movement".

[67] *Dokumenty Vneshnei Politiki SSSR*, xvii (1971), 150.

[68] For their reception see p. 124 below.

[69] *SSSR: Tsentral'nyi Ispolnitel'nyi Komitet 6 Sozyva: 4 Sessiya* (1933), No. 1, p. 27.

And the influential American journal *Foreign Affairs* published an article by Radek, which harped on the theme that "the main object for which Soviet diplomacy is fighting is *peace*", but offered "a positive answer to the question of the feasibility of an agreement between the Soviet Union and an imperialist Power which, for the sake of its own imperialist interests, was willing to help the Soviet Union in its struggle against other attacking imperialist Powers".[70]

[70] *Foreign Affairs* (N. Y.), January 1934, pp. 193–206.

CHAPTER 6

THE THIRTEENTH IKKI

It was at this crucial moment in the evolution of the Soviet attitude to Germany and to the western capitalist world that IKKI held its thirteenth session at the end of 1933. The hesitations and ambiguities which confronted it were ideological as well as practical. The bewilderment of Comintern in face of the Nazi victory in Germany stemmed not only from inability on the political level to decide on the course to be pursued, but from inability to analyse and understand a conflict of two ideologies resting on conceptions of the historical and political process so alien to each other as to preclude meaningful argument between them. The attempt to explain the Nazi phenomenon in terms of the Marxist concept of class struggle led to endless embarrassment. At moments Hitler was the spokesman—or the prisoner—of the big bourgeoisie which controlled industry and finance. At moments he was the leader of the petty bourgeoisie in revolt against the big Jewish merchants and financiers. Vestiges of socialism had crept, not only into the name of the party, but into its economic programme—an appeal to the oppressed, the unemployed, the helpless. The failure of the workers to provide effective resistance could not be excused simply by the split in the workers' movement or by the betrayal of the social-democratic leaders. The Nazi ideology, most crudely presented by Alfred Rosenberg, saw the historical process as a conflict not of class, but of race. It cut across the whole structure of the Marxist analysis. Unlike Marxism, it represented a regression into the past, not a leap forward into the future. Unlike Marxism, it stood for no universal ideal. In the event its glorification of the "Nordic" or "Aryan" race was narrowed down to the confines of the German nation and the Third Reich. But its attitude to the USSR suffered from no such inconsistency; it could dismiss the Slavs as an inferior race, and communism as an alien doctrine designed to introduce a divisive factor into the German body politic. The Nazi ideology remained a closed book to Moscow. Just as the west was blinded to its peculiar and specific quality by addiction to the liberal principles of conciliation and compromise, so the vision of the Soviet leaders was distorted by the attempt to diagnose the rise of Hitler in the Marxist terms of class struggle.

The thirteenth IKKI assembled on November 28, 1933; Pieck, who as leader of the KPD deputized for Thälmann, formally opened the proceedings, striking the three obligatory key-notes of the session: an invocation of "*socialist construction in the USSR*", an obeisance to Stalin in the form of a quotation from his works, and an optimistic reference to the "*new revolutionary upsurge*".[1] The debates were dominated by the establishment of the Nazi dictatorship in Germany, about which it was hard to find anything new to say; and Japan figured from time to time as a secondary disturbing factor. Kuusinen delivered the main report under the title "Fascism, the Danger of War, and the Tasks of Communist Parties". An analysis of the world economic crisis and the end of capitalist stabilization led to the familiar prediction of a "new phase of revolutions and wars". The contradictions of capitalism were fraught with the danger of war against the USSR. Japan and Germany had left the League of Nations, and Italy was preparing to do so—an early hint that the League might acquire a positive role in Soviet calculations. Kuusinen boldly denied that Fascism "impedes revolutionary development"; the hypothesis of the "new revolutionary upsurge" was invoked to justify an unconvincing eulogy of the KPD. Nothing was said to clarify relations with social-democracy: "The Fascisization of social-democracy proceeds at an accelerated pace"—a formula which permitted the assumption that it was not yet identical with Fascism. Kuusinen defended the March appeal of the presidium of IKKI to all parties of the Second International: "there are exceptional cases when Bolshevik tactics not only permit, but presuppose, an appeal even to social-Fascists who have a significant mass influence". But this approval was immediately qualified by a reference to "Right errors . . . in many countries". The "chief slogan" everywhere must be "For Soviet power".[2]

Pieck and Pollitt were honoured with invitations to deliver reports on their respective parties. Pieck's long speech was full of fiery rhetoric, and unusually empty of content. He stressed the European significance of German Fascism, and the threat of war against the USSR. He attacked the demagogy of the Nazi economic programme as a tool for exploitation of the workers. Fascism was a

[1] *XIII Plenum IKKI* (1934), pp. 1–3.
[2] *Ibid.* pp. 4–30.

form of monopoly capitalism, which was itself a form of capitalism in decline. He denounced the Neumann–Remmele group which dissociated the Nazi regime from bourgeois democracy by calling it a "dictatorship of the lumpenproletariat". He held social-democracy responsible for the Fascist dictatorship; and he ended by saluting the approaching fifteenth anniversary of the KPD, "founded by the never-to-be-forgotten Karl Liebknecht and Rosa Luxemburg". Injunctions regarding the united front were as confused as ever. But among the slogans recommended to the KPD the theme of national liberation now occupied a newly conspicuous place: "Workers of Germany, defend your proletarian fatherland", and "Communism, the worker-peasant republic, will destroy the Versailles peace".[3] Pollitt asserted that "the very policy which led in Germany to the rule of Hitler is the policy of British social-democracy", and devoted most of his speech to the problems of the united front in Britain.[4]

A note of resolute optimism permeated the debate. Even Browder, the United States delegate, who alleged that Roosevelt was leading the country on "the Fascist path", ended his speech with the prediction that "America will perhaps not be the last of the great capitalist countries of the world to place on the agenda the question of Soviet power, the question of proletarian revolution."[5] Nevertheless, some anxieties came to light. Pyatnitsky recorded that, of the parties belonging to Comintern, only 16 were "more or less legal", 7 were "semi-legal" and 38 "totally illegal"; and his review of the state of the parties revealed more defeats than achievements.[6] Of the Russian delegates Manuilsky was the most cautious. He admitted some revival in the economic situation "in particular capitalist countries (USA, Japan, Germany)". Since the twelfth IKKI membership of communist parties in capitalist countries "does not consistently advance", and the number of new recruits had not risen. Nevertheless Manuilsky rejected the precedents of 1848 and 1871 when reaction followed the defeat of

---

[3] *Ibid.* pp. 30–56. Pieck's report, together with extracts from the other principal speeches relating to Fascism in Germany, were published in German in *Der Faschismus in Deutschland* (Moscow, 1934); no German editions of the proceedings of the eleventh, twelfth and thirteenth IKKIs were ever published.

[4] *XIII Plenum IKKI* (1934), p. 61; for Pollitt's speech see pp. 229–230 below.

[5] *Ibid.* pp. 106, 111.

[6] *Ibid.* pp. 191–196; for his criticism of the French and British parties see pp. 187, 230 below.

revolutionary movements. No Bolshevik party could admit that the KPD had suffered defeat; that would mean to lose faith in Comintern. The existence of the USSR, which communists were pledged to defend, was a new factor; and these reflexions enabled him to end on a not very convincing note of confidence.[7] Kolarov attacked Fascist attempts to woo the peasantry (the original programme of the NSDAP had promised "confiscation of land without compensation"), and to set it in opposition to the proletariat. He called on communist parties, and especially the PCF, to devote more attention to party work among the peasants.[8]

Conciliatory utterances on the question of the united front were few. Knorin was eloquent on the doom of capitalism. Its contradictions had reached their most acute point in Germany and the Far East: "The capitalist world is drifting without rudder and without compass to its ruin. . . . Capitalism has outlived its time." But, as throughout the debate, Germany was the central theme. Germany, repeated Knorin, was "the weakest link in the chain of imperialist states"; in Germany "proletarian revolution is nearer than in any other country".

The victory of the German proletariat would mean the victory of the proletarian revolution everywhere in Europe, the defeat of the German proletariat would mean the collapse of the proletarian revolution in other European countries.

The recurrent *leitmotif* of the treachery and bankruptcy of German social-democracy had its counterpart in confidence in the KPD, in refusal to admit that it had suffered defeat, and in the call to lead the masses forward into revolution.[9] Bela Kun described the response of the Second International to the IKKI overture of March 1933 as "the customary slanderous offensive of the united enemies of revolutionary unity".[10] Lozovsky interpreted the united front as requiring communists to work in the Fascist trade unions in Italy, Germany and Poland, to agitate among the members, and to protest against the nomination of union leaders from above and against compulsory membership and payment of dues.[11] Vasiliev,

[7] *XIII Plenum IKKI* (1934), pp. 306–316.
[8] *Ibid.* pp. 438–446.
[9] *Ibid.* pp. 327–341.
[10] *Ibid.* p. 346; for the IKKI appeal see p. 85 above.
[11] *XIII Plenum IKKI* (1934), p. 385.

an important Comintern official, reasserted the campaign against social-democrats in all its former intensity, denouncing the "Right" or "opportunist" deviation which sought to "suppress or weaken the struggle against social-democracy". In order to overthrow Fascism, "the decisive blow in the immediate future must be directed against the social-democratic party".[12]

The plight and manifest impotence of the KPD saved it from more than perfunctory criticism. It was still obligatory to maintain that the tactics of the KPD had been correct, and that Hitler's victory had not been a defeat for communism, but a stimulus for a fresh upsurge. Remmele, who had come out actively against the complacent line laid down in the resolution of April 1,[13] was summoned to Moscow in advance of the session to appear before a "commission for the investigation of fractional work in the KPD" presided over by Marty. Here under pressure he made "several half-confessions"; and the commission recommended to the presidium of IKKI that he should be suspended from all work in the KPD. Remmele accepted the decision, and on November 23 sent a letter to the political secretariat of IKKI resigning his appointments as a member of IKKI and of its presidium. The commission continued, however, to press the matter. During the session of the thirteenth IKKI, it addressed a number of specific questions to Remmele on his various errors, but, on receiving from him a promise of reassuring answers, did not recommend his expulsion from the party; his recantation, dated January 13, 1934, was published some time after the session.[14] Heckert alone spoke in some detail at the session of the social policies of Nazism. Hitler had promised to liquidate unemployment by May 1, 1933. In fact, the number of unemployed had been reduced by two millions since he came to power, but productivity had declined. The sending of "agricultural assistants" to the countryside had ended in a fiasco. The "clever manoeuvres of Fascism" in the trade unions were merely designed to swallow up the unions altogether. Mockery did not veil the uneasy impression that Hitler had made some progress in wooing the workers. Abuse of social-democrats and of Remmele and Neumann completed the speech.[15]

[12] *Ibid.* pp. 413–414.
[13] See pp. 90–91 above.
[14] *XIII Plenum IKKI* (1934), pp. 567–568; *Rundschau*, No. 12, February 1, 1934, p. 464.
[15] *XIII Plenum IKKI* (1934), pp. 316–323.

The impact of the Nazi dictatorship on other communist parties was indirect, and the deductions drawn from it at the thirteenth IKKI confusing and hesitant.[16] But for the Czechoslovak party the immediate proximity of the Nazi terror, and the presence in Prague as refugees of the rump of the SPD leadership, made it a burning issue, and led to rift in the party. At the twelfth IKKI in September 1932, the Czechoslovak delegation had been heavily committed to the united front.[17] In October the party central committee had made another appeal to workers of all parties on a broad platform, while still ruling out a direct approach to social-democratic leaders;[18] and during the winter of 1932–1933 it claimed considerable success in mobilizing the masses in support of workers' demands.[19] When on March 5, 1933, Comintern issued its response to the overture of the Second International on joint action against Nazism, the moment seemed ripe for a fresh advance. At a session of the party central committee on March 11–13, 1933, Guttmann made the main report on the united front. He rejected the proposal of the SPD leaders for a "non-aggression" pact. The united front meant "a common struggle against the bourgeoisie, not silence in face of bourgeois policy". Nevertheless, some socialist workers believed that it was necessary to "win the leaders of socialist parties for the struggle"; and this Guttmann pronounced to be "in complete accord with the Comintern offer of a united front". After a lively debate the committee unanimously approved the text of an appeal for common action against Fascism addressed to the leaders of all socialist parties.[20] A few weeks later it went even further. On April 7 Gottwald telegraphed in its name to IKKI urging Comintern to put forward proposals to the Second International for a joint struggle against Fascism which would "make things more difficult for opponents of the united front".[21]

This bold initiative proved highly inopportune. A major pronouncement had just issued from Comintern on the affairs of the KPD. The SPD had further discredited itself by its subservience to Hitler; and the resolution of IKKI of April 1, 1933, was primarily

[16] For the PCF, CPGB and PCI see below.
[17] See p. 71 above.
[18] *Internationale Presse-Korrespondenz*, No. 87, October 21, 1932, pp. 2809–2810.
[19] *Iz Istorii Kominterna* (1970), p. 106.
[20] *Rundschau*, No. 5, March 18, 1933, pp. 127–128; for a long summary of Guttmann's report see *ibid.* No. 6, March 25, 1933, pp. 152–153.
[21] *Kommunisticheskii Internatsional: Kratkii Istoricheskii Ocherk* (1969), p. 354.

concerned to exonerate the KPD and place responsibility for the
catastrophe on the shoulders of the SPD.[22] A prompt reversal of
tactics on the part of the Czechoslovak party was called for. The
situation in Czechoslovakia was complicated by the existence of a
coalition government of bourgeois and social-democratic parties.
This made the social-democrats accomplices in all repressive
measures taken by the government; and the wavering and time-
serving Gottwald, in a speech in the Czechoslovak parliament on
April 27, 1933, delivered a violent attack on the SPD, which "by its
whole policy over the past 15 years prepared the way for the present
Fascist dictatorship of Hitler", and was openly going over to the
Fascist camp.[23]

Of this change of front the unlucky Guttmann was made the
scapegoat. On June 16, the party politburo, reacting to a decree
which conferred "exceptional powers" on the government, passed a
conventional resolution which denounced the social-Fascist leaders
of the socialist party and "the complete bankruptcy of the theory
and practice of the Second International", and did not mention the
united front.[24] Guttmann was accused of having taken up "an
opportunist position" in the German question; he had attempted to
organize joint protest demonstrations with Left social-democrats,
and had induced Reimann, who headed the Agitprop section of the
party, to conduct a campaign to this end in the party press. He was
expelled from the politburo.[25] The fact that he had acted with the
unanimous approval of the central committee, and that Gottwald—at any rate, openly—had not hitherto come out against
him, was passed over in silence. The eighth plenum of the party
central committee in October 1933 described the existing regime, a
coalition in which socialists participated, as a "Fascist dictatorship", demanded that "all opportunist and semi-opportunist
views of social-democracy" should be eradicated from the party,
and observed that the thesis of social-Fascism as substantially
identical with Fascism could not be regarded as "incorrect".[26] An
open letter addressed to "all worker members of social-democratic

[22] See p. 90 above.
[23] The speech was printed in *Rundschau*, No. 12, May 5, 1933, pp. 363–367.
[24] *Rundschau*, No. 22, June 30, 1933, pp. 746–747.
[25] *XIII Plenum IKKI* (1934), pp. 156–157; an article in the Comintern journal
denounced the errors committed in the Czechoslovak party journal
(*Kommunisticheskii Internatsional*, 1933, No. 24, pp. 31–37).
[26] Quoted from Czechoslovak party archives in *Iz Istorii Kominterna* (1970),
pp. 116, 119.

parties" attacked "your parties and your leaders" as social-Fascist, and called for a "united front of communism" against a "united front of Fascism".[27] A month later a ban placed by the authorities on the communist press provoked a resolution of the politburo which once more denounced the social-Fascists and the doctrine of the "lesser evil", protested against *opportunist underestimation of revolutionary prospects*", and called for a stepping up of illegal activity; the united front had dropped altogether out of sight.[28]

At the thirteenth IKKI the issue came to a head. Gottwald recited the offences of Guttmann and Reimann, who had failed to see that Nazism was a symptom of the weakness, not the strength, of capitalism, and had neglected the prospects of revolution. Pyatnitsky mentioned no names, but asserted that symptoms had appeared in the Czechoslovak delegation even at the twelfth IKKI of an inclination "to conceal the party identity in carrying out the tactics [of the united front]". He spoke of errors in the party press, and of failure to show up "the reactionary role of social-democrats and National-Socialists", and called on the leaders to "expose the opportunists in the party itself".[29] Reimann, whose speech was greeted with contemptuous interruptions, confessed his errors and denounced those of Guttmann. Knorin referred bitterly to the "sabotage" of Guttmann and Reimann, and accused Guttmann of seeking "unity for the sake of unity". Šverma, a faithful follower of Guttmann at the twelfth IKKI, now fiercely denounced him, and declared that his "opportunist assessment of the German events was only the result of a whole system of opportunist errors on the fundamental problems of our strategy and tactics".[30] A comprehensive resolution of the central committee of the Czechoslovak party, probably drafted in Moscow, called for "a clear front against opportunism", and offered a strict definition of the doctrine of the united front.[31]

---

[27] *Rundschau*, No. 41, November 3, 1933, pp. 1580–1581.

[28] *Ibid.* No. 50, December 25, 1933, pp. 1944–1945.

[29] *XIII Plenum IKKI* (1934), pp. 156–159, 186–188.

[30] *Ibid.* pp. 286–289, 334, 348, 507; for Guttmann's and Šverma's speeches at the twelfth IKKI see p. 71 above.

[31] *Rundschau*, No. 49, December 21, 1933, pp. 1885–1892. The party politburo issued an announcement, dated "Prague, December 20, 1933", that Guttmann had "completely broken with the revolutionary class struggle", and had "no longer any connexion with Comintern" (*ibid.* No. 2, January 4, 1934, p. 30); this was followed by another savage attack on Guttmann by Gottwald (*ibid.* No. 6, January 18, 1934, pp. 219–221)

What was new in the debates of the thirteenth IKKI, and clearly reflected the new turn in Soviet policy, was the alarm created by the aggressive nationalism of Hitler's programme, which gave a fresh twist to the familiar theme of the danger of war against the USSR. Pieck quoted *Mein Kampf* on Germany's need to acquire living-space "at the expense of Russia", and recalled Hugenberg's plan at the London economic conference of June 1932 for the colonization of the Ukraine. Richter, the second KPD delegate to speak, concentrated on "the struggle against Fascist chauvinism", and accused Hugenberg and Rosenberg of hatching "a plan to finance Ukrainian White-guard counter-revolution".[32] Martynov stressed, more powerfully than any other speaker, "the *specifically* Fascist variety of nationalism", and the need to counteract the support derived by Fascism from petty-bourgeois chauvinism".[33] Krevels, a member of the eastern secretariat of IKKI, identified "contemporary militant nationalism" as "a specific tool of mono-poly capital", adding that "the *leaders* of petty-bourgeois strata" were being consciously drawn into the movement. But he also concluded that militant Fascist nationalism was "inseparable from the colonial enslavement and oppression of weak, dependent nations, such as China, India and Indonesia", as well as from "the struggle for national liberation" in such countries as Poland, Czechoslovakia, Yugoslavia and Rumania.[34] The argument, if carried further, had awkward implications. Guttmann had ap-parently maintained that "as the result of national oppression in Czechoslovakia, national-revolutionary elements in the ranks of the peasantry and the petty bourgeoisie"—evidently the Sudeten German minority—"were turning to the Nazis as their only champions against national oppression". Reimann, eager to sep-arate himself from Guttmann, accused Czechoslovak social-democrats of "an approximation to the positions of bourgeois nationalism", and asserted that "a genuine revolutionary struggle for national liberation and the right of peoples for self-determination" could be pursued only under the banner of proletarian internationalism.[35] A Ukrainian nationalist movement

---

[32] *XIII Plenum IKKI* (1934), pp. 44, 162.

[33] *Ibid.* 476–482.

[34] *Ibid.* pp. 300–302.

[35] *Ibid.* pp. 288–289; for an article revealing the embarrassments of the German question in Czechoslovakia, and an ambiguous declaration by a communist deputy in the Czechoslovak parliament, see *Rundschau*, No. 47, December 7, 1933,

in Polish-occupied Western Ukraine was described by a Ukrainian delegate as "an anti-Soviet campaign . . . orchestrated by the conductor's baton of the Polish occupying authorities", since both German and Polish Fascists "look on the Western Ukraine as a base for an attack on the Soviet Ukraine"; and Kuusinen added that "the counter-revolutionary bourgeoisie of the Western Ukraine" dreamed of making it "a European Manchukuo".[36] Other speakers did not venture on ground so strewn with pitfalls.

It was less easy to evade discussion of the Versailles treaty and the territorial settlement imposed by it, which had become a burning issue in several European parties. Pieck in his report mentioned it only once in a quotation from the KPD resolution of October 10, which asserted that "the yoke of exploitation" imposed on German workers "in the interests of finance capital and the Junkers" was "heavier than Versailles".[37] The problem had been further complicated by an unexpected initiative of Hitler, who had held out to the Polish Ambassador in Berlin the olive-branch of a *détente* in German–Polish relations; and this conjured up in anxious Soviet minds the frightening vision of a bargain by which Poland would cede the corridor to Germany in return for German support of a Polish invasion of the Ukraine and a revival of the Polish aggression of 1920.[38] Lenski cunningly hesitated to decide between the view that Poland would serve as the advance base for a combined European offensive against the USSR and the view that war between Poland and Germany was imminent. Without mentioning Versailles, he quoted a resolution of the KPP which, recognizing that Upper Silesia and the Baltic corridor were key-points in the antagonism between Poland and Germany, proclaimed the right of those regions to self-determination—a right to be asserted against both Polish and German imperialism.[39] Thorez admitted that some sections of the PCF, like the SFIO, upheld the Versailles treaty and opposed the campaign denouncing it. But he treated these manifes-

---

pp. 1825–1826; Pieck at the seventh congress of Comintern in July 1935 blamed the Czechoslovak party for having allowed Henlein "to draw a majority of the Germans in Czechoslovakia into his [Nazi] party" (*ibid.* No. 37, August 14, 1935, p. 1766).

[36] *XIII Plenum IKKI* (1934), pp. 112, 581.
[37] *Ibid.* p. 40; for this resolution see pp. 100–101 above.
[38] *Rundschau*, No. 46, November 30, 1933, p. 1761.
[39] *XIII Plenum IKKI* (1934), p. 79; for the resolution see p. 267 below.

tations as breaches of the correct party line.[40] The Austrian delegate, Koplenig, spoke out more clearly on this issue than anyone. The Austrian social-democrats opposed the Nazi campaign for the unification of Austria with Germany, which was prohibited by the Versailles treaty, with a demand for the neutralization of Austria; the KPÖ opposed it with a demand for the creation of a Soviet Austria and its union with a Soviet Germany. For both parties, Versailles was a bulwark against Hitler.[41] Kuusinen, summing up the debate, touched obliquely on the question in the form of an attack on Trotsky. Trotsky was said to "brand the campaign to bring state frontiers in Europe into conformity with ethnographic frontiers as a 'revolutionary Utopia'". Hitler, however, had no such intention; he simply carried on "the German imperialist policy of expansion". No practical conclusion was drawn, and Versailles was not specifically mentioned. But Kuusinen made his point succinctly when he expressed the fear that the communist parties would not be strong enough "to convert a counter-revolutionary war against the USSR into a victory of the world proletarian revolution".[42]

Nothing said at the thirteenth IKKI was, however, more remarkable than what was left unsaid on a theme which for several weeks past had excited an intense emotional interest in western Europe—the Reichstag fire trial and Dimitrov's bold defiance of Göring. Pieck in opening the session spoke of Dimitrov as "a courageous Bolshevik, a stout revolutionary"; and the appointment of Dimitrov and Thälmann as members of the honorary presidium was received with "stormy applause".[43] Yet, of the two principal *rapporteurs* Kuusinen ignored the subject, and Pieck, in enlarging on Nazi brutalities, casually mentioned Göring's threats "to Dimitrov and the other comrades at the Leipzig trial".[44] Of later orators, Manuilsky in the peroration of a long speech observed that "Dimitrov in fetters has been transformed into a powerful herald summoning the workers of all countries beneath the banner of communism"; and Knorin criticized "our campaign" in support of the accused at Leipzig as far less effective than the campaign many

[40] *XIII Plenum IKKI* (1934), pp. 143–144; for the attitude of the PCF see pp. 185–186 below.
[41] *XIII Plenum IKKI* (1934), pp. 201–204.
[42] *Ibid.* pp. 580–581.
[43] *Ibid.* p. 3.
[44] *Ibid.* p. 50.

years earlier on behalf of Sacco and Vanzetti. Kuusinen in his concluding address quoted Dimitrov as having attributed the failure of the KPD to bring about a mass rising to the fact that "a majority of German workers still found themselves under the influence of the counter-revolutionary SPD"; and he reported, amid applause, that Dimitrov from his prison cell had sent a "revolutionary greeting" to the session.[45] Of the two Bulgarian delegates, one praised Dimitrov for his "Bolshevik steadfastness" at the Leipzig trial, and named him as "one of the leaders of our party and of the September rising [of 1923] in Bulgaria", the other gave a brief account of his earlier career. But neither hinted at any significant role to be played by him in the present or future of the BKP or of Comintern.[46] No other foreign delegate ventured into these still uncharted waters. Nobody mentioned the suspicion, now hardening into firm belief everywhere in the west, that the Reichstag fire had been the work of the Nazis themselves. Soviet policies were in the melting-pot, and no clear directive yet prescribed the judgment to be passed on these events.

The resolution adopted at the end of the session, which also did not mention the Leipzig trial, did rather more than justice to the inchoate character of the debate. Fascism, "born within the womb of bourgeois democracy", was "a means of saving capitalism from collapse". Though some differences existed between democracy and Fascism on "forms and methods", social-democracy was still "the chief social support of the bourgeoisie"; it had "helped the bourgeoisie, by splitting the working class, to prolong the existence of capitalism". But it was wrong to suppose that the victory of Fascism in Germany had enabled capitalism to strengthen its position or overcome its crisis. The task of the international proletariat was "to convert this crisis into the victory of the proletarian revolution", and the empty assurance of "a new revolutionary upsurge" in Germany was repeated. The international situation had "the character of the eve of a new world war", the threat of war being explicitly attributed to Japan and Germany. The resolution did, however, betray, more explicitly than any of the speeches, the shift in attitude in Moscow, incomplete and not yet openly proclaimed, to the Versailles treaty.

[45] *Ibid.* pp. 316, 338, 576, 581.
[46] *Ibid.* pp. 264, 544; for the divisions in the BKP see pp. 130–133 below.

> The Fascist government in Germany [it declared], the principal instigator of war in Europe, provokes disorder in Danzig, Austria, the Saar, the Baltic and Scandinavia, and attempts under the flag of the struggle against Versailles to forge a bloc for a new bloody repartition of Europe in the interests of German imperialism.

Communist parties were instructed to stand, as hitherto, "for the independence of colonies, for the liberation of dependent peoples". But "in the key centres of national contradictions" the prescription was qualified:

> Communists should struggle against imperialist occupation and oppression, for the right of self-determination (Upper Silesia, the Saar, northern Bohemia etc.), coming out in all these regions, and also in Austria and Danzig, against the chauvinism of their national bourgeoisie and against annexation to the murderous "third Reich" of German Fascism.

The resolution reverted in the conclusion to the call for a mass struggle against Fascism, and against war, and ended with a rhetorical appeal to "the *living example of the great country of the Soviets*".[47] The moment of the thirteenth IKKI found the Soviet leaders poised uneasily between long-standing and deeply rooted attitudes to Germany, to the western Powers and to the Versailles treaty, which they still hesitated to jettison, and new and unfamiliar vistas which they were beginning, tentatively and fearfully, to contemplate.

While the thirteenth IKKI was in session, growing apprehension of the course of German policy made itself felt in Moscow. Several speakers referred to the exodus of Japan and Germany from the League of Nations, but drew no specific conclusions from it. Radek, in an article in *Pravda* on December 4, 1933, issued a powerful warning that the increasingly insistent German demands for rearmament could lead to an arms race, which would end inevitably in a world war.[48] On December 25 Stalin, who had not

---

[47] *XIII Plenum IKKI* (1934), pp. 589–595.

[48] A further article by Radek entitled "Disarmament or War" appeared in *Rundschau*, No. 48, December 14, 1933, p. 1839; an anonymous article *ibid*. No. 49, December 21, 1933, pp. 1870–1871, accused Britain of supporting German rearmament in order to encourage German designs against the USSR.

broken silence for several months, gave an interview to Duranty, the correspondent of the *New York Times*. In response to a doubtless prearranged question whether his attitude to the League of Nations was "exclusively negative", Stalin replied, "Not always and not in all conditions"; and he went on to explain that, since the departure of Germany and Japan, "the League may become a certain factor in slowing down the outbreak of military actions or in preventing them", and that, if the League could facilitate the cause of peace, "then we are not against the League".[49]

Three days later Molotov included a substantial section on foreign policy in his statement to a session of TsIK; and on the following day Litvinov reported separately on foreign affairs. Molotov noted as achievements of the Soviet Government in the past year the agreement for mutual recognition with the United States, the conclusion of non-aggression pacts with neighbouring countries, and the establishment of "practical cooperation" with France. Echoing Stalin's remarks to Duranty, he spoke of "the role played by the League of Nations as a brake on the forces making for war". In a cautiously worded passage about Germany he denied that the Soviet Government had any desire to modify the "special place" which Germany had always occupied in Soviet foreign relations. The attempt to revise these relations came from "ruling circles in Germany", Hugenberg, Rosenberg and others, "the ideologues of militant National-Socialism". Litvinov elaborated the same points, significantly adding that, "if one can speak of diplomatic eras, we stand undoubtedly at present on a watershed of two". The people of the USSR and of France were united in a common love of peace. In Germany the change had come in 1932 with the installation of a new government whose leader (the reference was to Papen) "preached a *rapprochement* with the west for a common offensive against the Soviet Union". Since then a new turnover had "brought to power a party which professed the most extreme anti-Soviet ideas". On this showing, "Germany must not only re-conquer all territories separated from Germany by the Versailles treaty, not only conquer lands where there is in general a German minority, but with fire and sword clear a path for expansion to the east, not halting before the frontiers of the Soviet Union and the enslavement of the peoples of the Union". He even

[49] Stalin, *Sochineniya*, xiii, 280; on December 28, 1933, the Soviet Ambassador in Paris informed the French Government of the conditions on which the USSR would enter the League (*Dokumenty Vneshnei Politiki SSSR*, xvi (1970), 876–877).

touched on what was the most delicate point of all for Comintern:

> We have, of course, our opinion of the German regime, and are, of course, sensitive to the sufferings of our German comrades. But as Marxists we can least of all be reproached for allowing sentiment to rule over our policy. . . . We do not interfere in the internal affairs of Germany, or of other countries, and our relations with her are determined not by her internal, but by her external, policy.[50]

A few weeks earlier Litvinov had observed that the Germans raised the issue of Comintern only when they wished to "justify a worsening of relations" between Germany and the USSR.[51] Litvinov made clear his determination not to complicate these relations by raising it.

The seventeenth Russian party congress in January 1934 provided the occasion for a major policy speech by Stalin. It was his first public utterance on Germany since Hitler's *coup* a year earlier; and in the section of it devoted to foreign affairs he returned again and again to the German question. Germany's exit from the League of Nations, prefiguring a policy of *revanche*, had "given a new impetus . . . to the growth of armaments in Europe". To the reproach of a change in attitude to the Versailles treaty he replied that it was not for those who had "suffered the shame of the Brest peace" to celebrate Versailles, which might indeed be the source of a new war. But the change was on the German side—not in the change of regime (Fascism in Italy had not stood in the way of excellent relations between the USSR and Italy), but in the "new" aggressive policy towards the USSR. Dimitrov and the Leipzig trial were once more passed over in silence. The leaders, and perhaps Stalin in particular, had still not made up their minds how far to commit themselves to this campaign of predominantly western inspiration. Throughout the past year fear of Germany, and desire to maintain good relations with Germany, had been evenly balanced in Soviet policy and in Stalin's mind. Now the former factor had begun to predominate. The speech was noteworthy for

---

[50] *SSSR: Tsentral'nyi Ispolnitel'nyi Komitet 6 Sozyva: 4 Sessiya* (1934), No. 1, pp. 27–32, No. 3, pp. 1–24; both speeches, as a tribute to their importance, were included in *Dokumenty Vneshnei Politiki SSSR*, xvi (1970), 778–797.

[51] *Ibid.* xvi, 742; for Stresemann's similar tactics see *Socialism in One Country, 1924–1926*, Vol. 3, p. 68.

the cynically realistic tone characteristic of many of Stalin's later pronouncements:

> In our time one does not count with the weak, one counts only with the strong. . . . We were not oriented to Germany in the past any more than we are oriented now to Poland and France. We were oriented in the past, and are oriented in the present, to the USSR, and only to the USSR.[52]

Bukharin spoke in the debate of the counter-revolutionary threat to the USSR from German Fascism and Japanese imperialism, and quoted *Mein Kampf* and the writings of Rosenberg.[53] But few speakers touched on foreign affairs.

Manuilsky, who reported on the work of IKKI, did his best to translate Stalin's blunt hints into the language of Comintern. He too noted that Germany was arming, and could "today put into the field an army of a million". Germany had become "the chief instigator of war in Europe". In the United States, France and Britain, "so-called bourgeois democracy is not yet completely bankrupt". Today "no proletarian in the world would raise a finger, in case of war, to support *Fascist* Germany in a struggle against Versailles". "In Germany," he declared, "there has never been so profound an urge towards a fighting united front of the working class." Unlike Stalin, he spoke openly of "the burning of the Reichstag by Fascist *provocateurs*", and observed that "the world was delighted with Dimitrov's behaviour". But taunts against social-democracy continued, and the old formulas for the united front were not modified. Manuilsky gave no lead for a change of line in Comintern.[54] Heckert, speaking for the KPD, indulged in fulsome flattery of Stalin and of the USSR.[55] Chinese, Japanese, Spanish, Polish and British delegates (but no French delegate) spoke to equally little purpose. The incorrigible Knorin pronounced that, thanks to Soviet achievements, the years of crisis had been "years of the conversion of Comintern into a really united, solid monolithic party", whose solid and monolithic character could be shaken by no Guttmanns or Neumanns.[56] It was a symptom of the emptiness of

[52] Stalin, *Sochineniya*, xiii, 291, 299–306.
[53] *XVII S"ezd Vsesoyuznoi Kommunisticheskoi Partii (b)* (1934), pp. 127–128.
[54] *Ibid.* pp. 305–322.
[55] *Ibid.* pp. 331–333.
[56] *Ibid.* p. 344.

the debate that neither Stalin nor Manuilsky thought it necessary to avail himself of the traditional right to reply to it. Soviet diplomacy had begun to display its flexibility in face of the new threat from Nazi Germany. But, in the absence of any direction from above, some months longer were needed to break down resistance in Comintern to so sharp a reversal of its cherished attitudes and slogans.

Stalin's indecisive role in Comintern affairs at this time may be explained in part by a serious crisis in his leadership of the party— the only such crisis which he ever had to face after 1927. The years 1932 and 1933, when famine stalked the countryside in the wake of collectivization, were a terrible period in Soviet history. The policies pursued under Stalin indubitably provoked deep uneasiness among the leaders and in the rank and file of the party;[57] the so-called Ryutin group was denounced and expelled in October 1932. The search for an alternative leader must have been widely canvassed. Some of the critics may have thought of Kirov, the popular party chief in Leningrad; if so, he seems to have given them no encouragement. No ranking party member was willing to court the upheaval or the risks which a change in the leadership would have involved.[58] Just as there was no alternative programme, so there was no organized movement in favour of Kirov or of any other alternative leader.

[57] A "letter from Moscow" dated "beginning of October", published in *Byulleten' Oppozitsii* (Paris), No. 31, November 1932, p. 23, spoke of discontent among high party officials with Stalin's leadership and his prolonged silence; Stalin made no public policy statement between June 1931 and January 1933. Trotsky in March 1933 noted the currency, inside and outside the party, of the slogan "Down with Stalin", but rejected it as incorrect on the ground that "the question is not one of Stalin, but of his fraction", and that "the issue is not the removal of individuals, but a change in the system" (*ibid.* No. 33, March 1933, p. 9).

[58] V. Serge, *Portrait de Staline* (1940), pp. 94–95, relates an occasion in the Politburo when Stalin, overwhelmed by the weight of criticism and opposition, offered his resignation; after an embarrassed silence, Molotov reassured him that he had the confidence of the party, and the incident was closed. The episode is not precisely dated, but is placed between the suicide of Stalin's wife and the seventeenth party congress, i.e. some time in 1933. Serge's story rests on hearsay. But he was in Moscow at the time, moving in opposition circles; and his account, written only a few years later, deserves more credence than that of Medvedev (see p. 121, note 60 below), written nearly 30 years after the event. If not true, it was a plausible invention. Serge does not mention Kirov.

Stalin rode out the storm. The harvest of 1933 was the best for several years, and marked the end of the period of famine conditions in the countryside. Attention was focused on the second five-year plan. By the time the seventeenth party congress met in January 1934 the challenge to Stalin's leadership had faded. He made the customary report on behalf of the central committee and was greeted with an ovation. The tone of the speech was self-assured, but moderate and relatively benign, unusually free from personal vituperation. Every subsequent speaker unreservedly praised him;[59] and the unanimity of the views expressed enabled him to dispense with a reply to the debate. In the elections to the party central committee at the end of the congress some delegates—estimates of their numbers vary—refused to vote for Stalin; this last token of revolt was an empty gesture, since the total of nominations coincided with the total of seats available.[60] It was presumably in deference to the critics that the title of secretary-general formerly held by Stalin was dropped. Stalin was appointed as the first of four secretaries, the others being Kaganovich, Kirov and Zhdanov.[61] During the greater part of 1934 Stalin continued to feel his way, and comparative moderation prevailed. It was only after the assassination of Kirov on December 1—the most enigmatic event in this eventful decade—that the iron fist was allowed to appear.

Throughout this period, the oppressive anxieties of the home front, economic and political, were a leaden weight on party and Soviet officials, and on Stalin himself; only a handful of specialists in

[59] Past offenders who had been censured, but had not been expelled from the party, or had been reinstated in it, confessed their errors and proclaimed their loyalty to Stalin. Lominadze, Bukharin, Zinoviev and Kamenev were heard without interruptions, and sat down to polite applause; Rykov, Preobrazhensky and Tomsky were subject to constant heckling and abuse. Kirov, speaking at the end of the debate, poked fun at Bukharin, Rykov and Tomsky, hinting that their confessions had not been sincere (*XVII S"ezd Vsesoyuznoi Kommunisticheskoi Partii (b)* (1934), p. 253).

[60] R. Medvedev, *Let History Judge* (1971) pp. 155–156, reports that "270 delegates voted against Stalin"; the number is probably an exaggeration (nor could delegates "vote against"—they could only withhold their votes). The total number of voting delegates was 1227. According to a party history published in the period of sharp revulsion against Stalin after 1956, "many congress delegates, notably those who were acquainted with V. I. Lenin's testament, considered that the time had come to transfer Stalin from the post of secretary-general to other work" (*Istoriya KPSS* (2nd ed. 1961), p. 486); nothing of this appears in the long account of the congress in *Istoriya KPSS*, IV, ii (1971), 261–277.

[61] *Pravda*, February 11, 1934.

foreign relations were mainly preoccupied by the threat of Hitler's rise to power in Germany. Stalin was ready to leave the conduct of diplomacy in the reliable hands of Litvinov, who seems to have enjoyed his confidence.[62] The affairs of Comintern were more complex, and in the organization itself opinions were divided on the question of the united (or later "popular") front. Here Stalin, whose contempt for Comintern and for foreign communist parties was well known, did not rouse himself to intervene; his spokesman, Molotov, did not appear at the eleventh, twelfth and thirteenth sessions of IKKI in 1931, 1932 and 1933. Stalin's interview with Duranty in December 1933, his warning against Nazi Germany in his speech at the seventeenth party congress in January 1934, the diplomatic manoeuvres which followed, and the entry of the USSR into the League of Nations in September 1934, were evidently prompted by Litvinov; there is no sign that either he or Stalin paused to consider their implications for Comintern. In the Comintern hierarchy, the advocates of the united front, reinforced by the powerful pleadings of Dimitrov, slowly gained ground over their opponents; but no guidance came from above. It was not until December 1934 that Stalin seems at last to have declared himself for the popular front— and then not publicly.[63] One had to wait for Stalin's declaration of May 16, 1935, in the context of the Franco–Soviet pact, to call Comintern and the foreign parties finally and sharply to order, and to subordinate every other consideration to the defence of the USSR against German aggression.

[62] A prominent member of the League of Nations secretariat was struck by the degree of independence enjoyed by Litvinov at Geneva: "Litvinov rarely asked for time to consult his government; he seemed always ready to decide on the spot when to press his argument, when to propose a compromise or to resign himself to accepting the majority view. It was clear that he had at least as free a hand as was generally given to the Foreign Ministers of the democratic Powers" (F. P. Walters, *A History of the League of Nations* (1952), i, 358–359).

[63] See p. 145 below.

CHAPTER 7

DIVIDED COUNSELS

The thirteenth IKKI and the seventeenth Russian party congress were scarcely over when sharper and more unmistakable symptoms of the Fascist danger confronted Comintern. On February 6, 1934, an attempted *coup* in Paris by Right-wing groups of a Fascist complexion was narrowly averted, and excited strong revulsion among the parties of the Left and Centre. In Austria, six days after the abortive *coup* in Paris, the Heimwehr, backed by Dollfuss's Christian-Social government and by Mussolini, crushed the still powerful social-democrats in Vienna by military force.[1] *Pravda* concluded that the events in Austria and France proved the impossibility of any compromise between the dictatorship of the bourgeoisie and the dictatorship of the proletariat; while the bourgeoisie was "treading the road to war", the class struggle was taking on "ever sharper forms".[2] But the victimization of the Austrian social-democrats did not qualify their guilt. An appeal by IKKI to "proletarians of all countries" ended with the cry: "Down with Fascism and its accomplices, the Second International: Long live the proletarian world revolution".[3] The Fascist triumph in Austria was followed three months later by the seizure of power by Fascist parties in Latvia and Bulgaria.

The alarm created by the advance of Fascism all over Europe was intensified by the blood-bath in Germany on the night of June 30, 1934, when several hundred persons, thought to constitute a danger to Hitler's personal rule, were shot on his orders. They included Röhm, the commander of the Nazi para-military Sturm-abteilungen (SA), Gregor Strasser, once Hitler's rival for the leadership of the party, and Schleicher, the former Chancellor and head of the Reichswehr. The first communist diagnosis of the event was that the "monopolist big bourgeoisie" had crushed the "petty-bourgeois strata" represented in the SA.[4] More significantly,

---

[1] For these events see p. 189 below.
[2] *Pravda*, February 19, 1934.
[3] *Rundschau*, No. 20, March 8, 1934, pp. 711–712.
[4] *Rundschau*, No. 39, July 5, 1934, pp. 1541–1543.

perhaps, Hitler had surrendered his private army, the SA, into the control of the Reichswehr in return for the recognition by the Reichswehr of his supreme authority. The murder of Schleicher, and the acquiescence of the other Reichswehr generals in it, sealed a relation between the Reichswehr and the dictator which was undisturbed for several years. What now haunted Moscow was the vision of a well integrated Germany where military and economic power were welded into an iron popular dictatorship. The safeguard, on which reliance had so long been placed by Soviet leaders, of the secret bond of sympathy and cooperation between the Reichswehr and the Red Army, was now subject to the unpredictable will of the Nazi dictator.

Reactions in Moscow were, however, still halting and ambiguous. Stalin, in the Duranty interview and in his speech at the party congress in January 1934, had exhibited his alarm at Hitler's aggressive attitude, and encouraged Litvinov's increasingly successful moves to bring the USSR closer to the western Powers. But he showed no eagerness to extend this diplomatic change of front to the activities of Comintern. His reluctance to declare himself on this point prolonged an anomalous situation in which officials of Comintern spoke with different voices, and directives issued to communist parties were conflicting and indecisive. It was the pressure of external events rather than pressure from above in Moscow which eventually drove Comintern along the path of the united, and later of the popular, front.

The arrival of Dimitrov in Moscow on February 27, 1934, was a crucial turning-point. The same evening, with his comrades Popov and Tanev, he gave an interview to nearly a hundred Soviet and foreign journalists.[5] On the following day he spoke at a celebration of Krupskaya's sixty-fifth birthday.[6] *Pravda*, which no longer had any inhibitions about proclaiming that "the Fascists set fire to the Reichstag", extended "a Bolshevik, revolutionary greeting to comrades Dimitrov, Popov and Tanev, brave soldiers of the great party of Lenin and Stalin". Dimitrov's name had "become the symbol of the struggle of the proletarian masses in all countries", and Dimitrov had "drawn towards Comintern over a million new

---

[5] *Rundschau*, No. 20, March 8, 1934, pp. 753–755.
[6] *Pravda*, March 1, 1934.

workers".[7] The Leipzig trial, by providing a forum for his rugged and independent personality, had made him the symbol of a world-wide wave of indignation and protest against a monstrous regime; and the immense prestige which this brought to him gave him a standing and an influence in Moscow such as no other foreign communist ever attained.

Already in the autumn of 1932, Dimitrov, in his capacity as head of WEB, had pleaded in a letter to Moscow for "a revolutionary united front of the working class against the offensive of capital and Fascism", and argued that recognition of the leading role of the communist party should not be made a preliminary condition for "a common struggle of communist, social-democratic and other masses of workers".[8] Now, back in Moscow after his German ordeal and triumph, he pressed the case for a thorough-going revision of Comintern policy on the united front. On March 27, 1934, he wrote again to Rolland, and received a sympathetic but evasive reply.[9] He used a speech in honour of the memory of Blagoev, the father-founder of the Bulgarian Communist Party, to stress the difference between the original Bulgarian Tesnyaki or "Narrows" and the Bolsheviks, schooled by Lenin in a more flexible tradition, and to recall the party's notorious error in 1923, when it had failed to support Stambuliski against what he termed "a Fascist *coup*".[10] The moral was crystal clear. Nothing must be allowed to impede the unity of the anti-Fascist forces. Receiving foreign journalists in the sanatorium in which he was recuperating from the ordeal of his imprisonment and trial, he once more insisted on the hope of winning over the social-democratic workers for an anti-Fascist united front.[11]

Dimitrov's dramatic incursion not surprisingly evoked jealousies and resistance in the hard kernel of officials set in the rigid ways of Comintern orthodoxy. On April 7, 1934, Dimitrov attended a session of the Politburo at which he attributed the failure of

[7] *Pravda*, February 28, 1934; the same issue carried an article by Radek praising the "Dimitrov generation", raised in the tradition of Marx, Lenin and Stalin.

[8] Quoted from the archives in *Georgii Dimitrov: Vydayushchiisya Deyatel' Kommunisticheskogo Dvizheniya* (1972), p. 201.

[9] G. Dimitrov, *S'chineniya* (n.d.), ix, 403.

[10] G. Dimitrov, *Izbrannye Sochineniya* (1957), i, 371–374. For the 1923 *coup* see *The Interregnum, 1923–1924*, pp. 191–194; for the Tesnyaki see *The Bolshevik Revolution, 1917–1923*, Vol. 3, p. 145.

[11] *Rundschau*, No. 29, May 9, 1934, pp. 1127–1128.

communist parties to win the allegiance of the masses to "the system
of our propaganda, our incorrect approach to the European
workers". Stalin expressed scepticism, but apparently suggested
that Dimitrov should "head the work in Comintern" and promised
him support from the Politburo.[12] For some time, however, he
continued to be cold-shouldered and ignored. At an international
conference of editors of communist newspapers and journals held in
Moscow in April 1934, Bela Kun delivered a massive report
featuring "the struggle for Soviet power", "the struggle against
social-democracy" (the doctrine of "the lesser evil" was trounced
yet again), and "the struggle against imperialist war and for the
defence of the Soviet Union". "The struggle against Fascism" was
evasively handled; the party press was accused of separating
Fascism from social-democracy, and both from capitalism, instead
of "*concentrating on an attack on capitalism*". Neither the united front
nor Dimitrov was mentioned. Speeches by Pyatnitsky, Knorin and
Heckert did not diverge significantly from this pattern; no other
speeches were reported.[13]

Even in Comintern circles, however, other views began to be
heard, and controversy raged with increasing intensity throughout
the summer. On April 22, 1934, Dimitrov was appointed a member
of the political secretariat of IKKI, and replaced the intransigent
Knorin as director of its Central European section.[14] Shortly
afterwards he became a member of the presidium of IKKI, and
"headed the work of the preparatory commissions" for the seventh
congress.[15] Kuusinen, Manuilsky and the KPD delegate
Maddalena, were among those who supported Dimitrov; Manuilsky and the KPP delegate Bronkowski, in particular, urged the
importance of wooing not only workers', but petty-bourgeois and
peasant, parties. On the other side, Bela Kun, Lozovsky, Knorin
and Wang Ming continued to denounce social-democracy as the
chief prop of the bourgeoisie, to demand the maintenance of
independent Red trade unions, and to treat the new line as a "Right
deviation".[16] The sharp division of opinion paralysed action by

[12] B. Leibzon and K. Shirinya, *Povorot v Politike Kominterna* (2nd ed., 1975),
p. 93.
[13] *Rundschau*, No. 33, May 30, 1934, was devoted to a report of the conference.
[14] B. Leibzon and K. Shirinya, *Povorot v Politike Kominterna* (2nd ed.,
1975), pp. 90–91.
[15] *Istoriya KPSS*, IV (1971), ii, 310.
[16] *Kommunisticheskii Internatsional: Kratkii Istoricheskii Ocherk* (1969), pp. 379–380,
the authors of which had access to Comintern archives.

Comintern. When Thorez visited Moscow in May 1934, the dissident Doriot was attacking the leaders of the PCF for their resistance to a broad extension of the united front. Doriot was severely censured. Thorez returned to Paris, well briefed by Dimitrov, but without any official instructions.[17]

The ground was, however, slowly shifting. The thirteenth IKKI at the end of 1933 had instructed the presidium of IKKI, not later than June of the following year, to make preparations for a seventh Comintern congress (six years after its predecessor in 1928) by publishing an agenda, and appointing *rapporteurs* for the different topics.[18] The question was discussed in the political secretariat of IKKI on May 11, 1934, and on May 17 Manuilsky and Pyatnitsky communicated the results to the central committee of the Russian party, and asked for approval and advice. The Politburo on May 26 gave the signal to proceed, and appointed a commission headed by Stalin to supervise the operation.[19] Thus encouraged, the presidium of IKKI on May 28, 1934, named four *rapporteurs* for the congress. Pieck was to report on the activities of IKKI since the last congress (the traditional opening report), Dimitrov on "The Offensive of Fascism and the Tasks of Comintern in the Struggle for the Unity of the Working Class against Fascism", Togliatti on the dangers of imperialist war, and Manuilsky on socialist construction in the USSR. The choice of topics and *rapporteurs* was in itself a programme, and showed that, though opposition might not have been overcome, Dimitrov's campaign had begun to meet with approval in the highest quarters. Commissions, in which leading Comintern officials and representative foreign communists participated, were set up to discuss in advance the terms of the four reports.[20]

On June 14, 1934, Kuusinen opened the proceedings of the commission on Pieck's report with a speech pointing to the need for a change in tactics. Manuilsky, in his role as spokesman of the Russian party, developed the theme at length. He condemned current slogans as "abstract" and "schematic". It was foolish to underestimate the Fascist menace, and to treat the revolutionary

[17] For Thorez's interview with Dimitrov and the situation in the PCF see p. 191 below.

[18] *XIII Plenum IKKI* (1934), p. 597.

[19] *Voprosy Istorii KPSS*, 1975, No 8, pp. 52–53.

[20] *Rundschau*, No. 34, May 31, 1934, p. 1277; *Kommunisticheskii Internatsional*, 1934, No. 16, p. 64; *Voprosy Istorii KPSS*, 1965, No. 7, p. 88.

struggle as "a struggle of communists with social-democrats". A "more concrete" programme of action was needed: "not proletarian dictatorship, not socialism, but a programme which will lead the masses to the struggle for proletarian dictatorship and socialism".[21] No further report of the discussion has been published. But, throughout the debates of the commissions, Kun, Heckert, Lozovsky, Knorin and Pyatnitsky are said to have resisted any attempt to depart from the thesis which denounced social-democracy as the principal prop of the bourgeoisie.[22]

It was not till July 1, 1934, that Dimitrov submitted to the second commission an outline of his proposed report. It analysed "the national and social demagogy of Fascism", described the German regime as "a conspicuous lesson for the proletariat of all countries", spoke of "our relation to social-democracy in the period of the Fascist offensive" as a major problem, called for "a united front from above and below" and for "a united front in the trade union movement", cautiously mentioned "our relation to various strata of the petty bourgeoisie", and finally proposed "a reorganization of the whole mass work of communist parties . . . from the point of view of the struggle against Fascism". The outline was accompanied by a letter which explicitly challenged "the wholesale qualification of social-democracy as social-Fascism" and as "the chief social prop of the bourgeoisie". More boldly still, he proposed "a change in the methods of work and leadership of Comintern, taking into account that it is impossible to give operational directions on all questions from Moscow to all 65 sections of Comintern".[23] On the evening of July 2, he addressed the commission in support of his proposals, repeating that tactics and policy must be changed in the light of experience gained since the sixth congress. Marxist analysis, he claimed, was being "replaced by formulas and abstractions which take no account of the peculiarities of each country, each party and organization". He challenged the correctness of three current slogans: the classification of social-democrats as social-Fascists, the description of social-democracy as

[21] Quoted from archives in *Kommunisticheskii Internatsional: Kratkii Istoricheskii Ocherk* (1969), p. 377; K. Shirinya, *Strategiya i Taktika Kominterna* (1979), pp. 40–41.
[22] *Ibid.* pp. 43–44.
[23] *Voprosy Istorii KPSS*, 1965, No. 7, pp. 83–86; for an earlier draft of the outline see *ibid.* 1969, No. 4, pp. 80–81. The letter is described in *Kommunisticheskii Internatsional: Kratkii Istoricheskii Ocherk* (1969), p. 377, as "a letter to IKKI and the central committee of the VKP (b)".

the chief social prop of the bourgeoisie, and the qualification of Left social-democracy as the chief danger. The debate was probably heated, and appears to have gone on far into the night.[24]

The commission on Togliatti's report on the threat of imperialist war met on July 17, 1934. This identified Fascist aggression as the source of danger, and raised the question of the attitude of communists to national defence in countries opposed to Fascist aggression.[25] But, since all these questions turned on the same underlying issue of the united front between communists and other parties, and the same speakers confronted one another, the work of the commissions tended to merge in a single hard-fought debate, in which the well-worn crux was the attitude to be adopted to social-democrats. While Manuilsky and Kuusinen argued that the role of social-democracy had changed in many respects with the advent of Fascism, Kun, Lozovsky, Pyatnitsky and Heckert continued to denounce social-democracy as the prop of the bourgeoisie, and even to defend the formula of social-Fascism.[26] On July 31 Codovilla called for a united front in Spain.[27] On the same day Hevesi, a Hungarian representative, denounced the "Fascisization" of all bourgeois parties, including especially peasant parties; and Kolarov, drawing examples from the Balkans, angrily retorted that the whole peasant movement could not be written off as Fascist, and that an approach must be sought to the mass of poor peasants.[28] On August 3, the commission on Togliatti's report ended with a discussion of the relations between national and social demands in communist policy, of which no record has been published.[29] The despatch by IKKI on August 21 of a letter to the PCF urging

[24] *Voprosy Istorii KPSS*, 1965, No. 7, pp. 86–88; B. Leibzon and K. Shirinya, *Povorot v Politike Kominterna* (2nd ed., 1975), pp. 95–96; K. Shirinya, *Strategiya i Taktika Kominterna* (1979), pp. 42–43.

[25] *Ibid.* p. 43.

[26] *Voprosy Istorii KPSS*, 1975, No. 8, pp. 54–55; a cryptic passage in B. Leibzon and K. Shirinya, *Povorot v Politike Kominterna* (2nd ed., 1975), p. 186, suggests that Kun challenged the assumption that some capitalist countries would fight on the side of the USSR in case of war. At a debate in 1933 Kun, Madyar, Safarov and others are said to have protested against the absurdity of discussing which imperialist country would be less dangerous or treacherous than another (*ibid.* p. 191).

[27] See p. 312 below.

[28] K. Shirinya, *Strategiya i Taktika Kominterna* (1979), pp. 45–46; Kolarov was continuing his previous argument at the thirteenth IKKI (see p. 107 above).

[29] *Voprosy Istorii KPSS*, 1975, No. 8, p. 55.

"maximum development of the united front"[30] was followed by further debates in the preparatory commission on the Dimitrov report and resolution. Kuusinen insisted on the need for parties to change their attitude to the united front and to abandon "sectarian principles", and was supported by Manuilsky. Knorin and Varga drew attention to increasing state intervention in the economy of capitalist countries and the rise of state monopoly capitalism, which facilitated preparations for war.[31]

A peculiar, though minor, role in the controversy about the united front was played, thanks to Dimitrov's nationality, by the affairs of the Bulgarian Communist Party (BKP), whose unhappy and complex history was reflected in its record of perennial discord. It had been severely censured for its failure to support the resistance of Stambuliski's Peasant Union to the *coup* of June 9, 1923; and the abortive rising of September 1923 had been organized, on directives from Moscow, by Dimitrov and Kolarov under the banner of a united front between the BKP and the peasantry against the Tsarkov regime.[32] Since that time the BKP had been subjected to constant and brutal persecution, intensified after the bomb outrage in Sofia Cathedral in April 1925. In the years that followed, nominal leadership in the party was shared between a foreign bureau in Moscow, in which Dimitrov and Kolarov were the leading figures, and groups functioning illegally and precariously on Bulgarian soil, with occasional secret party conferences in Vienna or Berlin. The turn to the Left in Comintern after 1928 was reflected in current attitudes towards the BKP, and more sympathy was felt for the young activists who challenged the authority of the older leaders. Kolarov and Dimitrov continued to enjoy the protection of Comintern, but with somewhat diminished prestige. Kolarov was appointed director of the International Agrarian Institute in Moscow, and became the Comintern expert on peasant affairs. Dimitrov was sent in March 1929 to work in WEB in Berlin. When the eleventh IKKI met in March 1931, Kolarov spoke in general terms on the peasant question, and Dimitrov on the danger of war; neither touched on the specific problems of the BKP.[33]

[30] See p. 196 below.
[31] *Voprosy Istorii KPSS*, 1975, No. 8, p. 56.
[32] See *The Interregnum, 1923–1924*, pp. 194–195.
[33] *XI Plenum IKKI* (1932), i, 345–367, ii, 148–152.

But Iskrov, a Bulgarian youth leader, was also given the floor; and he seized the occasion to denounce both the social-democrats and the Bulgarian Peasant Union as being hand-in-glove with the bourgeoisie, and the Balkan "social-Fascists" who had recently welcomed representatives of the Second International and the Amsterdam International, as well as "a group of Trotskyists" which had recently made its appearance.[34] Controversial party issues were not raised by Bulgarian delegates at the twelfth IKKI in September 1932. By this time, however, rifts in the party could not be disguised. As was afterwards alleged by IKKI, "petty-bourgeois elements temporarily gained the upper hand" in the party leadership, and were responsible for "sectarian distortions of the Bolshevik line of Comintern" and for a "Leftist course", which was traced back to the heresy of the "Narrows" in the early days of the party.[35] But these verdicts were penned some time later, when the new line in Comintern had gained the upper hand. Dimitrov's young rivals could hardly have gone so far without friends and supporters in Moscow; divisions in the BKP reflected divisions in Comintern itself.

At the thirteenth IKKI at the end of November 1933 Kolarov again spoke of the peasant question in general, and did not mention the BKP.[36] Dimitrov was on trial in Leipzig. The two BKP delegates, Dybov and Iskrov, both paid formal tribute to Dimitrov, and both set to work to undermine his position. Dybov, in extolling the achievements of the party, denounced a "Right opportunist theory of the consolidation of the Fascist dictatorship in Bulgaria", which "would have dragged the party back, and condemned the proletariat to passivity and inaction", though he tactfully admitted "some Left sectarians were also rushing ahead". Iskrov praised the successes of the party in still more exaggerated terms; and his treatment of Dimitrov's defiance of the Nazi court as a call to the BKP for "a decisive mass struggle to win power and establish a proletarian dictatorship" was a piece of transparent sophistry.[37] It

[34] *Ibid.* ii, 178–183.
[35] *Die Kommunistische Internationale vor dem VII Weltkongress* (1935), pp. 397–398; many years later Kolarov described these proceedings in a heavily loaded pamphlet with the expressive title, *Protiv Levogo Sektanstva i Trotskizma v Bolgarii* (1949).
[36] For this speech see p. 107 above.
[37] *XIII Plenum IKKI* (1934), pp. 264–268, 543–549; for their tributes to Dimitrov see p. 115 above.

was left to Walecki, speaking in the name of the Balkan secretariat of
IKKI, to reproach the BKP with its failure to "convert into living
practice" the recognition of the poor and middle peasantry as "the
chief ally of the proletariat in its revolutionary struggle". He also
urged the party to struggle by all means against "the banning of
mass organizations and their press", such as the Workers' Party,
which, though it retained its legal status till May 1934, was
constantly harassed by the government.[38] These recommendations,
which accorded with the growing inclination in Comintern for
united front policy, were unlikely to prove acceptable to the
Bulgarian Left.

The Fascist *coup* in Sofia on May 19, 1934, transformed the
divisions in the distracted BKP. Dimitrov now enjoyed in Moscow a
prestige which could not be ignored; and the defeat of May 19
recalled memories of the party's traumatic failure of June 9, 1923.[39]
On May 22, following a meeting between Dimitrov and Iskrov,
now head of the foreign bureau of the BKP, the bureau addressed a
letter to the central committee of the party calling for resistance to
the "military-Fascist dictatorship" in cooperation with the peasants
and soldiers, and specifically referring to "the lesson of June 9". The
new line, reinforced by sharp criticism of the past leadership, was
not welcomed by rank-and-file members of the party in exile or in
the Bulgarian underground; and recriminations continued during
the summer.[40] It was not until August 14, 1934, that the political
secretatariat of IKKI, taking formal cognisance for the first time of
the events of May 19, condemned the activities of "Left sectarians"
in the BKP, and instructed the party to direct itself "to the masses,
to local and central organizations of the reformist trade unions and
of the Peasant Union, with proposals to establish a united front for
the struggle against Fascism". In a further discussion in the

[38] *XIII Plenum IKKI* (1934), p. 523.

[39] At the seventh Comintern congress more than a year later, when the official
line had been entirely reversed, the Bulgarian delegate Krumov declared that on
the occasion of May 19, 1934, the BKP, "under cover of revolutionary phrases, fell
in fact into opportunist passivity", and that "deplorable cases of disloyalty and
treachery" occurred in the party leadership; Kolarov claimed that the BKP had
fallen under the sway of "outspokenly sectarian elements" and had directed their
main attack on the social-democrats and on the Peasant Union (*Rundschau*, No. 50,
September 25, 1935, pp. 2146–2147, No. 60, October 30, 1935, pp. 2443–2446).

[40] The fullest available account of these events is in an article in *Georgii Dimitrov:
Vydayushchiisya Deyatel' Kommunisticheskogo Dvizheniya* (1972), pp. 474–476, the
author of which had access to archives.

following month, Dimitrov trenchantly argued that the platform of the BKP should be a platform of democratic rights and liberties, and that, instead of dismissing bourgeois democracy with terms of abuse, it should be utilized for the struggle against Fascism.[41] Such plain speaking was only just beginning to be heard in Comintern. It was not until January 1935 that an "enlarged plenum" of the central committee of the BKP was convened in Moscow. It adopted a resolution which, with "unsparing self-criticism", denounced "the grave political and tactical errors committed by the party leadership since 1933", which had led to "opportunist passivity" during and after the May 19 *coup*. The "anti-Fascist united front" was hitherto to be the aim of the party. Finally, the committee adopted a message of greeting to Dimitrov as its "universally beloved and authoritative leader", and "renewed" the party leadership by co-opting new members.[42]

One of the obstacles to progress was a rift in the exiled and dismembered KPD. A mammoth resolution of the party central committee in Paris of February 5, 1934, expressed unconditional approval of the decisions of the thirteenth IKKI, and conformed unreservedly to the line there laid down.[43] This involved a repudiation of Neumann, whose abject recantation of his errors was published by the central committee with the curt comment that he had still to "demonstrate his fidelity to the line of Comintern and the KPD through long practical work".[44] Since the thirteenth IKKI at the end of 1933, a nucleus of KPD leaders, of whom Pieck and Ulbricht were the most prominent, seems to have established itself permanently in Moscow. This group, which enjoyed the tacit support of IKKI, soon began to assert its independence of party headquarters in Paris, and leaned more or less openly towards the new line sponsored in Moscow by Dimitrov. A majority of the central committee and the politburo in Paris, which found leaders in Schubert and Schulte, clung firmly to the old orthodoxy.

[41] *Ibid.* pp. 476–480; K. Shirinya, *Strategiya i Taktika Kominterna* (1979), pp. 46–47, 50.

[42] *Rundschau*, No.15, March 28, 1935, pp. 788–789.

[43] *Rundschau*, No. 22, March 22, 1934, pp. 821–828; this was evidently the resolution said to have been drafted by the party politburo after a debate of several days (*ibid.* No. 15, February 15, 1934, p. 537).

[44] *Ibid.* No. 25, April 12, 1934, p. 942.

Believing that the proponents of change over-rated the strength and durability of the Nazi regime, they repeated the time-honoured slogans of the rising revolutionary wave and the German Soviet republic, and attacked any compromise with social-democratic or bourgeois parties on a platform of democratic rights as a betrayal of communist principles. "Fourteen years of social-democracy", declared a long manifesto of the party central committee of May 7, 1934, "ended in the morass of Fascism"; to support social-democracy meant "to stifle the proletarian revolution in embryo".[45] A clash between the two groups and the two opinions could scarcely be avoided.[46]

On July 9–10, 1934, the presidium of IKKI, now deeply involved in the controversy over Dimitrov's proposals, held a session to examine the German question.[47] Richter reported on behalf of the KPD. The events of June 30 in Germany showed that "the Fascist dictatorship is at the beginning of its crisis". After dwelling, however, in familiar terms on the "revolutionary upsurge of the broad masses of the working class" and on the collapse of the SPD, the speaker cautiously admitted that the KPD had enjoyed little success among social-democratic workers, and that "something in our tactics is not correct". One could not hope to win over these workers by sweeping attacks on the record of the SPD. Having ventured so far, Richter concluded with an appeal for the united front, and for "the leading, organizing role" of the KPD, which echoed the language of the thirteenth IKKI. Knorin attempted to redress the balance. He, too, admitted the failure of the KPD, but supplied a different diagnosis. "Our" formula that "social-democracy and Fascism are twin brethren", and that "social-democracy is the chief social prop of the bourgeoisie", was correct; it was still correct to call the SPD leader Wels a social-Fascist. The KPD propagandists had not shown sufficient energy to carry conviction to social-democratic workers. He concluded by calling

[45] *Ibid.* No. 36, June 14, 1934, pp. 1405–1408, 1425.
[46] For slanted accounts of the rift in the KPD see *Geschichte der Deutschen Arbeiterbewegung*, v (1966), 84–87; *Kommunisticheskii Internatsional: Kratkii Istoricheskii Ocherk* (1969), p. 385.
[47] In *Georgii Dimitrov: Vydayushchiisya Deyatel' Kommunisticheskogo Dvizheniya* (1972), p. 322, this is called "an extended session of the politburo of the central committee of the KPD, in which representatives from Germany and members of the presidium of IKKI took part"; the writer refers to archives, but does not quote them. Later the evidence for the establishment of a politburo of the KPD in Moscow becomes clear (see p. 142 below).

for "popularization of the programme of Soviet power in Germany as the sole salvation of the working masses". After further speeches, which were not reported, Pyatnitsky summed up. He professed himself "in absolute agreement with [Knorin's] whole speech". But his line was different. He congratulated the KPD on having "extraordinarily quickly reorganized its ranks and very quickly re-assembled its forces". Its most important task at present was to establish "the united front with social-democratic organizations" in the industrial centres. He praised the example set by the French and Austrian parties. He traced the weakness of the KPD back to its failure to mobilize "at least a part of the proletariat" against the Prussian *coup* of July 20, 1932. He disagreed—this was the only recorded expression of dissent in the debate—with a demand made by Lozovsky in his (unreported) speech that, at joint protest meetings against Fascism with social-democratic workers, the KPD should announce "our whole programme"; this resembled "the old method", and might be inappropriate in current conditions. The session did not, and was not expected to, record any formal conclusions.[48]

The sequel of these deliberations was a session of the central committee of the KPD, convened in Moscow and joined by "regional and factory officials" from the underground in Germany. This body, bypassing and tacitly superseding the committee in Paris, passed on August 1, 1934, a crucial resolution on the creation of "a united front of the worker masses in the struggle against the Hitler dictatorship". Taking its cue from the Hitler *putsch* of June 30, the committee called for "unity of action of communist and social-democratic workers" as well as of "opposition elements" in SA organizations, whose "disillusionment with Fascism" could be boldly utilized. Collaboration was needed to establish "free" trade unions and restore trade union unity. The party was pledged to seek unity "on the basis of the Comintern programme". But "a brotherly, comradely attitude" should be adopted to former social-democratic workers, and even to "the best part of the corps of [SPD]

---

[48] The speeches of Richter, Knorin and Pyatnitsky were published in reverse order in *Rundschau*, No. 47, August 23, 1934, pp. 1953–1963, No. 48, August 30, 1934, pp. 2017–2021; Pyatnitsky's speech was incomplete, but neither its conclusion nor the promised further speeches ever appeared. The debate, being restricted to secondary figures like Pyatnitsky and Richter, allowed for the ventilation of controversial opinions, and was not intended to produce any authoritative pronouncement.

officials".[49] It was a sharp reversal of earlier party attitudes; the KPD group in Moscow had finally embraced Dimitrov's conception of the united front. On August 2, in the preparatory commission for Dimitrov's report, the KPD delegate Schwab strongly condemned the identification of social-democracy with Fascism and the neglect of the national question in the struggle against the Fascist dictatorship.[50] An article by Ulbricht published in the *Rundschau*, which was signed "Walter" and purported to come from Berlin, contained an impassioned plea for trade union unity. It was claimed that illegal trade union groups, including workers of all parties, had been formed in Germany; where this happened, groups based on the RGO or on Red trade unions should abandon their separate organizations.[51] In the next two months negotiations took place between Ulbricht and a representative of the SPD, Aufhäuser, but ended only in a re-statement of their differences.[52]

It was events in other parties rather than pressure from Moscow which forced the pace. While in Moscow resistance to change, though being gradually eroded, was still stubborn and vocal, and Stalin sat on the fence, the French communists and socialists on July 27, 1934, signed an agreement for common action against Fascism; on August 18, the Italian communist and socialist parties in exile followed suit. In Britain, in the summer and autumn of 1934, the activities of Mosley's blackshirts had created new eagerness for a united front in the CPGB and in other Left parties.[53] Enthusiasm for united front policies was weak or non-existent in countries where political institutions of the Left had long been crushed under an iron dictatorship—Italy, Poland, Bulgaria. It was most powerful in

[49] *Rundschau*, No. 45, August 16, 1945, pp. 1867–1869; B. Leibzon and K. Shirinya, *Povorot v Politike Kominterna* (2nd ed., 1975), p. 114, admits that the resolution "in some places met with opposition from communists who regarded the turn towards unity of action as a concession to opportunism".

[50] K. Shirinya, *Strategiya i Taktika Kominterna* (1979), pp. 44–45.

[51] *Rundschau*, No. 44, August 9, 1934, pp. 1805–1806; the identity of the author was disclosed in *Geschichte der Deutschen Arbeiterbewegung*, v (1966), 88.

[52] *Ibid.* v, 91–92; Togliatti is said to have been critical of Ulbricht's handling of the negotiations with Aufhäuser, and regarded the KPD as "the weakest link in the chain of the united front policy" (P. Togliatti, *Opere*, III (1973), i, p. cci).

[53] For these developments see pp. 195 (PCF), 254 (PCI), 233–235 (CPGB) below; Dimitrov in his speech at the seventh congress (see pp. 412–413 below) said that the PCF "set an example to all the sections of Comintern in the application of the united front".

countries where a democratic tradition had bred familiarity with coalitions between political parties and groups of the Left—France, Britain, Austria and Czechoslovakia. For the communist parties in these countries resistance to Hitlerism was a more effective rallying cry than calls to overthrow the capitalist system. Above all the united front offered them an opportunity to emerge from the isolation to which the orthodoxy of Comintern had condemned them, and to play an active, sometimes a leading, role in the workers' movements of their respective countries.

These struggles in Comintern and in the communist parties took place against a diplomatic background which reflected more and more openly the shift in attitudes to Germany and to the Versailles treaty foreshadowed during the preceding winter at the thirteenth IKKI, at the December session of the TsIK of the USSR, and at the seventeenth Russian party congress.[54] The surprising *rapprochement* between Germany and Poland, marked by the signature on January 26, 1934, of a ten-year pact of mutual non-aggression, and by the cessation of propaganda for German territorial claims against Poland, seemed to carry a fresh threat to the USSR, and contributed to the increasing tension in Soviet–German relations.[55] The constant assurance that the deterioration in these relations was due to Hitler's aggressive foreign policy, and not to the character of the regime, was confirmed by the maintenance of cordial relations with Fascist Italy; the Soviet Ambassador in Rome told Mussolini in July 1934 that, if the hostility of Nazi Germany to the USSR were to change, "nothing would prevent the Soviet Government from continuing friendly collaboration with Germany in the spirit of the Rapallo and Berlin agreements".[56]

The counterpart of the growing tension between the USSR and Germany was the steady improvement during 1934 of Soviet

[54] See pp. 113–120 above.

[55] Notice of the impending signature of the pact seems to have been given to the Soviet Government only on the previous day, and to the French Government a few days earlier (*Dokumenty Vneshnei Politiki SSSR*, xvii (1971), 69, 99–100). For a protest of the KPP against the treaty between "the Fascist government of Pilsudski" and "the Fascist government of Hitler" see *Iz Istorii Mezhdunarodnoi Proletarskoi Solidarnasti*, v (1961), 192–195; for the Polish documents on the negotiation of the pact see J. Lipski, *Diplomat in Berlin* (1968), pp. 100–129.

[56] *Dokumenty Vneshnei Politiki SSSR*, xvii (1971), 471.

relations with France. In June the Soviet government established diplomatic relations with two of the *protégés* of France in the Little Entente, Czechoslovakia and Rumania;[57] and on November 2, the politburo authorized negotiations, if the opportunity offered, for an eastern pact, without the participation of Germany and Poland, with France and Czechoslovakia or with France alone.[58] Meanwhile, in September the USSR took a step, the possibility of which had first been adumbrated in Stalin's interview with Duranty in December 1933,[59] and with strong encouragement from France joined the League of Nations. This move, reinforced by the amicable relations now established with the United States, symbolized the integration of the USSR into a defensive front of the western Powers to resist the aggressive designs of Germany and Japan. But it embarrassed some party stalwarts in Moscow as well as in the foreign parties.[60] It may well have been confusion and divisions of opinion in Comintern, as well as the delicacy of the international situation, which prompted the presidium of IKKI on September 5, 1934, to postpone the seventh congress of Comintern, still projected for the autumn, till the first half of 1935.[61]

In this context the fate of the Saar territory became for a short time a burning question. The Versailles treaty had placed this rich coal-mining area under the administration of the League of Nations (and effectively under French control) for fifteen years, at the end of which its destination was to be determined by a plebiscite, due to be held in January 1935. It had long been common form in the KPD and the PCF, and in the Soviet press, to denounce the occupation of the Saar, together with other iniquities of the treaty, as an example of French or western imperialism. With the approach of the plebiscite, however, which would offer the population a choice between the restoration of territory to Germany, its annexation by France, and the maintenance of the *status quo*, doubts began to arise. For communists, a vote to bring the area under the Nazi dictatorship was unthinkable. To abstain from voting, and call for

[57] *Ibid.* xvii, 379–381; an article applauding this step appeared in *Pravda*, June 11, 1934.

[58] *Istoriya KPSS*, IV, ii (1971), 296.

[59] See p. 117 above.

[60] A defensive leading article on "The USSR and the League of Nations" appeared in *Kommunisticheskii Internatsional*, 1934, No. 26–27, pp. 3—11.

[61] *Rundschau*, No. 51, September 20, 1934, p. 2165; *Kommunisticheskii Internatsional*, 1934, No. 28, p. 3.

an independent Saar territory under a Soviet regime–hitherto the theme of party propaganda—would be an empty gesture. When the presidium of IKKI met in July 1934 to discuss the affairs of the KPD, the party central committee had already decided to abandon the slogan of "a Red Saar", and to advise Saar communists to vote for the *status quo*. But it was apparently slow to publicize so radical a reversal of its previous attitude.

At the session of the presidium, Richter, who at the thirteenth IKKI had come out for "the unification of a Red Saar with a Soviet Germany",[62] now spoke in neutral terms of "our struggle for the Saar, which also has great importance for our struggle to bring about the downfall of the Hitler dictatorship in Germany". Knorin, in an unusually conciliatory mood, praised the KPD for having abandoned the slogan " a Red Saar territory" in favour of a decision to vote in January for the *status quo*; a united front should be formed without any conditions other than readiness to vote for the *status quo*. Pyatnitsky in his summing-up concurred, but feared that the new line had not yet been thoroughly applied; "only just now have the communists in the Saar territory come to life".[63] The dropping of revolutionary slogans which had so long been obligatory did not come easy to German communists. It was not till the beginning of October that the central committee of the KPD issued a massive appeal to the workers of the Saar to vote for the *status quo* with the assurance that, after the fall of the Nazi dictatorship, a second plebiscite on the return of the Saar to Germany would be held.[64]

These influences cannot have failed to weight the balance in Comintern in favour of those who sought to promote an active anti-fascist line. At this moment a fresh warning of the encroachment of Fascism came from a remote corner of Europe. The formation on October 4, 1934, of a new Spanish Government with the participation of the Fascist party CEDA provoked armed socialist risings in Madrid and Barcelona, which were quickly put down, and a massive miners' strike in the Asturias region, which lasted for a fortnight amid scenes of violence and was eventually crushed with

[62] *XIII Plenum IKKI* (1934), p. 164.
[63] *Rundschau*, No. 47, August 23, 1934, pp. 1955, 1962, No. 48, August 30, 1934, p. 2020; for this session see pp. 134–135 above.
[64] *Rundschau*, No. 54, October 11, 1934, pp. 2378–2379.

great brutality by the armed forces.[65] At the height of this conflict, IKKI issued a call to the workers of all countries to support the Spanish workers, and also proposed negotiations with the Second International for a joint campaign.[66] On October 15 the political commission of IKKI sent to all parties a circular, said to have been drafted by Dimitrov, on preparations for the seventh congress, which defined the united front against Fascism and war as "the central link in a genuinely mass policy for the congress".[67] It was at this moment that Dimitrov drew up a memorandum, which secured the approval of IKKI, arguing that the increasing activity of communist parties called for a "concentration of operational directives" in the parties themselves, which worked in very varied conditions. But this was qualified by insistence on the need to "strengthen the general ideological–political direction of the communist movement by Comintern as the world party of the proletariat". The memorandum was submitted to Stalin, who replied on October 25 that he was in complete agreement with Dimitrov "regarding a review of the methods of work of the organs of Comintern, of their reorganization and of changes in their personal composition", and did not doubt that " the central committee of the VKP(B) will support you".[68] The exchange was not free from an element of vagueness and ambiguity. But it was a token of Dimitrov's enhanced prestige and influence with Stalin. He spoke out with a new confidence in an article in *Pravda* on November 8, 1934, in which he sharply criticized the opponents of the united front.

The way ahead was, however, still far from clear. On October 11, 1934, Cachin and Thorez, in the name of IKKI, but on whose initial instigation is uncertain, addressed a letter to the secretariat of the Second International offering a meeting to discuss ways and means of joint action by the two Internationals. The invitation was accepted, and Adler and Vandervelde met Cachin and Thorez in Brussels on October 15. The meeting was not a success. Adler and Vandervelde, suspicious as ever of communist tactics, wanted a discussion of the principles and conditions of collaboration; Cachin

[65] See p. 314 below.

[66] *Rundschau*, No. 54, October 11, 1934, p. 2331.

[67] *Voprosy Istorii KPSS*, 1975, No. 8, p. 57; K. Shirinya, *Strategiya i Taktika Kominterna* (1979), pp. 52–53.

[68] B. Leibzon and K. Shirinya, *Povorot v Politike Kominterna* (2nd ed., 1975), p. 97.

and Thorez wanted only to discuss the planning of a joint campaign. Adler and Vandervelde would only promise to refer the question to the executive of the Second International, due to meet in the following month—a form of procrastination which incensed the impatient Cachin and Thorez.[69] Opinion in the socialist and social-democratic parties was divided; and the meeting of the executive in Paris on November 13–17, 1934, was the scene of a long and angry debate. It was decided to revoke the ban placed in March 1933 on direct negotiations between socialist and communist parties, which had been flagrantly ignored by the French socialists. The executive by a majority vote rejected the proposal for direct negotiations with Comintern. But a powerful minority which favoured negotiations included Blum for the French, Nenni for the Italian, and Del Vayo and Largo Caballero for the Spanish, socialist parties, and Dan for the Mensheviks. An official letter recording the negative decision was sent to Cachin and Thorez; and the minority published a declaration of dissent.[70]

Nor was the battle in the KPD yet over. A majority of the politburo in Paris was in open conflict with the self-constituted central committee in Moscow, and enjoyed some, though fast diminishing, sympathy in Comintern circles. In spite of extravagant claims in Comintern literature, the activity of communist groups functioning illicitly in Germany seems to have been very restricted. But such contacts as could be maintained with them were more easily made from the west than from the east; the occasional issues of the *Rote Fahne* smuggled into Germany were printed in various western centres. It is probably true that the politburo in Paris was unwilling to publicize the pronouncements of the Moscow central committee.[71] But German workers, whether they had belonged to

[69] J. Braunthal, *History of the International* (Engl. transl. 1967), ii, 474–475; a record of the meeting published in *Protokoll der Verhandlungen zwischen den II und III Internationalen über die Unterstützung des heldenhaftes Kampfes der Werktätigen Spaniens* (Zurich, 1935) has not been available; an abbreviated record appeared in *Humanité*, November 8, 1934, a longer one in *Rundschau*, No. 60, November 15, 1934, pp. 2679–2687. Thorez's remarks are in *Oeuvres de Maurice Thorez*, II, vii (1952), 34–41.

[70] J. Braunthal, *History of the International* (Engl. transl. 1967), ii, 476–478; the letter and the minority declaration were published in *Rundschau*, No. 61, November 22, 1934, p. 2719, preceded by an ironical article by Bela Kun commenting on the proceedings. Longer critical accounts appeared in *ibid*. No. 62, November 28, 1934, pp. 2783–2784, No. 66, December 27, 1934, pp. 3061–3065. For the ban of March 1933 see pp. 85–86 above.

[71] *Gescheichte der Deutschen Arbeiterbewegung*, v (1966), p. 89.

the SPD or to the KPD, are less likely to have been impressed by the doctrinal differences between them than by the need for joint resistance to the impositions of the Nazi dictatorship. Brandler, now also an exile in Paris, made an approach to the Paris headquarters of the KPD, and was received by representatives of the politburo. But, since he continued to justify his past breach of party discipline on the score of abnormal conditions in the party, the conversations resulted only in the publication of a recriminatory open letter to Brandler in the illegal *Rote Fahne*.[72]

Meanwhile the contingent of important KPD members ensconced in Moscow began to arrogate to itself more and more openly the role of leadership, and to ignore the pretensions of the group in Paris. On October 27, 1934, what was described as a joint meeting of the political secretariat of IKKI and of the politburo of the KPD condemned the Paris group as "Left sectarian", and proclaimed its support for Pieck and Ulbricht.[73] In November a body unequivocally calling itself the politburo of the central committee of the KPD adopted a resolution on preparations for the seventh congress of Comintern, and named among other items on the agenda "the relations between Fascism and social-democracy", "the role of Germany as the principal instigator of war in Europe", "the Bolshevik struggle for unity of action and the unity of the working class", and "the problem of allies of the proletarian revolution".[74]

> It is understandable [wrote Ulbricht] that, in view of the necessity to adapt our tactics to changed conditions and overcome certain errors and weaknesses in our party work, some uncertainties in the organization and waverings in many comrades should come to light. Undoubtedly sectarian tendencies and deviations are at present the greatest danger in our party.[75]

But the conversion to the united front was not yet absolute. Both Pieck and Ulbricht in their appeals for a united front continued to attack not only the leadership of the SPD established in Prague, but "Left" dissidents in the SPD who attempted to preach a comprom-

[72] *Rundschau*, No. 54, October 11, 1934, p. 2370.
[73] *Georgii Dimitrov: Vydayuschiisya Deyatel' Kommunisticheskogo Dvizheniya* (1972), p. 324.
[74] *Kommunisticheskii Internatsional*, 1934, No. 35, pp. 31–33.
[75] *Rundschau*, No. 62, November 29, 1934, pp. 2806–2809.

ise between socialists and communists.[76] The cause of trade union unity was also not neglected. The central committee of the KPD issued an appeal beginning with the unaccustomed salutation "Colleagues", and addressed to "all social-democrats and all trade unionists"; since all trade unions in Germany had been crushed under the dictatorship, it was logical that trade unionists of whatever colour should combine against it.[77] But the solid structure of the reformist unions in western Europe and of the Amsterdam International could not be breached; and an article by Lozovsky was full of recriminations against their leaders whose obduracy was a bar to unity.[78]

Even the Czechoslovak party, in which Gottwald had at one time appeared as a protagonist of united front policies, continued to display ambivalent attitudes. On the eve of Masaryk's re-election as president of the republic in May 1934, the party central committee issued a manifesto with the heading "Not Masaryk, but Lenin".[79] One of the party leaders wrote ironically of Masaryk that, "the more he speaks, the better philosopher of capitalism and bourgeois society he shows himself".[80] The ninth plenum of the party central committee in June 1934 again branded social-democrats as social-Fascists, and an appeal to socialist leaders for common action against "the white terror" in Austria and Germany and against the dangers of imperialist war met with no response.[81] Gottwald, apparently under danger of arrest for subversive activities, was summoned to Moscow to work in Comintern;[82] and from this vantage-point he was able to direct the course of the party into safer paths. It was embarrassing that the views now gaining ground in Moscow were difficult to distinguish from those so recently advocated by the now discredited and expelled Guttmann. In an article in the Comintern journal Gottwald explained the party's reluctance to embrace united front tactics by "fear of repeating the opportunist errors of Guttmann", adding that this attitude had

[76] See, in particular, an article by Pieck criticizing the "platform" of a group calling itself a "Workers Circle of Revolutionary Socialists" (*ibid.* No. 63, December 6, 1934, pp. 2869–2876).

[77] *Ibid.* No. 61, November 22, 1934, pp. 2739–2740.

[78] *Ibid.* No. 62, November 29, 1934, pp. 2805–2806.

[79] *Ibid.* No. 31, May 24, 1934, p. 1214; Gottwald stood as communist candidate and received the votes of 38 deputies against Masaryk's 327.

[80] *Ibid.* No. 39, July 5, 1934, p. 1578.

[81] *Iz Istorii Kominterna* (1970), p. 120.

[82] *Ibid.* p. 129; he remained in Moscow till February 1936.

merely helped social-democracy by "its own tactical immobility and lack of flexibility". He ended the article with a defence against those party members who criticized the USSR for entering the League of Nations and forming "a coalition with capitalist states".[83] Thus prompted, the party politburo on November 22, 1934, adopted a resolution on preparations for the seventh congress;[84] and a few days later the tenth plenum of the central committee cautiously proclaimed its hostility "*to the whole social-democratic ideology, to all illusions of the social-democratic workers which are an obstacle to the class struggle*", but called for a "united struggle of the working class against national Fascism". It demanded self-determination for oppressed nationalities "always and everywhere", but denounced any plan to cede national territories to Germany, Poland or Hungary.[85] With Gottwald established in Moscow, no voice of dissent from Prague was likely to make itself heard.

The strange episode in the PCF, when a restraining hand was laid on Thorez's ambition to convert the united front into a "popular front",[86] showed that resistance to change was not yet dead in Comintern itself. On November 14, 1934, Bela Kun sent to the political secretariat of IKKI copies of a speech of Thorez to the central committee of the PCF published in *Humanité* under the headline "Sur la Voie du Parti Unique", and argued against the transformation of the united front into "a vulgar policy of blocs".[87] The issue came to a head at a session of the presidium of IKKI on December 9–19, 1934, at which all the major parties were represented and 170 persons are said to have been present. Thorez made a report on the work of the PCF in promoting "a united workers' and a broad popular front". The length of the session suggests that the debate was stubborn. Lozovsky and others are said to have reiterated the fear that the new policy would strengthen bourgeois-republican loyalties in the working class and hamper the development of "revolutionary strivings". Kuusinen and Manuilsky criticized this "sectarian and mechanistic approach to the solution of new problems". Kuusinen praised the contribution of the French communist youth league to the new policy. Manuilsky

---

[83] *Kommunisticheskii Internatsional*, 1934, No. 30, pp. 46–52.

[84] *Ibid.* 1934, No. 35, pp. 33–35.

[85] *Rundschau*, No. 66, December 27, 1934, pp. 3081–3087.

[86] See p. 199 below.

[87] B. Leibzon and K. Shirinya, *Povorot v Politike Kominterna* (2nd ed., 1975), p. 107; for the speech see p. 200 below.

described the tactics of the united front as "something new", designed to meet "different unique conditions in different countries", and stressed the importance of supporting the "partial" demands of the workers. The session registered its approval of the line of the PCF, and marked the adoption by Comintern of the slogan of the "popular front".[88] Since the murder of Kirov, just a week earlier, had spread turmoil and panic among the party leaders, it is not surprising that the proceedings showed no sign of any clear directive from above. But it seems to have been at this time that Stalin was finally persuaded to declare himself; according to Thorez, he "expressed satisfaction with the bold policy of unity of action pursued by our party, which, he emphasized, accords with the spirit of Leninism".[89] The political secretariat of IKKI on January 15, 1935, passed a resolution praising the PCF for having worked out "a programme of genuine demands for a popular front".[90] Thorez celebrated his triumph in a two-part article which appeared in the Comintern journal early in the first weeks of 1935. He boasted of the role of the PCF in encouraging the Amsterdam-Pleyel movement, and the united front agreement with the SFIO of July 1934, which had "slowed down the growth of Fascist elements". What was now required, however, was "an anti-Fascist front of the working class and of the middle strata"; and this popular front "cannot and should not put forward the integral programme of the communist party". The old animosity against social-democracy had disappeared. The united front was "an excellent school, in which communists learn to take account of the state of mind of tens and hundreds of thousands of workers".[91]

It remained to quell the one remaining centre of revolt—the dissident group in the KPD. A conference of the German commun-ist youth league, said to have been attended by forty underground youth workers from Germany, was held in Moscow in December 1934. It passed a resolution favouring cooperation with young

[88] *Kommunisticheskii Internatsional: Kratkii Istoricheskii Ocherk* (1969), pp.382–383; B. Leibzon and K. Shirinya, *Povorot v Politike Kominterna* (2nd ed., 1975), pp. 108–110. Extracts from the final speeches of Kuusinen and Manuilsky on December 19 were printed from the archives in *Voprosy Istorii KPSS*, 1969, No. 3, pp. 4–6.

[89] M. Thorez, *Fils du Peuple* (1960), p. 102; this passage did not appear in the first edition published in 1938.

[90] B. Leibzon and K. Shirinya, *Povorot v Politike Kominterna* (2nd ed., 1975), p. 110.

[91] *Kommunisticheskii Internatsional*, 1935, No. 2, pp. 14–21; No. 4, pp. 24–31.

social-democratic workers in the struggle against Fascism, and ended its proceedings with the appointment of a new central committee—a sure sign of past opposition.[92] This prepared the ground for a final effort to restore order in the distracted party. The political secretariat of Comintern once more reviewed the question in January 1935. The only speech to have been published, many years later, was that of Togliatti, who expounded the official line with characteristic tact. He detected a certain "provincialism" in the attitude of the KPD; Germany was "the weakest link in the application of the united front". He criticized Knorin by name—a sure sign that Knorin's influence and prestige were on the wane; and he reverted to the old issues of "sectarianism" and of Neumann's heresies. Finally he commended the example of the PCF.[93] At the end of the debate, on January 19, the political secretariat recommended the KPD "to discuss ways and possibilities of creating a broad anti-Fascist people's front" in Germany.[94] On January 30 the central committee of the KPD complied by passing a resolution which called comprehensively for a proletarian united front and national front for the overthrow of the Fascist dictatorship; those who resisted this course were pronounced guilty of "sectarianism" and "opportunist conciliationism". The ultimate goal was *"a people's revolution for a free socialist Germany under a Soviet government"*.[95] The last recalcitrant party, and the last open resistance in Comintern, had been overridden.

---

[92] *Geschichte der Deutschen Arbeiterbewegung*, v (1966), 93–94.

[93] P. Togliatti, *Opere, III* (1973), ii, 672–683.

[94] *Kommunisticheskii Internatsional: Kratkii Istoricheskii Ocherk* (1969), p. 385.

[95] *Kommunisticheskii Internatsional*, 1935, No. 7, pp. 45–52; *Rundschau*, No. 10, February 21, 1935, pp. 551–555. An article in the party press described the united front as "the lever for the popular front, the people's revolution" (*ibid.* No. 8, February 14, 1935, pp. 417–419).

CHAPTER 8

TO THE POPULAR FRONT

Throughout the dark winter of 1934–1935 ominous symptoms on the international scene helped to strengthen the growing consensus in communist parties and in Comintern in support of the popular front. The disarmament conference had been in its death-throes since the departure of Germany from Geneva in October 1933: Mussolini was about to launch an invasion of Ethiopia, and obtained from Laval in January 1935 a tacit undertaking to turn a blind eye to this enterprise; negotiations for a security pact to cover eastern Europe had come to a standstill; and the links which bound France to her allies in the Little Entente were visibly under strain. On March 4, 1935, the British Government published a paper on national defence, which drew attention specifically to the threat of German rearmament; and on the next day the French government announced an extension of the term of military service. On March 16 Hitler issued a decree reinstating compulsory military service in Germany—the final and open rejection of the military clauses of the Versailles treaty.[1] This was not allowed to stand in the way of an amicable visit to Berlin by Simon, the British Foreign Secretary, and Eden on March 25–26; the unfortunate impression created in Moscow by this show of conciliation lent point to the contrast frequently drawn in the Soviet press of the period between stiff French resistance to Hitler and the encouragement given by Britain to his aggressive designs. The impression was mitigated only in part when Eden alone went on from Berlin to Moscow. He was, however, enthusiastically received, and the opportunity was taken to press home the common interest of the USSR and of the western Powers, including Britain, in organizing resistance to German aggression. Further suspicions were aroused in Moscow in April, when Simon and Eden, Laval and Mussolini, meeting in conference at Stresa, seemed ready to ignore the USSR and to pave the way for fresh conciliation of Hitler.

[1] *Pravda*, March 17, 18, 1935, gave great prominence to this event, to reactions in Paris, London and Rome, and to demonstrations in Berlin, drawing special attention to the defiance of the Versailles treaty.

In this uneasy climate the advance to the popular front was slow and faltering. While enthusiasm mounted in many foreign parties, notably the PCF and CPGB, resistance in some quarters in the Comintern hierarchy was tenacious, and the dissensions which had plagued and paralysed Comintern throughout 1934 persisted in covert and attenuated forms. How reluctant had been the surrender in December 1934, and how deep the reservations about cooperation with the social-democrats, was seen in an unsigned leading article in the Comintern journal in the first weeks of 1935. "The victory of Fascism in Germany and Austria," declared the writer, ". . . demonstrated to the whole world the complete falsity of the theory, strategy and tactics of social-democracy." What had been revealed as bankrupt was "only the social-democratic, anti-Marxist theory of a 'peaceful', 'democratic' road to socialism". If the KPD had failed to rally the masses for the battle against Fascism, this was because a majority of the working class had followed social-democracy and rejected the revolutionary road. Nevertheless in some countries agreements had been reached between communist and social-democratic parties "for a common struggle against capital, Fascism and war". The article reached the enigmatic conclusion that "the tactics of the united front and the strengthening of the communist party itself are two closely inter-connected tasks".[2] An article by Pieck, perhaps designed as a reply to this complacent approach, observed that a forthcoming enquiry would ask how Fascism could have triumphed in Germany, and would demand to learn lessons from the failure.[3] Some time in the latter part of 1934 a commission had been set up by IKKI to draft resolutions for the seventh congress of Comintern.[4] The preparatory commissions on the second and the third points of the congress agenda were still dogged by controversy between those who accepted "the general democratic, anti-Fascist phase" as a normal process through which the revolutionary movement in capitalist countries had to pass, and those who held that "the struggle against Fascism must be directly linked with task of overthrowing the power of the bourgeoisie." Not much information is available about a meeting on March 4, 1935, at which the possibility of securing the

[2] *Kommunisticheskii Internatsional*, 1935, No. 3, pp. 3–11.

[3] *Ibid.* 1935, No. 9, pp. 6–24.

[4] For a note by Dimitrov for the commission dated January 4, 1935, see *Voprosy Istorii KPSS*, 1965, No. 4, pp. 81–82; B. Leibzon and K. Shirinya, *Povorot v Politike Kominterna* (2nd ed., 1975) p. 120, names Dimitrov, Manuilsky, Kuusinen and Pyatnitsky among members of the commission.

support of capitalist countries for the USSR in case of war against the Fascist regimes was once more called in question.[5] Agreement not being in sight, the presidium of IKKI decided on March 8 on a further postponement of the congress till the end of July.[6] Togliatti became at this time one of the firmest allies of Dimitrov. In a series of lectures to Italian students in the Lenin school between January and April 1935, he argued for a flexible approach; Fascism presented itself in different countries in different guises, and new tactics were appropriate to fight it.[7]

The traditional theses of IKKI for May 1, drafted some weeks in advance, did not differ substantially from those of previous years. The appeal for the united front of workers was couched in conventional terms. The theme of the "two worlds"—"the world of socialism and the world of capitalism"—was heavily stressed; and no hint of a "popular front" against Fascism embracing bourgeois elements was allowed to appear.[8] Dimitrov issued a personal message to all workers who had "struggled for my liberation from the bestial clutches of German Fascism", pleading for the creation of a "united proletarian front".[9] A separate May 1 proclamation issued in the name of French, German, British, Italian, Polish, Czechoslovak, Hungarian and Lithuanian communist parties recalled their past opposition to "the brigand treaty of Versailles"; it was in the same spirit that they now demanded the mobilization of the masses of workers against "the warlike provocation of the Fascist rulers of Germany" and against "those who prepare a new imperialist war".[10] Bela Kun in an article in the Comintern journal argued that the united front should be "a class front of the workers against capital".[11] Meanwhile Schubert and Schulte, who had led

---

[5] B. Leibzon and K. Shirinya, *Povorot v Politike Kominterna* (2nd ed., 1975), p. 186.

[6] *Voprosy Istorii KPSS*, 1975, No. 8, p. 60.

[7] P. Spriano, *Istoria del Partito Comunista Italiano*, iii (1970), 23–24; the lectures are in P. Togliatti, *Opere*, III (1973), ii, 533–671.

[8] *Rundschau*, No. 17, April 11, 1935, pp. 853–854; for a similar appeal from the executive of Profintern see *Ibid*. No. 18, April 18, 1935, pp. 917–918.

[9] *Pravda*, April 30, 1935.

[10] *Oeuvres de Maurice Thorez*, II, ix (1952), 12–13; the proclamation was quoted in an article in the French party journal defending the Franco-Soviet pact of May 2 (see pp. 151–152 below), but does not appear to have been published in the Comintern press.

[11] *Kommunisticheskii Internatsional*, 1935, No. 15, p. 13; according to *Kommunisticheskii Internatsional: Kratkii Istoricheskii Ocherk* (1969), p. 386, Kun "exhibited a definite tendency to sectarianism".

the opposition to the new line in the KPD, came to Moscow in April 1935, and in the course of a discussion with the Central European bureau of Comintern were said to have received support from Knorin and Pyatnitsky; Pieck wrote to Dimitrov on April 28, complaining of the continued activity of "sectarians".[12]

The decisive moment came when the two countries most immediately alarmed by Germany's growing strength and aggressiveness, the USSR and France, drew together, and concluded on May 2, 1935, a pact under which the two parties undertook to come to each other's aid in the event of either being subjected to aggression in contravention of the Covenant of the League of Nations. An explanatory protocol added that this obligation would remain valid, even if the Council of the League failed to make any recommendation.[13] The pact put a fresh strain on those stalwarts who had doubted whether the Soviet membership of the League of Nations was compatible with communist doctrine; the USSR had now entered into a special relation with an imperialist Power which went even beyond the Covenant of the League. Radek defended it in a long article which acclaimed it as "a new step by the USSR in the struggle for peace", and as evidence of "the enormous growth of the international influence of the USSR", and explained that, while the USSR would not enter into alliances with imperialist aims, it was always ready for relations with capitalist countries which sought peace, and would help to restrain imperialist Powers which at a given moment threaten peace.[14]

When, however, Laval visited Moscow a fortnight later,[15] the question was raised in a still more acute form. An agreed *communiqué* on his two-day conversations with Stalin, Molotov and Litvinov recorded their recognition of a common obligation "not to allow their means of national defence to weaken in any respect", and in particular announced that Stalin "understands and fully approves the policy of national defence pursued by France to maintain her

---

[12] Quoted from archives in *Georgii Dimitrov: Vydayushchiisya Deyatel' Kommunisticheskogo Dvizheniya* (1972), p. 380.

[13] For the pact and the protocol see *Dokumenty Vneshnei Politiki SSSR*, xviii (1973), 309–312; a similar pact between the USSR and Czechoslovakia was signed on May 16, 1935 (*ibid.* xviii, 332–336).

[14] *Pravda*, May 13, 1935.

[15] *Pravda*, May 14, 1935, which reported Laval's arrival and Litvinov's speech of welcome, devoted its leading article to the opening of the Moscow Metro.

armed forces at the level consonant with her security".[16] The *communiqué* caused peculiar embarrassment in the PCF, whose principles and practice had been deeply imbued with hostility to the armed forces.[17] But France was not a unique case. Support for the armed forces of an imperialist Power was difficult to reconcile with the professions of any communist party or of the Comintern itself. Trotsky, in a widely publicized article, denounced Stalin for his open abandonment of "proletarian internationalism" for "social-patriotism", and ended with the cry: "The Third International is dead! Long live the Fourth International!"[18]

It is tempting to dramatize the Franco–Soviet pact and the declaration of May 16, 1935, as marking an abrupt abandonment of the aim of world revolution inherent in Marxist and Bolshevik doctrine in favour of the diplomacy of defensive alliances sponsored by Litvinov—the decisive victory of Narkomindel over Comintern. But this would be an undue simplification. Faith in imminent revolution in Europe foundered in the German *débâcle* of 1923. Events in China in 1927 showed up the limitations on the aid which Comintern could or would render to revolution in a semi-colonial country. Henceforth world revolution became an article in a creed ritualistically recited on solemn public occasions, but no longer an item of living faith or a call to action. The place left vacant in the ideology of Comintern was taken by defence of the Soviet Union. The "twenty-one conditions" of 1920 had imposed on communist parties an obligation to give "unconditional support to any Soviet republic in its struggle against counter-revolutionary forces".[19] The principle of the defence of the USSR was inscribed in the programme of Comintern after the war scare of 1927 at its sixth congress

[16] The *communiqué* was published in *Pravda* and *Izvestiya*, May 16, 1935, in *Humanité* on May 17, 1935, and in the press of many countries.

[17] For the reaction in the PCF see pp. 203–205 below.

[18] The article first appeared in the French opposition journal *Vérité*, May 25, 1935, and is reprinted in L. Trotsky, *Oeuvres*, v (1979), 301–313. Representatives of Trotskyist groups in the Netherlands, the United States, France and Canada issued an "open letter" constituting themselves a committee to make preparations for the creation of a Fourth International (*Byulleten' Oppozitsii* (Paris), No. 44, June–July 1935, pp. 1–6), where it was significantly followed by Trotsky's letter of June 10 to the French workers (see p. 205 below). Trotsky had originally canvassed the idea of a Fourth International in October 1933 (*Byulleten' Oppozitsii* (Paris), No. 36–37, October 1933, pp. 1–12).

[19] See p. 4 above.

in 1928;[20] the argument that, since the USSR was the one country where the socialist revolution had been victorious, the prime duty of communist parties everywhere was to defend it against the assaults of its enemies, became common currency. When the world economic crisis of 1930 provoked fresh confirmation of the impending bankruptcy of the capitalist order, and revolution in central Europe seemed once more a possible or even likely contingency, Comintern soon began to sound a note of caution, and impatient revolutionary enthusiasm became a "Left" or "sectarian" deviation.[21] As the early prospects of world revolution receded from view, the theme of the defence of the USSR gained strength and prominence, and was well established at the twelfth and thirteenth IKKI in 1932 and 1933. What was new in 1934 and 1935 was the recognition that the defence of the USSR could be assured through the support, not of foreign communist parties too weak to overthrow, or seriously embarrass, their national governments, but of the governments of capitalist countries exposed to the same external menace as the USSR, and that the best service which parties could render would be to encourage governments to provide that support. It was an unexpected, but logical development, a product of the weakness of existing communist parties and of the miscalculations by the early Bolsheviks of revolutionary prospects in the capitalist world. After 1935 the defence of the USSR was the highest common factor in the programme of Comintern and the diplomatic manoeuvres of Narkomindel.

The Franco–Soviet agreement and the Stalin–Laval declaration marked at last the end of a prolonged period of hesitation and dissension in Comintern. In Moscow Stalin's personal commitment to the new policy was decisive. It was no longer possible to doubt where Stalin stood. But the provocative verdict of Humbert-Droz was not altogether without foundation:

> The united front and the popular front were imposed by the workers themselves, who thus gave the Comintern leadership and the German Stalinists the most sensational lesson in truth in the history of the workers' movement.[22]

[20] *Kommunisticheskii Internatsional v Dokumentakh* (1933), pp. 35–36.
[21] See pp. 11–12 above.
[22] J. Humbert-Droz, *Dix Ans de Lutte Antifasciste* (Neuchatel, 1972), p. 111.

A later party account depicted a hesitant and divided IKKI subjected to "daily" pressure in the form of resolutions from the central committee of the Russian party and of speeches of foreign delegates in the standing organs and preparatory commissions of IKKI.[23] No discussion of the question in the Russian party is recorded; a session of the party central committee on June 5–6, 1935, was concerned exclusively with internal affairs.[24] But, with all dissentient voices now silenced, some credit for the weight of enthusiasm generated on behalf of the popular front could be given to the pressure of foreign communist spokesmen on a divided Comintern hierarchy.

The seventh congress was now formally summoned for the end of July. Dimitrov was indefatigable in his efforts. On May 11, 1935, he addressed a mass meeting of foreign workers who had come to Moscow for the May 1 celebrations with a plea for the unity of the working class in the struggle against Fascism and war;[25] and he spoke on June 23 at an "international day" of proletarian solidarity against Fascism and preparations for war.[26] Pressure on the few recalcitrants was kept up till the last moment. Down to the summer of 1935 the leaders of the Hungarian party, presumably resident in Moscow under the aegis of Bela Kun, stoutly maintained that only a socialist revolution could overturn Fascism in Hungary, and that no place could be found for a broad anti-Fascist front working for democratic demands. Not till July 9 was a meeting arranged of Hungarian communists from the Lenin school, who for several days debated "theses containing a criticism of obsolete views on the most important questions of party policy".[27] Kun, writing in the Comintern journal, avoided a direct recantation of his past errors by concentrating on the immediate and tactical aspects of the programme. Nowhere was there "so immense a possibility of united

[23] *Voprosy Istorii KPSS*, 1975, No. 8, p. 59; for a jealous denial by a Comintern writer of the claim of some unspecified foreign communists that decisions taken by them were "a comparatively complete anticipation" of the decisions of the seventh congress see *Georgii Dimitrov: Vydayushchiisya Revolyutsioner-Leninets* (1974), p. 148. But later writers (e.g. B. Leibzon and K. Shirinya, *Povorot v Politike Kominterna* (2nd ed., 1975), p. 210) continue to credit the PCF with the conception of the popular front.

[24] *Pravda*, June 8, 1935.

[25] G. Dimitrov, *S'chineniya*, x (n.d.), 11–17.

[26] *Ibid.* x, 20–22.

[27] B. Leibzon and K. Shirinya, *Povorot v Politike Kominterna* (2nd ed., 1975), pp. 116–117.

action . . . as in the struggle against war", which brought together social-democrats, bourgeois pacifists and pacifist and anti-Fascist intellectuals. In case of war, the proletariat in capitalist countries must work not only "for the defeat of their own countries"—Lenin's historic slogan—but for the victory of the Soviet state.[28]

A leading article in the Comintern journal "On the Eve of the Seventh Congress" laid down its tasks in unambiguous terms. It was to "determine, on the basis of the united front of the proletariat . . . the creation of a powerful popular front against Fascism and war in all the capitalist countries".[29] The following issue of the journal greeted the congress with a new cover style. From the earliest days it had appeared with portraits of the three great prophets of communism, Marx, Engels and Lenin, surrounded by hammer and sickle. Now Stalin was added to the number of the apostles. The issue contained a brief appeal by Dimitrov, followed by articles by the leaders of the principal parties. The most noteworthy came from the pen of Togliatti, who celebrated the victory of the new line with sly malice:

> Let us say quite frankly that in the past a tendency prevailed in our parties to look at any unity within the framework of the united front from a very narrow point of view, and that the policy of the united front was interpreted and applied by Comintern in a sectarian way, only formally.[30]

The defeated paid the penalty. Of leading figures in Comintern, Knorin, Pyatnitsky and Kun perished in the purges; Manuilsky and Kuusinen—and, of course, Togliatti—survived.

Outside the USSR, the only country where preparations for a Comintern congress received widespread publicity and interest was the United States. The State Department was alerted for the first time to the projected congress by the announcement of a farewell dinner for the American delegates to take place in New York on June 8, 1935. It was not until July 2 that the United States Embassy in Moscow received information from the American journalist Louis Fischer, "obviously under instructions of some agency of the Soviet Government", that the congress would open "at the end of

---

[28] *Kommunisticheskii Internatsional*, 1935, No. 20–21, pp. 75–85.
[29] *Ibid.* 1935, No. 19, pp. 3–10.
[30] *Ibid.* 1935, No. 20–21, p. 56.

July or the beginning of August". Fischer raised the question whether the United States Government would regard attacks on it by American delegates at the congress as a breach of the undertaking given by Litvinov, when diplomatic relations were established in November 1933, with regard to hostile propaganda. The State Department, apprised of the question, answered it in the affirmative, and instructed Bullitt, the Ambassador in Moscow, to speak in this sense to Litvinov or to anyone else who might raise the issue, "emphasizing that the American people are most sensitive with respect to interference of foreign countries in their domestic affairs". Bullitt then broached the topic with Litvinov, who made the "jocose" reply that he knew nothing about the congress, and that Stalin knew nothing either. Somebody seems to have persuaded Bullitt that his remarks led Litvinov, Molotov and Voroshilov to protest to Stalin against the holding of the congress. But this speculation deserves no more credence than Litvinov's profession of ignorance.[31] The American protest was not taken seriously.

[31] *Foreign Relations of the United States: The Soviet Union, 1933–1935* (1952), pp. 217–223.

PART II

PARTIES AND FRONTS

CHAPTER 9

THE FRENCH COMMUNIST PARTY (PCF)

The turn to the Left in Comintern had been marked in 1929 in the PCF by the eclipse of its secretary Sémard and the emergence of a group of four young men—Barbé, Célor, Thorez and Frachon—among whom Comintern evidently hoped to find a future leader of the party.[1] The arrest of Thorez in June 1929 appeared to ease the advance of the ambitious Barbé as the strong man of the party. But his career received a sudden and unexpected check when the presidium of IKKI in February 1930 proclaimed a struggle against "Left" as well as Right opportunism. Though the warning related particularly to the KPD, and Merker was its main target,[2] the note of caution injected into Comintern policy by the presidium also affected other parties. Ferrat, the PCF delegate in Moscow, who leaned towards the Right of the party, instilled into the receptive ears of Comintern officials the idea that the time had come to break the domination of the party by the Left under Barbé's leadership.[3] The new mood—a return to a not so distant past before the "turn" of 1928—found many echoes in the party rank and file. At a conference of the PCF which sat from March 9 to 11, 1930, Vassart, a member of the politburo, who delivered the main report, repeated the warning against "Left sectarianism" pronounced by the presidium of IKKI, and incurred the charge, which he attempted to rebut in a second speech, of implying that the main task of the PCF was no longer to struggle against Right opportunism, but against

---

[1] *Foundations of a Planned Economy, 1926–1929*, Vol. 3, p. 528; for the particular favour shown to Barbé see *ibid.* Vol. 3, p. 503, note 144.

[2] See pp. 13–27 above.

[3] P. Robrieux, *Maurice Thorez* (1975), p. 129. Ferrat, in a work published under party auspices before his expulsion, observed that the party leadership in the first half of 1930 "came to believe . . . that the greatest attention should henceforth be paid to the struggle for the immediate demands of the working class, to the real practice of the tactics of the united front . . . and finally to the 'struggle on two fronts' against both the opportunist danger and the Leftist danger" (A. Ferrat, *Histoire du Parti Communiste Français* (1931), p. 255); he does not discuss his own role, or mention Barbé or Thorez.

the excesses of the Left.[4] Barbé was furious, and later accused
Vassart of having attempted, "under the pretext of struggling against
a lot of deviations and sectarian, mechanical, pseudo-Left
opinions", to "revise the general political line of the party".[5]
Underlying friction was, however, not allowed to come to the
surface, and the conference ended in a compromise.[6] An open letter
from the politburo to the party, the text of which was agreed after
discussion with Vassart, repeated the Comintern formula of "the
struggle on two fronts". But, after condemning "mechanical
sectarian exaggeration and 'Left' phrase-mongering", it called on
the party once more to "overcome all deviations from the party line,
especially by uprooting social-democratic opposition".[7] An instruction from the party central committee to party cells on the
forthcoming May 1 demonstrations, after condemning "the clearly
opportunist tendency" of the Right as the greatest danger, admitted
the existence of "another deviation", which consisted in the view
that all possibilities of legal action had been exhausted, and that the
party should "immediately go over to illegality". But this cautiously
balanced introductory passage may well have been added as an
after-thought, and had little relation to the remainder of the text,
which showed few signs of moderation. In face of intensified police
brutality ("*the preventive repression of Chiappe is replaced by the bloody
repression of Zörgiebel*") the proletariat was said to have "begun to go
over to the counter-offensive". "*The more violent the action, the more it
departs from the limits of legality, the better.*" The present struggle
"keeps too much on a *sentimental* plane". Preparations were in
progress for "the mass political strike of May 1, 1930"; the

---

[4] The conference was reported in *Humanité*, March 9–14, 1930.

[5] *Kommunisticheskii Internatsional*, No. 18, 1930, pp. 54–55; a belated report in
Internationale Presse-Korrespondenz, No. 50, June 13, 1930, pp. 1116–1117, evidently
written by a supporter of Barbé, accused Vassart of "weakening our struggle
against [Right] opportunism". The party central committee in July 1930 (see
p. 164 below) condemned as "particularly erroneous" the choice of Vassart as a
rapporteur at the conference (*Discours de Célor, Thorez et Barbé au Comité Central*
(1930), p. 54); Vassart's strength lay in the Paris regional organization.

[6] Barbé in an article in *Humanité*, March 14, 1930, denied any rift between
himself and Doriot; both were party candidates in the municipal elections in Saint-
Denis.

[7] The text of the letter has not been traced, but it was summarized and quoted in
the report in *Internationale Presse-Korrespondenz*. According to this report, the open
letter was not intended to "revise" the party line; there was no "sickness" in the
party, and "no real Left danger". For the discussions with Vassart see *Discours de
Célor, Thorez et Barbé au Comité Central* (1930), p. 14.

watchword should be *"Strike and demonstration, the conquest of the factory and the conquest of the street"*.[8]

At this moment, on April 24, 1930, Thorez was released from prison, and took his place among the party leaders.[9] Comintern was by this time seriously concerned at the brash militancy of the PCF. Nor was it reassuring when Bernard, a former member of the politburo, in an open letter to members of the party, denounced the "leadership of the class by the party" which was imposed *"against the will* of the working class".[10] A delegation of 16 leading members of the party was summoned to Moscow to attend a session of the French commission of IKKI at the end of May 1930. If the delegates had arrived with an intention to denounce Ferrat and the new campaign against the Left, the ranks were soon broken by Thorez—and perhaps others—who were ready to conform to the new Comintern line. When the commission met at the end of May, the major speeches were delivered by Thorez, Manuilsky and Barbé. Thorez in a model pronouncement obsequiously admitted the past errors of the party, and called for a great effort to end the decline in numbers and the rapid turnover in party membership. To win *"every worker"* for the party would, he concluded, not be possible "without applying the inner party line with Bolshevik firmness, without *the struggle on two fronts* against opportunist deviations, both *Right* and Left". Manuilsky, having started with a remark on the recent decline in the communist youth movement—an obvious dig at Barbé—embarked on a devastating exposure of the failures of the PCF. Membership had fallen in December 1929 to 39,000, a loss of 31 per cent since its peak in 1926; the circulation of *Humanité* had

[8] *Carnet du Militant*, No. 6, 1930, reprinted in *Le PCF pendant l'Entre-Deux-Guerres*, ed. L. Racine and N. Bodin (1972), pp. 182–187. According to A. Ferrat, *Histoire du Parti Communiste Français* (1931), pp. 245–247, police repression of the anti-war demonstrations of August 1, 1929 (see *Foundations of a Planned Economy, 1926–1929*, Vol. 3, pp. 530–531) was a landmark in the history of the party: "After August 1 the activity of the PCF entered a new phase. For the first time the party was *de facto* reduced to semi-illegality."

[9] Recriminations occurred afterwards on the circumstances of Thorez's release, which he secured by paying the fine imposed on him—allegedly in defiance of a party ruling; Thorez later asserted that "the Barbé–Célor group, in order to apply its nefarious policy, had decided to leave in prison those who might upset their plans" (M. Thorez, *Fils du Peuple* (1960), p. 73); Marty asserted that the Barbé group "multiplied reasons for not paying" (*Humanité*, December 19, 1931).

[10] The letter dated May 1930 was published in the *Byulleten' Oppozitsii* (Paris), No. 15–16, September–October 1930, pp. 46–48; Bernard and some confederates were expelled from the party.

decreased from 173,000 in 1927 to 145,000. The number of strikes had fallen. It was in France that Trotsky published his journals, and Rosmer had recruited 20 communists for his group. The prescriptions were vague. The slogan "Closer to the Masses" had a faded air. Manuilsky made several polite references to Thorez's speech, and snubbed Barbé, who had interrupted to excuse shortcomings on the ground that "we have not enough young cadres". He admitted the persistence of a "Right danger". But there was also another danger. It was not enough to "go to a social-democratic worker and shout in his face 'You are a social-Fascist' ". He ended with the call for "*the struggle on two fronts*". Survivals, moods, still existed which were "harmful for the development of the party". After this broadside Barbé's speech was very much of a rear-guard action. He feared that the formula of the struggle on two fronts would "bring confusion into the struggle within out party and prevent it from carrying out the struggle against the main danger". The theory that the struggle against opportunism was matched by a struggle against "a danger from the Left" was "absolutely false". He deprecated attacks on the party leadership, but managed to end with a polite peroration on the need of help from Comintern "to strengthen our party".[11]

Manuilsky had behind him the full weight of Comintern. Molotov also spoke, and presumably reinforced Manuilsky's position, though his speech does not appear to have been published.[12] But French resistance, perhaps from a majority of the delegation, was evidently stubborn; and it was not till June 16 that the text of a resolution was finally agreed. It insisted strongly on the practical demands of the workers, denouncing so-called "Leftists" who despised "the struggle for beef-steak" and treated all socialists as "running-dogs of the bourgeoisie". It urged the party to pay

[11] The summons to Moscow was related two years later by Kuusinen at the twelfth IKKI (*XII Plenum IKKI* (1933), ii. 8); for a few further details see P. Robrieux, *Maurice Thorez* (1975), pp. 129–130. The three speeches—no others were published—appeared in *Kommunisticheskii Internatsional*, 1930, No. 18, pp. 37–63; the date is fixed approximately by a reference in Barbé's speech to May 25 as "last Sunday" (*ibid.* p. 59). The session lasted several days; Manuilsky spoke three days after Thorez (*ibid.* p. 51). Barbé referred in his speech to a meeting held in Moscow "some time ago", at which a report was read on the PCF conference, and "some apparently not quite clear and, in our opinion, incorrect views" were expressed about the leadership of the party; no record has been found of this meeting, which may have been between Ferrat and officials of Comintern.

[12] *Discours de Célor, Thorez et Barbé au Comité Central* (1930), pp. 21, 23.

more attention to the unemployed, and—reverting to an old crux—
to "weld together French and foreign workers into a single
unbreakable bloc of class solidarity". The resolution ended by
setting targets for the forthcoming tenth anniversary of the PCF in
December. The party was exhorted to increase its membership to
55,000 (it now stood at 39,000), *Humanité* to raise its circulation
(now 140,000) to 200,000, and the CGTU unions to increase their
membership by 100,000 to 500,000.[13]

The future leadership and organization of the party were actively
discussed. Doriot, who had at one point threatened to resign his
membership of the politburo, but had been induced to come to
Moscow with the delegation, incurred fresh reproaches from
Thorez for his "individualist position". But Manuilsky succeeded in
composing the quarrel between the two men, and Doriot made a
conciliatory speech which, according to Barbé's concluding
remarks, held out hopes that he would "work effectively in the
leadership of the party".[14] In accordance with the current mood in
Comintern, no sanctions were imposed other than the dropping of
Vassart from the politburo. But it was recommended that the
membership of the politburo should be drastically reduced from 13
to 7 full members and from 4 to 2 candidates. These decisions would
have to be registered by the party itself. No formal notice was taken
of the emergence of Thorez. But Thorez, who made much of his
proletarian origins, looked more and more like the French counterpart of the German Thälmann. The situation was eased by the fact
that the ageing Sémard, who took no part in the discussions and
belonged to no faction, retained his post as secretary of the party.
But the seal was set on Thorez's future role when at the end of June
1930 he was selected to address the sixteenth congress of the Russian
party as fraternal delegate of the PCF. Now thoroughly schooled in
the current Comintern orthodoxy, he delivered a highly conventional speech to the congress, expressing perfect loyalty to the
Russian party and its leaders, and painting in somewhat too rosy
colours the achievements of the PCF. After praising the past

[13] No full text of the resolution has been traced; for a summary of it by Thorez in
the French edition of the journal of Comintern (it did not appear in the Russian
edition) see *Oeuvres de Maurice Thorez*, II, i (1950), 44–56; it was extensively quoted
by Kuusinen two years later in *XII Plenum IKKI* (1933), ii, 9.

[14] *Discours de Célor, Thorez et Barbé au Comité Central* (1930), pp. 33, 50–51; for the
quarrel and the intervention of Manuilsky, who told Doriot to be "more serious in
future", see G. Walter, *Histoire du Parti Communiste Français* (1948), p. 266.

victories of the party over "opportunists" of the Right, he ended with a brief but significant comment:

> But we must also struggle against different "Left" sectarians. As for you, the question poses itself for us also of a struggle on two fronts. We need now to maintain this clear line and to consolidate the organization.[15]

On the return of the French delegation from Moscow, the party central committee met on July 17–19, 1930, to give effect to the decisions which had been taken. The profession of unanimity among the leaders was maintained, Vassart being the common target of attack. Célor opened the session with a slightly uneasy report on the work of the politburo. He hinted that the theme of social-Fascism had been pressed too far. The united front had been abandoned; and this Leftism had brought about a divorce between the immediate demands of the workers and the slogans of the party. But he also denounced the passivity of the party in face of the development of Fascist policies, and called for a vigorous campaign against socialists, Trotskyists and members of the Parti Ouvrier Populaire (POP).[16] Thorez followed with a report on the discussions in Moscow which gave him the opportunity to insist on a theme conspicuously neglected by Célor—the dutiful dependence of the PCF on Comintern directives. Predictably more inclined than Célor to dwell on the recent decline in the influence and fortunes of the party, for which he escaped personal responsibility through his sojourn in prison, he rehearsed the current formulas as prescriptions for a revival: "our policy in regard to social-democracy" was the most important political and tactical question confronting the party. Thorez prostrated himself with crude obsequiousness before the dictates of Comintern:

> It is the method of Comintern at present to watch more attentively than ever over the policy of the parties, and to proceed

[15] *XVI S'ezd Vsesoyuznoi Kommunisticheskoi Partii (b)* (1931), pp. 448–449; a slightly abbreviated version of the speech, omitting some fulsome flattery of Stalin, is in *Oeuvres de Maurice Thorez*, II, i (1950), pp. 38–43. An article by Thorez on the congress in the party journal elaborated the theme of Right and Left directions (*ibid*, II, i, 64–71).

[16] *Discours de Célor, Thorez et Barbé au Comité Central* (1930), pp. 3–17; the POP was a small group founded by six members who had seceded from the PCF in November 1929.

in an altogether regular and consistent manner to an examination of the problems posed in the different parties. This has happened in the Polish, German, Italian and French parties.

The reorganization of the politburo of the PCF was handled in ambiguous language which pointed to the scope of Thorez's personal ambition:

> In agreement with Comintern we propose to create a secretariat which will realize the policy of the politburo, with a single responsible comrade from the politburo and comrades chosen to realize the policy of the politburo.[17]

It was a self-confident performance, based on the growing conviction that, if he listened attentively to the voice of Moscow, Comintern would uphold his supreme authority in the PCF. Of the 26 speeches delivered at the session only those of Célor, Thorez and Barbé were published. Barbé, chosen to wind up the debate, was more flexible than Célor, or perhaps more bent on preserving what was left of his diminishing prestige. He attacked Vassart again and again, patronized Doriot, and announced that Célor would be sent to work in the restive Paris regional organization. He denied that there was any crisis in the leadership of the party; the only crisis which required a new "turn" was in the relation of the party to the masses. He attacked Merker, whose failure to make contact with the workers pointed to a "theory of despair". He cited, frequently though rather less obsequiously than Thorez, the authority of Comintern; and he ended by exhorting the committee to vote unanimously for the resolution of Comintern and for the resolutions to be drafted on the basis of Célor's and Thorez's reports.[18]

The resolution on the tasks of the party bore the clear imprint of the promptings of Comintern mediated through the pliant Thorez. It accepted "without any reservation" the verdicts pronounced in the Moscow resolution. While claiming "certain positive results" for the work of the PCF, it was profuse in acknowledgement of failures and weaknesses; the party had neglected the united front, hesitated to apply the formula of "the struggle on two fronts", and distorted the "class against class" slogan. The resolution endorsed

[17] *Ibid.* pp. 18–38.
[18] *Ibid.* pp. 39–51.

the targets set by Comintern for the tenth anniversary of the party, though these may have seemed even less realistic in Paris than they had appeared in Moscow.[19] The membership of the politburo was reduced to seven—Barbé, Célor, Doriot, Frachon, Monmousseau, Sémard and Thorez.[20] An anonymous article in the party journal announced "a pitiless battle", not only against "social-democratic opportunism of the Right (still the most serious danger)", but also against the "sectarian pseudo-Left".[21] A further session of the party central committee at the end of October 1930 called for greater activity in carrying out the "turn in the party", and criticized the weakness of its work in recruiting new members and in the trade unions.[22] It was apparently on this occasion that Thorez was appointed sole secretary of the politburo, thus ending the vaunted fiction of collective leadership.[23] Sémard remained as titular secretary of the party, but was now quite without influence.

Friction between the PCF and the CGTU had been endemic since the adoption of the hard line by the party under Comintern pressure in 1929.[24] An article by Sémard attributed the trouble in the CGTU to Trotskyist influences. A so-called "Communist League" had been founded in April 1930; and a committee of "Left" communists in the CGTU raised the cry of trade union independence and opposed the practices of the "third period".[25] Several fresh issues arose in the latter part of 1930. The French Government had introduced for the first time a system of social insurance, contributions being payable by both employers and workers. The CGTU, like the reformist CGT, welcomed the innovation in principle, and campaigned for a reduction of workers'

[19] *Ibid.* pp. 52–64.

[20] G. Walter, *Histoire du Parti Communiste Français* (1948), p. 230; P. Robrieux, *Maurice Thorez* (1975), p. 133, substitutes Ferrat for Frachon.

[21] *Cahiers du Bolchévisme*, September 1930, p. 850.

[22] *Internationale Presse-Korrespondenz*, No. 92, November 4, 1930, p. 2249, No. 95, November 11, 1930, pp. 2352–2353, No. 96, November 14, 1931, p. 2373, No. 98, November 21, 1931, pp. 2419–2420. Thorez's later censure on the party at this time was unqualified: "a caricature of a party, a party reduced to impotence, vegetating, self-centred, instead of being the conscious, active vanguard of the working class" (M. Thorez, *Fils du Peuple* (1960), p. 74).

[23] *Le PCF pendant l'Entre-Deux-Guerres*, ed. L. Racine and N. Bodin (1972), p. 292; J. Fauvet, *Histoire du Parti Communiste Français* (1964), i. 92 (the statement, *ibid.* i, 110, that he was appointed secretary of the party in July 1930 is incorrect).

[24] See *Foundations of a Planned Economy, 1926–1929*, Vol. 3, pp. 531–533.

[25] *Internationale Presse-Korrespondenz*, No. 106, December 9, 1930, pp. 2612–2613.

contributions. The PCF, after some hesitation and confusion, condemned the law outright as a fraud at the expense of the workers and a device to raise the cost of living, since the employers would recoup themselves by raising the prices of their products. But the argument was far-fetched; and the slogan "Down with social insurance" did not appeal to the CGTU leaders or to many trade unionists.[26] In November 1930 a Left group in the CGT headed by Dumoulin issued what came to be known as "the manifesto of the 22" calling for a fusion of the CGT and the CGTU—a proposal which attracted some members of Red unions, but was denounced by the PCF and by Profintern in Moscow as a manoeuvre to disorganize the CGTU. The leaders of the CGTU were induced to issue a statement rejecting the proposal, and declaring that unity between the two federations could be realized only on the basis of the class struggle. But the statement, according to Lozovsky, received little publicity in the party and trade union press, and the agitation for the Dumoulin proposal continued.[27] According to a later verdict, "the 'Left' policy of the Barbé group" was responsible for "a false and dangerous orientation" in the PCF towards the unions. Only when this policy had been rejected did the party turn to the practical demands of the workers.[28]

At the end of January 1931 the central committee of the PCF, reinforced by representatives of Comintern and Profintern, met to consider the situation. It noted that the party had not yet, either in the trade union movement or in the youth organization, carried out the "decisive turn" prescribed by the committee at its July session. Its preoccupation with the CGTU was indicated by the announcement of "a broad trade union conference of the party" to be held on February 27.[29] When the conference met, Thorez delivered a major report full of the cautious compromise now acceptable in Comintern. It would be wrong to deny the exceptional severity of

[26] For a summary of this affair see Barbé's speech at the eleventh IKKI of March 1931 (*XI Plenum IKKI* (1932), i, 497–499); Guyot in an article in the party journal accused the Barbé group of having launched the slogan "Down with social insurance" instead of demanding social insurance exclusively at the cost of the employers (*Cahiers du Bolchévisme*, January 15, 1932, pp. 120–121).

[27] For Lozovsky's remarks see *XI Plenum IKKI* (1932), i, 418–419.

[28] *Die Kommunistische Internationale vor dem VII Weltkongress* (1935), p. 239.

[29] *Internationale Presse-Korrespondenz*, No. 12, February 10, 1931, pp. 333–335.

the economic crisis. On the other hand, to call it a "crisis of the regime" or a "crisis without escape" would lead to "an adventurist and putschist policy", if one believed it, or to "'fatalism', i.e. opportunism", if one treated it as mere words. The CGTU had not done enough. But the party also was not free from blame. "*One must know how to speak the language of the trade unions.*" On the other hand, the scepticism expressed by some delegates of the need for leadership of the unions by the party was a heresy. The conclusion was "a more serious struggle than ever on the two fronts, against Right opportunism and against 'Left sectarianism'". Vassart was once more attacked in the debate, and was the only delegate to vote against the resolution based on Thorez's report. But no rift between the leaders was allowed to appear. Thorez in his speech paid a passing tribute to Barbé, who was being hunted by the police, and was not present.[30]

Any complacency surviving in party circles in Paris was rudely shattered when the eleventh IKKI met in Moscow at the end of March 1931. What little Manuilsky had to say about the PCF in his main report was caustic. Where the other parties had made some advance since the tenth IKKI, the PCF had "moved backwards"; it had had no cause to suffer from "dizziness through success" in the past year. An "opportunist agency within the CGTU" had encouraged the Dumoulin proposals.[31] Thorez began his speech by approving "the severe but just criticism of the grave defects in the work of our party", and heaped flattery on his accuser. But he soon retreated to more congenial ground in denouncing French imperialism and the social-Fascism of the SFIO, whose press had vied with that of the SPD as to "who should go further in slander and aggressiveness" against the USSR. His attempt to minimize or explain away electoral failures of the PCF was less successful, and was subject to frequent interruptions. He tried the effect of pathos: "Great weaknesses, yes! Opportunism, No!" He concluded with praise for party work in the army and navy.[32]

---

[30] *Oeuvres de Maurice Thorez*, II, i (1950), 128–179; the tribute to Barbé was omitted from this version, but is quoted by P. Robrieux, *Maurice Thorez* (1975), p. 152, from a contemporary publication. Barbé was elected, with Stalin, Manuilsky, Thälmann and other distinguished figures, to the honorary presidium of the conference (*Humanité*, March 1, 1931). For a brief account of the conference see *Internationale Presse-Korrespondenz*, No. 21, March 6, 1931, pp. 557–558.

[31] *XI Plenum IKKI* (1932), i, 46–48, 68.

[32] *Ibid.* i, 188–203.

Subsequent references in the debate to the PCF were in a lower key. Pyatnitsky soothed the ruffled feelings of the French delegation by admitting that "as regards military work things are better in France than in any other party". But, now that France had become "the gendarme of the world, the organizer of intervention against the USSR", these efforts were manifestly inadequate. Pyatnitsky added that there had been "not a drop of self-criticism" in Thorez's speech, and that "this would have been very useful to the PCF".[33] Lozovsky sharply censured the party and the CGTU for their feeble reaction to the Dumoulin affair.[34] Barbé made a cringing speech in which he hinted at his past merits in combating opportunism, but unconditionally accepted current policies, deploring the lack of self-criticism in the PCF and its resentment of criticism from Comintern designed to "eliminate our weak sides".[35] The PCF escaped notice in the main resolution of the session.[36] But French imperialism was another matter. Stalin at the sixteenth Russian party congress in June 1930 had described "bourgeois France" as "the most aggressive and militarist country of all aggressive and militarist countries in the world".[37] This view still held. It was appropriate that Cachin should have been chosen to introduce at the eleventh IKKI a resolution on "The Strengthening of the Threat of Military Intervention against the USSR".[38] In retrospect, the most remarkable feature of the speech and of the resolution was that every major country was named as a potential source of aggression against the USSR, except Germany. Few people in 1931 could have imagined that within ten years Germany would possess either the will or the power for such an enterprise.

The performance of the French delegation at the eleventh IKKI left behind it a deep anxiety in Comintern about the capacities and prospects of the PCF. France at this time was still, in the eyes of Moscow, the most active, as well as the most hostile, of the

---

[33] *Ibid.* i, 225–227.
[34] See p. 167 above.
[35] *XI Plenum IKKI* (1932), i, 491–506.
[36] For this resolution see p. 38 above.
[37] For this speech see p. 18 above.
[38] *Kommunisticheskii Internatsional v Dokumentakh* (1933), pp. 966–972; for Cachin's speech in which he called France "the chief organizer of war against the Soviet Union" see *XI Plenum IKKI* (1932), ii, 3–39.

imperialist Powers. The ineffectiveness of the PCF, and lack of
control over its operations, presented a serious danger. The radical
youth leaders Barbé and Célor had been found wanting. Thorez's
role as their successor was consecrated by his election to the
presidium and to the political secretariat of IKKI.[39] But the new
leader on whom the mantle of Comintern had fallen was commended only by his ready subservience, and lacked both intel-
lectual weight and authority in the party. In the summer of 1931, to
provide the necessary stiffening, Fried, a Hungarian-born
communist, who after a troubled career as a hard-liner in the
Czechoslovak party had been recalled to Moscow to work in
Comintern, was appointed Comintern delegate to the PCF, and
sent to Paris, supported by a large international team which
included Walecki, the Pole, Anna Pauker, the Rumanian, and
Kheimo, the Finn.[40] Whether or not the arrival of the group
preceded the session of the party central committee on May 27,
1931, Thorez's long speech on that occasion was a model of
discretion, being confined almost entirely to pedantic repetition of
the conclusions, and of the very language, of IKKI, complete with
quotations from Lenin and Stalin. No names were mentioned, but a
few passages hinted at the subterranean struggle within the party.
The shortcomings of the PCF were attributed to past failure to pay
attention to the "pressing directives" of Comintern:

> The correctness of the resolutions of the International is
> recognized, the decisions of the central committee are approved,
> *but they are not applied.* This is what we must condemn as
> *"opportunism in practice".*

The struggle on two fronts must be conducted *"against Right
opportunism, the principal danger, and against Left phraseology*", which also
ends in opportunist passivity". The deadly charge of opportunism,
hitherto levelled against the Right, was made available for use
against the Left. A reference to "a certain tendency to substitute the
activity of one or a few comrades for the collective work of
responsible organizations" presaged the coming indictment of
Barbé and Célor for their promotion of a "group spirit". The only

---

[39] *XI Plenum IKKI* (1932), ii, 246.
[40] For Fried see *Voprosy Istorii KPSS*, No. 1, 1977, p. 77. Information about the
team in P. Robrieux, *Maurice Thorez* (1975), p. 145, seems to have come from
Ferrat; according to this source, Comintern hesitated in its choice of leader
between Thorez and Doriot, but found the latter's independence too dangerous.

decision announced by Thorez was the appointment of the veteran Marty as leader of the youth organization.[41] Marty's prestige would counter Barbé's predominance in the organization; and Barbé's loss of his power base would make it easier to bring about his downfall.[42]

The ground being thus prepared, Manuilsky himself arrived in Paris in July 1931 to administer the *coup*. The procedure was characteristic. The enemy camp was not to be taken by assault, but undermined from within. Guyot, a member of the youth organization and of the party central committee, one of Barbé's associates, was induced to recant and to denounce the "group". At a meeting of the politburo, attended by Manuilsky, he read a prepared statement expressing remorse for his collaboration with a group which constituted a danger to the party and to Comintern, and which had secretly prepared rebellion against Comintern decisions. Thorez professed a hypocritical surprise and shock at Guyot's revelations; other reactions are not recorded.[43] Barbé had a private interview with Manuilsky, and seems to have received the assurance that, if he gave no further trouble, no sanctions would be imposed. When Thorez opened the next session of the party central committee on August 26, 1931, he referred to "the group spirit which manifests itself even in the politburo", and appealed eloquently for open discussion in the party, but criticized nobody by name.[44] It seems clear that no open dissent was expressed. But the mood in the party was depressed. A leading article in *Humanité* on September 4 admitted that, in spite of the economic crisis the influence of the party had not increased, but "in some cases diminished". Thorez continued throughout the autumn to conduct a press campaign in favour of open discussion in the party.[45]

[41] *Oeuvres de Maurice Thorez*, II, ii (1950), 9–79; the passages quoted are on pp. 61, 63, 75. For a brief record of the session see *Internationale Presse-Korrespondenz*, No. 53, June 5, 1931, pp. 1235–1236.

[42] Marty's appointment had already been announced in *Humanité*, June 21, 1931, in an article by Thorez (*Oeuvres de Maurice Thorez*, II, i, 222–224).

[43] The scene is described in Barbé's unpublished memoirs (P. Robrieux, *Maurice Thorez* (1975), p. 148).

[44] It may be significant that the report of the speech in *Humanité*, September 5, 1931 (reprinted in *Oeuvres de Maurice Thorez*, II, ii (1950), 110–116), was confined to extracts and summaries; no full text is available. A brief note of the debate appeared in *Humanité*, September 10, 1931.

[45] Typical articles under the titles "Pas de 'Mannequins'" and "Enfin on va discuter" appeared in *Humanité*, August 14, September 1, 1931 (*Oeuvres de Maurice Thorez*, II, ii (1950), 102–104, 117–121).

Comintern was, however, unwilling to prolong this indeterminate situation. It was decided—by whom, or exactly when, remains uncertain—to charge Marty with an enquiry into the activities of the Barbé–Célor group, and to hold the enquiry in Moscow; Barbé and Célor were summoned to attend it. What happened at the inquiry is a matter of conjecture and of some subsequent, not particularly plausible, allegations. Barbé showed every sign of flexibility. In an article in *Humanité* on October 1, 1931, he praised the recent session of the party central committee, and denounced "group ideology and practice" as a "most dangerous aspect of sectarianism". Célor, on the other hand, proved obdurate and was roughly treated in Moscow. The existence of an *agent provocateur* in the youth organization was said to have been uncovered; and Célor was interrogated for twelve hours in an attempt to extract an admission of complicity. Later still, he was accused of having betrayed Thorez to the police, and thus to have been responsible for his imprisonment during the winter of 1929–1930.[46] While the enquiry was in progress in Moscow, Thorez published in *Humanité* on October 28, 1931, an article entitled "Political Characteristics of an Unprincipled Group", which was his first public attack on the group, though still without naming its members. The distinguishing mark of the group was said to be "mistrust as a general principle of the forces of the working class and the party". Its association with the youth organization recalled a past heresy of Trotsky, who had once called the youth "the barometer of the party".[47] This was followed by an article by Sémard which, once more without mentioning names, called for "the elimination of sectarianism".[48]

Pressure on members of the group was now extremely strong. Lozeray, in an article in *Humanité* on October 8 entitled "Against 'Groups' in the Party", abjectly repented his past errors and promised to reform. The next recantation came from Billoux, a youth leader, whose admission of sectarianism, "lack of faith in the party", and illicit action by the group in defiance of the Comintern

---

[46] L. Couturier, *Les "Grandes Affaires" du Parti Communiste Français* (1972), pp. 14–15, the work of a former insider, much inclined to malicious gossip; Thorez perpetuated the legend of his betrayal in his autobiography (*Fils du Peuple* (1960), p. 64).

[47] *Oeuvres de Maurice Thorez*, II, ii (1950), 172–175.

[48] *Humanité*, November 6, 1931.

line, appeared in *Humanité* on November 2.[49] At a congress of the CGTU a vocal minority, which wanted a less intransigent attitude to the CGT, was voted down by overwhelming majorities.[50] Towards the end of November Marty, having completed his mission in Moscow, returned to Paris.[51] On November 26 *Humanité* published an unsigned article accusing the group of an attempt "to mobilize its forces against the Comintern line", and containing an extract from a confession made by Barbé to the commission in Moscow. Barbé confirmed, in the language of total submission, that his group had pursued a sectarian policy opposed to the line of Comintern and of the party central committee, and had behaved in a conspiratorial manner.[52]

Marty made his report to a meeting of the central committee on December 2–5, 1931. Nobody defended the group. Doriot praised the "class against class" slogan, and declared that the bourgeoisie was the principal enemy, but also spoke of the struggle against social-democracy. Duclos denied that the condemnation of the group implied a move to the Right or any revision of "class against class" policy; and Thorez qualified his recent pronouncements in favour of open discussion by asserting that the party would never tolerate "the introduction and propagation in our ranks, in the guise of discussion, of opinions which have nothing in common with the elementary principles of communism".[53] In a resolution adopted at the end of debate, the group was convicted of a "veiled, underhand struggle against the party and Comintern"; for two years it had "kept in its hands all the positions of command in the party". Barbé and Célor were removed from the politburo, and deprived of their posts, as member and candidate member respectively, in the political secretariat of IKKI. Other members of the group were publicly censured. Only Guyot, in virtue of his

---

[49] Billoux had made himself notorious by a pamphlet published in March 1931 in which he had demanded a "combative" strike, and made fun of "the struggle for beef-steak" (L. Couturier, *Les "Grandes Affaires" du Parti Communiste Français* (1972), pp. 14–15).

[50] *Internationale Presse-Korrespondenz*, No. 110, November 20, 1931, pp. 2498–2499.

[51] His return was reported in *Humanité*, November 27, 1931.

[52] P. Robrieux, *Maurice Thorez* (1975), pp. 152–154; the full text of the confession appears not to have been published.

[53] *Humanité*, December 22, 1931.

collaboration in unmasking the group, escaped.[54] Considering the
terms in which their offences had been denounced, it was a mild
sentence, characteristic of the desire of Comintern at this time to
achieve its ends without resorting to overtly drastic action. But the
point was implacably driven home in an article in the party journal
by Stepanov, a member of the Comintern secretariat, using his
French pseudonym Chavaroche. The article dissected in scathing
terms the "group disease" introduced into the PCF by "the group
directed by Barbé", identified as "the group Barbé–Célor–
Lozeray". This "Left sectarian" group was to blame for the fact that
the PCF had lagged behind "the rhythm of events and the tasks of
the party"; the *"balance-sheet of the political and organizational work of
the group"* had been "negative in all respects".[55]

Simultaneously with these troubles in the PCF, there were
symptoms that all was not well in the CGTU. The agitation created
at the end of 1930 by the Dumoulin manifesto[56] had been quelled,
but not extinguished. In August 1931 Lozovsky summoned the
leaders to Moscow, and warned them that they were moving not
towards revolution, but towards the reformist CGT. That this fear
was not unjustified was shown at the CGTU congress in November
1931, when a substantial minority expressed the desire to seek
reunion with the CGT. The proposal was strongly resisted by the
leaders; and a railway worker named Rambaud, said to have been a
Freemason, threatened to split the CGTU on the issue.[57] The
minority was safely defeated. At a session of the central council of
Profintern which opened on December 5, 1931, Monmousseau
made a scathing report on the affair, from which it transpired that
the overtures of the minority had been repelled by CGT; and
Lozovsky, in his final speech, concluded that the defeat of the
minority represented "a progressive stage in the development and
construction of our forces in France".[58]

[54] *Ibid.* December 29, 1931; *Internationale Presse-Korrespondenz*, No. 1, January 5,
1932, pp. 26–28.
[55] *Cahiers du Bolchévisme*, January 1, 1932, pp. 33–43; an article by Guyot in the
following issue (*ibid.* January 15, 1932, pp. 120–123) dealt with the harm done by
the group to the youth league.
[56] See p. 167 above.
[57] *Internationale Presse-Korrespondenz*, No. 115, December 8, 1931, p. 2622, where
the minority were described as "agents of the bourgeoisie".
[58] *Ibid.* No. 117, December 15, 1931, pp. 2681–2682, No. 120, December 30,
1931, pp. 2797–2798.

The results of the purge in the PCF were confirmed at the seventh party congress which met from March 11 to 19, 1932. An article in the party journal on the eve of the congress once more held the Barbé–Célor group responsible for the weaknesses of the party. But it proclaimed that, "since the liquidation of the Barbé–Célor–Lozeray group, the party is resolutely turning . . . towards effective Bolshevization"; and it detected "a new drive (élan) of the workers towards the party and the CGTU", though it lamented that the membership still did not exceed 30,000.[59] The function of the congress was to establish the position of the PCF as a model party in the eyes of Moscow, and to establish Thorez as undisputed leader of the PCF. Thorez delivered an immensely long report—he is said to have spoken for four hours—in which he traversed the whole field in the current Comintern idiom of vituperation. Having expatiated on the economic crisis, on the Moscow trials of the "industrial party" and of the Mensheviks, on the role of French imperialism and on the danger of war against the USSR, he moved on to the issues which had divided the party in the recent past.

> In order to defeat the capitalist bourgeoisie which is the principal enemy, we must strike the stoutest blow at its principal social support, at our most dangerous enemy in the ranks of the working class: social-democracy.

The doctrine of the "lesser evil" was contemptuously rejected. Thorez admitted that the party had "lagged behind". The decline in membership was disquieting. Recruiting was not organized. Workers entered the party, but stayed only "six months, a year, two years". The party had not protested adequately against Japanese aggression in Manchuria, or against the Versailles system and the Young plan. The blame rested on the Barbé–Célor influence, on the failure to carry on "the struggle on two fronts" and to maintain contact with the masses. At the forthcoming elections to the Chamber the PCF must outdo its record of 1928; to predict a loss of votes was "a manifestation of opportunism".[60] The debate, in which 91 delegates took part, was distinguished by nothing but a total

---

[59] *Cahiers du Bolchévisme*, March 1, 1932, pp. 293–303.

[60] Thorez's report and reply to the debate, published in a pamphlet entitled *En Avant pour l'Issue Révolutionnaire de la Crise* (1932), are in *Oeuvres de Maurice Thorez*, II, iii (1951), 9–193.

absence of dissent. Servet, a former member of the Barbé–Célor group, dissociated himself from it, and denounced his one-time partners. Frachon, reporting on the trade unions, detected a "period of sectarianism", but added that "reformist tendencies" exhibited in the "appeal of the 22" had also not disappeared. Marty and Cachin spoke of the danger of war and denounced French imperialism. The appropriate resolutions were unanimously adopted, including a resolution approved by the politburo on electoral tactics. Communist candidates could not be withdrawn at the second ballot in favour of bourgeois or socialist party candidates, but might be withdrawn in favour of worker candidates not belonging to these parties. A central committee of 44 members was elected, and the membership of the politburo was raised from nine to eleven.[61] A manifesto issued by the congress denounced the SFIO and the reformist CGT for supporting the policies of the French bourgeoisie "under the cloak of pseudo-democracy".[62]

The elections of May 1932 were a disaster and humiliation for the PCF. The party had registered 1,085,000 votes in the elections of 1928, and leaders had talked of raising this to 1.5 million. In 1932 the PCF polled 800,000 votes, 35,000 less than it had secured even in 1924. Meanwhile the SFIO had increased its vote from 1,700,000 in 1928 to 1,950,000 in 1932. Cachin, Marty and Duclos of the PCF leaders lost their seats. Thorez saved his, through the support of socialists, it was alleged, at the second ballot. Blame for the *débâcle* could be placed on Left sectarianism. But the remedy was not apparent. The defeat had in no way modified the intransigent attitude of Comintern to cooperation with social-democrats. It was only "Right opportunists" who wanted a united front with the socialists. While admitting that the Herriot–Blum coalition marked a victory over Tardieu's reactionary policies, *Pravda* predicted that the new government would move towards the Right, and re-affirmed its faith that it was only the PCF which "mobilizes the masses for a real mass struggle against participation in intervention [against the USSR]".[63] Thorez dutifully read to the Chamber a declaration on behalf of the PCF attacking the Herriot government, which owed its existence to "the active cooperation of the social-

[61] The congress was summarily reported in *Internationale Presse-Korrespondenz*, No. 23, March 15, 1932, pp. 675–676, No. 24, March 18, 1932, p. 705, No. 25, March 23, 1932, pp. 744–746.

[62] *Humanité*, April 1, 1932.

[63] *Pravda*, June 6, 1932.

democrats".[64] During the summer of 1932 a diversion was created by the preparations for the Amsterdam peace congress, in which the PCF was deeply involved. But even this project, based on appeals for cooperation with socialists and other Left parties, was regarded with some misgivings in Moscow.[65]

The twelfth IKKI, meeting at the end of August 1932, found the PCF very much on the defensive. Kuusinen in his main report was more preoccupied by the threat of French imperialism than by the problems of the PCF. He quoted Doriot with approval on contact with the masses and their demands, and did not mention Thorez.[66] Thorez, whose prestige had been tarnished by electoral defeat, was not honoured with the role of co-*rapporteur*, but spoke early in the debate. He admitted that the party had "lagged behind", did not extenuate its failure at the elections, and confessed that some of its members had been lukewarm supporters of the campaigns against Versailles and against the war in Manchuria. But the party congress of March 1932 had uncovered these shortcomings and prepared it for a fresh advance.[67] Thorez was not, however, allowed to escape so easily. Pyatnitsky devoted a long section of his speech to the PCF, which in the past two years had given more trouble to the presidium and political secretariat of IKKI than any other party. He dwelt at length on the electoral fiasco. Many party members did not understand the "class against class" policy, and were opposed to the maintenance of communist candidates at the second ballot in elections. The congress of March 1932 had itself been "not at all bad". But its resolutions had been ignored, and had not even been published in *Humanité*.[68] The appointment of a high-level commission, presided over by Thälmann, to examine the affairs of the PCF and report to the presidium, did not arrest the flow of critical debate. Ferrat noted that "the 'Left' wing of the PCF" had "put a brake" on cooperation with the Herriot government after the elections. He called for "a mass movement against imperialist war" and for "systematic application of the united front from below,

[64] *Internationale Presse-Korrespondenz*, No. 49, June 14, 1932, pp. 1551–1552.
[65] See pp. 388–389 below.
[66] *XII Plenum IKKI* (1933), i, 21, 33–34.
[67] *Ibid.* i, 138–143.
[68] *Ibid.* ii. 8–14.

while avoiding sectarian 'Left' errors and opportunist errors". He spoke of a united front demonstration in Paris against imperialist war, at which 40,000 workers had been present. Gitton, the trade union representative, painted a gloomy picture of divisions in the CGTU. Some attempt had now been made to check the "sectarianism" of the Barbé group, which had wanted to turn the CGTU into a branch of the PCF. But the election results had "weighed heavily on the party from top to bottom", and the central committee had "not yet recovered from the blow".[69]

Doriot, speaking late in the debate with a frankness which must have added to Thorez's discomfiture, offered the most devastating exposure of the decline of the PCF in numbers and in voting power. Membership of the PCF had fallen in 1931 to 28,000 and of the CGTU to 290,000—little more than half of the peak figures in the nineteen-twenties. Doriot directed his main criticism against the Barbé group, and established his orthodoxy by denouncing the abandonment of "class against class" policies and declaring that "the opportunist danger should be in no way underestimated". He ended with a plea for collective leadership in the party and for help from Comintern in restoring it.[70] Kuusinen in his reply to the debate noted that the commission set up earlier in the session had not yet completed its labours, adding that "the present position in the leadership of the PCF gives ground for disquiet".[71] The brief reference to the PCF in the main resolution of the session was colourless. But the resolution on strike action observed with unusual harshness that the CGTU had "not only failed to extend its influence over strike struggles or to organize a broad movement of the unemployed, but in some places had even retreated from its former positions".[72] A sequel of the congress was the expulsion of Célor from the party. This was announced in a vindictive article by Cachin, which described him as "no ordinary traitor, but an extremely skilful dissimulator"; insinuation, rather than direct statement, pointed to his role as a police agent.[73] Barbé's submission

[69] *Ibid.* ii, 93–99, 151–155.

[70] *Ibid.* ii, 192–198. Membership of the PCF had been put at 39,000 in May 1930 (see p. 163 above), and at 30,000 in March 1932 (see p. 175 above); according to J. Duclos, *Mémoires*, i (1968), 349, it had risen from 30,000 to 34,000 at the time of the seventh party congress in March 1932.

[71] *XII Plenum IKKI* (1933), iii, 127–128.

[72] *Kommunisticheskii Internatsional v Dokumentakh* (1933), pp. 980, 986.

[73] *Humanité*, October 9, 1932; *Internationale Presse-Korrespondenz*, No. 84, October 11, 1932, pp. 2697–2698.

won him a temporary respite; he was praised by Duclos in *Humanité* as "an honest militant who deserves the confidence of the party".[74]

The party central committee met on October 22–25, 1932, to approve the decisions of the twelfth IKKI. Thorez had brought back from Moscow the impression that he was required to play the strong man and pursue the hard line. In an article in the party journal on the results of the twelfth IKKI, he insisted that capitalist stabilization was at an end, called for a "Bolshevik mass party", and denounced the "betrayals" of the socialists and the CGT.[75] At the central committee he began by affirming that the workers' movement was still in the midst of the "third period" inaugurated at the sixth Congress of Comintern in 1928. He admitted that the PCF and the CGTU were in a state of stagnation or regression, and proclaimed as the essential need work among the masses and work for the "*immediate demands* of the workers". But he was unyielding on the united front from below, which was bound up with the struggle against social-democracy:

> In the united front we must clearly mark out our inde-
> pendent position, we must absolutely criticize the false and very
> dangerous ideas developed by certain socialist militants who are
> involved in the Amsterdam united front.[76]

More dramatic was a demonstration of Franco–German soli-
darity on the occasion of the fifteenth anniversary of the Bolshevik revolution. A joint manifesto of the KPD and the PCF denouncing both the Versailles treaty and "imperialist rearmament" was published in the press of both parties, and was read by Thälmann at a "monster meeting" in Essen on October 25.[77] A public meeting was held at the Salle Bullier in Paris on October 31, 1932, at which Cachin spoke on socialist construction in the USSR and Thorez against Versailles. During the meeting Thälmann, who had come secretly to Paris, made an unannounced appearance, and amid frenetic applause denounced Versailles and French imperialism,

[74] *Humanité*, October 13, 1932.
[75] *Cahiers du Bolchévisme*, October 15, 1932, pp. 1247–1260.
[76] The session was reported in *Humanité*, October 27, 30, 31, 1932; Thorez's speech, somewhat abbreviated, is in *Oeuvres de Maurice Thorez*, II, iv (1951), 73–84.
[77] *Humanité*, October 26, 1932, where the manifesto was published under the heading "À bas Versailles"; *Internationale Presse-Korrespondenz*, No. 90, October 28, 1932, pp. 2869–2871.

declaring that communists would never recognize treaties concluded by French and German bourgeois capitalists. He was then
smuggled out of the hall before the police could discover his
presence.[78]

If the twelfth IKKI had failed to give a clear lead to the PCF, the
SFIO was beset by even sharper divisions. In spite of its electoral
triumph, its congress in July 1932 produced a split between a Right
faction, led by Renaudel, which wanted cooperation with the
unashamedly bourgeois Radical-Socialist Party, and a Left faction
led by Zyromski and Blum, which still hoped for a united front with
the PCF. The Right group was narrowly defeated; and so bitter was
the clash that Renaudel and some of his supporters seceded from the
SFIO to found, in November 1932, an independent socialist party.
These events created a ferment both in the SFIO and in the PCF,
and increased the pressure from rank-and-file members of both
parties for common action. The administrative council of the SFIO
issued a public appeal to workers of the Parisian region to set up a
"joint bureau" to plan joint meetings of the Left; and on December
1, 1932, Thorez broke new ground by addressing a letter to Faure,
the secretary of the SFIO, in the name of the politburo of the PCF.
The letter took note of the appeal, expressed agreement with the
proposal for a joint bureau to organize meetings, and suggested that
this might apply to a meeting planned to take place on the following
evening in the Salle Bullier in Paris, as well as to future meetings in
other centres. Thorez cautiously added that "there could be no
question, in such a discussion, of exchanging insults". But each side
could remain free to express its separate views.[79] A reply can hardly
have been expected in time for the PCF meeting on the following
day. Thorez devoted his speech at the meeting exclusively to the
question of the united front. He indulged in some awkward
reminders, referring to the complicity of the social democrats in the
war of 1914, and bluntly declaring that "the Second International is
dead". But he avoided abuse of the SFIO, spoke sympathetically of

[78] *Humanité*, October 31, November 1, 2, 1932; Thorez's speech is in *Oeuvres de Maurice Thorez*, II, iv (1951), 85–88, Thälmann's in *Internationale Presse-Korrespondenz*, No. 92, November 4, 1932, pp. 2941–2942. Vassart's unpublished memoirs add some picturesque details of the occasion, which he mis-dates "December" (*The Comintern: Historical Highlights*, ed. M. Drachkovitch and B. Lazitch (1966), p. 238).

[79] *Humanité*, December 2, 1932; *Oeuvres de Maurice Thorez*, II, iv (1951), 107–108.

common action at the Amsterdam congress, and ended in matter-of-fact style:

> We are ready to come to an agreement with the SFIO and the POP for the organization of these discussions, on places and dates, on joint bureaus, and on equal speaking time, in order to ensure freedom of expression to everyone.[80]

It was not until December 8 that Faure replied to Thorez's letter of December 1, simply reaffirming previous party pronouncements "on the problems of workers' unity". Nothing daunted, Thorez replied on December 12 that the PCF was willing to discuss the organization of meetings, "taking as a starting point the texts to which you refer", and proposed that meetings should take place in a large number of centres in the second half of January.[81]

This initiative by the volatile Thorez excited grave misgivings in Moscow. It is said to have been taken in the absence of Fried, who afterwards severely reprimanded Thorez for his rashness. What is certain is that later in December 1932 the leaders of the PCF were again summoned to attend a meeting of the French commission of IKKI, which discussed the issue of the united front. No published record of the proceedings exists. But, according to Ferrat, who was present, he, Manuilsky and Stepanov favoured a conciliatory line, while Fried, Marty, and the now chastened Thorez defended the hard line of unconditional hostility to social-democracy. Whatever views were exchanged, no clear decision seems to have been reached. But both sides united in a renewed denunciation of Barbé and his group.[82] The occasion was typical of the hesitations prevailing in Moscow at this time. Any movement towards a united front with socialists, in the PCF as in the KPD, though cautiously supported by Manuilsky, encountered stubborn suspicion and hostility from the group of stubborn hard-liners in Comintern.[83]

In Paris the flicker of expectation kindled by Thorez's correspondence with Faure died away. A few days after Hitler became Chancellor in Berlin, Thorez in a further letter to Faure of February

---

[80] *Ibid.* II, iv, 107–108; for the POP see p. 164 above.

[81] *Oeuvres de Maurice Thorez*, II, iv (1951), 133–134.

[82] For Ferrat's recollections of the meeting see P. Robrieux, *Maurice Thorez* (1975), p. 161; Thorez is said to have made an attack on Ferrat's recently published history of the PCF, which did not mention Thorez.

[83] See p. 126 above.

6, 1933, continued to propose joint public meetings, but reverted to the recriminations of the past, and observed that "the so-called policy of 'the lesser evil' of German social-democracy" had contributed to Hitler's rise to power.[84] Thorez's long report to the party central committee on February 11 betrayed something of the growing tensions in the party. Hitler's success had aggravated all the contradictions between Germany and France, and shaken the Versailles system. But communists must continue to wage "a passionate and systematic struggle" against Versailles, and resist the attempt of bourgeois and socialist parties to use the danger of a Fascist attack as a pretext to "justify their policy of armaments and provocation to war". The united front was once more defined in uncompromising terms; the pursuit of it must not prevent "an organized and systematic struggle against social-democracy, the SFIO and the CGT". The CGTU miners in the Moselle region were criticized for a strike agreement rashly concluded with CGT and Christian unions. On the other hand, some "sectarian" elements in the party had opposed participation in the Amsterdam movement as having nothing to do with communism, and others had failed to make suitable electoral bargains with socialists. A feature of the session was a report by Renaud Jean on work among the peasants, which had been neglected by the party for several years.[85]

Hitler's open assumption of dictatorial powers, and ruthless suppression of the KPD, at the beginning of March 1933 came as a sharper shock in France than in any other country. Something like panic overtook the PCF, which was afterwards accused of having fallen a victim to the "Trotskyist version" that the KPD had "capitulated".[86] On March 5, Comintern had sent a belated and guarded reply to an overture from the Second International; and on the following day the central committee of the PCF published an enthusiastic open letter to "socialist workers" and to the "administrative commission" of the SFIO, proposing "a national day of demonstrations" for workers of all political tendencies on

[84] *Oeuvres de Maurice Thorez*, II, iv (1951), 154–156.

[85] *Ibid.* II, iv, 157–218, V (1951), 11–16; Marty at the thirteenth IKKI in December 1933 recorded that this was the first occasion on which the PCF had "defined our position in the agrarian question" (*XIII Plenum IKKI* (1934), p. 392); the party claimed after 1933 to have "overcome its passivity" in work among the peasantry (*Die Kommunistische Internationale vor dem VII Weltkongress* (1935), p. 241).

[86] *XIII Plenum IKKI* (1934), p. 338.

behalf of the immediate demands of the workers and of aid to German workers.[87] This was followed a few days later by a similar appeal from the CGTU to the CGT and its leaders.[88] But these overtures carried no more weight than their predecessors; and the resolution of the presidium of IKKI of April 1 on the German situation re-introduced a note of ambiguity and restraint.[89] The usual May 1 proclamation of the PCF called eloquently for unity of action and the united front, but was accompanied by an article from Marty's pen on the bankruptcy of social-democracy.[90] The session of the party central committee in May 1933 reverted to the discontent of the French peasantry, and adopted a long resolution on the agrarian crisis. But its main business was with the German situation. Mindful of the line laid down in Moscow, the committee greeted "the great heroic struggle of the KPD", whose "policy before and at the moment of Hitler's seizure of power was perfectly correct". It roundly attacked the "anti-worker" policy of the Second International and taunted the SPD with their tolerance of the rise of Fascism. The break-up of the trade unions and arrest of a few of their leaders could not redeem "the treachery of the SPD and of the Second International". Their attempts, abetted by the renegade Trotsky, to put the blame on the KPD were designed to "shake the confidence of the workers in Comintern". The resolution ended with the usual denunciation of the Versailles treaty and of French imperialism.[91]

How little the PCF had yet moved in response to the German catastrophe was shown at the session of its central committee on July 14–18, 1933. Duclos reported on the united front, Gitton on the trade unions, Vassart on organization, and Ferrat on the German situation. Thorez wound up the proceedings in a speech which criticized the weakness of the debate, and which derived special significance from being delivered on the eve of a congress of the SFIO. It was devoted almost exclusively to the need to create a united front of workers against capitalism "without ever renouncing the battle against the socialist party and its policy of conformity with the interests of the bourgeoisie". The term "social-Fascist" was no

[87] *Humanité*, March 6, 1933; for the Comintern letter of March 5 see p. 85 above.
[88] *Rundschau*, No. 6, March 25, 1933, p. 151.
[89] See p. 91 above.
[90] *Humanité*, May 1, 1933.
[91] *Humanité*, May 13, 14, 1933; *Rundschau*, No. 14, May 19, 1933, pp. 436–437.

longer in use. But Fascism in France might "take the form of a grouping around this or that Left party". Only the PCF was truly international and "struggles against war in the spirit of re-volutionary defeatism": the leaders of the SFIO were still wedded to "national defence". The *clou* of the speech was to be found in its concluding passages. Here Thorez admitted that all was not "clear in the head of every member of the party", and that the party was "not ideologically proof against outside influences". Some party members, noting a diminution of hostility among socialist workers, "let themselves be influenced by the sentimental current of unity at all costs, and forget the criticism of the socialist party". He attempted to balance these broadsides against opportunism by an attack on the sectarianism which neglected the day-to-day demands of the workers (the "struggle on two fronts"). But it was clear on which side, in Thorez's estimation, the real danger lay.[92] After the socialist party congress, Thorez renewed the attack in an article in the party journal, denouncing the Second International as "an assembly of champions of the Versailles system and of the League of Nations". But he again expressed anxiety, repeating the same formula, that "our party is not ideologically proof against outside influences".[93]

During the summer of 1933 the atmosphere was insensibly modified by the growing cordiality of official Franco–Soviet relations: the two countries were drawn together by common fear of a revived German nationalism and of German rearmament. The ratification in May of the Franco-Soviet pact of non-aggression was greeted by Litvinov with unusual warmth.[94] On July 7, 1933, on a visit to Paris, Litvinov gave a statement to the press which, after dwelling on the well-known Soviet devotion to peace, observed that this was receiving "more and more understanding in France", and that Soviet political and economic interests "do not clash with the interests of France at any point in the world".[95] Herriot, the French Prime Minister, paid a visit of a fortnight's duration to the USSR at the end of August 1933; and this was followed by a visit of Cot, the

[92] *Ibid.* No. 26, July 28, 1933, p. 938; *Oeuvres de Maurice Thorez*, II, v (1951), 112–126.

[93] *Ibid.* II, v, 127–139.

[94] *Dokumenty Vneshnei Politiki SSSR*, xvi (1970), 303.

[95] *Dokumenty Vneshnei Politiki SSSR*, xvi (1970), 419–420.

Minister for Aviation, in mid-September. Both were received with every mark of enthusiasm.[96]

These manoeuvres of Soviet diplomacy were not reflected in any fresh directives from Comintern, and confronted the PCF with an embarrassing problem. It was the essence of any communist party in a capitalist country to be the enemy of its national government. But, while the KPD, in denouncing the Versailles treaty, could profess to champion national claims more courageously than the supine and submissive German government, the PCF, in pursuing the same policy, exposed itself to the reproach of betraying national interests or, more specifically, of being pro-German.[97] Now that the Soviet government was expressing a new-found sympathy for French national interests and policies, the intransigence of the PCF became increasingly anomalous and unpopular with the rank and file of its members. This dilemma occupied a large part of Thorez's report to a session of the central committee on October 20–22, 1933. He admitted that some party members had been so infected by bourgeois ideology as to reject the essential Comintern slogan: "Down with the Versailles treaty!" Some Paris workers even toyed with the idea that "it would perhaps be better to make war on Hitler at once". Thorez strove to show that the danger of war was not peculiar to Fascism; democracy also could "very well lead to war". French imperialism was still the enemy; and, "so long as the USSR is surrounded by capitalist states, it must use diplomacy to defend the dictatorship of the proletariat". Meanwhile Fascist tendencies were developing in France, and drew encouragement not only from the bourgeois parties, but from the SFIO, which continued to

[96] *Ibid.* xvi, 841, note 148, 856, note 218.

[97] Alsace-Lorraine had always been an embarrassment to the PCF (see *Foundations of a Planned Economy, 1926–1929*, Vol. 3, p. 473), especially since most of the inhabitants who agitated for autonomy or for the re-establishment of German institutions belonged politically to the Right; after 1933 they were more or less open Nazi sympathizers. Kuusinen, in his speech at the eleventh IKKI in March 1931, while including Alsace-Lorraine in the category of "oppressed European peoples", admitted that under French rule "the policy of assimilation is not pursued so persistently as it was formerly under Prussian imperialism" (*XI Plenum IKKI* (1932), i, 438–439). But the attitude of the PCF was unchanged; on April 4, 1933, Thorez delivered a speech in the Chamber in which he denounced "certain aspects of colonial exploitation of the people of Alsace-Lorraine", and called for their "absolute and unconditional independence" (*Oeuvres de Maurice Thorez*, II, v (1951), 60–87). For Nazi activities in Alsace-Lorraine see *Die Kommunistische Internationale vor dem VII Weltkongress* (1935), pp. 234–235.

slander the USSR. It was an uncomfortable and unconvincing performance.[98]

The affairs of the PCF received little attention at the thirteenth IKKI in November–December 1933. Kuusinen in his main report referred briefly to its "*Right errors*" and "opportunistic application of the tactics of the united front".[99] Thorez, schooled no doubt by Fried, gave a long and illuminating exposition of its problems. His starting-point was the international situation which, in the words of the thesis submitted by Kuusinen, "has the character of the eve of a new world war". France was in the centre of the contradictions between the major imperialist Powers. Her relations with Germany were marked by "a number of contradictory elements". Franco–Soviet relations were a special case, since external conditions, including "the pressure of the masses", had resulted in "the decision of France at the present moment to renounce arrant provocations . . . and support to counter-revolutionary conspirators". Yet "the deep hatred of imperialist France for the land of socialist construction remains as before"; and France "arms herself and organizes war in the name of 'security'". These ambiguities evidently puzzled the PCF, especially in its attempts to apply united front tactics. At a joint meeting with socialists and radicals at Troyes, communists proclaimed their "readiness to defend republican liberties, to uphold the conquests of 1789, against Fascism and especially against German Fascism". In the Nord department, a communist had voted for a socialist resolution expressing "loyalty to the bourgeois-democratic regime", and *Humanité* had printed the resolution without comment. The party organization in Marseilles had declared that "*the struggle against the Versailles treaty means aid for Hitler's cause*"; in Saint-Etienne, it had called for the abandonment of the slogan, "*Down with the Versailles treaty*". The PCF, declared Thorez, must profit by "the immense lesson given us by the establishment of a Fascist dictatorship in Germany"; it must follow "the line of Comintern . . . in questions of the united front". Only since the twelfth IKKI had it begun to give some attention to "the elementary needs of the workers". But the controversial implications of these injunctions were left unresolved.[100]

[98] Extracts only from the report were published in *Humanité* and in *Oeuvres de Maurice Thorez*, II, v (1951), 144–163.
[99] *XIII Plenum IKKI* (1934), p. 26.
[100] *Ibid.* pp. 142–153.

It was again left to Pyatnitsky to dilate, though in somewhat milder terms than at the twelfth IKKI, on the shortcomings of the PCF. Since the twelfth IKKI "serious opportunist errors" had been committed. Negotiations had been carried on not only with the central committee of the SFIO (this was correct), but also with the POP group which consisted of "renegades expelled from the communist party"; and, instead of organizing a united front of workers "on definite questions and a definite platform", vague discussions had been held between leaders on the principles of a united front. The same criticism applied to contacts between the CGTU and the CGT. But it emerged that the main problem arose in the field of international relations. The SFIO had raised a loud outcry over the renewal in May 1933 of the Soviet–German treaty of 1926, and demanded that the USSR, in sympathy with KPD, should break off relations with Fascist Germany. On the other hand, the warm reception given to Herriot in Moscow in August had been denounced by socialists as truckling to French imperialism. To these attacks the PCF, through the columns of *Humanité*, had replied feebly or not at all. Pyatnitsky stressed the change in the French attitude to the Soviet government in the past year, but did not directly raise the question of the Versailles treaty.[101] But his defence of Soviet foreign policy sounded hollow in French ears. Frachon and Marty, who also spoke in the debate, did not attempt to answer his criticisms, and contributed nothing to the issues involved, though Marty referred to French hegemony in Europe as being "conditioned by the Versailles treaty".[102] Nor did Kuusinen revert to the question in his closing speech; his final exhortation to the PCF was "to utilize the split in the socialist party to undermine the influence of the reformists".[103] The resolution of the thirteenth IKKI, which wrestled uneasily with the problems of German nationalism and the Versailles treaty,[104] barely mentioned the PCF. At this moment of indecision in Moscow, no clear counsel could be offered to the baffled and embarrassed French party. But this did not prevent Thorez returning to Paris in a mood of elation. In *Humanité* on January 7, 1934, he proclaimed "Soviet power" as the main watch-word of Comintern; and in an article in the party

[101] *Ibid.* pp. 176–184.
[102] *Ibid.* p. 389.
[103] *Ibid.* p. 582.
[104] See pp. 113–114 above.

journal he announced "a new step forward" on the basis of the
resolutions of the thirteenth IKKI.[105]

The central committee of the PCF met from January 22 to 25,
1934, to consider and endorse the conclusions of IKKI. Thorez
delivered a report which was published as a pamphlet under the
title *The Struggle for a Revolutionary Issue from the Crisis*. He showed
himself in no mood to abate the declared hostility of the party for the
SFIO:

> All the parties of the bourgeoisie, including the social-
> democratic fractions, cooperate in the work of Fascisiz-
> ation. . . . The task of social-democracy is to curb, to set up an
> obstacle to, the revolutionary movement of the masses.

The split in the SFIO was meaningless. Blum and Faure were
merely concerned "to dupe the workers for as long as possible by
means of so-called 'democratic' methods". Thorez admitted that
"the influence of the PCF and of the CGTU does not progress
sufficiently, and the total memberships do not grow". Nevertheless,
the party had been able to "rally a broad united front movement
against war and Fascism, bringing to its side thousands of socialist
workers and influencing elements of the petty bourgeoisie". A
eulogy of the united front from below included a friendly reference
to the work of "MOPR, MRP, Friends of the Soviet Union etc."[106]
Doriot called for a genuine united front, and spoke with biting
contempt of the half-hearted approaches made to Faure. His speech
was, however, not reported or mentioned in *Humanité*, and—to
make things worse—was printed in the dissident communist journal
Vérité.[107] The resolution adopted on Thorez's report called for
stronger action against Fascism and against the complicity of the
SFIO and of other "Left" parties in the repression of the workers,
and for an approach to socialist workers on the line of the Comintern
appeal of March 5, 1933.[108] The resolution, like the report, made no
reference to dissent within the party. But Doriot's frankness had
certainly earned him the sympathy of many delegates. An ill-timed

---

[105] *Oeuvres de Maurice Thorez*, II, v (1951), 203–224.
[106] *Oeuvres de Maurice Thorez*, II, v (1951), 225–268.
[107] Thorez indignantly recounted this six months later (*ibid.* II, vi (1951), 183).
[108] *Humanité*, January 24, 1934; *Rundschau*, No. 14, February 8, 1934,
pp. 526–527.

article by Marty headed "Pas d'Enervement" exhorted the party to remain calm in face of Fascist threats.[109]

This factitious calm was short-lived. The demon of Fascism was not so easily exorcized. On February 6, 1934, in a tense political situation extremist Right-wing groups rioted in the Place de la Concorde, and were with difficulty restrained by the police from bursting into the Palais Bourbon, where the Chamber of Deputies was in session. Twelve demonstrators were killed, and many more injured. Consternation reigned in all parties. Local organizations of the SFIO and the CGT and of the PCF and the CGTU respectively appear to have made overtures to one another to discuss common action for the defence of democratic institutions against Fascism. But at the top stiffer attitudes still prevailed. Marty, on the very eve of the Fascist rising, had appealed to the PCF to demonstrate "against the Fascist bands, against the government which encourages them, and against social-democracy which, by dividing the working class, seeks to weaken it".[110] A joint manifesto of the PCF, the CGTU and the communist youth league, published in *Humanité* on February 7, 1934, appealed to all workers to fight together against Fascism, but continued to denounce the SFIO for its failure to respond to previous appeals for a united front, for its role as a strike-breaker, and for its abandonment of the class struggle in favour of cooperation with capitalist parties. During the next few days joint demonstrations of workers against Fascism took place in many cities. But, as an uneasy calm returned to the French political scene, the impulse died away. A one-day general strike on February 12, sponsored both by the CGT and by the CGTU, temporarily brought socialists and communists together on the same platforms, but had no sequel. The two parties continued to confront each other in postures of mutual mistrust and hostility. Thorez, in an article in *Humanité* on March 20, pointedly declared that "it is under the leadership of the communist party, and in spite and in face of the socialist party, that fighting unity between communist and socialist proletarians will be forged".[111] In an article of April 19 he for the first time criticized Doriot by name.[112] It is clear that Doriot had

[109] *Humanité*, February 3, 1934.
[110] *Ibid.* February 6, 1934.
[111] *Oeuvres de Maurice Thorez*, II, vi (1951), 61.
[112] *Ibid.* II, vi, 91–92.

many silent sympathizers in the PCF. Barbé, nursing his wounds
and eager, perhaps, for revenge on Thorez, drew nearer to Doriot;
and loyal party organizations began to denounce "the Barbé–
Doriot group".[113] But the leaders dared not move without some
signal from Comintern headquarters.

Desire in Moscow to evade a troublesome dilemma was frustrated
by Doriot's determination to pursue his campaign. On April 11,
1934, strong in the support of a large majority of the Saint-Denis
section of the party, he addressed an open letter to IKKI
expounding the reasons for his dissent from the party line, and
asking for a ruling; and this he published in the local party organ.[114]
The Comintern secretariat, never enthusiastic about Thorez, and
perhaps divided against itself on the issue of policy, reacted with
surprising indulgence to this bold initiative. On April 23 it invited
the rivals to suspend their mutual hostilities, and to submit their
differences to Comintern, coming to Moscow to plead their cause.
Thorez promptly obeyed the summons. Doriot, now evidently
riding for a fall, refused to go, and indulged in a gesture which must
have infuriated his opponents. He resigned his post as mayor of
Saint-Denis, and then stood for re-election, challenging the party
central committee to put up a candidate against him; this it
prudently refrained from doing.[115] On April 26 he addressed a joint
communist–socialist meeting in Saint-Denis;[116] and on May 6, he
was triumphantly re-elected.

Doriot had left Comintern no option. On May 16, 1934, the
presidium of IKKI passed a resolution noting that Doriot had
defied its summons and continued his "struggle against the central
committee of the PCF". By his actions and his open letter Doriot
had placed himself "on the same road on which the counter-
revolutionary Trotsky stood in his day". The presidium decided to
"deprive Doriot of the protection of Comintern" and allow the
central committee of the PCF to take "all such measures of an
ideological and organizational character as it finds necessary to

---

[113] *Humanité*, April 23, 1934; Thorez at this time described Barbé as a former
"sectarian" who had become an "opportunist" (*Oeuvres de Maurice Thorez*, II, vi
(1951), 65–66).

[114] For extracts from the letter see *Le PCF pendant l'Entre-Deux-guerres*, ed.
N. Racine and L. Bodin (1972), pp. 215–219; it was also published as a pamphlet.

[115] These particulars may be gleaned from the *Pravda* article of May 23, 1934
(see below).

[116] L. Trotsky, *Oeuvres*, iv (April–December 1934) (1979), 17.

assure the unity of the party and a successful struggle against Fascism". The resolution was published in *Pravda* on May 23, 1934, accompanied by a long article detailing Doriot's offences. Doriot had had the right to appeal to Comintern. But to publish the appeal as a "platform" was to "enter on the inadmissible path of a fractional struggle against one's own party". The principle of the united front was once more enunciated in uncompromising terms. It meant a rupture of the working class with the bourgeoisie, and could not embrace social-democratic leaders who preached collaboration with the bourgeoisie. Surprisingly the article concluded that Doriot had not yet "completely passed into the enemy camp", and once more appealed to him to retreat from "the brink of the precipice"—a hint to the PCF to withhold the final sanction of expulsion. The decision marked, however, the reluctant abandonment of the view, long cherished in some circles in Comintern, that the vigorous and popular Doriot would make a better leader of the PCF than the docile and malleable Thorez.

During Thorez's stay in Moscow, on May 11, 1934, he had a meeting with Dimitrov, who urged on him the importance of breaking down "the wall between communist and social-democratic workers". Policy must "break away from the dogmatic formulas of the Zinoviev period". Common action by communist, social-democratic and other workers "against the bourgeoisie" was to be welcomed "even if at first everything does not go in conformity with our slogans".[117] But Dimitrov's word was not yet law in Comintern, and Thorez had learned to be cautious. He celebrated his return to Paris on May 23 with a speech in which he again denounced Doriot, though without indicating what action was to be taken against him. Nor did he foreshadow any new departure in party policy.[118]

By a paradox not infrequently illustrated in political life, the defeat of Doriot paved the way for an advance towards the policies

---

[117] B. Leibzon and K. Shirinya, *Povorot v Politike Kominterna* (2nd ed., 1975), pp. 93–94; a record of the meeting exists in the Comintern archives (*Kommunist*, 1972, No. 8, p. 20), but has not been published. *Humanité*, April 26, 1934, had published an interview given by Dimitrov to a French journalist in Moscow, cautiously commending a united front of workers, petty bourgeois and intellectuals against Fascism, and on June 2, 1934, published a fulsome letter of congratulation from Dimitrov to Cachin on his birthday; both these items are in G. Dimitrov, *S'chineniya*, ix (n.d.), 435–443, 471–473.

[118] *Humanité*, May 24, 1934.

for which he had stood. Opinion at the congress of the SFIO held in Toulouse in May 1934 was overwhelmingly in favour of the principle of a united front. But the acrimonious abuse of its leaders in which the leaders of the PCF saw fit to indulge was a serious obstacle; and the resolution presented by Blum was inconclusive. In Paris an anti-Fascist congress on May 20–21, presided over by Barbusse and attended by nearly 3500 delegates, received greetings from the PCF, and sent a telegram to the SFIO congress begging it to participate in common action against Fascism "on the basis of the Amsterdam movement".[119] On May 27 the annual commemoration in the Père-Lachaise cemetery of the executions which followed the suppression of the Paris Commune in May 1871 was transformed by the zeal of the PCF into a massive demonstration of support for Comintern, in which 100,000 workers, including socialists, anarchists and others, are said to have participated.[120] On the following day the PCF announced a national party conference for June 24 to discuss the question of the united front.[121] *Humanité* on May 31 printed a translation of the *Pravda* article of May 23 denouncing Doriot; but the front page of the same issue was occupied by an appeal to workers and socialists and to the administrative council of the SFIO for common action to secure the release of Thälmann and to vanquish Fascism. The note of recrimination about the past, though muted, was not absent; and the reply of the administrative council, while purporting to accept the overture "without reservation", demanded "an end to attacks directed against our respective organizations and leaders".[122] On June 15 Thorez spoke again in the Chamber on the desire of the PCF for common action. He drew attention to the fact that a majority of the SFIO supported national defence, to which the PCF was unalterably opposed, but did not appear to treat this as an obstacle.[123] In an article in the party journal of the same date he declared that "the organization of the united front to struggle against Fascism" was the sole item on the agenda of the forthcoming party conference. The workers wanted unity. But Thorez, with a clumsiness which seemed to belie any sincere desire for cooperation,

[119] *Rundschau*, No. 31, May 24, 1934, pp. 1223–1224; for the Amsterdam movement see pp. 387–394 below.

[120] *Humanité*, May 28, 1934.

[121] *Ibid.* May 29, 1934.

[122] *Populaire*, June 6, 1934.

[123] *Oeuvres de Maurice Thorez*, II, vi (1951), 124–129.

went on to refer contemptuously to "the Blums and the Jouhaux", the leaders of the SFIO and the CGT, who had begun to talk of unity, but stopped short of "unity of action and unity *tout court*".

> To chatter, to deceive the working class [he concluded], to keep it partially under their influence—that is to say, under the influence of the bourgeoisie, of which they are and remain the principal social support—such is the aim of the leaders of the social-reformist organizations.[124]

Outraged by these attacks the executive committee of the SFIO on June 20 wrote a letter to the PCF breaking off negotiations.[125]

A thoroughly confused atmosphere therefore prevailed when the party conference met at Ivry on June 23, 1934. Ever since Thorez's visit to Moscow in May, the supporters of the united front in Comintern had been increasingly uneasy about the conduct of affairs in the PCF; and on June 11 a letter was dispatched to Paris which was intended to give a lead to the conference.

> You should treat the task of creating a united front [ran the instruction] more broadly than any other party or organization whatever in the French working class. The whole force of mass actions of the working class should be concentrated against Fascism. In order to create an anti-Fascist front it is indispensable to work out a programme of demands which would be supported by the broadest masses. . . . It is indispensable to make an end of declarations which are often met with in the party press or in pronouncements of party organs that the party fights to abolish bourgeois democracy. Such empty and completely one-sided declarations are politically erroneous.[126]

The letter, though too late to affect Thorez's article of June 15, must have arrived in good time before the conference. But the obtuse

[124] *Ibid.* II, vi, 114–123; the article also attacked Doriot, who was assimilated to the Barbé–Célor group and compared with Trotsky.

[125] The letter, published in the socialist newspaper *Populaire* on June 21, 1934, is quoted in J. Braunthal, *History of the International*, ii (Engl. transl. 1967), 425, note 3.

[126] *Voprosy Istorii KPSS*, 1972, No. 1, p. 128; the full text was never published, and may have included reservations which weakened the force of the quoted passages. Vassart, at that time delegate of the PCF in Moscow, in his unpublished memoirs claimed to have participated in drafting it (*The Comintern: Historical Highlights*, ed. M. Drachkovitch and B. Lazitch (1966), pp. 246–247).

Thorez, unskilled in reading the finer nuances of Comintern vocabulary, failed to realize its intentions. His main report at the conference, an impassioned appeal for a united front, was full of naive self-congratulation, and was spiced with much niggling criticism of the hesitations of the SFIO and the CGT. The implication throughout was that the reluctant leaders of SFIO were being driven into the united front by the enthusiasm of their followers. The Toulouse congress of the SFIO was said to have been dominated by "an orientation towards Moscow". In a revealing passage, Thorez remarked that the demands of the Left must be so framed as "to *subject the SFIO and the CGT to so strong a pressure, so firm a control, on the part of the masses that they could not refuse to accept the struggle for these demands*".[127] It was a tactless performance, calculated to confirm the worst suspicions of Blum and his supporters.

By this time the advocates of the united front who were in the ascendant in Moscow had become thoroughly alarmed at what was going on in Paris. While the conference was in session, a telegraphic instruction arrived from Comintern which reversed the course of the proceedings.[128] On June 25, an open letter was addressed to the SFIO on behalf of the conference, accepting the SFIO's proposals for common meetings and a joint campaign against Fascism, and including the declaration that the two parties would "refrain mutually from all attacks, insults and criticisms against each other's organizations and party members".[129] The speech in which Thorez wound up the conference differed markedly in tone from that with which he had opened it. The united front, Thorez repeated, "is not a manoeuvre". Not only did the PCF desire "*at all costs* to realize unity of action with socialist workers against Fascism", and "*at all costs* the unity of the trade unions in one CGT", but also "to draw in the middle classes and snatch them from the demagogy of Fascism". The assurance that "we love our country" struck a further note of conciliation.[130] The same themes were pursued in a fulsome article

[127] *Oeuvres de Maurice Thorez*, II, vi (1951), 130–176.
[128] Vassart's unpublished memoirs, which show a naive eagerness to inflate his personal role, are the source for this telegram; according to his account, Manuilsky was furious with Fried for having failed to guide Thorez correctly, and threatened to remove him from his post in Paris (*The Comintern: Historical Highlights*, ed. M. Drachkovitch and B. Lazitch (1966), pp. 248–251). If this threat was made, it was not carried out; Fried remained in Paris throughout the nineteen-thirties as the mentor and intimate friend of Thorez (P. Robrieux, *Maurice Thorez* (1975), p. 184).
[129] *Humanité*, June 25, 1934; for the text of the letter see *ibid.* July 2, 1934.
[130] *Oeuvres de Maurice Thorez*, II, vi (1951), 177–192.

by Thorez in the party journal for July 1—a remarkable *volte-face* from his article in the preceding issue.[131]

Doriot gave the conference no opportunity to ignore him, if it had wished to do so. He did not appear, but wrote a letter complaining that, though he held a mandate entitling him to attend, no documents had been sent to him, and he felt himself "*de facto* excluded". A reply was drafted to the effect that he had "eliminated himself" by his absence.[132] Thorez denounced him in both his speeches, though the second contained yet another sentimental appeal to him "to bow to the decisions of our party and the International", and repeated that there was still time for him to "avoid the abyss into which he is slipping". The conference pronounced no formal sentence, but instructed the central committee to "pronounce on Doriot's expulsion".[133] Doriot was expelled from the party without any publicity on June 27, the day after the conference ended.[134]

Whatever misgivings may have lingered in the minds of some members of the SFIO, the way was now clear. On July 8, a massive joint socialist–communist demonstration took place in the Bois de Vincennes. The leaders of the two parties had a preliminary meeting on July 14. On the following day a special conference of the SFIO approved the agreement by an overwhelming majority of 3471 to 366 with 67 abstentions;[135] and the pact was finally signed without ceremony, in a small Paris restaurant, on July 27. It contained four points: unity of action and a joint campaign in defence of democratic liberties, against war preparations, against "the Fascist terror in Germany and Austria", and for the release of Thälmann and other anti-Fascists in prison; the organization of joint meetings and demonstrations; an agreement to refrain from mutual "attacks and criticisms", while reserving to each party "entire independence to develop its own propaganda, without insults or outrages against the other party"; and an undertaking by both parties to deal with objectors in their own ranks.[136] The

[131] *Cahiers du Bolchévisme*, July 1, 1934, pp. 771–780; this article, unlike its predecessor, was not reprinted in the collected works.

[132] *Humanité*, June 26, 1934.

[133] A brief and selective account of the conference appeared in *Rundschau*, No. 38, June 23, 1934, pp. 1533–1534, No. 39, July 5, 1934, pp. 1568–1569.

[134] G. Walter, *Histoire du Parti Communiste Français* (1948), p. 271.

[135] J. Braunthal, *History of the International*, ii (Engl. transl. 1967), 427–428.

[136] The text is reprinted, together with the original drafts put forward by both parties, in *Le PCF pendant l'Entre-Deux-guerres*, ed. N. Racine and L. Bodin (1972), pp. 221–224.

political secretariat of IKKI in a letter of August 21, 1934, approved the agreement, recommending to the PCF a "flexible and consistent policy" to develop the united front, a campaign for the fusion of the trade unions, and an electoral pact for the mutual withdrawal of candidates at the second ballot.[137] By way of completing the demonstration of its devotion to the new line, the PCF pronounced a belated sentence of expulsion on Barbé, whose "Left sectarian policy" had once "incited communist against social-democratic workers".[138]

A subsidiary aim of the sponsors of the united front was to heal the rift in the French trade union movement. A minority in the CGTU had always favoured moves towards reconciliation with the CGT, but had received no official encouragement.[139] After the events of February 1934, the executive of the CGTU on March 28 had made an appeal to workers belonging to CGT unions to join "unity committees" with their comrades of the CGTU for the pursuit of practical common ends.[140] This mild initiative foundered on the opposition of the CGT leaders. During the summer some slight progress was made; the railway workers in Marseilles formed a joint union. On October 8, the leaders of the CGT and the CGTU met— apparently for the first time—at the offices of the CGT. The CGT accepted unification of the railway unions, but rejected a proposal of the CGTU to draw up a general agreement on the process of unification, and to settle disputed points by a referendum of members.[141] Later, a CGTU proposal for a joint union of public servants seems to have met similar obstruction.[142] Pyatnitsky, in an interview published in the PCF journal, argued the case for a unified trade union movement.[143] But it is clear that the campaign for trade union unity lagged behind the drive for the united front of the PCF and the SFIO.

---

[137] *Kommunisticheskii Internatsional: Kratkii Istoricheskii Ocherk* (1969), p. 381; no archival reference is given for this item.

[138] *Rundschau*, No. 51, September 20, 1934, pp. 2191–2192.

[139] See *Foundations of a Planned Economy, 1926–1929*, Vol. 3, pp. 531–533.

[140] *Rundschau*, No. 27, April 26, 1934, pp. 1007–1008.

[141] *Ibid*. No. 54, October 11, 1934, pp. 2349–2350.

[142] *Ibid*. No. 65, December 20, 1934, p. 3009.

[143] *Cahiers du Bolchévisme*, November 1, 1934, pp. 1275–1283; Pyatnitsky claimed that there were already 166 unified trade unions in France, of which 105 were railway workers' unions.

Meanwhile, the coordinating committee set up by the agreement of July 27, 1934, continued to function; and on October 9 the PCF delegates submitted a programme designed to create a "broad united front" extending "to trade unions of workers, and to the masses belonging to cooperative groups of peasants, artisans, small traders and other elements of the middle classes".[144] On the following day a mass meeting was held at the Salle Bullier in Paris, at which Thorez, Marty and Duclos spoke for the PCF and Zyromski for the SFIO, and which issued a joint manifesto on cooperation in the regional elections. When at the party conference in June Thorez had mentioned "the middle classes" as potential recruits for the struggle against Fascism, nobody had paid much attention.[145] The inclination was strong to seek support wherever it could be found against the reactionary Doumergue government installed after the events of February 6. In an article in *Humanité* of September 9, Thorez argued that the "Français moyen", like the worker, was subjected to bourgeois exploitation, and enquired whether "most of the demands of the 'Français moyen', for which we ardently struggle, are not the specific demands of communism"; and a month later he wrote more specifically of the defence of "democratic liberties" and "popular liberties", and of "the struggle for bread and liberty".[146] This seemed plausible and harmless. But in his speech of October 10 in the Salle Bullier the appeal to the bourgeoisie, and no longer to the petty bourgeoisie in particular, became explicit, and was reinforced by the plea for an electoral alliance not only with the SFIO, but with the bourgeois Radical-Socialists. He also had extravagant praise for the role of Rolland and Barbusse in the Amsterdam movement and for the Amsterdam-Pleyel committee. But he balanced this wooing of bourgeois allies by an emphatic assertion of communist leadership:

We repeat that unity of action will lead to the creation of a single party of the working class, a party resting on a solid basis of doctrine—the dictatorship of the proletariat, the struggle for Soviet power, hostility to the lie of national defence—centralized

[144] *Oeuvres de Maurice Thorez*, II, vii (1952), 142–143.
[145] *Ibid.* II, vi, 17–19; for this speech see p. 194 above.
[146] *Oeuvres de Maurice Thorez*, II, vii (1952), 27–30.

and disciplined on the model of the glorious party of Lenin, a party worthy of the Communist International.[147]

Thorez's naive frankness was not calculated to lull the doubts of SFIO leaders about the possibility of equal partnership with the PCF.

The PCF, which so recently denounced cooperation even with socialists, had now embarked on a further transition—so smooth as to be perhaps in part unconscious—from the "united front" of workers, the embodiment of the "class against class" doctrine, to a comprehensive "front" of all men of goodwill committed to the defence of democracy against Fascism. The appeal was now explicitly extended to "the middle classes".[148] This apparent reversal of cherished principles and practice shocked many members of the SFIO; and the fact that it was still accompanied by eloquent protestations of loyalty to the USSR, and of a determination to work for a workers' and peasants' government at home, threw doubt on its sincerity. Nor was the alliance of the SFIO with the PCF regarded as worthy of imitation by other major social-democratic parties, or approved by the respected leaders of the Second International. The meeting of Thorez and Cachin in Brussels with Vandervelde and Adler on October 15, 1934, ended in an emphatic rejection of their plea for an international meeting to be addressed by representatives of the Second International and of Comintern.[149]

Unabashed by this set-back, Thorez proceeded boldly on his chosen path. A congress of the Radical-Socialist Party was to open on October 24, 1934, at Nantes. Some time before it, Duclos and Frachon, on behalf of the PCF, visited Herriot, the Radical-Socialist leader, now a minister in the Doumergue government. Herriot seems to have spoken frankly of his dissatisfaction with the government. What was said on either side about future relations between the two parties is not recorded.[150] But Thorez now conceived the bold plan of travelling to Nantes, and delivering there

[147] *Humanité*, October 11, 12, 1934; the speech was not reprinted in the collected works. For the "Amsterdam-Pleyel committee" see p. 394 below.

[148] The transition was eased by avoidance of the word "bourgeoisie" and substitution of "les classes moyennes".

[149] See p. 140 above.

[150] J. Duclos, *Mémoires*, i (1968), 419–420, is the sole source for this interview, which is not precisely dated.

on the eve of the congress an appeal for an alliance with the Radical-Socialists in a broad anti-Fascist popular front, which would also embrace the PCF and the SFIO.

The news of this project reached Moscow at a moment when keen controversy was raging in the Comintern hierarchy over preparations for the seventh congress, and when a handful of hard-liners were engaged in a rear-guard action against the application of united front policies. The prospect of this fresh extension of the united front seems to have aroused general uneasiness, swelled perhaps by recollections of Thorez's heavy-handed methods. On October 15, 1934, the day of the abortive meeting in Brussels, the political commission of IKKI in Moscow drew up instructions to the parties on preparations for the seventh congress of Comintern;[151] and this was followed up by a special instruction to the PCF recommending the creation of an anti-Fascist bloc, which might be called a "worker-peasant bloc" or a "bloc of labour". Given the divisions of opinion in Comintern, the text may have been equivocal; and it was decided to send representatives to Paris to ensure that the wishes of IKKI were correctly interpreted.[152] On the morning of October 24 Thorez received in his home in Ivry a Comintern delegation in the persons of Togliatti, Gottwald and Fried; Stepanov, who was to have been of the party, was indisposed. Togliatti, who spoke in their name, sought to deter Thorez from his rash initiative, which risked playing into the hands of the SFIO and prejudicing the PCF; Dimitrov and Manuilsky were quoted as fearing that such a manoeuvre would weaken the drive of the masses for the democratic and popular cause. It was evidently an embarrassing moment. Fried remained obstinately silent. Duclos, who was present, said nothing positive. Thorez was unmoved. He explained that he was just about to take the train for Nantes, that his speech was ready, and that he was not prepared to change a word of it. He had probably already given the summary of it to *Humanité*, where it appeared on the following day.[153]

---

[151] See p. 140 above.

[152] K. Shirinya, *Strategiya i Taktika Kominterna* (1979), p. 53; the text of the instruction has not been published.

[153] The scene is described in G. Cerreti, *Con Togliatti e Thorez* (1973), pp. 168–172; the author, an Italian member of the PCF, was present. J. Duclos, *Mémoires*, i (1968), 421, mentions the occasion, but names only Togliatti; Thorez (*Fils du Peuple* (1960), p. 102) speaks only of "the leader of a fraternal party". *Kommunisticheskii Internatsional: Kratkii Istoricheskii Ocherk* (1969), pp. 301–302, observes that "the decision of the PCF was in advance of the development of the views of some workers in Comintern", and that this accounted for the warning.

It was in these discouraging circumstances that the "popular front" was conceived and brought to birth. The first public use of the term seems to have been in an article by Cachin in *Humanité* on October 24, 1934, written in preparation for a joint mass meeting in Paris on that evening, which was addressed by Cachin and Duclos and by Blum and Zyromski, and was attended by 3000 workers.[154] On the same evening, Thorez in Nantes made the prepared appeal for a broad popular front, in which communists would take their place, to defend their beloved country against reaction and Fascism.[155] Addressed to a bourgeois party with a long tradition of participation in "national" governments, the speech set the seal on the altered character of the quest for a united front against Fascism. Eloquent articles by Cachin in support of the popular front in its new guise appeared in *Humanité* on October 26 and 27.

When the central committee of the PCF met on November 1, 1934, Thorez opened his speech with a reference to the entry of the USSR into the League of Nations, which he treated as part of the struggle against Fascism. Fascism was still "the principal danger". In an unexpected digression he broached the theme of a single workers' party (the "parti unique"), while admitting that this had been used by adversaries as "a weapon against the united front". But he also renewed the appeal to "the middle classes", whose claims would be considered in detail in "the programme of the popular front". The purpose was *"in the struggle against Fascism to seal the alliance of the working class and the middle classes"*. The programme of the popular front would concern itself with "the defence of the democratic freedoms" and with their extension. The PCF had travelled far beyond its grudging acceptance of partnership with the SFIO, and was openly seeking alliances outside the traditional workers' parties of the Left.[156] An article by Thorez entitled "For

[154] *Humanité*, October 24, 25, 1934. Vassart, followed by D. Desanti, *L'Internationale Communiste* (1970), p. 192, and P. Robrieux, *Maurice Thorez* (1975), p. 194, attributed the invention of the term to Fried. It was certainly coined in French; the Russian "narodnyi front" is a slightly awkward translation, and the German equivalent "Volksfront" as distinguished from the united front (Einheitsfront) never came into common use. For subsequent elaborations of the phrase by Thorez see pp. 205–206 below.

[155] G. Walter, *Histoire du Parti Communiste Français* (1948), pp. 284–285. An abbreviated version of the speech appeared in *Humanité*, October 25, 1934; it was not printed in the collected works.

[156] *Oeuvres de Maurice Thorez*, II, vii (1952), 52–89; the speech was published in a pamphlet entitled *Les Communistes et le Front Populaire*.

the Alliance with the Middle Classes" appeared in the next issue of the party journal.[157] First reactions in Moscow to Thorez's bold gesture of defiance were mixed.[158] Togliatti, in a characteristically tortuous letter to Manuilsky, attempted to justify the hesitations felt in Moscow about the transition to the popular front. Thorez should in the first instance have launched an appeal to the masses in the form of a programme of concrete demands. As a result of this failure, the popular front had become simply a "formula", and the initiative had been left in the hands of the SFIO. Togliatti cunningly put the blame on Fried, with whom, as he doubtless knew, Manuilsky was on bad terms.[159]

The situation was further complicated by the resignation of the Doumergue government on November 8, 1934, and its replacement by a new coalition under Flandin, which marked a move to the Left. Thorez greeted it with an ambivalent speech in the Chamber, in which he proclaimed both the defence of democratic freedoms and the establishment of "Soviet power" as the goal. In his speech to the party central committee on November 1 he had named the USSR as "the country of socialism, liberty and peace". He now ended by calling for "the triumph, against the capitalist front of Fascism and war, of the popular front of labour, liberty and peace".[160] This became the final form of the slogan. Friction, however, quickly arose between the two partners to the July pact, partly over the conditional support which the SFIO was prepared to give to Flandin's bourgeois government, partly over the PCF's positive proposals, which included the formation of "popular front committees" in factories and in the villages, and the summoning of a conference of the socialist parties of six western countries to discuss the extension of the popular front.[161] But the two major bones of contention between communists and socialists were the questions of national defence and of Alsace-Lorraine. Thorez in a speech in the Chamber denounced "the lie of national defence", and demanded

[157] *Ibid.* II, vii, 113–121.

[158] See p. 199 above.

[159] P. Togliatti, *Opere*, III (1973), i, pp. cxci–cxciii; for Manuilsky's quarrel with Fried see p. 194, note 128 above.

[160] *Oeuvres de Maurice Thorez*, II, vii (1952), 91–112.

[161] A letter from the PCF and a reply from the SFIO were followed by a further PCF letter of December 9 propounding its proposals; the letters were not published, but an account of the dispute was given by Thorez to a party meeting of the Paris region on December 20, 1934 (*ibid.* II, vii, 142–171).

"the free disposition of the peoples of Alsace and Lorraine"; and in *Humanité* he named the two questions as obstacles to the realization of "a united front of the working class".[162] After the reprisals which followed the murder of Kirov in Leningrad on December 1, attacks on the USSR in the socialist press provided a fresh source of protest by the PCF.[163] But in Moscow Thorez's prestige now stood high. The meeting of the presidium of IKKI on December 9–10, 1934, was his moment of triumph. He was invited to deliver a report on the experience of the PCF, which was held up as a model for other parties to follow in the pursuit of the popular front.[164]

Collaboration between the PCF and the SFIO, more effective at lower party levels than between the leaders, continued during the first months of 1935. The unity of the working class was the constant theme of communist pronouncements. But the wooing of the "middle classes" and of the intellectuals was not forgotten; and Thorez once more celebrated "the fruitful work of the magnificent Amsterdam-Pleyel movement".[165] Cautious support was extended to Flandin's national government, whose diplomatic relations with the Soviet Government were progressively more cordial. Thorez in an article in the party journal of March 1935 kept up the pressure for a fusion of the CGTU and the CGT.[166] The national committees of both these organizations met later in the month. In the course of the negotiations the CGTU expressed its willingness to accept a stipulation, demanded by the CGT, that the communists should refrain from constituting party fractions in the joint unions. The PCF was induced to approve this condition, while continuing to regard it as "an extraordinarily far-reaching concession".[167] It proved, however, insufficient to prevent a breakdown of the negotiations. While the CGTU pronounced enthusiastically for trade union unity and for the creation of joint unions, the CGT

---

[162] *Ibid.* II, vii, 124, 131.

[163] *Ibid.* II, vii, 166–171, 175–179.

[164] See p. 145 above.

[165] *Oeuvres de Maurice Thorez*, II, viii (1952), 84.

[166] *Ibid.* II, viii, 91–97.

[167] *Rundschau*, No. 58, October 23, 1935, p. 2376. Lozovsky at the seventh congress of Comintern gave his approval to the concession, though obviously with some reluctance (*ibid.* No. 62, November 6, 1935, p. 2496); according to B. Leibzon and K. Shirinya, *Povorot v Politike Kominterna* (2nd ed., 1975), p. 227, the question was debated in the preparatory commission for the congress.

resisted it on the plea of maintaining the independence of the unions of any political party.[168]

The heritage of the past could not be so easily abandoned; and friendly overtures were incongruously accompanied by a flow of petty recriminations. In *Humanité* on February 13, 1935, Thorez recited difficulties said to have been placed by the SFIO in several constituencies in the way of common lists for the muncipal elections.[169] Duclos quoted the warning example of MacDonald's treachery to the Labour Party in support of the thesis that a working class party must be based on the principle of democratic centralism.[170] Blum caused offence by recalling the *volte-face* in the attitude of the PCF in the previous June; and the socialist newspaper, citing the opinion of Faure, asserted bluntly that "the offers of unity of action made to us are the result of an order given to the PCF by Russia", and might be reversed at any time.[171] The PCF kept up the pressure. In April Thorez, not very convincingly, revived the slogan of a single workers' party. But he also complained that none of the other parties of the Second International accepted the principle of the united front.[172] The municipal and national elections of May 1935 were, however, a triumph for the Left. Cooperation between parties in this practical sphere proved easier than in any other. The PCF, in spite of occasional disputes with the SFIO about the mutual withdrawal of candidates in the second ballot, gained ground everywhere, and became the largest party in Paris and in the department of the Seine. Thorez, in a speech in the Salle Bullier on May 17, hailed the results as a vindication of the popular front, and repeated the call for "the defence of bread, peace and liberty".[173]

It was at this moment that the Franco–Soviet pact of May 2, 1935, and the Stalin–Laval declaration of May 16,[174] impinged on the progress of the PCF towards the realization of the popular front.

[168] For Thorez's remarks see *Oeuvres de Maurice Thorez*, II, viii (1952), 169–172, 174–175.
[169] *Ibid.* II, viii, 71–74.
[170] *Cahiers du Bolchévisme*, April 1, 1935 (editorial).
[171] *Oeuvres de Maurice Thorez*, II, viii (1952), 83–85, 129–131.
[172] *Ibid.* II, viii, 174–176, 182–185.
[173] *Ibid.* II, viii, 197–207.
[174] See pp. 150–151 above.

An article in *Humanité* on April 16 had already expressed the view that, in default of the agreement for general disarmament proposed at Geneva by the USSR, "the method most likely to constitute an obstacle to war is that of pacts by which the Powers will undertake to boycott the aggressor", and called for the speedy conclusion of such a pact between France and the USSR; and in its propaganda for the elections the PCF had proclaimed that "the most sacred duty of proletarians of the whole world is to ensure the defeat of aggressors against the country of socialism and of all their allies".[175] The signature of the pact on May 2 was, therefore, no surprise, and was easily digested. As Thorez explained in his speech of May 17:

> If war . . . broke out against the Soviet Union, and an imperialist state, for the sake of some interests of its own, ranged itself on the side of the Soviet Union, the war would not be a war between two imperialist camps, for it would be monstrous to treat as an imperialist camp the camp in which the country of socialism, the country of the working class, finds itself.[176]

The declaration of May 16, however, though a logical outcome of the pact, was another matter. The PCF had been congratulated in the past on its record of activity in the armed forces[177]—a record matched by no other party. More recently national defence had been one of the issues dividing the PCF from the SFIO.[178] The sharp and abrupt reversal of long-cherished attitudes required by Stalin's demand for support of French governmental policies on national defence and rearmament shocked many loyal party members. On the day after its publication, Thorez, at the end of his speech in the Salle Bullier celebrating the party's electoral triumphs, read the text of the declaration, and defended it in a confused and tortuous argument. If some capitalist countries acted in concert with the land of socialism, "their action *objectively* serves the cause of peace" and "*objectively* serves the cause of the proletariat", the two causes being inseparable. Thorez repeated over and over again the charge that German Fascism was a threat to peace, and the pledge to defend the USSR by all means, but did not directly mention the issue of

[175] *Humanité*, April 21, 1935.
[176] *Oeuvres de Maurice Thorez*, II, ix (1952), 17.
[177] See p. 169 above.
[178] See p. 192 above.

military service.[179] At the end of the speech, an audience of 5000 rapturously acclaimed the pact.[180]

Next day, in a leading article in *Humanité*, Vaillant-Couturier faced the problem more bluntly. He admitted that "Stalin's words resounded like a thunder-clap", and would be exploited "in bad faith" by the class enemy. But Stalin, at a time when "Hitler gets ready to attack our socialist fatherland", had spoken "like a statesman and a Bolshevik". French communists were not allies of the "armament magnates", and did not seek a "holy alliance" with the bourgeoisie. But it was necessary "to give full force to the pact"; the reader was advised to "seek no other meaning in Stalin's words".[181] Next day the Fête Jeanne d'Arc, a great patriotic occasion, was celebrated by a demonstration of 200,000 workers of both parties at the Mur des Fédérés.[182] The Stalin–Laval declaration undoubtedly caused, as Marty later admitted, "some confusion in the French party for a short time".[183] But little evidence of this appeared in print; and overt protest was confined mainly to dissident Left groups more or less directly associated with Trotsky. On June 10, on the eve of his expulsion from France—a by-product of the increasingly warm relations between the French and Soviet Governments—Trotsky addressed an open letter of protest to the French workers under the title "Stalin's Treachery and the International Revolution".[184]

Meanwhile intensive propaganda continued for the popular front; the phrase had now replaced the united front in current French political terminology. On May 29, 1935, the PCF submitted to the communist–socialist unity committee what was described as a "charter of unity for the French working class". It was in fact a plea for a "single party of the proletariat", which was to constitute "an alliance of working men and women with peasant workers, small traders, artisans, intellectuals, of all toiling people" for the purpose

[179] *Oeuvres de Maurice Thorez*, II, ix (1952), 9–22.
[180] *Humanité*, May 18, 1935.
[181] *Ibid.* May 18, 1935.
[182] *Ibid.* May 20, 1935.
[183] *Rundschau*, No. 72, December 11, 1935, p. 2769. The story in G. Lefranc, *Histoire du Front Populaire* (1965), p. 28, and elsewhere, that Marty, then editor of *Humanité*, refused to print the *communiqué* till he received specific instructions from the politburo to do so is perhaps apocryphal; the fact that the declaration was originally issued in Moscow is sufficient to explain its appearance in *Humanité* one day later than in the Soviet press.
[184] *Byulleten' Oppozitsii* (Paris), No. 44, July 1935, pp. 6–10.

of "overthrowing bourgeois domination and installing the worker-peasant government".[185] It was a propaganda gesture without prospect of success and was quickly forgotten. Thorez in a report to the central committee of the PCF on June 1–2, 1935, attributed the successes of the party at the elections to electoral bargains with socialists, and occasionally with radicals. He ended with the usual appeal for the popular front, for democratic liberties, for peace, and against Fascism at home and abroad. In a confused and embarrassed passage he rounded on "our adversaries", who "want to make trouble", those who cried: "Down with the two years [of military service]. Down with armaments credits!" The PCF was against the "two years" as an instrument of imperialism. But the contingency of war against the USSR had to be taken into account. "We listened to Stalin because he has shown by all his acts that he was a revolutionary". The watchword remained: "We shall do everything to defend the Soviet Union and to defend peace."[186] The Flandin government fell on June 1, and was succeeded, after an interval of confusion, by a government headed by Laval; it cannot have helped that one of the socialist ministers was Frossard, once a renegade from the PCF. The congress of the SFIO at Mulhouse on June 9–12 embraced the united front with the PCF, but had some scruples about cooperation in a popular front with bourgeois parties; a compromise resolution moved by the moderate Blum admitted that the SFIO did not rule out such cooperation. Thorez in an article in *Humanité* on June 30 continued to flatter the Radical-Socialist Party, which he called "the greatest of the parties" and "the one which exercises the greatest influence on the political life of the country";[187] and he was rewarded three days later when the executive committee of the party decided to join the massive popular front demonstration organized by the PCF for July 14.[188]

Everything was now concentrated on preparations for July 14, and for its celebration as the first public appearance of the popular front, described as a Rassemblement Populaire, on the French political scene. A preliminary meeting was called on June 8, 1935, by a representative of the Amsterdam-Pleyel movement, and on

---

[185] J. Duclos, *Mémoires*, ii (1969), 41; the full text appeared in *Humanité*, June 5, 1935.

[186] *Oeuvres de Maurice Thorez*, II, ix (1952), 28–54; these "extracts" from the speech appeared in *Humanité*, June 5, 1935.

[187] *Oeuvres de Maurice Thorez*, II, ix (1952), 79–81.

[188] *Humanité*, July 4, 1935.

June 17 a committee of organization was set up which included representatives of political parties, of the two trade union federations, the CGTU and the CGT, and of a number of non-political bodies of a Left complexion, of which the Amsterdam-Pleyel movement and the Ligue des Droits de l'Homme were the most important.[189] A summons to the demonstration was issued in the name of 48 organizations.[190] The occasion turned into a vast spontaneous demonstration of apprehension and protest against the rise of Fascism in France and against the menace of German Fascism. It was said to have been attended by 500,000 people. Among those present, apart from the leaders of the PCF and prominent Left-wing intellectuals, were Blum, Daladier and Jouhaux, the president of the CGT. "La Marseillaise" and the Internationale were both sung; and the participants, amid scenes of enthusiasm, subscribed to an oath "to defend the democratic liberties won by the people of France, to give bread to the workers, work to the young, and to the world the great peace of mankind". Blum, who had approached the proceedings with some scepticism, wrote on the following day in the newspaper of the SFIO, the *Populaire*, that he had "never been present at such a spectacle", and that "perhaps Paris has never seen the like". Similar demonstrations were held in other centres.[191] It was a triumph for the PCF and for Thorez, who could now appear with the halo of a victor at the seventh congress of Comintern in Moscow later in the month.

[189] G. Lefranc, *Histoire du Front Populaire* (1974), pp. 76–78; it is not clear whether all the organizations said to be represented on the committee had already committed themselves. Duclos in an appeal in the PCF party journal attributed the initiative to the "Amsterdam-Pleyel movement created by Henri Barbusse and Romain Rolland" (*Cahiers de Bolchevisme*, July 1, 1935, p. 715); the movement was said to be supported at this time by 150 anti-Fascist committees (J. Duclos, *Mémoires*, ii (1969), 14). Thorez at the seventh congress of Comintern a month later said that "the Amsterdam-Pleyel committee took the initiative in the Rassemblement Populaire of July 14" (*Oeuvres de Maurice Thorez*, II, ix (1952), 134); since Rabaté, an active communist, was one of the Amsterdam-Pleyel representatives on the organizing committee, the hand of the PCF in the initiative may be confidently inferred.

[190] J. Duclos, *Mémoires*, ii (1969), 46.

[191] The occasion was reported in *Humanité*, July 14, 15, 16, 1935, and throughout the press; M. Thorez, *France Today and the Popular Front* (1936), pp. 186–190, provides a vivid self-congratulatory account. For later narratives see J. Fauvet, *Histoire du Parti Communiste Français*, i (1964), 116–117, and G. Lefranc, *Histoire du Front Populaire* (1974), pp. 82–86.

CHAPTER 10

THE BRITISH COMMUNIST PARTY (CPGB)

The purge of the leadership of the CPGB in the latter part of 1929,[1] and the inauguration of the *Daily Worker* on January 1, 1930, were intended to breathe new life into the frail frame of the CPGB. Any such hopes entertained by Comintern, and no doubt by some party stalwarts, were disappointed. The ensuing year, while symptoms of economic crisis multiplied all round, was empty of achievement for the party. The presidium of IKKI in February 1930 dubbed the British Labour government "anti-proletarian" and "social-Fascist", declared that the CPGB could perform its tasks only by transforming itself into "a mass communist party", and adjured it to "put an end to the passivity and sectarianism" which hindered recruitment.[2] Campbell, now submissive to discipline from Moscow, spoke as a fraternal delegate at the Russian party congress in June 1930. He described Britain as "one of the classic countries of social-Fascism", praised the leadership of Comintern, and followed the current fashion by denouncing Left as well as Right deviations.[3] But exhortations from Moscow fell on barren soil. Rust, the editor of the *Daily Worker*, admitted that its circulation was "very low and unsatisfactory", and party membership "small and stagnant", and made the usual appeal for "ruthless war against opportunism in practice, against Right-wing passivity and Left sectarianism".[4] At the end of 1930 the membership of the CPGB had fallen to 2550—its lowest figure since the early nineteen-twenties.[5]

Even more serious was the decay of the National Minority Movement (NMM) and the National Unemployed Workers' Committee Movement (NUWCM), which had formerly represented mass movements of workers.[6] At the fifth congress of Profintern in August 1930, Lozovsky bluntly described the trade union

---

[1] See *Foundations of a Planned Economy, 1926–1929*, Vol. 3, pp. 393–397.
[2] *Kommunisticheskii Internatsional v Dokumentakh* (1933), pp. 931–934.
[3] *XVI S"ezd Vsesoyuznoi Kommunisticheskoi Partii (b)* (1930), pp. 450–451.
[4] *Communist Review*, No. 6, 1930, p. 258.
[5] *Internationale Presse-Korrespondenz*, No. 32, April 19, 1932, p. 990.
[6] See *Foundations of a Planned Economy, 1926–1929*, Vol. 3, pp. 394–395.

situation in Britain as "very bad"; the NMM had "no basis" and very little organization. But he also issued a warning against those who wished to create new Red unions in Britain.[7] Allison, who led the British delegation at the congress, dwelt on the difficulties of converting the NMM into a mass organization to lead the workers; and Hannington, while speaking at length on the problem of unemployment, admitted the weakness of the party in dealing with it and did not mention the NUWCM. Only the veteran Tom Mann attempted a highly unrealistic defence of the NMM, and claimed that it represented 200,000 workers.[8] Heller of the Profintern secretariat depicted members of the NMM as "afraid of isolation", incapable of leading "*a struggle for the street*", and willing to "apply only legal, parliamentary methods".[9]

Heckert, who introduced a long resolution on the NMM, politely attributed its errors to "the old leadership", which had not been displaced till the autumn of 1929.[10] The resolution noted the decreasing membership of the NMM, its "isolation from the masses" and "open resistance", even after its last congress in August 1929, to the "new line". Its "Right opportunist errors" included "trade union legalism", and failure to expose "the social-Fascist development of the bureaucracy and the treacherous role of the pseudo-Left"; among its "Left sectarian errors" were the calling of strikes without preparation and the inopportune use of the slogan of "the struggle for power". It was instructed to "formulate a broad united front programme of action" in the shape of a Workers' Charter designed to embody the "simple and popular demands" of the workers. The activity of the NMM in the reformist trade unions was to be maintained and strengthened. On the other hand, great emphasis was laid throughout the resolution on the role of "independent leadership" to be exercized by the NMM in the trade union movement; and energetic support was to be given to the only two "Red" trade union organizations in Britain—the United Mineworkers' Union of Scotland and the United Clothing Workers' Union in London. Nobody in Moscow detected any incompatibility between these diverse instructions. The NUWCM got short shrift. It was to be "reorganized as an integral part of the NMM under its

---

[7] *Protokoll des V Kongresses der Roten Gewerkschaftsinternationale* (1930), i, 73, 510.
[8] *Ibid.* i, 189–190, 216–219, 329–331.
[9] *Ibid.* ii, 65.
[10] *Ibid.* ii, 283–285.

direct leadership", and "opportunist tendencies" which hindered its development into a mass organization firmly resisted.[11]

The British delegates returned to London in chastened mood; and the NMM, eager to carry out the instructions of Profintern, proceeded to draft and issue a Workers' Charter, which represented not the full communist programme, but a catalogue of practical demands of the workers. A review in the *Daily Worker* of September 10, 1930, attributed its authorship to the party leader, Pollitt. Sold at one penny a copy, it had some success. But it was overshadowed by a short-lived sensation in British politics, the formation by Mosley of a new political party of the Left, purporting to stand on a more radical platform than the Labour Party. Though Mosley's appeal was mainly to intellectuals, he succeeded in recruiting the volatile Cook, the former miners' leader, whose association with Maxton had once been a source of embarrassment to the ILP.[12] The new party soon developed Fascist overtones which alienated some of its original supporters, but broadened its appeal to a dissatisfied section of the middle class.

During the winter of 1930–1931 the gathering economic crisis brought a series of lock-outs and strikes, notably among the miners, still embittered by the experience of 1926. A strike of Welsh miners produced a serious rift in the communist ranks. Horner, the communist president of the South Wales Miners Federation was at loggerheads with local representatives of the NMM, who in their eagerness to apply the principle of "independent leadership" attempted to set up separate strike committees which had no truck with the "reformist" trade unions. Horner in exasperation wrote to Moscow on January 21, 1931, complaining that the Miners Federation was being ignored, and that the "artificial" strike committees set up by the NMM were simply "NMM groups" completely isolated from the mass of strikers.[13] On January 23 the party central committee adopted a resolution which seemed less critical of Horner than of the NMM. It recorded that "the independent role of the party during the strike was almost completely non-existent"; the party did not "clearly formulate the basic tasks", and had not applied the directives of the fifth congress of Profintern. It had failed to "link the general line with concrete

[11] *Ibid.* ii, 350–356.

[12] See *Foundations of a Planned Economy, 1926–1929*, Vol. 3, pp. 369–370.

[13] This account comes from a denunciation of Horner in the *Daily Worker*, March 10, 1931.

issues of the workers' struggle for their immediate demands", and had assumed that "the only way out of the crisis for the British coal mining industry is the overthrow of capitalism and the nationalization of the main branches of industry".[14] The matter could not, however, be allowed to rest there. On March 14, the party central committee, having considered a long report from the politburo, perhaps prompted from Moscow, on Horner's delinquencies, passed a resolution summoning him to confess his errors and to submit himself to the decisions of the party.[15]

The CPGB sustained further critical scrutiny at the eleventh IKKI in March–April 1931. Manuilsky accused it of a mechanical approach to the class struggle. It had neglected work in the trade unions and the "immediate demands of the working class". By "most unsuccessfully politicizing" the NMM, it had reduced it to "a basis no broader than that of the party". Pyatnitsky attacked its slogans as "abstract."[16] Pollitt expatiated on the severity of the crisis in Britain, and on the popular campaign for "military intervention against the Soviet Union" and for an "economic blockade", and denounced the Labour Party which fulfilled the same "dangerous role" as the SPD in Germany. Mosley's "new party" was composed of people who professed to have come from the extreme Left, but represented "the first form of an openly Fascist organization against the workers". The "pseudo-'Left'" of the ILP must also be combated and exposed. Nevertheless sectarianism had penetrated the ranks of the CPGB: "nine-tenths of our members are so disposed that, if a new worker, especially a worker from the ILP, is not ready to swallow whole the 21 conditions of Comintern, they call him a social-Fascist". He ended by criticizing Horner, whom he accused of "opportunist passivity", "lack of faith in independent leadership", and disagreement with the new line of Comintern. It was a dispiriting performance. The other main British speaker, Arnot, dealt exclusively with India—a theme rendered topical by the impending Round Table Conference in London.[17] Lozovsky castigated both the CPGB and the NMM for their failure to lead the massive strike movement; they remained "outside" the workers'

[14] *Daily Worker*, January 28, 1931; the formula of "the only way out" was condemned by Comintern (*Kommunisticheskii Internatsional*, 1931, No. 8, pp. 4–5).
[15] For the report and the text of the resolution see *Communist Review*, No. 4, 1931, pp. 145–157.
[16] *XI Plenum IKKI* (1932), i, 48, 229.
[17] *Ibid*. i, 203–216, 390–398.

struggle. Britain was the weakest, as Germany was the strongest, link in the revolutionary chain.[18]

The only activity of the CPGB which both satisfied Profintern and had some modest prospect of popular success was the campaign for the Workers' Charter. The party organized charter committees in main centres throughout the country, and summoned a National Charter Convention to meet in London on April 12, 1931. On the eve of the convention the *Daily Worker* published an open letter from the executive bureau of Profintern addressed to the members of the NMM and "the revolutionary workers of Great Britain". It heartily condemned "the Labour government and the trade union bureaucracy" for having "helped the capitalists to attack the workers", and added that "the most despicable part" had been played by ILP leaders such as Maxton and Brockway, who criticized the Labour government in words and supported it in deeds. But the NMM was "still dangerously isolated from the mass of workers, still meeting the needs of the working class struggle all too ineffectively, still lagging dangerously behind the mass struggles of the workers". It had failed to provide "class leadership" in the strikes. Its addiction to "trade union legalism" and its "resistance to the line of independent leadership" were symbolized in Horner's "opportunist" attitude. The Workers' Charter was a programme of action designed to unite the broad masses of the workers; the Charter convention must "lay the greatest emphasis upon the preparation, under the leadership of the NMM, of the economic struggle".[19]

The convention met on April 12 with three items on its agenda: the economic struggles and the Workers' Charter, colonial oppression (India was particularly in view), and the danger of war against the USSR. It mustered 788 delegates. Mann presided, and Pollitt was the principal speaker. The Workers' Charter was said to have sold 120,000 copies.[20] But, in spite of the enthusiasm generated on this score, it was afterwards admitted that the charter had "not succeeded in leading and organizing the workers in the struggle against the enemy".[21] The NMM continued to languish. In May 1931 the CPGB, anxious to retrieve its credit, issued a manifesto on the crisis entitled *The Way Out*. The capitalist system was breaking

[18] *Ibid.* i, 216–217.
[19] *Daily Worker*, April 11, 1931.
[20] *Ibid.* April 13, 1931; *Labour Monthly*, No. 5, 1931, pp. 283–286.
[21] *Ibid.* No. 6, 1931, p. 341.

down everywhere. In Britain, where the crisis was at its most acute, the political parties were united in their determination "to save capitalism by sacrificing the workers". This was the policy also pursued by the Labour government, "the betrayers of the working class, warmongers, colonial murderers, wage cutters and creators of unemployment", and by the ILP. The solution could be found only in a "workers' dictatorship", which would be "realized by the workers themselves through their own workers' councils elected from the factories".[22] But the manifesto raised no echo. Horner once more proved a source of embarrassment, making a statement to the central committee which fell short of a complete admission of his errors, and was said to display opposition to the "class against class" line. The committee was unwilling to resort to extreme measures, and left it to the party politburo "to apply disciplinary action if necessary, in conjunction with the International".[23]

While the economic situation grew more and more desperate, and swelled the discontent of the workers, the CPGB relapsed into impotence, and its voice was barely audible in the tumult. The *Daily Worker* showed no signs of rivalling the circulation or the popularity of *Humanité* or the *Rote Fahne*. In the late summer of 1931 the economic and financial crisis boiled over into a parliamentary crisis. The Labour Party split. On August 24 the Labour government resigned, and was succeeded by an all-party coalition government, Ramsay MacDonald remaining as Prime Minister, and the sole opposition being constituted by a rump of the Labour Party. In September the naval mutiny at Invergordon hastened the climax; and on September 21, two days after Japan had launched an occupation of Manchuria, the Bank of England announced the suspension of gold payments.[24] The reaction of the CPGB to these dramatic events was predictable. An open letter from the central committee to members of the party of August 28 denounced the pressure on wages and on the social services, and "the sham-opposition role of Henderson and of the general council of the TUC".[25] On September 19–20 the party central committee listened

---

[22] *To Fascism or Communism?* (CPGB, May 1931), pp. 26–31.
[23] *Daily Worker*, June 9, 1931.
[24] For these events see p. 45 above.
[25] *Internationale Presse-Korrespondenz*, No. 85, September 1, 1931, pp. 1915–1916; extracts appeared in the *Daily Worker*, August 28, 1931.

to a report from the politburo, which diagnosed in the fall of the "so-called" Labour government "the bankruptcy of reformism", and in the revolt of the sailors "the revolutionization of the masses". The Labour Party had followed a "conscious social-Fascist" line, and the national government would now resort to "Fascist measures of class rule". Unhappily the CPGB had been weak and unprepared. What was needed was a new approach to the workers—to broaden the NUWCM, to build up the NMM, and to use the charter campaign as the basis for a united front.[26] But the prospect, seen from Moscow, looked more exciting than at any time since 1926.

> Now it has begun [wrote *Pravda* on October 9, 1931]. The working class, in mass demonstrations, in fights and clashes with the police, is freeing itself from the bonds of its age-long illusions about parliamentary democracy, from its belief in the leaders of the parliamentary "opposition" and the trade unions.

Party membership had risen from its low point of 2550 at the end of 1930 to 3000 in June 1931 and to over 6000 in November.[27] But the number was pitiably small, and any encouragement derived from it was quickly disappointed. In the parliamentary election on October 27, 14 million votes were cast for the national government and 6.5 millions for the Labour opposition. The 26 communist candidates received 75,000 votes in all, and none of them won a seat.[28]

It was a harsh demonstration of the inability of the CPGB to win the support of the worker, even in face of a major crisis of capitalism. *Pravda*, with a faith in things not seen, discovered that "the basis of social-Fascist influence is constantly narrowing, the ground for communist influence is expanding".[29] The *Daily Worker* looked forward to "a new Conservative government of hunger and war", and deduced "the bankruptcy of the parliamentary weapon for the worker".[30] Dutt headed an article on the election result "The

[26] *Communist Review*, No. 8, 1931, pp. 417–432 (apparently an abbreviated text); for passages relating to the ILP see p. 218 below. For an attempt by Pollitt to galvanize the charter committee into action see *Labour Monthly*, No. 10, 1931, pp. 616–623.

[27] *Internationale Presse-Korrespondenz*, No. 32, April 19, 1932, p. 990.

[28] For the CPGB's election manifesto, which invited the working class to "fight its *way out of the crisis of capitalism*", and held up the Soviet Union as a model, see *Communist Review*, No. 11–12, 1931, pp. 441–448.

[29] *Pravda*, October 29, 1931.

[30] *Daily Worker*, October 31, 1931.

Defeat of the Labour Party".[31] The same themes reappeared in a resolution of the party central committee, which argued that it was not the working class, but "the Labour Party, ILP and TUC leadership and policy" which had been defeated.[32] But such pretences reassured nobody. The British delegates to the eighth session of the central council of Profintern in December 1931 were severely mauled. Allan, the secretary of the NMM, sought such consolation as he could find in "the radicalization of the masses", and the success of work among the unemployed, but could not avoid the hard fact of the NMM's "isolation from the masses". One of the secretaries of Profintern retorted that, in spite of the apparently propitious situation in Britain, the NMM was "one of the weakest links in the chain" and was successful only among the unemployed, most of whom were not members of unions. Pollitt alleged that Profintern had given no help to the NMM in its work in reformist unions—a charge indignantly denied by Lozovsky.[33]

The resolution adopted by the central committee of the CPGB in January 1932, reflecting the current uncertainties in Moscow, was a repetition of formulas no more likely to prove effective than they had been in the past. The starting point was the contradiction between "the increasing radicalization of the workers" and the isolation of the CPGB and its failure to rally the mass of workers. This was attributed to the party's failure to make clear *"the demarcation in principle between its line and the reformist line"*. Without unmasking the Labour Party and ILP as "agents of the enemy in the camp of the working class", no "revolutionary mass work could succeed." Emphasis on the need to work in the factories and in the reformist trade unions did not imply any weakening in the intransigence of the party line; the NMM was "to be made into a real trade union opposition with a broad mass basis in the factories and the trade unions."[34] To work within the trade union movement, while seeking to break down its allegiance to the Labour

[31] *Internationale Presse-Korrespondenz*, No. 104, November 3, 1931, pp. 2327–2329.
[32] *Communist Review*, No. 11–12, 1931, pp. 492–504.
[33] For this session see p. 48 above. For Allan's speech and the Profintern reply see *Internationale Presse-Korrespondenz*, No. 120, December 30, 1931, pp. 2793–2794, for Lozovsky's reply to Pollitt *ibid.* p. 2798; Pollitt's speech was not reported—a sign of sharp disapproval. Hannington was said to have been elected to the presidium of the session, and Horner to have spoken against imperialism (*ibid.* No. 115, December 8, 1931, p. 2639), but no speeches by either were reported.
[34] *Communist Review*, No. 2, 1932, pp. 55–69.

Party, and while supporting dissident Red trade unions, was not a realistic policy. Nor did it unite the rank and file of the CPGB. In April an article in the party journal detected in the ranks of the party "two forms of resistance to the resolution: conscious, more or less open, and passive unconscious, resistance".[35]

In spite of official reassurances, the failure of the party to make any appeal to the masses of workers bred uneasiness in the rank and file. In the autumn of 1931 a group of party members in south London came across some issues of the American Trotskyist journal, the *Militant*, and were impressed by Trotsky's trenchant criticism of Comintern, and in particular of its handling of the Nazi menace in Germany. Groves, the leader of the group, wrote to Trotsky expressing sympathy with his views. Trotsky replied on November 10, 1931 urging the formation of a British group of the International Left Opposition; and the main part of his letter was published in the *Militant* of December 5.[36] But the malcontents were not yet prepared for open defiance of the party; and the incipient revolt simmered throughout the winter. It was not till April 1, 1932, that the "Balham Group" sent to the party authorities a resolution criticizing party policy in the trade unions, and in international questions, and calling for a party congress. This was published with a reply from the party secretariat in the *Daily Worker* on April 14. The group made play with a remark attributed to Lozovsky at the eighth session of the central council of Profintern in the previous December that "we want to explode the trade union apparatus and destroy it".[37] In June 9 and 10, 1932, the *Daily Worker* published a long article by Lozovsky, who accused the Balham group of seeking to "contrast work in the factories to work in the trade unions"; he added that the remark attributed to him had been wrongly translated.[38] It was not until later in the summer that the clash with the Balham group came into the open. The group issued in May the first number of a fly-sheet *The Communist*, and finally burned its boats in an open letter of July 27 to Pollitt professing its loyalty to Trotsky and the Left Opposition.[39] In August Groves and another

[35] *Ibid.* No. 4, 1932, p. 179.
[36] R. Groves, *The Balham Group* (1974), pp. 46–49; the full text of the letter is in *Writings of L. Trotsky, 1930–1931* (1973), p. 344.
[37] R. Groves, *The Balham Group* (1974), pp. 54–56.
[38] The remark had appeared in the *RILU Magazine*; but it is unlikely that the wily Lozovsky would have expressed himself in such crude terms.
[39] R. Groves, *The Balham Group* (1974), pp. 86–90.

leader of the group were interviewed by Pollitt and Gallacher, and having repeated their defiance were expelled from the party; other expulsions followed later.[40]

Meanwhile the party leaders dealt more cavalierly with a more formidable opponent. Murphy had long been a thorn in their side, but had hitherto successfully courted the favour of Moscow.[41] This was now presumably withdrawn. On May 10, 1932, on the flimsy pretext of an article in the April number of the *Communist Review*, of which he was editor, advocating efforts to improve British trade with the USSR, the party politburo decided to expel him from the party.[42] Murphy compounded his offence by publishing in the ILP journal *New Leader* on May 20 an article entitled "Why I left the CP", which provoked a retort from Campbell three days later in the *Daily Worker* on "Murphy in the Arms of the ILP".

The economic and political crisis which had caused these heart-searchings in the CPGB had struck with equal force the Independent Labour Party (ILP). Since 1928 the relation of the ILP to the CPGB had been a source of mutual embarrassment.[43] In particular, since Maxton's withdrawal from the League against Imperialism in the following year, the ILP had been regarded with suspicion and hostility in communist circles as one of those "'Left' social-democratic" parties which were branded by Comintern as especially dangerous. Pollitt at the eleventh IKKI in March 1931 had spoken contemptuously of the ILP "with its programme of revolutionary phrases, trying by various illusions to draw the workers away from the daily struggle".[44] The ILP, which had once played a significant role in the rise of the British labour movement, had become in recent years a ginger group within the Labour Party, more representative of intellectuals than of organized workers. Now, as the crisis deepened, disillusionment in its ranks with the timid and faltering policies of the Labour Party grew apace, and provoked a demand to sever time-honoured links with it by a formal process of disaffiliation. The issue was raised at the annual

[40] *Ibid.* pp. 67–69.

[41] See *Foundations of a Planned Economy, 1926–1929*, Vol. 3, pp. 378–379, 389.

[42] *Internationale Presse-Korrespondenz*, No. 38, May 10, 1932, p. 1168, No. 40, May 13, pp. 1244–1245; *Communist Review*, No. 4, 1932, pp. 163–168. The politburo's refutation of Murphy's heresy appeared in the *Daily Worker*, May 10, 1932; for Murphy's own version see J. T. Murphy, *New Horizons* (1941), pp. 297–304.

[43] See *Foundations of a Planned Economy, 1926–1929*, Vol. 3, pp. 369–372.

[44] *XI Plenum IKKI* (1932), i, 208; for this speech see p. 211 above.

conference of the ILP in April 1931, but shelved. The CPGB professed no great interest in these moves. Dutt in an article on the eve of the conference noted the emergence of a demand for disaffiliation from the Labour Party as "*the most important new development in the ILP*". But he reminded his readers that "the Mosley group derives straight from the ILP", and concluded that the ILP, "*even if separated from the Labour Party, provides no answer to the problem of those workers who are seeking for an independent policy of socialism and class struggle*".[45]

The break-up of the Labour government in August 1931 in no way mollified the attitude of the CPGB to the ILP. Its pronouncement on the September crisis[46] contained a fierce denunciation of the ILP, which was described as "a social-Fascist party basically on the lines of the Labour Party", and was said "despite many revolutionary words" to be pursuing "capitalist social-Fascist policy"; and six weeks later the verdict of the CPGB on the results of the October elections complained that "the exposure of the 'Left' leaders—and especially of the ILP—has not been carried far enough", and condemned "the move towards pacts with the ILP" as "a sign of opportunist tendencies in the party, which have revealed themselves also in the central committee".[47] The sweeping victory of the MacDonald coalition government in the elections of October 1931 increased the ferment in the ILP; but its council decided once more to wait and see.[48] Meanwhile abuse of the ILP and insistence on its role as "an inseparable part of British social-Fascism" again marked the CPGB resolution of January 1932.[49] An article in the Comintern journal on "The CPGB and Social-Fascism" dealt in conventional terms with the doctrine of the lesser evil and the tactics of the united front, and ended with a bitter attack on the leaders of the ILP,[50] and an article in the Comintern news-sheet entitled "The ILP in the Services of Imperialism" harped on the charge that it merely hindered workers from understanding "the real position in which they find themselves, and

[45] *Labour Monthly*, No. 4, 1931, pp. 204–208.
[46] See p. 213 above.
[47] For this declaration see p. 215 above; which members of the central committee exhibited these "opportunist tendencies" is not known.
[48] *New Leader*, November 13, 1931.
[49] For this resolution see p. 215 above.
[50] *Kommunisticheskii Internatsional*, 1932, No. 5, pp. 56–63.

the right methods which must be brought to bear on the struggle against imperialist war".[51]

It was not till the summer of 1932 that, following the cultivation of united front policies in Germany, the tide began to turn in the CPGB. A resolution of the party central committee of June 1932, while purporting to censure the weakness of a majority of the party in carrying out the January resolution, altered the emphasis. It opened with a passage on the international situation and the danger of imperialist war against the USSR. But it also protested against "the tendency to limit our work only to the old methods of political generalizations and slogans", and called for more attention to the concrete demands—"'small' and partial demands"—of the workers. The "united front of the working class against hunger and war" acquired a new prominence; and, while this implied no weakening of the fight against reformist leaders "who are the principal enemies and disorganizers of a united front of the workers", the tone of denunciation was much milder and less obsessive than before. To work in the reformist unions was a major task of the party.[52] It was a straw in the wind. The change of mood did not, however, sensibly affect attitudes to the ILP, which was due to hold a special conference at Bradford at the end of July 1932 to consider the question of disaffiliation from the Labour Party. Three days before the conference the *Daily Worker* published a vehement attack on the ILP; its most heinous sin seemed to be its campaign for disarmament, which would simply "lay the frontiers of the USSR open to the imperialists". The same issue printed a letter from an ILP supporter of disaffilation, who expressed "admiration of the bold working-class lead you give", but complained of a "sectarian attitude" which tended to "confuse and alienate comrades who might otherwise be won for the revolutionary class struggle".[53] The moral was reinforced by a manifesto addressed to delegates at the conference. The CPGB offered cooperation "with those ILP workers who follow up the disaffiliation policy by being prepared to build the unity of the workers in a struggle around immediate demands directed against unemployment, wage cuts and war". But the manifesto included a reminder that, "in being prepared to unite

[51] *Internationale Presse-Korrespondenz*, No. 34, April 27, 1932, p. 1156.
[52] *Communist Review*, July 1932, pp. 311–317; for an abbreviated version of Pollitt's speech introducing the resolution see *ibid.* pp. 318–324.
[53] *Daily Worker*, July 27, 1932.

with other workers around an immediate policy directed against the capitalist offensive, we do not cease to be communists"; and it warned the ILP leaders against any attempt to create a new middle force between the Labour Party and communism.[54]

When the conference met, Brockway, the chairman of the ILP, strongly supported disaffiliation, but none the less delivered a blunt criticism of the CPGB:

> The rigidity of mind and method of the British Communist Party makes it incapable of appealing to the mass of the British working class or of adopting policies applicable to the British situation. It speaks of a united front of revolutionary socialists only to destroy it in practice.

After a stubborn debate, the conference voted to disaffiliate from the Labour Party by a majority of 241 to 142.[55] The result was not greeted by the *Daily Worker* with unalloyed enthusiasm: "The ILP leaders have not disaffiliated from their life-long policy. The leopard does not change his spots even if he comes out of his cage." And there was nothing to justify the view that, even in Britain, "the capitalist class can be got rid of by other means than a forcible revolution".[56] Meanwhile, Pollitt, initiating a discussion in preparation for the twelfth congress of the CPGB, announced for the end of October, continued to press the theme of work in the reformist unions, and urged that "every ounce of our energy should be used to make the trade union organizations of the workers strong and powerful weapons in their daily fight".[57]

At this turning-point in the affairs of the CPGB, the twelfth IKKI met in Moscow on August 27, 1932. Kuusinen in his main report scarcely mentioned the CPGB, but referred contemptuously to the attempt of "40 British communists without mass support", in the South Wales miners' strike of January 1931, to set themselves up as the "central strike committee"; this he called "a game of spillikins", thus unconsciously endorsing Horner's heretical attitude at the time.[58] Pollitt was now duly impressed by the break-away of the ILP from the Labour Party; it would "be wrong to underestimate in the

[54] *Ibid.* July 30, 1932.
[55] The proceedings were reported in *New Leader*, August 5, 1932.
[56] *Daily Worker*, August 2, 1932.
[57] *Ibid.* August 20, 1932.
[58] *XII Plenum IKKI* (1933), i, 30; for this episode see p. 213 above.

slightest degree the importance of this decision". He recalled that the CPGB in its June resolution had called for "the organization of a broad united front of the working class". This was still the main task, though care must be taken "not to create the impression that there are no fundamental differences between our party and ILP". Pollitt enthusiastically echoed Kuusinen's verdict on the South Wales strike, and spent much time discussing strike policy. But he scarcely mentioned the NMM, and spoke frankly of the weakness of the party in the trade unions. At the annual congress of the TUC, then in session at Newcastle, only four out of more than 700 delegates were communists. The party had not won over a majority of the unemployed. Its membership had not increased; only 25 per cent of members "actively apply the resolution of the central committee", while the rest "cling to the old, sectarian routine".[59] The moral of the speech was the need for change. But the character of the change was not very clearly defined.

The rest of the debate made it clear that, of the alternative "Right" and "Left" dangers to which communist parties were prone, it was a "Left sectarian" attitude which now constituted the most serious heresy in the CPGB. Pyatnitsky praised Pollitt's speech as "far more concrete than on previous occasions". Where the party concentrated on the practical demands of the workers, it was successful; where it merely discussed principles, it lost influence.[60] Lozovsky dismissed the CPGB briefly and pungently. The NMM had not grown; activity in the reformist trade unions was "in a catastrophic state". It was necessary "*to change methods of work*". In Britain "we lag behind further than anywhere".[61] Gusev accused the CPGB of a "*sectarian approach to the masses*", quoted a number of recent articles hostile to the ILP from the *Daily Worker*, and asked: "Is it really possible with such a tactical line to organize a united front with workers of the ILP and the Labour Party?"[62] The resolution at the end of the session briefly called on the CPGB for "work in the reformist trade unions and in the factories, mobilizing the masses for the struggle on the basis of the united front from below".[63]

[59] *XII Plenum IKKI* (1933), i, 129–138.
[60] *Ibid.* ii, 26–29.
[61] *Ibid.* ii, 163–164.
[62] *Ibid.* ii, 201–202.
[63] *Kommunisticheskii Internatsional v Dokumentakh* (1933), p. 980; for the general tenour of the resolution see pp. 73–74 above.

The signals from Moscow were too confused and ambiguous to be read promptly in London, where sharp controversy broke out in the CPGB in advance of its impending twelfth party congress. Before the session of IKKI ended, Dutt published an article in the *Daily Worker* protesting against the tendency "to reverse our whole trade union line" and "to preach confidence in the reformist trade union machine as organs of the working class struggle", and a few days later followed this up with another article which denounced "the constant habit in our party to move in straight lines from one opposite to another".[64] This was countered by Allan, the secretary of the NMM, who attributed its weakness to "contempt for trade union work largely resulting from party influence", and by Gallacher who boldly asserted that Pollitt's line "will enable us to go forward", whereas Dutt's line "will throw us back once again into the morass of sectarianism".[65] Pollitt committed himself uncompromisingly to the new approach in an article headed "We Must Win the Support of Organized Trade Unionists".[66] One of the curiosities of the pre-congress discussion was the publication in the *Daily Worker* of a letter from a member of the ILP fiercely attacking the inflexible and unscrupulous tactics of the CPGB, together with a rebuttal of the charges by the party secretariat.[67]

By the time the twelfth congress of the CPGB finally opened on November 12, 1932, order was restored. The party politburo had drafted and published in advance the main resolutions to be submitted to the congress.[68] Pollitt wound up the pre-congress discussion in an article which, quoting liberally from the decisions of the twelfth IKKI, referred to "the danger of Right mistakes" as "always the main danger", but more emphatically demanded "a ruthless war on every remaining vestige of sectarianism in our party".[69] On the day the congress began, an article by Dutt admitted the need for "revolutionary mass work" to end the isolation of the party in the factories and in the unions, and for a discriminating attitude to the ILP.[70] The speeches at the congress, which lasted for four days and was attended by 249 delegates, were

[64] *Daily Worker*, September 14, 19, 1932.
[65] *Ibid.* September 19, 21, 1932.
[66] *Ibid.* September 26, 1932.
[67] *Ibid.* November 4, 1932.
[68] *Ibid.* October 18, 19, 31, 1932.
[69] *Ibid.* November 7, 1932.
[70] *Ibid.* November 12, 1932.

uneventful. Pollitt opened on a sombre note, predicting that this might be the last congress "before a new imperialist slaughter". He claimed that the twelfth IKKI had shown the workers "concretely the way out"; but he added once more that it was necessary "to overcome sectarianism and divorce from the growing mass movement", and to pursue the struggle for all "partial demands". He asked, and failed to answer, why the treacherous social-democratic leaders "still possess an enormous influence", and why the CPGB had lagged behind in the revolutionary upsurge. He put the present party membership at 5400, but admitted that the turnover was heavy, and that most of the new members were unemployed; the unemployed now accounted for 60 per cent of the membership. The expulsion of Murphy and of the Balham Group was recorded with suitable expressions of indignation at their heresies. Campbell spoke mainly on the threat of war. Rust discussed how to strengthen the *Daily Worker*, of which he was the editor, and also attempted to rebut the ILP's favourite charge against the CPGB of "rigidity". Speeches from the floor were not reported in detail. Two delegates from the central committee of the KPD brought greetings and admonitions. An Irish delegate called Ireland "the weak spot in the chain of British imperialism". Pollitt's closing speech, reported in full, was repetitive and hortatory.[71]

The congress issued a manifesto denouncing the Labour Party, praising the USSR, and especially urging ILP workers to join "our ranks".[72] The main resolution adopted on Pollitt's report attacked "the social-Fascist role and policy of the Labour Party", and observed that the ILP, though disaffiliated from the Labour Party, "continues the same fundamental policy". The CPGB must continue to struggle against "the Labour Party, the TUC leaders and particularly the ILP". Its January resolution had laid down the line for party work in the trade unions and factories and among the masses, but had been inadequately applied. The goal was a united front of workers to be achieved by concentration on their "everyday economic and political interests". A resolution on the trade unions exposed the familiar dilemma. "Revolutionary mass work in the reformist trade unions" was demanded side by side with support for "unofficial trade union movements", as well as with NMM "groups and sections" in order to build up a "revolutionary trade union

[71] Speeches were reported *ibid.* November 14–19, 24, 28, 1932.
[72] *Ibid.* November 15, 1932.

opposition". Party fractions in the NUWCM should be strengthened in order to make it the "core" of the unemployed movement. A long resolution was devoted to the danger of war against the USSR, in which British imperialism figured as the major culprit. An ingenious argument was based on the premiss that the British Government was "pursuing an aggressive warlike policy against its leading imperialist rival, the USA":

> *The danger of a new imperialist war between Britain and the USA at the same time intensifies the danger of direct military intervention in the Soviet Union.*
>
> *The more antagonisms between the two great imperialist giants develop, the more there develops a tendency to settle their differences temporarily at the expense of the USSR.*

The supply of munitions to the Japanese was a particular target of attack. The ILP, having denounced Japan as the sole aggressor, paid lip service to mass action against the transport of munitions; but only its rank and file, in contrast with its "leading officials", were ready to cooperate. The CPGB was exhorted "to develop a great united front movement of the workers against war on the lines of the Amsterdam anti-war congress", to dispel pacifist illusions, and to engage in "mass anti-militarist activity". Other resolutions endorsed the decisions of the twelfth IKKI, approved the expulsion from the Russian party of Zinoviev, Kamenev and members of the alleged counter-revolutionary group which had been unearthed in the Soviet Union, and dealt with the training of new party cadres.[73]

Hitler's accession to power in Germany produced in Britain the same slow, stunned reaction as elsewhere. The Comintern reply of March 5, 1933, to the appeal of the Second International for common action[74] was published in the *Daily Worker* three days later; and the CPGB responded promptly to the recommendation it contained by addressing an offer of cooperation to the leaders of the

[73] The resolutions, in addition to those published before the congress (see p. 222 above), appeared in the *Daily Worker*, November 17, 21, 22, 24, December 1, 1932; the resolution on the danger of war (*ibid.* November 24, 1932) had been considerably amplified and strengthened since the publication of its first draft on November 1.

[74] See p. 85 above.

Labour Party, the TUC, the ILP and the Cooperative Party.[75] The
ILP replied favourably on March 13; and four days later conversations began.[76] They were not interrupted by the receipt of negative
replies to the CPGB approach from the Labour Party and from the
TUC;[77] and at the end of the month an exchange of letters between
Pollitt and the secretary of the ILP registered the modest progress
achieved. Agreement had been reached for concerted action, down
to and including May 1, on resistance to Fascism and war, and on
support for German and Austrian victims of Fascism. But the ILP
had reservations on more specific issues, such as the means test and
the supply of munitions to China: these were to be referred to its
forthcoming annual conference at Derby.[78] The decline in membership of the ILP, which had persisted since 1930,[79] had initially been
due to the ambiguity of its role within the Labour Party. But it was
now intensified by sharp divisions on the issue of relations with the
CPGB. A successful joint mass demonstration of April 2 breathed
defiance of the Labour Party and the TUC.[80] But the conversations
had masked an essential difference in purpose. A majority of the ILP
wanted joint action with the CPGB; the CPGB wanted a merger
which would mean the absorption of the ILP into the CPGB.

The hectoring tone of an appeal addressed by the CPGB to
members of the ILP on the eve of the conference which opened at
Derby on April 17, 1933, gave the moderates little chance of
blurring the issue:

[75] *Daily Worker*, March 11, 1933; *Rundschau*, No. 6, March 25, 1933, p. 150.

[76] *Daily Worker*, March 14, 18, 1933; Brockway described the friendly personal
tone of the conversations between Maxton and himself for the ILP and Pollitt and
Campbell (or Gallacher) for the CPGB. Pollitt, who was "a skilful and persuasive
negotiator", said to Maxton, whom he addressed as Jimmy: "It's all very well to
have principles, but the test of any course is its success. The CPGB has failed to
build a mass revolutionary party. So has the ILP. Together we can do it . . . unite
our forces, the ILP and the CPGB, and we can make a movement in this country
which will change history" (F. Brockway, *Inside the Left* (1942), pp. 248–249).

[77] *Daily Worker*, March 24, 1933. The Labour Party, in a letter beginning "Dear
Comrades", replied that "it was not felt necessary to meet", and that before any
discussions took place Comintern should respond to the appeal of the Second
International of February 19, 1933 for direct negotiations; the TUC, in a reply
addressed "Dear Sirs", curtly declined the invitation.

[78] *Ibid.* April 4, 1933.

[79] For figures from various sources see H. Pelling, *The British Communist Party*
(1958), p. 192.

[80] *Daily Worker*, April 3, 1933.

You are becoming more and more convinced that the Communist Party has consistently followed the path of the revolutionary mass struggle. You are asking the question: Can there be two revolutionary parties? Common sense tells you that two parties, both professing to lead the militant struggle of the workers to socialism, is an absurdity.

The ILP leadership was accused of failing to "declare for a clear revolutionary Marxist position"; and "we unhesitatingly call on all ILPers to come into the ranks of the CP, and make it a powerful section of the Communist International".[81] The debate at the conference was sharp and sometimes bitter. A motion to "approach the secretariat of the Communist International with a view to ascertaining in what way the ILP may assist in the work of the International" was carried by the narrow majority of 83 to 79.[82] The decision was regarded with misgivings by senior members of the ILP, and was followed by several resignations.

In Moscow the CPGB appeared to have scored a considerable victory. On April 30, 1933, the secretariat of IKKI telegraphed to the ILP offering direct talks, and promising that the united front would prove "a turning-point in the history of the British labour movement and would open up an international perspective for the revolutionary workers of the ILP".[83] Encouragement was forthcoming from a joint CPGB–ILP demonstration which attracted a crowd of 100,000 in Hyde Park on May 7, and applauded a declaration of its determination to fight Fascism and to support "the principle of working-class dictatorship as exhibited in the Soviet Union".[84] Discussions proceeded between the CPGB and the ILP, apparently with some holding back on the part of the latter; and on May 18, the ILP wrote in some confusion to Moscow enquiring in what form IKKI envisaged the cooperation of the ILP with Comintern.[85] The Comintern leaders took their time, and replied on June 21 in a lengthy letter of admonition. Great emphasis was

[81] *Daily Worker*, April 17, 1933.

[82] *New Leader*, April 21, 1933 (supplement); the conference, as Pollitt said at the thirteenth IKKI, "reflected the dissension which had started in the ranks of the ILP" (*XIII Plenum IKKI* (1934), p. 70).

[83] *Daily Worker*, May 3, 1933, *New Leader*, May 5, 1933, *Rundschau*, No. 12, May 5, 1933, p. 374.

[84] *Daily Worker*, May 8, 1933.

[85] F. Brockway, *Inside the Left* (1942), p. 249; the letter does not appear to have been published, but was cited in the IKKI reply of June 21.

laid not only on the practical collaboration of the ILP with the CPGB, but on the need for a total break with the Labour Party and the Second International, "the greatest social prop of the bourgeoisie in the working class". On these conditions, even though the ILP "does not at present accept the standpoint of the programme of Comintern", a "real revolutionary collaboration" with the CPGB and Comintern could be established. The writers professed to know that "many members" of the ILP were studying the Comintern programme, and hinted that this might one day lead to the formation of "a single strong mass communist party".[86]

When this missive arrived from Moscow, enthusiasm in both parties for the cause of unity was on the ebb, and reservations were being made. In the CPGB, if Pollitt had been won over whole-heartedly for the united front, Dutt shared the misgivings still felt by some stalwarts in Comintern about the new line.[87] Some members of the ILP were shocked by the cynical eagerness of the Soviet Government to maintain friendly relations with Berlin and by the renewal of the 1926 Soviet–German treaty of friendship. Brockway, in an article in the party journal in June, argued that Comintern "has become so concentrated upon what it regards as the interests of Soviet Russia that it is seriously compromising revolutionary policy in other parts of the world". Another article a fortnight later was still more explicit:

> The core of my case against the Communist International as an adequate instrument of the international working class is that it is not an International at all. It is almost exclusively the Russian Communist Party.[88]

With this mood prevailing even among leaders who had approved the approach to Moscow, the ILP returned a polite but tart reply to the letter of June 21, attributing "the present catastrophic position of the workers' movement" impartially to "the failure both of the Second International and of the Communist International". It was

---

[86] *Daily Worker*, June 26, 1933, *Rundschau*, No. 22, June 30, 1933, pp. 761–762.

[87] Dutt's "Notes of the Month" in *Labour Monthly*, No. 7, 1933, pp. 403–421, consisted of a blistering attack on social-democracy. "The chains and prison-house of Fascism" were linked with "the poison gas and stranglehold of social-democracy"; and "*the slogan of 'democracy versus dictatorship'*" was described as "*a direct slogan for the preparation of war*".

[88] *New Leader*, June 15, 30, 1933.

silent on relations with the Labour Party, but offered a continuance of collaboration in the campaign against capitalism, imperialism and war, and proposed a world congress of workers' organizations to consider the problems of collaboration "on a revolutionary-socialist basis".[89]

The summer vacation may have accounted for Comintern's delay in countering this ambiguous broadside. The answer when it came, on September 17, 1933, was long and argumentative. It emphatically rejected the proposal for a comprehensive congress for the purpose of creating "an all-embracing International"; this repeated the line of thought which had led to the formation of the ill-fated Two-and-a-half International in 1921. The customary denunciation of the Second International led up to a bitter indictment of the SPD and its capitulation to Hitler. This was followed by an attack on Brockway's "slanderous statements" about the USSR, which were "quite as bad as the anti-Soviet attacks made by Citrine at the Trades Union Congress". A clear distinction was drawn between two distinct tendencies at work in the ILP:

> Many members of the party are for the new line outlined by the Derby conference, but many leaders are for the old reformist line. . . . *In short, many members of your party are revolutionary, but many leaders are reformists.*

The one symptom of a less intransigent attitude, and of a desire to keep the negotiations alive, was that the demand for the fusion of the ILP with the CPGB was not repeated. The ILP was invited to join Comintern, under art. 18 of its statute, as a "sympathizing party" with "the right to a consultative vote".[90] But the negotiations were in fact dead, though Comintern and the CPGB were obviously determined to avoid the onus of making a break. The departure of Brockway early in October 1933 on a visit to the United States may have been responsible for a lull in the correspondence. But the tone of the *New Leader* grew less and less conciliatory. Maxton, in an article in February 1933 protesting against the refusal to admit Trotsky to Britain, had called him a "most honoured man" and the "greatest individual menace to the capitalist order".[91] In October

[89] *Daily Worker*, July 10, 1933; *Rundschau*, No. 25, July 21, 1933, p. 914.
[90] *Daily Worker*, September 23, 1932.
[91] *New Leader*, February 17, 1933.

the *New Leader* published an interview with Trotsky calling for a new International, and in the following month an article by Thalheimer on the impossibility of reforming Comintern.[92] This was a declaration of war.

The thirteenth IKKI opened in Moscow at the end of November 1933. Pollitt began his report with a long analysis of the economic crisis, followed by a fierce attack on British foreign policy.

> *The whole foreign policy of the national government* is plainly directed against America, the strongest imperialist rival of Britain, but for all that the most serious warlike preparation is being carried on against the Soviet Union.

Indulgence towards Japan and towards Hitler were key-notes of this policy. A brief warning against the "strong tendency to under-estimate the movement of the British Union of Fascists led by Sir Oswald Mosley", who was "moving quite in the footsteps of Hitler and Mussolini", led up to a bitter denunciation of the government, whose policy was "the very same policy which led Germany to the rule of Hitler"; this was "the lesson which we must bring home to the whole working class". Pollitt then turned to questions of the united front. The CPGB had approached the Labour Party, the TUC, the Cooperative Party and the ILP with a proposal for a meeting to discuss the formation of a united front. Only the ILP had accepted the invitation; and cooperation had gone no further than a few joint meetings on special occasions. A detailed and discouraging account of negotiations with the ILP during the past year ended with the usual warning against both "opportunist errors" and "Left sectarianism", and with the enigmatic admission of a tendency in the party "to consider that, in view of our work on the formation of a united front, the principal slogan of all party work, 'class against class', should be temporarily abandoned". Surprisingly, in view of Horner's record as a dissident, Pollitt hailed as a great success his election as secretary of the South Wales Miners Federation. A word of praise was reserved for the propaganda conducted by the Friends of the Soviet Union. The NUWCM, which had 40,000 paying members and 350 branches, had done good work in organizing

[92] *Ibid.* October 13, November 3, 1933.

opposition to the new government legislation on unemployment, and in preparing for a protest march and a congress to be held in February 1934. But the NUWCM had its defects. It tended to become a "trade union" of the unemployed, and to neglect the fundamental aim of revolution. Party influence in it was weak; and it did nothing to promote the formation of a united front with the reformist unions, to which it remained hostile. The report ended with a schematic enumeration of the tasks of the party, including the injunction "to win the ILP for a united communist party on the lines of the Communist International".[93]

The rest of the debate offered few consolations to the CPGB. Pyatnitsky attributed the vote of the ILP for disaffiliation from the Labour Party to the propaganda of the *Daily Worker* and the NUWCM. But his remarks about the CPGB were uniformly uncomplimentary. It had not taken advantage of the split in the ILP, or of the correspondence of Comintern with the ILP, to recruit new members. It had not exposed the manoeuvres of the ILP leaders who had availed themselves of the "counter-revolutionary services of Trotsky" to discredit Comintern.[94] Rust abjectly confessed the sins of the CPGB and lauded the wisdom of Comintern. The ILP was seeking an alliance with the Trotskyists, and wanted to set up a Two-and-a-half or a Fourth International. Gallacher also accepted Pyatnitsky's criticisms, and condemned the party for failing to "overcome reformist illusions". While praising its conformity to the Comintern line, he contrived to maintain some show of independence, and was attacked later in the debate for opposing a proposed economic boycott of Germany.[95] Heckert bitterly denounced Brockway, who for all his Left professions was hostile to the USSR and found collaborators in Trotsky, Thalheimer and Brandler; the ILP had something in common with the

[93] The original English text of Pollitt's speech is not known to exist; it was published in German in *Rundschau*, No. 4, January 13, 1934, pp. 131–142, in Russian in *XIII Plenum IKKI* (1934), pp. 56–77. The German text reads like a literal translation of the typescript from which Pollitt presumably read his speech; the Russian text probably represents what the Russian interpreter and the Russian stenographers made of a speech containing a good many unfamiliar names and references, and is helped out by snatches of Comintern vocabulary not found in the German version. The differences are in some passages substantial, but do not appear to be politically significant. The warning against Mosley's Fascist movement has oddly dropped out of the Russian text.

[94] *XIII Plenum IKKI* (1934), pp. 189–191.

[95] *Ibid.* pp. 215–217, 297–300, 303.

Neumann–Remmele group in the KPD.[96] Kuusinen in summing up also attacked Gallacher. But his strictures on the CPGB were milder than Pyatnitsky's, and his concluding exhortations purely conventional.[97] The CPGB, like other parties, emerged from this enigmatic session chastened, but without any clear directive to shape its future course.

On January 8, 1934, the council of the ILP at last replied to IKKI's letter of September 17. It accepted the principle of a united front to defend the USSR, to resist capitalism, Fascism and war, and to promote the aim of "revolutionary socialism". But it pointedly asked whether the ILP, if it affiliated to Comintern, would be free to criticize the policies of Comintern and of the CPGB; and it ended with a sharp attack on the current practices of IKKI, which, instead of applying "working-class democracy" within the International, exercised a monopoly of control over the policies and leadership of foreign parties, and had in fact substituted an exclusively Russian leadership for "a real collective international leadership". Another sensitive nerve-point was relentlessly exposed: the USSR concluded treaties of "*friendship* with governments which had distinguished themselves as the most ferocious executioners of Comintern's own members".[98] It was not an answer calculated to appease Comintern. The *Daily Worker* ironically commented that the ILP leaders, having spent most of their lives as advocates of "reformism", now "suddenly announced themselves to the world as reformers of Comintern".[99] Manuilsky seized the occasion of a speech at the seventeenth Russian party congress later in the month to bracket Brockway with Trotsky, Frossard and other renegades, and to pour scorn on his proposal to create a new International; "Lenin is not replaced by Brockwayism". Rust, who spoke as a fraternal delegate of the CPGB, accused the " 'Left'-reformist" leaders of the ILP of having "concluded an alliance with Trotsky in order to form a new International, and to provide themselves with a regular supply of anti-Soviet defamatory materials".[100]

The reply of IKKI, once more signed by Kuusinen, was despatched on February 20, 1934. The January letter of the ILP

---

[96] *Ibid.* p. 322.
[97] *Ibid.* pp. 579–580, 582; for Kuusinen's speech see p. 105 above.
[98] The letter was published in the *New Leader*, January 12, 1934.
[99] *Daily Worker*, January 9, 1934.
[100] *XVII S"ezd Vsesoyuznoi Kommunisticheskoi Partii (b)* (1934), pp. 321–322, 340.

was said to "consist for the most part of anti-communist and anti-Soviet slanders". Brockway, as the author of the letter and of numerous articles critical of Comintern, was singled out for bitter attack as "a Left-reformist pacifist" and "in full agreement with the slander campaign of the counter-revolutionary traitor Trotsky". The letter was incompatible with three major aims. It rejected the defence of the USSR against the danger of war by condemning the Soviet policy of peaceful relations with other states. It rejected the slogan of Soviet power by contrasting the dictatorship of the proletariat with "working-class democracy". It rejected the principle of centralized organization which any party sympathizing with Comintern was obliged to accept. The assumption was made throughout that the rank and file of the ILP remained faithful to the Derby conference decision to seek affiliation to Comintern, but had been diverted from its course by its reformist leaders. Brockway's comment that "the purpose of splitting the party was clearer than ever" was not unfair.[101]

The ILP held its annual conference in York on March 30–April 3, 1934. By this time disillusionment with the dictatorial tactics of Comintern and the CPGB had begun to spread from the leaders to some of the branches, notably in South Wales and Lancashire, where the communists were most active.[102] The council submitted a mildly worded resolution which, in spite of the attitude of IKKI, "which makes affiliation or sympathetic affiliation [to Comintern] impossible in present circumstances", declared the readiness of the ILP "to associate with Comintern in all efforts which, in the view of the ILP, further the revolutionary struggle of the workers"; and it committed the ILP to "approaching the two Internationals and all other sections of the working class to urge united action against Fascism, war and capitalist attacks". Several amendments were proposed: one for immediate sympathetic affiliation; another to send a delegation to Moscow to discuss the doubts of members; another to continue cooperation on the basis of the *status quo*; yet another to found a Fourth International. All these were rejected by large majorities, and the resolution was carried by 102 votes to 64.[103] The conclusion drawn by the central committee of the CPGB

[101] *Rundschau*, No. 19, March 1, 1934, pp. 701–703; F. Brockway, *Inside the Left* (1942), p. 251.

[102] F. Brockway, *Inside the Left* (1942), p. 252.

[103] The proceedings were reported in the *New Leader*, April 6, 1934; the ILP had refused to admit a "fraternal delegate" of the CPGB (*Daily Worker*, April 2, 1934),

from the conference was "the imperative necessity of strengthening the struggle against the 'Left' reformists in Britain and winning over the revolutionary workers for the class line of revolutionary struggle".[104]

The eventful year 1934 brought little encouragement to the CPGB. Its membership had not risen since 1932. A "hunger march" of the unemployed on February 24–25 culminating in a large demonstration in Hyde Park seems to have owed nothing to communist initiative. On the eve of the march, Pollitt and Mann were arrested on a charge of seditious speeches delivered a week earlier. After the demonstration they were released on bail, and the charges against them were subsequently dropped.[105] When Mosley's blackshirts staged their first mass demonstration, at Olympia on June 7, the CPGB organized a march against them. Scuffles occurred, and a few "anti-Fascists" were arrested. But, though this was hailed by the *Daily Worker* as a "great anti-Fascist victory", the demonstration was evidently more impressive than the attempts to discredit it.[106] The announcement of a blackshirt rally in Hyde Park on September 9, however, provoked a large counter-demonstration of marchers against Fascism and war, at which Pollitt spoke, and which apparently swamped the blackshirt demonstration. This was boycotted by the Labour Party.[107]

Fear of the rise of a powerful Fascist movement in Britain now began to affect the whole British Left, and not least the CPGB. Nowhere in western Europe more conspicuously than in Britain was Dimitrov accepted, in virtue of his defiance of the Nazi court, as an outstanding symbol of resistance to Fascism. The signals from Moscow were still ambiguous. But Pyatnitsky at the session of the presidium of IKKI in July 1934 grudgingly attributed such meagre success as the British party had enjoyed to the NUWCM, which "stands under the influence of the CPGB"—the one organization

---

but *Labour Monthly*, No. 41, 1934, pp. 273–279, carried a full account of the conference. The ILP Guild of Youth, which stood well to the Left of the leaders, voted for "sympathetic affiliation" to Comintern (*New Leader*, May 25, 1934).

[104] *Rundschau*, No. 25, April 12, 1934, pp. 944–945.
[105] *Daily Worker*, February 24, 26, April 13, 1934.
[106] *Ibid.* June 7, 8, 9, 1934.
[107] *Ibid.* September 10, 1934.

initiated by the CPGB which had made a successful appeal to non-communist workers.[108] Nor, in spite of past rebuffs, was the hope abandoned of wooing the allegiance of ILP members from their obdurate leaders. In August branches of the CPGB, presumably prompted from Moscow, wrote to branches of the ILP in the same locality inviting them to send delegates to the forthcoming seventh congress of Comintern, announced at this time for the latter part of 1934. The ILP wrote to the CPGB protesting against the approach to sections of the ILP as a breach of accepted procedure, but adding that an invitation to the party leadership to send a delegation to the congress would have been welcomed. The CPGB replied denying that the approach to the sections had been in any way improper, but promising that, if the ILP wished to be represented at the congress, its request would be passed on to Comintern.[109] This half-hearted exchange apparently had no sequel. The ILP journal applauded the arrangements for a meeting in Brussels between representatives of the Second and Third Internationals.[110] On October 14 the CPGB organised a protest meeting in Hyde Park against the bloody repression of striking miners in Spain; and on October 17, the CPGB and the ILP addressed a joint letter to the Foreign Secretary in support of the Spanish republican government threatened by the encroachments of Fascism.[111] But ambivalence continued to dog this uneasy relationship. In November the ILP journal reported a meeting of the ILP council with Pollitt to discuss united front tactics, but a week later published an article by Brockway once more denouncing the Soviet policies of alliance with imperialist Powers.[112]

By this time the pressure for effective united front measures in the CPGB was intense; and the remaining voices of opposition in Moscow and in the KPD were being gradually silenced. Municipal elections in many parts of Britain were due to take place on November 1, 1934. In advance of them the CPGB issued a

[108] *Rundschau*, No. 47, August 23, 1934, pp. 1957–1958; for this session see p. 134 above.

[109] For this odd episode see *Daily Worker*, August 23, 1934, *New Leader*, August 24, 1934; extracts from the ILP letter and the CPGB reply appeared in *Rundschau*, No. 50, September 13, 1934, p. 2125.

[110] *New Leader*, October 19, 1934; for this meeting see pp. 140–141 above.

[111] *Daily Worker*, October 15, 18, 1934; for events in Spain see pp. 313–317 below.

[112] *New Leader*, November 16, 23, 1934.

manifesto urging communists, in constituencies where there was no CPGB candidate, to vote for candidates of other Left parties.[113] Communist successes were few and modest; but the communist press was able to applaud sweeping Labour gains at the expense of the Conservatives. Dutt, hitherto the protagonist in the CPGB of the hard line, celebrated the occasion with an article in which he proclaimed his conversion to the new policy. The change since 1929 and 1931, when the CPGB had instructed its members to spoil their ballot papers by writing "communist" on them, was, he explained, a change of tactics, not of principle. The Labour victories at the municipal elections were the symptom of a wish for a united front. Everything now turned on the need for a united front of the working class against Fascism and the danger of war.[114] An announcement was made by the party politburo of a party congress to be held in February 1935;[115] and during the next two months the columns of the *Daily Worker* were filled with outbursts of enthusiasm for the united front.

From this time onwards the CPGB made unremitting efforts to build a united front against Fascism and the threat of war in partnership with members of other Left parties. On January 26, 1935, what was described as "a united front conference" was held in London. It was sponsored by the *Labour Monthly*, the journal edited by Dutt, but not officially by the CPGB. The chairman and the two principal speakers were members of the Labour Party. Of 257 delegates only 17 came from the CPGB, though many of the 66 trade union delegates were probably communists; 40 delegates belonged to the Labour Party, and 32 to the ILP. Public interest was great, and many would-be participants had to be turned away.[116] At this juncture the thirteenth congress of the CPGB duly assembled on February 2, 1935. Pollitt's report opened with the recognition of the menace of Fascism and war as the "keynote" of the situation; and, as the main task of the congress, the "building of the united front" was set beside the party's "historic role—the carrying through of a workers' revolution, the establishment of a

[113] *Daily Worker*, October 20, 1934.

[114] *Ibid.* November 10, 1934; the article, in token of its importance, was translated in *Rundschau*, No. 58, November 8, p. 2584. An article of similar tenour appeared in Dutt's *Labour Monthly*, No. 12, 1934, pp. 711–727.

[115] *Daily Worker*, November 10, 1934.

[116] The conference was announced in *Labour Monthly*, No. 1, 1935, p. 3; a report on it appeared *ibid.* No. 3, 1935, pp. 188–200.

workers' dictatorship and the building of a Soviet Britain". After this ritual pronouncement Pollitt turned his attention to the international scene, and praised the peace policy of the Soviet Union, though this must not be used "to build up pacifist illusions in the working class or trust in the League of Nations as an instrument to prevent war". He drew an alarming picture, backed by many quotations, of the rise of Fascism in Britain, which was not confined to Mosley's blackshirts. Hence the urgent need for the united front, which was not "a cunning manoeuvre", but in the interest of the whole working class. The electoral policy of voting for Labour candidates where no communist candidate had been put up was simply an *extension* of the united front, and implied no "support of reformism". Social-democracy was still denounced as everywhere paving the way to Fascism. The main appeal was to the rank and file of the Labour Party. But a special passage was devoted to the uneasy, but still hopeful, wooing of the ILP. In the peroration, the CPGB was hailed as "the party of Lenin, Stalin and Dimitrov".[117]

The proceedings of the congress did no more than enlarge on Pollitt's report. The other major report, by Campbell on the "economic struggles", pointed to the conclusion that it was necessary to "bring down the barrier presented by the four rebel reformist unions". No voice of dissent appears to have been heard throughout the congress.[118] The first resolution of the congress on "The Communist Party and the United Front" echoed the terms of Pollitt's report. The second carried the same message into the trade unions, calling for a campaign "for the fusion of the Red International of Labour Unions and the International Federation of Trade Unions", though it did not omit to praise the break-away United Mineworkers of Scotland, on the specious plea that it was working for "the fusion of all unions in Scotland into one union for all Scottish mine workers". The third appealed for a mass communist party, and condemned sectarianism; and the fourth was the conventional plea for the liberation of colonial and semi-colonial peoples from "foreign domination and all forms of capitalist exploitation".[119] Finally, the congress adopted a manifesto calling, in spite of the opposition of leaders of the ILP and

[117] *Harry Pollitt Speaks* (CPGB, n.d. [1935]), pp. 3–45.

[118] It was extensively reported in *Daily Worker*, February 2–6, 1935; *Kommunisticheskii Internatsional*, No. 8, pp. 11–21, printed an extract from Pollitt's closing speech.

[119] *Harry Pollitt Speaks* (CPGB, n.d. [1935]), pp. 47–79.

TUC, for a united front of workers to break the capitalist dictatorship and overthrow the National government.[120] On March 17, Pollitt attended a session of the presidium of IKKI in Moscow at which British affairs were discussed. Pollitt's line met with approval, and "the practice of putting forward demands unacceptable to Labour Party workers as conditions for unity of action" was condemned.[121] Doubts, however, had not been quite silenced. The Comintern journal in the spring of 1935 published an article by Dutt which, while not challenging the new line, recalled pronouncements of Comintern from the sixth congress of 1928 onwards, on "social-Fascism" and "the identity of bourgeois democracy with Fascism"; and this was answered in the following issue by the Netherlands communist Van Lieuw.[122] The debate was conducted in polite and highly theoretical language. But it revealed the element of muted dissent still existing within the CPGB and in Comintern.

International events once more forced the pace. When in March 1935 the decree of Hitler re-introducing conscription in Germany as part of a programme of intensive rearmament was followed by Simon's and Eden's visit to Berlin,[123] this gesture of appeasement was the occasion of much heart-searching in Left circles in Britain, and provoked a furious manifesto from the central committee of the CPGB, which deduced that "the aim of British foreign policy is war against the Soviet Union".[124] The annual conference of the ILP in April showed deep divisions on the perennial issue of relations with the CPGB; and Maxton's suggestion of "a new workers' party . . . with the ILP and the Communist Party as its central core" won no favour on either side.[125] But opinion on the Left was on the move. A second united front conference was held in May, with 311 delegates, of whom only 22 represented the CPGB;[126] and at the end of June Henderson shared the platform with Gallacher of the CPGB at a well publicized peace congress, followed by a mass meeting in Trafalgar Square.[127] These demonstrations were the

[120] *Daily Worker*, February 9, 1935.
[121] B. Leibzon and K. Shirinya, *Povorot v Politike Kominterna* (2nd ed., 1975), p. 113.
[122] *Kommunisticheskii Internatsional*, 1935, No. 10, pp. 26–45, No. 11, pp. 34–39.
[123] See p. 147 above.
[124] *Rundschau*, No. 15, March 28, 1935, p. 773.
[125] *Ibid.* No. 20, May 3, 1935, pp. 1020–1021.
[126] *Labour Monthly*, No. 6, 1935, pp. 373–386.
[127] *Daily Worker*, June 29, 1935.

starting-point of a powerful and popular campaign, directed primarily against Nazism, but not without pacifist undertones, in which Left intellectuals played a prominent part, and which eventually led many of them into the CPGB. The foundations of the popular front in Britain had been well and truly laid before the seventh congress of Comintern convened in Moscow in July 1935.[128]

[128] A CPGB resolution in preparation for the congress appeared in *Kommunisticheskii Internatsional*, 1935, No. 16–17, pp. 69–72.

CHAPTER 11

THE ITALIAN COMMUNIST PARTY (PCI)

The Italian Communist Party (PCI) was in a desperate plight at the end of 1929.[1] A harsh and powerful dictatorship crushed all its attempts to remain active in Italy. Its leadership, operating mainly from Paris, was torn by internal dissensions. At a meeting of the party politburo in September 1929 Togliatti, already suspect in Moscow of lukewarmness in dealing with Tasca and the Right, had expounded the demand of Comintern for more radical policies, and more contact with the masses, which could only mean an extension of work within Italy. These views incurred much criticism, and failed to convince a majority of the politburo. When however the central committee met, Togliatti's skill in manoeuvre once more prevailed. Portraying Tasca as a disciple of Bukharin, he pointed out that dissenters from the Comintern line would inevitably become "potential allies" of Tasca; and the committee shelved its differences in a unanimous vote for Tasca's expulsion from the party.[2] The truce was short-lived. At the end of December 1929 Longo, a supporter of Togliatti, submitted a set of drastic proposals to the party politburo. The concentration abroad of all the organs and operations of the party was to be terminated, and steps taken to bring back the headquarters of the party to Italian soil. The project was strongly resisted by Leonetti, Ravazzoli and Tresso, who begged the leaders to count the cost of such an adventure. The three found supporters in the central committee. On January 15, 1930, Silone, who lived in Switzerland and had taken no part in the discussions, submitted a memorandum, under his pseudonym Pasquini, in which, without identifying himself with the three, he argued that a return to work in Italy would be suicidal; this attitude was denounced by Togliatti's supporters as "a further development of Tasca's ideas". The rift was

[1] See *Foundations of a Planned Economy, 1926–1929*, Vol. 3, pp. 560–561.
[2] *Kommunisticheskii Internatsional*, 1930, No. 16–17, pp. 123–124 (an article written by Grieco under the pseudonym Garlandi); for Togliatti's two speeches in the committee see P. Togliatti, *Opere*, III (1973), i, 9–77. For an account from the point of view of the opposition see *Byulleten' Oppozitsii* (Paris), No. 15–16, September–October 1930, p. 40.

grave, and was embittered by personal attacks on Togliatti as an opportunist. Togliatti and several other leaders were summoned to Moscow to attend the session of the enlarged presidium of IKKI which opened on February 8, 1930.[3]

Togliatti was prominent throughout the session. He spoke on Manuilsky's report, mechanically echoing both Manuilsky's denunciation of social-democracy and his warning against phrasemaking "from the Left".[4] He delivered a long report on the PCI, humbly confessing past weaknesses and hesitations and welcoming the radicalization imposed by the new Comintern line. But he admitted that deviations still existed in the party; in particular, many comrades refused to see the imminent danger of war. Without naming Silone he referred to one comrade whose views amounted to a "liquidation of the party"; others also agreed with him and must be sternly fought.[5] The verdict was registered in a long mandatory resolution of the session on the tasks of the PCI. The tone was radical and militant. While the economic crisis was said to have bred increased dissatisfaction with Fascism, the illusion that it could be replaced by a period of bourgeois democracy was "the defeatist ideology of opportunism". What had been "placed on the agenda" was "the socialist proletarian character of the revolution". Hence the fundamental task was "to win a majority of the working class in town and country"; the danger was rift with the masses. After this unrealistic diagnosis, the central committee of the PCI was accused of failing to mobilize party opinion against Tasca's "Right-opportunist" position. Silone's memorandum constituted an "opportunist platform" pointing to the liquidation of the party. But, while the Right danger was the greatest, the party was also warned against "'Left' tendencies", which recalled Bordiga's "anarcho-liquidationist" policies. No concrete action was proposed. But the resolution was an endorsement, in terms of current Comintern vocabulary, of Togliatti's careful balancing act.[6]

[3] P. Spriano, *Storia del Partito Comunista Italiano*, ii (1969), 239–244.

[4] P. Togliatti, *Opere*, III (1973), i, 148–158; for Manuilsky's report see p. 9 above.

[5] P. Togliatti, *Opere*, III (1973), i, 159–187; *Kommunisticheskii Internatsional*, 1930, No. 7, pp. 28–40.

[6] *Kommunisticheskii Internatsional v Dokumentakh* (1933), pp. 934–944. Silone (*alias* Pasquini) was the only dissident named in the resolution; this doubtless prompted Grieco's not quite correct remark that he "became, perhaps against his will, the leader of the new opposition" (*Kommunisticheskii Internatsional*, 1930, No. 16–17, p. 127).

He celebrated his victory in a defiant closing speech:

> It is said that no majority exists in our central committee. Yes, comrades, it does exist; but, if there were no majority in our central committee—a majority for the line of Comintern and of all its sections—it would be created.[7]

The return of the delegates from Moscow was followed by a tense session of the party central committee held at Liège on March 20–23, 1930. The dissentients made a direct attack on Togliatti, whom they accused of "adventurism" and of outrunning even the behests of IKKI (he had raised the slogan of the "political mass strike"). The proceedings ended in the rout of the opposition. Tresso, Leonetti and Ravazzoli were expelled from the politburo, Silone from the central committee, and Bordiga, who was still in prison in Italy, from the party.[8] But all that remained of Longo's original project to transfer party activities to Italian soil was a decision to send Camilla Ravera into Italy to organize party cells. She survived there for less than two months before being picked up by the police, and sentenced to fifteen years' imprisonment.[9] Communist work in the trade unions, like other party work in Italy, was at a standstill. But a communist rump of the Confederazione Generale del Lavoro (CGL), firmly dissociated, not only from the majority of the unions under D'Arragona which had sought an accommodation with the Fascist regime, but from the anti-Fascist CGL under Buozzi in Paris which was affiliated to the Amsterdam International, was represented for the first time at the fifth congress of Profintern in Moscow in August 1930, where its principal delegate described "the various phases of the struggle of capitalism and of social-democracy against the Italian proletariat" as "an instructive example for the workers of all countries".[10]

---

[7] P. Togliatti, *Opere*, III (1973), i, 188–193; *Kommunisticheskii Internatsional*, 1930, No. 7, pp. 40–43.

[8] *Internationale Presse-Korrespondenz*, No. 36, April 25, 1930, pp. 825–826; further details are in P. Spriano, *Storia del Partito Comunista Italiano*, ii (1969), 246–250, and in Grieco's article in *Kommunisticheskii Internatsional*, 1930, No. 16–17, pp. 130–131, which reproached the PCI with sluggishness (*zapazdanie*) in carrying out Comintern decisions. No proceedings of the session were published.

[9] A. Gobetti, *Camilla Ravera: Vita in Carcere e al Confino* (1969), pp. 50–54.

[10] *Protokoll des V Kongresses der Roten Gewerkschaftsinternationale* (1930), i, 203–204; for the split in the CGL see *Foundations of a Planned Economy, 1926–1929*, Vol. 3, pp. 543–546.

These depressing conditions, so far at variance with the optimistic boasts and exhortations of Comintern, deepened the rift caused by the sanctions against the dissidents, who evidently enjoyed much sympathy in the party. In April 1930 Leonetti, Ravazzoli and Tresso approached Rosmer, Trotsky's foremost French supporter; and on April 25 *Vérité*, the French opposition journal, published the first of three articles attacking the PCI leadership which, though signed by a new pen-name, were recognizably the work of Leonetti.[11] On May 5 the three wrote directly to Trotsky.[12] This was a burning of boats. At an enlarged session of the central committee on June 9, Tresso—Leonetti and Ravazzoli having already been expelled from the committee—made a defiant declaration; and the three were duly expelled from the party, Tresso recording the only adverse vote. Comintern in its new mood of moderation, or perhaps piqued that Togliatti had taken the matter into his own hands and not awaited instructions, was uneasy at the decision, and would have liked further discussion with the three. Togliatti was summoned to Moscow in July to attend the session of an Italian commission of IKKI.[13]

Togliatti delivered his report on July 19, 1930, to a highly critical audience. He was frequently interrupted by searching questions from Manuilsky, and from time to time also by Molotov, Stepanov and Vasiliev. He attempted to paint a reassuring picture of the state of the PCI. The "new turn" had been almost achieved, party activity had increased; "great organizational work" had been undertaken. By way of contrast Togliatti exaggerated—perhaps deliberately—the "extremely grave" situation of the past winter, when the split in the leadership made "common work" impossible, and paralysed the party apparatus which "reeled" under the blow. Now the three main dissidents had formed a bloc with Trotsky; they were " no longer comrades guilty of a deviation, but counter-

[11] P. Spriano, *Storia del Partito Comunista Italiano*, ii (1969), 257–258; this open act of defiance was reported to Comintern on April 30 (P. Togliatti, *Opere*, III (1973), i, 277).

[12] The letter does not appear to have been published; but Trotsky published his reply of May 24 some months later in *Byulleten' Oppozitsii* (Paris), No. 15–16, September–October 1930, pp. 35–38. He welcomed the prospect of cooperation with them, but disclaimed any special knowledge of Italian affairs; he expressed the view that "*Fascism has not liquidated social-democracy, but has on the contrary preserved it*", and that social-democracy might have a role to play in overthrowing it.

[13] P. Spriano, *Storia del Partito Comunista Italiano*, ii (1969), 259–261.

revolutionaries"—a "segment of a counter-revolutionary formation, the Trotskyist opposition". Their expulsion had been delayed as long as possible, but was inevitable; if they had been summoned to Moscow, they would have refused to come. Togliatti ended with a plea to his judges to understand the position of the PCI as an illegal party.[14]

Manuilsky made a sour reply, designed largely to expose the deficiencies of the PCI, which was "completely isolated from the [workers'] movement". In phrases which recalled his criticism a year earlier of the CPGB, he now described the PCI as consisting of "closed circles of friends, evidently old comrades", of groups formed "on a basis of personal acquaintance". He did not share Togliatti's optimism that the expulsion of the three would strengthen party work. He praised the party leaders for raising the question of the mass political strike, but thought that they had done so "too abstractly". The familiar keynote of the speech was the need for contact with the masses. But Manuilsky did not broach the vexed question of the transfer of the party organization to Italy.[15] The *fait accompli* of the expulsions had to be accepted. Togliatti had scored his point.[16] The verdict was made all the more inescapable by the publication in *Vérité*, while Togliatti was away in Moscow, of an "open letter of the new Italian opposition" signed by the three and by Recchia (*alias* Teresa), who was still a candidate member of the party central committee. The writers denounced "*the profoundly false and opportunist*" line of the party leaders, and the policies and methods of Comintern. They rejected the prognosis of an immediate and inevitable transition in Italy from Fascism to the dictatorship of the proletariat. They demanded free discussion of disputed questions in the party, and the re-instatement of those expelled in the past for defending Bordiga's position (though not apparently of

[14] P. Togliatti, *Opere*, III (1973), i, 248–280.

[15] *Kommunisticheskii Internatsional*, No. 22 (252), 1930, pp. 38–49; other speeches must have been delivered, but were not published or reported. For Manuilsky's criticism of the CPGB see *Foundations of a Planned Economy, 1926–1929*, Vol. 3, p. 392.

[16] The personal bitterness between Manuilsky and Togliatti engendered by these exchanges is shown in a letter of September 22, 1930, from Berti, who had succeeded Grieco as delegate of the PCI in Moscow, and Togliatti's reply of October 15, 1930; Manuilsky had called the PCI "the party of Machiavelli", and Togliatti protested that the "brutality" of Comintern had aggravated the crisis in the PCI due to the "turn" to the Left and the expulsion for the three (quoted from the party archives in the introduction to P. Togliatti, *Opere*, III (1973), i, pp. xcv–xcvii).

Bordiga himself, whose expulsion they themselves had so recently endorsed); and they declared their solidarity with "*the international Left opposition*".[17]

The expulsions were a blow to a divided and dispirited party, and left behind them a bitterness which was felt for many years to come.[18] The dissidents clearly enjoyed much popularity and support in the party, and the accumulation of authority in Togliatti's hands was increasingly resented. Gramsci and Terracini, serving long sentences in a Fascist prison,[19] both expressed sympathy with the rebels, and indignation at their precipitate expulsion.[20] The open defiance of the party by the expelled dissidents strengthened Togliatti's position. His precarious relations with Comintern in the past two years were succeeded by slow growth, if not of mutual confidence, at least of mutual toleration. He was recognized in Moscow as irreplaceable if discipline and cohesion were to be maintained in the troublesome PCI; and he for his part accepted the obligation of unconditional submission to the rulings of Comintern, though he sought to retain a measure of independence by restricting to a minimum his involvement in the affairs of Comintern or of other parties. On one point his orthodoxy was unimpeachable. He applauded without reservation the achievements of the Soviet regime, and proclaimed with enthusiasm the duty of communists everywhere to rally to the defence of the USSR.[21]

[17] An abbreviated translation of the letter appeared in *Byulleten' Oppozitsii* (Paris), No. 15–16, September–October 1930, pp. 39–44.

[18] P. Spriano, *Storia del Partito Comunista Italiano*, ii (1969), 262–286.

[19] See *Foundations of a Planned Economy, 1926–1929*, Vol. 3, pp. 540, 549.

[20] According to a story related many years later, Gramsci's brother Gennaro visited him in prison in July 1930 and gave him the news of the expulsions; but, on his return to Paris, he deemed it prudent to suppress his brother's hostile reaction, and simply told Togliatti that Gramsci agreed with him (G. Fiori, *Antonio Gramsci* (Engl. transl. 1970), pp. 252–253; the original Italian work was published in 1965). If Togliatti had nevertheless some inkling of the truth, this would help, together with Gramsci's letter of October 1926 (see *Foundations of a Planned Economy, 1926–1929*, Vol. 3, pp. 536–537), to account for the disappearance of Gramsci's name from party and Comintern literature for many years. An article by Togliatti of January 1931 celebrating the tenth anniversary of the PCI and reviewing its history did not mention Gramsci (P. Togliatti, *Opere*, III (1973), i, 311–323). For Terracini's letter to the party see P. Spriano, *Storia del Partito Comunista Italiano*, ii (1969), 263–265; both imprisoned leaders resented the imposition on the PCI by Comintern of "third period" policies unsuited to it, and did not recognize the pressures which induced Togliatti to submit to them.

[21] P. Togliatti, *Opere*, III (1973), i, 302–307.

It may have been the desire to avoid another confrontation with Manuilsky which impelled Togliatti to absent himself from the eleventh IKKI which met in Moscow at the end of March 1931. Grieco, the sole Italian delegate, while professing complete agreement with Manuilsky's report, contrived to give a radical turn to his speech. Reaffirming the hard line of the "third period" proclaimed by the sixth congress and the tenth IKKI, he deprecated talk of a "new formula" or a "fourth period". He denounced the "opportunists" in the politburo who had now been expelled from the party, linking them with Tasca. He welcomed the formula of "the transformation of the economic crisis into a revolutionary crisis"; and in conclusion he expressed disapproval of "some of our comrades" who foresaw the possibility of "an interval between the fall of Fascism and the struggle of the proletariat", i.e. a return to bourgeois democracy.[22] The speech was not very well received. Manuilsky reproached Grieco with holding that Fascism was an historically inevitable stage of the bourgeois dictatorship, and could be overthrown only when capitalism was destroyed. This discouraged the mobilisation of the proletariat for "partial battles" which might weaken the Fascist regime and wring from the bourgeoisie concessions to the oppressed masses.[23] The PCI was barely mentioned in the resolutions of the eleventh IKKI, and was the only major party not represented in the debate on the war danger. But Grieco was duly re-elected to the presidium at the end of the session; and Togliatti was elected in his absence to the political secretariat.[24] Nothing irretrievable had happened.

A fourth congress of the PCI, its first since the Lyons congress of January 1926,[25] was held in great secrecy in April 1931 near Cologne. It was attended by 56 delegates, of whom 28 managed to arrive from Italy; but Secchia, the youth leader, who had been sent into Italy to organize the operation, was caught by the police.[26] Heckert was present as Comintern delegate. Togliatti made the

[22] *XI Plenum IKKI* (1932), i, 305–314.

[23] *Ibid.* i, 602, 609.

[24] *Ibid.* ii, 246; Togliatti had lost his membership of the political secretariat at the eighth IKKI in 1927 (*Desyat' Let Kominterna v Tsifrakh* (1929), pp. 327–328), at which his attitude had left much to be desired (see *Foundations of a Planned Economy, 1926–1929*, Vol. 3, pp. 146–147).

[25] See *Socialism in One Country, 1924–1926*, Vol. 3, pp. 369–371.

[26] P. Secchia, *L'Azione Svolta dal Partito Comunista in Italia* (1970), p. 379; according to this account the number of persons belonging to the underground "centre" in Italy at this time was only about 30 (*ibid.* p. 375).

main report, and once more condemned opportunism, explaining that there could be no return to bourgeois democracy in Italy. He was, however, duly cautious about the early prospects of proletarian revolution. Silone was once more denounced for his temporizing attitude and his refusal to submit unreservedly to party decisions. Shortly after the congress, by arrangement between the PCI and the Swiss party, in which as a resident in Switzerland he was now registered, he was expelled from the party.[27] But the PCI was evidently still regarded with some mistrust in Comintern, and Togliatti was once more summoned to Moscow to report to the Latin secretariat. This he did on July 15–16, 1931. He expressed confidence in the success of the congress and the prospects of the party. After the expulsion of the three, "the little group of opportunists" had "completely disappeared from the political scene". At the time of the congress in April party membership had numbered 4500; it had now risen to 5700 or 6000. On the united front, Togliatti pressed the distinction between social-democratic leaders and workers, and wanted cooperation with workers who were anti-Fascist "in an instinctive way".[28] No record of the meeting was published. It may be assumed that Togliatti's report was received with equanimity, though without enthusiasm. A resolution was passed instructing the party to work in "Fascist mass organizations"; this was described as the way to overcome "sectarianism", and bring the PCI closer to the masses. But it was later alleged that little had been done to carry out these ambitious directives.[29]

It was probably on this occasion that pressure was put on Togliatti in Moscow to come out publicly in support of the decision that the KPD should take part in the plebiscite of August 9, 1931, on the demand for the dissolution of the Prussian Landtag.[30] Togliatti was clearly reluctant to become involved, and may have secretly doubted the wisdom of the decision, but could not refuse what was

[27] P. Spriano, *Storia del Partito Comunista Italiano*, ii (1969), 308–324. No record of the congress was published; but a summary of the proceedings, together with abbreviated versions of Togliatti's report and reply to the debate, appear in P. Togliatti, *Opere*, III (1973), i, 341–353.

[28] *Ibid.* III, i, 362–399.

[29] *Die Kommunistische Internationale vor dem VII Weltkongress* (1935), p. 283; the principal organizations in question were the trade unions, the Dopolavoro and the cooperatives.

[30] See p. 42 above.

tantamount to an order. A short unsigned article appeared in the issue of the party journal *Stato Operaio* for July–August endorsing the action of the KPD. But doubts were expressed when the central committee of the PCI met in August; and on September 3, Togliatti unburdened himself in a letter to Dozza, the delegate of the PCI in Moscow, the substance of which was doubtless intended for communication to the Comintern secretariat. He was apologetic about the slight and "superficial" article in *Stato Operaio*, but complained that the PCI had not sufficient information to take a stand; nor had it been realized that the question was so important that other sections of Comintern were required to pronounce on it.[31] The same blend of formal compliance and non-committal caution was exhibited in an anonymous article in *Stato Operaio* on Stalin's letter of October 1931 to *Proletarskaya Revolyutsiya*. The writer (undoubtedly Togliatti) praised the letter extravagantly, but failed to discuss its contents in detail, treating it in general terms as directed "against ideological contraband" and against any relaxation of "the ideological purity of the party".[32]

Togliatti's prudent reluctance to involve the PCI in controversial issues was never more marked than in the first months of 1932. Articles on the Japanese aggression in Manchuria, on the futilities of the disarmament conference and on the struggle against imperialist war[33] were safe ground. But this could not divert attention from the desperate plight of the party in Italy. In March 1932 Longo reported to the party central committee that the party really existed only in Emilia and Tuscany; of its 5000 members only 300 were workers in factories employing over 100 workers. In the same month all the members of the Centro Interno were arrested, and received long prison sentences. The PCI had become not an underground party, but a party in prison.[34] On May 4, 1932, Togliatti wrote a letter in the name of the party central committee to party members imprisoned in Ponza commenting on the affairs of the party. He referred to the fourth party congress held a year earlier, denounced the oppositionists who had been expelled, and cited the letter of

[31] The article is in P. Togliatti, *Opere*, III (1973), i, 404–409. The letter to Dozza is quoted *ibid*. III, i, pp. ci–cvi; in the same letter Togliatti criticized Thorez's policy in the PCF, which was causing concern in Moscow (see pp. 170–171 above) but expressed doubt about the wisdom of publishing an article about it.

[32] *Ibid*. III, i, 451–456; for Stalin's letter see Note A, pp. 428–432 below.

[33] P. Togliatti, *Opere*, III (1973), ii, 14–22, 41–51.

[34] P. Spriano, *Storia del Partito Comunista Italiano*, ii (1949), 352–355.

"comrade Stalin, the head of the International". A few weeks later he managed to send through secret channels a reply to a letter which Terracini had smuggled out of prison, and which evidently expressed concern at the discussions and expulsions in the party. Togliatti pleaded that Terracini did not realize what had happened to some former Russian and foreign party leaders. The role of individuals must not be exalted above the party line; and the elimination of deviators was a source not of weakness but of strength.[35] It was at best a half-truth. But Togliatti never wavered in his conviction that defiance of Comintern was not a viable alternative. By outward show of total subservience to Moscow Togliatti did succeed in preserving a certain independence for the PCI in Italian affairs, and staving off Manuilsky's frequent attempts to intervene. Togliatti was the only leader of an important party who was not a nominee of Comintern.

Meanwhile preparations were going forward in Moscow for the twelfth IKKI due to be held later in the summer. On April 17, 1932, Dozza, prompted no doubt by Comintern officials, wrote to the secretariat of the PCI in Paris complaining of the "isolation" and "nationalism" of the party which seemed to remain "apart". It should contribute articles to Comintern journals, send delegates to congresses of other parties, and in general participate in the work of Comintern. The PCI had given offence by sending Jacopo, a junior member of its central committee, and not Togliatti or Grieco, to represent it at the session of the central committee of the KPD in February 1932. Togliatti in reply pleaded the practical problems: lack of adequate information, lack of time, lack of personnel.[36] But behind these excuses Comintern not unjustly suspected Togliatti's wily determination to avoid involvement in the controversies which were dividing other parties. Three Italian delegates attended the peace congress at Amsterdam in August 1932.[37] But the interest of the PCI in the anti-war campaign had always been minimal.

When the twelfth IKKI met at the end of August 1932, Kuusinen mildly reproved the PCI for the weakness of its work among the masses, especially in the trade unions; and Manuilsky distinguished Fascism in "semi-agrarian" Italy, where it had been able to crush

[35] P. Togliatti, *Opere*, III (1973), ii, 59–85; it is not clear whether Togliatti was replying to Terracini's letter of 1930 protesting against the expulsions (see p. 244, note 20 above), or to a more recent letter.

[36] P. Togliatti, *Opere*, III (1973), i, pp. lxxxiii–lxxxiv.

[37] P. Spriano, *Storia del Partito Comunista Italiano*, ii (1969), 372.

the workers' movement in a few months, from Fascism in Germany with its large proletariat and powerful communist party.[38] Togliatti was on the defensive. He began by briefly excusing the alleged isolation of the PCI from other parties and from Comintern on the score of its illegal status. He referred in general terms to "opportunist survivals" after the sixth congress, which had led to parties being "taken unawares" by the "mass movement". Much of his speech was devoted to the differences between Italian and German Fascism. The sixth congress had said that "Italian Fascism . . . created the classic type of a Fascist regime". But Lenski's reference to Italian Fascism as "classic Fascism" was questionable, and led to errors in the assessment of the German situation. Trotsky, for example, treated the Papen regime as "a state *coup* (perevorot), half plebeian, half military and dynastic, like the march on Rome", and conducted "a propaganda of panic, defeatism and provocation . . . in different countries". (Togliatti, when he found himself in an embarrassing position, often extricated himself by attacking Trotsky.) In Germany Togliatti predicted that "we are on the eve of civil war", and that "the KPD may face rapid development and sudden overturns". Clearly no such prospect existed in Italy. Togliatti concluded by admitting three mistakes of the PCI: weakness in united front tactics, a too defensive attitude which failed to prepare for revolutionary action, and a belief, now said to be eradicated, that Fascism would discredit and destroy itself.[39] The resolution adopted at the end of the session briefly urged the PCI "to come out of the deep underground by developing a mass struggle against the Fascist dictatorship", and "to strengthen mass illegal work", infiltrating Fascist organizations,

[38] *XII Plenum IKKI* (1933), i, 36, 161–162.

[39] Togliatti spoke in French; an Italian version of the speech is in the archives of the PCI (P. Togliatti, *Opere*, III (1973), ii, 104–128), a Russian version in the official record of the session (*XII Plenum IKKI* (1933), i, 168–177). The Russian version omits some passages in the Italian version, including the apologia for the isolation of the PCI, and Togliatti's endorsement of the attack on Humbert-Droz (see p. 285 below); and unnamed "comrades" (and not Lenski personally, as in the Italian version) are credited in the Russian version with the erroneous view of Italian Fascism. On the other hand, some passages in the Italian version are elaborated in greater detail in the Russian version. Togliatti may have had the opportunity to correct his text for the official publication. Excerpts from the speech appeared in the September number of *Stato Operaio* under the title "Against False Analogies between the German and the Italian Situation".

including the "bogus trade unions".[40] It was not a very realistic
programme.

The winter of 1932–1933, which witnessed the death agony of the
Weimar republic, brought no mitigation of the sufferings of the
PCI; and events in Germany made little impact on it. It was not till
March 3, after the Reichstag fire and its sequel, that Togliatti broke
silence in the party journal. He found the roots of Hitler's victory in
the Versailles treaty and in the "fifteen-year-old policy of social-
democracy", linking the defeat with the notorious betrayal of
August 4, 1914. Nobody but the counter-revolutionary Trotsky,
"blinded by his anti-communist hatred", could believe that social-
democracy would fight Fascism. The article was remarkable only
for its ostentatious praise of the KPD, "about whose heroic
tenacious struggle we are just beginning to learn", and for the
virulence of its abuse of Trotsky and of the social-democrats.
Togliatti would go to any lengths in seeking the favour of Moscow
on an issue which involved no commitment relating to the PCI.[41] A
few days later the response of Comintern, grudging but not wholly
negative, to an appeal from the Second International for a united
front against Fascism[42] reached Paris. On March 10, Togliatti
submitted to the party politburo a draft appeal to Italian socialists
for a united front. Less controversy seems to have been excited by
the proposed text than by the question of to whom it should be
addressed. The decision was taken to address it to all parties and
groups of the Left, and it was issued in this form on March 14.[43] But
this did not deter Togliatti from publishing at the beginning of April
a further article on "The Ruin of Social-democracy", which
attacked both the Right-wing socialists led by Nenni and the Left-
wing group led by Roselli, whose journal *Giustizia e Libertà*,
published in Paris, had become a rallying point for Left-wing

[40] *Kommunisticheskii Internatsional v Dokumentakh* (1933), p. 980.

[41] P. Togliatti, *Opere*, III (1973), ii, 176–184. In a further article in July
Togliatti again tried to rescue the KPD from the contempt heaped on it by Trotsky
and others, and reverted to his favourite theme of the difference between Italian
and German Fascism; German Fascism had been far more of a mass movement,
and it had been infinitely more difficult for the German than for the Italian
working class to fight Fascism (*ibid.* III, ii, 225–235).

[42] See p. 85 above.

[43] P. Spriano, *Storia del Partito Comunista Italiano*, ii (1969), 377.

intellectuals.[44] Mussolini doubtless drew encouragement from Hitler's triumph. The spring and summer of 1933 was a period of fierce repression, of mass arrests and trials of communists, which virtually extinguished the party as a force on Italian soil.[45]

The persecution of Italian communists did not diminish either the eagerness of Comintern to sow dissension between the two Fascist dictatorships,[46] or the efforts of the Soviet Government to improve its relations with Italy. A trade agreement was signed on May 6, 1933, with a mutual exchange of compliments between Mussolini and the Soviet Ambassador;[47] and this was followed on September 2 by the signature of a non-aggression treaty on the lines of the Franco–Soviet treaty of the previous year, its main clause providing that neither party should enter into any international agreement designed to impose economic or financial restrictions on the trade of the other.[48] It was an affair of no great consequence, but it served as a debating point in the feud between socialists and communists. Nenni at the conference of the Second International in August 1933 asked whether Moscow, "having concluded pacts of friendship with Mussolini's Italy, Pilsudski's Poland and Hitler's Germany, could refuse to conclude a pact of friendship with the socialist workers". But the conference rejected Nenni's proposal to approach Comintern once again with a proposal for a joint conference to organize a common campaign against Fascism, and adopted an anodyne resolution to "use all appropriate means to encourage a united front".[49]

Though Togliatti did not hesitate to denounce Nenni, and to hail the Italian treaty as "one of a series of brilliant successes in Soviet foreign policy",[50] the PCI continued to enjoy scant credit in Moscow. At an acrimonious meeting of the Italian commission of IKKI in November 1933, Pyatnitsky and the youth leader Chemodanov criticized the passivity of the PCI, and Togliatti tartly

[44] P. Togliatti, *Opere*, III (1973), ii, 185–192.

[45] P. Spriano, *Storia del Partito Comunista Italiano*, ii (1969), 398–407; the report of IKKI to the seventh congress of Comintern referred to "the extraordinarily severe blow" suffered by the PCI "in the middle of 1933" (*Die Kommunistische Internationale vor dem VII Weltkongress* (1935), p. 284).

[46] For the use of the question of the South Tirol for this purpose see p. 24 above.

[47] *Dokumenty Vneshnei Politiki SSSR*, xvi (1970), 284–287.

[48] *Ibid.* xvi, 494–496; for the Franco–Soviet treaty of 1931 see p. 44 above.

[49] J. Braunthal, *History of the International*, ii (Engl. transl. 1967), 400–401; for this conference see p. 94 above.

[50] P. Togliatti, *Opere*, III (1977), ii, 251–254.

rejoined that "when comrade Chemodanov says that our task is to break the power of the state . . . and create Soviets, what he says is correct, but he is only making propaganda".[51] At the thirteenth IKKI, which opened at the end of November, Vasiliev, a member of the Comintern secretariat, again blamed the central committee of the PCI for its neglect of underground party cells in Italy, where activity had rapidly declined.[52] But Italy and the PCI attracted little or no attention in the debates or in the resolution adopted at the end of the session. The interminable discussions about the nature of Fascism revolved, not unnaturally, round its German manifestation. Togliatti's long speech characteristically evaded practical issues, and conformed to current Comintern orthodoxies. He stressed once more the differences between German and Italian Fascism. He denounced Neumann and Remmele, Nenni and Trotsky. He rejected both the view that Nazism was "a form of dictatorship of the petty bourgeoisie or the lumpenproletariat", and the view that it was an intermediate stage between capitalism and socialism. He was fulsomely laudatory of the KPD; Hitler's rise to power had "compelled it to retreat, but not shattered it". He concluded by offering to the PCI and the Italian proletariat "*the German prospect*, the prospect of the growing influence of the communist party, the prospect of broader and broader mass battles, in which our party will know how to take its place". Grieco, speaking more briefly, also claimed that "the influence of the party is growing".[53] Nobody contested these comforting illusions, though a Profintern delegate later in the debate spoke of "*the loss of years*, during which our Italian comrades, in spite of timely and exhaustive resolutions of Comintern and Profintern, were quite unable to understand and recognize the need to work within Fascist trade unions".[54]

Events in France and Austria in February 1934 heralded a new Fascist offensive. Togliatti in an article in March on "The March of Fascism in France" blamed the "paralysing" and "nefarious"

[51] P. Spriano, *Storia del Partito Comunista Italiano*, ii (1969), 407–408, quoting archives; the long resolution of the party central committee in *Rundschau*, No. 43, November 17, 1933, pp. 1669–1674, was presumably a sequel of this discussion.

[52] *XIII Plenum IKKI* (1934), p. 414.

[53] *XIII Plenum IKKI* (1934), pp. 92–104, 271; on the day on which Grieco spoke, Litvinov had a friendly meeting with Mussolini in Rome (*Dokumenty Vneshnei Politiki SSSR*, xvi (1970), 712–714).

[54] *XIII Plenum IKKI* (1934), p. 452.

influence of the SFIO for the attempted Fascist *coup*; that influence had now, however, been "liquidated" thanks to the courageous action of the PCF.[55] But progress was slow and reluctant. A long resolution of the party central committee endorsed the conclusions of the thirteenth IKKI, denounced the corporate state, Fascism and preparations for war, but said nothing to conciliate the socialists;[56] and a declaration of May 26, 1934, which reverted to the theme of the united front, continued to attack them for their collaboration with the capitalists.[57] But the tide in Moscow was now setting towards a new approach—for Italy as for France. At a meeting of the Latin secretariat of Comintern in May 1934 (Dozza and Gennari being present, but not Togliatti), Manuilsky launched a ferocious attack on the failure of the PCI to conduct an effective struggle against Fascism. The party membership had fallen from 7000 in 1932 to 2400; the reprisals of 1933 had struck deep. The party was cut off from the masses: "You are *émigrés* even when you are in your own country". Pyatnitsky capped Manuilsky's epigram by calling the PCI "a terrorist group without the terrorism". Nothing was left for the Italian delegates but to abase themselves, and confess to the sectarian errors of their past record.[58] It was a particularly brutal way of formulating the demand to set a new course.

The gradual evolution of the PCI, as of other parties, towards the united front must be read in the light of the rapidly changing international scene. In June 1934 Mussolini and Hitler had a historic meeting in Venice, which laid the foundation of what came to be known as the "Rome–Berlin axis". The smooth development of the alliance was momentarily interrupted by rivalry over the fate of Austria. On July 24, the Austrian Chancellor, Dollfuss, a *protégé* of Mussolini, who manifestly preferred Italian to German patronage, was assassinated by Austrian Nazis.[59] Mussolini, suspecting an attempt at a Nazi take-over, ostentatiously moved troops up to the Austrian frontier; and threats of war circulated round Europe. Hitler, whatever his original intentions may have been, preferred

[55] P. Togliatti, *Opere*, III (1973), ii, 363–373.

[56] *Rundschau*, No. 28, May 3, 1934, pp. 1059–1061, No. 29, May 9, 1934, pp. 1113–1114, No. 30, May 17, 1934, p. 1160.

[57] P. Spriano, *Storia del Partito Comunista Italiano*, ii (1969), 390, note 4.

[58] *Ibid.* ii, 408–409; this was evidently the meeting on which Grieco reported somewhat later to members of the party in prison in Ponza (*ibid.* ii, 410).

[59] See p. 279 below.

caution, disowned the *coup* against Dollfuss, and sent Papen as ambassador to Vienna to mend relations. Togliatti speculated on the possibility of Mussolini drawing closer to France as a counter-weight to his involvement with Hitler.[60] But no such movement occurred. The alliance was still too valuable to both dictators to be jeopardized; and Hitler postponed his designs on Austria for another four years.

It was in these conditions that progress was slowly made in the PCI towards acceptance of the principle of the united front. At the end of June 1934 a firm directive had been given by Comintern to the PCF to seek an accommodation with French socialists;[61] and in the following month Togliatti, in an article in the party journal entitled "For Unity of Action of the Proletariat", signalled a significant change of mood in the PCI. The successes of the united front in France had had "an enormous resonance". The congress of the SFIO had accepted by an overwhelming majority the proposal of the PCF for an alliance which would represent "the most important moment in the development of the class struggle in France and in Europe". Had such common action been taken in Germany on July 20, 1932, or January 30, 1933, Fascism could not have triumphed; the failure was due to the refusal of the social-democrats. Togliatti drew the moral for Italy:

> *We want to realize the united front.* We sincerely believe that the PSI feels the importance and the urgency of uniting the forces of all Italian proletarians against Fascism and against war. . . . *Our intention is to do everything to make a firm pact of common action with the PSI.*[62]

A meeting between Longo and Nenni at the end of July 1934 produced a joint manifesto pledging the PCI and the PSI to "oppose with all their might the crime of war"; this was published in the press of both parties. After further negotiations a pact for common action was signed on August 17, 1934. This admitted the existence of "fundamental divergences of doctrine, tactics and method", which did not, however, preclude cooperation to resist Fascism and war.

[60] *Rundschau*, No. 51, September 20, 1934, pp. 2197–2198.
[61] See p. 194 above.
[62] P. Togliatti, *Opere*, III (1973), ii, 399–403; for a further article in praise of the united front in France see *ibid*. III, ii, 413–417.

The difficulties of reaching even this tentative agreement were shown by two separate declarations made respectively by the parties to it. The PSI noted that the PCI had "broken with the theory of social-Fascism". The PCI, while affirming its commitment to common action in the future, recalled the past collaboration of the PSI with "bourgeois forces".[63] As Togliatti wrote a few weeks later, communists in the interests of the united front could make "some concessions of form, but never of *principle*, never of *content*".[64] Grieco in a letter of September 5, 1934, to party members in prison defended the "new line" as the product of self-criticism in face of rebukes in the IKKI commission. The pact with the PSI had been concluded on the French model and "for certain limited objectives". Grieco presented the agreement not as a change of front but as an enlargement of the old "common action from below." The breaking of the ice between communist and socialist workers would encourage "the conquest of a majority of the proletariat by the PCI".[65] In the first months of 1935 the Rome–Berlin axis was confirmed and strengthened, and a new configuration began to emerge in world affairs. The two Fascist regimes confronted an anti-Fascist front consisting of France and Britain, with the United States in the background, to which the USSR was rapidly gravitating. But the immediate result of these developments was to magnify the determination and the ruthlessness of Mussolini's rule; and they brought no relief to the exiled and impotent PCI. Togliatti played a prominent part at the seventh congress of Comintern in July–August 1935. But the PCI was less concerned than any other major party in the changed policies proclaimed by it.

[63] P. Spriano, *Storia del Partito Comunista Italiano*, ii (1969), 393–394; the texts are in *Rundschau*, No. 49, September 6, 1934, pp. 2075–2077.

[64] P. Togliatti, *Opere*, III (1973), ii, 448. According to B. Leibzon and K. Shirinya, *Povorot v Politike Kominterna* (2nd ed., 1975), p. 84, the parties differed on "questions of the overthrow of the Fascist dictatorship and the creation of a new regime"; Manuilsky at the thirteenth IKKI had rejected "the opinion that a Fascist dictatorship can be replaced only by a proletarian dictatorship" (*XIII Plenum IKKI* (1934), p. 315).

[65] P. Spriano, *Storia del Partito Comunista Italiano*, ii (1969), pp. 410–411.

CHAPTER 12

THE POLISH COMMUNIST PARTY (KPP)

While the Polish economy wilted under the first impact of the world crisis, the storms of the nineteen-twenties in the Polish party were succeeded, after the settlement imposed at the sixth plenum of its central committee in June 1929,[1] by a spurious calm in its affairs. The docility of its leader, Lenski, matched that of Thälmann and Thorez. The seventh plenum of its central committee in February 1930 drew some satisfaction from the growing impact of the economic crisis in Poland. It dutifully recited the formulas just prescribed by the presidium of IKKI: the mobilization of the masses for revolutionary action and for the defence of the USSR, the denunciation of Right deviators (Kostrzewa, Stefański and Brand were named), and a less obtrusive warning against "ultra-Left tendencies".[2] A further resolution of June 1930, adopting the correct Comintern vocabulary, spoke of "the struggle on two fronts",[3] and Lenski in the same month told the Russian party congress that "our Rightists" had arrived at "ultra-'Left' conclusions", without attempting to identify the offenders or the nature of the offence.[4] A bone of contention—on which opinions were divided in Comintern—was allowed to appear at the fifth congress of Profintern in August 1930, when Henrykowski condemned the "false line" adopted in 1929 of "the *immediate* formation of revolutionary trade unions", which had prevented effective communist participation in a strike of metal workers in Warsaw; and another Polish delegate expressed mistrust of the German RGO.[5]

---

[1] See *Foundations of a Planned Economy, 1926–1929*, Vol. 3, pp. 584–585.

[2] *KPP: Uchwały i Rezolucje*, iii (1956), 52–74; the resolution of the presidium (see pp. 9–11 above) had mentioned that one in three Polish workers were unemployed as a result of the economic crisis (*Kommunisticheskii Internatsional v Dokumentakh* (1933), p. 917).

[3] *KPP: Uchwały i Rezolucje*, iii (1956), 99.

[4] *XVI S"ezd Vsesoyuznoi Kommunisticheskoi Partii (b)* (1930), p. 457.

[5] *Protokoll des Fünften Kongresses der Roten Gewerkschaftsinternationale* (1930), i, 419, 460. For the divisions in Comintern see *Foundations of a Planned Economy, 1926–1929*, Vol. 3, p. 582.

The fifth congress of the KPP was held at Peterhof near Leningrad at the end of August 1930.[6] The party at this time claimed 7000 members at liberty, with an almost equal number in prison; of these 30 per cent were classified as factory workers, 45 per cent as workers in small concerns or intelligentsia, 25 per cent as peasants.[7] A message of greeting from the central committee of the Russian party congratulated the KPP on having defeated the "Right deviationists, Trotskyists and ultra-Left semi-Trotskyists" in its midst, and hailed it as a "Bolshevik-modelled, monolithic party";[8] and the congress sought to justify these exaggerated encomiums in a long and wordy resolution which repeated and amplified the current formulas of Comintern. It condemned the views of Stefański and Próchniak (Kostrzewa and Brand were not present), which had already been denounced a year earlier at the sixth plenum; these implied a discrimination between social-democracy and Fascism, and acceptance of the former as having a potentially revolutionary role. The resolution also confessed to weakness in applying united front tactics and in wooing the unemployed, and spoke several times of the struggle "on two fronts" and of the danger of ultra-Left as well as of Right tendencies in the party. But the Left was nowhere defined or identified.[9] The resolution on economic affairs admitted that the decision of the fifth plenum in 1928 to move towards the immediate creation of Red trade unions had weakened work in the PPS unions. The absence of positive conclusions reflected the confusions and ambiguities prevailing in Moscow on this question.[10] But Knorin's election as a member of the party central committee[11] guaranteed conformity with the decisions of IKKI.

The most dramatic event in Poland in the autumn of 1930 was the brief assumption by Pilsudski of the office of Prime Minister, which he used to launch a severe campaign of repression against dissidents in his own party, the PPS, and against the leaders of the national parties in the Western Ukraine and Belorussia. Some hundreds of these were lodged in the fortress of Brest-Litovsk, where they were subjected to a regime of extreme brutality. Few members of the

[6] The venue is named in J. Kowalski, *Trudne Lata* (1966), p. 145.
[7] *KPP: Uchwaly i Rezolucje*, iii (1956), 103–104.
[8] *Ibid.* iii, 109–110.
[9] *Ibid.* iii, 111–155.
[10] *Ibid.* iii, 169–171.
[11] J. Kowalski, *Trudne Lata* (1966), p. 160.

KPP were involved, and the party failed to join the Left PPS in its campaign of protest. The party central committee meeting in January 1931 repeated the call of the party congress in August 1930 for revolutionary action by the masses: "the Polish proletariat may confront a revolutionary situation earlier than the proletariat of other capitalist countries". But the savagery of Pilsudski's reprisals against the Left did not modify the refusal of the KPP to make common cause with the PPS. To exploit the ferment in the PPS would have been to pander to "illusions" about the nature of social-Fascism. Common action with the Left PPS was ruled out:

> To the Brest-Litovsk campaign which seeks to make the Centre-Left leaders into heroes of the anti-Fascist struggle we must oppose broad action by the masses against Fascist terror, against punitive expeditions.[12]

The committee passed a separate resolution on party preparations to meet the danger of an imperialist war of intervention against the USSR.[13]

Polish affairs did not attract much attention at the eleventh IKKI in Moscow in March 1931. Manuilsky bracketed Poland with Italy as "Fascist states", and treated social-Fascism as "the agent of Fascism in the working class".[14] Lenski drew such encouragement as was possible from the epidemic of strikes in Poland, from *"the wave of demonstrations of unemployed"*, and from "the symptoms of a revolutionary upsurge in the countryside". He celebrated the achievements of the KPP, "including the KPZU and KPZB", in the struggle for national liberation; and he cited rather more cautiously the campaign of Polish and German workers in Upper Silesia using the slogan of "self-determination to the point of separation", and similar campaigns in Danzig and in "the Lithuanian lands seized by Poland". He ended with the curt dismissal of "a handful of Warsaw renegades", who had adopted "the Right-

---

[12] *KPP: Uchwaly i Rezolucje*, iii (1956), 277–293; the "punitive expeditions" were those undertaken in the Western Ukraine and Belorussia. To this passage the editors in 1956 appended a note that the KPP had been wrong to differentiate action in defence of Centre-Left leaders from action in defence of "revolutionary workers and peasants"; this had made it more difficult for the KPP to launch a really broad campaign against Fascist terror (*ibid.* iii, 289).

[13] *Ibid.* iii, pp. 295–300.

[14] *XI Plenum IKKI* (1932), i, 35, 38.

opportunist anti-party position of Warski and Kostrzewa".[15] The only other Polish speaker, Henrykowski, called for "a struggle against social-Fascism and national-Fascism", and denounced the "Left" manoeuvres of the tricksters of the PPS.[16] The main resolution classified Poland among "the vassal states of French and English imperialism". But it concluded optimistically that the industrial and agrarian crisis in Poland, unemployment of workers, impoverishment of the peasantry, created "the pre-conditions of a revolutionary crisis"; discontent "in the lower ranks of the social-Fascist parties" was matched by "a strengthening of the communist party".[17] The central committee of the KPP meeting in July 1931 endorsed the decisions of IKKI, adding a condemnation of the Hoover reparations plan which had just been announced.[18] Later in the year Stalin's letter to *Proletarskaya Revolyutsiya*, which connected the name of Rosa Luxemburg with current ideological deviations in communist parties, inspired a resolution of the central committee of the KPP violently attacking Luxemburgism as the source of past and present heresies in the party.[19] But this episode had no significance other than to demonstrate the now total subservience of the KPP to the dictates of Moscow.

It was, however, the inescapable German question which swayed and dominated the policies and pronouncements of Comintern. Proximity to Germany made the KPP more sensitive than any other party, except the KPD, to the problems posed by the rise of Hitler. The German presidential election of March–April 1932, followed by Hindenburg's dismissal of Brüning and appointment of Papen as Chancellor, heightened the tension. A Polish move at the end of April to establish a military base in the port of Danzig was denounced by the KPP as "a new step on the road to intervention against the USSR".[20] In this atmosphere of increasing alarm an article appeared in a Yiddish literary journal, *Literarishe Tribune*, which, though published legally, was closely affiliated to the illegal

[15] *Ibid.*, i, 106–139.

[16] *Ibid.* i, 339–345.

[17] *Kommunisticheskii Internatsional v Dokumentakh* (1933), pp. 956, 959.

[18] *KPP: Uchwaly i Rezolucje* (1956), ii, 304–324; *Internationale Presse-Korrespondenz*, No. 81, August 18, 1931, pp. 1827–1828.

[19] For this episode see Note A, pp. 428–432 below.

[20] *Internationale Presse-Korrespondenz*, No. 37, May 7, 1932, pp. 1123–1124.

KPP, under the title "The Danger of Barbarism over Europe". Its author was Isaac Deutscher, a young party member writing under the pseudonym Krakowski. The argument of the article was that "the Marxist sector of the German workers in the present correlation of forces in the country is not capable by itself of repelling the offensive of Hitlerite barbarism", and should therefore seek "allies in this struggle, even if those allies are hesitant, inconsistent, temporary". Social-democracy "is at the present moment interested in the struggle against Hitlerism", but "is not capable of conducting that struggle independently". The article made a sensation and attracted extensive support. In June 1932 Deutscher was expelled from the party, though the party leaders were unable to prevent the circulation of the offending issue of the journal.[21]

Meanwhile a group of Deutscher's sympathizers, encouraged by the response to its views, drafted a memorandum addressed to the party secretariat and to the secretariat of Comintern, in which it openly advocated cooperation not only with the SPD in Germany, but with the PPS Left in Poland. The party leaders are said to have described it as a "Trotskyist revival" of Kostrzewa's former position.[22] The movement does not seem initially to have had any link with Trotsky, or to have been influenced by his opinions.[23] But when Trotsky, then engaged in a lone campaign to persuade the KPD to seek an alliance with the SPD against Hitler, heard of a

[21] J. Kowalski, *Trudne Lata* (1966), pp. 312–317, supplemented by Deutscher's own account in *Les Temps Modernes*, No. 145 (March 1958), pp. 1633, 1666–1667, and I. Deutscher, *Marxism in Our Time* (1972), pp. 113–160. No copy of the article has been found, and it is known only from quotations in *Kommunisticheskii Internatsional*, 1932, No. 35–36, pp. 22–23.

[22] J. Kowalski, *Trudne Lata* (1966), p. 317; in a circular letter of June 25, 1932, to members of the party the central committee rebutted the views expressed in the memorandum, and reaffirmed "the role of social-democracy as the chief bulwark of the bourgeoisie in the worker masses" (quoted by Lenski in *XII Plenum IKKI* (1933), i, 79–80). For the condemnation of Kostrzewa in 1929 see *Foundations of a Planned Economy, 1926–1929*, Vol. 3, pp. 583–585; the stigma of "Trotskyism" was rendered plausible by her share of responsibility for the support given to Trotsky by the central committee of the KPP in December 1923 (see *The Interregnum, 1923–1924*, pp. 234–235).

[23] At the ninth IKKI in February 1928, which resounded with denunciations of Trotskyism, Purman, the Polish delegate, boasted that no Trotskyist group had ever existed in the KPP (*Internationale Presse-Korrespondenz*, No. 18, February 23, 1928, p. 388); until the *Byulleten' Oppozitsii* began to appear in Paris in 1929, and pamphlets by Trotsky were published in various languages, his views were probably little known in Poland.

group propounding similar views in the KPP, he published in his journal a "Greeting to the Polish Left Opposition", dated August 31, 1932. Dissociating himself sharply from Walecki and Kostrzewa as semi-Mensheviks, he hailed the rise of a Polish group of "Bolshevik Leftists", who would have to fear persecution from Stalin as well as from Pilsudski. He noted that opposition literature was being translated into Polish and Yiddish: "some brochures have managed to get through the needle's eye of the Polish censorship". And he ended by warmly greeting "our Polish co-thinkers".[24] The movement thus acquired, from both friends and enemies, an association with Trotskyism which it did not originally possess.

However grave the challenge to the leaders of the KPP, no haste was shown to pronounce on it in Moscow. Lenski in his speech at the twelfth IKKI early in September 1932 was preoccupied by the German imbroglio.[25] But he was at pains to depict a comparatively rosy situation in the KPP. The economic crisis had deepened; discontent among the workers was shown by an increasing wave of strikes, and was fanned by rising unemployment. This was sufficient to justify the customary diagnosis of a "new revolutionary upsurge". Lenski dealt lightly with the minor instances of dissent in the party. He poured scorn on the "anti-reformist phraseology" of the PPS, which purported to preach democracy and a worker-peasant government. He spoke contemptuously of the "fractional platform" of a group of "Right swindlers", who demanded a united front with social-Fascists; this was the policy which had been advocated by "the Right group of Brandler in the KPD and of Kostrzewa in Poland", and was now beginning to "revive in a different form among, it is true, isolated activists, who are ready to accept as genuine coin the new manoeuvres of social-democracy".[26] Another Polish delegate spoke of "the platform of Right fractionalists", which treated the PPS as "a force which will be compelled to struggle against Fascism", and as "an ally with whom we can go a part of the way"; this was "a platform of Right deviators who are

[24] Byulleten' Oppozitsii (Paris), No. 29–30, September 1932, pp. 18–19.

[25] See p. 74 above.

[26] XII Plenum IKKI (1933), i, 78–96. For figures of the increased number of strikes in Poland at this time see Die Kommunistische Internationale vor dem VII Weltkongress (1935), p. 340; on the other hand, "the party organizations often devote their chief attention to the creation of Red trade unions, frequently even in cases where these unions have no prospect of becoming mass organizations" (ibid. p. 342).

coalescing with Trotskyism".[27] Knorin spoke sarcastically of those
who wanted the united front "from below and from above", and
added that "in Poland there are such Rightists who come out
against the leadership of the party". But the movement was not
mentioned in the brief injunctions to the KPP included in the
resolution of the session.[28]

The question of the Western Ukrainian and Western Belorussian
parties (KPZU and KPZB) continued to give trouble. The fifth
congress of the KPP in August 1930 and the second plenum of its
central committee in February 1931 dutifully denounced the Polish
"occupation" of the Western Ukraine ("East Galicia") and
Western Belorussia, and rehearsed the formula of self-determination to the point of secession and union with the adjacent Soviet
republics.[29] The third plenum in July 1931, perhaps under pressure
from Comintern, devoted a separate resolution to the "National
Liberation Movement", in which it called on the party "to intensify
the struggle not only of the Ukrainians and Belorussians, but also of
the masses of Jewish, German, and Lithuanian people". The
Lithuanians were offered "self-determination to the point of
secession". In Upper Silesia, the demand was to mobilize both
German and Polish workers against their oppressors, and to stamp
out national hatreds between peoples (including anti-Semitism).[30]

These professions were, however, still regarded with mistrust in
Moscow. Kuusinen, in a remarkable digression in his speech at the
twelfth IKKI, noted the existence in Poland of "a 'national-
communist' group", whose ancestry he traced back to 1920, "at the
time of the advance of the Red Army on Warsaw". It was notorious
that "nationalist prejudices and tendencies still exist in the ranks of
the Polish working class"; and the party's struggle against these,

---

[27] *XII Plenum IKKI* (1933), ii, 34.

[28] *Kommunisticheskii Internatsional v Dokumentakh* (1933), p. 980.

[29] *KPP: Uchwały i Rezolucje*, iii (1956), 148, 282–288; for the earlier history of the
question see *Foundations of a Planned Economy, 1926–1929*, Vol. 3, pp. 586–593.

[30] *KPP: Uchwały i Rezolucje*, iii (1956), 333–340; the party continued to wage
war on anti-Semitism, but in 1931–1932 had also to carry on "a successful struggle
against ideological survivals of Bundism and Zionism which made themselves felt
among some leading members of the Jewish bureau, who had come over from
Jewish nationalist petty bourgeois parties" (*Die Kommunistische Internationale vor dem
VII Weltkongress* (1935), p. 357). For a further protest against "the occupation by
Polish imperialism" of the Western Ukraine and the activities of Pilsudski agents
there see *Internationale Presse-Korrespondenz*, No. 89, September 15, 1931, pp. 2007–
2008.

"especially of late", was a "weak point". Kuusinen called for "an unsparing struggle against the persecution by Polish imperialism of different nationalities, the persecution of Ukrainians, Belorussians, etc." His hearers must have known that his words could have applied to examples of Polish imperialism in Upper Silesia, Danzig and the so-called "Polish corridor". But he refrained from any mention of these, perhaps as unduly provocative, perhaps as irrelevant in present conditions.[31] Manuilsky subtly remarked that Poland was both "a bridge to the proletarian revolution in Germany" and "an outpost in the encirclement of the USSR, a mailed fist of world imperialism",[32] but ventured no further into the minefield of Polish nationalism, which was also avoided by the Polish delegates. The resolution at the end of the session called summarily for "mobilization of the broadest masses in town and country against the criminal policy of an anti-Soviet war" and for "a stubborn ideological struggle against the nationalist prejudices of Polish workers, peasants and petty bourgeoisie".[33]

A month later the sixth congress of the KPP met at Mogilev in the Belorussian SSR in a confident mood. The membership of the KPP was returned at 17,200; this excluded several thousand communists serving long terms of imprisonment, but included 3500 and 3400 members of the KPZU and KPZB respectively.[34] Spurred perhaps by Trotsky's endorsement of the programme of the dissidents, the congress pronounced it "indispensable to strengthen the struggle against Trotskyism, which grows up in the soil of Kostrzewism". The platform of "the Trotskyist group in Poland" was said to reflect basically Rightist conceptions of the independent role of the petty bourgeoisie, and of recognition of the PPS and its present allies as an embodiment of bourgeois democracy, and a potential "temporary ally" for the KPP. The "fractional group" of "Trotskyist contrabandists" was even said to be associated with opposition groups in the USSR.[35] The draft programme approved in principle by the congress, whose main provisions were closely modelled on the

[31] *XII Plenum IKKI* (1933), ii, 36.
[32] *Ibid.* i, 160. The incidence of Polish nationalism in the KPP must have been tempered by the survival of the Luxemburgist tradition among its older members, and by the very high proportion of Jews in the party leadership; for the influx of Jews into the KPP see *Foundations of a Planned Economy, 1926–1929*, Vol. 3, p. 576.
[33] *Kommunisticheskii Internatsional v Dokumentakh* (1933), p. 980.
[34] *Die Kommunistische Internationale vor dem VII Weltkongress* (1935), pp. 338–339.
[35] *KPP: Uchwaly i Rezolucje*, iii (1956), 377–378.

programme of Comintern, contained a paragraph rejecting the view that "social-democracy or its Left wing can play an objectively revolutionary or two-edged role", and describing Trotskyism as "a variant of social-Fascism".[36] These conclusions were endorsed in the journal of Comintern, which now also published a detailed account of "the formation of a Kostrzewa–Trotskyist group" in the KPP.[37]

The congress also responded to the injunctions of Comintern by adopting a comprehensive resolution on "the struggle against Polish imperialism and national oppression". This repeated the old prescriptions for the KPZU and KPZB, but insisted that the national question could be solved only by proletarian revolution, and unification with the Soviet republics. It had a special section denouncing anti-Semitism. Its main novelty was a final section devoted to the struggle against national oppression in Upper Silesia and the "coastal region", this being a reference to the Kashub minority in the Polish corridor; the Kashubs were a primitive peasant group, speaking a Slav dialect, whose national aspirations were of a shadowy kind. The industrial development of Upper Silesia made the German proletariat ripe for the class struggle against the bourgeoisie, which was reinforced by the struggle against the Versailles system. Whether or not the claim for self-determination to the point of secession was. explicitly made, the implication was obvious, and must have aroused misgivings in some sections of the KPP.[38]

Next to the KPD, the KPP was the party most directly affected by Hitler's seizure of power at the beginning of 1933. Since 1930 persecution by the Polish authorities had effectively prevented any overt party activities on Polish soil. The politburo and party headquarters were established in Berlin, while a so-called "internal secretariat" and—intermittently—a party central committee fun-

---

[36] *Ibid.* iii, 404.

[37] *Kommunisticheskii Internatsional*, 1932, No. 35–36, pp. 10–11, 21–26; according to B. Leibzon and K, Shirinya, *Povorot v Politike Kominterna* (2nd ed., 1975), p. 217, Kostrzewa wrote to IKKI "at the end of 1932" protesting against the application of the term "social-Fascists".

[38] *KPP: Uchwaly i Rezolucje*, iii (1956), 379–394. Omission marks occur in two places in the final section, and the full text has never been published; according to J. Kowalski, *Trudne Lata* (1966), p. 331, it included a demand for self-determination for both Upper Silesia and the Kashubs.

ctioned illicitly in Poland. The Comintern directive of March 5, 1933, opening the way to joint action with the parties of the Second International against Fascism was eagerly welcomed by the internal secretariat, which on March 7 issued an open letter to the PPS, the Bund and other Left organizations proposing common action to defend the German workers and to create a united front against the Polish regime. It also undertook to refrain from polemics against the PPS.[39] The last recorded act of the KPP politburo in Berlin was a communication to the internal secretariat designed to restrain this ill-judged ardour. The politburo took the view that the motive of the Comintern initiative was to unmask the socialists, and to dispel the illusion of the workers that agreement between leaders could provide a solid basis for the struggle against Fascism.[40] But the situation of Polish communists in Berlin was now untenable. Lenski was arrested, and released a few days later—apparently as a result of Soviet diplomatic intervention. The politburo and the party headquarters found a home in Copenhagen; and the publication of the party journal *Nowy Przegląd* was transferred from Gleiwitz in German Upper Silesia to Danzig, where another party centre was also set up. In January 1934, as the danger mounted, all these activities were moved to Prague.[41]

Some progress was made by the KPP during 1933 towards closer relations with other parties. In a textile strike in Lodz in March 1933, "in spite of the opposition of trade union bureaucrats from the PPS", a united front was formed in the strike committees in the factories.[42] The congress of the PPS in April 1933 decisively rejected the united front with the KPP, though in Poland, as in other countries, spontaneous cooperation at lower levels was more readily achieved than agreement between leaders.[43] In the following month a congress of the peasant party Stronnictwo Ludowe made radical pronouncements, and some of its members are said to have

[39] *Rundschau*, No. 6, March 25, 1933, p. 150; for the Comintern directive of March 5 see p. 85 above.

[40] J. Kowalski, *Trudne Lata* (1966), pp. 408–410; according to Lenski, the KPP appeal of March 7 was "a tactical move", which "compelled the PPS to show its hand, and come out openly against a united front with the communists" (*XIII Plenum IKKI* (1934), p. 86). The KPP was afterwards reproached for having failed to utilize the appeal and its rejection by the PPS for "a broad mass campaign" (*Die Kommunistische Internationale vor dem VII Weltkongress* (1935), p. 346).

[41] J. Kowalski, *Trudne Lata* (1966), p. 410.

[42] *Die Kommunistische Internationale vor dem VII Weltkongress* (1935), pp. 345–346.

[43] J. Kowalski, *Trudne Lata* (1966), pp. 414–418.

called for a united front with the KPP. But the KPP, like the PPS, was wary of involvement in peasant insurgency, which could not easily be linked with the struggle of industrial workers.[44] A resolution of the party central committee in June was full of recrimination against the PPS and the Bund, and denounced "Right-wing Trotskyists" who wanted an alliance with social-democrats.[45] In July the KPP in conjunction with MOPR organized a "week of aid for victims of Fascism in Germany", which seems to have attracted sympathy and support from the PPS and the trade unions.[46] But it is clear that cooperation between the parties remained fitful and spontaneous and did not involve the leaders on either side.

The first serious attempt from Moscow to diagnose the consequences for Polish communists of Hitler's supremacy in Germany came through Narkomindel rather than through Comintern channels. As early as March 1933 those responsible for Soviet international relations had become increasingly uneasy about the implications of Hitler's ambitions for a resurgence of German power; and Radek, in a famous article in May, had thrown doubts on the consequences of a revision of the Versailles treaty, hitherto a major plank both in Soviet and Comintern propaganda. But a visit by Radek to Poland a few weeks later produced no tangible results;[47] and, in the absence of any fresh directive from Comintern, where opinions were still sharply divided, the KPP line was not substantially modified during the greater part of 1933. The KPP was reproached by the PPS, not only with its demand for the secession of the Western Ukraine and of Western Belorussia, but with its rejection of Polish claims to Pomerania ("self-determination for the Kashubs") and to Upper Silesia.[48] The central committee of the KPP met in Moscow, on the eve of the thirteenth IKKI, on November 24–25, 1933;[49] and it was presumably on this occasion that it attempted, not perhaps without prompting from Comintern,

[44] *Ibid.* pp. 456–461.
[45] *KPP: Uchwaly i Rezolucje*, iii (1956), 464–479.
[46] J. Kowalski, *Trudne Lata* (1966), p. 494.
[47] For Radek's article and his Polish visit see p. 96 above.
[48] J. Kowalski, *Trudne Lata* (1966), p. 413.
[49] *Ibid.* pp. 509–510; Mitskevich-Kapsukas was present as representative of IKKI.

to refute the taunt that the demand for self-determination for Upper Silesia and for the corridor was tantamount to a demand for their cession to Fascist Germany:

> Upper Silesia and the seaboard corridor are key-points in the now exacerbated Polish and German imperialism . . . In this situation our party considers itself all the more bound to press the right of the seaboard and Upper Silesian populations to self-determination, a right whose edge is directed against the Polish and German imperialisms, against the Fascist dictatorships of Pilsudski and Hitler . . . *This slogan can be translated into practice only through a struggle both against Polish imperialism, which has seized Upper Silesia and the seaboard corridor by force, and against German imperialism, which wants to unite them with Germany by force.*[50]

The explanation carried conviction probably to few members even of the KPP.

The record of the KPP, as presented to the thirteenth IKKI in November–December 1933, was not impressive. Lenski began with the international situation, and noted signs of Hitler's growing inclination to come to terms with Pilsudski at the expense of the USSR and as a prelude to a *rapprochement* with France. In Poland he diagnosed in conventional terms "an accelerated, though very uneven, rise of the revolutionary upsurge". But he admitted "opportunist errors", failure to realize the united front of workers, and weakness of the revolutionary movement in the trade unions. A widespread peasant revolt had occurred in central Galicia; but "we had not yet learned how to become the general staff of the rising". The "nationalist-opportunist conceptions of Skrypnik" were blamed for tactical errors of the KPZU.[51] Próchniak argued that Pilsudski, unlike Hitler and Mussolini, had no "mass Fascist base" of his own, and found support in "the old historic parties of the Polish bourgeoisie", including the PPS and the party organizations of the oppressed nationalities.[52] Henrykowski, the trade union

---

[50] The only published source for this declaration is Lenski's speech at the thirteenth IKKI on November 29, 1933 (*XIII Plenum IKKI* (1934) p. 79); if it was included in a resolution adopted at the meeting of November 24–25, it was omitted from the text eventually published in January 1934 (see p. 268, note 54 below).

[51] *XIII Plenum IKKI* (1934), pp. 77–91.

[52] *Ibid.* pp. 223–225; for his exposure of alleged "Pilsudski agents" in the party see p. 271 below.

representative, admitted that the party, in view of its illegal status and persecution by the authorities, had not been able to place itself at the head of the current waves of strikes.[53] In Moscow profound concern with the role of Poland on the international scene was not matched by any lively interest in the internal troubles of the KPP.

After the session the central committee of KPP refurbished the resolution adopted at its meeting of November 24–25, 1933, prefaced it by an introduction stressing its complete conformity with the decisions of IKKI, and issued it under the date January 1934. It recognized the campaign against war, linked with the campaign against all forms of Polish chauvinism and nationalism (including anti-Semitism), as the most important task of the KPP at the present moment. It called for more decisive action in the trade unions, and for the coordination of the workers' movement with peasant struggles and struggles for national liberation. It was also confronted with the problems of the KPZU, which remained precariously balanced on a razor edge between the Ukrainian nationalism promoted by Skrypnik, especially dangerous owing to its subterranean contact with nationalists in the Soviet Ukraine, and Polish chauvinism exhibited in a lack of enthusiasm among some members of the KPP for the right of the Western Ukraine to self-determination. The resolution urged the new leadership of the KPZU (a "severe crisis" had been ended only by a "renewal" of the leadership) to purge the party of "alien elements".[54]

The winter of 1933–1934, which saw the beginning of a reversal of traditional attitudes in Moscow, was also eventful for the KPP. Prognostications of an approach by Hitler to Poland were fulfilled when a ten-year pact of non-aggression and mutual aid between Germany and Poland was signed in Warsaw on January 26, 1934.[55] A protest from the KPP headed "Down with the Anti-Soviet Warmongers" accused the partners to the pact of planning a joint attack on the USSR.[56] The abortive Fascist riot in Paris and the successful Fascist *coup* in Vienna followed in the first days of February.[57] These

[53] *XIII Plenum IKKI* (1934), pp. 366–367.

[54] *KPP: Uchwały i Rezolucje*, iii (1956), 481–491; *Rundschau*, No. 12, February 1, 1934, pp. 463–464; *Die Kommunistische Internationale vor dem VII Weltkongress* (1935), p. 357. For the circumstances of its publication see J. Kowalski, *Trudne Lata* (1966), pp. 509–510.

[55] See p. 137 above.

[56] J. Kowalski, *Trudne Lata* (1966), p. 490.

[57] See p. 123 above.

events, together with the impression created by Dimitrov's bold defiance of the Nazi court at Leipzig, intensified the ferment in the Polish Left. The PPS at a congress in January 1934 had adopted a platform which spoke of "the dictatorship of the working masses" and of "revolutionary methods of struggle".[58] But this was not enough. Supporters in the PPS of a united anti-Fascist front with the KPP seceded from the PPS and, not without some assistance from the KPP, founded a Workers' Socialist Party. On both sides, the rank and file showed itself more eager than the leaders to bury the hatchet of past quarrels. A group in the KPP proposed to open the way to the united front by withdrawing the label of "social-Fascists" applied to the PPS, but found themselves condemned as Trotskyists and police agents. Altogether 80 oppositionists are said to have been expelled from the KPP in the spring of 1934, and 170 from the youth league.[59] An open letter addressed by the KPP to the members and the central committee of the PPS, the Bund and the German SPD does not seem to have marked any fresh advance;[60] the KPP and the PPS held separate demonstrations on May 1.[61] A resolution of the party central committee in June 1934 demanded that the open letter of the previous April should be brought to the attention of workers and trade unionists. But the main purpose was still to unmask their social-Fascist leaders; differences of principle must not be blurred by forming opportunist blocs with social-Fascists.[62]

Tension increased rapidly during the summer of 1934.[63] A new para-military organization, the Obóz Narodowo-Radykalny (ONR), enjoying the toleration or patronage of the government, engaged in demonstrations and acts of violence against the Left. A visit from Goebbels in June stressed the good relations between Poland and Germany, and encouraged imitation of the Nazi model. In the same month a cluster of concentration camps were established at Bereza in eastern Poland, to which members of the KPP and PPS were consigned in large numbers, and which became the scene of notorious barbarities and tortures.[64] These pressures,

[58] *Die Kommunistische Internationale vor dem VII Weltkongress* (1935), p. 346.
[59] J. Kowalski, *Trudne Lata* (1966), pp. 422–430.
[60] *KPP: Uchwaly i Rezolucje*, iii (1956), 513; the text has not been found.
[61] J. Kowalski, *Trudne Lata* (1966), p. 551.
[62] *KPP: Uchwaly i Rezolucje*, iii (1956), 513–515.
[63] For a somewhat one-sided account of this period see *Die Kommunistische Internationale vor dem VII Weltkongress* (1935), pp. 347–349.
[64] The number of political prisoners at the end of 1934 was put at 16,000 (J. Kowalski, *Trudne Lata* (1966), p. 630).

combined with the example of the pact concluded in July between the PCF and the SFIO in France,[65] gave a renewed impetus to projects of a united front against Fascism. But resistance to the new line was not dead in the KPP,[66] and subsequent communist accounts which put the blame for slow progress exclusively on the PPS may be misleading. In July 1934, when Dimitrov had opened his campaign for the popular front in Moscow, the central committee of the KPP, stressing the alliance of the Polish bourgeoisie with "the bloody Hitler government" against the USSR, appealed for joint action against the Fascist terror to workers of all parties and groups, including the PPS, the Workers' Socialist Party and the Jewish Bund; and a further appeal two months later in similar terms accused the Pilsudski regime of collusion with Japanese aggression.[67] Negotiations were opened with the Jewish Bund, which apparently laid down the condition that the KPP should cease to apply the label "social-Fascist" to parties of the Left.[68]

The PPS leaders continued to resist these overtures with the utmost bitterness. What was described as a "secret circular of the Warsaw committee of the PPS" of August 22, 1934, complained that the KPP "represents the official line of Stalinist policy in Comintern, i.e. the foreign policy of Soviet Russia, full of treaties and pacts even with Fascist states". This was the party which "for some time past has been bombarding our committee with united front proposals", the "insincerity and humbug" of which was obvious to all. The circular roundly condemned the French socialists for having broken ranks by coming to terms with the PCF.[69] A further appeal from the KPP in October attempted to refute these charges, and ended by once more extending "a fraternal hand to all workers who want to struggle against Fascism, reaction and imperialist war". This was accompanied by an indignant article by Lenski, who alleged, probably with reason, that

[65] See p. 195 above.

[66] J. Kowalski, *Kommunistyczna Partia Polski, 1935–1938* (1975), p. 105, lists the KPP, with the Hungarian and Bulgarian parties, as "initially" opposed to the new line.

[67] *Rundschau*, No. 47, August 23, 1934, pp. 1966–1967, No. 50, September 13, 1934, pp. 2159–2161.

[68] J. Kowalski, *Trudne Lata* (1966), pp. 603–605.

[69] For extracts from the circular see *Rundschau*, No. 55, October 18, 1934, p. 2411.

many local PPS organizations had come out in support of a united front with the KPP.[70] A further pronouncement of the KPP deplored the breakdown of negotiations with the Bund, and called for their immediate resumption.[71] These reiterated appeals did not conceal deep uneasiness in the ranks of the KPP.

An illegal party constantly harassed by the authorities, and restricted to underground activities, was always liable to infiltration by agents of the secret police. Since about 1931 a party member named Mützenmacher, who rose to be a candidate member of the central committee and a member of the secretariat, had been in police pay and betrayed other party members to the police. In 1933, fearing exposure, the authorities withdrew him from the party under cover of a faked murder. But he continued to work for the authorities, and in 1934 he published a critical history of the KPP under the pen-name Regula.[72] The prevalence of espionage, and suspicion of it even where it did not exist, added to the demoralization of the party. When opposition groups appeared within the party, it was all too easy to hint that they were police agents as well as Trotskyists. Próchniak at the thirteenth IKKI in November 1933 claimed that the "purging of the party of ideologically alien elements" was being carried on "simultaneously with a process of purging it of direct Pilsudski agents", whose infiltration had resulted "in deviations from Bolshevism, as well as in fractional strife". He quoted two "examples". More than two years earlier the "notorious Pilsudskist" Wojewódzki had been expelled from the party; and more than a year ago Sochacki had been "removed from operational work . . . as an ideologically alien individual".[73] Though no direct accusation was made, the insinuation was unmistakable that they had been police spies. The speech gave a

---

[70] *Ibid.* No. 55, October 18, 1934, pp. 2409–2411.

[71] *Ibid.* No. 57, November 1, 1934, pp. 2547–2548.

[72] J. Kowalski, *Trudne Lata* (1966), pp. 635–637; according to this account, he was employed by the Gestapo in Poland during the war, and later by the Polish government in exile in London. For Regula's history see *Socialism in One Country, 1924–1926*, Vol. 3, p. 184, note 3.

[73] *XIII Plenum IKKI* (1934), p. 224; Sochacki's approach to Pilsudski in May 1926 (see *Foundations of a Planned Economy, 1926–1929*, Vol. 3, p. 563, note 5) may have been brought up against him.

sinister foretaste of later accusations of treachery within the KPP. The Polish fraternal delegate at the seventeenth congress of the Russian party in January 1934 spoke of "the discovery of a counter-revolutionary agency in the Ukraine and the blow struck at Skrypnik's nationalist deviation".[74]

As the controversy about the united front grew sharper, the miasma of suspicion thickened. In August 1934 the KPP central committee published a statement alleging that Żarski, a member of the committee, together with his wife, had entered the party in 1919 or 1920 as Pilsudski's agents, and had worked for the official military organization (POW), which also had links with the PPS. An accompanying article signed Albert (i.e Żytlowski) claimed that those former members of the PPS who had left it after 1918 to join the KPP had done so as agents of the POW or of the PPS; Sochacki was denounced as an *agent provocateur*, not only in the KPP but in the KPZU, and accused of having set up a spy centre for the POW in the Soviet Ukraine.[75] This campaign was accompanied by attacks, said to have been conducted by "security organs of the USSR", on Polish political *émigrés* in the Soviet Union;[76] and a sinister link between oppositions in the Polish and Russian parties was forged in a further statement of the KPP central committee, which alleged that "Pilsudskism and the secret police give very strong support not only to nationalist, but to other currents and deviations hostile to communism in the KPP, including ultra-Left and Trotskyist elements which were actively attacking Comintern and the VKP (B)".[77]

The charge against the PPS of complicity with Pilsudski's secret police in infiltrating the KPP did nothing to further the cause of the united front, and provided its opponents in the PPS with a formidable argument for the indignant rejection of overtures from the KPP.[78] In January 1935 the central committee of the KPP, evidently prompted from Moscow, adopted a half-hearted directive in preparation for the seventh congress of Comintern. Changes in the working class were said to require "a change of tactics". This

[74] *XVII S"ezd Vsesoyuznoi Kommunisticheskoi Partii (b)* (1934), p. 338.
[75] *Nowy Przegląd*, 1934, No. 8.
[76] J. Kowalski, *Trudne Lata* (1966), p. 628.
[77] *Nowy Przegląd*, 1934, No. 9–10.
[78] References to the detection of these agents in the ranks of the KPP, and to the use made of these revelations in PPS propaganda, occur in the KPP manifesto of October 1934 and in Lenski's article (see pp. 270–271 above).

implied stronger insistence on the united front, though definitions of it remained discreetly vague. A warning was issued against deviations in the party and against "the doubts of some comrades about the united front". The study of Comintern and party literature was recommended.[79] But, as elsewhere, the rank and file was in advance of its leaders. On February 17, 1935, a large workers' congress, organized by the PPS and the Bund, met in Warsaw. Of nearly 500 delegates, 300 represented the PPS, 100 the Bund, and 60 the KPP; the presidium of ten contained one communist. Its results were ambiguous. It decided to set up united front committees in factories and other places of work and among the unemployed. But its published manifesto was confined to practical demands of the workers, and did not raise the question of the united front against Fascism.[80] The PPS once more refused a KPP proposal for a joint demonstration on May 1; and the KPP procession was fired on by the police.[81] On May 12, Pilsudski died, and his funeral became a political issue for the Left. The decision of the PPS to be represented at it on the score of Pilsudski's earlier achievements aroused indignation among those party members who supported the united front with the communists.[82]

In June 1935, with the seventh congress of Comintern already in sight, further moves were made. Even now opposition is said to have come not only from the PPS, but from some elements in the KPP which were guilty of "opportunist attitudes and errors".[83] A Polish representative of Comintern, Izydorczyk by name, was sent from Moscow to stimulate the lagging conversations between KPP and PPS; the latter put forward a proposal for a non-aggression pact between the two parties.[84] Some communists are said to have come out at this time with the slogan of a constituent assembly, which would restore democratic rights to the people.[85] The KPP politburo proclaimed that "the task of the moment is a popular anti-Fascist

---

[79] KPP: Uchwaly i Rezolucje, iii (1956), 521–527; it also appeared in Kommunisticheskii Internatsional, 1935, No. 5–6, pp. 66–69.

[80] Die Kommunistische Internationale vor dem VII Weltkongress (1935), p. 349; J. Kowalski, Trudne Lata (1966), pp. 692–693.

[81] Ibid. pp. 709, 715.

[82] Ibid. pp. 717–720.

[83] Die Kommunistische Internationale vor dem VII Weltkongress (1935), pp. 350–351.

[84] J. Kowalski, Kommunistyczna Partia Polski, 1935–1938 (1975), p. 126.

[85] B. Leibzon and K. Shirinya, Povorot v Politike Kominterna (2nd ed., 1975), p. 244.

front, a front in the struggle for freedom, bread, work and peace"—
an imitation of the PCF formula of the popular front; and the party
central committee announced its readiness to cooperate to these
ends with any organization of toilers. Negotiations took place on
June 3–4 between delegates of the KPP and the PPS. The PPS
declined any "written pact", but agreed on joint action in support
of a series of political strikes which began on June 19. But the
movement was unsuccessful—allegedly owing to the defection of
the PPS.[86] In the following month a delegation of the KPP 24
strong attended the seventh congress of Comintern to support the
world-wide call for a popular front against Fascism and war.[87]

[86] J. Kowalski, *Komunistyczna Partia Polski, 1935–1938* (1975), pp. 27–28; for the
variations in the French formula see p. 201 above.
[87] J. Kowalski, *Komunistyczna Partia Polski, 1935–1938* (1975), p. 109.

CHAPTER 13

THE AUSTRIAN COMMUNIST PARTY (KPÖ)

The rump state of Austria, created by the peace settlement of 1919 out of the ruins of the Austro–Hungarian empire, led a precarious existence throughout the nineteen-twenties, and suffered the full weight of the economic crisis after 1930. German-speaking and overshadowed by Germany, Austria was prohibited by treaty from uniting with Germany; and the two states were prevented in 1931 from forming a customs union.[1] In a predominantly Catholic country the Christian-Social Party provided the core of the government. A party created by the Heimwehr, a para-military organization representing the dispossessed aristocratic, military and official strata of the old empire, won a handful of seats at the elections to the National Assembly in November 1930, and entered into a coalition with the Christian-Social Party. A National-Socialist Party still had few adherents. The Austrian Social-Democratic Party (SPÖ) formed a powerful opposition, winning two-fifths of the votes at the 1930 elections. Like the SPD in Germany, it was a well organized mass party, possessing a para-military organization, the Schutzbund, a more powerful counter-part of the SPD Reichsbanner. Unlike the SPD, however, it faced no serious communist challenge, and retained the undivided loyalty of virtually the whole body of workers.

The Austrian Communist Party (KPÖ), though it attracted some perhaps undeserved publicity at the time of the Vienna insurrection of 1927,[2] remained a small sect without representation in the National Assembly. Its membership increased during 1930 from 1500 to 2600.[3] Since 1930, when after many splits Koplenig, a faithful disciple of Comintern orthodoxy, became its established leader, it had punctually mirrored the gestures, and repeated the slogans, of Comintern and of the KPD. It branded the Christian-Social government as a Fascist dictatorship, and the SPÖ as social-

---

[1] See pp. 40, 43 above.
[2] See *Foundations of a Planned Economy, 1926–1929*, Vol. 3, pp. 149–151.
[3] *XI Plenum IKKI* (1932), i, 316; the SPÖ numbered about 600,000.

Fascist, and confessed its own "sectarian" errors; "we placed too much hope on the spontaneity of the masses", said Koplenig at the eleventh IKKI in March 1931.[4] At its eleventh congress in June 1931, which was attended by an unnamed representative of the KPD, it decided that the KPÖ must unmask the "bourgeois class policy" of the SPÖ. It adopted, in imitation of the KPD manifesto of the previous August, a manifesto on "The Social and National Liberation of the Austrian People", which demanded the right of self-determination and denounced "the robber peace of Saint Germain and Versailles".[5] In November 1931, a letter from WEB warned the KPÖ of the dangers both "of Right opportunism and of Left phraseology and sectarianism"; and Dimitrov, as leader of WEB, attended a meeting of the party politburo at the end of the month and a session of the central committee in January 1932.[6] As a result of these efforts the committee, once more following the example of the KPD, but perhaps with rather more conviction, initiated a campaign for a united front with the workers' parties.[7] The campaign continued spasmodically during the year. But, in view of the small size of the party, it remained unreal and insignificant, even in comparison with its German model. Koplenig at the twelfth IKKI in September 1932 was still careful to couple the united front with "the struggle against social-democracy".[8] The session produced no direct guidance for the KPÖ. But the paragraph of the resolution relating to the KPD looked forward to a Soviet Germany which would pave the way for a voluntary union of Austria with it.[9] The patriotic protest against the Versailles treaty, with its ban on the *Anschluss* of Austria to Germany, was upheld.

The death agony of the Austrian Left began when, on March 7, 1933, a few days after Hitler's triumph, Dollfuss, the Christian-Social Chancellor, dismissed the National Assembly, and instituted a dictatorship. The moment coincided with the reply sent by

[4] *XI Plenum IKKI* (1932), i, 314.

[5] *Internationale Presse-Korrespondenz*, No. 68, July 14, 1931, pp. 1529–1530; *Voprosy Istorii KPSS*, 1964, No. 2, p. 99. For the KPD manifesto see p. 24 above.

[6] *Georgii Dimitrov: Vydayushchiisya Deyatel' Kommunisticheskogo Dvizheniya* (1972), p. 117.

[7] *Internationale Presse-Korrespondenz*, No. 14, February 16, 1932, p. 374; the KPÖ was said to have further increased its membership during 1931, reaching a total of 6800 by the end of that year (*ibid.* No. 32, April 19, 1932, p. 991).

[8] *XII Plenum IKKI* (1933), i, 180–181.

[9] For this paragraph see p. 73 above.

Comintern on March 5 to the overture of the Second International; and the KPÖ, interpreting this as a licence to proceed with the united front tactics, addressed an open letter to the SPÖ and to the social-democratic and free trade unions, and to their leaders, inviting them to form "a fighting proletarian united front" against the regime, which had taken "a decisive step to the establishment of a Fascist dictatorship".[10] But the move had come too late. Dollfuss installed a rigorous press censorship, and proceeded to widespread arrests of communists; the KPÖ was formally banned in May 1933.[11] The social-democratic Schutzbund was also banned. But the SPÖ itself was not yet attacked, and like the SPD sealed its own fate by its failure to resist.

A distinctive feature of the situation was the hidden rivalry between Hitler and Mussolini for control over Austria. The Austrian Nazis, though increasing in numbers, were not yet strong enough to provide a base for effective action. The Heimwehr, supported by the Catholic Church and by Mussolini, its lavish paymaster, became the dominant political force. Outside Vienna, the social-democratic stronghold, it reigned supreme; and its strong-arm tactics did not differ greatly from those of the Nazis. The course of events provoked a series of pronouncements by IKKI and by the KPÖ, which merely revealed their own impotence. At the thirteenth IKKI in December 1933 Koplenig noted anxiously that Austria had become the crossroads for all the current "imperialist contradictions", exposed the weakness of the social-democrats, and predicted the "radicalization of the masses" and a "new revolutionary upsurge". His one significant pronouncement was that the KPÖ had "come out openly and definitely against union with Hitlerite Germany".[12] A lengthy resolution adopted by the party central committee after the session laid down as the first task of the party "the struggle against the imperialist war-fever" and the exposure of national chauvinism; the party was also to undertake "stronger and continuous work among social-democratic workers to unmask and shatter the treacherous manoeuvres of social-democracy".[13]

The Heimwehr, egged on by Mussolini, was now impatient to go

---

[10] *Rundschau*, No. 6, March 25, 1933, pp. 149–150.
[11] *Rundschau*, No. 17, June 2, 1933, p. 526.
[12] *XIII Plenum IKKI* (1934), pp. 201–205.
[13] *Rundschau*, No. 15, February 15, 1934, pp. 571–574.

into action. On February 12, 1934, it embarked on a systematic
search for arms in the possession of the workers, and shooting began.
The now illegal Schutzbund was no match for the well-equipped
Heimwehr with all the authority and resources of the government
behind it. Artillery was brought up to demolish the last social-
democratic stronghold in Vienna, blocks of workers' apartments.
There were many casualties, and reprisals were thorough and
ruthless. The reaction of *Pravda* was predictable:

> The Austrian social-democrats, like their German friends,
> helped to prepare the triumph of Fascism. They supported every
> reactionary government, and helped them faithfully in their
> struggle against the revolutionary elements in the Austrian
> workers' movement.[14]

A message of sympathy from the PCF referred to the attempted
Fascist *coup* a few days earlier in Paris, and hailed "the common
struggle of the proletarians of Paris and Vienna".[15] An appeal of the
KPÖ against "Heimwehr-and-Hitler-Fascism" was addressed
comprehensively to "workers, members of the Schutzbund and
comrades".[16] "The facts indisputably prove", wrote Gottwald,
"that the Austrian social-democrats have brought the Austrian
workers under the yoke of Fascist dictatorship".[17] The verdict of
IKKI, which blamed both German and Austrian Fascism, led up to
an all too familiar conclusion: "the united front can be welded only
in a relentless struggle to destroy the perfidious Second International".[18] A month later a group of former leading members
of the SPÖ headed by Ernst Fischer, who had taken refuge in
Prague, announced their adhesion to the KPÖ.[19] A conference of
the KPÖ in Vienna in June 1934, attended by 94 delegates,
celebrated the adhesion of this "Red front" to the party, and
undertook to resist "the economic and political assaults of
Fascism".[20] Several units of the Schutzbund which had regrouped
in Prague accepted an invitation to find an asylum in Moscow,

[14] *Pravda*, February 14, 1934.
[15] *Humanité*, February 14, 1934.
[16] *Rundschau*, No. 17, February 22, 1934, pp. 597–598.
[17] *Ibid*. No. 19, March 1, 1934, pp. 663–665.
[18] *Ibid*. No. 20, March 8, 1934, pp. 711–712.
[19] *Ibid*. No. 27, April 26, 1934, pp. 993–994.
[20] *Ibid*. No. 40, July 12, 1934, pp. 1614–1616.

where they served for some time as a living testimony to the virtues of the united front.[21] But these demonstrations of solidarity did not mask the severity of the blow which had been struck at the tottering structure of European communism and the European Left. Fascism, open and undisguised, was installed at a key-point in central Europe.

The peculiar orientation of Austrian Fascism, its dependence on the Catholic Church and on Italy, sharply differentiated it from German Nazism as represented by the Austrian Nazi party.[22] The assassination of Dollfuss on July 25, 1934, by Austrian Nazis sparked off a crisis, in which Mussolini and Hitler confronted each other as rivals for a dominant control over Austria. But the tension was short-lived. Hitler's tactical retreat quickly restored, and even cemented, the threatened "Rome–Berlin axis".[23] These claims, following the secessions from the SPÖ, gave a fresh impetus to the movement for a united front of the Left. Difficult negotiations took place with leaders of the SPÖ, and an agreement was reached, in face of some opposition, to set up a standing joint committee to organize united action.[24] Knorin, in the Comintern journal, while continuing to stress the "differences of principle" between the KPÖ and the socialists, hailed the agreement as progress towards the establishment of a mass communist party in Austria.[25] In August the central committee of the KPÖ announced the forthcoming twelfth party congress, which would proclaim "*the struggle for the dictatorship of the proletariat, for a Soviet Austria*", and—more realistically, perhaps—the campaign "*for one goal, one party, against any splitting of the working class*", associated with the "*daily struggle for wages and bread*".[26] By this time the membership of the party had risen to 16,000, and the illegal *Rote Fahne* boasted a circulation of 40,000.[27]

According to a party *communiqué*, the congress was held in

[21] For an open letter from one of these units see *ibid.* No. 41, July 19, 1934, p. 1689.

[22] Koplenig, at the seventh congress of Comintern in 1935, dwelt at length on the contrast between "German Fascism" and "Austrian Fascism" (*Rundschau*, No. 60, October 30, 1935, p. 2436).

[23] For these events see pp. 253–254 above.

[24] *Voprosy Istorii KPSS*, 1972, No. 3, pp. 112–113.

[25] *Kommunisticheskii Internatsional*, 1934, No. 19, pp. 3–10.

[26] *Rundschau*, No. 47, August 23, 1934, pp. 1963–1964.

[27] *Voprosy Istorii KPSS*, 1972, No. 3, p. 112.

Salzburg at the end of September 1934 with about 70 participants. More than two-thirds of the delegates had joined the KPÖ since the February *coup*; and of the party central committee elected at the end of the proceedings about half had joined the KPÖ since February, and were former officials of the SPÖ.[28] If these figures are correct, the proportion of defections of social-democrats to the communist party at this time was higher in Austria than elsewhere. The main report at the congress was delivered by Koplenig as secretary of the party. The Schutzbund, he declared, by its heroic resistance to the Fascist onslaught in February had "saved the honour of the Austrian working class". But this action was in no sense "*a merit of social-democratic leadership*", since it was "in contradiction with their own policy". But he refrained from personal abuse of the SPÖ leaders. The whole report was an extended plea for the united front; this was "*no manoeuvre*", but "*a necessary condition of the proletarian class struggle*". The most important task of the KPÖ was "to bring home to the masses a *recognition of the necessity and possibility of partial struggles*"; this was the way to "*strengthen the confidence of the masses in the party*". The congress marked "*a decisive turning-point in the history of the KPÖ*". Before February 1934 it had been a small party. Now it was "in many respects a new party", strong in its union with the masses of workers and with "the best revolutionary core of the old SPÖ". The main resolution of the congress faithfully rehearsed these conclusions; and the congress also adopted a resolution on the trade unions, and an appeal to workers, petty bourgeois and intellectuals who had been seduced into National-Socialist organizations.[29] After the congress Koplenig and another member of the central committee, Fürnberg, travelled to Moscow, attended a session of the presidium of IKKI, visited Dimitrov, and received encouragement to persevere in the new course.[30]

The distinctive advantage which the KPÖ could draw from the international situation was the opportunity to combine social and national elements in its programme. The proletarian united front was also a national front for the defence of Austrian independence

[28] *Rundschau*, No. 53, October 4, 1934, p. 2301.

[29] *Ibid.* No. 53, October 4, 1934, pp. 2305–2312, No. 55, October 18, 1934, pp. 2425–2429; for Koplenig's report see *ibid.* No. 63, December 6, 1934, pp. 2881–2887.

[30] *Voprosy Istorii KPSS*, 1972, No. 3, p. 113; a speech by a KPÖ delegate at the presidium of IKKI on October 11, celebrating the achievements of the party, was published in *Kommunisticheskii Internatsional*, 1934, No. 35, pp. 44–49.

against German Fascism. Early in 1935 the KPÖ adopted a programme, allegedly at the instance of Comintern, which emphasized its opposition to the Anschluss with Germany: "We love Austria, and fight for its independence".[31] From this time the KPÖ became a model party in the eyes of Moscow. *Pravda* on the eve of the seventh congress of Comintern praised the modest, but substantial, achievement of the KPÖ. The events of February 1934 had dealt a heavy blow to social-democracy; but fear of Fascism still fed the reformist illusions of the mass of workers. Nevertheless February 1934 had marked a "beginning of a great turn of the masses towards communism". This had come about because the KPÖ had fought with the Schutzbund on the barricades, and was a major tribute to the united front proclaimed by the KPÖ at the congress in September 1934.[32] It was something of a paradox that the principles of the united front should have found the readiest acceptance and application in a country where opportunities for practical resistance to Fascist rule were negligible.

[31] B. Leibzon and K. Shirinya, *Povorot v Politike Kominterna* (2nd ed., 1975), p. 311.

[32] *Pravda*, July 22, 1935.

CHAPTER 14

THE SWISS COMMUNIST PARTY

The small but intellectually active Swiss party had never attracted much attention in Moscow, but became a minor source of embarrassment when, at the end of 1929, an influential member named Bringolf founded a break-away group in Schaffhausen, and established relations with the Brandler opposition in Germany.[1] It did not help that Bringolf was a friend of Humbert-Droz, the Swiss member of the Comintern secretariat, whose dissident attitudes had been under attack since 1928.[2] Humbert-Droz, after his return from Latin America in the autumn of 1929, and after Bukharin's final disgrace, had made a declaration renouncing his erroneous views and submitting to the discipline of Comintern.[3] A year later, under threat of expulsion from the party, he made a further abject and hypocritical recantation of his "false and dangerously conciliationist attitude towards Right elements", and promised to conform to the party line "not only out of discipline, but in the firm conviction that it is the only possible one".[4] Thanks to this act of self-abasement he was reprieved, and despatched at the end of 1930 on a mission to Spain, which occupied him for the next six months.[5] In the autumn of 1931 he was back in Switzerland, stood in the national elections of October as a communist candidate in his native town of La-Chaux-de-Fonds, and fell foul of the Swiss authorities. In November 1931 Comintern took a decision to attach him to the Swiss party for a period of six months, his mandate being to strengthen the work of the party after its electoral fiasco, and in particular to intensify the struggle against "Left" socialists, and against the Schaffhausen

---

[1] J. Humbert-Droz, *De Lénine à Staline* (Neuchatel, 1971), pp. 401–402.
[2] See *Foundations of a Planned Economy, 1926–1929*, Vol. 3, pp. 452–453.
[3] See *ibid.* Vol. 3, p. 256.
[4] *Internationale Presse-Korrespondenz*, No. 92, November 4, 1930, pp. 2248–2249; Humbert-Droz reproduced the statement in his memoirs, but maintained a studied silence about the occasion and date, remarking only that he had "no recollection of his political activity in 1930" (Humbert-Droz, *De Lénine à Staline* (Neuchatel, 1971), pp. 400–402).
[5] See p. 293 below.

dissidents.[6] The decision was prompted perhaps more by desire to be rid of a turbulent official, whose public expulsion would have created a scandal, than by any grave concern with the affairs of the Swiss party. Early in 1932 Humbert-Droz became secretary of the party.

Scarcely was Humbert-Droz installed in new party headquarters in Zurich when a highly critical letter was received from the political secretariat of Comintern. The Swiss party was reproached, among other things, with its failure to make any progress "in the struggle against social-democracy or in the development of a broad united front aimed at social-democratic workers". It had also "completely neglected the directives of the political secretariat on the question of the struggle against renegades". This provoked a lengthy argumentative reply, drafted by Humbert-Droz, from the party politburo, ending with a request for further instructions in time for the next politburo meeting on June 4–5, 1932. The instructions were not sent. Nor is Comintern likely to have been mollified by a proposal of Humbert-Droz to respond amicably to an overture from Bringolf for discussions on his re-admission to the party.[7] When, however, rioting workers clashed with the police in Zurich, Humbert-Droz dutifully hailed it as "a sign of the growing radicalization of the masses".[8]

The approach of the twelfth IKKI brought matters to a head. The Swiss party central committee adopted an immensely long resolution, drafted by Humbert-Droz, for submission to the secretariat in Moscow in advance of the session. Much of it repeated current Comintern doctrine in familiar Comintern phraseology. But sharp notes of dissent were audible to the attentive ear. Communist parties had failed to realize "a broad united front", or to win over the masses of workers who had left social-democratic parties or were unemployed; election results had revealed "stagnation or even a marked decline of communist influence".

Too often [the document continued] our policy has given the impression that our principal enemy was social-democracy and not the bourgeoisie. Too often our struggle has the exclusive

[6] J. Humbert-Droz, *Dix Ans de Lutte Antifasciste* (Neuchatel, 1972), pp. 9–11; the text of the decision does not seem to have been published elsewhere.

[7] *Ibid.* pp. 29–34; the communication from the Comintern secretariat was not published, and is known only from the text of the reply.

[8] *Internationale Presse-Korrespondenz*, No. 51, June 21, 1932, pp. 1611–1612.

character of an anti-social-democratic policy instead of a fierce struggle against capitalism. Our united front policy has remained a phrase, a formula, without any effort to achieve real contact and common action with social-democratic workers.

The party should conduct its struggle against the bourgeoisie "by practising a broad united front policy with social-democratic, Christian and non-party workers".[9] Neither the length nor the content of the document will have assured it a patient reading in Moscow.

When the three Swiss delegates, Humbert-Droz, Müller and Giorgio, arrived in Moscow in the middle of August 1932, they had a cool reception. A commission, which included Pyatnitsky, Bela Kun, Remmele and Neumann, was set up to deal with the affairs of the Swiss party; the moving spirit was apparently Knorin, now in charge of Central Europe in the Comintern secretariat. In a six-hour session on August 11, 1932, Humbert-Droz was confronted by a sweeping indictment of his record, beginning with his support for conciliation in the KPD at the end of 1928. He was now accused of seeking a bargain with social-democrats, in particular with the Genevese Left socialist Nicole. The errors of the Swiss resolution were brought home to him. Humbert-Droz wilted under the violence of the attack. He was not prepared for a mortal combat which could end only with his expulsion. At a further session of the commission on August 14 he once more presented his "mea culpa", and performed the ritual ceremony of self-flagellation. He admitted that the resolution lacked "a truly revolutionary orientation", and was permeated with "subconscious opportunism". Knorin was appeased, and Humbert-Droz felt that the trouble was over.[10]

Experience should have taught him that repentant sinners were not so lightly treated. The leading article in the issue of the Comintern journal which appeared on the eve of the session of IKKI was devoted to a vitriolic analysis of Humbert-Droz's offences, and concluded with the charge that the resolution

---

[9] The resolution was not published in full, but an abbreviated version can be found in J. Humbert-Droz, *Dix Ans de Lutte Antifasciste* (Neuchatel, 1972), pp. 34–47; some passages quoted by Thälmann and Humbert-Droz in their speeches at the twelfth IKKI were not included in this version.

[10] J. Humbert-Droz, *Dix Ans de Lutte Antifasciste* (Neuchatel, 1972), pp. 49–52.

submitted to IKKI was "an *international platform* of the Right".[11]
When the twelfth IKKI met, Kuusinen avoided any mention of
Swiss affairs in his opening report. But Thälmann spoke of the error
committed by the Swiss party under Humbert-Droz's "opportunist
influence", and challenged Humbert-Droz to "explain here the
political principles which impelled him to put forward such a
platform".[12] The victim had no option but to repeat his confession
of error publicly in the plenary session. He did so at inordinate
length, denouncing the peccant resolution as "fundamentally
erroneous" and "opportunist", but claiming that no member of the
party intended to "set up a platform opposed to the line of the
Communist International". The party wanted to "escape from its
sectarian narrowness, from its opportunist passivity"; Humbert-
Droz criticized his own past indulgence for Bringolf and Nicole, and
called for "absolute clarity of our political line in relation to social-
democracy, and in particular to Left social-democracy".[13] Müller,
the second Swiss delegate, spoke more briefly, placing the sole
responsibility for the resolution on Humbert-Droz, and exonerat-
ing the party central committee, which had not understood its
malign significance. His tone was more abject even than that of
Humbert-Droz.[14]

The process of humiliation had now gone far enough. Later in the
session, Knorin, in a speech devoted entirely to Germany, struck a
side-blow at Humbert-Droz, who had "burnt his fingers on the
German question" by pretending that the presidential and Prussian
elections demonstrated the failure of the Comintern line; and his old
enemy, Gusev, declared that his views led to a "defeatist, capitu-
lationist strategy", and to capitulation in face of Fascism".[15] But the
Swiss misdemeanour was not mentioned in the resolutions of the
session. The verdict was pronounced later in a resolution of the
Swiss commission. This recited in detail Humbert–Droz's offences
from 1928 onward, but accepted the assurances and promises of

[11] *Kommunisticheskii Internatsional*, 1932, No. 24, pp. 3–7. The article was entitled
"The Bolshevik Broadside against Opportunism"; its author was probably Knorin.
According to J. Humbert-Droz, *Dix Ans de Lutte Antifasciste* (Neuchatel, 1972),
p. 64, it appeared on September 1, just after the session had begun.
[12] *XII Plenum IKKI* (1933), i, 69–70.
[13] *Ibid*. i, 192–200.
[14] *Ibid*. ii, 49–51.
[15] *Ibid*. ii, 69, 198; for the controversy between Gusev and Humbert-Droz in
1928 see *Foundations of a Planned Economy, 1926–1929*, Vol. 3, pp. 977–978.

amendment received from all three Swiss delegates. The party central committee was instructed to conduct a vigorous campaign to reverse its past errors; and Humbert-Droz in particular was to "unmask" the opportunist policies which he had fastened on the party. The delegates, battered into submission, returned quietly to Switzerland; and Humbert-Droz published yet another contrite article in the party press.[16]

The year following the twelfth IKKI was a time of bewilderment for the Swiss party and for Humbert-Droz. On November 9, 1932, riots occurred in Geneva between socialist and Right-wing parties. The police fired and some twenty socialists and a few communists were killed. In the wave of indignation which ensued, Humbert-Droz, faithful to the Comintern line, was compelled to refuse all cooperation with the socialists; and this policy found so little favour with Geneva communists that the party there was reduced to a tiny faction. An awkward feature of the situation was that Nicole, the leader of the Geneva socialists, had been an ardent advocate of cooperation with the communists, and in the previous year had attended the Amsterdam peace congress. After the establishment of Hitler's dictatorship in Germany, Humbert-Droz for a time made contact with German dissident communist *émigrés* in Zurich. But he soon withdrew from an involvement which seemed likely to damage his image in Moscow, and throughout the year, on his own showing, "publicly expounded the policy of the International" at meetings and in the party newspaper, and "only in private conversations stated my real opinion".[17]

When Humbert-Droz reached Moscow at the end of November 1933 for the thirteenth IKKI, he met with a frosty welcome. Not much was said in open session. But Pyatnitsky apparently blamed him for the success of the socialists, and the communist fiasco, in the recent Geneva elections.[18] Müller, who spoke as leader of the Swiss delegation, was careful to dissociate himself from the resolution presented by Humbert-Droz a year earlier to the twelfth IKKI, which

[16] J. Humbert-Droz, *Dix Ans de Lutte Antifasciste* (Neuchatel, 1972), pp. 65–70.
[17] *Ibid.* pp. 88–90, 95.
[18] Humbert-Droz wrote to his wife on December 2 that "Pyatnitsky this morning launched an attack on me . . . holding me responsible for the fact that the social-democrats won 46 per cent of the votes at Geneva" (*ibid.* p. 96). Pyatnitsky did speak on the morning of that day; but no such passage appeared in the official record of the speech (*XIII Plenum IKKI* (1934), pp. 173–200).

contested "the presence of a revolutionary upsurge of the masses". He claimed that progress had been made in winning over socialist workers for a united front, and poked fun at Nicole with his "revolutionary phrases".[19] Humbert-Droz's original intention not to speak was shaken by Knorin, who taunted "the ultra-silent comrade Humbert-Droz" with having been induced by "Leftists" to believe that Comintern "by its reply to the appeal of the Second International initiated new tactics in the question of the united front", and made a fierce attack on "'Left' social-democrats of the type of Nicole".[20] Thus provoked, Humbert-Droz belatedly delivered a long speech which once more alternated between self-defence and self-abasement, and can have satisfied nobody. It was punctuated by cries of disapproval from the other Swiss delegates.[21] The affairs of the Swiss party were left in the same fog of uncertainty which enveloped those of more important parties; and the Swiss delegates returned home without further guidance. An authoritative article published after the session made no concessions. The Swiss bourgeoisie was said to be pursuing the Fascisization of the country in league with the social-democrats: special condemnation was reserved for the "Left" social-democratic followers of Nicole who controlled the canton of Geneva. "Opportunism" on this issue was still hindering the evolution of the Swiss Communist Party into a "Bolshevik mass party".[22]

The growing menace of Fascism created alarm throughout Switzerland, but brought about no change in the official policy of the Swiss Communist Party. Since the membership of the Swiss party at this time did not exceed 2000 and of the Red trade unions 4000, while the social-democratic party counted 40,000 members and the reformist trade unions 250,000,[23] the formation of an anti-Fascist front seemed to depend on initiatives within the social-democratic party rather than on action by the communists. A congress against war and Fascism, held at Zurich on May 29, 1934, was said to have produced demonstrations by socialist workers in favour of a united front with the communists, and to have discredited the socialist leaders who obstructed it.[24] In the autumn

[19] *Ibid.* pp. 276–278.
[20] *Ibid.* p. 340; for the "reply" referred to see p. 85 above.
[21] *XIII Plenum IKKI* (1934), pp. 406–411.
[22] *Rundschau*, No. 17, February 22, 1934, pp. 612–613.
[23] *Kommunisticheskii Internatsional*, 1935, No. 7, p. 9.
[24] *Rundschau*, No. 36, June 14, 1934, p. 1484.

of 1934 the Swiss Communist Party demanded a referendum on a proposed law prolonging the period of compulsory military training. While the social-democratic leaders opposed the demand, it was supported by a sufficient number of non-communist voters to validate the demand; and the social-democratic party at its congress in Lucerne in January 1935 decided by a large majority of 343 to 200 to vote against the law. When the referendum was eventually held on February 24, 1935, the law was approved by a majority of 501,434 to 429,520. But the size of the minority, sponsored jointly by social-democrats and communists, represented a gain for the communist party and for the principles of a united front.[25]

Nevertheless, when the time came, the Swiss party seems to have been taken aback by the sudden switch in the Comintern line. An article by Thorez extolling the popular front in its most extended form, which appeared in the French edition of the Comintern journal at the beginning of March, was a landmark for the Swiss party.[26] In Basel a coalition of social-democrats and communists overthrew the bourgeois government of the canton; and a massive joint demonstration was held on May 1. Contacts between the two parties were established in Zurich and Geneva.[27] As successive pronouncements from Moscow demonstrated the extent of change, the relief of Humbert-Droz and his supporters knew no bounds. He departed for Moscow with the other Swiss delegates to the seventh congress, "with a fairly light heart, and satisfied to discover that Comintern accepted—though rather late, too late in my opinion—the policy which I had recommended in 1928 and 1932, and which it had so vigorously condemned".[28]

---

[25] J. Humbert-Droz, *Dix Ans de Lutte Antifasciste* (Neuchatel, 1972), pp. 123–124.
[26] *Ibid.* pp. 114–117; for Thorez's article see p. 145 above.
[27] *Rundschau*, No. 49, September 21, 1935. pp. 2138–2139.
[28] J. Humbert-Droz, *Dix Ans de Lutte Antifasciste* (Neuchatel, 1972), p. 129.

CHAPTER 15

THE SPANISH COMMUNIST PARTY (PCE)

The Spanish Communist Party (PCE), which was founded in 1921 and held its first two congresses in 1922 and 1923, had from the first to compete for the allegiance of the workers with the established Spanish Socialist Workers' Party (PSOE) and its trade union organization (UGT), as well as with the older and more powerful anarchist-syndicalist trade union organization (CNT), linked with an underground anarchist federation (FAI). After 1923 it was subjected, together with the rest of the Left, to the harsh and repressive rule of Primo de Rivera, which deprived it of any means of legal activity. In these conditions it remained a small sect of a few hundred members.[1] The only Spaniard to earn some prestige in Moscow was Nin, who worked for many years in Profintern, where he proved something of a trouble-maker.[2] In August 1929 the third congress of the PCE, held in Paris, endorsed the decisions taken by the sixth congress of Comintern a year earlier. But the occasion was a pure formality without practical consequences for anyone.

The Iberian peninsula, under strictly autocratic regimes dominated by the powerful influence of the Catholic Church, had remained a backwater in western Europe. In Spain, industry, centred in the Catalan city of Barcelona, expanded slowly. Agriculture stagnated, being conducted mainly in the form of large *latifundia* employing the low-paid labour of peasants who were either altogether landless or unable to scrape a bare subsistence from their paltry holdings. During the nineteen-twenties the ferment of discontent spread among radical intellectuals preaching the cause of bourgeois democracy, among workers striving to organize for protection against employers, and among peasants, less articulate, but even more ruthlessly exploited. For a long time a self-

---

[1] A PSOE leader declared in the spring of 1930 that the PCE was "totally unknown" in Spain (*Kommunisticheskii Internatsional*, 1930, No. 13–14, p. 99); according to an apparently authoritative article in the Soviet press the PCE "at the moment of the overthrow of the monarchy [i.e. April 1931] did not have even a thousand members" (*Mirovoe Khozyaistvo i Mirovaya Politika*, 1934, No. 11, p. 8).

[2] See *Foundations of a Planned Economy, 1926–1929*, Vol. 3, pp. 189–191.

confident and apparently impregnable autocracy stifled every symptom of revolt. But a first rift in the situation occurred in January 1930 with the overthrow of the dictatorship of Primo de Rivera, and his replacement as Prime Minister by Berenguer, who promised the restoration of constitutional freedoms. This gesture, designed to allay the restiveness of a bourgeois democratic middle class, had little appeal for the seriously fragmented workers' movement. The anarchist CNT had some two million members, the socialist UGT, affiliated to the PSOE, more than a million. The tiny PCE, led by Bullejos, scarcely impinged on the scene.

Events in Spain had hitherto rarely engaged the attention of Comintern. The Comintern press recorded the disorders which followed the downfall of Primo de Rivera, but found no encouragement in his replacement by Berenguer's "reactionary-monarchist-clerical dictatorship";[3] and the change seems to have passed unnoticed at the session of the presidium of IKKI in Moscow in the following month. An article in the Comintern journal, written (no doubt, in the absence of a reliable Spaniard) by the Italian representative in IKKI, Grieco, contained only empty platitudes and unrealistic exhortations to the PCE.[4] Early in March, however, after preliminary discussions with Comintern representatives in Paris, the PCE held a party conference in a village near Bilbao, referred to in the records as "the Pamplona conference". It was attended by a Comintern delegate, an unnamed member of the KPD, who played a conspicuous role in the proceedings. Everyone agreed that revolution was on the march in Spain. But controversy turned on the well-worn theme of the character of the revolution. If it was still in the stage of a bourgeois democratic revolution against the remnants of feudalism (whose existence in Spain could hardly be denied), it would be the duty of communists to lend support to bourgeois democratic parties. If, on the other hand, the dictatorship of Primo de Rivera and Berenguer had reached the stage of finance capitalism, communists should already fix their sights on the coming proletarian revolution. The latter hypothesis accorded better with the prescriptions of the sixth Comintern congress of 1928, and was supported by the Comintern delegate. But many members of the PCE, including its leader Bullejos, leaned to the former view. In these conditions, the political resolution adopted by

[3] *Internationale Presse-Korrespondenz*, No. 11, January 31, 1930, p. 247.
[4] *Kommunisticheskii Internatsional*, 1930, No. 4, pp. 25–31.

the conference was a compromise. The principles of the sixth congress were firmly enunciated. A "democratic transformation of the dictatorship" was pronounced impossible, and the party was urged to win the masses away from the democratic opposition. The conference endorsed the aim proclaimed at the third party congress in the previous year: "the establishment of a democratic dictator-ship of workers and peasants on the basis of worker and peasant Soviets, finding its expression in a worker-peasant government". But sections of the resolution relating to the actual situation were apparently less satisfying to Comintern orthodoxy. Nor had the PCE any achievements to its credit. In the main industrial centre, Barcelona, the workers' movement was dominated almost exclus-ively by anarchists; and support offered by the PCE to the claims of Catalonia and the Basque provinces to independence was lukewarm.[5]

Uneasiness in Comintern was revealed in a summons to Bullejos to attend a meeting of WEB in Berlin. Dimitrov presided, and the discussion lasted for two days. Some compromise was reached;[6] but no record appeared in the Comintern press. Meanwhile trouble had arisen from another quarter. The Catalan federation of the PCE, based on Barcelona, the strongest local party organization, and the one which could boast the highest proportion of industrial workers among its members, claimed an independent role in the party which may also have reflected strains of Catalan nationalism. The leader Maurín, a founder member of the PCE, was married to a sister of the French dissident Souvarine[7]—a circumstance which encouraged the suspicion that his loyalty to Comintern was not beyond question. Nin, who in September 1930 returned from Moscow to Spain, provided a fresh focus of discontent in the PCE, organizing a group of Left communists with the title (in Catalan) of Esquerra Comunista, which later became the Marxist Workers' Unity Party (POUM). He quickly established relations with Maurín and

[5] The main sources for the conference are J. Bullejos, *La Comintern en España* (Mexico, 1972), pp. 98–100; E. Comín Colomer, *Historia del Partido Comunista de España*, i (1963), pp. 218–219 (this is an "official" history published under the Franco regime, which prints a number of PCE documents, presumably from police archives), and an article by Grieco in *Kommunisticheskii Internatsional*, 1930, No. 13–14, pp. 99–107, which quotes selectively from the resolution; the full text of the resolution was not published.

[6] J. Bullejos, *La Comintern en España* (Mexico, 1972), p. 100.

[7] See *Socialism in One Country, 1926–1929*, Vol. 3, 155–156.

entered into correspondence with Trotsky in Prinkipo.[8] The party central committee condemned the "fractional activity" of Trotskyist elements inside and outside the party who sought to transform it into a "second socialist party" and to come to terms with bourgeois republicans, and expelled several unnamed offenders.[9]

Increasing symptoms of unrest persuaded Comintern that serious attention must be paid to the troubles of the PCE. In the spring of 1930 a high-powered Comintern delegation, consisting of Duclos, the PCF leader, Rabaté of the French CGTU, who represented Profintern, and Woog, a Swiss member of the Comintern secretariat, was dispatched to Spain. Some friction evidently occurred between the commission and the party leaders, Bullejos, Trilla and Adame, whose methods, according to Duclos, were "authoritarian and marked by a sectarianism which helped to isolate the party".[10] The task was complicated by the arrest on August 23, 1930, of Bullejos and other party leaders, who appear however to have enjoyed the regime of political prisoners and communicated freely with the outside world. The main bone of contention was trade union policy. The delegates had come with firm instructions from Profintern to create a new "unitary" trade union confederation on the lines of the German trade union opposition (RGO). The PCE leaders protested that this would nullify their efforts to penetrate the anarcho-syndicalist CNT, the most powerful trade union federation in Spain. But their objections were overruled.[11] Whatever the result of these measures, the rising wave of strikes and violence towards the close of the year, culminating in an attempted republican *coup* by a handful of young officers, encouraged *Pravda* to celebrate "the powerful growth of the revolutionary workers' movement", and to believe that the

[8] For Maurín and Nin see V. Alba, *Dos Revolucionarios: Joaquin Maurín, Andreu Nin* (1975), pp. 99–158, 351–358; selections from Trotsky's correspondence with Nin beginning with a letter from Trotsky of September 13, 1930, and a letter from Nin of October 21, 1930, were published in L. Trotsky, *The Spanish Revolution (1931–39)* (1973), pp. 369–400.

[9] *Internationale Presse-Korrespondenz*, No. 82, September 30, 1930, p. 2032. According to Nin, Maurín was expelled at this time for refusing to make a declaration "against Trotskyism", and the Catalan party federation, having declared their solidarity with him, was also expelled (L. Trotsky, *The Spanish Revolution (1931–39)* (1973), p. 370). But this report seems to have been premature; Maurín was not expelled till the summer of 1931 (see p. 299 below).

[10] J. Duclos, *Mémoires*, i (1968), 317.

[11] J. Bullejos, *La Comintern en España* (Mexico, 1972), pp. 101–103.

Spanish workers were "ever more rapidly adopting the programme and slogans of the PCE", and had "become conscious of its role as leader in the revolution".[12]

In January 1931, Humbert-Droz arrived in Barcelona to replace Duclos.[13] The conditions of his appointment suggest that it was inspired rather by desire to remove a trouble-maker from Moscow than by any particular preoccupation with developments in Spain. He carried credentials only from Profintern, and was instructed to confine himself to trade union affairs. His first impressions were bleak. He found "nothing, nothing, nothing", and "what there is divided, sub-divided, impotent". In Barcelona there were less than 50 official communists, of whom only a dozen were active, though Maurín had 700 followers who constituted a quasi-independent Catalonian communist federation. It was the first time, wrote Humbert-Droz, that he had been instructed "to set in motion a movement which did not exist". Duclos had authorized him to act in his place as head of the Comintern delegation. But this authorization was not endorsed from Moscow; and Humbert-Droz bombarded Manuilsky with protests against his indeterminate status.[14] All the members of the politburo of the PCE except one were in prison. But this did not prevent them from issuing instructions to the party, including a demand to abstain from participation in the forthcoming municipal elections, which Humbert-Droz thought misguided, and a call for early revolutionary action, which he thought unrealistic.

The release of the prisoners in March 1931 increased the tension. A strong mutual antipathy sprang up between Humbert-Droz and Bullejos.[15] The Comintern delegation in Barcelona now consisted of Humbert-Droz and Rabaté, Duclos being still absent in Paris, and Woog having been deported by the police. After two days' argument Bullejos bowed to Humbert-Droz's insistence that the PCE should participate in the municipal elections fixed for April 12. But this was the extent of Humbert-Droz's success. The party central committee decided, against his opinion, to transfer the party

[12] *Pravda*, December 17, 1930.
[13] J. Duclos, *Mémoires*, i (1968), 335.
[14] J. Humbert-Droz, *De Lénine à Staline* (Neuchatel, 1971), pp. 403–412.
[15] Humbert-Droz in his memoirs described Bullejos as "the prototype of a Stalinist with 'revolutionary' slogans but very opportunist tactics" (*ibid.* p. 415); the narrative of events in J. Bullejos, *La Comintern en España* (Mexico, 1972), pp. 111–119, does not, however, differ substantially from that of Humbert-Droz.

headquarters from Barcelona to Madrid; and controversy was resumed on the issue, now vital for electoral tactics, of the character of the revolution. Humbert-Droz, apparently without further consulting Moscow, argued that the PCE was confronted by a bourgeois revolution against a feudal regime, and should at this stage give support to the republicans. Bullejos, modifying his attitude a year earlier, now held that the regime in Spain was already in essence bourgeois-capitalist, and that the PCE should call for a worker-peasant revolution—a slogan implying opposition to the bourgeois republican parties. Both Humbert-Droz and Bullejos wrote to Moscow expounding their views.[16]

While, however, this controversy was in progress, Manuilsky at the eleventh IKKI in Moscow, unknown to Humbert-Droz, had declared that the presence in Spain of "*deep survivals of feudalism*" did not justify the view that "a typical bourgeois democratic revolution is ripening". On the contrary, the regime was already "bound up with the whole system of finance capital and imperialism", and "*the moving forces of the Spanish revolution can be only the proletariat and the peasantry*".[17] Trilla, the PCE's representative in Moscow, and the only Spanish delegate to speak at the session, had evidently been well schooled in the current Comintern line. On the one hand, "a group of responsible comrades", holding that the seizure of power was the party's "fundamental task and central slogan", had advocated abstention from the elections; this error had persisted for two months. On the other hand, the party central committee now maintained that the Spanish bourgeoisie was engaged in a historic struggle against a feudal regime, and merited support; but, having correctly decided to participate in the elections on this basis, it had put forward false and confusing slogans.[18] Confusion in Comintern about Spanish affairs matched the confusion prevailing among the party leaders in Spain.

---

[16] J. Humbert-Droz, *De Lénine à Staline* (Neuchatel, 1971), pp. 440, 446–448; J. Bullejos, *La Comintern en España* (Mexico, 1972), pp. 113–119. Bullejos bitterly accused Humbert-Droz of fomenting hostility to him in the party (*ibid.* p. 159).

[17] *XI Plenum IKKI* (1932), i, 52–53.

[18] *Ibid.* i, 530–531. Humbert-Droz complained that, while Trilla in Moscow had briefed Bullejos on the correct line, he had received no information from Manuilsky (J. Humbert-Droz, *De Lénine à Staline* (Neuchatel, 1971), p. 449); Trilla informed Bullejos that Comintern approved his line, though "not in its entirety" (J. Bullejos, *La Comintern en España* (Mexico, 1972), p. 114).

The elections of April 12, 1931, were a fiasco for the PCE; Bullejos could console himself only with the reflexion that its aim had been not to win votes, but "to present itself to the masses as an independent party".[19] But they were a triumph for republicans, radicals and socialists, whose sweeping victories, coming on top of a long period of strikes and violence, rocked the monarchy to its foundations. Two days later, Alfonso XIII, intimidated by fierce displays of anti-monarchist feeling, abdicated and left the country; and a republic was proclaimed amid scenes of enthusiasm and sporadic disorder. A coalition government was formed with Alcadá Zamora, a conservative republican, as Prime Minister. It included three socialists, Prieto as Minister of Finance, Fernandez de los Rios as Minister of Justice, and Largo Caballero, the secretary-general of the UGT, as Minister of Labour. But these events brought nothing but humiliation for the PCE, revealing "the extreme weakness of the party, its complete isolation, its minute influence on the masses".[20] Its first reaction to the abdication was a murmur of confused and discordant voices, scarcely heard amid the general enthusiasm of the proclamation of the republic. Communists are said to have taken the lead in a popular movement to release prisoners from the jails. But when communists attempted to address the crowds or distribute leaflets, they were "hissed, shouted down, and received with a threatening hostility".[21] May day demonstrations in Seville, Barcelona and Bilbao led to clashes of workers with the police, in some of which communists were involved. But their following remained insignificant compared with that of the anarchists and socialists.[22]

The dramatic events of April 1931 could not, however, be ignored by the communist world. A few days after the abdication, the PCI was holding its fourth congress in Germany. Some delegates wished, like other Italian anti-Fascist parties, to hail the Spanish republic with enthusiasm. But the majority were content to accept Togliatti's more cautious verdict. Spain was not like Italy. Survivals

---

[19] J. Bullejos, *La Comintern en España* (Mexico, 1972), p. 122.

[20] J. Humbert-Droz, *De Lénine a Staline* (Neuchatel, 1971), p. 451.

[21] The most vivid description of the scene is in a letter from Humbert-Droz to Manuilsky (J. Humbert-Droz, *De Lénine à Staline* (Neuchatel, 1971), pp. 451–453).

[22] J. Bullejos, *La Comintern en España* (Mexico, 1972), pp. 124–126, describes various demonstrations including a joint one in Barcelona shared by the PCE with the anarchist CNT and Maurín's Workers' and Peasants' Bloc; but one suspects that the role of the PCE was small.

of feudalism were still powerful. What had been achieved was at best a bourgeois revolution, and not a victory for the proletarian cause.[23] Bullejos, in an article in the Comintern press, explained that the new bourgeois government was seeking to mobilize its forces "against the proletariat and the peasantry", and exhorted the masses to cast off "democratic illusions" and "march to the conquest of their own republic, the republic of workers', peasants' and soldiers' Soviets".[24] The confusion of reactions in Comintern was reflected in a two-part article in *Pravda* which concluded that it would be "incorrect to characterize the Spanish revolution in its present stage as a socialist revolution", and that "the most immediate task is a worker-peasant revolution against the landlords and the bourgeoisie".[25] A few days later a leading article in *Pravda* instructed the PCE to work for such objectives as "the disarming of reactionaries, the arming of the proletariat, election of factory and workshop committees, . . . the seven-hour working day etc." It claimed optimistically that *"democratic illusions are passing away, and the movement is in transition to a higher plane"*. But it evaded any definition of the attitude to be adopted to the republican government, and gave no directives on participation in the forthcoming elections to the Cortes.[26] Finally the central committee of the PCE issued a belated appeal addressed to "Workers! Soldiers! Comrades!", whom it urged to take up the struggle for "Soviets of Workers and Peasants" and for a "workers' and peasants' republic".[27]

Humbert-Droz, disowned and disillusioned, left for Moscow at the end of April 1931, and a few days later Trilla arrived from Moscow. Doubtless instructed by him in the latest orthodoxy in Comintern, the PCE put out on May 11 what appears to have been its first manifesto since the proclamation of the republic. The provocation was a monarchist demonstration on the previous day which had led to violent clashes with the Left. The manifesto denounced a republican government which protected monarchists

[23] P. Spriano, *Storia del Partito Comunista Italiano*, ii (1969), 309–310; for this congress see pp. 245–246 above. Togliatti's views were expounded in an article in the party journal (P. Togliatti, *Opere*, II (1973), i, 328–340).

[24] *Internationale Presse-Korrespondenz*, No. 41, May 5, 1931, pp. 985–986; the article may have originally appeared in a Spanish communist publication.

[25] *Pravda*, May 7, 10, 1931.

[26] *Ibid.* May 14, 1931.

[27] *Internationale Presse-Korrespondenz*, No. 47, May 21, 1931, pp. 1122–1123.

and allowed the "odious civil guard" to fire on the people. Among its demands were the disarmament of the civil guard, the armament of the people and the expulsion of the religious orders.[28] But Trilla had also brought with him a summons for Bullejos to present himself in Moscow for a meeting of the political commission of IKKI. The session, which was attended by all the leading members of the Comintern hierarchy, as well as by Pieck, Togliatti and Thorez, lasted for three days. It was not an agreeable occasion. To condemn the failures and shortcomings of the PCE was easy enough. But agreement was not so readily reached on the instructions to be given to it; and the long IKKI letter of May 21, in which they were eventually embodied, reflected the wide variety of opinions and reservations, and made up in emphasis what it lacked in clarity. "*The party as a whole,*" it began, "*and its leadership in particular, has not understood the profound significance of the events of April 14.*" These events had shown the desire of the masses for revolutionary change which the new government had failed to satisfy. It was wrong to cry "Long live the republic"—that was the slogan of Trotskyists and Maurinists—but also wrong to cry "Down with the republic". The demand for Soviets was correct as a distant prospect, but not as a call for immediate action. The PCE should in no circumstances form an alliance with other parties; the letter recalled "the Bolshevik slogan: Fight together, but march separately". Nor should the party support the republican government. Its task was to unmask the pretensions of the Left, and, "first of all, to smash the anarcho-syndicalist and socialist leaders who still have a great influence on the working class".[29]

Trotsky's reaction to these events was prompt and emphatic; more than any other observer he was alive to the analogy of the Russian revolution. The Spanish communist workers were still too weak to seize power by themselves; what was required was "a broad and bold policy of a united front". The PCE should put forward

[28] J. Bullejos, *La Comintern en España* (Mexico, 1972), pp. 127–130.

[29] E. Comín Colomer, *Historia del Partido Comunista de España*, i (1965), 287–301, which prints the text from police archives; it had not been previously published. For some account of the discussions see J. Bullejos, *La Comintern en España* (Mexico, 1972), pp. 121–134; Humbert-Droz treats the occasion as a victory of his views over those of Bullejos, "who recommended the party to struggle against the republican government and for its replacement by a worker-peasant government"—a highly tendentious interpretation of the letter of May 21, which he does not mention (J. Humbert-Droz, *De Lénine à Staline* (Neuchatel 1971), p. 454).

"the most radical democratic slogans". But its main demand should be for a workers' Soviet, "the most natural, most open, most honest and most healthy form" of a united front of workers, which by gaining the confidence of the workers would "open the era of the socialist revolution"—the familiar theme of permanent revolution.[30] A few days later he addressed a letter to the politburo in Moscow predicting that the continued confusion in the PCE would lead "to the establishment in Spain of *genuine Fascism* in the style of Mussolini"; this was predictably ignored.[31] In a lengthy article at the end of May 1931 Trotsky summed up his conclusions. It had been right to boycott elections to the Cortes under Alfonso; to boycott them under the republic was a different matter. The PCE should not shrink from putting forward such democratic demands as votes for men and women at the age of 18, a single chamber constitution, national self-determination (important for Catalonia) and agrarian reform. The point at issue was "not the struggle for power, but the struggle for the masses".[32] Meanwhile Comintern, conscious perhaps of the inadequacy of its instructions, especially in view of the impending elections to the Spanish Cortes on June 28, 1931, took the desperate step of sending yet another delegation to Spain. It consisted of Stöcker, a German, Purman, a Pole, neither of whom knew anything of the country, and Humbert-Droz. The delegation arrived in Madrid on June 5. The only member of the original Duclos delegation still in Spain was Rabaté, who spoke fluent Spanish and served as interpreter. But since he spoke no German, and Stöcker had no language but his own, communication must have been difficult. The mission proved a complete fiasco.[33] About the same time, Koltsov, one of the editors of *Pravda*, arrived in Spain to report on the elections.[34]

The electoral campaign of the PCE, presumably conducted under the guidance of the Comintern delegation, declared "against the dictatorship of Primo de Rivera and Berenguer and for the republic". But it roundly attacked the socialists, its aim being to

[30] *Byulleten' Oppozitsii* (Paris), No. 21–22, May–June 1931, pp. 18–19; these notes, entitled "The Ten Commandments of the Spanish Communist", were dated April 15, 1931—four days after the proclamation of the Spanish republic.

[31] *Ibid.* No. 21–22, May–June 1931, p. 17.

[32] *Ibid.* No. 21–22, May–June, 1931, pp. 2–11.

[33] J. Humbert-Droz, *De Lénine à Staline* (Neuchatel, 1971), pp. 455–457; J. Bullejos, *La Comintern en España* (Mexico, 1972), pp. 150–152.

[34] E. Comín Colomer, *Historia del Partido Comunista de España*, i (1965), 353.

mobilize the masses against "the government of *provocateurs*", against "social-democrats, anarchists and opportunists of all kinds", and for a "revolutionary dictatorship of proletariat and peasantry", with the ultimate goal of a "Soviet Iberian federation" and the dictatorship of the proletariat.[35] The campaign was marred by an untoward episode. In March 1931 Maurín and Nin had come together and founded a Worker-Peasant Bloc (Bloc Obrer i Camperol) which, without breaking away from the PCE, virtually substituted itself for the Catalan federation of the party, and put forward its own list of candidates for the elections. During the campaign Maurín made a provocative speech in Madrid, in which he denounced Comintern for attempting to apply to other countries the "Russian formula of revolution", and held it responsible for past failures in Germany, Bulgaria and China.[36] In due course Maurín was expelled from the party, taking with him the whole Catalan federation, and leaving the PCE without any organization, and with only a minute handful of followers, in the major industrial city of Barcelona.[37]

The elections took place on June 28, 1931, and passed off peacefully. Of 466 seats in the new Cortes the government coalition won 383; socialists held 116 of these, making them the largest single party. The opposition consisted of a motley collection of small extreme Right, and extreme Left, parties, together with 14 Basque and 3 Catalan representatives. The anarchists refrained from voting. The PCE, though it won no seats, did well to receive a total, excluding Catalonia, of 190,000 votes. In Catalonia, it was paralysed by the schism of Maurín's group, which put up its own candidates and secured 92,000 votes.[38] *Pravda* attributed the weakness of the PCE to anarcho-syndicalist influence over the workers; the CNT was "one of the chief props of the radical-socialist

---

[35] *Internationale Presse-Korrespondenz*, No. 57, June 16, 1931, pp. 1300–1301; no text of a programme has been found.

[36] E. Comín Colomer, *Historia del Partido Comunista de España*, i (1965), 386.

[37] For the situation in Barcelona see p. 293 above. Nin vacillated between Maurín and the PCE, writing to Trotsky on July 13, 1931, that Maurín's "electoral campaign . . . had little of a communist nature" (L. Trotsky, *The Spanish Revolution (1931–39)* (1973), p. 376); what appears to have been the platform of the Maurín group was severely criticized by Trotsky in *Byulleten' Oppozitsii* (Paris), No. 23, August 1931, pp. 16–18.

[38] E. Comín Colomer, *Historia del Partido Comunista de España*, i (1965) 304–305; J. Humbert-Droz, *De Lénine à Staline* (Neuchatel, 1971), p. 457, records his abortive attempt to patch up the quarrel with the Maurín group.

bloc".[39] The Comintern delegation, frustrated on all sides, took its leave, Humbert-Droz being assigned to duty with the Swiss party.[40]

These developments were not calculated to relieve anxieties in Comintern. In October 1931 the PCE leaders once more visited Moscow to listen to another broadside from Manuilsky, who, in a speech full of irony, accused them of having failed to engage in self-criticism after the IKKI letter of the previous May. "Spontaneous movements" of peasants and workers were rife in Spain, but where was the party? What existed in the PCE was not democracy, but the "petty tyranny" of local bosses. The present leadership was "an obstacle to the Bolshevization of the party". Manuilsky called for a party congress which, after another open letter and discussions with the Latin secretariat, would have to deal with the agrarian and trade union questions and with party organization.[41] The PCE leaders are likely to have been more angered than edified by these wholesale reproaches.

Meanwhile the first ostensible task of the government whose authority had been confirmed by the June elections was to draft a constitution. The graver issues confronting it were demands for social and agrarian reform, and for autonomy for Catalonia. Any zeal displayed by the socialists in support of these demands was curbed by their radical allies. Already in August 1931 *Pravda* concluded that the republican-socialist government was "*as like a military dictatorship as one egg to another*".[42] Alcadá Zamora resigned as Prime Minister in October to become President of the Republic, and was succeeded by Azaña; and a republican constitution was adopted on December 9. This did nothing to calm the rising wave of disorder. The elections had been followed by a week of strikes in Seville which cost several lives. Barcelona was the scene of a general

[39] *Pravda*, July 4, 1931; Trotsky also wrote of "the syndicalist traditions of the Spanish proletariat" as "one of the chief obstacles in the way of the development of the revolution" (*Byulleten' Oppozitsii* (Paris), No. 25–26, November–December 1931, p. 1).

[40] See p. 282 above.

[41] The speech was not published, and was translated in E. Comín Colomer, *Historia del Partido Comunista en España*, i (1965), 355–368, from police archives; nothing else is known of the proceedings.

[42] *Pravda*, August 7, 1931; according to the Spanish delegate at the twelfth IKKI a year later a "counter-revolutionary bourgeois-landlord dictatorship" disguised itself in democratic forms (*XII Plenum IKKI* (1933), ii, 85).

strike in September, and a further general strike was proclaimed in January 1932. Peasant discontent was less articulate, but not less deep. In these events the PCE played no visible part, though its membership was said to have increased from 3000 to 7000 in the summer of 1931.[43] But this was far from satisfying critical observers in Comintern. The party congress had been fixed for March 1932; and the party was invited to send a delegation to Moscow for schooling by the Spanish commission of IKKI.

The session took place in January 1932, and Bullejos and his three colleagues had once more to face an unflattering reception. The Comintern leaders were present, together with Togliatti, Pieck and Ulbricht, Doriot and Barbé. Manuilsky led the attack, in which Pyatnitsky, Lozovsky and Togliatti joined. The Spaniards refused to confess their guilt and attempted to refute Manuilsky's arguments.[44] The conclusions were registered in a letter to the party, oddly issued in the name, not of IKKI but of WEB. It characterized the republican regime as a "bourgeois-landlord bloc", brought into power "with the active participation of socialists and anarcho-syndicalists". The PSOE played "the chief role in the counter-revolutionary bloc of bewildering the masses". The PCE had achieved "some political and organizational successes". Membership during the past year had risen from 1500 to 10,000, and it had established a daily newspaper, the *Mundo Obrero*. But the rest of the letter was devoted to an unsparing analysis of its errors. It had failed to appreciate "the immense political significance of the economic, social and political survivals of feudalism in Spain". On the other hand, it had failed to grasp the counter-revolutionary role of the bourgeoisie in the ripening bourgeois democratic revolution, and the need for the proletariat "as the one truly revolutionary class" to take the lead. "Passivity" and "sectarianism" had marked the attitude of the PCE to the formation of Soviets, to the agrarian, trade union and national questions. It had not reacted strongly enough to the Trotskyist and Maurín oppositions; an attempt should be made to win the Maurínists, though not Maurín himself, back into the party.[45]

[43] J. Bullejos, *La Comintern en España* (Mexico, 1972), p. 155; an article in *Internationale Presse-Korrespondenz*, No. 96, October 6, 1931, p. 2163, claimed an increasing number of supporters in Madrid.

[44] J. Bullejos, *La Comintern en España* (Mexico, 1972), pp. 160–163.

[45] *Internationale Presse-Korrespondenz*, No. 4, January 15, 1932, pp. 91–95; *Kommunisticheskii Internatsional*, 1931, No. 2–3, pp. 38–45; E. Comín Colomer,

Bullejos, before leaving Moscow, was introduced by Pyatnitsky to Maevsky, newly appointed TASS representative in Spain, who would serve as a personal link between him and Stalin.[46] It was an odd gesture, presumably meant as a mark of favour. But it had no sequel. A new Comintern representative arrived in Spain in the person of Codovilla, who had long worked in Comintern, mainly on Latin American affairs.[47] This did not improve matters. Bullejos and his colleagues, outraged by the hectoring tone in which Comintern customarily addressed foreign parties, treated the WEB letter as an insult, and threatened to resign at the forthcoming congress. The threat was taken seriously. On the eve of the congress, Codovilla received a telegram from IKKI instructing him to refuse to accept the resignations of Bullejos and his supporter Adame, and to re-elect them to the central committee. A similar telegram was addressed personally to Bullejos and Adame, who also received an appeal from Trilla and Vega, the two Spaniards remaining in Moscow, assuring them that the attitude of IKKI had changed in their favour.[48] Evidently Comintern, with much else on its hands, was in no mood to court an upheaval in the distant PCE.

On March 17, 1932, 201 delegates with voting rights, and about 1000 others, met in Seville for the fourth congress of the PCE, which was also attended by a fraternal delegate of the PCF. No record was published of the debates. But the proceedings were said to have been unanimous except for some scuffles with a group of Trotskyist delegates from Madrid, who were apparently turned out. A resolution was adopted which condemned three types of deviation, "opportunist", "sectarian", and "Trotskyist"; this, according to Bullejos, followed the line of the WEB letter of January. What, however, was at stake was the control of the party. The Comintern delegate (presumably Codovilla) did not speak in the public sessions of the congress, and evidently had instructions to avoid extreme

Historia del Partido Comunista de España, i (1965), 368–382: none of these versions is dated. A long unsigned article further elaborating the points in the WEB letter appeared in *Kommunisticheskii Internatsional*, 1931, No. 2–3, pp. 20–37.

[46] J. Bullejos, *La Comintern en España* (Mexico, 1972), p. 163.

[47] See *Foundations of a Planned Economy, 1926–1929*, Vol. 3, p. 967. P. Neruda, *Confieso que he Vivido* (Buenos Aires, 2nd ed., 1974), pp. 421–422, describes him as an "egotistical" and "authoritarian" figure, who, "bulky and brimming over, seemed always to take up the whole room, the whole table, all the surroundings"; he remained in charge of the PCE till 1937.

[48] J. Bullejos, *La Comintern en España* (Mexico, 1972), pp. 164–166.

measures. A compromise was reached, no doubt after hard bargaining behind the scenes. Bullejos and his group withdrew their resignations. In the election of the party politburo at the end of the congress, Bullejos remained as secretary-general, and Adame in charge of trade union affairs; Hurtado became secretary for organization, and Dolores Ibárruri (later known as "La Pasionaria") for women's affairs. Hurtado was the nominee of the Comintern delegation, which also insisted on the inclusion of Astigarrabia and Mije Garcia as assistants to Adame. Bullejos described the result as a defeat for the Comintern delegation. Duclos, present as delegate of the PCF, diagnosed it more plausibly as a "great turning-point" leading up to the replacement of the old leadership later in the year.[49] After the congress the headquarters of the party politburo were transferred back to Barcelona, the ostensible motive for the change being the need to counter the activities of Maurín's Workers' and Peasants' Bloc; the central committee remained in Madrid. A few weeks later Bullejos and several other members of the politburo were arrested. Bullejos utilized his stay in prison to draft a proposed manifesto on "the revolutionary defence of the republic", which was rejected by the Comintern delegation.[50]

The events of the summer of 1932 and the persistence of unrest throughout the country strained the delicate balance of the coalition government. The moderates were stubbornly opposed to any far-reaching agrarian reform; the socialists were uneasy at the repression by the civil guard of workers' strikes and demonstrations. But the PSOE itself was divided. Besteiro, the veteran party leader, who was not in the government, counted as a Rightist and a reformist. Prieto, the Minister of Justice, and Fernandez de los Ríos, the Minister of Finance, headed a centre group; and Largo Caballero, the Minister of Labour, stood furthest on the Left. The situation was already tense when, on August 10, Sanjurjo, a veteran general of the monarchy, attempted a military *coup d'état*—the first overt move from the Right since the proclamation of the republic.

[49] The sources for the congress are a brief report in *Rundschau*, No. 25, March 23, 1932, pp. 746–747, a contemporary account by Bullejos, *ibid.* No. 30, April 12, 1932, p. 906, and the much later account in J. Bullejos, *La Comintern en España* (Mexico, 1972), pp. 166–167; see also J. Duclos, *Mémoires*, ii (1969), 96–97.

[50] J. Bullejos, *La Comintern en España* (Mexico, 1972), pp. 183–184, 190–191. This version should be accepted with caution; Bullejos seems to have wavered in his attitude to the republican regime.

The *coup* was easily put down by forces loyal to the government, but excited a confused reaction in the ranks of the PCE. Bullejos, now released from prison, induced the party central committee, in an underground news-sheet *La Palabra*, to issue an appeal to the masses to rally to the defence of the republic.[51] The crisis brought back Codovilla in haste from Moscow. On August 18 a meeting of the politburo was convened in Barcelona—apparently without informing Bullejos, who was in Madrid. Adame and Vega, another of Bullejos's supporters, attended, but made a noisy exit when they discovered what was afoot. A politburo resolution of August 19 suspended Bullejos, Adame and Vega from their party functions pending a final decision of Comintern. The Comintern delegation made a statement in which it disclaimed any desire to interfere in the affairs of the party except for the purpose of creating "a collective and united leadership", and accused Bullejos, Adame and Vega of having pursued, ever since the Seville congress, "an open struggle against the Comintern delegation and its policy" and "a conscious struggle against the policy of Comintern".[52]

The twelfth IKKI met in Moscow on August 27, 1932, and Hurtado and Mije Garcia attended it as delegates of the PCE. Comintern spokesmen at the session firmly rejected any inclination to treat the Spanish revolution as bourgeois democratic, or to accord any measure of sympathy or support to the republican government. Kuusinen reproached the PCE with failure to bring home to the worker-peasant masses the importance of the slogan of Soviets "as a slogan of action". Lenski described Spain as the country "where the development of economic and political strikes has advanced furthest". Manuilsky more cautiously canvassed the possibility that in Spain "we may succeed in winning over a majority of the working class in a time of great revolutionary upheavals".[53] Hurtado detailed the succession of strikes and disorders in Spain since the proclamation of the republic on April 14, 1931, as proof of the counter-revolutionary character of the regime. In a brief reference to the abortive Sanjurjo *coup* he admitted that the PCE had missed the opportunity to call for the formation of Soviets. He denounced the PSOE, the UGT, and Largo Caballero in person as social-Fascists. The anarchists were

[51] *Ibid.* pp. 191–192.
[52] *Ibid.* pp. 199–200; E. Comín Colomer, *Historia del Partido Comunista de España*, i (1965), 446–448.
[53] *XII Plenum IKKI* (1933), i, 26, 91, 166.

said to be working in league with the reformists. Finally, he attacked the two dissident communist groups, one led by Maurín who was "carrying on a struggle against Comintern . . . for the benefit of the bourgeoisie", and "a group of Trotskyists led by Nin", which sought to discredit Comintern and gave "conscious support to the counter-revolution". He claimed that the membership of the PCE had risen from 1200–1400 at the time of the eleventh IKKI in 1931 to 15,000–16,000, and was increasing its influence. The fourth party congress in March 1932 had affirmed the principle of the united front. But two opposite mistakes had been made in applying it. Either its importance had been under-estimated, or it had been treated in "a sentimental way", which neglected the need to win over "the masses now under the influence of social-Fascist and anarcho-reformist leaders".[54] Kuusinen, in winding up the debate, drew encouragement from the conviction that the Spanish revolution "does not allow itself to be crushed by any violence or any demagogy of the bourgeois-social-democratic counter-revolution". The resolution adopted at the end of the session called on the PCE to "steer its course for the dictatorship of the proletariat and the peasantry in the form of Soviets".[55] While IKKI was still in session, *Pravda* celebrated the defeat of Sanjurjo in an article entitled "The Workers Conquer the Generals", but added that "the PCE strives to carry on its struggle . . . against *coups* from the Right in such a way as not to render a shade of support to the present counter-revolutionary government".[56] As in Germany the doctrine of the "lesser evil" was contemptuously rejected.

The question of the leadership of the PCE had not been resolved. Comintern, faithful to its habit of postponing for as long as possible the application of disciplinary measures to foreign parties, summoned Bullejos, Adame and Vega to Moscow. Hurtado and Mije Garcia had already left when they arrived. According to Bullejos, Manuilsky and Duclos received them "with great surprise", having perhaps expected them to make things easier by disobeying the summons. Discussions took place in a hastily constituted Spanish commission, three young Spaniards from the Lenin school being brought in to support the official line. Manuilsky offered a

---

[54] *Ibid.* ii, 83–93.

[55] *Ibid.* iii, 120; *Kommunisticheskii Internatsional v Dokumentakh* (1933), p. 980.

[56] *Pravda*, September 9, 1932; the article was bitterly criticized by Trotsky in *Byulleten' Oppozitsii* (Paris), No. 31, November 1932, pp. 25–28.

compromise which would have left Bullejos as secretary of the party in Spain, while his chief supporters were assigned to work in Moscow. While this argument was in progress, news reached Moscow that the politburo of the PCE, convened by Hurtado and Mije Garcia, had on October 5 passed a resolution condemning Bullejos and his supporters as a "sectarian group", and quoting a pronouncement of Manuilsky to that effect; the resolution had been published in the party newspaper *Frente Rojo*. After this, no alternative option remained. On October 31 the commission, presided over by Bela Kun, passed a sentence of expulsion from Comintern, which was communicated to the offenders on the following day by Duclos.[57] The resolution accused the group of four—Adame, Trilla, Bullejos and Vega—of having repeatedly defied party decisions, including the resolution of the politburo of October 5.

The expulsion of the dissidents was confirmed a few days later by a vote of the party central committee in Madrid.[58] A manifesto of IKKI addressed to the "workers, peasants and communists of Spain" denounced the four for stubborn opposition to the creation of a mass party, and to "a joint struggle with honest revolutionary anarchist and socialist workers", directed against "the bourgeois agrarian counter-revolution".[59] The KPD was moved, for no very obvious reason, to pass a resolution expressing approval of their expulsion.[60] A later Comintern account described the four as a "sectarian-doctrinaire group", which alienated the masses from the party by raising the slogan "Down with the Bourgeois Republic!", and by demanding the immediate separation of the three national regions—Catalonia, the Basque region, and Galicia.[61] What was achieved was the elimination of a small group whose independence of mind made them insufficiently submissive to Comintern directives. After their condemnation, the four were not for some weeks allowed to leave Moscow, and it was not till December that they returned to Spain. Here Díaz had been appointed secretary-general of the PCE, and Hurtado and Mije Garcia held important

---

[57] J. Bullejos, *La Comintern en España* (Mexico, 1972), pp. 203–206; E. Comín Colomer, *Historia del Partido Comunista de España*, i (1965), 456–458.

[58] *Internationale Presse-Korrespondenz*, No. 91, November 1, 1932, p. 2900, No. 94, November 11, 1932, p. 3024.

[59] *Ibid.* No. 93, November 8, 1932, pp. 2998–2999.

[60] *Ibid.* No. 96, November 15, 1932, p. 3063.

[61] *Kommunisticheskii Internatsional: Kratkii Istoricheskii Ocherk* (1969), p. 340.

posts in the politburo. The Comintern delegation was reinforced by the arrival of Neumann, whose short stay was, however, marked only by a few articles in the party press.[62]

The year 1933, which opened with Hitler's assumption of power in Berlin and the Dollfuss *coup* in Vienna, was a time of growing tension throughout Europe, and of the rising strength and self-assurance of parties and groups of the Right. In Spain an anarchist rising in January in the province of Cadiz was put down with a massive display of force, including bombing from the air and a large number of executions. The savagery of the repression outraged the Left, and disturbed the uneasy balance between Left and Right on which the Azaña government rested. In February 1933 a number of Right groups coalesced to form a Confederacion Español de Derechas Autónomas (CEDA) under the leadership of a young and ambitious politician Gil Robles. The new party professed loyalty to the republic, but was strongly Catholic, and modelled on the dictatorship of Dollfuss rather than of Hitler. It did not formally adopt, but did not reject, the label of Fascism. Azaña, now subject to intolerable and irreconcilable pressures from Left and Right, resigned in July, and was succeeded by Martinez Barrio, a colourless figure who struggled vainly to maintain the compromise. One of the last acts of the Azaña government was to establish normal diplomatic relations with the USSR.[63]

The drastic purge imposed on the leadership of the PCE by Comintern at the end of 1932 had not equipped it to navigate these treacherous waters. The Comintern appeal of March 6, 1933, for a united front of communist and other Left parties to resist Fascism caused the PCE to issue an open letter addressed to the PSOE, the UGT and the CNT, proposing the formation of joint anti-Fascist committees and of a united anti-Fascist militia of workers and peasants.[64] But the enthusiasm in Comintern for this initiative was

[62] J. Bullejos, *La Comintern en España* (Mexico, 1972), pp. 206–208; Neumann had at this time fallen out of favour in Comintern, but had not yet been officially condemned (see pp. 75–76 above).

[63] *Dokumenty Vneshnei Politiki SSSR*, xvi (1970), 464.

[64] *Rundschau*, No. 6, March 25, 1933, p. 150. B. Leibzon and K. Shirinya, *Povorot v Politike Kominterna* (2nd ed., 1975), p. 81, dates the letter March 18, 1933, and cites a further appeal of April 8; the PSOE and UGT apparently did not reply, and the CNT spoke of the "tricks" and "impudent pretensions" of the PCE.

limited. An article on the tasks of the PCE by the Comintern spokesman Stepanov (using his pseudonym Chavaroche) struck an equivocal note. The party was criticized for its failure to "*prepare* the workers and peasants for the seizure of power". The slogan of Soviets had been mistakenly and prematurely applied. Above all it was not the Right, but the republican government which was responsible for the "January events", and which constituted "the bulwark of the real counter-revolution". The united front had faded silently from view.[65] An "enlarged plenum" of the party central committee, mustering 94 delegates, met in Madrid on April 7–10, 1933. The party congratulated itself on being rid of "the group of traitors—Adame, Bullejos and Trilla". But its positive achievements were less apparent. Its many weaknesses included insufficient penetration of the factories; 90 per cent of its members were not enrolled in factory cells. Sectarianism had not yet been completely rooted out. One unnamed delegate "proposed an unconditional united front, and demanded a revision of the political line of Comintern, since this line had suffered bankruptcy in Germany". He was condemned as a Trotskyist, and summarily expelled.[66]

The summer of 1933 was a period of continuous governmental crisis. In September Lerroux, a republican radical who was on bad terms with his former socialist allies, formed a government. An appeal of the central committee of the PCE addressed to workers and peasants described its role as the same as that of the previous Azaña government: "a counter-revolutionary dictatorship of capitalists and landlords". It called for "a united front instead of fatal splitting, and the organization of revolution by all forces".[67] Lerroux did not command a majority in the Cortes, and new elections were fixed for November 19. The PCE issued an elaborate programme, calling for a worker-peasant government, confiscation of land without compensation, the conventional workers' demands, and national liberation for Catalonia, the Basque country and Galicia, even to the point of secession from the Spanish state.[68] The result of the elections was a sharp swing to the Right. Successful

[65] *Rundschau*, No. 12, May 5, 1933, pp. 359–361; the article is not dated, but was evidently written before the session of the party central committee in April.

[66] *Ibid*. No. 13, May 12, 1933, pp. 397–398; the episode of the Trotskyist was recalled at the thirteenth IKKI later in the year (*XIII Plenum IKKI* (1934), pp. 458–459).

[67] *Rundschau*, No. 35, September 22, 1933, pp. 1357–1358.

[68] E. Comín Colomer, *Historia del Partido Comunista de España*, i (1965), 598–600.

candidates of the Left numbered only 99, of whom 58 were socialists; this low figure was apparently due in part to the refusal of the socialists to make electoral bargains with other republican parties. The Centre which supported Lerroux gained 167 seats, Lerroux's own Radical party accounting for 104. 207 seats went to various groups of the Right, of which CEDA was by far the largest and most formidable. Lerroux now ruled by grace of the Right. The PCE claimed to have received 400,000 votes, and won one seat. A statement addressed by the party central committee to "workers, peasants and all the exploited" made the best of it. It noted with satisfaction "the defeat of the republican socialist bloc" and admitted "the temporary electoral success" of "Fascism and reaction". But the conclusion breathed optimism: "The revolution goes on and expands, since none of its fundamental problems has been solved, or can be solved, within the present regime".[69]

When the thirteenth IKKI opened in Moscow at the end of November 1933, a few days after the elections, the Spanish delegation had not yet arrived. Kuusinen referred fleetingly in his report to strikes and peasant disorders in Spain, and Knorin produced the crisp verdict that "Spanish social-democracy, like German social-democracy, will surrender power to the Fascists, unless the Spanish communists rapidly isolate it from the masses".[70] On December 9, Hernández, the chief Spanish delegate, an associate of the new party leader Díaz, and editor of its journal, *Mundo Obrero*, presented an inconclusive view of the turbulent Spanish situation. He admitted that the elections of November 19 had increased the voting strength of the Right, but quoted Gil Robles as saying that "our hour has not yet come". He said nothing of the communist vote, but recognized that the election results reflected "weak leadership [of the PCE] in the economic struggles of the militant masses". He reserved his fiercest attacks for Largo Caballero, "the leader of Spanish social-democracy" and "the head executioner of the Spanish revolution", who quoted Lenin and posed as "the Spanish Lenin". But he claimed an anti-Fascist demonstration in Madrid on August 18 as a victory for the united front. He noted the need to struggle against "another mass organization", the anarchists, as a "specific peculiarity" of the Spanish scene. Later in the debate Ibárruri, in a loudly applauded

[69] *Rundschau*, No. 46, November 30, 1933, p. 1778.
[70] *XIII Plenum IKKI* (1934), pp. 3, 24, 333.

speech, spoke eloquently of workers' strikes and peasants' risings.[71] Characteristically for this unsatisfactory session, Togliatti summed up by facing both ways. The revolts of workers and peasants in Spain had been "insufficiently organized and coordinated", and were in that sense "premature". But they provided "brilliant confirmation of the correctness of our revolutionary perspective". The resolution adopted at the end of the session confined itself to the remark that in Spain "revolution and counter-revolution have come to grips".[72] At the seventeenth Russian party congress in January 1934 Manuilsky attacked Largo Caballero for pretending that "between us and the communists there are no differences at all"; and Ibárruri, speaking as fraternal delegate of the PCE, expatiated on the duty of communist parties to rally to the defence of the USSR.[73]

The rising tide of Fascism all over Europe in the first half of 1934 brought fresh self-confidence and aggressiveness to the Spanish Right, and especially to CEDA, whose leader Gil Robles visited Hitler and expressed unstinted admiration for the Catholic dictatorship of Dollfuss. In the PSOE, Largo Caballero distinguished himself by militant utterances which alarmed more moderate sections of the party. The anarchists remained aloof and uncooperative. The PCE optimistically announced its sponsorship of an anti-Fascist campaign which was said to have been enthusiastically taken up by the Spanish workers.[74] Early in 1934 a separate Communist Party of Catalonia was founded, and held its first congress in Barcelona—an attempt to assert the principle of national self-determination for Catalonia, and to wrest the leadership of the workers of Barcelona from the anarchists and from Maurín's opposition group.[75] In April a congress of 135 delegates claiming to represent 180,000 organized workers from all parts of Spain met in Madrid to found a communist trade union federation, the Confederación General del Trabajo Unitaria (CGTU), af-

[71] *Ibid.* pp. 458–465, 525–531; the versions of the two speeches in E. Comín Colomer, *Historia del Partido Comunista de España,* i (1965), 626–642, show many variants from the Russian text.
[72] *XIII Plenum IKKI* (1934), pp. 585, 591.
[73] *XVII S"ezd Vsesoyuznoi Kommunisticheskoi Partii (b)* (1934), pp. 315, 333–335.
[74] *Rundschau,* No. 27, April 26, 1934, p. 991.
[75] *Ibid.* No. 36, June 14, 1934, pp. 1394–1395.

filiated to Profintern. About 50 trade unions, some of them formerly belonging to the CNT or the UGT, were said to have joined the new federation.[76] But there is little evidence that the PCE played any significant part in fomenting the strikes and disorders persisting everywhere in Spain at this time.

The PSOE was also not inactive. In Barcelona, encouraged perhaps by the activities of Maurín's worker-peasant union, it created the first of a number of "workers' alliances", designed to broaden its appeal by enlisting workers of any or no party on a Left platform. At a time when socialists were still being denounced as social-Fascists, this innovation could excite only hostility in the PCE; the first congress of the Communist Party of Catalonia described it as "an abortion" and "an alliance against the united front and the revolution". In hard fact the PSOE, like the PCE, wanted a united front under its own sponsorship and control; and the workers' alliances were designed, as the PCE well knew, to serve this purpose. During the summer of 1934, with political tension rising everywhere in Spain, appeals for a united front from the PCE were met by invitations from the PSOE to join the workers' alliances, which were in turn indignantly rejected by the PCE.[77] These exchanges did not prevent numerous demonstrations of protest against the growing Fascist menace in which workers of all groups, including anarchists, were associated. A youth congress in Madrid against Fascism and war on July 15–16, for which the PCE claimed responsibility, was attended by 326 delegates including representatives of the UGT and CNT.[78] But the leadership of the PCE showed no sign of wavering in its hostility to the PSOE, and appeared to enjoy the unqualified support of Moscow. The Comintern journal in a leading article attempted to answer the question, "How can the Revolution in Spain Conquer?" It admitted that the PCE was "not for the present a great mass party". But it believed that the idea of a revolutionary seizure of power, *"in the same way in which the Russian Bolsheviks achieved it"*, was making progress even among anarchist workers. Though it recognized the existence of "great oppositions of principle" between the leaders of the PCE and PSOE, these need be "no barrier to creation of the united front of a struggle against

[76] *Ibid.* No. 38, June 28, 1934, pp. 1517–1518.
[77] *Ibid.* No. 53, October 4, 1934, pp. 2289–2290.
[78] E. Comín Colomer, *Historia del Partido Comunista de España*, i (1965), 136–137, 146–148.

Fascism". But the article went on to expound these differences at
length, and was particularly vehement in its attacks on Largo
Caballero, whose pretensions to be "the Spanish Lenin" continued
to rile Moscow.[79]

By this time, however, other voices were beginning to be heard in
Comintern. The movement, stimulated by Dimitrov's tireless
activity, for the united anti-Fascist front was gathering strength;
and on July 31 Codovilla spoke in the commission for the
preparation of Dimitrov's report at the seventh congress. He
"subjected to sharp criticism the sectarian errors of the PCE
committed at the moment of the bourgeois democratic revolution",
and "raised the question of the need to create in the country an anti-
Fascist bloc and a union of all anti-Fascist forces".[80] It came,
however, as something of a shock in Madrid, when Codovilla,
accompanied or followed by Stepanov, arrived back from Moscow
with a directive that the new united front line required the PCE to
join the workers' alliances. So abrupt a reversal of established
principle and practice was difficult to digest. The issue was debated
at what was probably a stormy meeting of the party central
committee on September 11–12, 1934. The committee bowed to the
inevitable, and endorsed the directive in a long and slightly
ambiguous resolution. It hailed "the wave of enthusiasm" for "our
slogan of the united front". It complained that the workers'
alliances were *"organs of only one of the main moving forces of the
revolution, the proletariat"*, and that they should be transformed into
worker-peasant alliances, based on factory committees and peasant
committes. Communists should enter the alliances, and create
alliances where they did not exist. But this should not prevent them,
within these organizations, from upholding "the policy and tactics
of the communist party".[81] The adoption of this resolution was
followed two days later by a meeting in Madrid organized jointly by
the communist and socialist youth leagues, and said to have been
attended by 90,000 workers.[82] The problem of the united front,
however, presented itself in Spain in a unique form. Elsewhere the
prospect of a united workers' front against Fascism depended on

[79] *Kommunisticheskii Internatsional*, 1934, No. 25, pp. 3–10.

[80] *Voprosy Istorii KPSS*, 1975, No. 8, p. 55.

[81] *Kommunisticheskii Internatsional*, 1935, No. 13–14, pp. 75–78; the resolution
was published in the party newspaper *Mundo Obrero*, September 17, 1934.

[82] *Rundschau*, No. 53, October 4, 1934, p. 2390.

relations between communist and socialist workers and parties. In Spain it turned primarily on relations between socialist and anarchist workers and their respective trade union federations (UGT and CNT); the contribution of the PCE and its nascent trade union organization, the CGTU, was subsidiary, and only marginally affected the situation. What the PCE said and did about the united front was more important to itself than to the workers' movement as a whole.

Meanwhile Spain was moving rapidly towards a state of anarchy. In the summer of 1934 Lerroux, under pressure of the mounting disorders, stood down as Prime Minister in favour of another member of his party, Samper. Samper, less ruthless and less capable than Lerroux, failed to stem the tide of disruption. On September 29 the secretariat of the PCE warned its members that "the blackest elements of reaction" were plotting to establish a Fascist dictatorship, and urged them to "be prepared for anything, so as not to be taken unawares";[83] and on October 2 the PCE issued a far-ranging "Platform of a Soviet Regime". This included the confiscation of landlords', church and state land, and its redistribution to the peasants, the confiscation and nationalization of large-scale industry, a seven- or six-hour day for workers, self-determination for Catalonia, the Basques and Galicia, and the liberation of Morocco and the other colonies. The worker-peasant government would be supported by "the broad masses of workers, peasants and soldiers" and by "*the worker-peasant alliances*".[84] Two days later Lerroux was recalled at the head of a new government, which for the first time included three members of CEDA. The appointment of CEDA ministers was correctly interpreted by the Left as a prelude to policies of repression and to the establishment of a quasi-Fascist dictatorship. A proclamation of the PCE announced that Lerroux and Gil Robles "want to establish a regime of Hitler and Mussolini".[85] Massive strikes took place in Madrid and in other industrial cities, and an independent Catalan state within a "federal Spanish republic" was proclaimed in Barcelona. The movement was largely spontaneous and unorganized. But socialists, communists, the worker-peasant bloc and the workers' alliances were all in evidence. The anarchist CNT held aloof. Troops were

[83] *Kommunisticheskii Internatsional*, 1935, No. 13–14, pp. 80–81.
[84] *Ibid.* 1934, No. 31 pp. 40–44.
[85] *Ibid.* 1935, No. 13–14, p. 79.

called in; and the disturbances were put down within a matter of hours everywhere except in the province of Asturias, where the miners, better organized than the other workers, took possession of mines and factories, and occupied the provincial capital, Oviedo. Attempts to dislodge them having failed, crack troops were brought over from Morocco; and a rising general, Franco, was put in charge of the operation. After nearly a fortnight of civil war all over Asturias, the rebels were crushed. Some thousands perished in the fighting, or in the savage reprisals which followed. Isolated pockets of resistance were gradually mopped up by the triumphant army; and the winter of 1934–35 was occupied by a long series of arrests, interrogations under torture, and executions of those suspected of complicity in the revolt. Franco earned his reputation, on the Right as the saviour of his country, on the Left as the butcher of the workers. Many leaders of the PSOE, including Largo Caballero, were thrown into prison. Azaña, the former Prime Minister, was arrested, but subsequently released. Díaz, the leader of the PCE, escaped arrest—probably because he was too inconspicuous to attract the attention of the authorities.

The bloody defeat of the Asturias miners, and the prospective emergence of yet another Fascist regime in Europe, sent a shudder through the ranks of Comintern. While the struggle was still raging, IKKI issued an appeal addressed to the Second International and the working men and women of all countries. It depicted the whole military might of "Spain's Fascist-monarchist reaction" falling upon the working class and the peasantry, ranged for battle "under the leadership of the workers' alliance, which realizes unity between communists and socialists and has sealed this alliance with the blood shed in the struggle". It called on the Second International for "immediate action in common" to support the Spanish proletariat, and instructed Cachin to make contact with the International for this purpose.[86] The Communist Party of Catalonia circulated a broadsheet proclaiming that, "in spite of the bloody repression, in spite of hundreds of summary executions, the counter-revolution has not triumphed", and that "a precious weapon for the revolution" had been forged: the workers' alliance.[87] The central committee of the PCE in a more comprehensive verdict, addressed to the "workers and peasants of Spain, Catalonia, the Basque

[86] *Rundschau*, No. 54, October 11, 1934; for the Cachin–Thorez meeting with Vandervelde and Adler at which Cachin read part of this appeal see p. 140 above.

[87] *Rundschau*, No. 56, October 25, 1934, p. 2502.

country and Galicia", hailed "the heroic proletariat of Asturias", but referred ominously to "our differences of opinion" in the party on questions of tactics and organization. The political and organizational preparations for the revolution had fallen short, and "*the powerful forces of the countryside*" had not been fully drawn into the struggle. "Unity and iron discipline" had been absent. Companys, the leader of the Catalan republic, was ungenerously condemned as one of those "wavering personalities . . . who, out of fear of a people's revolution, capitulate to the enemy forces". The workers' alliances were obliquely mentioned only in the rhetorical peroration:

> Long live the workers' and peasants' government!
> Long live the Soviets!
> Long live the proletariat united in the alliances of workers and peasants!
> Long live the world revolution and its general staff, the Communist International!
> Long live the Communist Party of Spain![88]

Togliatti, in an article in the Comintern news-sheet, characteristically evaded the contentious issues, did not mention the workers' alliances, blamed the socialist, and especially the anarchist, leaders for the defeat, and ended with the improbable hypothesis that an energetic campaign by the PCE against imperialism would have made it impossible to bring troops back from Morocco to crush the rebellion.[89] The executive committee of MOPR appealed to its sections throughout the world to come to the aid of the victims of the Spanish terror. Contributions were reported from the Soviet trade unions; and protest demonstrations were held in many countries.[90] The revolt of the miners of Asturias had brought Spain into the picture of international revolution and resistance to the onset of Fascism.

Throughout Spain conservatives, and even bourgeois radicals, had been badly frightened; and opinion moved sharply to the

---

[88] *Ibid.* No. 58, November 8, 1934, pp. 2578–2579; for a manifesto of the Spanish Red trade union federation attacking the "anti-Marxist" leaders of other unions see *ibid.* p. 2618.

[89] *Ibid.* No. 58, November 8, 1934, pp. 2575–2577; the article is also in P. Togliatti, *Opere*, III (1973), ii, 489–497.

[90] *Rundschau*, No. 63, December 6, 1934, pp. 2857–2859.

Right. The hour of CEDA was at hand. By March 1935 the slaughter seemed to the few remaining moderates to have gone far enough. The president commuted death sentences on two socialist deputies from Asturias and on Companys, who had proclaimed the Catalan republic. The three CEDA ministers resigned from the government in protest against this leniency, thus provoking a crisis which dragged on for two months. It was finally resolved on May 6, 1935, by increasing the number of CEDA ministers in a re-constituted government from three to five, including the formidable Gil Robles as Minister for War.

The crisis promoted some spontaneous cooperation between parties of the Left. In March 1935 the PSOE, the PCE and other Left organizations are reported to have cooperated in a joint committee set up to aid victims of the reprisals.[91] In May the undisguised advance towards a Fascist regime marked by Gil Robles's appointment caused consternation in the Left. The PCE was moved to issue an appeal to all Left parties and organizations to form an anti-Fascist popular bloc, whose programme would include the resignation of the government and fresh elections, the restoration of democratic liberties, confiscation of large estates, self-determination for Catalans and Basques and liberation of Morocco, and the dissolution of Fascist organizations.[92] The programme, designed to appeal not only to workers and peasants but to radical democrats, marked a transition from the "united" to the "popular" front already pioneered by Dimitrov in Moscow.

The appeal from the party was followed, or accompanied, by a Comintern manifesto addressed to "the Socialist, Communist, Anarchist and Syndicalist Toilers of Spain", as well as to "the toilers of Catalonia, the Basque country and Morocco", and signed jointly by Díaz, Marty and Togliatti. Lamenting that the initial victory achieved by the Asturias miners had "slipped from the hands of the Spanish workers", the manifesto exhorted the PCE to learn the lessons of the Bolshevik revolution of 1917. It censured the PSOE

[91] J. Duclos, *Mémoires*, ii (1969), 103; according to a Spanish delegate at the seventh congress of Comintern, the initiative was taken at a meeting of MOPR in Madrid (*Rundschau*, No. 50, September 25, 1935, p. 2160).

[92] E. Comín Colomer, *Historia del Partido Comunista de España*, i (1965), 435–436; Hernández, at the seventh congress of Comintern, referred to a joint committee · with the socialists which had drafted an appeal on these lines (*Rundschau*, No. 60, October 30, 1935, p. 2431); it is not clear whether this refers to the same or another appeal.

which, ever since the fall of the monarchy in April 1931, had followed not the revolutionary path, but "the reformist path of collaboration with the bourgeoisie"; and it criticized Largo Caballero by name for failing to purge the party of extreme reformist elements. Its most bitter strictures were reserved for the anarchists, who had been guilty of "open treason" during the Asturias rising. Finally it blamed the PCE for having failed, after 1931, to deal with the problems of the worker-peasant alliance and of the united front. It demanded "unity of action" between socialists and communists at national and local level, "a complete anti-Fascist popular front" for "the establishment of a provisional revolutionary government", and for a unique, truly revolutionary, party of the proletariat.[93] The manifesto was a more sophisticated document, and contained more hidden reservations, than the simple proposal of a common programme in the party appeal. It probably reflected the divided opinions still current in Comintern in the spring of 1935.[94]

The conception of a broad "popular" anti-Fascist front embodied in these appeals was launched by Díaz at a mass meeting in a Madrid cinema on June 2, 1935—perhaps the first effective appearance of the PCE on the stage of Spanish Left-wing politics.[95] It presented an embarrassing dilemma to the PSOE. Besteiro, the veteran party leader, had finally discredited himself by his refusal to support the October risings; and Prieto had emerged as the leader of the Right or moderate wing of the PSOE. Largo Caballero remained the dominant figure on the revolutionary Left. But, while Prieto worked for a united anti-Fascist front with bourgeois radical defenders of the republic, of whom Azaña himself was the representative figure, and while Largo Caballero wanted a united anti-Fascist front between the PSOE and the PCE, neither Prieto nor Largo Caballero was initially prepared for the communist plan of a popular front embracing all three groups; Largo Caballero, in

[93] *Kommunisticheskii Internatsional*, 1935, No. 13–14, pp. 4–15; E. Comín Colomer, *Historia del Partido Comunista de España*, i (1965), 437–455, which plausibly attributes the authorship to Togliatti. Neither this nor the party appeal is dated; but both, on internal evidence, were issued in May 1935.

[94] See pp. 148–150 above.

[95] Memoirs of Díaz, quoted in P. Preston, *The Coming of the Spanish Civil War* (1978), pp. 142–143; B. Leibzon and K. Shirinya, *Povorot v Politike Kominterna* (2nd ed., 1975), p. 112. *Kommunisticheskii Internatsional: Kratkii Istoricheskii Ocherk* (1969), p. 384, claims that the PCE "was able in the summer of 1935 to achieve real successes in the struggle to form a popular front".

particular, quoting texts from Marx and Lenin, attacked the
readiness of the PCE for an alliance with the bourgeoisie as treason
to the workers, and subservience to the dictates of Moscow. The
confusion in the leadership of the PSOE reflected the total confusion
of Spanish politics in the summer of 1935. Stop-gap ministry
succeeded stop-gap ministry, while Azaña struggled to hold
together the crumbling fabric of the republic. Gil Robles and
CEDA, though professedly loyal to the republic and restricting itself
to constitutional action, became more vocal and more openly
Fascist in the attempt to break out of the existing impasse. The
Falangists, representing the monarchist tradition of Primo de
Rivera, whose son was now leader of the movement, emerged for the
first time since 1931 as a credible force of the extreme Right. In July
Díaz, Mije Garcia, Martínez and Ibárruri set out for Moscow to
share in the general enthusiasm for the popular front at the seventh
congress of Comintern.[96]

---

[96] According to E. Comín Colomer, *Historia del Partido Comunista de España*, i
(1965), 513, the Spanish delegation included refugees who had fled to the USSR
after the Asturias disaster.

CHAPTER 16

THE FAR EAST

(a) PARTY AND SOVIETS IN CHINA

While the Chinese Communist Party (CCP), decimated by Chiang
Kai-shek's relentless persecution, and demoralized by the defection
of Ch'en Tu-hsiu,[1] languished under Li Li-san's erratic leadership,
the peasant Soviets and the Red Army in southern China continued
to make progress. At the beginning of January 1930, what Mao Tse-
tung called the "ninth party conference of the Fourth Red Army"
met in Kut'ien in western Fukien.[2] Mao's authority at this time
seems to have rested primarily on his leadership of what was called
the General Front Committee of the Red armies; and the main
purpose of the conference was to strengthen his authority and to
vindicate his independence of the party centre in Shanghai. The
draft resolution prepared by Mao in advance for submission to the
conference displayed his habitual deftness in professing strict
submission to Marxist ideology and to party injunctions. Errors
were said to have arisen from "non-proletarian ideas in the
communist party organization in the Fourth Red Army", due to its
recruitment from "peasants and other elements of petty-bourgeois
origin". But the diagnosis of these errors bore marks of a sturdy
independence. Some comrades neglected "the political tasks of the
revolution", and adopted a purely military point of view; this
led them to indulge in "revolutionary impetuosity". "Ultra-
democracy" and "absolute egalitarianism" were also condemned;
and the draft ended with a further denunciation of "putschism",
described as "a combination of lumpenproletarian and petty-
bourgeois ideology".[3] This was an unmistakeable attack on the hard

[1] See *Foundations of a Planned Economy, 1926–1929*, Vol. 3, pp. 889–893.
[2] E. Snow, *Red Star over China* (3rd ed., 1972), p. 198; for a full and somewhat
speculative review of the sources for this conference see J. Rue, *Mao Tse-tung in
Opposition: 1927–1935* (1966), pp. 171–188. According to A. Smedley, *The Great
Road* (1956), p. 267, the conference was convened for January 1, 1930, the date of
Chu Teh's arrival in Kut'ien.
[3] *Selected Works of Mao Tse-tung*, i (1954), 105–115; the text was not published
till 1949, and it is not clear whether it is identical with the text of the resolution as

line preached by Li Li-san in Shanghai, and stood far closer to the
views which emerged at the presidium of IKKI in Moscow in
February 1930,[4] and of which Mao can have had no knowledge.

Exactly what happened at the Kut'ien conference is uncertain. A
sharp struggle evidently occurred, as a result of which a number of
party leaders and Red Army commanders, said by Mao to belong to
a "Trotskyist faction" (an implausible attribution), were removed
from their posts.[5] The procedure was probably ruthless. But there is
no reason to doubt that it strengthened the authority of Mao Tse-
tung and Chu Teh over the Red Army and the Soviets, and their
independent attitude to the CCP leadership in Shanghai. During
the conference Mao published one of his most famous articles "A
Single Spark Can Start a Prairie Fire". Professedly designed to
counteract pessimistic tendencies in the party, it repeated the
warning against the "revolutionary impetuosity" of comrades who
"overestimate the subjective forces of the revolution", but deprecated the opposite fallacy of underestimating these forces.
Significantly it quoted two passages from the letter of April 5, 1929,
to the party central committee, in which Mao had defined and
defended the independent status of the Red Army organizations.[6]

The sequel of the Kut'ien conference was an important regional
party conference which met in south Kiangsi on February 7, 1930,
and was attended by 70 or 80 delegates representing 30 party
organizations. The most controversial business of the conference
was the adoption of a land law. In south-west Kiangsi at this time 40
per cent of the land was said to be held by large landlords, 30 per
cent by religious institutions, and only 30 per cent by poor peasants.
The "opportunism" of those who resisted land re-distribution was
overcome; and drastic measures were enacted for the confiscation of
estates and the distribution of the land to poor peasants. But it was
easier to proclaim the principle than to apply it, and it is doubtful
whether much was achieved at this time. The most momentous
decision taken by the conference was to set up a provincial Kiangsi

---

adopted by the conference. This edition of Mao's *Selected Works* in four volumes
in English was published in London and New York in 1954–1956; an edition in
English published in Peking in 1961–1965 used a different translation, and some
items included in one edition are not found in the other.

[4] See pp. 10–12 above.

[5] E. Snow, *Red Star over China* (3rd ed., 1972), pp. 198–199.

[6] *Selected Works of Mao Tse-tung*, i (1954), pp. 116–128; for the letter of April 5,
1929, see *Foundations of a Planned Economy, 1926–1929*, Vol. 3, p. 889.

Soviet Government with an elected regional congress of Soviets and an executive committee of 17 members. The establishment of a government on the Russian Soviet model was a notable step in the organization of the areas occupied by the Red Army.[7]

The lack of contact between the central organs of the CCP leading a precarious existence in Shanghai and the Red Army and Soviets in south China masked a fundamental opposition and rivalry between them. The principle that the industrial workers must lead the revolutionary struggle, and that the peasants could be no more than their allies, was increasingly difficult to match with fact. Official party pronouncements were based on two palpable illusions. In China the party did not lead the proletariat, and neither the party nor the proletariat led the peasantry. The latest Comintern directive to the CCP of October 26, 1929, had been primarily concerned with the struggle against imperialism. But, in the context of general criticism of the party's ineffectiveness, it mentioned "the regions where Mao Tse-tung and Ho Lung are active", and insisted that "the fundamental and chief task of the communist party is to win a *leading* role in the revolutionary movement".[8] On February 26, 1930, the party central committee issued an important pronouncement on the familiar theme of "the rising revolutionary tide". Professing to detect an advance in the numbers and organization of the party in cities and in industrial enterprises, it offered the ambitious assurance that "an initial victory can be scored in one or several provinces, especially in the area of Wuhan and neighbouring provinces". But this would demand a change of direction:

> The troops commanded by Chu Teh and Mao Tse-tung and those in western Hupei still cling to their old-fashioned ideas of

[7] E. Snow, *Red Star over China* (3rd ed., 1972), p. 199; *Sovety v Kitae*, ed. E. Johanson and O. Taube (1933), pp. 227–244. The latter account, the fullest available, is a report by a CCP "instructor" dated October 1930. It is unlikely that any representative of the central committee was present at the conference; little or no information about events in south China seems to have reached the committee in the first half of 1930, and certainly none percolated to Moscow (see p. 326 below). A report of "the delegation of the Soviet region of south-west Kiangsi to the first Chinese Congress of Soviets" was published belatedly in the autumn of 1930 in *Kommunisticheskii Internatsional*, 1930, No. 25, pp. 37–43. For a translation of the agrarian law of February 1930 see J. Rue, *Mao Tse-tung in Opposition: 1927–1935* (1966), pp. 300–304.

[8] *Strategiya i Taktika Kominterna* (1934), p. 257; for this letter of IKKI see *Foundations of a Planned Economy, 1926–1929*, Vol. 3, pp. 902–903.

evasive dispersion. . . . Both strategically and tactically, the troops must push towards key cities and major transportation lines to wreck the enemy's vital positions.[9]

Thus was laid the foundation of what came to be known as "the Li Li-san line"—the demand for an offensive by the Red Army against major cities and industrial centres—which clashed with Mao's cherished conception of guerrilla tactics. Li's attempt to take control was apparent in the issue, at the same moment, of a summons by the central committee of the CCP, jointly with the All-China Labour Federation, for a conference of delegates from the Soviet areas to be held in Shanghai.[10]

The three months which elapsed between the summons and the meeting of the conference at the end of May were filled with a series of shrill exhortations from the centre. On April 3, 1930, the central committee addressed an instruction to the Red Youth Army's Front Committee explaining that the primary task of the Red Army was now "to make decisive thrusts into central cities"; the most obvious area for these thrusts were "the provinces of Hunan, Hupei and Kiangsi with Wuhan as the central focus". Victory in Wuhan would be "the beginning of victory for the revolution in the whole country". The letter concluded in peremptory terms: "The central committee has decided that comrade Mao Tse-tung should come to attend the national Soviet conference. He must comply with the decision of the central committee".[11] Successive articles by Li Li-san in the party press suggested that he had opponents who were not altogether happy about the implications of his appeal. To believe that "the forces of the peasantry, particularly of the Red Army, have outstripped the forces of the workers" was, he argued, a deviation betraying "lack of faith in the strength of the working class". Li rejected as nonsense "talk of 'encircling the city with country', or of relying on the Red Army to take the cities". No strategy could depart from the great principle that "the proletariat

---

[9] W. Kuo, *Analytical History of Chinese Communist Party*, ii (Taiwan, 1968), 109–112.

[10] B. I. Schwartz, *Chinese Communism and the Rise of Mao* (1951), pp. 140–141.

[11] W. Kuo, *Analytical History of Chinese Communist Party*, ii (Taiwan, 1968), 38–42; a further letter of April 26, 1930, again insisted on the necessity of Mao's presence in Shanghai (*ibid*. ii, 42–44). For both these letters see also Hsiao Tso-liang, *Power Relations within the Chinese Communist Movement* (1961), pp. 14–18.

is the leader of the revolution, the peasantry its ally".[12] What seemed important to Li was that the Red Army, in carrying out its revolutionary function, should be subject to the orders and the control of the party. Such submission would symbolize the leadership of the proletariat in the revolution. How Mao reacted to these attempts to place the Red Army under the tutelage of the CCP can only be guessed. It seems likely that other Red Army leaders may have chafed under Mao's cautious policy, and that the internal dissensions which later split the Red Army began at this time. In any case, Mao pursued his usual tactics of avoiding confrontation. He did not make the journey to Shanghai.

Nothing that came out of Moscow at this time threw any light on the dilemma. An article by Madyar, a Comintern official, noted that "the remains of the Kiangsi group and the troops of Chang Fa-kwei"—an oddly out-of-date description—were "preparing themselves to strike a blow against Nanking". He was aware that "the wave of partisan warfare and peasant risings is higher than that of workers' strikes and demonstrations", and that "an agrarian revolution is going forward". But the CCP knew that "peasants without workers cannot conquer", and that it must put itself at the head of the peasant movement.[13] Mif, the head of the eastern secretariat, referred in an article in *Pravda* to the very large proportion of lumpenproletarian elements in the Chinese Red Armies, and concluded by recognizing that "the partisan movement is developing in areas far removed from the basic industrial centres, and the problem of the leadership of the peasant movement by the workers is still far from being resolved".[14] Another Soviet expert on China celebrated the victories of "the army of Chu Teh" and of another general, P'eng Teh-huai, but recognized that it was rural districts rather than towns which had been overrun. He looked forward to "the congress of representatives of the Soviet regions of China summoned by the CCP", the function of which would be "to establish the close fighting cooperation between the partisans, partisan warfare and the actions of the industrial proletariat".[15] None of these articles named Mao Tse-tung. Ironically the only

[12] For these articles see B. I. Schwartz, *The Chinese Revolution and the Rise of Mao* (1951), pp. 138–139.

[13] *Internationale Presse-Korrespondenz*, No. 32, April 8, 1930, pp. 748–749.

[14] *Pravda*, April 28, 1930.

[15] *Internationale Presse-Korrespondenz*, No. 43, May 20, 1930, pp. 944–945.

mention of Mao in the Comintern press at this time was an obituary notice hailing him as "a Bolshevik and a champion of the Chinese proletariat in the full sense of the word".[16]

An advance article by an unidentified Chinese on "The First Congress of Representatives of the Soviet Regions in China" appeared in the Comintern journal in April;[17] and the conference met in Shanghai on May 30, 1930. Reports were made by delegations from various Soviet areas.[18] It adopted a resolution on the constitution and tasks of a Soviet government, a provisional land law, a labour law, an appeal for the defence of the USSR, and a manifesto calling for the early convocation of a first All-China Congress of Soviets.[19] But the conference attracted little attention in Moscow; and the journal of the China Institute of the Communist Academy, which belatedly published its resolutions, preceded them with a devastatingly critical commentary. The conference "completely forgot the lagging section of the Chinese revolution, the workers' movement in the cities", neglected the organization of government, the trade unions and the poor peasants, and failed to grasp the importance of the territorial expansion of the Soviet movement. Its agrarian pronouncements had been inconsistent, and laid too much stress on the break-up of estates and their conversion into Sovkhozy and kolkhozy. It had been guilty of "both Right errors and 'Left' twists (zagiby)".[20] The Soviets in southern China continued to make progress. In the summer of 1930, there were well over a hundred Soviet district committees—71 in Kiangsi alone—covering a population of 30 or 40 millions.[21] But the towns, including the cities of northern Kiangsi, Nanchang, Kiuhiang and Kanchow, remained firmly in Chiang's hands. Evidently the conference had done nothing to cement relations between the CCP in Shanghai and the Soviet areas, or between them and the authorities in Moscow.

[16] *Ibid.* No. 26, March 18, 1930, p. 634; the source of the report of Mao's death has not been traced.

[17] *Kommunisticheskii Internatsional*, 1930, No. 9, pp. 8–16.

[18] Reports from Kwangsi and eastern Kwangtung are in *Sovety v Kitae*, ed. E. Johanson and O. Taube (1933), pp. 195–200, 320–324, and from Kiangsi in *Kommunisticheskii Internatsional*, 1930, No. 25, pp. 37–44.

[19] *Problemy Kitaya*, No. 4–5 (1930), pp. 176–198.

[20] *Ibid.* No. 4–5 (1930), pp. 172–176. Hsiang at the third plenum of the CCP in September 1930 referred to friction which had occurred at the conference between Li Li-san and Ho Meng-hsiang, presumably over the labour law; this is plausible in view of the relations between the two men (see pp. 329–330 below).

[21] *Problemy Kitaya*, No. 4–5 (1930), p. 167.

The sequel of the conference was a long policy statement adopted by the politburo of the CCP on June 1, 1930, which was treated in subsequent party history as a victory for Li Li-san's disastrous "Left" line. Bearing the significant title "The New Revolutionary Wave and Preliminary Victory in One or Several Provinces", it boldly proclaimed that, China being "the weakest link in the ruling chain of world imperialism", the Chinese revolution might be the first to break out, "setting off the world revolution and the final decisive class war". On the other hand, "the victory of socialism in the Chinese revolution will be inseparable from world revolution"; support from "the already victorious proletariat of the Soviet Union" would be the decisive factor. The resolution conceded the importance of "the great revolutionary role of the peasantry", and "the birth of the Red Army in the agrarian revolution"; this was said to be a special feature of China. But it would be "a highly erroneous concept" to "use the country to encircle the cities" and to "rely on the Red Army to occupy the cities"; the role of the urban proletariat was fundamental. Nevertheless, the most pressing task was "a vigorous expansion of the Red Army", which was urged to conduct "attacks on the major forces of the enemy, assaults on key cities and lines of communication". The "guerrilla tactics" of the past, which consisted in attacking, but not occupying, cities and making no attempt to set up Soviets in them, were roundly condemned. The aim must be "the seizure of political power and the establishment of a national-revolutionary regime in co-ordination with armed uprisings in key cities".[22] More than a month later, on July 21, 1930, the party central committee issued a circular reaffirming these conclusions. The revolutionary upsurge was "moving ahead at a quickened tempo to a new climax". The workers should organize general political strikes in the cities. The Red Army should "concentrate on large-scale battles to annihilate enemy forces", and "converge on major target areas".[23] Coming at a moment when preparations were being made for an assault on Changsha, the capital of Hunan, to be followed by attacks on Nanchang, the capital of Kiangsi, and Wuhan, the capital of

[22] C. Brandt, B. I. Schwartz and J. K. Fairbank, *A Documentary History of Chinese Communism* (1952), pp. 184–200; W. Kuo, *Analytical History of Chinese Communist Party*, ii (Taiwan, 1968), 113–116. For the verdict in the party resolution of April 20, 1945, on party history see *Selected Works of Mao Tse-tung*, iv (1956), 178.
[23] W. Kuo, *Analytical History of Chinese Communist Party*, ii (Taiwan, 1968), 142–146.

Hupei, these pronouncements read like a desperate attempt to maintain the fiction of party control over these operations, and to reconcile them with the doctrine of proletarian leadership in the revolution.

The sixteenth Russian party congress meeting in Moscow at the end of June 1930 revealed only the deep ignorance of Chinese affairs prevailing among the Soviet leaders and their indifference to the dilemma which plagued the CCP. Stalin made one bare reference to China in his massive report to the congress: "They say that a Soviet government has already been formed there. I think, if that is true, there is nothing surprising about that."[24] Molotov thought that "reports of the organization of a peasant Soviet Government" were "quite plausible".[25] A Chinese delegate mentioned the "first congress of Soviet regions", but added that "the Soviet Government has not yet taken hold of the industrial centres", and that "the link between the workers' movement and peasant warfare is still not at all strong". Mif, admittedly having nothing to go on but press reports, claimed that the number of Red Army men had risen from 60,000 with 38,982 rifles at the beginning of April to 75,000 with 57,000 rifles at the end of the month. He then fell back on a routine denunciation of Ch'en Tu-hsiu, "formerly an arrant opportunist, now a Trotskyist".[26] The resolution of the congress on the affairs of IKKI confirmed the diagnosis of the Chinese revolution as a "revolution of workers, peasants and the urban poor under the banner of Soviets and the leadership of the working class".[27]

Within a few days of the end of the congress, fresh news from China must have reached Moscow. On July 23, 1930, IKKI issued a long resolution on the Chinese question. It did not mention the CCP resolution of June 11, the text of which may have not yet reached Moscow. But, while echoing some of the same phrases, it heavily qualified the emphasis. Having begun with a routine salute

[24] Stalin, *Sochineniya*, xii, 251.
[25] *XVI S"ezd Vsesoyuznoi Kommunisticheskoi Partii (b)* (1931), p. 416.
[26] *Ibid.* pp. 436, 468–469.
[27] *KPSS v Rezolyutsiyakh* (1954), iii, 34; Trotsky ridiculed the idea that "Chinese peasants, without the participation of the industrial centres and without the leadership of the communist party, had created a Soviet government" (*Byulleten' Oppozitsii* (Paris), No. 15–16, September–October 1930, p. 17).

to the "new upsurge", it went on to affirm that "so far there is no objectively revolutionary situation in China as a whole", and that "the waves of the workers' and peasants' movements have not yet merged into one". It was the task of the party "to organize and direct the activities of a central Soviet Government". For this purpose it was "essential to concentrate on forming and strengthening the Red Army, so that in the future, when military and political conditions present the opportunity, it may be able to capture one or several industrial and administrative centres". But the phrase "in the future" did not suggest imminent military operations; and the insistent demand for "complete control and leadership of the Red Army" by the party and for "proletarian hegemony" was scarcely realistic. The resolution went on to rehearse the familiar theme that the bourgeois democratic stage of the Chinese revolution was not yet exhausted, and that the immediate goal was the "revolutionary-democratic dictatorship of the proletariat and peasantry". Unlike the CCP pronouncements, it was not a call for action. It sounded the note of caution and restraint characteristic of Comintern policy at this time. But, if it was not an endorsement of the so-called "Li Li-san line", it was equally not a denunciation. It was a waiting move.[28]

Whatever the import of the resolution, it cannot have reached China when, on the night of July 27–28, 1930, a Red Army 17,000 strong, though with only 10, 000 rifles, delivered a successful assault on Changsha. Its commander was P'eng Te-huai, said to be a rival of Mao and a supporter of Li Li-san. Another army led by Chu Teh, with Mao as political commissar, advanced on Nanchang; and a third army was detailed for an attack on Wuhan. P'eng's army remained long enough in occupation of Changsha to proclaim, on July 29, 1930, a local Soviet Government; and *Pravda* declared that "Changsha under Soviet rule means that the Soviet revolution has captured its first great city", adding that this was "a damaging blow to the Right renegades", and especially to Trotsky, who had predicted a long period of reaction in China.[29] But the hopes on which these operations were based, that the workers in the cities

[28] *Strategiya i Taktika Kominterna* (1934), pp. 272–281, where it is dated "June"; but mis-dating occurs elsewhere in this volume (see *Foundations of a Planned Economy, 1926–1929*, Vol. 3, p. 965, note 429, and p. 334, note 52 below). Differences between this resolution and the CCP resolution of June 11 are usefully tabulated in Hsiao Tso-liang, *Power Relations within the Chinese Communist Movement* (1961), pp. 25–26.

[29] *Pravda*, July 31, 1930.

would eagerly rally to the support of the Red Army and the Soviets, were disappointed. Kuomintang troops still in Changsha rose against the intruders. They were soon reinforced; and the Red Army beat an ignominious retreat. By August 6 governmental authority had been restored, and executions of local communists and workers were proceeding. After this defeat, the projected attacks on Nanchang and Wuhan were abandoned. A further assault on Changsha was attempted a month later, but failed.[30] The withdrawal of the Red Army was a direct and deliberate defiance of Li Li-san's call to continue offensive action.

The Changsha fiasco fanned the discontent which had long smouldered in the party. While Hsiang retained the post of party secretary to which he had been appointed by the sixth party congress in 1928, the real power was in the hands of Li Li-san who controlled the party organization, and whose dictatorial methods incurred resentment.[31] A fresh focus of discord was provided by a group of young party members in their twenties, commonly spoken of as "the 28 Bolsheviks" or "the returned students",[32] back early in 1930 from Moscow, where they had studied in the Sun Yat-sen university. Their leaders were Ch'en Shao-yü, commonly known by his pseudonym Wang Ming, and Ch'iu Pang-hsien, known as Po Ku. They had presumably been schooled by Mif, a former director of the university, now in effective control of Chinese affairs in Comintern. There is no explicit evidence that they were sent back to China for the purpose of challenging Li's policies or leadership. [33] But the young men were energetic and ambitious, and a clash soon occurred. Four of them dissented from the politburo resolution of June 11—allegedly on the ground of its demand for "armed

[30] An account, said to have been written by Wang Ming, and published by the CCP in its information bulletin, is in *Sovety v Kitae*, ed. E. Johanson and O. Taube (1933), pp. 201–211; other accounts differ in detail, but the general picture is clear.

[31] See *Foundations of a Planned Economy, 1926–1929*, Vol. 3, pp. 884–885.

[32] The latter term had been familiar for many years in the Chinese vocabulary to denote young Chinese educated abroad, who on their return to China propagated western ideas and literature.

[33] Wang Ming already had to his credit a pamphlet entitled *Armed Risings*, in which he called for the occupation of urban centres by the Red Army (quoted in B. I. Schwartz, *Chinese Communism and the Rise of Mao* (1952), pp. 149–150). When Mif visited China in 1927 (see *Foundations of a Planned Economy, 1926–1929*, Vol. 3, p. 792, note 66), Wang Ming accompanied him as interpreter; from this time he became Mif's favourite disciple at the Sun Yat-sen university, and owed his rise to power to Mif's patronage (Wang Fan-hsi, *Chinese Revolutionary* (1980), p. 64).

uprisings throughout the country"—and circulated a pamphlet by Wang entitled "Two Lines". The politburo, at Li's instigation, not unnaturally convicted the rebels of "fractionalism" and "Right opportunism", placed Wang on probation as a party member—a form of suspension—for six months and severely censured the other three.[34]

The other main opposition to Li came from the Kiangsu provincial party committee, which had a long record of dissent,[35] and continued to accuse the party central committee of adventurism, and of neglecting the urban workers and the trade unions. At the fifth congress of Profintern in Moscow in August 1930 a Chinese delegate drew a highly optimistic picture of the trade union movement, claiming that membership of the All-China Labour Federation had grown from 36,000 in 1929 to 69,000 in March 1930, and that "millions and millions" of peasants in southern China were fighting "under the leadership of the proletariat".[36] But another Chinese delegate admitted "the development of the workers' struggle still lags behind the development of the peasant movement"; and the most realistic pronouncement at the congress was that of Safarov, who said that there were only two forces in China—the Kuomintang army and the peasant movement —and that one would swallow up the other.[37] The resolutions of the congress were ambivalent. The main resolution admitted that the Chinese Red unions had "no real feeling for the mass of the workers", and that an "opportunist-liquidationist view" of the unions prevailed, though a special resolution on the Chinese unions ended with the slogan: "Down with the Kuomintang unions! Set up Red unions in all factories".[38] But these were empty aspirations. The failure of the CCP to make any serious impact on the trade unions was fatal to the influence of the Kiangsu group. Its present leaders, Ho Meng-hsiang, a trade union organizer and one of the

[34] W. Kuo, *Analytical History of Chinese Communist Party*, ii (Taiwan, 1968), 147–148, 194–195; the evidence for this episode dates from the period after Li's disgrace, and should be treated with some caution. Wang Fan-hsi, *Chinese Revolutionary* (1980), p. 116, notes that "most of the older generation of party activists were contemptuous" of the returned students, and that Wang Ming had been offered "a very lowly position in the propaganda department under Li Li-san" (*ibid.* p. 150).

[35] See *Foundations of a Planned Economy, 1926–1929*, Vol. 3, pp. 834–835, 865, 885–886.

[36] *Protokoll des V Kongresses der Roten Gewerkschaftsinternationale* (1931), ii, 23–26.

[37] *Ibid.* i, 406, ii, 81.

[38] *Ibid.* ii, 366–367, 406.

founder members of the party, and Lo Chang-lung, carried on the tradition of hostility to Li's leadership. At the beginning of September 1930 Ho addressed a letter to the party politburo openly attacking Li's policies and methods, and claiming that the central committee had diverged from the Comintern line.[39] But, unlike the "28 Bolsheviks", the Kiangsu group never gained the ear of Moscow, and incurred the damning reproach of "Right opportunism" and "liquidationism".

In Moscow, where Chinese problems were still little understood, the Changsha affair seems to have made no immediate impact. An article in the Comintern journal published early in August 1930, and entitled "On the Threshold of a New Revolution in China", continued to explain that "the Soviet movement must by the very logic of the struggle direct itself to the capture of the industrial and administrative urban centres".[40] But the sequel soon alerted Comintern to the hazards of Li Li-san's rash ambitions. The Li Li-san line began to be seen in Moscow as one of these ultra-Left deviations which it had become the fashion to condemn. The complexities of the Chinese situation were increasingly apparent. A brief note in the Comintern journal explained that

> imperialist intervention . . . feudal fragmentation of the country, division of "spheres of influence" between different imperialist Powers, uneven development of the peasant movement in different parts of the country, lagging of the tempo of the workers' movement behind that of the peasant movement, determine that at the present time the chief task is the creation and strengthening of a Soviet Government.[41]

The caution conveyed in the Comintern resolution of July 23, 1930, was not enough; and at a meeting of the political commission of IKKI at the end of August Kuusinen spelt out in unmistakeable terms the need for patience:

[39] Hsiao Tso-liang, *Power Relations within the Chinese Communist Movement* (1961), pp. 50–53.

[40] *Kommunisticheskii Internatsional*, 1930, No. 22, pp. 9–17.

[41] *Ibid.* 1930, No. 25, p. 37; the note preceded the report of the Kiangsi delegation to the first congress of Soviets (see p. 324, note 17 above).

When a territorial base has really been created, when the Red Army has been strengthened, then it will be possible and necessary to face the task of capturing one or several big industrial centres or, in general, the big cities.[42]

Since Chou En-lai had recently arrived from China as leader of the CCP delegation at the sixteenth Russian party congress in June, and was a known supporter of Mao's cautious strategy, it is fair to suspect his influence behind this pronouncement.[43] Chou and Ch'ü Ch'iu-pai were both despatched to China to take part in the third plenum of the central committee of the CCP to be held at the end of September. To judge by the sequel, their mission was to restrain the aggressive policies adopted under Li's leadership rather than to seek a direct confrontation with him. No personal campaign against him had yet been launched in Moscow. Comintern at this time hoped to gain its end by persuasion, not by disciplinary measures.[44]

The third plenum of September 24–28, 1930, held at Lushan in north Kiangsi, was the first party assembly since the sixth congress in Moscow more than two years earlier; 14 members of the party central committee and 22 other party members were present. Ch'ü Ch'iu-pai presided. Hsiang Chung-fa opened the proceedings with an optimistic account of the party record. The revolutionary wave was rising. Fifty million Chinese now lived under Soviet rule; 100,000 workers were enrolled in Red trade unions; party member-

[42] *Kommunisticheskii Internatsional: Kratkii Istoricheskii Ocherk* (1969), p. 362.

[43] According to Chang Kuo-t'ao, Chou "took over practically all the business of the Chinese delegation" to the exclusion of himself and Ch'ü Ch'iu-pai (Hsiao Tso-liang, *Power Relations within the Chinese Communist Movement* (1961), p. 61); Chang and Ch'ü had been resident in Moscow since 1928 (see *Foundations of a Planned Economy, 1926–1929*, Vol. 3, pp. 874–875).

[44] Mif was no doubt largely responsible for shaping Comintern policy in China at this time; but the assumption made by many commentators that he conducted a campaign against Li Li-san throughout 1930, and that "the 28 Bolsheviks" were used by him for this purpose is not supported by evidence. The statement in B. I. Schwartz, *Chinese Communism and the Rise of Mao* (1951), pp. 149, 207, followed by many subsequent writers, that Mif accompanied the "returned students" to China in the spring of 1930 rests on an unreliable source, and is disproved by Mif's speech at the sixteenth Russian party congress in June (see p. 326 above), which shows that he had not been in China recently, and was not well informed about events there; nor was Mif present at the third plenum in September (see pp. 333–334 below). The decision to remove Li was not taken in Moscow till October, i.e. after the third plenum; Mif then went to China to enforce it.

ship exceeded 120,000. The party had not been blameless. It had overestimated the revolutionary situation, and made "strategical and tactical errors" in the agrarian and trade union questions. But these had been corrected under the guidance of Comintern—an evident reference to the directive of July 23. Hsiang's condemnation was reserved for Ch'en Tu-hsiu and the Trotskyists, and for Ho and the Kiangsu faction. Complacency could hardly have gone further.[45] Chou En-lai's report on the tasks of the party was more sophisticated, but its conclusions were not substantially different. Chou firmly dissociated himself from the Right, denouncing "Bukharin and others" who had indulged in talk about "organized capitalism, United States exceptionalism, and Indian decolonization". He celebrated the "agrarian revolution" which had brought 50 million people in south China under the rule of Soviets, and noted an upsurge of revolutionary struggles in the cities. But mainly he was on the defensive. He quoted the Comintern directive of July 23, and declared himself vigorously opposed to "any attempts to distort the line of the International". He admitted that the CCP had committed tactical errors, though not errors of principle. In the Soviet areas its guidance had been inadequate, and it had failed to consolidate and centralize the direction of the Red Army. On the other hand, the central committee had had "too mechanical a concept" of a central Soviet Government necessarily located in one of the major cities. Of the 120,000 members of the party only 2000 were workers; this was an admitted source of weakness. But Chou's main shafts were directed against the Right; he rejected "irritating remarks . . . such as those of comrade Ho Meng-hsiang about Li Li-san-ism"; this was the nearest he came to recognizing current criticism of Li. Chou ended by recalling the familiar thesis that the Chinese revolution was still in its democratic stage; it was dangerous to suppose that, "once we have won the industrial cities, the revolution will immediately assume a socialist character".[46]

Li Li-san followed, expressing complete agreement with Hsiang's and Chou's reports and with the Comintern line. Evidently conscious that he was under covert attack, however, Li admitted

[45] Hsiao Tso-liang, *Power Relations within the Chinese Communist Movement* (1961), pp. 60–61, 73.

[46] *Ibid.* pp. 63–64; an abbreviated translation of the report is in C. Brandt, B. I. Schwartz and J. K. Fairbank, *Documentary History of Chinese Communism* (1957), pp. 200–208.

"personal" errors on a number of issues. He had overestimated the readiness of the workers for "armed uprisings", and the prospect of "a nationwide revolutionary high tide". The party had failed to work for the immediate establishment of a Soviet government, preferring to await victory in one or more key cities. Finally, by way of asserting the identity of the party line with that of Comintern, he vigorously assailed the Right, and in particular the "liquidationist" Kiangsu clique.[47] An unnamed representative of Comintern also spoke; but his intervention seems to have been oddly inconclusive.[48] None of the "returned students" group is known to have taken part in the debate; Wang was under sentence of suspension. Ch'ü Ch'iu-pai summed up, and presented a draft resolution which was duly adopted. Ch'ü followed Chou's line fairly closely. While speaking of the struggle on two fronts, he treated the Right deviation as the main danger, and attacked both Ho Meng-hsiang, the leader of the Kiangsu group, and Chang Kuo-t'ao, still absent in Moscow, as Rightists. The resolution reaffirmed the fidelity of the CCP leadership to the Comintern directive of July 23, and stressed the distinction between a "rising tide" of revolution and an "objectively revolutionary situation". The Comintern directive had asserted that the former existed in China, and the latter did not. The resolution repeated both statements in reverse order—a change of emphasis which may have been intentional, and may have attracted unfavourable notice in Moscow, where such minutiae were well understood.[49]

The proceedings of the third plenum were hailed in China as a defeat for "Right opportunism" and a victory for the Comintern

---

[47] A full summary of Li's speech is in R. Thornton, *The Comintern and the Chinese Communists* (1969), pp. 193–197; for the Kiangsu group see pp. 329–330 above.

[48] No text was published, and a later statement by Chou that it attacked the Li Li-san leadership for having "adopted an erroneous adventurist policy, and moved on to the path of an anti-Comintern struggle" (R. Thornton, *The Comintern and the Chinese Communists* (1969), p. 197) is highly dubious. If the representative in question was Ewert (see p. 356 below), his mild character and low rating in Comintern may help to account for his lack of authority; it is significant that blame for the fiasco of the third plenum subsequently fell not on him, but on Chou and Ch'ü.

[49] Hsiao Tso-liang, *Power Relations within the Chinese Communist Movement* (1961), pp. 66–70. According to W. Kuo, *Analytical History of Chinese Communist Party*, ii (Taiwan, 1968), 151–152, 193–194, a request was made to the political secretariat of IKKI to send Chang back to China; this information presumably came from Chang himself.

line.[50] In Moscow they caused acute irritation. Chou En-lai and Ch'ü Ch'iu-pai had been less than half-hearted in discharging their mission.[51] The lessons of the Changsha fiasco had now been thoroughly digested; and it was an outrage that, at a time when Comintern was more and more concerned to curb projects of imminent revolution, and to interpret "the struggle on two fronts" in terms of a campaign against excesses of the Left, Li Li-san's reckless ardour should have escaped formal condemnation or public sanction. It was decided to remove Li from the scene by summoning him to Moscow, and to send Mif to China to call the peccant CCP leaders to order. A letter from IKKI was drafted dissecting Li's errors at length and in detail. Li had overestimated the revolutionary upsurge, had overlooked the extent to which the peasant movement had outstripped the workers' movement, and pressed for attacks on cities, on Wuhan as well as on Changsha. His views were branded as non-Marxist, non-Leninist and quasi-Trotskyist.

The letter apparently reached the CCP on November 16, 1930,[52] and threw the party into a state of confusion. Li Li-san left hastily for Moscow. At a conference of leaders on November 22, described as the meeting of an "enlarged politburo", Wang Ming and other members of the returned students' group denounced the decisions of the third plenum, and demanded an open party discussion of Li's errors. The embarrassed Chou En-lai, while opposing their extreme views, admitted that errors had been committed, and Ch'ü Ch'iu-pai said that he had committed errors under the influence of Chou. The conclusion reached was that the line of the third plenum was basically correct, but that it had not pointed out all Li's errors. Three days later the politburo adopted a more precise resolution condemning the third plenum for having "failed to expose thoroughly the semi-Trotskyist character of comrade Li Li-san's line, which contradicts the line of Comintern", and on

[50] B. I. Schwartz, *Chinese Communism and the Rise of Mao* (1951), p. 154; Hsiao Tso-liang, *Power Relations within the Chinese Communist Movement* (1961), p. 73.

[51] The supposition that Chou and Ch'ü deliberately neglected or qualified their instructions is scarcely plausible. The instructions were doubtless based on the IKKI resolution of July 23; and they probably left Moscow before news arrived of the final abandonment of the Changsha venture (see p. 328 above).

[52] Chinese sources date the letter November 16; according to H. Isaacs, *The Tragedy of the Chinese Revolution* (1938), p. 407, this was the date of its receipt. The text first published in Russian some years later (*Strategiya i Taktika Kominterna* (1934), pp. 283–290) dates it "October 1930".

December 11 decided to circulate the relevant documents to party branches.[53] On December 16 the reaction was carried several steps further. The suspension inflicted on Wang Ming, and the censure on his three colleagues, for their criticism of the Li Li-san line in June was cancelled, and denounced as an example of "the punitive patriarchal system" operated by Li; the views expressed by Ho Meng-hsiang were recognized as "generally correct", and the disciplinary measures taken against him and his group withdrawn.[54] Wang Ming had emerged triumphant on a platform which both denounced Li and criticized the party leaders who had condoned his policy at the third plenum.[55]

On this state of panic-stricken confusion in the CCP Mif descended in the later part of December. The preoccupation of Comintern was plainly recorded in an article in *Pravda* on December 25, 1930, which diagnosed "hesitations of a 'Left' semi-Trotskyist character" in the CCP. Some of its leading workers wished "to start immediately the struggle for power, ignoring the necessity of strengthening Soviet power in the regions occupied by the Red Army"; they also—this appeared to be an allusion to Ho's critics—sought "to restrain the economic struggle of the workers and dissolve the revolutionary trade unions". The first sign of Mif's handiwork in China was a circular of the central committee of the CCP of December 26, 1930, calling on the party to "bolshevize and unite itself in an uncompromising struggle against the Li Li-san line". The origin of the line was traced back to "putschism before the sixth congress"—a clear reference to the Canton rising, which was cited elsewhere in the circular as "the most conspicuous evidence of failure". From the time of the June 11 resolution to the third plenum the party central committee had worked "on a principle of perpetuating putschist adventurism"; and, though the third plenum had "discontinued agitation for nation-wide armed risings", it had "repeated and perpetuated the errors of Li Li-san's

[53] Hsiao Tso-liang, *Power Relations within the Chinese Communist Movement* (1961), pp. 93–94; R. Thornton, *The Comintern and the Chinese Communists* (1969), pp. 209–210; W. Kuo, *Analytical History of Chinese Communist Party*, ii (Taiwan, 1968), 173–178.

[54] *Ibid.* ii, 194–196; Hsiao Tso-liang, *Power Relations within the Chinese Communist Movement* (1961), pp. 94–95; R. Thornton, *The Comintern and the Chinese Communists* (1969), p. 212.

[55] This point was emphasized in a rather confused account of the episode in the resolution on party history of April 20, 1945 (*Selected Works of Mao Tse-tung*, iv (1956), 180–181).

line in the leadership of the party". The politburo now wished to confess its errors openly to the whole party. Finally the circular looked forward to a seventh party congress to "tackle all the basic political problems".[56] The presidium of IKKI, in the person of Manuilsky, decided, however, that a full party congress would be premature, and that a further session of the party central committee should be substituted for it.[57]

A "fourth plenum" of the central committee of the CCP was accordingly convened for January 7, 1931. The flexible Chou En-lai, adept at eating his own words, seems to have been Mif's principal coadjutor in these proceedings.[58] Li's removal left a vacuum which had to be filled. Ho Meng-hsiang made known his views in a pamphlet, in which he insisted on the supremacy of the proletariat, and on the need to win over the masses and to encourage economic strikes. Ch'ü Ch'iu-pai staked out his claim in a letter to the party which was afterwards condemned as "compromising".[59] But no claimant could stand up against the

[56] W. Kuo, *Analytical History of Chinese Communist Party*, ii (Taiwan, 1968), 197–201.

[57] *Ibid.* ii, 203.

[58] The evidence for Chou's role is the first sentence in the published version of the IKKI letter received on November 16, 1930 (see p. 334, note 52 above): "After a report by comrade M. the politburo cancelled its previous decisions and adhered to the decisions worked out in full agreement with the delegates of the central committee of the CCP" (comrade M. was the Russian cover-name of Chou En-lai—see *Foundations of a Planned Economy, 1926–1929*, Vol. 3, p. 867). This document provides a puzzle, any solution of which must remain conjectural. Its core is a long-winded and argumentative refutation of the views and policies of Li Li-san; this presumably constituted the original IKKI letter. In the published version it is, however, prefaced by two paragraphs and followed by four concluding paragraphs recording the satisfaction of IKKI at the reversal of policy by the CCP; these can have been written only after the receipt of the letter, and probably after Mif's arrival in China, and were presumably added in order to convey the impression that the reversal had been initiated by the CCP and not merely imposed on it by Comintern. The concluding paragraphs differ substantially in style from what had gone before, being curt and much sharper in tone: Li was said to have propagated theories "about Chinese exceptionalism, about the fact that Comintern did not understand the trend of development of the Chinese revolution", and to have declared that "the discipline of Comintern was one thing, and loyalty to the Chinese revolution another". The letter seems to have been published for the first time in 1931 in a Chinese collection of documents.

[59] B. I. Schwartz, *Chinese Communism and the Rise of Mao* (1952), pp. 164–165. According to Chang Kuo-t'ao, *The Rise of the Chinese Communist Party*, ii (1972), 156–157, Mif at first tried to woo the support of Ho in the struggle against Li; but this attempt broke down owing to divisions in the Kiangsu group, some of whom preferred Li to Mif and Wang Ming.

Wang Ming group, which now enjoyed through the patronage of Mif the decisive support of Comintern. After a stormy debate,[60] the fourth plenum adopted a resolution denouncing, in highly imaginative detail, Li's "anti-Leninist, adventurist line", and concentrating its attack on the party politburo resolution of June 11, 1930, and the resolution of the third plenum. The Changsha disaster was attributed directly to the errors of Li's leadership, which had issued "the premature, adventurist and dogmatic instruction to seize big cities", and "completely neglected the task of establishing a strong Soviet base". The politburo resolution of November 25 had, indeed, condemned the Li Li-san line, but errors were now detected both in it and in a subsequent letter to the party. It was imperative to "re-examine the membership of the politburo so as to secure correct leadership of the party". In conclusion, the party was exhorted "to convene a congress of Soviet deputies and to organize workers and peasants against the threatened invasion of the Soviet Union". The resolution was carried by a majority vote against fierce opposition, 16 of the 39 delegates voting in the minority.[61]

The sequel of the fourth plenum and of Li's disgrace was a complete take-over of the party organization by Mif's nominees, and its unconditional subordination to Comintern—a result achieved at about the same time in other parties. Hsiang Chung-fa remained as titular secretary of the party. But Wang Ming succeeded Li as the strong man in the leadership. Li and Ch'ü Ch'iu-pai were dropped from the politburo. Chou En-lai was rewarded for his prompt abandonment of Li Li-san, and of the stand which he had himself taken at the third plenum, by retaining an honoured place in the leadership, but was sent to work in the Soviet areas. Apart from Li, the main victims of the plenum were members of the Kiangsu group, who were branded as Right opportunists and completely routed. Boldly they attempted to resist, set up an emergency committee, and on January 17, 1931, issued a manifesto protesting against the decisions of the plenum. A few days later British municipal police broke up a meeting of the committee, and

[60] For some picturesque details from Chinese sources see R. Thornton, *The Comintern and the Chinese Communists* (1969), pp. 212–216.

[61] W. Kuo, *Analytical History of Chinese Communist Party*, ii (Taiwan, 1968), 204–210; Hsiao Tso-liang, *Power Relations within the Chinese Communist Movement* (1961), pp. 114–118; for an English translation of the resolution see C. Brandt, B. I. Schwartz and J. K. Fairbank, *A Documentary History of Chinese Communism* (1952), pp. 209–216.

handed over the participants to the Kuomintang authorities, who executed Ho Meng-hsiang and 24 of his followers. Suspicion was rife that they had been betrayed to the authorities by the CCP leadership.[62] Lo Chang-lung, Ho's principal lieutenant and author of a pamphlet attacking the fourth plenum, was expelled from the party. Ch'ü Ch'iu-pai issued a statement in which he accused himself of "cowardly, corrupt opportunism".[63] He never regained any authority in the party.

Concurrently with Li's condemnation by the central committee of the CCP, Comintern conducted its own inquisition. The eastern department, having cross-examined Li on his arrival in Moscow, made a damaging report to the presidium of IKKI.[64] This was the prelude to a major session of the presidium, in which all the leading officials of Comintern took part. Li began by reiterating and elaborating in still more abject terms the confession which he had already made to the eastern department. Kuchumov, replacing the absent Mif, repeated the now familiar indictment, and was followed by another member of the eastern department, Madyar. Madyar and Pyatnitsky both indicted Lominadze, who had exercised a malign influence on Li and Ch'ü ever since 1927. Chang Kuo-t'ao made his contribution by accusing Li of both Right and Left deviations, and denounced Ch'ü as "two-faced". Ts'ai Ho-shin, while confessing his own errors, also attacked Ch'ü. Among other orators were Bela Kun, Manuilsky and Kuusinen. Li, in a concluding speech, once more abased himself before his prosecutors, adding the detail that Chou En-lai and Ch'ü Ch'iu-pai had advised him at the time of the third plenum not to make any public confession of his errors since this would weaken the prestige of the leadership.[65] Li Li-san was not allowed to return to China, but was not otherwise penalized. He re-emerged many years later.

The principal feature of the change registered at the fourth

[62] W. Kuo, *Analytical History of Chinese Communist Party*, ii (Taiwan, 1968), 210–213; B. I. Schwartz, *Chinese Communism and the Rise of Mao* (1951), p. 166.

[63] Hsiao Tso-liang, *Power Relations within the Chinese Communist Movement* (1961), pp. 135–138.

[64] *Ibid*, pp. 27–28; Li's recantation on this occasion appeared in an English translation in *Report to the Oriental Bureau of the Comintern* (n.d.).

[65] Hsiao Tso-liang, *Power Relations within the Chinese Communist Movement* (1961), pp. 79–82; J. Rue, *Mao Tse-tung in Opposition: 1927–1935* (1966), p. 241; what appears to be the text of Kuchumov's speech is in *Kommunisticheskii Internatsional*, 1931, No. 1–2, pp. 36–43.

plenum in January 1931 was the replacement of a leader whose personality aroused mistrust in Moscow and among some of his colleagues by a leader of guaranteed fidelity to Comintern. But, though Wang Ming was afterwards condemned, like Li, as a Left sectarian, the change coincided with a certain shift in policy or emphasis. Li had always stood, as the doctrine of the leadership of the proletariat in the revolution required, for control by the party of what was done in the Soviet areas, including the operations of the Red Army. He seems for a time to have had more success than might have been expected; Mao later said that "the Li Li-san line . . . was sufficiently influential to force acceptance to some extent in the Red Army against the judgment of its field command".[66] Li had also, in the quest for a proletarian base, pressed for attacks by the Red Army not only on Changsha, but on other cities. The failure at Changsha in July 1930 came at a moment when Comintern, alarmed by symptoms of mounting crisis in Europe, was turning towards policies of caution and restraint. This mood soon percolated into its attitude towards the CCP. The elimination of the Kiangsu group weakened the specifically proletarian element in the party. It was safer to await and watch developments in the Soviet areas, and to come to terms with them, rather than seek to promote military adventures. Fewer predictions were heard of the imminence of revolution. To talk of a "revolutionary upsurge" did not imply the existence of a revolutionary situation. The period of Wang Ming's leadership was mainly a period of passivity for the CCP, marked by ready compliance with every wish of Comintern. The Shanghai conference of representatives of the Soviet areas[67] had proposed the convening of an All-China Congress of Soviets and the formation of a Soviet Government in the following November; and preparatory discussions proceeded in Shanghai during the summer.[68] The project ran into difficulties, and was first postponed from November to December, and then shelved.[69]

[66] E. Snow, *Red Star over China* (1938), p. 178; Mao may, however, in 1937 have been glad to blame the long discredited Li for dissensions in the Red Army which had other causes.

[67] See p. 324 above.

[68] Hsiao Tso-liang, *Power Relations within the Chinese Communist Movement* (1961), pp. 39–49.

[69] *Internationale Presse-Korrespondenz*, No. 89, October 24, 1930, p. 2174; among the documents prepared for the congress was an appeal from the presidium to the "workers, peasants and oppressed and exploited masses of China" (*ibid.* No. 95, November 11, 1930, pp. 2347–2348).

These first attempts to create a Soviet Government had encountered opposition from groups in Kiangsi which came to be
known as "the A-B (Anti-Bolshevik) League". Resistance to Mao's
growing personal ascendancy, and rivalry between military leaders,
probably played their part; rumours were current of friction
between Mao and P'eng, the general who had led the assault on
Changsha in July 1930. Controversy occurred on the moot question
of agrarian policy. Sometimes the A-B League was said to act as a
cloak for landlords and *kulaks*; it consisted of "representatives of
exploiting elements", and "formed organizing centres for remnants
of landlord and usurer strata remaining in Soviet territory".
Sometimes it was said to stand, in opposition to Mao's more
moderate line, for the confiscation and equal distribution of all land,
or for collective farming. Later, when Li had been finally
discredited, the league was alleged to have embraced the Li Li-san
line.[70] What is clear is that, as the Red Army grew in strength, and
the area under Soviet rule expanded, Mao's authority was subjected
to a dramatic assault. In December 1930 a serious clash began at
Fukien, which had the character both of a political rebellion and of
a military mutiny. According to Mao's own subsequent account,
the twentieth army "rose in open revolt, arrested the chairman of
the Kiangsi Soviet, and attacked us politically on the basis of the Li
Li-san line".[71] Whatever the origins and ramifications of the affair,
Mao emerged victorious and with enhanced authority, but at the
cost of savage fighting and much blood-letting.[72]

[70] The first mention of the league in Comintern literature is in an article in
Kommunisticheskii Internatsional, 1930, No. 25, pp. 37–38; the most detailed accounts
come from highly biased reports in *Sovety v Kitae*, ed. E. Johanson and O. Taube
(1933), pp. 16, 244–245, 255–256, 273. How far it was an organized movement is
not clear. O. Braun, *Chinesische Aufzeichnungen* (1973), pp. 74–75, offers a plausible
account of the fluctuations in Mao's attitude to the agrarian question. The first
slogan was "Everything for the front"—a form of war communism. This was
followed by "Everything for the peasant"—a version of NEP. This in turn was
corrected by Mao's "Left" insistence on the class division within the peasantry. But
all these attitudes served to "water down" the doctrine of the leading rôle of the
workers in the party.

[71] E. Snow, *Red Star over China* (1938), p. 182.

[72] For accounts of this obscure episode see Hsiao Tso-liang, *Power Relations within
the Chinese Communist Movement* (1961), pp. 98–113; W. Kuo, *Analytical History of
Chinese Communist Party*, ii (Taiwan, 1968), 298–307; B. I. Schwartz, *Chinese
Communism and the Rise of Mao* (1951), pp. 175–177; J. Chen, *Mao and the Chinese
Revolution* (1965), pp. 164–165; J. Rue, *Mao Tse-tung in Opposition* (1966), pp. 231–
235; P. Vladimirov, *Osobii Raion Kitaya* (1973), pp. 218, 222–232, which prints
some contemporary documents. *Ex post facto* attempts to associate it with Li and his
policies are highly dubious.

The situation remained, however, precarious so long as the Red Army was exposed to a constant threat from Kuomintang forces. In December 1930 Chiang Kai-shek decided that the time had come to restore the authority of the nationalist government over these remote and rebellious regions, and launched a campaign to encircle and destroy the Red Army; and this was followed by "second" and "third" campaigns in February and June 1931. These attacks secured only temporary successes, and the Red Army brought them to a standstill.[73] But the struggle against enemies within and without may have brought home to Mao the potential value of closer relations with the CCP and with its masters in Moscow at a time when Comintern for its part was disposed to take a more tolerant view of Mao's independent policies in the Soviet areas. The decision to transfer Chou En-lai to south China[74] may have been prompted by desire to remove a contentious figure from party headquarters in Shanghai. But, reinforced by a decision to establish a central party bureau for the Soviet areas in Juichin, it served as a means of bringing about closer contact between Mao and the party leadership, and perhaps of strengthening the leading role of the party.[75] Under Chou's efficient and energetic management the central bureau was not likely to remain idle. Several party directives were issued prescribing measures of support for the Red Army in its struggle against nationalist forces.[76]

The eleventh IKKI which met in Moscow at the end of March 1931 paid scant attention to Chinese affairs. Manuilsky claimed

[73] For a summary Soviet account of the three campaigns which preceded the Japanese incursion into Manchuria, see *Rundschau*, No. 24, July 14, 1933, pp. 851–852; in the spring of 1931 the Comintern press reported that "the wife of Mao Tse-tung, the leader of the Fourth Army", had been captured and executed by Kuomintang forces (*Internationale Presse-Korrespondenz*, No. 39–40, April 28, 1931, p. 979). The third campaign was launched from Nanchang on June 22, 1931, by Chiang in person, accompanied by German military advisers, 35 divisions being deployed (*Sovety v Kitae*, ed. E. Johanson and O. Taube (1933), p. 15); it initially penetrated deep into the Soviet area, but was driven back (*Internationale Presse-Korrespondenz*, No. 84, August 28, 1931, p. 814).

[74] See p. 337 above.

[75] O. Braun, *Chinesische Aufzeichnungen* (1973), p. 4 dates Chou's transfer "end of 1931", but connects it with Wang's departure for Moscow, which took place in September (see p. 344 below); Chou was certainly in Juichin in time for the preparations for the Congress of Soviets which opened on November 7 (Hsiao Tso-liang, *Power Relations within the Chinese Communist Movement* (1961), pp. 150–151).

[76] Three such directives of January 20, May 9, and June 1931 are cited in W. Kuo, *Analytical History of Chinese Communist Party*, ii (Taiwan, 1968), 237–245.

that "*the organization of Soviets and the Red Army* in territories with a population of tens of millions" provided "*a solid base for the hegemony of the proletariat in the national revolutionary movement*". He attacked the "Leftist error" of the Li Li-san group, which had drawn "*putschist conclusions*" from the fact of "*the beginnings of a revolutionary situation in China and in the whole world*". The solitary Chinese delegate who spoke in the debate echoed these sentiments, but admitted that the workers' movement had significantly lagged behind the peasant movement.[77] Neumann, in a rare and uncomfortable allusion to the past, admitted that the Canton commune of December 1927 had "ended in heavy and bloody defeat", but added: "Not two years passed since that blow, and we could already count on tens of millions of people in Soviet territory under Soviet government.[78] A brief passage about China in the main resolution of the session rejoiced at "the organization of Soviets and a Red Army in a territory with a population of tens of millions", and added the cryptic assurance that "the fact of the formation of Soviets and the Red Army determines the success of the hegemony of the proletariat in the national revolutionary movement".[79] In the debate on the danger of war a Chinese delegate drew attention to the encroachments of Japanese imperialism in Manchuria, and added that "the American imperialists are also strengthening their influence in Manchuria and preparing their intervention against the USSR".[80] But this was not mentioned in the resolution adopted at the end of the debate. An article by Mif in the Russian party journal reiterated "the slogan of the agrarian revolution, the destruction of imperialist rule, the overthrow of the counter-revolutionary Kuomintang government, and the establishment of a revolutionary government of worker-peasant Soviets", and condemned equally Right opportunists who depreciated the importance of the Soviet movement and "Left" opportunist elements which sought to "push the party on the path of unprepared, premature, putschist armed risings in the big industrial centres of the country".[81]

---

[77] *XI Plenum IKKI* (1932), i, 53–54, 71, 264.

[78] *Ibid.* i, 487.

[79] *Kommunisticheskii Internatsional v Dokumentakh* (1933), p. 959.

[80] *XI Plenum IKKI* (1932), ii, 109.

[81] *Bol'shevik*, No. 13, July 15, 1931, pp. 67–79; *Byulleten' Oppozitsii* (Paris), No. 23, August 1931, p. 23, reported the arrest in Shanghai in May 1931 of Ch'en Tu-hsiu, the former CCP leader who had been expelled from the party in 1929 (see *Foundations of a Planned Economy, 1926–1929*, Vol. 3, p. 904), and of 12 other "Left" communists.

The year 1931 witnessed some progress in welding together the two elements in the Chinese revolutionary movement. In June Hsiang Chung-fa, the secretary of the CCP, was arrested in Shanghai and executed. He was succeeded by the more colourful and aggressive Wang Ming, who had been a power in the party ever since the fourth plenum. About the same time, the presidium of IKKI issued a long and verbose resolution, which managed to accommodate a wide variety of opinions, but revealed little understanding of the situation on the spot. It lamented the weakness of the CCP in non-Soviet areas, and the absence of party work in the trade unions. But it recorded with satisfaction that "the peasant war under proletarian leadership ever more systematically realized through the communist party, embraces more and more new regions". (The unrealistic formula of proletarian and party leadership was repeated *ad nauseam* throughout the text.) Li Li-san was once more accused of "a policy of adventurist putschism"; and a struggle on two fronts was called for against " 'Left' opportunism", as well as against "Right opportunism" with its "lack of faith in the forces of the revolution". But the last section of the resolution showed where the greatest emphasis now rested. "The paramount task of the movement is to strengthen and reinforce the Red Army." Its ranks should be filled with "workers, *batraks*, coolies, poor and middle peasants"; and it ("first and foremost, its officer corps") should be cleansed of "plainly *kulak* and gentry elements". Soviet democracy must be "brought to life", and "a central Soviet government formed in the most secure region". The concluding sentence affirmed that "the cause of the Chinese Soviets is the cause of the whole international proletariat".[82] It is not clear that the resolution was directed against Mao, or designed to weaken his hold over the Soviet areas. But when in September 1931 the party politburo sent a circular directive to all Soviet areas, criticizing the guerrilla tactics hitherto pursued, and demanding the reorganization of the Red Army into a regular army in preparation for a major offensive against the Kuomintang forces,[83] this was an

[82] *Strategiya i Taktika Kominterna* (1934), pp. 294–312. It is here dated August 26, 1931 (perhaps the date of its first publication in Russian), but it appeared in a Chinese party journal in July (Hsiao Tso-liang, *Power Relations within the Chinese Communist Movement* (1961), pp. 155–157); the misdating is characteristic (see p. 327, note 28 above).

[83] J. Rue, *Mao Tse-tung in Opposition: 1927–1935* (1966), p. 245. This appears to be the resolution of September 20, 1931, referred to in the resolution on party

unmistakable challenge to Mao's authority. In the same month, Wang Ming was recalled to Moscow, and succeeded as party secretary by his lieutenant, Po Ku.[84]

While the Soviets and the Red Army were consolidating their power in the south, the situation throughout China was over-shadowed by the Japanese *coup* of September 18–19, 1931, leading within a few weeks to the total occupation by Japanese forces of Manchuria and the CER. The sensitiveness of the USSR to events on its border with northern China outstripped, as always, its concern with other parts of China. But resistance was impossible, and the Soviet reaction was confined to a flood of protests through diplomatic and Comintern channels. On September 22, both Japanese and Chinese communist parties issued declarations of protest against the act of aggression by Japanese imperialism.[85] *Pravda* on September 25 assumed the complicity of the other imperialist Powers, which would be eager to share the booty; nothing could save China but "a worker-peasant revolution under the leadership of the CCP". A statement issued by WEB observed that "the blow struck by the Japanese Government has been met fairly benevolently by the other imperialists", who were also seeking "a way out of the world crisis by dividing up and plundering China"; and this was followed by a similar protest from the League against Imperialism.[86] The eventual impact of these events on the international constellation of forces still lay in the future. The Sino–Soviet clash in Manchuria at the end of 1929 had already sown the seeds of a common interest between the USSR and the western Powers.[87] Now American and British indignation at the Japanese incursion into Manchuria, matching the sharp reaction in Moscow, opened a vista which both sides were at first reluctant to

---

history of April 20, 1945, in which the mistakes of the new "Left" line first found expression (*Selected Works of Mao Tse-tung*, iv (1956), 184).

[84] J. Rue, *Mao in Opposition: 1927–1935* (1966), p. 246; *Selected Works of Mao Tse-tung*, iv (1956), 185.

[85] *Internationale Presse-Korrespondenz*, No. 97, October 9, 1931, p. 2182.

[86] *Ibid.* No. 93, September 29, 1931, pp. 2080–2081; for two letters from Dimitrov, the head of WEB, to IKKI urging that communist parties should be mobilized for the campaign against imperialist war see *Georgii Dimitrov: Vydayushchiisya Deyatel' Kommunisticheskogo Dvizheniya* (1972), p. 109.

[87] See *Foundations of a Planned Economy, 1926–1929*, Vol. 3, pp. 907–908.

recognize,[88] and which for a long time produced no tangible results.

Meanwhile Chinese communists were concerned mainly with the repercussions of the affair on the Chinese nationalist government. The CCP in its protest of September 22 denounced the *coup* as the beginning of an imperialist offensive against the USSR, and urged the revolutionary masses both to rally to the defence of the USSR and to form a united front from below to overthrow the Kuomintang government.[89] Three days later seven Soviet governments in the Soviet areas issued a statement in still more heated terms, which referred to the preparation of a second world war, taunted "the Kuomintang bureaucrats and militarists" with policies of "non-resistance" and appeals for "calm", and bracketed the imperialists and Kuomintang as joint targets of attack.[90] The emphasis in Comintern shifted from preoccupation with struggles for leadership within the CCP to the potentialities of armed resistance now being developed in the south. Mif in an article on the tasks of the CCP stressed the importance of the Chinese Red Army, and described the Soviets as "the genuinely revolutionary form of the dictatorship of the working class and the peasantry".[91]

It was, however, important that the cause of national liberation from the imperialist yoke which had presided at the birth of the CCP should not be forgotten. The customary IKKI manifesto on the anniversary of the revolution in November 1931 contained an inflammatory passage on events in Manchuria. The Japanese aggression was said to have had the blessing of "French imperialists", and blame was indiscriminately laid on British and American imperialism, on the League of Nations, and finally on Chiang Kai-shek and Kuomintang as "servants of the imperialists". The concluding appeal ran:

> *Support actively your Chinese brothers in their struggle against Japanese occupation, against the League of Nations, against the treacherous Kuomintang, against Chiang Kai-shek, for a united independent China.*[92]

[88] A curious fencing-match between Litvinov and the British chargé d'affaires a few days after the event is recorded in *Dokumenty Vneshnei Politiki SSSR*, xiv (1968), 537; both carefully veiled the coincidence of their reactions to the Japanese aggression. *Izvestiya* on September 26 compared the American reaction favourably with that of the League of Nations.

[89] *Internationale Presse-Korrespondenz*, No. 97, October 9, 1931, p. 2182.

[90] *Sovety v Kitae*, ed. E. Johanson and O. Taube (1933), pp. 446–448.

[91] *Problemy Kitaya*, No. 8–9 (1931), pp. 3–27.

[92] *Pravda*, November 6, 1931.

A Comintern instruction to the CCP of December 1931 called for "a national revolutionary war to oppose Japanese imperialists and all other imperialists, in order to win the liberation of the Chinese nation and to promote the independence and unification of China", but pronounced a revolution to overthrow Kuomintang to be "the pre-requisite of the triumph of the national revolutionary war against imperialism".[93] A CCP resolution, presumably issued in response to this instruction, described the Manchurian affair as "a beginning of the dismemberment and colonization of China by the imperialist Powers", but optimistically concluded that it would "greatly facilitate the Soviet movement and the Red Army struggle, and ripen the conditions for the nation-wide revolution", which would bring about "the collapse and bankruptcy of Kuomintang rule".[94] The conception of national resistance to Japanese aggression had eclipsed the concept of social revolution in Comintern thinking. But for Chinese communists Kuomintang was still the implacable enemy. Trotsky, writing at the end of 1931, also believed that "the necessity of defence against the Japanese aggressors will be directed more and more against the Kuomintang regime".[95]

The next major event in Juichin was the convocation of a party conference to prepare for the first All-China Congress of Soviets, postponed from the previous year,[96] and now announced for November 7, 1931. The occasion was marked by a determined, and largely successful, attempt by the Po Ku group, now reinforced by the versatile Chou En-lai and perhaps enjoying direct encouragement from Moscow, to discredit Mao's leadership and wrest control of the party machine from his hands. The resolution of the conference attacked the party agrarian programme of February 7, 1930, as unduly indulgent to the well-to-do peasant, and firmly declared that the agrarian revolution must be led by the proletariat; denounced "class alien" elements in Soviet institutions and in the trade unions; and, criticizing the guerrilla tactics of the Red Army, demanded a strategy of taking over urban centres and establishing revolutionary bases—a revival of something like the Li Li-san

---

[93] W. Kuo, *Analytical History of Chinese Communist Party*, ii (Taiwan, 1968), 413–414.

[94] *Ibid.* ii, 372–373.

[95] *Byulleten' Oppozitsii* (Paris), No. 25–26, November–December 1931, p. 4.

[96] See p. 339 above.

programme now sponsored by Chou.[97] It was the beginning of a gradual eclipse of Mao's pre-eminence in the Chinese revolutionary movement which lasted for three years. Chou En-lai, who had already displayed his dislike, or perhaps jealousy, of Mao at the sixth party congress in 1928,[98] seems to have played a leading part in the process.

The first All-China Congress of Soviets opened in Juichin on November 7, 1931, the fourteenth anniversary of the Russian October revolution. The fiasco of the previous year had been retrieved. The congress mustered 610 delegates from Soviets in Kiangsi and Fukien, and outlying Soviets in Hunan, Hupei and Kwangsi, from Red trade unions and from the CCP; and a torchlight procession on the first evening was said to have been attended by a crowd of 10,000.[99] The confusion spread in the ranks of Kuomintang by the Japanese aggression in Manchuria had brought to a standstill the third nationalist offensive against the Soviet regions; and this respite bred an atmosphere of euphoria. The congress adopted a draft constitution which described the Soviet republic (according to Lenin's formula of 1905, but not of 1917) as a "democratic dictatorship of workers and peasants", but was otherwise precisely modelled on the Russian precedent, even to the paradoxical extent of "reserving to the proletariat special privileges in elections to Soviets (election of a proportionally larger number of delegates)"; a draft agrarian law reaffirming the principle of confiscation and redistribution of land; a draft labour code based on the most advanced principles; and a draft law on economic and financial policy.[100] The "provisional government" set up by the congress issued a manifesto declaring its solidarity with the USSR, and demanding the annulment of the unequal treaties, the withdrawal of foreign troops, and the confiscation of foreign enterprises; the last paragraph protested against "the robber war of the Japanese in Manchuria".[101] These enactments and pronounce-

[97] J. Rue, *Mao Tse-tung in Opposition: 1927–1935* (1966), pp. 247–248; the resolution on party history of April 20, 1945, referred to the conference as having "replaced the former correct party and military leadership" (*Selected Works of Mao Tse-tung*, iv (1956), 185).

[98] See *Foundations of a Planned Economy, 1926–1929*, Vol. 3, p. 867.

[99] *Sovety v Kitae*, ed. E. Johanson and O. Taube (1933), pp. 417–418.

[100] *Ibid.* pp. 419–434; the texts, apparently drafted before the congress, are also in *Problemy Kitaya*, No. 8–9 (1931), pp. 191–205.

[101] *Sovety v Kitae*, ed. E. Johanson and O. Taube (1933), pp. 444–446.

ments were a response to popular enthusiasm, and served to generate and perpetuate it. But they had little immediate application. The elections at the end of the congress were more significant. They showed that, notwithstanding the virtual take-over of the party machine, the prestige of Mao and his supporters in the Soviets was still too firmly entrenched to be shaken. The congress, following Russian precedent, elected a central executive committee of 63, which in turn appointed a Council of People's Commissars; Mao became president of both bodies, with Hsiang Ying, and Chang Kuo-t'ao, both veteran members of the central committee of the CCP, as vice-presidents.[102] A Bureau of State Political Protection, a counterpart of the Cheka, was set up by a decree of January 27, 1932, signed by Mao, Hsiang and Chang, and said to have been approved by the congress.[103] A struggle for power still lay ahead, and would turn on the control of the Red Army. But during the years 1932–1934 Mao seems to have lost all authority in the party.

The nationalist government in Nanking had looked on helplessly while Japanese forces took possession of Manchuria. In Shanghai some students demonstrated; an attempt was made to organize a boycott of Japanese goods; and strikes occurred in Japanese-owned textile factories. These provocations were the pretext for the landing in Shanghai on January 28, 1932, of a substantial contingent of Japanese troops. The CCP responded with a manifesto of January 31, which maintained that "all groupings of Kuomintang, the whole Chinese bourgeoisie, are abettors of Japanese imperialism", and that "in order to overthrow imperialism it is necessary to overthrow the tool of imperialism, the Chinese imperialism, the Chinese Kuomintang".[104] A ferocious party proclamation of

[102] Hsiao Tso-liang, *Power Relations within the Chinese Communist Movement* (1961), p. 173.

[103] W. Kuo, *Analytical History of Chinese Communist Party*, ii (Taiwan, 1968), 349–353; the only party post retained by Mao was that of secretary of the party group in the Soviet administration (*ibid.* ii, 484).

[104] *Sovety v Kitae*, ed. E. Johanson and O. Taube (1933), pp. 448–450; *Kommunisticheskii Internatsional: Kratkii Istoricheskii Ocherk* (1969), p. 364, criticizes the leadership of the CCP for not taking into account the fact that "many strata of the people who had arisen to struggle against the Japanese aggressors" had not yet lost faith in Kuomintang, blame being laid on "sectarian elements in the CCP" which believed in "an immediately revolutionary situation".

February 2 called for a general strike of workers, students, soldiers and police, and begged "revolutionary soldiers" to kill their officers and "unite with armed civilians to defeat the imperialists and Kuomintang".[105] Unexpectedly for the communists, and apparently against or without orders from Chiang Kai-shek, the Kuomintang nineteenth army, which was stationed in Shanghai, attempted to resist the Japanese invaders; and strikes and sporadic fighting continued for some weeks. This spontaneous outburst of Kuomintang resistance did not mollify the CCP leaders. A further manifesto of February 16 declared that the "Kuomintang militarists", under the pretence of resisting the Japanese, were deceiving "the heroic revolutionary people", and preparing the way for a sell-out to the imperialists.[106] It is not clear that communists played any prominent part in these events.[107] A scathing rebuke administered by the party central committee to the Kiangsu provincial party committee, whose domain included Shanghai, alleged that the latter had failed to take any action against the Japanese "imperialist occupation of Shanghai", that local party membership was decreasing, and party influence over the masses weakening.[108]

In the Soviet regions of the south, indignation at Japanese aggression in Manchuria and Shanghai was a slower and less spontaneous growth. An article in a party journal early in 1932 alleged that "the party in the Soviet areas knew only the agrarian revolution, not the national revolution".[109] The party committee in

[105] W. Kuo, *Analytical History of Chinese Communist Party*, ii (Taiwan, 1968), 414–416.

[106] *Ibid.* ii, 416–418.

[107] At the twelfth IKKI in August 1932 the Japanese delegate boldly attributed the resistance in Shanghai to "the heroic struggle of soldiers, workers and the poor of Shanghai under the leadership of the CCP"; Wang Ming more modestly described it as having "mainly a spontaneous character", but praised the CCP for organizing "a general strike in all Japanese enterprises—altogether about 60,000 workers" (*XII Plenum IKKI* (1933), iii, 10, 20–21). The claim that the CCP instigated the strikes and the resistance of Kuomintang forces to the Japanese incursion was dismissed by an eye-witness as "a palpable falsehood" (H. Isaacs, *The Tragedy of the Chinese Revolution* (1938), p. 431); the account in *Die Kommunistische Internationale vor dem VII Weltkongress* (1935), pp. 559–560, of mass demonstrations against Kuomintang, against Japanese and other imperialists, and against the League of Nations, is unrealistic.

[108] W. Kuo, *Analytical History of Chinese Communist Party*, ii (Taiwan, 1968), 374–375.

[109] *Ibid.* ii, 374–375.

Juichin was, however, thoroughly bellicose. In a proclamation of January 31, 1932, it described "all Kuomintang groups, the whole Chinese bourgeoisie" as "accomplices of Japanese imperialism". The purported defiance of Chiang by Kuomintang leaders eager to fight the Japanese was merely a device "to deceive the working masses, to deceive the Chinese people". The only force arrayed against Japanese and world imperialism was the communist party, which now issued the call: "Down with Kuomintang which has betrayed Shanghai to the imperialists". A further manifesto of February 26 urged the masses and the soldiers to take the power into their own hands, and to form a revolutionary-military committee to carry on the struggle.[110] Nothing here was likely to mitigate Chiang's eagerness to crush the insurgents. But it was also logical for the Red Army and the Soviets to be more preoccupied by the immediate threat from the nationalist armies than by Japan's more remote offensive. Collaboration between nationalists and communists against the Japanese aggressor would not at this time have seemed even a remote possibility.

The Japanese incursion at Shanghai in January 1932 was followed by the installation in Manchuria of the Japanese puppet state of Manchukuo. Tension mounted in Moscow. The Japanese action provoked two leading articles in the journal of Comintern early in 1932. A warning was sounded that the world was "drifting towards imperialist war"; and communist parties were urged to disrupt war production in capitalist countries and impede the shipment of arms to the Far East.[111] Apathy in the CCP and the Chinese Soviets on the Japanese question caused concern in Comintern; in March 1932 a long article by Wang Ming, carrying every mark of official inspiration, appeared in the Russian party journal. Wang attacked Right opportunists, who "do not understand that a war of national liberation is at present the necessary form of the struggle of the Chinese people". Victory of the "anti-imperialist revolution" was a condition of the victory of the "agrarian revolution". The balance was maintained by a concluding criticism of remnants of the "Left" Li Li-san line, which also prejudiced the anti-imperialist struggle.[112]

[110] *Sovety v Kitae*, ed. E. Johanson and O. Taube (1933), pp. 448–452.

[111] *Kommunisticheskii Internatsional*, 1932, No. 4, pp. 3–9, No. 6, pp. 3–9.

[112] *Bol'shevik*, No. 5–6, March 31, 1932, pp. 26–41; Wang was employed at this time as an instructor in the Communist University of Toilers of the East; a lecture delivered by him there on April 27, 1932, on party history, heavily attacking the Li Li-san line, was published in *Revolyutsionnyi Vostok*, 1932, No. 3–4, pp. 144–159.

An almost simultaneous response came from Juichin. On April 5, Mao and Chu Teh in the name of the Chinese Soviet Government issued a declaration of war against Japan.[113] Chou, in articles in the party press which must have been read with gratification in Moscow, harped on two main themes: the danger of war against the USSR inherent in Japanese aggression, and the call to strengthen the Red Army for greater military activity.[114] The same two themes were rehearsed in a party directive of May 1932, which severely criticized the lack in the Soviet areas of "a sufficient appraisal of the political situation" and "the errors committed by the Soviet Government". The Red Army was urged to mobilize against expected "new imperialist Kuomintang attacks". The directive was a strong covert attack on Mao's leadership, and was remarkable not only for a personal tribute to Chou (under his *alias* Wu Hao), who was said, since coming to Juichin, to have corrected "fully or partially" certain unspecified errors of the past, but for a reversion to a demand of the Li Li-san period to "seize one or two key cities in order to win a victory for the revolution" in one or several provinces.[115] Later reports have spread much confusion over the relations at this time between Chou and Mao. But these months saw the beginning of a steady process which transferred the supreme authority over the Red Army from Mao to Chou.[116]

The mood of optimism prevailing in Juichin in the first months of 1932 was quickly shattered. Chiang Kai-shek, having recovered from the first shock of the Japanese incursion, was determined not to allow this episode to distract him from the more congenial task of subduing the recalcitrant Soviet areas in the south. In January 1932 he came to terms with the pliant Wang Ching-wei, formerly leader of the Left Kuomintang and long Chiang's rival. Eugene Chen, the Foreign Minister in the nationalist government, resigned and left China, being succeeded by Wang Ching-wei. It was significant that the nationalist government had never demanded the recall of the Japanese Ambassador, and remained in friendly relations with him.

[113] *Programmnye Dokumenty Kitaiskikh Sovetov* (1935), pp. 90–93.

[114] Hsiao Tso-liang, *Power Relations within the Chinese Communist Movement* (1961), pp. 201–202, 207–208.

[115] W. Kuo, *Analytical History of Chinese Communist Party*, ii (Taiwan, 1968), 419–421.

[116] O. Braun, *Chinesische Aufzeichnungen* (1973), p. 83, attributes Chou's success in part to the fact that many Red Army officers were former pupils of his in the Whampoa Military Academy.

The fighting in Shanghai had petered out, and a truce was arranged. Chiang was free to undertake his fourth campaign against the Soviet areas, which was launched in greater force than its predecessors in June 1932.[117] Much of the weight of this offensive was directed against the so-called Fourth Army of Fourth Corps, to which Chang Kuo-t'ao, newly returned from Moscow, was attached as political commissar. The Fourth Army had already been split off by Chiang's offensive in 1931 from the main forces of the Red Army and from the Soviet territory in Kiangsi, and maintained itself in precarious isolation in eastern Hupei, controlling an area with a population of some three million, and mustering a strength of 12,000 to 15,000 men. From here it was driven out by Chiang's fourth campaign in July 1932, and proceeded westward through Huan into Shensi, and thence into northern Szechwan, where it at length found a resting-place, unmolested by Kuomintang forces.[118] This achievement was used to justify the dubious claim that the Kuomintang offensive had been beaten off, and that the area under Soviet rule had been increased, now embracing a population of 79 millions.[119]

The greatest concentration of Kuomintang forces, however, estimated at 250,000 to 300,000 men, was used in the summer of 1932 to encircle the central Soviet region from west, north and

[117] For two CCP manifestos of June 18 and 22 on "the imperialist-Kuomintang fourth encirclement campaign" see W. Kuo, *Analytical History of Chinese Communist Party*, ii (Taiwan, 1968), 430–433. Subsequent communist accounts distinguished a minor attack of March 1932 as the "fourth" and the campaign launched in June–July 1932 as the "fifth", Kuomintang offensive (*Rundschau*, No. 24, July 14, 1932, pp. 851–852); this led to confusion later, when the final campaign of the autumn of 1933 was sometimes called the "sixth", e.g. by Wang Ming at the thirteenth IKKI (*XIII Plenum IKKI* (1934), p. 122) and by Mao himself at the second Chinese Congress of Soviets (see p. 365, note 159 below). In the eventual official reckoning, the "fourth" offensive was defeated in the spring of 1933, and the "fifth" opened in the autumn of that year (*Selected Works of Mao Tse-tung*, iv (1956), 186).

[118] See Chang Kuo-t'ao, *The Rise of the Chinese Communist Party*, ii (1972), 313, for a sketch-map showing these movements; this work contains the most detailed available account of the experiences of the Fourth Army. The party central committee, on learning of the move into Szechwan, is said to have sent a telegram condemning it as "Right escapism" (*ibid.* ii, 332–333). But the report is dubious; radio communication was precarious, and the terminology belongs to a later period. Chang treats the offensive against the Fourth Army as the main element in Chiang's fourth encirclement campaign (*ibid.* ii, 295); this is partly confirmed by O. Braun, *Chinesische Aufzeichnungen* (1973), p. 32.

[119] *Rundschau*, No. 6, December 1, 1932, p. 114, No. 24, July 14, 1933, p. 852.

east.[120] The weight of the assault took the defenders by surprise; and a conference of party and military leaders under the auspices of the central party bureau was hastily convened at Ningtu in central Kiangsi. It produced a direct confrontation between Mao, who clung to the guerrilla tactics by which the Red Army had been built up, and which were now branded as "military opportunism" and "passive defence", and Chou, who wished to forestall attacks by massed counter-attacks—tactics described as "halting the enemy beyond the gate". Mao is said to have been criticized for "Left sectarian" errors in his attitude to large-scale and middle peasants and in the institution of a "terror regime". Chou was victorious. Mao remained as president of the Soviet Government and as a member of the party bureau and of the military revolutionary council, but lost his hitherto dominant position and his control of military strategy, being confined to work in the Soviet administration. As usual, he appears to have yielded without a struggle, awaiting a subsequent opportunity for a comeback.[121] Following the conference, directives were published on the expansion of the Red Army (its numbers were to double in three months) and the incorporation in it of local armed levies.[122]

The twelfth IKKI meeting in August 1932, though heavily preoccupied with the threat of war against the USSR, brought dangerously nearer by the Japanese aggression, paid little attention to Chinese affairs. Kuusinen hailed "the *Red Army* of the Chinese Soviet government" as "the one true army for the defence of the independence of the country"; and Manuilsky spoke of China "with its vast Soviet territory, with its invincible Red Army".[123] Wang Ming said that China was the scene "*both of revolution and of war*". The Chinese Soviet Government was "really a government of

[120] See O. Braun, *Chinesische Aufzeichnungen* (1973), pp. 31–34, for a full, but still confused, account of the fourth encirclement campaign, with an inadequate sketch-map.

[121] The best summary account of the Ningtu conference, of which no records were ever published, is in O. Braun, *Chinesische Aufzeichnungen* (1973), p. 28; see also E. Snow, *Red Star over China* (1938), p. 185, and the sources cited in Hsiao Tso-liang, *Power Relations within the Chinese Communist Movement* (1961), pp. 210–211. The party resolution of April 20, 1945, referred to the conference as a landmark in the erroneous policy adopted in these years (*Selected Works of Mao Tse-tung*, iv (1956), 185).

[122] W. Kuo, *Analytical History of Chinese Communist Party*, ii (Taiwan, 1968), 450–451.

[123] *XII Plenum IKKI* (1933), i, 22, 160.

workers, peasants and all toilers under the leadership of the proletariat". But the picture was marred by the presence in the Soviet regions of "counter-revolutionary organizations", some of which had raised the slogan "Soviet power without Bolsheviks". Wang asserted that the fourth plenum of the CCP had produced "a radical turn-about in the question of the agrarian revolution", and praised the activity of the party in the strike movement.[124] The passages referring to the Far East in the main resolution of the session were devoted primarily to denunciation of imperialism and Japanese aggression. But the "development of the Soviet movement" and the "great successes of the heroic Chinese Red Army" were duly celebrated; and the task of the CCP was "the mobilization of the masses under the slogan of the national-revolutionary struggle against Japanese and other imperialists for the independence and unification of China".[125] The same national note was heard in the resolution against the danger of war, which called on the CCP for a "revolutionary war of national liberation for the independence, unification and unity of China, against the imperialists and for the overthrow of the agency of imperialism, Kuomintang". The resolution reproached the communist parties of the imperialist countries with their failure to "prevent by re-volutionary action the transport of armies to China and of military supplies to Japan", which it attributed to "an opportunistic underestimate of the Far Eastern war", and to "a Leftish-fatalistic light-minded attitude to the war".[126] The proceedings of the twelfth IKKI marked a significant turn towards the theme of national liberation in China, but entailed no relaxation of hostility to the Kuomintang regime, which was consistently treated as a tool of imperialist aggression. The session betrayed little knowledge of, or interest in, conditions in the Soviet regions, and the subsequent use of the resolution by Po Ku to support a "forward and offensive line" in the strategy of the Red Army[127] had no relation to its original purpose.

The debates of the twelfth IKKI showed no trace of a new current of thought which was just setting in among those concerned in Moscow with the conduct of foreign affairs. Fear of an offensive against the USSR was the all-prevailing anxiety. But the Japanese

[124] *Ibid.* i, 144–157.
[125] *Kommunisticheskii Internatsional v Dokumentakh* (1933), pp. 973–982.
[126] *Ibid.* p. 992; for this resolution see p. 73 above.
[127] See p. 357 below.

aggression incontrovertibly offered a threat to the integrity of Chinese territory as well as to the USSR; and the only power existing in China which might resist the threat was concentrated, not in the Soviet regions, but at Nanking, where Chiang Kai-shek exercised a precarious authority over a large part of China, including the great cities. Since 1929 the Soviet Government had had no official relations with any Chinese Government, and had remained implacably hostile to Chiang Kai-shek, the butcher of Chinese communists, and to the nationalist government in Nanking, which enjoyed regular diplomatic relations with the western Powers. This self-imposed isolation no longer seemed consonant with Soviet interests. In December 1932 an agreement was reached between Moscow and Nanking for mutual recognition and the exchange of ambassadors.[128] At the very moment when Chiang's armies were fighting to destroy the newly established Chinese Soviet Government and the Red Army in the South, it was a paradoxical gesture. Yet it was consistent with the view expounded in Moscow in the nineteen-twenties, and shortly to be repeated when Hitler seized power in Germany, that the official relations of the Soviet Government with the German Government were not affected by any treatment meted out by the German Government to German communists.[129] The same logic applied to Soviet diplomatic relations with Nanking. But the Soviet *volte-face* of December 1932 in China had another perhaps unsuspected dimension. The western representatives in Nanking were engaged in quiet, but persistent, pressure on Chiang to stiffen his resistance to the Japanese invaders. It was difficult to believe that a Soviet Ambassador in Nanking could remain wholly aloof from this process, even though Comintern at the same time was vociferously preaching that resistance to Chiang was an integral and necessary part of resistance to Japanese imperialism. This was one of several cases in which Narkomindel and Comintern continued for a time to pursue different and apparently incompatible lines of action side by side, without any overt conflict arising between them. It is, however, noticeable that in this period it was the policy of Narkomindel rather than of Comintern which, after a lengthy

---

[128] *Dokumenty Vneshnei Politiki SSSR*, xv (1969), 680–682. The original approach had been made to Litvinov six months earlier by the Chinese delegate in Geneva; a suggestion for a non-aggression pact was rejected by the politburo in Moscow (*ibid.* xv, 780–781).

[129] See p. 98 above.

interval of uncertainty and confusion, became the nucleus of a concerted policy.

About the time of the twelfth IKKI a new Comintern representative, a military adviser, was sent out to reinforce the central committee of the CCP in Shanghai. He was Otto Braun, a German communist, who had just taken a course at the Frunze Military Academy in Moscow. Comintern was represented in Shanghai at that time by Ewert, who had been ousted from work in the KPD owing to his support for the "conciliationist" Meyer, and by Russian representatives of OMS (the communications and secret intelligence section of Comintern); and two Americans represented Profintern and KIM.[130] Ewert put Braun in touch with Po Ku and other leaders of the CCP, and also with the American Agnes Smedley, who maintained contact not only with Chinese communists, but with Ts'ai T'ing-k'ai, the commander of the Kuomintang nineteenth army which had put up an abortive resistance to the Japanese incursion in January 1932.[131] For some time Braun seems to have been content to study the complex Chinese scene, and took no initiative.

In south China stubborn fighting between the Red Army and Kuomintang forces engaged in the fourth encirclement campaign went on throughout the winter of 1932–1933. The invaders advanced far into Kiangsi. Appeals to the civilian population, emergency decrees on mobilization, and promised reforms in administration, revealed a desperate military situation.[132] The imminence of military disaster sharpened the dissensions between the leaders revealed at the Ningtu conference in the previous August. Mao retained his political role as president of the council of commissars, and was not openly attacked.[133] But a powerful military group, led or instigated by Chou En-lai, blamed Mao's

[130] O. Braun, *Chinesische Aufzeichnungen* (1973), pp. 10–12. For Ewert see *Foundations of a Planned Economy, 1926–1929*, Vol. 3, p. 461; the Profintern representative was presumably Browder (see *ibid.* Vol. 3, p. 1040).

[131] O. Braun, *Chinesische Aufzeichnungen* (1973), pp. 11–12.

[132] Several party and Soviet documents are summarized in Hsiao Tso-liang, *Power Relations within the Chinese Communist Movement* (1961), pp. 214–217.

[133] For obscure and conflicting reports on this episode see Jerome Chen, *Mao and the Chinese Revolution* (1965), pp. 176–177; in the autumn of 1932 Mao fell ill, and spent some time in hospital.

guerrilla tactics for the defeats of the Red Army. A savage campaign was mounted against Lo Ming, the Red Army commander in Fukien, who was a supporter of Mao, and was said to have a brother of Mao on his staff. He was now accused of clinging, in defiance of the Ningtu decisions, to Mao's discredited guerrilla tactics. A party resolution of February 15, 1933, condemned his "opportunist line", and relieved him of his party posts. The campaign against him was spearheaded by Po Ku—a clear indication that the party machine was now working hand in glove with Chou En-lai; Po, in a speech which was published in a party journal, offered selective quotations from the resolution of the twelfth IKKI as proof of Comintern support for the "forward and offensive" strategy.[134] This was followed by another campaign evidently designed to discredit and isolate Mao, an attack on bureaucracy of which Teng Tzu-hui, the finance minister, and Ho Shu-heng, another official of the Soviet Government, both associates of Mao, were the principal targets. Mao throughout this time seems to have pursued his usual tactics of yielding silently to superior force. Teng was reduced to the rank of vice-minister, and Ho dismissed from his office.[135]

In Moscow interest in Chinese affairs was concentrated on the threat to the USSR from the north. An article by Wang Ming in the Comintern journal criticized the weakness of CCP in Manchuria, and called for "a broad anti-imperialist, anti-Japanese front", though the usual juggling with the conceptions of the united front "from below" and "from above" obscured the question of whether support was invited from any groups or units of Kuomintang.[136] In Shanghai the attention of the central committee of the CCP was directed to the Soviet regime in the south. Po Ku and the other leaders were alarmed by the attempt of the ruling group in Juichin to exclude Mao, whose "great influence and support in the central Soviet region" brought with it the danger of a split, and advised it to

[134] For documents condemning the Lo Ming line see Hsiao Tso-liang, *Power Relations within the Chinese Communist Movement* (1961), pp. 230–246; W. Kuo, *Analytical History of Chinese Communist Party*, ii (Taiwan, 1968), 486–493. For the IKKI resolution see p. 354 above.

[135] W. Kuo, *Analytical History of Chinese Communist Party*, ii (Taiwan, 1968), 504–508.

[136] *Kommunisticheskii Internatsional*, 1933, No. 4–5, pp. 8–17. O. Braun, *Chinesische Aufzeichnungen* (1973), p. 71, quoting an IKKI directive of January 1933, envisaged "possible alliance with opposition groupings or military units of Kuomintang in the national-revolutionary struggle for freedom"; if this is correct, it probably related to the situation in Manchuria.

resort to methods of persuasion and to draw Mao back into the common work. Ewert shared this view, which is said to have been approved by IKKI. In pursuit of this end, it was decided in the spring of 1933 to transfer the party headquarters to Juichin, leaving only a subsidiary bureau in Shanghai.[137] The predominant motive for the change was determination to establish a firmer control over what went on in the Soviet region. But it might also be said to have marked the eclipse of the proletarian element in the CCP, especially since the defeat of the Kiangsu group, and recognition of the now major role of the Soviets and the Red Army, both overwhelmingly composed of peasants.[138] On either view it made for a closer identification of the party machine with the Red Army and the Soviet Government. Ewert did not accompany the south-bound travellers, and presumably returned soon afterwards to Europe. Braun also remained temporarily in Shanghai, but moved to Juichin later in the year.[139]

Meanwhile the spring of 1933 witnessed a dramatic improvement in the fortunes of the Red Army. The Kuomintang invaders had over-reached themselves; and, by one of those sudden reversals characteristic of this form of warfare, they were soon in full retreat, pursued by the Red Army as far as the approaches to the Kuomintang stronghold of Nanchang in north Kiangsi, so that Mao could boast later of the "annihilation" of the Kuomintang offensive.[140] Chiang Kai-shek was, however, not a man to accept failure. In the late summer of 1933 he launched his fifth and final campaign against the Soviet areas. By this time, he not only enjoyed a large measure of foreign sympathy and support, but had gathered round him at Nanking some hundreds of foreign military advisers.

[137] O. Braun, *Chinesische Aufzeichnungen* (1973), pp. 28–29; this source is decisive for the date of the transfer. For earlier conflicting evidence on the date see Hsiao Tso-liang, *Power Relations within the Chinese Communist Movement* (1961), pp. 161–162; some of the sources there cited evidently confused it with the establishment of a party bureau in Juichin in 1931 (see p. 341 above).

[138] According to official statistics of 1934 the central Red Army group was made up of 66 per cent peasants, 30 per cent workers and 4 per cent "others"; but the peasant element was probably understated, and the category of "workers" was both vague and comprehensive (O. Braun, *Chinesische Aufzeichnungen* (1973), pp. 58–59). 20 per cent of those enrolled in the Red Army were party members (*ibid.* p. 24).

[139] See p. 362 below.

[140] *Internationale Presse-Korrespondenz*, No. 43, November 17, 1933, pp. 1690–1691.

The most numerous contingent were German officers, headed by three senior generals, Seeckt, Wetzell and Kriebel; but there were also Americans, including the famous aviator Lindbergh.[141] Arms and munitions reached Nanking from all over the world, being financed by American and British loans; 850 aeroplanes were said to have been ordered in the United States, of which 150 had been delivered.[142] The German advisers not only provided tactical instruction, but worked out a new plan of campaign, under which the Kuomintang armies were schooled to avoid sporadic engagements with the enemy, but to set up a ring of fortified points (so-called "block-houses") on the fringes of enemy territory. These were to serve as bases with assured communications from which further advances could be made to crush the enemy piecemeal.[143] The military talents of Chou or Mao were no match for those of Chiang's professional advisers.

A succession of cries for help betrayed the state of alarm in Juichin. The first appears to have come on July 24, 1933, in the form of a summons from the party to mobilize the whole population against the renewed offensive. This was repeated on October 18, when "the decisive battle" was said to have begun.[144] On September 6 a long rhetorical proclamation, signed by Mao as president of the executive committee of the Soviet republic and by Chu Teh as commander-in-chief of the Red Army, was addressed "to the toilers of the whole world with an appeal to struggle against imperialist intervention in China". Speaking in the name of the "workers, peasants, town and country poor, revolutionary soldiers and intellectuals of China", it pilloried "Kuomintang with Chiang Kai-shek and Wang Ching-wei at its head", which had launched its "sixth successive campaign against our free Soviet China". Neither the Japanese imperialists, who had occupied whole provinces of China, nor the western imperialists who supplied Chiang with arms and money, were spared; and a special place in the roll of infamy was reserved for Fascist Germany, which had sent to Nanking "seventy military specialists with Seeckt at their head". The appeal

[141] O. Braun, *Chinesische Aufzeichnungen* (1973), p. 32.
[142] *XIII Plenum IKKI* (1934), p. 22; according to O. Braun, in an article written in 1934 (see p. 368 below), the Kuomintang army "strengthens its weak infantry by an air arm". Bombings of Red Army positions from the air are mentioned from time to time in the records, but do not seem to have become a decisive factor.
[143] O. Braun, *Chinesische Aufzeichnungen* (1973), pp. 60–62.
[144] W. Kuo, *Analytical History of Chinese Communist Party*, ii (Taiwan, 1968), 543.

ended on the note of "the international solidarity of the proletariat and of the oppressed peoples of the whole world".[145] On the occasion of the second anniversary of the first Chinese Congress of Soviets, a report of the central committee of the Chinese Soviet Government denounced the "merciless and incessant civil war", and dwelt on the need to strengthen the Red Army at all costs", in order to "annihilate the sixth campaign of Kuomintang and the imperialists.[146]

The initial stages of the operation were interrupted by an unforeseen episode—one of those incalculable hazards typical of this form of warfare. When Chiang made his peace with the Japanese invaders in Shanghai in January 1932, and called off the resistance offered by the Kuomintang nineteenth army,[147] he transferred that army to the southern coastal provinces of Fukien, where it would take part in the encirclement of the Red Army and the Soviet regions. Once established in Fukien, however, the nineteenth army, demoralized and wavering in its loyalty to Chiang, appears to have relapsed into a passive role, and played no further part in the fighting. At CCP headquarters in Shanghai the reaction to the nineteenth army's resistance in January 1932 had been ambivalent, and this issue continued to divide the party. Braun, arriving in Shanghai in the autumn of 1932, claims to have taken the view that the nineteenth army in Fukien should be wooed as a potential ally in the campaign against Japan and, by implication, against Chiang Kai-shek. But when a superior officer in the Soviet intelligence, Manfred Stern, *alias* Fred, who later functioned in Spain under the title of General Kleber, visited Shanghai in the spring of 1933, he overruled Braun, insisting that the nineteenth army, like other Kuomintang units, should be treated as an enemy force, and by illusory promises of massive Soviet support encouraged the Red Army to adopt offensive tactics. Ewert at first supported Braun, but then wavered. The same division or confusion of opinions is said to have prevailed in Juichin, where the politburo and the revolutionary military council eventually came round to the intransigent line endorsed by Stern in Shanghai, and prepared for an offensive against Fukien.[148] But the question took a

---

[145] *Kommunisticheskii Internatsional*, 1933, No. 28, pp. 22–24.
[146] *Rundschau*, No. 15, February 15, 1934, pp. 554–556.
[147] See p. 349 above.
[148] O. Braun, *Chinesische Aufzeichnungen* (1973), pp. 40–42.

fresh turn when, in October 1933, a local Kuomintang leader Ch'en Ming-shu and the army commander Ts'ai T'ing-k'ai planned a revolt against Chiang, and sent a delegate to Juichin to negotiate with the Soviet Government. There, on October 26, 1933, what was called a "preliminary anti-Japanese, anti-Chiang agreement" was signed, under which the two parties undertook to suspend hostilities against one another, and to prepare for military action against Chiang and against the Japanese. On the strength of this agreement, the rebels summoned a conference at Foochow, the capital of Fukien, and on November 20 proclaimed an independent government.[149]

No sooner had this been done, however, than recriminations broke out in the Soviet camp. The agreement of October 26 seemed to represent too sharp a reversal of the party line and of the Comintern tradition of implacable hostility to Kuomintang. It excited resentment, more perhaps in party than in Soviet, but most of all in military, circles. According to Braun, who at this crucial moment made the journey from Shanghai to Juichin, what Ts'ai wanted was confined to a non-aggression pact between the two armies and the fixing of a demarcation line between them, since he at this time feared the incursion of the Red Army into his territory quite as much as that of Chiang's forces.[150] Whatever the explanation or excuse, no military support from the Red Army reached the Fukien rebels; and on December 5, 1933, the party central committee adopted a resolution to the effect that the Fukien government "could not distinguish itself from any counter-revolutionary Kuomintang government", and that any attempt to find "a third road between revolution and counter-revolution is doomed to failure".[151] A telegram of December 20 from the Soviet Government to the Fukien rebels, signed by Mao and Chu Teh, was less harsh in tone, though in substance equally negative. It reproached the Fukien regime with its failure to take "positive action against Japan and against Chiang Kai-shek", but declared readiness, should such action be taken, "to conclude a military

[149] W. Kuo, *Analytical History of Chinese Communist Party*, ii (Taiwan, 1968), 554; Hsiao Tso-liang, *Power Relations within the Chinese Communist Movement* (1961), pp. 248–249.

[150] O. Braun, *Chinesische Aufzeichnungen* (1973), p. 87.

[151] W. Kuo, *Analytical History of Chinese Communist Party*, ii (Taiwan, 1968), 554–555; this appears to be identical with the proclamation of December 13 in *Internationale Presse-Korrespondenz*, No. 17, February 22, 1934, p. 628.

agreement for fighting purposes". On January 13, 1934, the Soviet Government sent a further telegram exhorting the Fukien authorities to "mobilize the masses" for resistance to Kuomintang and "expose the sham democracy" of the Fukien regime.[152] By this time, however, the cause of the rebels was hopeless. A few days later troops loyal to Chiang Kai-shek recaptured Foochow, and crushed the revolt. Its end was celebrated in a further statement by the CCP on January 26, which showed no mercy to the defeated. The collapse of the Fukien revolt was said to prove "the correctness of the stand" taken by the CCP, and the futility of "the search for a third road"—i.e. a compromise between the CCP and Kuomintang. The revolutionary slogans put out by the rebels had been only "a smoke-screen to deceive the people".[153]

The transfer of Braun, the Comintern military adviser, from Shanghai to Juichin, while the Fukien controversy was at its height, was the beginning of a period during which he played an active, but enigmatic role in the affairs of the CCP and the Red Army. In Shanghai he had advocated an accommodation with the nineteenth army; but in Juichin he remained aloof from the debates. An understanding seems to have been reached that he would confine himself to strategy and military organization, and "refrain from any intervention in the political leadership". In form he adhered to this understanding. But political and military issues were rarely separable, and Braun soon drifted into the camp of Chou En-lai and Po Ku, and not into that of Mao. The language problem may have played some part here. Braun spoke Russian, and so also did Chou and Po; Mao did not. Braun had the habit of attending meetings of

---

[152] Hsiao Tso-liang, *Power Relations within the Chinese Communist Movement* (1961), pp. 253–254.

[153] *Ibid.* pp. 254–255; W. Kuo, *Analytical History of Chinese Communist Party*, ii (Taiwan, 1968), 556–557. Mao probably hedged; according to O. Braun, *Chinesische Aufzeichnungen* (1973), p. 42, he gave his support to the course adopted. Later, with the substantial aid of hindsight, Mao described the "failure to unite" with the rebels as a "costly mistake", which he attributed to Braun's "advice" (E. Snow, *Red Star over China* (3rd ed., 1972), p. 411). Mif, in the heyday of the popular front, explained that the CCP "failed to make good use of the favourable conditions created by the Fukien incident", and that many of its members did not understand the significance of establishing a popular united front against imperialism" (P. Mif, *Fifteen Years of Heroic Struggle* (Moscow, 1935), p. 105). *Kommunisticheskii Internatsional: Kratkii Istorcheskii Ocherk* (1969), p. 387, attributes the error to "adventurism, a 'Left' deviation", and holds it responsible for the "huge losses" incurred by the Red Army in the subsequent fighting.

the politburo when military questions were on the agenda. But Chou and Po discussed his military proposals with him in advance, and presented them on his behalf to the Revolutionary Military Council. According to Braun, Po tried to enhance his own authority by attributing to Braun wide-ranging full powers, which he did not possess.[154]

The collapse of the Fukien revolt coincided with the meeting of the fifth plenum of the CCP in Juichin in January 1934. Some factitious encouragement may have been generated by the figures of party membership, which had risen from some 3500 at the time of the fourth plenum in January 1931 to 20,000 at the end of 1933; the change was, no doubt, due mainly to the move to Juichin. It was claimed, more questionably, that the proportion of workers in the party had risen from 7 to 20 per cent.[155] The proceedings of the plenum were dominated by Po Ku. The main resolution, adopted on his report, praised the decisions of the fourth plenum of January 1931, and the subsequent achievements of the CCP in conformity with the line laid down by Comintern. It gave a radical twist to the diagnosis in the resolution of the twelfth IKKI of "a transitional period leading to a new stage of revolution and war". China's development had reached the stage of a direct revolutionary situation; a Soviet republic was the only alternative to a continuation of colonial subjection. The demand for a strengthening of party work and of the Red Army led to a denunciation both of "Left opportunism and sectarianism" and of "Right opportunists" who professed verbal agreement with the party, but took covert action against it, and who, in a phrase quoted from Kaganovich, would "eventually go the way of traitors". The plenum also adopted a resolution on economic work in the Soviet regions, and instructions to the party delegates at the forthcoming second Congress of Soviets.[156]

What remains uncertain is the relation of Mao to these proceedings. Braun was not present at the session, but his account

[154] O. Braun, *Chinesische Aufzeichnungen* (1973), pp. 50–53; Braun in his memoirs claims to have been embarrassed by his dissent from what he calls Stern's "adventurous plan for an offensive", which he was bound officially to support (*ibid.* pp. 68, 89–90, 139); but hindsight may have helped to suggest this excuse.

[155] *Internationale Presse-Korrespondenz*, No. 57, December 29, 1933, pp. 1309–1310.

[156] W. Kuo, *Analytical History of Chinese Communist Party*, ii (Taiwan, 1968), 559–561; Hsiao Tso-liang, *Power Relations within the Chinese Communist Movement* (1961), pp. 261–263. Po's report was not published, but its substance was no doubt

seems less biassed against Mao than the other second-hand sources. He claims that, since the Ningtu conference, "better and closer contact was established between the central leadership and local and military leaders who were predominantly under Mao's influence", and that Po worked to restore good relations with Mao. But he admits that these efforts were partly frustrated by Mao's aloofness, and quotes Po's sarcastic comment on the "diplomatic illness" with which Mao excused his absence from the plenum.[157] Other sources suggest that Po's quotation from Kaganovich about "traitors" was aimed directly at Mao, and assert that the plenum condemned Mao's agrarian policies. It is clear that Mao's standing in the party suffered some further diminution. According to some accounts he was not re-elected to the politburo; according to Braun he remained a member of the politburo, but was excluded from its inner committee or secretariat. Mao's own later verdict was that the fifth plenum "marked the height" of the Left line led by "the two doctrinaires" (Po and Wang Ming), and was responsible for the military disasters of the summer of 1934.[158]

The second Chinese Congress of Soviets met in Juichin, immediately after the fifth plenum of the CCP, on January 22, 1934. Mao, in his capacity as president of the Council of People's Commissars, made the main report. He was once more careful not to stray beyond the limits of current orthodoxy. He pointed to the Fukien revolt as a symptom of the disintegration of Kuomintang, but justified non-intervention on the ground that any attempt to find a middle way between Kuomintang and the Soviets was bound to fail. In the name of the congress he proposed "an agreement with all anti-Japanese volunteer units for a joint struggle against Japan and Kuomintang". The congress passed a resolution on the Red Army which declared it to be the only armed force capable of resisting Japanese aggression, and the decisive lever in the whole Chinese revolutionary movement, as well as a number of resolutions on political, economic and constitutional questions. But it came to a premature end when the Kuomintang forces which had suppressed the Fukien rising began to threaten Soviet territory. On January 29

reproduced in an article by him in the party journal, which included both the quotation from the twelfth IKKI and from Kaganovich (*ibid.* pp. 263–264). Po continued to quote the twelfth IKKI held more than a year earlier; the thirteenth IKKI concluded its deliberations a month before the fifth plenum, but no information about it had evidently yet reached Juichin.

[157] O. Braun, *Chinesische Aufzeichnungen* (1973), pp. 69–70.
[158] *Selected Works of Mao Tse-tung*, iv (1956), 186–187.

Mao made a call for urgent mobilization of all available forces, and announced that the congress would end on February 1, 1934. In spite of the prominent part played by Mao, the proceedings were clearly dominated by Po Ku as secretary of the party. Mao was allowed to retain the honorific post of president of the central executive committee of Soviets, but was replaced as president of the Council of People's Commissars by Chang Wen-t'ien, a member of the returned students group. Chu Teh remained as Commissar for military affairs, but was now overshadowed by Chou En-lai, who enjoyed the support of Po Ku and the party machine.[159] It was the lowest point in Mao's fortunes.

Little information reached Moscow about the course of events in the Soviet areas of southern China;[160] and the thirteenth IKKI, meeting at the end of November 1933, was too much absorbed in dangers nearer home to give much attention to it. Kuusinen in his main report took note of the "anti-imperialist war" being conducted both against the Japanese in Manchuria and against Chiang Kai-shek in "Kuomintang China", and accused the western Powers of supplying Chiang with aeroplanes, artillery, tanks and materials for chemical warfare.[161] Wang Ming delivered a wholly conventional speech, celebrating the victories of the Red Army, and denouncing Japanese imperialism and Chiang Kai-shek who had long abandoned any pretence of resisting it. He claimed that membership of the CCP had risen during the year from 300,000 to 410,600; this included an increase from 30,000 to 60,000 in non-Soviet China, though it was admitted that half of these had no contact with party headquarters "owing to the furious White terror". He referred to the fourth CCP plenum of January 1931 as the turning-point at which the party had abandoned its past

---

[159] Hsiao Tso-liang, *Power Relations within the Chinese Communist Movement* (1961), pp. 266–281; W. Kuo, *Analytical History of Chinese Communist Party*, ii (Taiwan, 1968), 567–570; O. Braun, *Chinesische Aufzeichnungen* (1973), pp. 70–72. For a much abbreviated extract from Mao's report see C. Brandt, B. I. Schwartz and J. K. Fairbank, *A Documentary History of Chinese Communism* (1952), pp. 226–239; for the appeal to "anti-Japanese volunteer units" see *Programmnye Dokumenty Kitaiskikh Sovetov* (1935), pp. 100–102.

[160] A similar ignorance prevailed in western Europe; the Comintern press reprinted an article from *The Times*, November 13, 1933, by a rare correspondent who had actually visited the region (*Rundschau*, No. 43, November 17, 1933, pp. 1691–1692).

[161] *XIII Plenum IKKI* (1934), pp. 16–17.

deviations from the Comintern line, though he admitted the
persistence of Right and "Left" errors among party and Soviet
workers in the Soviet areas.[162] Pyatnitsky declared that "the
successes achieved by the CCP under conditions of war and
revolution should serve as an example to all parties"; and
Manuilsky exuded confidence:

> The Japanese imperialists understand that, in the event of
> aggression against the USSR, 400 million Chinese will be set in
> motion, and that the Chinese Soviets will stand at the head of a
> movement for the liberation of China from the yoke of the
> imperialists.[163]

The resolution, which was primarily concerned with the struggle
against Fascism, recognized the Chinese revolution as "a large
element in the world revolution", and defined the Chinese Soviet
Government as "the state form of the revolutionary-democratic
dictatorship of the proletariat and peasantry, which guarantees the
growing of the bourgeois-democratic revolution into a socialist
revolution".[164]

A similar air of interested detachment pervaded other pronouncements in Moscow on the obscure Chinese situation. At the
session of TsIK which overlapped with the thirteenth IKKI,
Litvinov observed that the Chinese people were the victims "both of
the assault of foreign enemies and of deep internal dissensions", and
declared that the Soviet Government, in accordance with the
principle of non-intervention, "follows its struggle for independence
and national unity with the greatest sympathy". He did not
mention the Chinese Soviets.[165] A month later Manuilsky, in his
report to the seventeenth Russian party congress, devoted a section
to the CCP and the Chinese Soviet Government, claiming that the
party had increased its membership in the past year from 120,000 to
416,000, and "administers a Soviet state embracing a territory of
700,000 square kilometres, larger than France or Germany", and
that the Red Army now numbered 350,000 effectives, together with

---

[162] *Ibid.* pp. 116–126.
[163] *Ibid.* pp. 174, 313.
[164] *Ibid.* pp. 589–595; for this resolution see p. 115 above.
[165] *Dokumenty Vneshnei Politiki SSSR*, xvi (1970), 791, where the speech is
reprinted from the official record.

600,000 "partisans".[166] Wang Ming celebrated these achievements at fulsome length, though, doubtless referring to recent events in Fukien, he admitted that "numerous counter-revolutionary conspiracies and risings organized by agents of Kuomintang and of the imperialists have occurred in several Soviet regions".[167] In April 1934, when the records of the thirteenth IKKI had eventually reached Kiangsi, the central committee of the CCP formally endorsed its resolution, stressing the need "to link the anti-Fascist struggle with campaigns to counter the enemy's fifth encirclement offensive, and to fight for the victory of Soviets all over China".[168]

These pronouncements bore little relation to what was happening in Kiangsi, where the debate on strategy and tactics continued. After the fifth party plenum in January 1934 Mao, though he apparently remained a member of the military revolutionary council, remained silent on military affairs. But Chou, in a highly optimistic article evidently designed to discredit Mao's advocacy of guerrilla warfare, maintained that what he called "protracted warfare" (i.e. a war of attrition) with mass formations was favourable to the Red Army and would ensure its victory over Chiang's offensive.[169] Chou's self-confidence was misplaced. Chiang, having crushed the Fukien rebellion, again turned his attention to Soviet-held territory. In April a pitched battle was fought round the town of Kwangchang in central Kiangsi; and, though in Moscow Bela Kun misguidedly celebrated the defeat of "the German Fascist officers",[170] the engagement ended in a rout of the Red Army.[171] The disaster cannot have enhanced Chou's prestige, and must have cast some doubt on the validity of his campaign to discredit Mao. A series of articles, appeals and proclamations from party, Red Army

---

[166] *XVII S"ezd Vsesoyuznoi Kommunisticheskoi Partii (b)* (1934), p. 317.

[167] *Ibid.* pp. 323–328.

[168] Hsiao Tso-liang, *Power Relations within the Chinese Communist Movement* (1961), p. 283; W. Kuo, *Analytical History of Chinese Communist Party*, ii (Taiwan, 1968), 605–606.

[169] The article is summarized in *China Quarterly*, xliii (July–September 1970), 32–34.

[170] *Rundschau*, No. 39, July 5, 1934, pp. 1582–1583.

[171] For a summary account see W. Kuo, *Analytical History of Chinese Communist Party*, ii (Taiwan, 1968), 609–610; according to O. Braun, *Chinesische Aufzeichnungen* (1973), pp. 96–97, the decision to fight at Kwangchang was taken unanimously by a meeting of the military revolutionary council at which Mao was present.

and Soviet authorities[172] testified to the desperate plight of the regime.

It seems to have been at this moment that Braun emerged in an independent role as military adviser. At the end of March 1934 he began to put forward in the revolutionary military council a tactical plan which, while rejecting Mao's concept of guerrilla warfare, also diverged widely, though this does not seem to have been openly said, from Chou's plan of mass formation and a war of attrition. Braun wanted tactics which would lure the enemy forces out of their strong points, and then expose them to "short surprise blows" and "great leaps".[173] These views were embodied in an article published in the Chinese military journal on the eve of the Kwangchang battle over the pen-name Hua Fu.[174] As the military situation grew more desperate, controversy about tactics continued. During the summer Braun published no fewer than seven further articles in the military journal, while Chou pursued his campaign in favour of "protracted warfare", only in August paying lip-service to the catchword of "short, swift thrusts".[175] Mao refrained from any public utterance. But it is not surprising that he and his supporters should have engaged in "a partly open, partly concealed, struggle" against "the military *troika*" consisting of Chou, Po Ku and Braun, holding them responsible for the "catastrophe" of Kwangchang.[176]

The situation was now untenable. The area occupied by the Red Army and the Soviet Government was almost entirely surrounded by hostile territory, and the area was being steadily contracted on the north by well-organized Kuomintang armies. At what precise moment the decision was taken to break through the encirclement

[172] Several of these are summarized in Hsiao Tso-liang, *Power Relations within the Chinese Communist Movement* (1961), pp. 284–301.

[173] O. Braun, *Chinesische Aufzeichnungen* (1973), p. 96.

[174] The article presents problems of translation; originally written by Braun in Russian, it was first published in Chinese in the journal and by Braun in his memoirs in German (*ibid.* pp. 368–372). A summary of the article made from its Chinese text in *China Quarterly*, xliii (July–September 1970, 34–35) quotes the phrase "short, swift thrusts", with its Chinese equivalent, as the key to Braun's tactics and the catch-word round which argument later revolved. The German version contains no precisely equivalent phrase, but the substance is the same; Braun wrote in somewhat convoluted language, probably in order to avoid an open clash with Chou.

[175] For notes on these articles see *ibid.* xliii, 32–39.

[176] O. Braun, *Chinesische Aufzeichnungen* (1973), p. 99; Braun's story as it progresses becomes more and more hostile to Mao.

at all costs, to abandon the base in Kiangsi, and to transfer the Red
Army and the Soviet Government to more remote regions of China,
where Chiang Kai-shek's authority was not established, is not
certain; in a sense, the decision imposed itself by degrees. Braun
claims to have submitted a plan at the beginning of May 1934 to
prepare for a break-through by the main forces and "operations in
the enemy's deep rear by independent units".[177] In July 1934 Po Ku
advocated the immediate formation of a detachment of the Red
Army to combat Japanese imperialism, and a decree of the Soviet
Government signed by Mao and Chu ordered the vanguard of the
Red Army to march north to fight the Japanese aggressors. The
plan, which looked no more than a desperate gesture of defiance,
was also endorsed by Chou En-lai.[178] The detachment marched
north through Fukien into territory unoccupied by Kuomintang
forces, and apparently had some short-lived success in harassing
their rear. The move was later hailed as the birth of the concept
which eventually took shape in the Long March, and it may have
served in part as a cover for that operation. An enigmatic
"programme" published in the name of Chou in July placed all the
emphasis on the campaign against the Japanese, and hinted at
cessation of hostilities against the Kuomintang forces.[179]

Uncertainty about when, and in what circumstances, the final
decision to evacuate the Soviet areas in Kiangsi was taken is
matched by uncertainty about when, and in what form, news of the
decision reached Moscow. No published document of Comintern,
now or later, betrays any advance knowledge of it.[180] By the end of
the summer it had been decided that the Red Army should march
out through a gap in the Kuomintang encirclement in the south-
western corner of Kiangsi. The plan, as far as any destination was
thought of, was to effect a junction with the Red Army which had

[177] Ibid. p. 101; the statement that Mao opposed the proposal to break through
the encirclement (ibid. p. 99) appears to relate to the period before the Kwangchang
defeat.

[178] Hsiao Tso-liang, Power Relations within the Chinese Communist Movement (1961),
pp. 291–295.

[179] Ibid. p. 295.

[180] Braun's statement that the plan was "communicated in its broad outlines in
IKKI through the Comintern representative in Shanghai, and confirmed by it" is
followed by the sceptical qualification: "At any rate, that is what Po Ku told me"
(O. Braun, Chinesische Aufzeichnungen (1973), p. 102); if consultation took place,
Braun would surely have known of it, and not have had to rely on Po for second-
hand information.

retreated from Honan through Hupei into distant Szechwan. Still
more remotely the intention to march north in order to fight the
Japanese was proclaimed from time to time. It was, as Braun
observed, "a chief political slogan, but in no way the military-
strategic conception of the party and army leadership".[181] A
desperate appeal was signed by Chou En-lai on September 4, 1934,
for the mobilization of all available recruits from "the worker-
peasant masses".[182] On October 3, the Soviet Government and the
central committee of the CCP jointly issued a proclamation "to all
people in the Soviet area for the development of guerrilla
warfare".[183] No public announcement was made of the intention of
the Red Army to abandon the area. But the collapse of the strategy
of massed resistance and counter-offensive planned by Chou, and
approved by Po Ku, could not be disguised; and the reversion to the
guerrilla tactics of dispersal which Mao had always advocated must
have restored and enhanced Mao's prestige.[184] Chu Teh took
command of the Red Army, with Mao as political commissar. The
ever adaptable Chou succeeded Chu as president of the revolutionary military council, with Braun, the German military adviser, at his
side. Po Ku claimed a leading part in the operation as secretary of
the party. In face of the emergency all factions seem to have been
momentarily reconciled. The evacuation was completed in good
order about the middle of October. A small detachment was left
behind to organize guerrilla resistance to the advancing nationalist
forces. But the immediate sequel appears to have been a peasant
jacquerie, which resulted in the killing of landlords and rich peasants,
and of some party members.[185] Early in November Juichin was
occupied by Chiang's advancing armies.

---

[181] O. Braun, *Chinesische Aufzeichnungen* (1973), p. 108.

[182] W. Kuo, *Analytical History of Chinese Communist Party*, ii (Taiwan, 1968),
634–636.

[183] *Ibid.* ii, 636–638.

[184] Reports about Mao's status at this time are obscure and contradictory; it was
Mao who apparently made the announcement of the decision to evacuate the area
(Hsiao Tso-liang, *Power Relations within the Chinese Communist Movement* (1961),
pp. 291–297). According to one account (J. Chen, *Mao and the Chinese Revolution*
(1965), p. 183), Mao was seriously ill with malaria during August and September;
but this, if true, may have been a tactical withdrawal, like his illness of the previous
year (see p. 364 above).

[185] W. Kuo, *Analytical History of Chinese Communist Party*, ii (Taiwan, 1968),
620–621.

Meanwhile, a horde said to have been 130,000 strong, comprising some 90,000 Red Army men and a large number of party and Soviet officials and other auxiliaries and camp followers, marched westward through the remote and inhospitable fastnesses of southern Hunan and northern Kwangsi into Kweichow, engaging in battles with hostile forces and suffering incalculable losses and hardships, to open a fresh chapter in the history of the CCP and of the Chinese revolution. It was the Long March which finally established Mao Tse-tung as the supreme authority in army, party and Soviet, and sealed the reputation which he had initially won as creator of the Red Army. Paradoxically, he was not a military figure. On Braun he made "the impression of a thinker and poet rather than of a politician and soldier". He had never travelled abroad, and knew no foreign language, expressing himself readily in homely Chinese proverbs and aphorisms. He seemed a man of the people, and "based his influence on a long-standing tradition of common armed struggle through which he had firmly become one with the peasants". His knowledge of Marxism was limited by his linguistic deficiencies, and his understanding of it was never profound. When he spoke of the "proletariat" he appears to have thought of the poor and oppressed of all classes and occupations, and in the countryside rather than in the factories. His repetition of conventional formulas, such as the leadership of the workers, was without content.[186] He combined these characteristics with determination and ruthlessness in pursuit of his aims and great skill in manoeuvre. He preferred, where necessary, to yield to superior forces and wait for the moment to strike back when victory was within his grasp.

A crucial moment in the Long March arrived when at the end of 1934 the marchers forced a crossing of the Wu river, a tributary of the upper Yangtse. This opened the way to the north; and in the first days of January 1935, without further resistance, they occupied Tsunyi, a town in northern Kweichow. Here they paused to regroup, reorganize, and consider their future strategy. The stay at Tsunyi was marked by an important party conference.[187] No record of its debates appears to have been preserved. But the result was a

---

[186] O. Braun, *Chinesische Aufzeichnungen* (1973), pp. 79–80.

[187] In the resolution adopted by it (see below) it is described as "an enlarged conference of the politburo"; according to Braun's very hostile account (*ibid.* pp. 131–132), two-thirds of the 35–40 participants were not members of the party central committee or politburo, but were members of the Soviet Government or officers in the Red Army invited by Mao.

sudden and dramatic reversal of the progressive decline in Mao's authority, status and prestige over the past four years, and his reinstatement as undisputed leader of the party, the government and the Red Army. The magnitude of the disaster suffered under the leaders who had dominated military strategy for more than two years, and had rejected Mao's earlier tactics, must have created profound and widespread discontent in party and Red Army ranks. The details of the intrigues and the hard bargaining which went to produce the *volte-face* will probably never be known. But the key may plausibly be found in a shift in the attitude of Chou En-lai, who now abandoned his former ally Po Ku, and his military mentor Braun, and concluded an alliance with Mao, which lasted throughout the rest of the Long March, and for many years afterwards. Chou had on previous occasions exhibited the supple and slippery qualities of an eel. But Mao's determination, his hold on the loyalty of the masses, and his ability to turn defeat into victory were scarcely less remarkable. What happened at Tsunyi was nothing less than a miniature *coup d'état*.

Po Ku, as secretary of the party, delivered the main report of the session, and was followed by Chou with a report on military affairs. Neither found anything to criticize in the conduct of military operations or in the decision to evacuate the Soviet area in Kiangsi; and both expressed faith in the future. But, while Po praised the work of the party, and attributed the losses of the Red Army exclusively to the overwhelming strength of Chiang, supported by the imperialist Powers, Chou went out of his way to censure the party for its failure to carry out propaganda among the enemy forces, for its defective organization of partisan detachments and for other tactical errors. The divergence between them was the cue for Mao's intervention. In a long speech read from a prepared manuscript, he launched a powerful attack on Po Ku and Braun (under his pen-name Hua Fu), whose false tactics he held responsible for the disasters sustained by the Red Army. He mentioned Chou's report, but carefully refrained from any criticism of it.[188]

Mao's speech provided the basis for a momentous resolution adopted by the session on January 8, 1935—its only published document.[189] The resolution began by referring to the report of Po Ku (here called "comrade XX") and the supplementary report of

[188] *Ibid.* pp. 135–136.

[189] Braun called the resolution "a re-drafted and worked over version of Mao Tse-tung's speech", and even suspected that the text as published was a

Chou En-lai (called "comrade XXX") on the fifth encirclement campaign. The supplementary report was not characterized, or even mentioned again. But Po's report was described as "fundamentally incorrect"; and much of the resolution was devoted to the exposure of his errors. The inability of the party leadership to repel the fifth encirclement campaign was due to its failure to "expand guerrilla tactics" and its resort to tactics of "pure defence". Praise was reserved for the tactics previously pursued under Mao's leadership; the Red Army was said to be "specially skilled at destroying the enemy in mobile warfare". Fierce attacks were made by name on "Hua Fu" (i.e. Braun), whose theory of "short, swift thrusts" was said to have led to a "policy of pure defence", and who was convicted of "opportunist tendencies". The resolution reverted to the Fukien incident of December 1933. The aim should have been "the exploitation of every conflict among the reactionaries, actively widening the cleavages between them", and support should have been given to the nineteenth Route Army, however reactionary its character. The blame for rejecting this policy was laid squarely on comrade XX. An odd feature of the resolution was the quotation of three otherwise unrecorded instructions from Comintern of October 1933 and February and June 1934. But understanding in Moscow of what was happening in southern China was limited; the resolution of the twelfth IKKI had already been misleadingly invoked by Po Ku in support of his policies.[190] What was significant in the quotations was Mao's desire at this time to avoid any political rift with Moscow, and to maintain the fiction of the conformity of his proceedings with the prescriptions of Comintern. The resolution was careful to criticize Braun as a military expert, not as an emissary of Comintern. The aim of the party was now "to found a new Soviet in the vast territories of Yunnan, Kweichow and Szechwan, to recover our lost Soviets, to unite the Red Armies and Soviets at various places in the country into one entity, and to turn the struggles of the workers and peasants of our country into a triumphant great revolution". Throughout the resolution Kuomintang was treated as the sole enemy, and no allusion made to warfare against Japan, though the Comintern

"subsequently drafted" text of the speech (ibid. pp. 138, 147); an English translation by J. Chen in China Quarterly, xi (October–December 1969), 1–17, is followed by a commentary (marred by failure to identify the persons referred to), and an account (pp. 37–38) of the circumstances of its publication several years later.

[190] See p. 363 above.

instruction of June 1934 was quoted as calling for the "consolidation and expansion" of the Red Army, "while awaiting the opportunity for a large-scale offensive against imperialism and Kuomintang". After the session Mao sent an envoy to Moscow to report on the proceedings; but the envoy did not reach his destination till after the seventh congress of Comintern in August, and, having to travel through hostile territory, carried no documents. The text of the Tsunyi resolution is said to have been communicated to IKKI only in 1939.[191]

The achievement of the Tsunyi meeting, as celebrated in later party history, was to reverse the "Left" course which had prevailed in the party since the fourth plenum of 1931. In a sweeping indictment this was described as the "third" Left line in the history of the party, its errors being traced back to the Li Li-san line of 1930, and even to the "emergency meeting" of the central committee on August 7, 1927.[192] At the time Mao was more circumspect. The denunciation of Po Ku and "Hua Fu" in the Tsunyi resolution, though unsparing, was directed exclusively against their errors of military leadership; and, though these were attributed to "specific Right opportunism" in the party, no allusion was made to what were later recognized as "Left" deviations over the past four years. Po Ku's errors, it was admitted, "did not amount to a whole mistaken political line", though they might develop into one if he persisted in them. The main achievement of the conference was the assertion of Mao's supreme authority. Mao was elected to the standing committee of the politburo, and soon became its effective head; Chang Wen-t'ien (alias Lo Fu), who, though one of the original 28 Bolsheviks, had evidently changed sides, succeeded Po Ku as secretary-general of the party, though Po apparently remained a member of the politburo and secretary of the party central committee. Mao replaced Chou En-lai as president of the revolutionary military council, but Chou remained a member of it.[193] Chu Teh remained commander of the army; he seems to have

[191] O. Braun, *Chinesische Aufzeichnungen* (1973), p. 146; since the exodus from Kiangsi communications with Shanghai, and through Shanghai with Moscow, had been completely severed (*ibid.* p. 111).

[192] *Selected Works of Mao Tse-tung*, iv (1956), 176–187; for the session of August 7, 1927, see *Foundations of a Planned Economy, 1926–1929*, Vol. 3, pp. 824–828.

[193] E. Snow, *Red Star over China* (3rd ed., 1972), p. 489 (note appended by Snow to the second edition; Mao in his reminiscences to Snow did not mention the Tsunyi conference); O. Braun, *Chinesische Aufzeichnungen* (1976), p. 144.

followed Chou both in criticizing Mao during 1933 and 1934 and in rallying to him at the Tsunyi conference.[194] For the rest of the Long March, Mao enjoyed the confidence of the army and the loyalty of his subordinates.

The army and the Soviet and party administrations settled down in and around Tsunyi for more than three months, while future plans were debated. It is possible that, before the Long March from Kiangsi began, the remote fastnesses of north-western China were thought of as the ultimate destination. Mao certainly toyed from time to time with the prospect of establishing direct contact with Soviet territory and obtaining aid from the USSR.[195] But it is by no means certain that any firm decision on the point was taken, even at Tsunyi. The immediate objective was to effect a junction with the Red Fourth Army, which had established a Soviet area in northern Szechwan.[196] In April 1935 the First Army at length moved out of Tsunyi. Kuomintang forces were in firm possession of southern Szechwan; and the First Army was compelled to re-cross the Wu river, and make a long detour through Yunan. It crossed the upper Yangtse, here called the Tatu river—a legendary exploit of the Long March—and marched northwards along the western border of Szechwan, finally reaching Mao-kung in the extreme north-western corner of the province. In these operations little resistance was encountered. But, though casualties through enemy action were small, heavy losses occurred through sickness and exhaustion. Of the army of 90,000 which set out from Kiangsi in the previous autumn, only 10,000 were said to have reached Mao-kung.[197] Some thousands of local volunteers had, however, been recruited; and Braun records that discipline and morale remained surprisingly

[194] Chu Teh is described by Braun as "a legendary hero of the civil war, but at the same time an undemanding and modest man"; he contented himself with the role of military commander, and no longer played an independent or decisive part in events (*ibid*. p. 84).

[195] According to Chang Kuo-t'ao, *The Rise of the Chinese Communist Party*, ii (1972), 383, Mao stated in June 1935 that, before the departure from Kiangsi, Comintern had telegraphed instructions "to go towards Outer Mongolia", but that Chang Wen-t'ien qualified this by adding the words "in case of extreme necessity". The story is dubious; it is not clear that Comintern had prior knowledge of the evacuation. For the so-called "north-western theory", i.e. withdrawal to the north-western provinces, advocated by Borodin and others in 1927, see *Foundations of a Planned Economy, 1926–1929*, Vol. 3, pp. 780–781.

[196] See p. 373 above.

[197] Chang Kuo-t'ao, *The Rise of the Chinese Communist Party*, ii (1972), 379.

high. Disaffection with Mao's leadership was, however, heard in some quarters; Po Ku and Braun were among those who would have preferred to consolidate their positions in the south, and abandon the march to remote regions in the west and north. But Chou and Chu Teh remained loyal to Mao.[198] In June the long planned dramatic meeting between the main army and the Fourth Army, and between Mao and Chang, took place at Mao-kung.

The sequel is not difficult to explain, though much of what happened is obscure and controversial.[199] The enthusiasm generated by the project of a united Red Army soon evaporated; the question of who should be the supreme commander seems not to have been resolved. Mao and Chang had never been close associates, and formed a temperamentally uncongenial pair.[200] Each sought to extol the achievements of his own army, and was not unduly impressed by those of the other. Jealousy and friction between the two armies was not confined to the leaders. Within a few days these incompatibilities found expression in a serious difference of opinion about future action. Mao wished to continue the northward advance of the army into Shensi. Chang more cautiously proposed to suspend the advance and to establish a secure Soviet base in western Szechwan. Agreement, could not be reached, and tempers were frayed. At the beginning of August a compromise was finally reached. No open break occurred. The two armies separated, Mao to continue the northward march, Chang to consolidate his positions in Szechwan. An unexpected feature of the parting was that Chu Teh remained with Chang.[201]

[198] O. Braun, *Chinesische Aufzeichnungen* (1973), pp. 157-159.

[199] The two detailed accounts by participants (Chang Kuo-t'ao, *The Rise of the Chinese Communist Party*, ii (1972), 374-428; O. Braun, *Chinesische Aufzeichnungen* (1973), pp. 169-186) are hostile to Mao, Chang being particularly bitter; the Maoist account, recorded in later party resolutions and official histories, briefly dismissed Chang as a "flightist" and a "deviationist", who finally left the CCP in 1938.

[200] Braun described Chang as "a big, imposing man in his forties", who "received us like a host receiving guests" (*ibid.* p. 170).

[201] Chu Teh afterwards refused to discuss this episode, and the account in A. Smedley, *The Great Road* (1956), pp. 328-332, derived indirectly from him, is highly confused; Chu claims to have broken almost at once with Chang, and to have remained for a year as his "virtual prisoner". According to Chang Kuo-t'ao, *The Rise of the Chinese Communist Party*, ii (1972), 167-168, the communist youth league and members of the party hostile to Mao had at one time hoped to use Chu Teh against him. Chang narrates a long conversation with Chu at Mao-kung, full of disillusionment with the achievements of the Red Army and of criticisms of Mao (*ibid.* ii, 379-383).

At the very moment when Mao and Chang and their respective armies met and parted at Mao-kung, delegates were assembling in Moscow for the seventh congress of Comintern. It is difficult to imagine two gatherings more dissimilar in composition, outlook and purpose. Nobody in north-western Szechwan is likely to have heard of the congress. In Moscow nobody had any clear impression of what was going on in these remote Chinese regions. The seventh congress sounded loudly the call for a united front against Fascism. In China, the logic of this appeal would have been a reconciliation between the warring Chinese factions and the formation of a common front to repel Japanese aggression. But nobody at the congress ventured to spell out that conclusion, though it seems to have made some headway behind the scenes.[202] For Mao and his followers, if it had occurred to them, it would have been totally unrealistic. Resistance to Japan was a slogan empty of practical content.[203] The armies of Chiang Kai-shek and Kuomintang, from whose clutches they had so hardly and so recently escaped, constituted the main visible threat to their survival. The moment still lay ahead when the threat from Japan would come to dominate every other issue on the Chinese scene.

(b) THE JAPANESE COMMUNIST PARTY

Attempts by Comintern to intervene in Japanese affairs during this period provided an almost continuous record of failure. After the crushing blows of 1929,[204] a group of stalwarts met secretly in January 1930 to set up a new party organization.[205] About the same time, WEB in Berlin addressed a communication to the Japanese party congratulating it on the exclusion of "reformist elements" from its ranks, and warning it against all forms of "liquidationism" and "legalism", i.e. movements to dissolve the illegal party or to set up a legal party in its place. This was followed by an instruction on tactics to be followed in the forthcoming elections on February 20, 1930; the party was to stand on the uncompromising platform of "a

[202] For the proceedings of the congress see pp. 421–423 below.
[203] According to Chang-Kuo-t'ao, *The Rise of the Chinese Communist Party*, ii (1972), 384, the question of "going north to resist Japan" was not raised by Mao in the discussions at Mao-kung.
[204] See *Foundations of a Planned Economy, 1926–1929*, Vol. 3, pp. 624–625.
[205] G. Beckmann and Okuba Genji, *The Japanese Communist Party, 1922–1945* (1969), p. 189.

revolutionary worker-peasant government based on Soviets", and
put forward partial demands on the basis of "united front tactics
only from below".[206] But there is no evidence of the receipt of these
messages by the party, or of any effective communication between it
and Comintern at this time. When the elections took place, all but
one of the candidates put forward by the party were in prison, and
were disqualified; the one remaining candidate received 3000
votes.[207]

It seems to have been the indefatigable Lozovsky who decided
that something ought to be done. The fifth congress of Profintern in
August 1930, though it threw no fresh light on the situation in
Japan, produced a full-length resolution on the Japanese revolutionary trade unions. It did not conceal their desperate plight.
Of five million industrial workers, only 320,000 were organized in
any unions at all. The revolutionary Hyogikai, which had once had
35,000 members, had been forcibly disbanded; and the Zemkyo, the
trade union council which replaced it, was reduced to a few
thousands and had been driven completely underground. The
movement, in the terminology now current in Moscow, had been
guilty both of "Right-opportunist legalism" and of "Left-sectarian
deviation"; the latter meant that it had identified itself with the
communist party, and failed to appeal to the masses as a non-party
organization. Nothing, however, was offered as a remedy for these
failings but a spate of conventional rhetoric.[208]

No major instruction to the Japanese party had issued from
Comintern since the theses of 1927, which had been the work of
Bukharin.[209] Since then much had changed. In the autumn of 1930
Comintern and Profintern collaborated in the drafting of a new
instruction based on the well-worn theme that the coming proletarian revolution would also "include a broad range of bourgeois-
democratic tasks". A Moscow-trained Japanese communist,
Kazama, was selected to return to Tokyo with this message, which
would, it was hoped, breathe fresh life into the dispirited party.

[206] *Internationale Presse-Korrespondenz*, No. 7, January 21, 1930, pp. 144–145;
No. 14, February 7, 1930, p. 327.

[207] G. Beckmann and Okuba Genji, *The Japanese Communist Party, 1922–1945*
(1969), p. 191.

[208] *Resolutions of the Fifth Congress of the RILU* (1931), pp. 141–151; for discussions
in a Japanese Commission of the congress, which were not published in Russian, see
G. Beckmann and Okuba Genji, *The Japanese Communist Party, 1922–1945* (1969),
p. 197.

[209] See *Foundations of a Planned Economy, 1926–1929*, Vol. 3, pp. 618–619.

Since Kazama, for reasons of security took nothing with him in writing, and is said on arrival to have consulted other communists in and out of prison, it is not clear how far the theses published early in 1931 in the revived party journal *Red Flag* corresponded with the original text drafted in Moscow six months earlier.[210] What distinguished the theses of 1931 from the Bukharin theses of 1927 was the firm insistence, justified by the onset of the world economic crisis, on the temporary nature of the stabilization achieved by the capitalist system, the prominence assigned to Japanese imperialism and to the threat of war against the USSR, and the emphasis, dictated by the total suppression of the legal party, on illegal activities. The new text pointed the way confidently to the socialist, proletarian revolution, which would also realize the tasks of the bourgeois democratic and agrarian revolutions; these were relegated to a subsidiary and incidental role. It denounced social-democrats as social-Fascists. It ended with the conventional denunciation of "extreme Left sectarianism" as well as of Right opportunism. But the general intention, in contrast with the 1927 theses, was to mark a shift to the Left.[211]

None of this had much relevance to what was happening in Japan, where a tiny handful of devoted communists struggled to maintain some kind of party organization in face of constant arrests, sometimes ending in confession and recantation. Some of the surviving leaders found the new theses unrealistic, and preferred the more moderate text of 1927. In Comintern, too, a more cautious mood was beginning to prevail. Japanese affairs were not discussed at the eleventh IKKI in March 1931, nor did any Japanese delegate take part in the debates. But, when a Japanese communist named Nosaka arrived in Moscow in the summer of 1931, he learned that the 1931 theses were already suspect.[212] The reaction against "Left sectarianism" had gained strength. Problems of the united front were beginning to loom large in Comintern debates. In 1931 the Japanese party "failed to draw a line in practice between the

[210] G. Beckmann and Okuba Genji, *The Japanese Communist Party, 1922–1945* (1969), pp. 198–205.

[211] For a translation of the theses see *ibid.* pp. 309–331. According to Japanese sources quoted *ibid.* p. 229, the neglect of the peasantry in the theses was later condemned as showing "semi-Trotskyist tendencies"; the blame was laid on Safarov, an old Bolshevik who had worked as an expert on eastern affairs throughout the nineteen-twenties, and who after 1933 was branded as a Trotskyist.

[212] *Ibid.* p. 229.

activity of the party and the activity of Left trade unions and other mass organizations". For example, when a League of Unemployed was set up, the party wished to make "definite political convictions" a condition for enrolment in it.[213] In the autumn of 1931 the Japanese *coup* in Manchuria spread alarm in Moscow, and concentrated the attention of Comintern on anything that might shake the authority of the imperialist regime in Tokyo rather than on remote and unrealistic prospects of a Japanese proletarian revolution. Among the numerous protests against this flagrant act of aggression[214] was a declaration signed by the three leading Japanese communists in Moscow, Katayama, Nosaka and Yamamoto.[215] But one consequence of the commotion caused by this event in Japan was an intensification of persecution of the struggling Japanese underground party. In the summer of 1932 it was described as having an elaborate organization on paper, but claimed only "over 400" members.[216]

It was in these conditions that Kuusinen, on March 2, 1932, made a report to the presidium of IKKI on "Japanese Imperialism and the Character of the Japanese Revolution". Japanese imperialism rested on a combination of a weak monopoly capitalism with "powerful survivals of feudalism". The "monarchical state apparatus" served as "a strong framework for the existing dictatorship of the class of exploiters". The war in Manchuria had "opened revolutionary perspectives" in Japan. But, when Kuusinen attempted to define "the chief task of the coming stage of the Japanese revolution", the goals set before it were carefully limited: the overthrow of the monarchy, the liquidation of the estates of the big landlords, the seven-hour working day, and the control of banks and large production enterprises through Soviets of workers and peasants. These were aims which characterized the bourgeois democratic revolution. Kuusinen recognized that the Japanese party was "terribly weak", and exhortations to engage in more vigorous action rang hollow.[217] A few days later the presidium of IKKI adopted a new set of theses on the tasks of the Japanese party which were widely publicized in the summer of 1932. The theses

[213] *Sovremennaya Yaponiya* (1934), i, 136.
[214] See pp. 344–345 above.
[215] *Internationale Presse-Korrespondenz*, No. 95, October 2, 1931, pp. 2138–2139.
[216] G. Beckmann and Okuba Genji, *The Japanese Communist Party, 1922–1945* (1969), p. 255.
[217] *Mirovoe Khozyaistvo i Mirovaya Politika*, 1932, No. 6, pp. 3–14, reprinted in *Sovremennaya Yaponiya* (1934), i, 26–38.

leaned heavily on the theme of Japanese imperialism, and instructed the party "to combine the struggle against war with the struggle of workers, peasants and all toilers against their economic and political enslavement in order to convert the imperialist war into civil war and overthrow the bourgeois-landlord monarchy". It was emphasized that "the path to the dictatorship of the proletariat in present Japanese conditions can only be through a bourgeois-democratic revolution", and the recommended slogan was: "People's revolution against imperialist war and the police monarchy, for rice, land, freedom and a workers' and peasants' government".[218]

The twelfth IKKI in August 1932 could no longer afford to repeat the neglect of Japan displayed at the eleventh IKKI eighteen months earlier. Kuusinen in his report observed that Japanese imperialism was "very aggressive, but internally not strong". Class rule rested on three elements—monopoly capitalism, the monarchy and feudal ownership of land. Japan was "deeply infected with remnant of feudalism"; and this encouraged the speculation that it might soon "find itself in the condition of a revolutionary crisis".[219] Nosaka, using the name Okano, in a lengthy speech on conditions in Japan, endorsed Kuusinen's conclusions; he also introduced a separate debate on the war in the Far East.[220] The veteran Katayama, appearing for the last time on a Comintern platform, congratulated "the Red Army of the Chinese Soviets" on its victories "against Japanese imperialism and the armies of the Chinese militarists, supported by the imperialists of the whole world".[221] But these proceedings in Moscow were followed by wholesale arrests in Japan of the few devoted communists still at liberty, facilitated by the infiltration of party organizations by police informers, and by confessions extracted under torture from those arrested. Nor had the 1932 theses put an end to dissent in the party. The leadership, having crushed the "sectarian" and "adventurist" Left by insisting on the bourgeois democratic aims of the present

---

[218] G. Beckmann and Okuba Genji, *The Japanese Communist Party, 1922–1945* (1969), pp. 230–231; for an English translation of the theses see *ibid.* pp. 332–351. No Russian text has been found, but the theses were published in *Internationale Presse-Korrespondenz*, No. 42, May 20, 1932, pp. 1303–1310, apparently in the form in which they were communicated to the Japanese party by WEB.

[219] *XII Plenum IKKI* (1933), i, 22–23.

[220] *Ibid.* ii, 35–42, iii, 1–14.

[221] *Ibid.* iii, 78; Katayama died in November 1933.

stage of the revolution, was said to have opened the door to the opposite Right opportunist heresy. A group in the party wished the Zemkyo to abandon such political slogans as "the struggle against imperialist war, against the bourgeois-landlord government, for a worker-peasant government, and for the defence of the USSR and of the Chinese Soviets", and devote itself to the practical demands of the workers.[222]

A fresh blow now fell on the troubled and fragmented party. In October 1932, Sano Manabu and Nabeyana, who had in the past played important roles in the leadership of the party,[223] and who had been under arrest since 1929, were brought to trial and sentenced to life imprisonment. In the summer of 1933 they defected from the party, and made a public statement denouncing its policies and those of Comintern. The statement had a markedly patriotic flavour. Comintern understood nothing of conditions in Japan, where the "imperial system" had never been a "system of exploitation and oppression"; and the form of revolution would vary "according to factors peculiar to each country".[224] In Moscow, Katayama, Nosaka and Yamamoto issued, in the name of Comintern, a cry of protest against these "shameless traitors and provocateurs".[225] But these defections were followed by others, and it was clear that national chauvinism, stimulated by the achievements of the Japanese army in Manchuria and in China, had begun to make inroads on the Japanese Left. The long-standing communist demand for the liberation of Korea and Formosa from Japanese rule also became a stumbling-block. But by this time communications between Comintern and the rump of the struggling Japanese party had almost ceased to exist.

Throughout the year 1933 the growing menace of Hitler had suggested a sinister parallel between an aggressive Germany in the west and Japanese aggression in the east. An article in the Comintern news-sheet, echoing protests against Hitler's plans to revise the Versailles treaty, accused Japan of having resorted to the sword to revise the Washington treaties of 1921.[226] In May 1933 Litvinov,

---

[222] *Sovremennaya Yaponiya* (1934), i, 136–137.

[223] See *Foundations of a Planned Economy, 1926–1929*, Vol. 3, pp. 617–618, 622–624.

[224] G. Beckmann and Okuba Genji, *The Japanese Communist Party, 1922–1945* (1969), pp. 245–249.

[225] *Rundschau*, No. 32, September 1, 1933, pp. 1227–1228.

[226] *Rundschau*, No. 8, April 7, 1933, pp. 194–195.

certainly not without the authority of the politburo, took an unexpected initiative. Harassed by repeated clashes between Soviet and Japanese officials on the CER, he informed the Japanese Ambassador in Moscow orally of the willingness of the USSR to negotiate the sale of the railway to Japan[227]—the symptom of an anxious desire to remove every tangible source of friction—though it required two years of intermittent negotiations, mingled with recriminations, to bring the deal to a conclusion. Kuusinen's report at the thirteenth IKKI at the end of November 1933 was devoted mainly to Europe. He spoke of Japan in the context of the world economic crisis, and of the growth of armaments and of the danger of war, and bracketed Japanese with German "aggressive militarism".[228] He dismissed the Japanese Communist Party with a curt reference to the "treason of Sano and Nabeyana", and with the empty reassurance: "Fascism is growing, but the Japanese Communist Party is also growing".[229] Pyatnitsky did rather better. He recognized that it was difficult for "the small Japanese communist party" to raise "the question of the defeat of the fatherland and of the conversion of the imperialist war into civil war", but praised its brave attempts to do so.[230] Katayama had died on the eve of the session, and Nosaka (*alias* Okano) headed the Japanese delegates. Reacting sharply against the two "traitors" (whom, however, he did not name), he openly denounced the Japanese monarchy as Fascist. He spoke of the mass arrests of communists, but gave a wholly unrealistic picture of the state of the party. He appealed to Japanese communists to "turn the coming imperialist war into civil war", and to organize mass strikes and demonstrations against the war budget on the basis of the united front. But the plea for common action was qualified, in accordance with the orthodoxy still prevailing in Comintern, by denunciation of "the Fascisization of social-democracy". At the end of the session, Nosaka was appointed to the presidium of IKKI in succession to Katayama.[231] In the following month, he informed the seventeenth Russian party congress, where he spoke as a fraternal delegate, that in the past

[227] *Dokumenty Vneshnei Politiki SSSR*, xvi (1970), 831–832, note 114. Proposals to hand over the CER to Japan had been current for many years, and had been frequently denied (see *Foundations of a Planned Economy, 1926–1929*, Vol. 3, p. 907, note 438); a rumour of such a project was denied in *Izvestiya*, December 24, 1932.

[228] For this report see p. 105 above.

[229] *XIII Plenum IKKI* (1934), p. 24.

[230] *Ibid.* p. 174.

[231] *Ibid.* pp. 205–215, 570.

three years 60,000 communists sympathizers had been arrested in
Japan, 27,000 of them in Tokyo, and that 50 of the "best comrades"
had been executed.[232]

The multiplying symptoms of Japanese aggression provoked the
same alarms and hesitations in Moscow as the mounting threat of
Fascism in Europe. Stalin at the seventeenth party congress spoke in
cautious language of the bad relations between the USSR and
Japan; Manuilsky more bluntly called Japan and Germany "the
clenched fist of world bourgeois reaction".[233] In the spring of 1934
Comintern despatched Nosaka to New York, where he remained for
the rest of the year, writing pamphlets on Japanese militarism and
Japanese Fascism for underground circulation at home.[234] It was a
significant mission, designed both to encourage the Japanese party
with hopes of American support and to induce the American party
to fan the flame of American hostility to Japan. During the year
increasingly shrill denunciations of Japanese aggression poured
from the Soviet press and from the Comintern press of several
countries. But signs of any direct contact with Japan were absent.
Reports of communist activities in the armed forces and in
munitions factories carry little conviction. The Japanese Communist Party had been virtually extinguished, and any known communist went in daily fear of arrest. Other parties and organizations of the
Left had been engulfed in the current wave of chauvinism. United
front policies designed for specific European conditions were
meaningless in Japan. As preparations for the seventh congress of
Comintern went forward in Moscow, the Comintern journal in the
spring of 1935 published an article by Yamamoto (using the *alias*
Tanaka) appealing for a "broad united front in Japan".[235] But on
the eve of the congress an anonymous article in the same journal
reverted to the theme of "unity from below", and specifically
rejected unity with the leaders of a recently formed Social Masses
Party, who hoped to achieve reform by legal means and by appeals
to the existing authorities.[236] It is noteworthy that none of the three
Japanese delegates to the seventh congress—Nosaka, Yamamoto
and Kobayashi—had been in Japan for several years past.

[232] *XVII S"ezd Vsesoyuznoi Kommunisticheskoi Partii (b)* (1934), p. 330.
[233] Stalin, *Sochineniya*, xiii, 304–305; *XVII S"ezd Vsesoyuznoi Kommunisticheskoi
Partii (b)* (1934), p. 312.
[234] G. Beckmann and Okuba Genji, *The Japanese Communist Party, 1922–1945*
(1969), p. 254.
[235] *Kommunisticheskii Internatsional*, 1935, No. 5–6, pp. 31–39.
[236] *Ibid.* 1935, No. 15, pp. 43–54.

CHAPTER 17

FRONTS AND MOVEMENTS

With the adoption of the new Comintern line at its sixth congress in 1928, and the waning of Münzenberg's prestige, the activity of the auxiliary organizations and "fronts" designed to rally the support of the non-communist Left slowly declined, and non-communist members drifted away. The Friends of the Soviet Union, more than two years after its foundation,[1] held a second international congress at Essen in March 1930. Münzenberg presided and directed the proceedings, and Bell, the delegate of the CPGB, spoke eloquently on the danger of war against the USSR.[2] But the proceedings were lifeless, and the experiment was not repeated. At the fifth congress of Profintern in August 1930, Šmeral somewhat unexpectedly spoke as a delegate of the League against Imperialism, explaining that, since the congress in Frankfurt in 1929, the league was no longer "a fighting alliance between the national bourgeoisie of colonial countries and the masses of the international proletariat", but "a united revolutionary mass organization".[3] The transformation became evident when the executive committee of the league met in Berlin in May 1931; Nehru and other non-communist members had resigned from the committee, and were formally expelled on this occasion. The committee issued a protest against mass terror in China, and executions in Lahore, and called for an international recruiting week for the league on June 21–28.[4] The response appears to have been insignificant.

---

[1] See *Foundations of a Planned Economy, 1926–1929*, Vol. 3, pp. 307–310.

[2] For an incomplete report on the proceedings see *Internationale Presse-Korrespondenz*, No. 28, March 25, 1930, pp. 681–685; a continuation was promised, but did not appear. The only European country where the national society of Friends of the Soviet Union retained some spontaneous vitality was Britain; meetings in Plymouth and London were reported in *Daily Worker*, December 3, 1930, February 18, 1931.

[3] *Protokoll des V Kongresses der Roten Gewerkschaftsinternationale* (1930), ii, 52; for the Frankfurt congress see *Foundations of a Planned Economy, 1926–1929*, Vol. 3, pp. 305–307.

[4] *Internationale Presse-Korrespondenz*, No. 48, May 27, 1931, p. 1142. *Kommunisticheskii Internatsional: Kratkii Istoricheskii Ocherk* (1969), p. 366, admits that

385

If, however, the campaign against imperialism had ceased to yield results, the prospect of an international campaign against war looked more promising. The sixth congress of Comintern in 1928 had set the precedent of celebrating August 1, the anniversary of the outbreak of war in 1914, as a day of protest pointing to the renewed danger of war, and especially of war against the USSR.[5] The approach of the "day" in 1930 was heralded by an issue of the Comintern journal devoted entirely to articles on this theme. A leading article exhorted communists to "broaden the fighting front" of peace, and invoked Stalin's speech at the sixteenth Russian party congress on the threat of war and the Soviet policy of peace.[6] The most vigorous article, signed Alfred, apparently from the pen of Togliatti, was entitled "Against Indifference in the Question of the War Danger". The writer admitted that the question had been neglected since the previous year, and argued that to pretend that it was "unpopular among the working masses" was to deny the necessity of "*a special struggle against war*". On the contrary, war was just as much a matter of *industry and railways* as of armies; workers in industry should publicize the way in which their enterprises were furthering military production, and so alert the world to the danger of war.[7] On December 11, 1930, a "committee for the defence of the Soviet Union against imperialist war-mongers" issued a manifesto signed by Gorky, Upton Sinclair, Barbusse and Münzenberg.[8] The eleventh IKKI in March 1931 devoted a lengthy debate, introduced by Cachin, to the danger of imperialist war, and adopted a resolution which linked a call to the proletariat of the world to ward off the threat to the USSR with "the preservation of peace among nations".[9] In preparation for the anniversary of August 1, the Comintern journal once more raised the slogan of "a broadening of the fighting front against military intervention".[10]

"certain decisions of the league made cooperation with national-reformist organizations" difficult, but also attributed its decline to "Left sectarian errors of a number of eastern communist parties"; it was not formally liquidated till 1935.

[5] See *Foundations of a Planned Economy, 1926–1929*, Vol. 3, pp. 245–246.

[6] *Kommunisticheskii Internatsional*, 1930, No. 19–20, pp. 3–16.

[7] *Ibid.* 1930, No. 19–20, pp. 40–48. The identification of "Alfred" with Togliatti (see M. Drachkovitch and B. Lazitch, *Biographical Dictionary of the Comintern* (1973), p. xxxvii) is virtually certain; Togliatti later used the name Alfredo in dealings with the PCE.

[8] *Iz Istorii Mezhdunarodnoi Proletarskoi Solidarnosti*, iv (1960), 187–188.

[9] See p. 38 above.

[10] *Kommunisticheskii Internatsional*, 1931, No. 19–20, pp. 4–9.

These initiatives, though they had no immediate sequel, proved timely. The Japanese incursion into Manchuria in the autumn of 1931 shocked the western world into consciousness of the danger of another major war, and intensified Soviet fears of an attack on the USSR. At first the familiar bogey of a combination of the imperialist countries against the USSR still prevailed.[11] But, as the hostility of the western Powers to the Japanese venture became apparent, a different picture emerged. The horror of a renewal of war provoked in the west by the Japanese action in Manchuria could be brought into line with the more specific Soviet fears of aggression against the USSR. On March 9, 1932, the political commission of IKKI instructed WEB to organize in Berlin a conference of communist parties to plan a campaign against imperialist war, which would become "the starting-point of an effort to win over new masses by party slogans". The conference took place on March 30–31, being attended among others by Thälmann, Pieck, Thorez, Monmousseau, Pollitt and Lenski, and issued an appeal to the workers of all countries to join in the struggle against the danger of war.[12]

The notion of a world-wide campaign against war, into which broad strata of the Left in western countries, both workers and intellectuals, could be drawn, on the model of the joint campaign against imperialism, was probably the brain-child of Münzenberg.[13] But France was the country where the anti-war movement of the Left was most highly developed; and Barbusse and Rolland, whose pacifist record went back to the war of 1914, were key figures. The first overture seems to have been made in a visit of Thorez to Barbusse in the spring of 1932;[14] and shortly afterwards Münzenberg announced plans for an international congress at Geneva to be attended by "personalities closely linked with MRP", among whom he named Gorky, Rolland, Dreiser, Einstein, Dos Passos, Mme Sun Yat-sen, and Barbusse. Within a few days a

[11] See p. 344 above.
[12] *Georgii Dimitrov: Vydayushchiisya Deyatel' Kommunisticheskogo Dvizheniya* (1972), p. 110.
[13] Later Soviet accounts, written when Münzenberg was a discredited figure, assigned an important role in the proceedings to Dimitrov (*ibid.* pp. 110–114); but Dimitrov is rarely mentioned in contemporary sources, which constantly refer to Münzenberg.
[14] M. Thorez, *Fils du Peuple* (1960), pp. 79–80; J. Fauvet, *Histoire du Parti Communiste Français*, i (1964), 116–117, dates the meeting April 5, 1932.

committee had been set up in Geneva, which fixed July 28 as the
date of the congress.[15] On May 27 *Humanité* published an appeal by
Rolland and Barbusse to "all men and women irrespective of their
political views", as well as to all workers' and mass organizations, to
rally to the international anti-war congress. At the end of June the
manifesto signed by Rolland and Barbusse spoke eloquently of the
recrudescence of war and militarism; "a new world war threatens
us". Though the immediate target of these warlike preparations was
the USSR, "war against the USSR means world war". The
manifesto summoned "an international congress to make war on
war" to be held at Geneva on July 28, 1932.[16]

A broadly based popular campaign against war was bound to
excite misgivings in Moscow. For Comintern pacifism had long
been a delicate issue. Ever since the danger of imperialist war had
been a recurrent theme, the distinguishing line between the
campaign against imperialist war and an unconditional pacifism,
which no communist could accept, had been increasingly difficult
to draw. On the eve of the eighth IKKI in May 1927 a proposal of the
Italian delegation, led by Togliatti, to put forward the slogan of a
"struggle for peace" was indignantly rebutted by Manuilsky as "a
Trotskyist deviation";[17] and the main resolution adopted at the end
of the session put the question of the danger of war in a nutshell by
concentrating on "the defence of the Russian and Chinese
revolutions".[18] The debate on the danger of war at the sixth
congress of Comintern in 1928 revealed the same embarrassments.
The resolution which ended the debate reinforced the demand for
the defence of the Russian and Chinese revolutions, but described
pacifism as "a poisoned weapon of imperialism".[19] Moreover, as the
danger of imperialist war against the USSR had now narrowed

[15] *Internationale Presse-Korrespondenz*, No. 38, May 10, 1932, pp. 1181–1182, No.
43, May 24, 1932, p. 1339; an account in B. Gross, *Willi Münzenberg* (Engl. transl.
1974), pp. 223–227 is based on personal recollections.
[16] *Humanité*, June 26, 1932
[17] P. Togliatti, *Opere*, II (1972), pp. cxlii–cxliii. Togliatti was in disfavour at the
eighth IKKI on other grounds (see *Foundations of a Planned Economy, 1926–1929*, Vol.
3, p. 146); his strictly orthodox article of 1930 denouncing indifference to the war
danger (see p. 386 above) was doubtless part of the process of rehabilitation.
[18] *Kommunisticheskii Internatsional v Dokumentakh* (1933), pp. 699–717.
[19] See *Foundations of a Planned Economy, 1926–1929*, Vol. 3, pp. 211–213;
Kommunisticheskii Internatsional v Dokumentakh (1933), p. 826.

down to the specific danger of aggression by German or Japanese imperialism, so communist mistrust of pacifist ideology was reinforced by hostility to a creed which might weaken the military resistance of the western democratic countries to Germany and Japan.

Hesitations and divided opinions in Moscow were revealed in an article in the Comintern journal entitled "On the Inopportune Application of the Peace Slogan". The writer was Togliatti, using the pen-name Alfred, who, now restored to favour, was doubtless eager to efface any impression left by his earlier indiscretion on the subject; and it was qualified in an editorial note as a discussion article. Togliatti reminded those French and German communists who engaged in pacifist propaganda that the issue was not "peace" as such; communists could not call for the maintenance of the current "imperialist" or "capitalist" peace. He roundly criticized an article in the KPD journal which, in celebrating Litvinov's successes at Geneva, claimed that "the chief essence of communism is peace", and that "the struggle for peace forms the background of all revolutionary strategy and tactics in the present period".[20] Thorez, in a cautious article in *Humanité*, followed suit, issuing a warning against the "petty-bourgeois pacifism" which inspired some of the sponsors of the congress; nor was it right to treat Germany, "exploited by French imperialism" on a level with France. But the struggle against pacifism should not prevent communists from taking part in the congress.[21] Meanwhile the project was ill received by other sectors of the Left. It was boycotted by the Second International as a communist device.[22] Trotsky, in an open letter on the project dated June 14, 1932, derided both the silence of Comintern and Profintern, which left the initiative to petty-bourgeois pacifists, and the failure to form a united front in Germany against the pressing danger of Fascism.[23] The International Antimilitarist Commission, a pacifist organization having its headquarters in the Netherlands, complained that what had been announced as a congress against war was being transformed

[20] *Kommunisticheskii Internatsional*, 1932, No. 13, pp. 3–8; the offending phrases occurred in *Die Internationale*, No. 4, February 15, 1932, p. 179. For the identification of Alfred with Togliatti see p. 386, note 7 above.

[21] *Humanité*, June 28, 1932; *Oeuvres de Maurice Thorez*, II, iv (1951), 12–15.

[22] According to B. Gross, *Willi Münzenberg* (Engl. transl. 1974), p. 223, Barbusse rashly approached Adler and received a sharp refusal.

[23] *Byulleten' Oppozitsii* (Paris), No. 28, July 1932, pp. 6–8.

into a congress for the defence of the USSR and China.[24]

The Swiss Government having raised objections, the venue of the congress was changed from Geneva to Amsterdam, where it assembled on August 27, 1932.[25] Delegates numbered 2196 from 27 countries; of these 1865 were workers, 290 were social-democrats who defied the ban of the Second International and risked expulsion from their parties, and 830 were communists. Only one delegation failed to appear: the Netherlands Government had refused permission to Gorky and Shvernik, the Soviet delegates, to enter the country. Barbusse opened the congress and delivered the main address. Messages were read from Rolland (who was too ill to attend), Zetkin, Gorky and Einstein. Anonymous representatives of the German workers, of the French "colonial proletariat" and of the French peasantry, and an Italian sailor, addressed the congress. Three Comintern stalwarts—Katayama, Cachin and Heckert—spoke. As the debate dragged on, Münzenberg intervened to express impatience with the inconclusive character of the oratory, and to outline the terms of a prospective manifesto of the congress. The proceedings ended on August 29 with a valedictory address by Barbusse, with the adoption of a manifesto and of several resolutions, and with the announcement of a galaxy of distinguished names constituting a "world committee against imperialist war". The manifesto ranged far and wide. It denounced the wars, and the preparations for war, for which capitalism was responsible. It rejected the Versailles system and the doctrine that Germany was solely to blame for the war of 1914, and it branded France as the leading imperialist Power. It issued warnings against pacifism, against the League of Nations and against the Second International, and it ended with a solemn pledge never again to break the "formidable unity" of the exploited classes in resisting war.[26] The congress also elected an "international committee for

[24] The commission issued several protest bulletins during the congress.

[25] Dimitrov is credited with the choice of Amsterdam (*Georgii Dimitrov: Vydayushchiisya Deyatel' Kommunisticheskogo Dvizheniya* (1972), p. 111).

[26] The proceedings were reported daily in *Humanité*; see also *Internationale Presse-Korrespondenz*, No. 72, August 30, 1932, pp. 2309–2316, No. 75, September 9, 1932, pp. 2411–2412, No. 76, September 13, 1932, pp. 2444–2445. Münzenberg's speech was listed with other speeches in *Rundschau*, No. 3, September 1, 1932, p. 41, but was reported only in Bulletin No. 108 of the International Antimilitarist Commission; its omission from other records is significant. For Dimitrov's role see *Georgii Dimitrov: Vydayushchiisya Deyatel' Kommunisticheskogo Dvizheniya* (1972) pp. 111–112; he did not speak at the congress, but was probably busy behind the scenes.

the struggle against imperialist war" on which the Soviet delegates were Gorky, Shvernik and Stasova.[27] After the congress a mass anti-war demonstration was held in Paris, and the speeches which Gorky and Shvernik were to have delivered at the congress were read.[28]

Reactions in Moscow to the congress were oddly mixed. On its opening day, *Pravda* devoted to it a leading article and the bulk of its front page, describing it as a "war against imperialist war", and attacking those who decried it as a "Comintern manoeuvre". The principal speeches were reported, anti-war demonstrations took place in Moscow and Leningrad, and Barbusse's address and the congress manifesto were printed in full.[29] But this enthusiasm did not penetrate to the Comintern hierarchy. Kuusinen, who opened the twelfth IKKI in Moscow on the day of the opening of the congress in Amsterdam, did not mention it. Ever wary of the danger of an infiltration of pacifism into communist doctrine, he seized the occasion to warn the French and German parties that "the struggle for peace" was a pacifist, not a revolutionary, slogan. He reminded the PCF that France was "the country where the pacifist illusion plays a greater role than in any other country in the world"; and he condemned the article in the KPD journal already criticized by Togliatti.[30] Thorez maintained a discreet silence. Ferrat observed that preparations for the Amsterdam congress had led to the formation of committees to resist imperialist war, and had promoted the cause of the united front; and Doriot hailed them as symptoms of "a deep anti-war movement" in France.[31] It was perhaps significant that both stood on the Right of the PCF, and were shortly to be expelled from it.

The peace movement had, however, been too successful to be ignored. On October 15, 1932, the political secretariat of IKKI instructed Dimitrov in Berlin to take charge of the international committee set up by the congress under the presidency of Barbusse to pursue the campaign against imperialist war—probably a move to wrest control of the movement from the now suspect hands of Münzenberg, and to ensure that it was directed into the right

[27] *Iz Istorii Mezhdunarodnoi Proletarskoi Solidarnosti*, v (1961), 38, note 1.

[28] *Pravda*, September 4, 1932; *Internationale Presse-Korrespondenz*, No. 74, September 6, 1932, pp. 2385–2387. Both speeches were published in a pamphlet *La Voix de l'URSS à Amsterdam* (n.d. [1932]).

[29] *Pravda*, August 27, 28, 30, 31, September 15, 1932.

[30] *XII Plenum IKKI* (1933), i, 24; for Togliatti's criticism see p. 389 above.

[31] *XII Plenum IKKI* (1933), ii, 99, 193.

channels.[32] An anti-war conference of European communist parties under the presidency of Dimitrov met secretly somewhere in the Ruhr area of Germany (it was referred to as the "Essen conference") on December 30, 1932, and drafted a manifesto recommending "mass mobilization against the production and transport of war materials", coordination with the Amsterdam anti-war movement while observing "the non-party character of that movement", and "mobilization of the masses against the Versailles system . . . against the rearmament of Germany and chauvinistic and militaristic incitements".[33] This was followed by a meeting of the Amsterdam international committee in Paris presided over by Barbusse, at which Dimitrov, Shvernik and Stasova formed the Soviet delegation,[34] and which adopted an elaborate resolution on the struggle against imperialist war, and issued a separate declaration on the war in the Far East.[35]

Hitler's victory in Germany stimulated the demand for common action to resist the spread of Fascism, especially in France, the source of most "united front" initiatives at this time, and the rallying-point of German refugees from the Nazi terror.[36] Plans in Moscow to put Dimitrov in charge of the Amsterdam international committee were frustrated by his arrest in Berlin on March 9, 1933;[37] and it was once more Münzenberg who started a movement to repeat the success of the Amsterdam congress, Barbusse being again cast for a conspicuous role. A projected anti-Fascist workers' congress in Prague on April 16–17, 1933, had been prohibited by the Czechoslovak Government. [38] But the congress eventually took place in Paris in the Salle Pleyel on June 4–6. It was a formidable, if somewhat miscellaneous, gathering. According to one account, more than 3000 delegates represented three million European

[32] *Georgii Dimitrov: Vydayushchiisya Deyatel' Kommunisticheskogo Dvizheniya* (1972), p. 113.

[33] *Die Rote Fahne*, January 10, 1933; *Geschichte der Deutschen Arbeiterbewegung*, iv (1966), 377; *Die Anti-Faschistische Aktion* (1965), pp. 328–331.

[34] *Georgii Dimitrov: Vydayushchiisya Deyatel' Kommunisticheskogo Dvizheniya* (1972), p. 114; B. Gross, *Willi Münzenberg* (Engl. transl. 1974), p. 240.

[35] *Humanité*, January 6, 14, 1933.

[36] For a graphic account of Münzenberg's efforts to organize anti-Nazi activity in Paris and elsewhere see B. Gross, *Willi Münzenberg* (Engl. transl. 1974), pp. 241–246.

[37] See p. 88 above.

[38] *Rundschau*, No. 7, March 31, 1933, pp. 181–182, No. 10, April 20, 1933, p. 292.

workers; according to another, 1200 communists were present, 500 social-democrats and nearly 2000 non-party workers. Two-thirds of the delegates were French, but 120 Germans arrived from Nazi Germany. Of the delegates 87 per cent registered as factory workers. But 500 students were said to have been present, and they "organized a separate discussion".[39] A Trotskyist group which had proposed to attend was refused admission.[40]

The congress was opened by Racamond, the secretary of the CGTU—a plain indication of its communist sponsorship.[41] The main report was delivered by Florin, the leader of the German delegation, speaking under the name of Müller. Barbusse then spoke on behalf of the Amsterdam movement, and was followed by orators from several other countries. At the second session, Bergery, a former vice-president of the Radical-Socialist Party, introduced a jarring note by proclaiming his loyalty to the united front, but protesting against "the subordination of the French leadership of the anti-Fascists to an international organization". Doriot retorted that "anyone who wants to set national limits to the anti-Fascist struggle increases the danger that developments in Italy and Germany may be repeated in his own country", and that "the proletariat must take the lead". But the main division at the congress was between broad and narrow conceptions of the united front. A German delegate using the name Maier, who attacked Bergery, devoted most of a long speech to a denunciation of SPD leaders who had been willing to compromise with Hitler; and Cachin asked how one could have a united front with men like Blum and Jouhaux, "who work directly for war". The manifesto of the congress proclaimed that *"the international advance of Fascism announces an immediate transition to imperialist war"*, and that *"Fascism is an international danger for the workers of all countries"*. Even "in the so-called democratic countries" the development of Fascism into a mass movement could be prevented only by a struggle "against one's own bourgeoisie, against one's own capitalism": *"the struggle against Fascism cannot be conducted without breaking completely with workers' cooperation with the bourgeoisie, without an implacable revolutionary*

---

[39] *Rundschau*, No. 18, June 9, 1933, pp. 590–594; *Kommunisticheskii Internatsional*, 1933, No. 19–20, pp. 92–94.

[40] *Byulleten' Oppozitsii* (Paris), No. 35, July 1933, p. 31.

[41] *Kommunisticheskii Internatsional: Kratkii Istoricheskii Ocherk* (1969), p. 354, records that the congress was convened "on the initiative of the communists".

struggle." A separate appeal was made to trade unionists of all European countries; and it was decided to set up a "standing committee for the unity of workers against Fascism".[42] Two months later the anti-Fascist committee was amalgamated with the anti-war bureau set up by the Amsterdam congress in the previous year.[43]

Münzenberg's skilled and practised hand was visible in the organization of these events; and the funds necessary to mount them certainly came from Moscow. The opening of the congress in the Salle Pleyel was briefly, but prominently, reported in *Pravda* on June 6, 1933. But the divided counsels prevailing in Comintern on questions of the united front affected official attitudes to what came to be known as "the Amsterdam-Pleyel movement". Comintern and Russian party leaders remained aloof—a caution due, not so much to unwillingness to compromise the proceedings by revealing their communist inspiration, as to mistrust in the highest quarters in Moscow of a popular bourgeois "pacifist" crusade, and hesitation to endorse policies of open cooperation, not only with socialist parties (the "united front"), but also with bourgeois parties of the Left (the "popular front"). It was noteworthy that the thirteenth IKKI, meeting at the end of November 1933, which virtually ignored the Leipzig trial and the widespread interest and indignation aroused by it in western countries, and registered no sensible advance on the issue of the united front,[44] also took no cognisance of the Amsterdam and Paris congresses.

[42] For the proceedings see *Rundschau*, No. 18, June 9, 1933, pp. 590–594; for the manifesto *ibid.* No. 20, June 15, 1933, pp. 663–664; for the full text of Maier's speech *ibid.* No. 21, June 23, 1933, pp. 709–710; for the appeal to the trade unions *ibid.* No. 22, June 30, 1933, pp. 757–758. *Kommunisticheskii Internatsional*, 1933, No. 19–20, pp. 92–99, contains a Soviet account of the congress, and prints "a scheme of organization and plan of work" of the standing committee, concluding with an appeal to support the "international week" from June 17 to 25 proclaimed by MOPR on behalf of political prisoners (see p. 395 below). The controversial Bergery soon left the movement and attacked the popular front as a "communist manoeuvre" (J. Duclos, *Mémoires*, ii (1969), 55–56). Florin's identity is established by *Geschichte der Deutschen Arbeiterbewegung*, v (1966), 37; and some further details are in D. Desanti, *L'Internationale Communiste* (1970), pp. 199–200, including the statement that a representative of Comintern attended the congress, but was dissuaded by Thorez from speaking.

[43] *Rundschau*, No. 32, September 1, 1933, pp. 1219–1221.

[44] See pp. 115–116 above.

Throughout this period, International Workers' Aid (MRP or IAH) and International Red Aid (MOPR or IRH), the earliest and most successful of Münzenberg's creations,[45] led a fitful and precarious existence. A "world congress" of MRP was held in Moscow in October 1931. It was opened by Münzenberg, and Ledebour, Zetkin and Remmele spoke. In the absence of any leading Russian party or Soviet personality, the Soviet delegates were led by a senior trade union official, Abolin, who pleaded for aid to "the hungry in the Volga region".[46] In May 1932 the central committee of MRP designated June 12 as its annual day of "international solidarity", and issued an appeal to unite against hunger, war and Fascism.[47] Thereafter it lapsed into obscurity. A shell remained in Moscow, and its annual appeals for "solidarity" continued to appear. But its strength had always been in Germany, and its effective role expired with the advent of Nazi rule.

MOPR, dedicated to the relief of martyrs of the revolution, fared better. The fresh waves of persecution and terrorism set in motion by the rise of Nazism in Germany gave a stimulus to its prestige and flagging activities. At the twelfth IKKI in August 1932 Kuusinen cited statistics of victims of the class terror; and Stasova made a report on the work of MOPR, and announced a forthcoming congress to celebrate its tenth anniversary which would coincide with the fifteenth anniversary of the Bolshevik revolution. The report revealed some impatience with party members who fled from their native countries in face of persecution, and were unwilling to engage in underground work there. Stasova made little attempt to disguise the fact that MOPR was now essentially a party organization directed from Moscow.[48] The congress was held in Moscow from November 10 to 25, 1932. Katayama opened the proceedings, and a manifesto was issued in honour of the "victims of capitalist class justice". The galaxy of orators who graced the occasion included Stasova, Bela Kun and Manuilsky, Zetkin and

[45] See *Foundations of a Planned Economy, 1926–1929*, Vol. 3, pp. 269–280.

[46] The congress was reported in *Internationale Presse-Korrespondenz*, No. 98, October 13, 1931, pp. 2217–2219, No. 99, October 16, 1931, pp. 2235–2236.

[47] *Ibid*. No. 40, May 13, 1932, p. 1235, No. 44, May 27, 1932, p. 1368; for an appeal issued jointly by MRP and the KPD, and for demonstrations in several countries, see *Iz Istorii Mezhdunarodnoi Proletarskoi Solidarnosti*, iv (1960), 440–444.

[48] *XII Plenum IKKI* (1933), i, 40, ii, 188–191; MOPR claimed at this time to have 11.5 million members, of whom 8.2 millions were in the USSR (*Internationale Presse-Korrespondenz*, No. 89, October 27, 1932, p. 2850).

PARTIES AND FRONTS

Pieck, Marty, and Münzenberg, who devoted most of his speech to the campaign against war.[49] In June 1933 the executive committee of MOPR called for a "week" of aid for victims of the white terror in Germany, and was backed up by a personal appeal from Clara Zetkin; and an "international solidarity day" on their behalf was proclaimed for June 11.[50] At the thirteenth IKKI in November 1933, Pyatnitsky noted the existence "in Germany and other countries" of such institutions as MOPR, MRP, the Friends of the Soviet Union, Red sport organizations and the RGO, but only in order to complain that their membership remained "one and the same", and that they had no appeal to the "broad masses". Stasova, as she had done at the twelfth IKKI, reported on MOPR, and claimed an increase in its membership and activities.[51] But no other delegate manifested any interest.

The revival and extension of united front tactics in the following year led to renewed activity in "the Amsterdam movement". An "international bureau" of the joint committee against war and Fascism was convened in Paris on April 21–22, 1934, to prepare for a revival of the campaign; Barbusse was once more the principal speaker.[52] On May 15 an appeal was issued in the name of the "world committee against imperialist war and Fascism"; and on May 21 Barbusse opened a two-day French anti-Fascist congress. 3487 delegates were said to have been elected by 32,000 workers and peasants, and included a substantial number of socialists as well as communists.[53] A few days later the indefatigable Barbusse presided over a meeting in Paris of an international committee to agitate for the release of Thälmann from a Nazi jail.[54] A joint appeal was issued by the central committees of the French, British, German and Polish

[49] Ibid. No. 96, November 10, 1932, pp. 2705–2706, No. 97, November 18, 1932, p. 3117, No. 102, December 6, 1932, pp. 3247–3249, No. 104, December 13, 1932, pp. 3329–3331, No. 108, December 29, 1932, p. 3457. The congress does not seem to have been reported in Pravda.
[50] Rundschau, No. 17, June 2, 1933, pp. 537–540, 549–552; the same issue carried (p. 535) a report of tortures at the Sonnenberg concentration camp.
[51] XIII Plenum IKKI (1934), pp. 193–194, 402–406; a further congress of MOPR was held in Moscow in March 1934, and received a message of greeting from Dimitrov, fresh from his triumph in the Nazi court (Rundschau, No. 22, March 22, 1934, p. 841).
[52] Rundschau, No. 26, April 19, 1934, p. 980.
[53] Ibid. No. 31, May 24, 1934, pp. 1221–1224, No. 35, June 7, 1934, pp. 1355–1356.
[54] Ibid. No. 35, June 7, 1934, pp. 1343–1344.

communist parties to celebrate the twentieth anniversary of the outbreak of war in 1914 as part of an international campaign against war and Fascism;[55] and the international bureau of the world committee met on July 30 to issue a manifesto which, beginning with a reference to the murder of Dollfuss a few days earlier, reiterated the familiar theme with ever increasing vehemence.[56] The approach of the anniversary of the armistice of November 11, 1918, provoked yet another appeal from the world committee.[57] Throughout 1934 hatred of Nazism and alarm at its potentially aggressive policies spread rapidly in the western world. The campaign promoted from Moscow, and conducted through the western communist parties, the world committee headed by Barbusse and other organizations, may not have contributed much directly to this process. But it served powerfully to reinforce the sense of an interest common to the USSR, to western communist parties and to the western democracies in defence against Fascism and the danger of another war. Other opportunities of mobilizing a world-wide protest against Fascism were not neglected. MRP proclaimed another "international solidarity day" on June 3, 1934, which received messages from such diverse personalities as Dimitrov, Pollitt and the secretary of the central council of Soviet trade unions. It called loudly for the release of Thälmann, Torgler, Ossietsky and other political prisoners of the Nazi regime, and for resistance to "social reactionary" policies.[58] MRP is said to have given aid to strikers in several countries. In August 1934 MOPR organized in Moscow a women's conference against war and Fascism.[59]

As Hitler's barely disguised plans of conquest created growing apprehension throughout Europe, and as the long announced, but twice postponed, seventh congress of Comintern came nearer, little pressure from Moscow was required to fan enthusiasm among workers and radical intellectuals in western countries (the two groups were blended in different proportions in different countries) for the united front against Fascism and war. In December 1934 the central committee of MOPR issued yet another appeal in which the

[55] *Ibid.* No. 39, July 5, 1934, pp. 1557–1558.

[56] *Ibid.* No. 47, August 23, 1934, pp. 1979–1981.

[57] *Ibid.* No. 56, October 25, 1934, pp. 2495–2496.

[58] *Ibid.* No. 30, May 17, 1934, pp. 1153–1155, No. 34, May 31, 1934, pp. 1316–1319.

[59] *Ibid.* No. 45, August 16, 1934, pp. 1886–1888.

united front of the Amsterdam-Pleyel movement was linked with the campaign of protest against "the social reaction and the hunger policy" of the Nazi regime.[60] The annual "international solidarity day" was announced for June 23, 1935, and greeted by a message from Dimitrov.[61] It is doubtful how much impact these gestures had on the Left in western countries.[62] The Amsterdam-Pleyel movement showed more signs of life. The world committee against war and Fascism issued an appeal to workers, peasants and intellectuals for demonstrations against war in the first week of August 1935, addressing itself especially to workers in the armament industries and in transport.[63] The intellectuals were not neglected. An international congress of writers for the defence of culture, at which an address from the absent Gorky was read, met in Paris on June 21–25.[64]

The seventh congress of Comintern represented in some ways the achievement of the purpose for which all the "fronts" of the past fifteen years had been created: the formulation of an aim which had an immediate appeal to progressive elements in the capitalist world, but at the same time served the ultimate ends of communism. The "fronts" of the nineteen-twenties fell short of their purpose because no aim propounded by them was powerful enough in the long run to overcome the contradictions inherent in the original conception; they were unmasked sooner or later as no more than agencies to promote the cause of communist revolution. The threat of war from Germany and Japan, and the Amsterdam movement which arose in response to it, for the first time forged a link of common interest between the USSR and the western democracies powerful enough to transcend the divisions of ideology and ultimate purpose between them. The Amsterdam congress, remarked a subsequent Soviet commentator, was "the first serious step towards overcoming the opposition of social-democratic parties to the united front".[65] It is

---

[60] *Ibid.* No. 2, January 10, 1935, pp. 83–84.

[61] Ibid. No. 22, May 16, 1935, pp. 1115–1116, No. 25, June 6, 1935, p. 1257.

[62] See *ibid.* No. 23, May 23, 1935, for Münzenberg's reply to a Swedish complaint that MRP was simply a communist organization.

[63] *Ibid.* No. 32, July 25, 1935, pp. 1583–1584; the writer who reported this initiative from Paris remarked severely that the time had come "not only to talk about peace", but "to *act* against war".

[64] *Trud*, June 16, 1935, *Pravda*, June 24, 1935.

[65] B. Leibzon and K. Shirinya, *Povorot v Politike Kominterna* (2nd ed., 1975), p. 183.

significant that the Amsterdam congress and the Amsterdam-Pleyel movement were constantly praised by speakers at the seventh congress.[66] Two representatives of the communist fraction in the executive committee of MOPR, which retained some credit by its championship of victims of the Fascist terror, spoke briefly of its work;[67] and Dimitrov in his reply to the debate on his report sounded a personal note of gratitude: "Any of us who has sat in prison knows from immediate experience the immense importance of the activity of MOPR".[68] Nobody mentioned the other fronts. They continued to exist for a few years longer. But the flame of international enthusiasm for the USSR kindled at the seventh congress largely superseded their less spectacular efforts and made them superfluous.

[66] Barbusse was in Moscow, but apparently too ill to attend the congress; he died there on August 30, 1935. His body lay in state for three days, and was then transported to Paris, where a large public funeral took place on September 7.

[67] *Rundschau*, No. 62, November 6, 1935, p. 2505, No. 74, December 18, 1935, pp. 2848–2849.

[68] *Ibid.* No. 66, November 19, 1935, p. 2608.

PART III

CHAPTER 18

THE SEVENTH CONGRESS

The seventh congress of Comintern opened on the evening of July 25, 1935, almost exactly seven years since its predecessor, in the Pillar Hall of the trade union building in Moscow.[1] Comintern at this time recognized 76 member parties, including 19 "sympathizing" parties which had not accepted the formal conditions of membership; 65 parties claiming a membership of over three millions (almost double the figure announced at the sixth congress in 1928) were represented at the congress by 513 delegates, of whom 371 were delegates with full voting rights, and 53 per cent were classified as workers.[2] Stalin's absence from the congress followed precedent and was unremarkable. His lack of enthusiasm for Comintern and for foreign communists was notorious. At the first four congresses of Comintern his absence had not even been noticed. At the fifth congress in 1924, held at the moment when he

---

[1] The seventh was the only congress of Comintern of which no complete stenographic record was ever published. Only the principal speeches were reported in *Pravda*; but all speeches (with perhaps a few exceptions) were reproduced in successive issues of the *Rundschau*, where most of them appeared twice—in a "telegraphic report" on the day after delivery, and in a "full report" somewhat later. The "full report" is normally not only much longer than the "telegraphic report", but more polished, and shows signs of editing; but such variations as occur do not seem to have any other significance. This remains the most convenient conspectus of the proceedings. After the congress the principal speeches were published in Russian as pamphlets (for a list of these see W. Sworakowski, *The Communist International and its Front Organizations* (Stanford, 1965), pp. 198–201); and some of the foreign parties published the speeches of their leaders in their respective languages in pamphlet form. Some of these versions are longer than the press reports, and probably represent the texts actually read by the speakers at the congress. The resolutions of the congress, as well as all Dimitrov's speeches, were published promptly in several languages. In February 1939 the Comintern secretariat belatedly published an "abbreviated stenographic protocol" of the congress in English, German and French (but not in Russian); the abbreviation consisted in the omission of all but a small and careful selection of speeches, as well as in the curtailment of those selected.

[2] For these and other particulars see the report of the mandates commission in *Rundschau*, No. 43, August 29, 1935, p. 1974.

was seeking to establish his power, he was active in the corridors, and spoke in some of the commissions, but did not appear in the plenary sessions.[3] During the sixth congress in 1928, which saw the down-grading of Bukharin, he was ostentatiously absent on vacation, though his directing hand was unconcealed. At the seventh congress his absence positively enhanced his supremacy; he received the frenzied applause of the audience without even showing himself in person. The absence of Bukharin was conspicuous for a different reason. Though he had enjoyed a partial reprieve, and worked as editor of *Izvestiya*, and on the drafting commission for a new constitution, he was never again allowed, after 1928, to concern himself with Comintern affairs. His name was not mentioned at the seventh congress.

When the congress assembled, Pieck's introductory speech was followed by formal speeches of several other delegates, by the election of a presidium, and by the decision to send a message of greeting to Stalin. Every mention of Stalin's name was hailed with "tumultuous applause".[4] On the following day Pieck delivered the traditional report on the work of IKKI since the previous congress.[5] It rehearsed familiar themes in conventional terms, denouncing social-democracy, criticizing sectarian errors of the principal communist parties, and registering the turn to the united front in 1934. Pieck praised the continued resistance of the KPD "in spite of frequent disorganization of the central leadership by the Gestapo and the gruesome mediaeval terror"; and he sought consolation for "the defeat of the German proletariat" in the resistance to Fascism by the workers in Austria, France and Spain. It required some effrontery, considering the recent divisions in the KPD, and the methods by which the breach had been healed, to claim that, whereas at the time of the sixth congress many parties had been split by fractional struggles, "we stand today united in closed ranks as never before." The report ended with an eloquent appeal to unite against Fascism and war in alliance with the USSR.[6]

[3] See *Socialism in One Country, 1924–1926*, Vol. 3, p. 92.

[4] *Rundschau*, No. 35, August 7, 1935, pp. 1693–1702.

[5] For the choice of *rapporteurs* see p. 127 above.

[6] *Ibid.* No. 37, August 14, 1935, pp. 1753–1774. The version in the Moscow editions of 1939 is almost complete; the few omissions include a criticism of the German working class, blinded by the SPD, for its passivity in face of the Nazi offensive (pp. 1761–1762), a quotation from Stalin in 1934 predicting "a rapid ripening of the revolutionary crisis" (p. 1763), and a long passage about China (see p. 418 below).

Representatives of every important delegation, including several Germans, spoke in the ensuing discussion, which occupied almost a week.[7] One unexpected clash occurred. Pieck had sharply criticized the CPGB for "sectarianism" in its trade union work; it had pursued "such clumsy and sectarian tactics that the Minority Movement really fell to pieces". Campbell in the debate struck back with some asperity, tracing back the sectarianism to the uncompromising "Strasbourg" resolution of 1929 and to the theory of "social-Fascism", both since disowned; and he went on to reproach IKKI, in veiled terms, for its delay in adopting united front policies.[8] Other speakers criticized their own parties but studiously spared Comintern. Pieck in his reply to the debate pointed out to Campbell that the eleventh and twelfth IKKIs had already denounced sectarianism and insisted on work in the reformist unions, and added tartly that past criticism of Right opportunism in the CPGB should not be construed as approval of sectarian errors.[9]

Pieck's report and the debate on it were, however, only the curtain-raiser for Dimitrov's report on the struggle for the unity of the working class against Fascism, which came next on the agenda, and was the key event of the congress. Pieck had accorded only a passing mention to Dimitrov. But his appearance on the platform was greeted with a "storm of applause", and with the singing of the Internationale, oddly led by the Chinese delegation, "in all languages of the world". The report, well stocked with quotations from Lenin and Stalin, contained no unexpected novelties. But the outspoken vigour of the orator's personality imparted a certain freshness to the familiar *clichés*. Dimitrov began with a long analysis of Fascism, which was neither a dictatorship of the bourgeoisie nor of the petty bourgeoisie, but a terrorist dictatorship of finance capital, replacing the regime of bourgeois democracy. He displayed a deeper understanding of the Nazi appeal than was common among the leaders of Comintern:

Fascism not only inflames deep-rooted prejudices in the masses, but plays on the best feelings of the masses, on their sense

[7] Detailed reports appeared in special issues of the *Rundschau*, Nos. 42, 49, 50, 54; of the thirty or more speeches only five were included in the Moscow editions of 1939.

[8] *Ibid.* No. 42, August 27, 1935, pp. 2372–2375; for the "Strasbourg" resolution see *Foundations of a Planned Economy, 1926–1929*, Vol. 3, pp. 238–239.

[9] *Rundschau*, No. 54, October 8, 1935, pp. 2267–2270.

of justice, and sometimes even on their revolutionary traditions. . . . The German Fascists . . . try to exploit the faith in revolution, the urge towards socialism, which lives in the hearts of the broad masses of German workers.

Throughout the speech, implied criticism of Comintern was masked in criticism of foreign parties. Since the sixth congress in 1928 parties had been eager to expel "Right opportunists"; but "the campaign against *sectarianism* was carried on less successfully, or often was not carried on at all". The error of June 9, 1923, in Bulgaria, and the "May error" of 1926 in Poland, as well as the policies of the KPD, were cited as instances of "sectarian narrowness". This led up to a comprehensive appeal for a united front, which would unite the workers of both Second and Third Internationals, and draw into itself the peasants, the urban petty-bourgeois and the intellectuals, who were equally the victims of Fascism, the goal being "the creation of a *broad anti-Fascist popular front on the basis of the proletarian united front*". It was not a matter of indifference whether the bourgeois dictatorship "takes a democratic or a Fascist form". Dimitrov was prepared to "defend every inch of the democratic achievements won in the past by the working class", though this did not mean that they would "adopt the same attitude to bourgeois democracy in all circumstances". He cited Lenin's well-known article of 1914 "On the National Pride of the Great Russians" in support of the thesis that communists are not "*believers in national nihilism*" and do not ridicule all national feelings of the broad working masses; and he reproved the KPD for having "underestimated the feeling of national humiliation and the indignation of the masses against Versailles". Finally, he announced that "the Communist International and its sections are ready to take up negotiations with the Second International and its sections for the restoration of the unity of the working class in the struggle against the capitalist offensive, against Fascism, and against the danger of imperialist war". The word "revolution" scarcely appeared throughout the report. But an eloquent peroration ended with a call "*to sweep Fascism, and with it capitalism, from the face of the earth*". The ovation which had greeted Dimitrov's appearance was repeated when he sat down, and his name was coupled with Stalin's in the shouts of applause.[10]

[10] *Rundschau*, No. 39, August 18, 1935, pp. 1825–1847; the speech was promptly published in several languages, and escaped abbreviation in the Moscow editions of 1939. For the quotation from Lenin see *Polnoe Sobranie Sochinenii*, xxvi, 110.

From this moment, the impressive figure of Dimitrov dominated the congress. Thorez, in view of the pre-eminent role of the PCF in the birth of the popular front, had the honour of opening the discussion of Dimitrov's report. Again and again he eulogized Dimitrov, paid tribute to the Amsterdam-Pleyel movement, and ended with the ritual homage to Stalin. But his main theme was the triumphant evolution of the PCF. After the victory over the "sectarianism" of the Barbé–Célor group, and the criticisms levelled at the party by the twelfth IKKI in 1932, it had advanced by steady stages to the united, and then the popular, front against Fascism and against the threat of imperialist war against the USSR. It had become the standard bearer of the glorious national revolutionary tradition. "We will not abandon to our enemies [exclaimed Thorez] the tricolour, the flag of the great French revolution, or the Marseillaise, the song of the soldiers of the Convention." Thorez was one of the few who noted that Dimitrov had admitted the possibility of communist support for an anti-Fascist bourgeois government. Trotskyists, POPists and Doriot came under attack. It was a wholly conventional performance.[11] Gitton, the trade union spokesman in the PCF, reiterated later in the debate the plea already made by Thorez for trade union unity, and hoped for a merger of the CGTU and CGT at their forthcoming congresses.[12]

Pollitt, who spoke after Thorez for the CPGB, covered familiar ground: the maturing revolutionary crisis, the class struggle in Austria and Spain, the menace of Fascism and war, the growing strength of the USSR. He trounced the Labour Party and the Second International for their opposition to the united front, and wistfully hoped that the Revolutionary Policy Committee of the ILP might yet win over the "revolutionary workers" in that party. The purpose of the united front was the defeat of the national government and its replacement by a Labour government "not as an end in itself, *but as a means to an end*". The best hope of common action lay in the struggle against unemployment, which appealed to the trade unions, and in the struggle against Facism and war, which

---

[11] The most complete text of Thorez's speech is the one published in the French edition of the Comintern journal and in a pamphlet, reprinted in *Oeuvres de Maurice Thorez*, II, ix (1952), 95–153, and translated into English and German in the 1939 editions; the German version in *Rundschau*, No. 56, October 16, 1935, pp. 2305–2312, was evidently made from stenographic records, and contains some not very important omissions and variants. For the POP see p. 164 above.

[12] *Rundschau*, No. 58, October 23, 1935, pp. 2375–2378.

also drew in "the intelligentsia and the professional classes"; the CPGB must take the lead in the peace movement and "help it to realize its objective in preventing war".[13] Dutt, making his only appearance at a major Comintern gathering in Moscow, spoke later in the debate. He avoided any personal confession of error, but admitted that the "tendency" to brand "every contemporary reactionary phenomenon in the whole world", including the whole camp of the bourgeoisie, as "Fascist", had had "fairly serious consequences", and had led to hesitations in recognizing a broad united front as "the decisive demand for combating Fascism.[14]

Apart from Pieck, who spoke in the name of Comintern rather than of the KPD, the German delegates played an inconspicuous role at the congress. Florin in the debate on Dimitrov's report admitted the weakness of the KPD approach to the united front since 1932, and spoke of "sectarian errors after the establishment of the Hitler dictatorship". But he made no direct reference to divisions in the party, and unhesitatingly embraced the programme of "the struggle for peace, freedom and bread" and "the struggle for democratic people's rights against Fascism". This way led to an "anti-Fascist popular front".[15] Ulbricht, still masquerading as "Walter", who had a longer record of advocacy of the united front, was more incisive, and apparently evoked more enthusiastic applause. It depended on "the decisive overcoming of sectarianism" in the KPD, "how soon we shall succeed in eliminating movements of opposition on a large scale and in developing the struggle for democratic freedoms". He frequently quoted Dimitrov, and credited the German working class with "a deep longing for unity". A plea for trade union unity led to a guarded criticism of Profintern for not having made a quick enough transition from the methods of the RGO to a "broad activity in the trade unions for a policy of class struggle". But both Florin and

[13] The most complete text of the speech is the one published by the CPGB under the title *Unity against the National Government: Harry Pollitt's Speech* and included in a composite volume entitled *Report of the Seventh World Congress of the Communist International* (1936). The text in *Rundschau*, No. 56, October 16, 1935, pp. 2312–2316 is abbreviated, and some passages have been substantially re-written, probably owing to misunderstandings by interpreters or stenographers; the text in the 1939 editions has been further abbreviated from the *Rundschau* version.

[14] *Rundschau*, No. 58, October 23, 1935, pp. 2372–2375.

[15] *Ibid.* No. 56, October 16, 1935, pp. 2319–2322; the speech is considerably abbreviated in the 1939 editions.

Ulbricht found time to attack the SPD leaders congregated in Prague.[16]

More than 60 delegates in all spoke in the debate on Dimitrov's report. Lenski pointed to the illegal status of the KPP throughout its existence, and argued that the revolutionary movement in Poland was riddled with internal contradictions, between employed workers and the unemployed, between urban workers and peasants, between the Polish proletariat and the national movements in the Western Ukraine and Western Belorussia. He claimed, however, that united front tactics "in a new style" had been introduced in February 1934, and that the party had achieved successes in its strike policy and its appeal to the peasantry. He admitted that some parties, including the KPP, had wrongly attacked bourgeois democracy at a time when Fascism was already in power or was on the point of attaining it.[17] Gottwald, speaking on behalf of a party which had for some time displayed leanings towards a united front policy, and of a country which now recognised the need for good relations with the USSR, had an easier task. Communists did not approve of the participation of social-democrats in the bourgeois government. But the defence of the bourgeois democratic republic against the threat of Fascism was another matter; and he appealed for "the creation of a broad popular front against the capitalist offensive, against Fascism, for peace and against imperialist war, a popular front of labour, freedom and peace". He reminded the congress that the Czechoslovak Communist Party had won 850,000 votes in the recent elections; and he particularly condemned the oppression by the Czechoslovak Government of the German and Ukrainian national minorities.[18] For the PCI Grieco, emulating the orators of the PCF, struck a patriotic note: "Precisely because we are the heirs of great patriots like Garibaldi, we are against all imperialist war, and against all oppression of other peoples".[19] The

[16] *Ibid.* No. 58, October 23, 1935, pp. 2282–2285; neither Ulbricht's speech nor those of minor German delegates were included in the 1939 editions.

[17] *Ibid.* No. 56, October 16, 1935, pp. 2315–2318; this speech, and a comment on it by Dimitrov in his reply to the debate, did not appear in the 1939 editions of the proceedings, Lenski having been purged in the meanwhile.

[18] *Ibid.* No. 58, October 23, 1935, pp. 2392–2395.

[19] *Ibid.* No. 62, November 6, 1935, pp. 2499–2500; the brevity of the record suggests that this speech has been considerably abbreviated. Dozza (alias Furini), speaking earlier on Pieck's report, attributed the Fascist victory in 1922 to "the isolation [of the PCI] from the strata of workers who ought to have been its allies" (*ibid.* No. 50, September 25, 1935, p. 2161).

leader of the Spanish delegation, who spoke under the name
Ventura, celebrated the progress of the united front and of the
workers' and peasants' alliances in Spain, and made a formal appeal
to "Largo Caballero and his friends" to work together with the PCE
for the creation of a united revolutionary party of the proletariat".[20]
For the Swiss delegation Müller celebrated the success of united front
tactics based on the defence of democratic traditions and liberties
against Fascism, and deplored the resistance of Right trade union
leaders to the united front and to trade union unity.[21] Humbert-
Droz was deterred from speaking.[22] He would not have had the
tact to refrain from pointing out the identity of the policies now adopted with those for which he had been condemned in the past.

The two Comintern leaders who had from the first shown most
favour for the new policy, Manuilsky and Kuusinen, did not speak
in this debate. Manuilsky commemorated the fortieth anniversary
of the death of Engels, which occurred during the session, with a
long disquisition on contributions to Marxist theory from Engels,
through Lenin, to Stalin—an odd excrescence on the proceedings.[23]
Kuusinen reserved himself for the third item on the agenda,
Togliatti's report on the danger of imperialist war. Kolarov called
on the parties to overcome "sectarian" prejudices and recognize the
role of the peasantry in a united front against Fascism and war.[24]
Gopner, another Comintern official, blamed "sectarianism" for "an
underestimate of work among intellectuals" who were looked on
almost as "Right opportunists"; this was perhaps a faint criticism of
the devaluation in recent years of Münzenberg's activities.[25] The
speeches of those members of IKKI who had obstructed the
adoption of the new line must have been heard with curious
attention by those in the know. Bela Kun, speaking as a Hungarian
delegate, and silently abjuring his past heresies, declared that the

[20] *Ibid.* No. 60, October 30, 1945. Pieck in his report had sent greetings to "the
leader of the Spanish socialists, Largo Caballero, who is languishing in jail" (*ibid.*
No. 37, August 14, 1935, p. 1763); both these mentions were omitted from the 1939
editions.
[21] *Ibid.* No. 65, November 18, 1935, p. 2590.
[22] For his account of the congress in letters to his wife see J. Humbert-Droz, *Dix
Ans de Lutte Antifasciste* (Neuchatel, 1972), pp. 129–134.
[23] *Rundschau*, No. 40, August 20, 1935, pp. 1849–1859; the speech was included
in the 1939 edition of the proceedings.
[24] *Ibid.* No. 60, October 30, 1935, pp. 2443–2446.
[25] *Ibid.* No. 62, November 6, 1935, pp. 2513–2514; for Münzenberg see p. 385
above.

united front could not be restricted to workers who believed that only a proletarian revolution could relieve the miseries of the working class, but must embrace social-democratic and reformist workers who did not share these views. Rather grudgingly perhaps he admitted that "bourgeois democracy represents a different blend of deceit and violence from Fascism". Pyatnitsky, without so much as hinting at any change of line, spoke exclusively of the opportunity presented to communists by mass unemployment everywhere in Europe.[26] Knorin, the most stubborn adversary in Comintern of the new line, did not speak in this debate.

The astute Lozovsky had always injected a spice of ambiguity into his pronouncements. His conversion sounded less abrupt, and therefore more plausible. The movement for a united front between trade unions lagged behind the corresponding movement in the parties; and Lozovsky's lack of enthusiasm for the united front between parties or between Comintern and the Second International may have been a retarding factor. But Profintern had always professed the purpose, not of splitting the trade union movement, but of re-uniting it; the rider that this could occur only under communist leadership was more often understood than openly expressed. On March 7, 1935, when the united front campaign was in full swing, the bureau of Profintern addressed to the bureau of IFTU a proposal for common action: (1) to organize joint demonstrations on May 1 "against Fascism, the capitalist offensive and war"; (2) to promote the fusion of French and Spanish trade unions; (3) to promote a revival of the free trade unions in Germany.[27] This drew a conventional reply which reiterated earlier decisions of IFTU congresses and insisted on adherence to the Amsterdam International as the road to trade union unity.[28] No further steps towards unification of the trade unions, either on the national or international plane, were taken before the seventh

[26] Rundschau, No. 56, October 16, 1935, pp. 2323–2327; both speeches were excluded from the 1939 editions. Revai, like Kun a Hungarian official of Comintern, did not speak at the congress, but wrote to Dimitrov protesting against his "extremely dangerous" proposals, which substituted "the transitional programme of a popular front" for a proletarian dictatorship and a Soviet government (Georgii Dimitrov: Vydayushchiisya Revolyutsioner-Leninets (1974), p. 151).

[27] Rundschau, No. 13, March 14, 1935, p. 713; Kommunisticheskii Internatsional, 1935, No. 9, pp. 4–5; the German text is addressed to "Kollegen", the Russian to "Grazhdane".

[28] Rundschau, No. 17, April 11, 1935, p. 869.

congress, though joint action between workers belonging to Amsterdam and Profintern unions was sometimes achieved, especially in France and Czechoslovakia. But Dimitrov in his report had referred in laudatory terms to the Profintern initiative; and this gave some substance to Lozovsky's rhetorical appeal for trade union unity, formerly used mainly as a weapon of attack against the Amsterdam International. Lozovsky made some concessions. He admitted that the RGO in Germany, while it had had "positive sides" in the past, "cannot today serve as a model for the organization of our forces in the reformist trade unions". The notion that the illegal trade unions in Fascist countries, including Germany, should remain "organizations of cadres" was attributed to Brandler and the social-democrats. What was required was to build "mass organizations" embracing all workers irrespective of party. But he had little to say about the campaign against war, or cooperation with other peace-loving nations. "Unity of the international trade union movement on the basis of the class struggle" remained the goal.[29]

The long debate ended at last; and Dimitrov in his reply sought to apply in practice the principles announced in his report. While proclaiming the need for "the weapon of Marxist–Leninist analysis", he condemned those who used such slogans as "a revolutionary way out of the crisis" without regard to concrete conditions, and lost "the broad perspective of the struggle"; and later in the speech he aroused the mirth of the audience by derisively quoting such well-worn phrases as "the conquest of a majority of the working class" and "to raise the struggle to a higher stage". He reverted to the crux of the popular front—the relation of communists to bourgeois democracy; and he found a quotation from an article of Lenin of 1916:

> It would be a radical error to suppose that the struggle for democracy can divert the proletariat from the socialist revolution. . . . Just as one cannot have a victorious socialism without realizing full democracy, so the proletariat cannot prepare itself for victory over the bourgeoisie without waging a comprehensive, consistent and revolutionary struggle for democracy.[30]

[29] *Ibid.* No. 62, November 6, 1935, pp. 2495–2499. This speech did not appear in the 1939 editions; by that time Profintern had been liquidated, though Lozovsky personally survived.

[30] Lenin, *Polnoe Sobranie Sochinenii*, xxvii, 253.

Dimitrov envisaged progress through successive stages: the united front from below beginning in the localities; the united front from above; unity of the trade unions; the drawing into the front of other anti-Fascist parties; and, finally, "the fully developed popular front from above and below". He tackled the complex question of the potential formation of a united front government. In Fascist countries, this could be conceived as part of the process of overthrowing the Fascist dictatorship. In bourgeois democratic countries, a popular front government might be the prelude to a democratic dictatorship of workers and peasants. The relation of communists to bourgeois democracy was "not in all conditions the same". Dimitrov ended by stressing the international significance of the movement: "Never has the public opinion of the world displayed so lively an interest in an international communist congress as in our present congress." Another eloquent peroration, which once more included an invocation of Stalin's name, was followed by an ovation which lasted "for 15 or 20 minutes".[31] The sincerity of the enthusiasm, and the strength of Dimitrov's dominance over his audience, need not be doubted. Delegates could feel that he had broken out of the doctrinal strait-jacket which had so long inhibited their efforts to win the support of their compatriots, and provided the platform for a mass appeal which would end their painful isolation. "Dimitrov's report and reply to the debate," proclaimed *Pravda*, "are among the most important documents of the workers' movement."[32]

Togliatti came next with his report on the obligations of communist parties in face of the danger of imperialist wars. The Japanese adventure in Manchuria, the collapse of the Versailles system and the Nazi menace in Europe, the Italian invasion of Abyssinia, all sounded a note of warning. The most contentious passage in the report was the defence of the "peace policy" of the USSR, involving its entry into the League of Nations, the pacts with France and Czechoslovakia, and the encouragement given to the military build-up of capitalist countries opposed to Nazi Germany. Togliatti was an able and persuasive advocate. He bolstered his argument with copious quotations from Lenin, who (in turn quoting Engels) had recognized the legitimacy of "wars of defence" on behalf of an already victorious socialist regime. Lenin had

[31] *Rundschau*, No. 66, November 19, 1935, pp. 2601–2610.
[32] *Pravda*, August 15, 1935.

subscribed to the principle of "military agreements with one imperialist coalition against another in cases where such an agreement, without undermining the foundations of Soviet power, could strengthen its position and paralyse the pressure of some imperialist Power on it"; and he added, harking back to Brest-Litovsk, that, "by utilizing the mutual contradictions between the imperialist Powers, we were able to hold on even at that time when the Red Army was not yet formed". Togliatti rejected the "demagogy" of the pacifist movement in some of its manifestations. "We are no anarchists", he exclaimed, and "boycott of mobilization, boycott of the army, sabotage in the factories, refusal of military service etc.—all these are not our forms of the struggle against war". He ended with an impassioned appeal to the workers of the world to rally to the defence of the USSR in the event of imperialist aggression against it, and with a tribute to Stalin, fulsome even by the standards of the seventh congress:

> We have a leader, comrade Stalin, of whom we know that always, in the most difficult moments, he has ever found the line which led to victory; our leader is comrade Stalin who, during the years of the civil war, was sent by Lenin to all those fronts where victory seemed to be eluding the workers of the USSR. And everywhere, from Perm to Tsaritsyn, from Petrograd to the southern front, he restored the position, defeated the enemy, and made victory secure.[33]

Tito, who met Togliatti for the first time at the end of the congress, paid tribute many years later to his "critical spirit" and "rare intelligence"; he was "not like other leaders who thought that all and everything was going well".[34] An unusually wide gulf separated Togliatti's private from his public utterances.

The discussion on Togliatti's report was less impressive than that which followed Dimitrov's. Less than half the number of delegates

---

[33] *Rundschau*, No. 52, October 2, 1935, pp. 2197–2218; P. Togliatti, *Opere*, III (1973), ii, 730–805. The quotations from Lenin, dating from 1916, 1918 and 1920, are in *Polnoe Sobranie Sochinenii*, xxx, 133, xxxvi, 323, xlii, 100; the Engels quotation was from a letter to Kautsky of September 12, 1882.

[34] Interview in the Yugoslav party journal *Politika* reprinted in *Unità*, August 23, 1970. Tito was present at the congress, but did not speak; the leader of the Yugoslav delegation was Gorkić, who made a colourless speech (*Rundschau*, No. 60, October 30, 1935, pp. 2441–2443).

spoke; most of these were delegates of lower standing. The most important of them was Marty. The PCF was the party which had been most disturbed by the implications of the Franco–Soviet pact; and Marty bluntly attacked "certain renegades" who criticized the pact as "an alliance between a proletarian government and an imperialist government". He gave unqualified and enthusiastic support to the pact, though he admitted that this did not imply confidence in the government of Laval, who had recently concluded an agreement in Rome giving Mussolini a free hand in Abyssinia—a point conveniently ignored by Togliatti. But nothing was missing in Marty's final invocation of the glories of the Red Army, and of the national tradition of the revolutionary armies of France.[35] Shields, a CPGB delegate, accused the British Government of furthering and supporting German rearmament; and a Spanish delegate accused the Spanish Government of seeking an alliance with "the English–German–Japanese bloc".[36] Two Comintern delegates who had not taken part in the debate on Dimitrov's report now spoke: Knorin and Kuusinen. Knorin did not refer to past controversies, remained on safe ground in advocating the defence of the USSR against the Nazi menace, and paid a personal tribute to Dimitrov. Kuusinen was mainly concerned to extend to the youth organizations the appeal made by Togliatti to the parties, though he admitted that they had to fear competition from Fascist youth organizations which purported to speak in the name of the young generation and to pay more attention than the communists to its immediate interests. While nobody in the debate had challenged Togliatti's conclusions, he found it necessary in his reply to refute those "rotten, fatalistic assumptions which result from an over-simplified interpretation of Marx's correct assertion of the inseparability of capitalism from war", and therefore dismiss as hopeless the struggle for peace.[37] The resolution on the report expressly repudiated "the slanderous assertion that communists desire war, expecting it to

[35] *Ibid.* No. 72, December 11, 1935, pp. 2765–2771; some stylistic amendments, but no changes of substance, were made in the 1939 editions.

[36] *Ibid.* No. 72, December 11, 1935, pp. 2772–2773, 2792.

[37] For the debate and Togliatti's reply see *ibid.* No. 72, December 11, 1935, pp. 2765–2796, No. 74, December 18, 1935, pp. 2845–2859; Togliatti's reply in *Opere*, III (1973), ii, 806–814, is erroneously described as the closing speech of the congress. Marty's and Kuusinen's speeches appeared in the 1939 editions; Knorin had been liquidated in the meanwhile, and none of the other speeches were thought worth reprinting in 1939.

bring about revolution". It contained the only reference in the resolutions of the congress to Mussolini's impending invasion of Abyssinia, which was said to be creating "a new tension in relations between the imperialist Great Powers".

The fourth and last report was Manuilsky's on the "Achievements of Socialist Construction in the Soviet Union". He found no difficulty in contrasting the immense advance to socialism registered in the USSR since the last congress seven years earlier— the victory of socialism in one country, which he was careful to attribute to both Lenin and Stalin—with the crisis of decaying capitalism, which had brought in its train mass unemployment and the threat of imperialist war. Communist parties were adjured to seek allies in "the main masses of the peasantry, the urban petty bourgeoisie threatened with ruin, the intellectuals etc.". The struggle was for genuine people's democracy, for the freedom of nations, and above all peace among nations. Echoing Togliatti, he contemptuously dismissed "fatalistic assumptions that it is impossible to prevent war, that the struggle against the preparation of war is futile".[38] Manuilsky had left little unsaid, and the congress was entering its fourth week. No discussion of this report was deemed necessary; only Marty responded "in the name of several delegates" with a brief eulogy of the USSR and of the victory of socialism.[39]

Resolutions on the four reports had been drafted many weeks in advance.[40] The resolution on Pieck's report was adopted at the end of the debate on it on August 1, 1935. When all the debates were over, the congress adjourned for two days while the finishing touches were put on the resolutions on the other three reports. These were finally adopted on August 20; and the resolutions were promptly published in several languages.[41] Since the original drafts were not published, it is uncertain what changes were made at the congress. But it is known that, at the instance of the Russian delegation, references to a current "revolutionary crisis" were removed, and other indiscretions corrected "in the same spirit". The headline of one section of the main resolution "Fascism and the Growth of Revolutionary Forces" was amended to read "Fascism

[38] *Rundschau*, No. 47, September 18, 1935, pp. 2073–2087; the report appeared unabbreviated in the 1939 editions.
[39] *Ibid*. No. 74, December 18, 1935, pp. 2859–2860.
[40] See p. 148, note 4 above.
[41] They appeared in *Rundschau*, No. 45, September 11, 1935, pp. 2029–2040.

and the Working Class".[42] Nuances of terminology are difficult to detect. But Pieck's opening report contained uninhibited expressions of faith in the impending revolution such as are not found in the other reports;[43] and the resolution on his report, while it echoed the call for "the united front of the proletariat and the popular front of all workers against the capitalist offensive, against Fascism and the danger of a new war", alone ended with an appeal to unite the workers under the influence of communist parties in order "in this way to create the conditions which are necessary for the victory of the proletarian revolution".

With the appearance of Dimitrov on the congress platform, the emphasis shifted. The main target was no longer bourgeois capitalism, but Fascist imperialism; the anti-Fascist front was no longer exclusively proletarian. Even the ritual invocation of proletarian revolution in the peroration of his report carried a significant preface:

> We should be no revolutionary Marxist–Leninists, no true disciples of Marx–Engels–Lenin–Stalin, if we did not adjust our policy and tactics to the changed situation and to the reorientations which are taking place in the workers' movement.[44]

In this spirit the resolution on Dimitrov's report concentrated on the major practical objectives:

> The defence of the immediate economic and political interests of the working class, its defence against Fascism, must be the starting-point, and constitute the chief content, of the united front of workers in all capitalist countries.

Sectarian errors in the trade union movement were to be eliminated, and communists were to struggle "in every country and on an international scale for unified class trade unions as one of the most important bulwarks of the working class against the offensive

[42] K. Shirinya, *Strategiya i Taktika Kominterna* (1979), pp. 65, 73, quoting archives.

[43] References by Pieck to the ripening of revolutionary crises in Germany, Poland, China and Spain (*Rundschau*, No. 37, August 14, 1935, pp. 1757–1758) were omitted from the 1939 editions of the proceedings—perhaps because none of these hopes had been realized.

[44] *Rundschau*, No. 39, August 17, 1935, p. 1846.

of capital and of Fascism". The resolution led up to an unprecedented offer to "*enter into negotiations with the Second International*" in order to promote "unity of action of the working class" against "the offensive of capital, Fascism, and the danger of imperialist war". Neither Togliatti nor Manuilsky had occasion to broach the theme of world revolution; and the resolutions on their respective reports did little more than summarize what they had said.

The seventh congress was primarily a European occasion, with Japanese expansionism as a Far Eastern counterpart to German expansionism in Europe. But the problem of fitting the traditional call for the liberation of colonial peoples from the yoke of imperialism into the framework of a world-wide anti-Fascist popular front could not be altogether avoided. The ground had been prepared in an unusually outspoken article by a member of the Far Eastern section of the Comintern secretariat in the Comintern journal entitled "The Struggle for a United Anti-Imperialist Front in Colonial and Semi-Colonial Countries". The struggle of communist parties in the colonial world was now aimed "primarily against imperialism"; every effort should be directed to "the creation of a broad anti-imperialist front". Such slogans as "Soviet power" or "confiscation of landlords' land without compensation" should be avoided if they stood in the way of "joint action with the national bourgeoisie against imperialism".[45] At the congress Dimitrov hailed "the oppressed nations of the colonies and semi-colonies" as allies of the proletariat, and appealed for "an anti-imperialist united front".[46] Wang Ming devoted the first part of a long speech (the second part dealt exclusively with China) to the familiar theme of the oppressed peoples of colonial countries, and tediously harked back to the forgotten heresies of "decolonization", propounded by "renegades (Roy etc.)", and "organized capitalism".[47] Two delegates spoke in the name of the "Arab countries". The first,

[45] *Kommunisticheskii Internatsional*, 1935, No. 20–21, pp. 103–111.

[46] *Rundschau*, No. 39, August 17, 1935, pp. 1831, 1840.

[47] The general part of the speech was briefly reported *ibid.* No. 38, August 15, 1935, pp. 1791–1792, the Chinese section far more fully *ibid.* No. 58, October 23, 1935, pp. 2385–2390. A version which differed widely in many passages from the *Rundschau* version appeared in the 1939 editions of the proceedings (*VII Kongress der Kommunistischen Internationale* (Moscow, 1939), pp. 278–310); the speech was published as a pamphlet in Russian after the congress, and may have been rewritten for this occasion. For the heresies cited, both associated with Bukharin, see *Foundations of a Planned Economy, 1926–1929*, Vol. 3, pp. 923–927.

adhering unimpeachably to the new line, referred to "the coming democratic-bourgeois revolution" in Arab lands, and urged communists to "support anti-imperialist demands put forward by reformist nationalists". The second argued that, if the imperialists dragged the Arab countries into war, communists should try to convert that war into "a victorious anti-imperialist war of national liberation".[48] The speech of an Egyptian delegate was not reported, presumably because he rejected a united front with the national bourgeoisie.[49]

Care was taken not to ruffle the susceptibilities of those imperialist Powers whose support Comintern was seeking to woo for the anti-Fascist front. The records fail to reveal the presence of any Indian or Indonesian delegate at the congress. Delegates of Syria and of Indo-China addressed it; but the brief published records of their speeches do not refer to the suffering of their peoples under French imperialist rule.[50] The question was avoided by all the delegates from countries possessing colonies except the Netherlands delegate, who in the debate on Togliatti's report showed some embarrassment over his nation's "colonial possessions in the Far East and in America", the defence of which was "dependent on the imperialist Great Powers".[51] The Brazilian delegate, the most articulate among several Latin American orators, admitted that it was only in the previous autumn that the Brazilian party had taken its "first, still rather insecure and indeterminate, steps towards a united anti-imperialist popular front" by joining with other parties in an "Alliance of National Liberation".[52] None of these utterances

[48] *Rundschau*, No. 60, October 30, 1935, p. 2447, No. 72, December 11, 1935, p. 2789; the second delegate, Yussef, had spoken previously in the name of the Palestine communist party, mentioning "English imperialism", but directing his main protest against the Jewish leadership of the party, which resisted "Arabization" (*ibid*. No. 54, October 8, 1965, p. 2261).

[49] B. Leibzon and K. Shirinya, *Povorot v Politike Kominterna* (2nd ed., 1975), pp. 272–273; the Egyptian party was said at this time to have been paralysed by an "ultra-Left deviation" (*ibid*. p. 280).

[50] *Rundschau*, No. 49, September 24, 1935, pp. 2141–2142, No. 50, September 25, 1935, pp. 2145–2146.

[51] *Ibid*. No. 72, December 11, 1935, p. 2784.

[52] *Ibid*. No. 62, November 6, 1935, pp. 2491–2492. The reference is to a congress of Latin American communist parties at Montevideo in October 1934, at which the principal speeches were delivered by the Brazilian and Cuban delegates; hostility to the United States as the protagonist of imperialism seems to have been the main unifying theme (*Kommunisticheskii Internatsional*, 1935, No. 9, pp. 25–52). Its decisions were formally ratified by the central committee of the Brazilian party in May 1935 (*ibid*. 1935, No. 26, p. 60).

excited any interest at the congress. The call in the resolution on Dimitrov's report for a struggle "against the increasing imperialist exploitation, against cruel enslavement, for the expulsion of the imperialists, for national independence" was routine business. This was the year of the liquidation of the long moribund League against Imperialism.[53]

China was another matter. In the world spectrum as seen from Moscow, China could never be a negligible factor; and her current role as the victim of an act of imperialist aggression which also threatened the USSR heightened the tension. The liberation of the Chinese people from the imperialist yoke was an essential element in the programme of a communist party, especially now that Japan was pilloried as a major Fascist Power. But the slogan of a united popular or national front against the Fascist aggression was difficult to invoke in a situation where the "national" Chinese Government in Nanking was not only less than lukewarm in its resistance to the Japanese invader, but was also engaged in a war of extermination against the CCP, the Red Army and the Chinese Soviet Government. In these conditions, it was particularly embarrassing that the elusive CCP, since its withdrawal into the Soviet region in 1933, had shown little eagerness to comply with the directives of Comintern, and that all communication between the CCP and Moscow had now been severed. Comintern had no authorized or reliable spokesman in China.

The gap had somehow to be filled. When Hitler crushed the KPD, and a group of its leaders, having taken refuge in Paris, sought to assert their independence of Comintern, the secretariat moved quickly to establish a new party central committee and politburo in Moscow.[54] A similar device was now employed to supply the deficiency of the CCP. Apparently while the seventh congress of Comintern was in session, a manifesto addressed to "all citizens, all sons and daughters of our fatherland" was issued in Moscow in the name of the central executive committee of the Chinese Soviet Republic and the central committee of the CCP. It contained an emotional appeal to organize national resistance to Japan. Chiang Kai-shek, Wang Ching-wei and their followers were denounced as traitors to their country. But a solemn assurance was offered by the Chinese Soviet Government and the CCP that "if the Kuomintang

[53] See p. 385, note 4 above.
[54] See p. 142 above.

armies will stop the offensive against our Soviet regions, if they will carry on the struggle against Japanese imperialism", then the Red Army "will be the first to stretch out a hand for a joint armed struggle to save the fatherland". The manifesto ended by calling for an "All-China United People's Government of National Defence" and an "All-China United Anti-Japanese Army".[55] A historian who had access to Comintern archives later hinted at some of the pressures applied at this time:

> At the congress a potential anti-imperialist, anti-feudal pro-gramme for China was discussed, and advice was given to revise certain measures of the CCP, in order to impart to its policy at the present stage an outspokenly popular national character.[56]

What however emerged most clearly from the debates of the seventh congress of Comintern was an almost total ignorance, or lack of understanding, of Chinese affairs. The report prepared by IKKI for the congress admitted "the loss of a substantial part of the central Soviet region", but argued not unreasonably that "the strategic plan of General von Seeckt and Chiang Kai-shek" to destroy the Red Army had been defeated.[57] Even this relatively sober estimate had, however, not been digested, or perhaps read, by most of the delegates. Pieck in his opening report to the congress professed to believe that all the Kuomintang offensives against the

---

[55] *Kommunisticheskii Internatsional*, 1935, No. 33–34, pp. 106–111, where a Chinese journal, presumably published in Moscow, is cited as the source; *Rundschau*, No. 71, December 5, 1935, pp, 2755–2757. O. Braun, *Chinesische Aufzeichnungen* (1973), pp. 183–184, describes the manifesto as being "in sharp contradiction to the decisions of the Mao-kung conferences", and dates it August 1, 1935; this is the sole authority for the date, which may be regarded with some scepticism. The manifesto was not mentioned at the seventh congress, and no publication of it earlier than November 1935 has been traced. Another document was, however, certainly published at the time of the congress. *Rundschau*, No. 34, August 1, 1935, p. 1690, printed a declaration purporting to emanate from "a united peoples' front" against "Japanese imperialism and its accomplice Chiang Kai-shek". It also celebrated "the victorious march" of the Red Army which had extended Soviet authority to 19 provinces. It bore the signature of Mao Tse-tung and Chang Kuo-t'ao for the Soviet Government, and Chu Teh and Chou En-lai for the Red Army, and was dated June 15, 1935—a moment when the two Red armies were converging in Szechwan. Neither the original of this remarkable forgery, nor any reference to it in subsequent literature, has been found.

[56] *Kommunisticheskii Internatsional: Kratkii Istoricheskii Ocherk* (1969), p. 413.

[57] *Kommunistische Internationale vor dem VII Weltkongress* (1935), p. 552.

Soviet regions had been triumphantly beaten off. A Chinese "representative of the Soviet areas" painted a rosy picture, ignoring altogether the abandonment of the whole Kiangsi region in the previous autumn; another unidentified Chinese delegate mentioned the withdrawal, but refused to admit that the Red Army had sustained a defeat.[58] Dimitrov, though not personally involved in Far Eastern affairs, could not avoid the Chinese imbroglio in his report, and called briefly for "the broadest anti-imperialist united front against Japanese imperialism and its Chinese agents, together with all organized forces in China which are ready really to carry on the struggle to save their country and their people".[59]

The major pronouncement on China was reserved for Wang Ming in his capacity as delegate of the CCP to IKKI. He declared that China, as the result of Japanese aggression, was passing through "an unprecedented national crisis"; and he denounced Chiang Kai-shek, Wang Ching-wei and other Kuomintang leaders as "traitors to their country". He condemned the past errors of the CCP in failing to support the nationalist army which had attempted to oppose the Japanese landing in Shanghai in January 1932, and again to support the rebellious nationalist army in Fukien at the end of 1933. Some comrades, he added, did not understand that the anti-imperialist united front had to be applied in a new way. But Wang's knowledge of current events in China was apparently as slight as that of other delegates. He managed to depict the withdrawal of the Red Army from "the former central Soviet region" and its "heroic march from Kiangsi to north-west China" as "a new great victory"; and he cited Mao Tse-tung (whose name was greeted with applause), Chu Teh and Po Ku indiscriminately in a long list of "party and state leaders". Otherwise the only member of the CCP mentioned in the speech was the long discredited Li Li-san, who was once more the target of fierce denunciation. The key-note of the later published version of the speech was an injunction to the CCP, "*in common with the Chinese Government, to approach the whole Chinese people, all parties, groups, armies, mass organizations, and all known political figures engaged in public life, with the offer to organize together with us an all-China united people's government of national defence*". But it is doubtful whether these words

---

[58] *Rundschau*, No. 37, August 14, 1935, p. 1766, No. 49, September 24, 1935, pp. 2136–2138, 2143.

[59] *Ibid.* No. 39, August 17, 1935, p. 1840.

were uttered at the congress itself.[60] In any case, no appeal was addressed at the congress to Kuomintang, since the resolution on Dimitrov's report was directed "against Japanese imperialism and its Chinese lackeys"; and the resolution on Togliatti's report named Kuomintang with "Japanese and other imperialists" as enemies of "the Red Army of the Soviet Government". The issue of relations with Kuomintang, like others arising from the complex situation in the Far East, was not raised at the congress.[61] For the Japanese delegation, Nosaka (*alias* Okano) confined himself to a fanciful picture of the prowess of the Japanese party, and Yamamoto (*alias* Tanaka) celebrated its advance towards a realization of the united front, while admitting that "sectarianism is not yet overcome".[62]

The last duty of the seventh and last congress of Comintern was, as usual, and ironically in retrospect, to elect an IKKI to serve until the next congress, and to instruct it to prepare amendments to the statutes in time for the next congress, which was destined never to take place.[63] After the adoption of the resolutions, Dimitrov appropriately closed the proceedings with another eloquent speech amid scenes of frenzied enthusiasm.[64] The newly elected IKKI met at once to elect a presidium and a secretariat. Stalin, Manuilsky, Kuusinen and Dimitrov were elected to a presidium of nineteen, together with leaders of the principal parties, Thorez, Cachin and Marty, Pieck, Pollitt, Togliatti, Gottwald, Lenski and Wang Ming; Lozovsky, who had been a full member of IKKI and of its presidium for many years, was reduced to the rank of candidate member of both. Bela Kun, though re-elected to IKKI, was dropped from the presidium. Dimitrov was appointed secretary-

[60] This passage does not appear in the *Rundschau* text (see p. 422, note 58 above), but is in the 1939 editions (*VII Kongress der Kommunistischen Internationale* (1939), p. 285).

[61] Dimitrov a year later remarked that Comintern had been "two or three years late" in applying the new policy to China (*Georgii Dimitrov: Vydayushchiisya Deyatel' Kommunisticheskogo Dvizheniya* (1972), p. 202.

[62] *Rundschau*, No. 49, September 24, 1935, pp. 2122–2126, No. 62, November 6, 1935, pp. 2511–2512.

[63] For the elections to IKKI see *Pravda*, August 21, 1935; Pyatnitsky and Knorin significantly lost their membership. The resolution was published with the other resolutions of the congress, but was not included in the 1939 editions.

[64] For the final scene see *Rundschau*, No. 43, August 29, 1935, pp. 1974–1975, for Dimitrov's speech *ibid*. No. 74, December 18, 1935, pp. 2861–2864.

general, the other secretaries being Manuilsky, Kuusinen, Togliatti, Pieck, Marty and Gottwald.[65] *Pravda*, as the congress closed, summed up its achievements. It had been a congress of "genuine Bolshevik self-criticism", which had proclaimed a change in tactics. It had announced "the triumph of unity between the proletariat of the country of victorious socialism, the Soviet Union, and the proletariat of the capitalist world still struggling for its liberation". It had "laid the foundations for a comprehensive mobilization of the forces of all workers for the struggle against capital, such as had never been seen in the history of the struggle of the working class".[66] One question had been passed over rather lightly at the congress. Two days after its close, the organizers convened an "international trade union conference" to plead the cause of trade union unity. Lozovsky made a report, 60 delegates spoke in the discussion, and Kuusinen in winding up the debate pointed out that only the PCF had made some progress towards trade union unity; other parties had formulated no concrete plans.[67]

Nobody in retrospect will deny that the seventh congress marked a turning-point in the history of Comintern. But the question of whether the policies promulgated by it were the logical culmination of what had gone before, or a sharp reversal of the principles to which the institution had hitherto been pledged, is less easy to answer. No speaker even hinted that the congress was rejecting or revising the conclusions of its predecessor. The congress was nicely balanced between desire to demonstrate the continuity of the new with the old, and desire to acclaim fruitful innovations in the practice of the parties and of Comintern. Very many orators invoked the authority of Lenin, and quoted passages from his works in justification of the stand taken at the congress. Lenin, while criticizing the concessions made in 1922 to the spurious "Two-and-a-half International", had nevertheless proclaimed and introduced into the party vocabulary "the tactics of the united front".[68] But he had also prepared the way for tactical compromise with national

---

[65] *Rundschau*, No. 43, August 29, 1935, p. 1973.
[66] *Pravda*, August 21, 1935.
[67] *Voprosy Istorii KPSS*, 1969, No. 3, pp. 3, 6–9.
[68] Lenin, *Polnoe Sobranie Sochinenii*, xlv, 144; for Lenin's article see *The Bolshevik Revolution, 1917–1923*, Vol. 3, p. 411.

allegiances and with bourgeois democracy.[69] The resolution on Dimitrov's report alluded to another famous article of Lenin when it described "sectarianism" as "no longer an 'infantile disease' of the communist movement, but a deeply rooted defect". Not much help could be found in Stalin's rare and evasive pronouncements on the united front. But the editors of the Comintern journal disinterred an interview by him in 1925 to a member of the KPD in which he had exhorted the party "to combine in its work an uncompromising revolutionary ardour (not to be confused with revolutionary adventurism) with a maximum of flexibility and manoeuvrability (not to be confused with conformism)". This was solemnly rehearsed in an article in the Comintern journal on the eve of the congress as guidance on how to "master all forms of struggle and organization", and win over the toiling masses under the leadership of the proletariat for the overthrow of capitalism.[70] The quotation was repeated in Dimitrov's report to the congress[71]—a tribute not so much to its relevance as to the lack of other material.

If however the conformity of the policies and prescriptions now proclaimed with those of the past was still implied and asserted, enthusiasm for the new course that was being set emerged more and more clearly as the keynote of the congress. It was this which inspired the frenzied and prolonged ovations—such as had been heard at no previous congress—which greeted Dimitrov's utterances. The new course, which would enable communist parties to emerge from their isolation and cooperate with other Left parties and groups in the struggle against Fascism, had implications which were not clearly stated. In opposition to those who, like Kun, believed that capitalism itself, and not its incidental offshoot Fascism, should still be the main target of attack, Dimitrov, in unpublished notes for his report at the congress, argued that "the proletarian revolution—proletarian in its character and in its driving forces—may begin as a people's anti-Fascist revolution led by the proletariat".[72] What was not said was that the new course implied the postponement of the pursuit of proletarian revolution in favour of an aim—the defeat of Fascism—which, though perhaps a

[69] For Dimitrov's and Togliatti's quotations from Lenin see pp. 412–414 above.

[70] *Kommunisticheskii Internatsional*, 1935, No. 21–22, p. 11; for the interview, which was published in *Pravda*, February 3, 1925, see Stalin, *Sochineniya*, vii, 39.

[71] *Rundschau*, No. 39, August 17, 1935, p. 1845.

[72] *Georgii Dimitrov: Vydayuschiisya Revolyutsioner–Leninets* (1974), p. 149; for Kun's views see pp. 128–129 above.

necessary prelude to proletarian revolution, was not in itself revolutionary, and could be pursued in alliance with declared enemies of revolution. The logical outcome of this unconfessed dilemma was the silent relegation of the proletarian revolution to as inconspicuous a place as was decently possible in the proceedings and resolutions of the seventh congress. Lenin's "united front" had been designed to hasten the advent of the proletarian revolution. Dimitrov's "popular front" was designed to keep the proletarian revolution in abeyance in order to deal with the pressing emergency of Fascism. It is not surprising that the conclusion was unpalatable to some stalwarts in Comintern, and to Trotsky and his followers, as well as to a group of dissident socialists from ten countries, who met in London under the aegis of the ILP while the seventh congress was in progress, condemned both the Second and the Third Internationals, urged workers to reject all calls for unity with the capitalist class or with capitalist governments, and proclaimed that "the results of the October revolution in the USSR can be defended only through the development of revolutionary policy and activity in all countries".[73]

In official circles outside the USSR the proceedings had attracted little interest. Only the American press gleefully reported the attacks on their country by American delegates at the congress, and whipped up the indignation of a sensitive sector of public opinion. At the end of the congress Bullitt delivered a note to the Soviet Government protesting against "this flagrant violation" of the Soviet pledges of non-interference in the affairs of the United States, and received in reply from Narkomindel the expected disclaimer of responsibility for the proceedings of Comintern. The Secretary of State in Washington issued a solemn warning to the Soviet Government of the consequences of "permitting activities in its territory involving interference in the internal affairs of the United States".[74] There the matter rested. The press of other countries had paid scant attention to the congress; and their diplomatic representatives in Moscow confined themselves to verbal protests, or ignored the whole affair.

The removal of world revolution from the centre of the stage to the wings permanently affected the status of Comintern, though the

---

[73] *New Leader*, August 16, 1935.

[74] *Foreign Relations of the United States: the Soviet Union, 1933–1939* (1952), pp. 250–259; *Dokumenty Vneshnei Politiki SSSR*, xviii (1972), 474–477.

consequences of the shift were perhaps not noticed in the enthusiasm of the congress. World revolution had always played a cardinal role in Bolshevik ideology; and to dismantle or degrade the institution which stood for it would at this stage have been unthinkable.[75] But the seventh congress had brought into the open the deep-seated trend, long apparent to the discerning critic, to identify the aims of Comintern with the policies of the USSR; and, after the paradoxical success of the congress, the institution seemed to have lost its reality. It was significant that no further congress, and no major session of IKKI, was ever again summoned. Comintern continued to discharge subordinate functions, while the spotlight of publicity was directed elsewhere. Trotsky's verdict that the seventh congress would "pass into history as the liquidation congress" of Comintern[76] was not altogether unfair. The seventh congress pointed the way to the *dénouement* of 1943.

[75] Trotsky wrote in July 1935 that Stalin could not have abandoned Comintern unless he had been prepared "to appear in the character of a consistent Bonaparte, i.e. break openly with the tradition of October and place some kind of crown on his head" (*Byulleten' Oppozitsii* (Paris), No. 44, July 1935, p. 13).

[76] *Ibid.* No. 46, December 1935, p. 12.

NOTE A

STALIN'S LETTER TO *PROLETARSKAYA REVOLYUTSIYA*

A curious episode of 1931–1932 illustrates both the constant preoccupation in Moscow with the German question and the personal adulation of Stalin now becoming mandatory in foreign communist parties. The hard line adopted by Comintern in 1928, and the sharpening of hostilities between communists and social-democrats, led to a burst of historical research into relations between Bolsheviks and social-democrats before 1914. At the end of 1928, the Lenin Institute set up a group of historians to study the role of the Bolsheviks in the pre-war socialist movement, and the Communist Academy a group on German social-democracy; the secretary of the latter group was a young party historian named Slutsky. From 1929 onwards these questions were ventilated in several controversial articles in *Proletarskaya Revolyutsiya*, a journal published under party auspices and devoted mainly to the history of the revolution, and *Istorik-Marksist*, the journal of the Society of Marxist historians, as well as in debates of the Institute of Red Professors. The embarrassment underlying these discussions, which could not be totally concealed, was that Lenin before 1914 accepted the authority of Kautsky, then widely recognized as the leading exponent of Marxist orthodoxy and theorist of the SPD, and showed little sympathy for those, including both Rosa Luxemburg and Radek, who criticized the party leadership from the Left.[1] In the autumn of 1930 *Proletarskaya Revolyutsiya* published an article by Slutsky mildly criticizing Lenin for having underestimated the danger of "centrism" in the SPD (Kautsky) and failed consistently to support the Left wing (Luxemburg, Parvus); Slutsky hinted that this attitude was influenced by "fractional considerations", i.e. the struggle of the Bolsheviks against the Mensheviks. An editorial note was appended to the article treating it as a serious contribution to the discussion, but recording disagreement "on the question of Lenin's appraisal of international opportunism".[2]

That Slutsky's article became a historical landmark was due to extraneous circumstances. Since the end of 1928 literature had been subjected to firm party control exercised through the Russian Association of Proletarian Writers (RAPP).[3] Economic research had been harnessed to the orthodoxy of the Five-Year Plan. But no attempt had yet been made to impose ideological uniformity on such learned disciplines as history and philosophy. During the nineteen-twenties Pokrovsky had been recognized as the doyen of Marxist historians. By 1929 not only had bourgeois historians been silenced, but younger Marxists were beginning to challenge Pokrovsky's orthodoxy; and during the next two years violent controversies raged between rival schools on questions of Russian historical

---

[1] For these developments see an article by John Barber in *Soviet Studies*, xxviii (1976), No. 1, pp. 27–29.

[2] *Proletarskaya Revolyutsiya*, 1930, No. 6, pp. 38–73.

[3] See *Foundations of a Planned Economy, 1926–1929*, Vol. 2, pp. 413–418.

428

development. In 1931 the imputation of Trotskyism was introduced into the debate.[4] *Proletarskaya Revolyutsiya* published a long reply to Slutsky by another member of the Communist Academy group defending Lenin against the charge of undue indulgence to "centrism". This for the first time detected a Trotskyist taint in Slutsky's argument.[5]

The polemical tone of these exchanges, and the sly attempt to associate opponents with political heterodoxy, invited intervention by the party authorities, particularly in a period of acute tension in the economy and in the party.[6] In the autumn of 1931, when a purge of historians in the Communist Academy and in the Academy of Sciences was already in progress,[7] the party central committee addressed a protest to *Proletarskaya Revolyutsiya* against its publication a year earlier of Slutsky's article, though why this article was singled out as a target has never been explained. At what point Stalin personally intervened is not clear. But in October 1931 *Proletarskaya Revolyutsiya* published a lengthy letter from him, angrily attacking both Slutsky and the editorial board which had published his article. Slutsky had not explicitly drawn any moral from his criticism. But Stalin now did so by asserting that "what had impelled the editorial board to take this incorrect step" was "a rotten liberalism which has at present some currency among one section of the Bolsheviks". The Left German social-democrats, Rosa Luxemburg and Parvus, had "invented the Utopian and semi-Menshevik scheme of permanent revolution", which had been "taken up by Trotsky . . . and turned into a weapon in the struggle against Leninism".[8]

Apart from the obsessive denunciation of Trotskyism, with which every form of opposition was now identified, the violent language of the letter was oblique to the point of ambiguity, and its positive content obscure. Its importance was, however, underlined in an address by Kaganovich on December 1, 1931, to the Institute of Red Professors on the tenth anniversary of its foundation. Kaganovich repeated and embroidered on Stalin's diatribe without adding anything new. He denounced Slutsky's "slanderous Trotskyist attempt" to pervert history by censuring Lenin for failure to support "so-called Left social-democrats of the type of Rosa Luxemburg", whose errors, in spite of her "great services", could not be condoned.[9] But no positive guidance was offered. The purpose of the exercise was not to enunciate new doctrine, but to curb free-ranging ideological debate, and to insist on rigid conformity. Hitherto some latitude had been allowed, in peripheral

[4] See *Soviet Studies*, xxviii (1976), No. 1, pp. 37–39.

[5] *Proletarskaya Revolyutsiya*, 1931, No. 2–3, pp. 22–53, No. 4–5, pp. 35–79.

[6] Two public trials of managers and engineers accused of sabotage (the so-called "industrial party" and "Menshevik" trials) were held in 1930 and 1931, and two dissident groups (Lominadze–Shatskin–Syrtsov and the Ryutin group) were exposed and expelled from the party; for these events see p. 23 above.

[7] Pokrovsky died under a cloud in April 1932; he was eulogized by Thälmann in his opening speech to the twelfth IKKI in August 1932 (*XII Plenum IKKI* (1933), i, 2), but was not officially rehabilitated for nearly thirty years.

[8] Stalin, *Sochineniya*, xiii, 84–102. It was originally published in *Proletarskaya Revolyutsiya*, 1931, No. 6, pp. 1–12; the same issue carried (p. 199) an obsequious note by the editors abjectly apologising for their error, and undertaking that the future work of the journal would be governed by Stalin's principles. A translation of the letter appeared in *Internationale Presse-Korrespondenz*, No. 110, November 20, 1931, pp. 2435–2458.

[9] *Ibid.*, No. 117, December 15, 1931, pp. 2661–2668.

and specialist journals, to the expression of a variety of views, provided party policy and party pronouncements were not directly criticized. Henceforth any independent opinion was frowned on, and scholarship was firmly held in leading-strings. Stalin's letter was the crowning item in a campaign which included among its targets both Pokrovsky and historians immediately associated with him, and Deborin, the leading Marxist philosopher.

But it had also wider implications. Translations of the letter and of Kaganovich's address in the Comintern news-sheet were followed by an article of Popov, a party historian, entitled "The Idealization of Luxemburgism is the Banner of our Enemies", identifying Brandler and Thalheimer, who had led the KPD to bankruptcy in 1923, as "disciples of Rosa Luxemburg".[10] The hint was taken. Stalin's letter appeared on the agenda of both the Polish and the German parties. Both had wavered on the question of cooperation with Left socialists and social-democrats; and the letter could be construed as a sharp reminder of the danger of such entanglements. But more significantly these parties shared the heritage of Rosa Luxemburg. Her errors had been admitted and discussed. She had differed from Lenin on party organization in 1903; the economic analysis in her major work *The Accumulation of Capital* had been contested; her views on the national question were heretical; she had criticized the October revolution. But she remained none the less the symbol of a powerful revolutionary tradition in the two parties with which she had been associated. Ever since the "Bolshevization" of the foreign parties had been proclaimed in Moscow, apprehension had been intermittently felt of the survival of "Luxemburgism" as an independent school of thought within the revolutionary movement, inimical to the conception of a monolithic "Leninist" International. These fears became real and insistent when Trotsky challenged this conception in the name of an international, European, not specifically Russian, revolutionary tradition, and linked Stalin's ambition to create an International on the Russian model with Stalin's doctrine of socialism in one country. Henceforth Luxemburgism could be seen as a variant of Trotskyism. It became part of the campaign against Trotsky to discredit Luxemburg; and this was the main moral of Stalin's letter for the two parties in which her memory was still a living force.

The Polish party was the first to take the field. In December 1931 the central committee of the KPP, hailing Stalin's letter as "of permanent importance for the whole of Comintern", made it the starting-point for a slashing attack on "Luxemburgism", which, identified with the names of Trotsky and Brandler, and of Warski and Kostrzewa, had been responsible for the past errors of the party.[11] Rosa Luxemburg's opinions had sometimes in the nineteen-twenties been a bone of contention in the KPP as well as in Comintern.[12] But she had always been honoured as one of the creators of the KPP and of its traditions. The unbridled denunciation to which she was now subjected was a symbol of total submission to Stalin's masterful will. The party journal *Z Pola Walki*, the Polish counterpart of *Proletarskaya Revolyutsiya*, was prudently closed down.

The reception of the letter in the KPD was marked by the same self-prostrating eagerness to comply with instructions whose text was difficult to decipher. On

[10] *Internationale Presse-Korrespondenz*, No. 117, December 15, 1931, pp. 2677–2679.

[11] *KPP: Uchwały i Rezolucje*, iii (1956), 341–347.

[12] See *Socialism in One Country, 1924–1926*, Vol. 3, pp. 187, 201–202, 1003–1005; *Foundations of a Planned Economy, 1926–1929*, Vol. 3, pp. 584–585.

January 8, 1932, the *Rote Fahne* published a long statement by the central
committee of the KPD, which unequivocally associated the campaign against Rosa
Luxemburg with the burning issue of current policy. Stalin's letter was said to bind
the party "to the most strenuous struggle against the social-democratic influences
in the revolutionary movement, against Centrist and Luxemburgist survivals in the
party"; Luxemburg was branded as a "Left radical", and Slutsky as a "masked
Trotskyist".[13] But ambiguities remained. For some years, it had been the practice
in Comintern to link the anniversary of the death of Luxemburg and Liebknecht on
January 15 with that of Lenin's death on January 21 in a joint commemoration of
"the three Ls".[14] In 1932 an article in *Pravda* on January 7 preparing the way for
the Lenin anniversary did not mention Luxemburg or Liebknecht. But the KPD
was evidently reluctant to let the association go by default. A translation of the
article which appeared in the Comintern news-sheet was headed "Lenin–
Luxemburg–Liebknecht Campaign", and was immediately followed by an article
by Heckert commemorating the two German martyrs.[15]

Thälmann, in his report to the party central committee in February 1932,
handled the question with some embarrassment. Rosa Luxemburg's errors could
not be excused, yet she and other Leftists of pre-war social-democracy could not be
denied their revolutionary record: "Rosa Luxemburg and the others belong to
us".[16] This was followed by an unsigned article in the party journal on Stalin's
letter, which "teaches us to use Bolshevik weapons in the struggle against social-
Fascism, against the SPD and its 'Left' section, against the SAP and Trotskyism,
against opportunism in general". It referred in passing to Rosa Luxemburg's
errors. It was full of quotations from Lenin, but like other commentaries failed to
quote Stalin's letter itself, so that the specific content of the admonition remained
vague and ambiguous.[17]

By the time the twelfth IKKI met in Moscow at the end of August 1932, Stalin's
letter was nearly a year old; and Thälmann did not revert to it in his main report.
The KPD had now hesitatingly embarked on a programme of "anti-Fascist
action", involving an increased emphasis on the principles and practice of the
united front.[18] Ulbricht, in his contribution to the debate on Thälmann's report,
boldly claimed that Stalin's letter had been directed against "*neglect and
underestimate of the united front and of mass work*", and took issue with the statement in
the *Rote Fahne* at the time of its publication as being "in clear contradiction with the

[13] Reprinted in *Internationale Presse-Korrespondenz*, No. 3, January 12, 1932, pp. 70–72.

[14] See, for example, *Internationale Presse-Korrespondenz*, No. 4, January 16, 1930, pp. 125–
126.

[15] *Ibid.* No. 3, January 12, 1932, pp. 65–66.

[16] *Der Revolutionäre Ausweg und die KPD* (1932), pp. 71, 94; for this report see p. 50
above.

[17] *Die Internationale*, No. 3, March 1932, pp. 134–137. The article also reminded the
Communist Youth League of an article by Thälmann devoted to its work in the previous issue
of the journal; the league had evidently been exhibiting its customary recalcitrance to party
discipline, and was exhorted by Thälmann "to pursue with far greater energy the campaign
to explain the errors of Rosa Luxemburg and Karl Liebknecht", and to study "the towering
role of Lenin and of the Leninist Communist Youth League of the Soviet Union" (*ibid.* No. 2,
February 1932, p. 90). For SAP see p. 41 above; one of its leaders, Frölich, who had been
expelled from the KPD in 1928, was a disciple of Luxemburg and later her biographer.

[18] See p. 56 above.

context of the letter".[19] Thälmann in his reply to the debate retired to safer ground, limiting himself to the assertion that Stalin's letter "rendered to all parties, and especially to us in Germany, great help in the struggle against Right opportunism and 'Left' sectarianism, against hidden survivals of Luxemburgism and Trotskyism".[20] The resolution adopted at the end of the session called, with studied vagueness, for "an unremitting struggle against all perversions of Marxism–Leninism", and for purity of party theory, in the spirit of the indications in Stalin's letter".[21] So much flexibility demonstrated that, whatever purpose the letter was originally designed to serve in Soviet domestic affairs, its relevance to foreign communist parties was to insist, not so much on any particular policy, as on prompt and unqualified obedience to mandates issuing from Moscow. The last shot in the campaign was an article by Martynov in the journal of Comintern which, reverting to the lessons to be learnt from Stalin's letter, maintained that there was no difference of principle between the opportunism of the "Centrists" and the opportunism of Luxemburg and Liebknecht. There could be "no other communism than that which fights under the banner of Marx and Engels, of Lenin and Stalin", and attempts to "refurbish" this banner whether from the "Left" or from the Right must be sternly rejected.[22] The campaign deprived the Polish and German parties of the one figure-head of an independent revolutionary tradition which could be set up against the monopoly of revolutionary orthodoxy claimed by the Russian party and by Comintern in the name of Lenin. The Nazi menace was not mentioned throughout the argument.

Other parties were less directly involved in the controversy. The letter was published in December 1931 in the Italian party journal *Stato Operaio*, with a fulsome introductory article by Togliatti, who declared it to be "of the greatest political importance . . . for all parties of the International". He contrived to connect the heresies denounced in it with the deviations in the PCI, and found in Rosa Luxemburg's errors the main elements of Bordigism;[23] and he returned briefly to the same theme in a letter addressed to members of the PCI in prison a few months later.[24] But Togliatti was perhaps more concerned to refurbish his own slightly tarnished image in the eyes of Comintern than to probe the meaning of Stalin's pronouncement. Thorez in the French party journal described the letter as "of primordial importance for the PCF", and hailed it in his speech to the seventh party congress in March 1932 as a warning against "social-democratic Guesdist and Jaurèsist survivals" in the party.[25] Communist parties in countries where Luxemburg was no more than a historic name were able to avoid the issue altogether.

[19] *XII Plenum IKKI* (1933), i, 120; for the *Rote Fahne* statement see p. 431 above.

[20] *XII Plenum IKKI* (1933), iii, 109.

[21] *Kommunisticheskii Internatsional v Dokumentakh* (1933), p. 982.

[22] *Kommunisticheskii Internatsional*, 1933, No. 2, pp. 12–23; the article was provoked by a cautious defence of Luxemburg which ran through three successive issues of *Internationale Presse-Korrespondenz*, No. 96, November 15, 1932, pp. 3081–3085, No. 97, November 18, 1932, pp. 3109–3118, No. 98, November 22, 1932, pp. 3147–3153, and was written by its editor, the Hungarian communist Alpari.

[23] P. Togliatti, *Opere*, III (1973), i, 451–456.

[24] *Ibid.* iii, ii, 62.

[25] *Cahiers du Bolchévisme*, March 1, 1932, p. 301; *Oeuvres de Maurice Thorez*, II, iii (1951), 175.

TROTSKY AND THE RISE OF HITLER

Trotsky maintained during the period of Hitler's rise to power so persistent and, for the most part, so prescient a commentary on the course of events in Germany as to deserve record. His first broadside, which did not deal directly with Germany, was an article entitled "The 'Third Period' of the Errors of Comintern" which occupied the whole issue of the *Byulleten' Oppozitsii* for January 1930. Trotsky rejected the new line announced by Comintern at its sixth congress of 1928 and thereafter. He did not accept the hypothesis of the final "end of capitalist stabilization"; the economic crisis was a cyclical slump which capitalism might still survive. He saw no evidence for the alleged radicalization of the masses and mounting wave of revolution. The constantly repeated prediction of an imminent danger of war defeated itself. Finally, Trotsky wished to return to the "united front" as preached by Lenin.[1] Molotov at the sixteenth party congress in June 1930 swept aside these views with the usual charge of pessimism and lack of faith, and called Trotsky "the bard of American 'prosperity'".[2]

The sensational Nazi gains in the Saxon elections of June 1930 prompted Trotsky to grapple seriously with the German situation. He began by taunting Comintern with the contradictions of its policy. At a moment when the international crisis was becoming acute, Comintern had begun to signal caution: this signified "the abandonment of the tactics of the 'third period' in favour of the tactics of the 'second period'". If the communist party was "*the party of revolutionary hope*", Fascism was "*a party of counter-revolutionary despair*". Fascism was a real danger in Germany owing to the failure of the KPD; this was "the old tragic contradiction between a mature revolutionary situation on the one hand and the strategic impotence of the revolutionary party on the other". Nevertheless, Trotsky recognized that the role of the KPD in the immediate future must be defensive, not offensive. "The policy of a united front of the workers against Fascism" and the abandonment of the harmful "theory and practice of 'social-Fascism'" were the needs of the moment.[3] The article contained the kernel of nearly everything which Trotsky was to write in the next two years about the Nazi menace.

Trotsky's next assault was provoked by the participation of the KPD in the Prussian plebiscite of August 1931.[4] The formation of "a united front with the Fascists" was an easy target for attack; but he also raised the dominant practical issue:

---

[1] *Byulleten' Oppozitsii* (Paris), No. 8, January 1930, pp. 2–22.

[2] *XVI S"ezd Vsesoyuznoi Kommunisticheskoi Partii (b)* (1930), p. 412.

[3] *Byulleten' Oppozitsii* (Paris), No. 17–18, November–December 1930, pp. 45–54; the article was dated September 26, 1930.

[4] See p. 42 above.

   The problem comes down to the relation of forces. To take to the streets with
the slogan "Down with the Brüning–Braun government", when in the existing
relation of forces this government can be replaced only by a Hitler–Hugenberg
government, is pure adventurism.

Trotsky went on to denounce the ideological underpinning of cooperation with the
Nazis. Thälmann's adoption of the slogan of a "people's revolution" was a further
retreat from the proletarian revolution and the proletarian united front.[5] This was
followed later in the year by an article in which Trotsky, after briefly reviewing the
prospects in Spain, Britain, France, the United States and the Far East, reverted to
Germany as the key to the international situation. Everything turned directly
and immediately on the question which would be victorious in Germany:
communism or Fascism. The rise of Fascism had two causes: the grave social crisis
and the revolutionary weakness of the proletariat. The weakness of the proletariat
had also two causes: the continued strength of the SPD as "the agency of capitalism
in the ranks of the proletariat", and the failure of the central direction of the KPD
and of Comintern to rally the workers. Trotsky reproached the leaders in Moscow
with their silence and passivity; paralysed by their internal problems, they wanted
only to be left in peace. He ventured on the firm prediction that "the victory of
Fascism in Germany would inevitably bring about war against the USSR". Once
Hitler was installed in power, France, Britain and the United States would support
his campaign against the USSR as they had once supported Kolchak, Denikin and
Wrangel.[6]
   Trotsky's fullest analysis of the German situation at this time was contained in a
substantial pamphlet entitled *Et maintenant?*, written in January 1932 and
published in several languages—his first appeal to a broad international audience.
Social-democracy he described as, "in spite of its working-class composition,
entirely a bourgeois party", serving bourgeois ends. But this did not justify the
identification of social-democracy with Fascism ("social-Fascism"). The contradiction between them was, it was true, not "an opposition of two classes", but of
"different systems of the rule of one and the same class". Social-democracy leaned
on the workers, Fascism on the petty bourgeoisie; social-democracy sought to work
through parliament, Fascism to destroy parliament. The Brüning government,
legislating by decree, "dances on a tight-rope between two irreconcilable camps",
and balances between the Fascist petty bourgeoisie and the workers' organizations—a caricature of Bonapartism. Trotsky gave the name of "ultimatism"
to the demand of the KPD for a united front only with workers who accepted in
advance the condition of supreme communist leadership. A Soviet of workers,
irrespective of party commitment, was *"the highest form of united front"* at the
moment of the struggle for power. The thesis of some communists that Hitler, if he
came to power, would quickly discredit himself and pave the way for proletarian
revolution was a dangerous illusion. Given the solidarity of the workers'
organizations the situation was not desperate; the united front was an effective

   [5] *Byulleten' Oppozitsii* (Paris), No. 24, September 1931, pp. 3–13; for the "people's
revolution" see pp. 25–27 above.
   [6] *Byulleten' Oppozitsii* (Paris), No. 25–26, November–December 1931, pp. 1–9; the
prediction of the inevitability of war if Hitler came to power was repeated by Trotsky in an
article in the American magazine *Forum*, April 15, 1932.

weapon of defence. Only when the masses of workers had abandoned "reformism" would agreements with social-democracy lose their meaning.[7]

The successive crises of 1932—Hindenburg's re-election as president, the dismissal of Brüning, his replacement by Papen, Papen's dismissal of the Prussian Government, and the fresh Nazi advance in the Reichstag elections of July 31— stung Trotsky into a fresh wave of protest. Another pamphlet, written in August and September and again published in several languages, defined the Papen regime, which leaned on the support of Schleicher and the Reichswehr, as Bonapartist (Brüning had been pre-Bonapartist). The petty bourgeoisie was divided between converts to National Socialism and those who, like millions of workers, still clung to the traditions of bourgeois democracy. Bonapartism still tried to balance between the Nazis and the workers; but these were two irreconcilable opposites. Any conceivable combination with Hitler must lead to the swallowing up by Fascism of the bureaucracy, of the courts, of the police and of the army. The analysis ended with a desperate plea for "the renaissance of the International".[8]

Even when, on January 30, 1933, Hitler became Chancellor, Trotsky, in common with most foreign observers, hesitated to recognize Hitler's victory as complete. In an article of February 5 headed "Before the Decision" he noted that "the government Hugenberg–Hitler contains within itself a complex system of contradictions". The combination was "extremely precarious", and could not last for long. The crisis would continue to "develop in the direction of Fascism"; but "the principal levers of power are not in Hitler's hands". What had happened was "a very severe blow for the working class", but not yet "an irretrievable defeat". He called on the KPD and "the Stalinist fraction" to reverse their tactics, and proclaim an unconditional united front with social-democracy and with the reformist trade unions.[9]

The savage blow struck by Hitler when, after the Reichstag fire and the elections, he seized full power and exterminated the KPD and the SPD, as well as all workers' organizations, stunned Trotsky as it stunned the world at large, though much that he had written foreshadowed it. An appeal to social-democrats for an effective united front was a belated response;[10] and a summons to prepare "the defence of proletarian positions" in countries adjacent to Germany was scarcely more realistic.[11] But in June 1933 Trotsky penned a brief and cogent analysis of the phenomenon of National Socialism. Hitler he saw as a personification of "the infuriated petty bourgeois". Recurrent economic crises since the war had borne as heavily on the petty bourgeois as on the workers; and they had found leadership in the lower and middle officer corps of the old army, soured by defeat. Hitler had no programme—less even than Mussolini. He appealed only to the sense of betrayal and the thirst for vengeance. The cult of the individual and the cult of

[7] The French text of this now rare pamphlet is in L. Trotsky, *Écrits, 1928–1940*, iii (1959), 109–230.

[8] *Ibid.* iii, 261–320; some sections of the pamphlet appeared in *Byulleten' Oppozitsii* (Paris), No. 29–30, September 1932, pp. 24–31. For a further analysis of "German Bonapartism" see *ibid*. No. 32, December 1932, pp. 4–7.

[9] *Ibid.* No. 33, March 1933, pp. 18–22, where it is incorrectly dated January 5 (though followed by a postscript dated February 6); the French translation in L. Trotsky, *Écrits, 1928–1940*, iii (1959), 341–350 is correctly dated.

[10] *Ibid.* iii, 353–374.

[11] *Byulleten' Oppozitsii* (Paris), No. 34, May 1933, pp. 7–11.

class was replaced by the cult of race and nation, economic materialism by "zoological materialism". Hitler's coup was not a revolution, or even a counter-revolution, since the social system remained intact. Fascism had climbed to power on the backs of the petty bourgeoisie, but the result was "the most inexorable dictatorship of monopoly capital, whose only resource could be to fasten responsibility for calamities at home on external enemies". Trotsky ended with a prediction:

> The interval which separates us from a new European catastrophe is determined by the time required for the rearmament of Germany. It is not a question of months; but equally it is not a question of decades. A few years suffice for Europe to be once more precipitated into war, if Hitler is not stopped in time by internal forces within Germany.[12]

Both Trotsky's diagnosis and his foresight were astonishingly acute. He was also right in exposing the ineptitude of the policies pursued by Comintern, and at its behest by the KPD. But, given these premises, he was wrong on one point. He had refused to believe that Hitler could come to power without resistance from the German workers and without an interlude of civil war. Perhaps he now shrank from pressing the analysis further. The German proletariat had failed to raise the standard of revolution in 1914. Even in the hour of defeat, and with the Russian example to spur it on, its revolutionary efforts in the bleak winter of 1918–1919 had been half-hearted, and had soon petered out. Nor in the years between the two wars was the spark of proletarian revolution alive in any of the major capitalist countries. If Trotsky did not share the view of Comintern that the passivity of the workers was due to the corruption or treachery of their leaders, he said nothing to refute it. He did not lose faith in the revolutionary destiny of the proletariat as the prime mover in the overthrow of capitalism. The logic of his next move rested on the hypothesis that the bankruptcy of Comintern was the source of the failure. He declared that the Third International was dead, and planned the foundation of a Fourth International.[13]

[12] L. Trotsky, *Écrits, 1928–1940*, iii (1959), 391–399.
[13] For Trotsky's appeals for a Fourth International see p. 229 above; the Fourth International was not founded until September 1938.

INDEX

Edward Hallett Carr was born in 1892 and educated at Merchant Taylors' School, London, and Trinity College, Cambridge. After joining the Foreign Office (1916) to work in Paris and Riga, he was appointed Assistant Adviser on League of Nations Affairs, First Secretary in the Foreign Office and, for one year during World War II, Director of Foreign Publicity at the Ministry of Information in London. From 1941 to 1946, he served simultaneously as Wilson Professor of International Politics at the University College of Wales and as Assistant Editor for *The Times*, eventually settling in Oxford as a Fellow at Trinity College in Cambridge.

Shortly before the publication of this book, in November of 1982, E.H. Carr died in Cambridge. He had been at work on a sequel to *Twilight of the Comintern*, which deals with the world's reaction to the Spanish Civil War.